Agile Systems with
Reusable Patterns of Business Knowledge

A Component-Based Approach

For a listing of recent titles in the *Artech House Computing Library,* turn to the back of this book.

Agile Systems with Reusable Patterns of Business Knowledge

A Component-Based Approach

Amit Mitra
Amar Gupta

ARTECH HOUSE

BOSTON | LONDON
artechhouse.com

Library of Congress Cataloging-in-Publication Data
Mitra, Amit, 1949–
    Agile systems with reuseable patterns of business knowledge : a component-based approach /
Amit Mitra, Amar Gupta.
        p.   cm.
    Includes bibliographical references and index.
    ISBN 1-58053-988-2 (alk. paper)
    1. Management information systems.   2. Knowledge management.   3. Business logicitics.
I. Gupta, Amar.   II. Title.

British Library Cataloguing in Publication Data
Mitra, Amit
    Agile systems with reusable patterns of business knowledge: a component-based approach.
    —(Artech House computing library)
    1. Knowledge management—Data processing   2. Information technology
    I. Title   II. Gupta, Amar
    658.4'038'011
    ISBN-10   1-58053-988-2

Cover design by Igor Valdman

International Standard Book Number: 1-58053-988-2

10 9 8 7 6 5 4 3 2 1

This book is dedicated to my mother, Sevati Mitra,
my wife, Snigdha Mitra,
and my daughters, Tanya and Trishna,
who helped make this book better in many ways!
—Amit Mitra

This book is dedicated to my mother, Urmila Devi,
my wife, Poonam Gupta,
and my daughter, Amita,
the three women who have enhanced my life in many ways!
—Amar Gupta

Additional materials and supplementary chapters are available at:

http://www.artechhouse.com/ Default.Asp?Frame=Book.Asp&Book=1-58053-988-2.

From here, click on the link to our Web site and enter Mitra as the user name and Gupta as the password to access this material.

Throughout this book, this Web site will be referred to as "our Web site."

Contents

Foreword

Over 15 years ago I wrote in my preface to Information Systems Planning: "The world is becoming an interlaced network of computerized corporations. As electronic data interchange among corporations grows with intercorporate networks, so the windows of opportunity become shorter. In such a world the corporation in which data processing is a mess, with spaghetti code, uncoordinated data, and long application backlogs, will not be able to compete. The techniques of information engineering are vital to a competitive corporation."

The passage of time has not only proven this to be painfully true, but has also shown that this was more than a prophecy—it has become the driving force in the global knowledge economy as intercorporate networks gave way to the World Wide Web and the global economy flourished on global ideation, information, global communication, and extended enterprises that consisted of supply chains that girded our planet.

In order to create an integrated archipelago of knowledge-based assets in such an environment, one needs to develop new paradigms that can help us transcend borders of various kinds, thereby addressing the individual needs of an increasingly diverse set of users of such systems. By providing effective on-off ramps to the emerging information highways, one can establish very sophisticated knowledge infrastructure that mitigates the problems of departmental, organizational, and national boundaries. A number of new paradigms to help achieve this goal are delineated in this insightful book by Amit Mitra and Amar Gupta.

When we switch "on" a light today, we expect the room to light up immediately. We do not think about where the electricity was generated or how it was distributed from there to our office. We hope that, in the years to come, we will be able to obtain similar instantaneous results to questions that we pose, irrespective of their scope and complexity. We expect such insights will be provided without our having to bother about which organizations are involved or how the underlying computation or communication processes will be performed. In our quest to attain such a tomorrow, I believe the ideas proposed in this new book are extremely relevant and timely.

James Martin
Chairman Emeritus, Headstrong Corporation
Bermuda
September 2005

Preface

This book is part of a series. The series addresses automated support for business process resilience and information systems agility. A companion book, *Creating Agile Business Systems with Reusable Knowledge*, published by Cambridge University Press, addresses the generic structure of knowledge and how it is configured from shared components. This book addresses how *business* knowledge is configured from shared components. You do not need to read the companion book to understand this one, but the structures and patterns in this book emerge as polymorphisms of those in its companion. The two books collectively cover the components from which business knowledge is configured. Practice does not always require perfection: The patterns in this book will suffice to accelerate and automate the design of resilient business processes and information models, which will support agile business practices and information systems; the patterns in the other book will sharpen and perfect these templates to make them even more resilient.

Resilience and agility have become critical for the long-term success of business. However, most business process engineering and requirements analysis methodologies discount innovation and agility; they address only operational efficiency and economics. The global economy is rapidly moving from the industrial era to the knowledge economy. As the industrial economy gives way to the global knowledge economy, innovation and automated coordination of business knowledge are beginning to have a profound impact on the way business is being done. The forces being unleashed will have a deep and fundamental impact on almost all aspects of human enterprise. Competition is not only between individual enterprises, but today it is also between supply chains that gird the globe. It will be a tumultuous, frenetic, and chimerical century in search of customer value, driven by innovation, research, and the need for global excellence.

Both books in the series address this need: flexibility of business processes and the absorption of new learning through specially crafted components of normalized knowledge. The intent is to automatically align information systems with the business process, by showing how systems may be reduced to automated expressions of business processes. Together, the two books develop a paradigm for automated support of innovation of new products and processes. The books do this by describing how information systems can automatically adapt to change by reusing and reconfiguring components of shared knowledge. (See Figure P.1. This book has been called Book 2 in Figure P.1. The companion book has been called Book 1 in Figure P.1.)

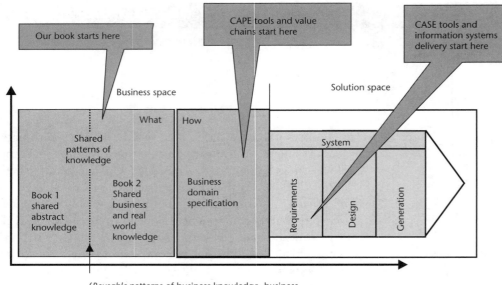

Figure P.1   Reusing business knowledge: the two books.

These books describe component technology, but are different from most approaches to the topic. The components in these books are not traditional I/T components. Rather, they are shared components of knowledge from which patterns of business knowledge are assembled. Business processes and supporting information systems configured from these components will be extremely flexible, configurable, and coordinated. They will help information architects and business process designers develop agile processes and resilient systems.

The books lay the foundation of a new computing paradigm—a paradigm in which computers manipulate meanings, not program code or blind symbols. Computers of the future, built on the principles described in the book, will operate on the plane of meanings—a little like we do.

The fundamental premise of both books is that meanings are patterns of information. *Creating Agile Business Systems with Reusable Knowledge* demonstrates how this happens. It also shows how it is possible to create new patterns of information from old patterns, by adding information to them. For instance, adding information to the meaning of "Person" might turn that person into "Parent." Thus, meanings can be built brick by brick by combining patterns of information. It is also possible to automate this process. Thus, it is possible to treat components of knowledge as patterns of information, and then *automatically* configure business processes and supporting information systems from these components. This book builds on this concept, described in detail in *Creating Agile Business Systems with Reusable Knowledge*. It applies the theory and uses the abstractions described in its companion book to build patterns of shared *business* knowledge.

Knowledge rarely stands still. New learning continually calls for new patterns, new meanings, shifting scopes, altered contexts, and new ways of doing things. In other words, processes, models, and systems must continually change and adapt.

Change can be chaotic. For this reason, it is rarely automated, and is usually time consuming, risky, and labor intensive. The two books taken together show how automation might facilitate change in step with new information.

To minimize the chaotic effects of change and to automatically propagate impacts to the right places in a business model, components of knowledge must be defined in a special way. The companion book shows how automation may then assemble new knowledge, assisted by the right components, brick by brick, by adding information to build new patterns from old patterns. Processes and information systems built in this manner will automatically absorb and adapt to new knowledge and expanded scopes. The impact of change will be minimized, and information systems, assisted by the right automation, will automatically wrap themselves around the new rules. This can be a critical advantage in an intensely competitive business environment, where competitive advantage depends on bringing new ideas to market quickly.

The key to designing components that will minimize the impact of change is to normalize information in special patterns. These normalized patterns will be components of business knowledge that may be configured in special ways to create additional knowledge. Thus, the business meanings in this book may be held in specific components, and the information will not be replicated in diverse uncontrolled forms and formats. The impact of change will then be contained and automatically driven to the right places when components are reconfigured. Together, the two books provide the complete paradigm for normalizing shared business knowledge.

Patterns of business knowledge are built from simple, very basic commonsense facts that cross multiple scopes. In order to normalize information, the information payload of the most basic components of common knowledge must necessarily be small and elementary. The most basic components are thus abstract. These abstractions are the focus of *Creating Agile Business Systems with Reusable Knowledge*. That book also elaborates on *rules* for assembling components to create new, flexible components and subassemblies. Naturally, these rules also will be components subject to the same laws. Thus, *Creating Agile Business Systems with Reusable Knowledge* is the theoretical basis for this book.

This book has richer, more concrete patterns that carry business meanings. These patterns are derived from the basic components described in its companion book by adding new layers of information. It is a little like the reverse of peeling an onion. If we are blind to the patterns in the companion book, then information will not be perfectly normalized. The core of the onion will not be addressed, and the impact of change will not be completely contained.

However, practitioners do not always have to aim for perfection to make an impact. Even if the abstract patterns of the companion book are not recognized, the patterns in this book can help jump start systems integration, business intelligence, and information architecture, helping reduce time to market. On the other hand, advanced readers and those who would like to either automate or perfect the process should also read the companion book. Without the theory in it, fully automating the alignment between business process and information systems will not be possible. Knowledge will not be normalized with requisite precision, and chaotic impacts of change will not be precisely controllable. More human intervention, judgment, intuition, and manual intervention will be required. This is certainly viable. Subjectivity and chaotic impacts still will be far less than if one started with a blank slate. The use of prefabricated models will still compress time to market, but to a lesser extent than if the process was fully supported and automated with the abstract, core patterns in the companion book. Thus, this book can be valuable to practitioners who have not read the companion book, but the companion book will help them polish and perfect their components further.

Similarly, designers of automated tools who read the companion book will have the option of using this book to enhance their tools with the prefabricated patterns here. These patterns are commonly used subassemblies of the core components described in the companion book, pertinent to the universe of business: they can provide prefabricated templates to designers of process models, data models, and object models. This is how the two books enhance each other.

In these books, you will find the framework that serves as the direct bridge between business process engineering and systems engineering—a proven framework that works for every industry and business application, from telecommunications to insurance, from financial services to manufacturing, and beyond.

In the following chapters, we will show not only how this framework works in practice, but also how it actually anticipates key requirements even before users articulate them.

Where will it eventually lead? In the short term, it can make your business more agile. It will provide reusable models, processes, and business knowledge components to compress your time to market new or improved products, services, and processes. It will also show you how you can compress systems development and integration times. However, it is the vision at the end of this journey that is the most fascinating of all. The concepts in this series can provide the foundation of disciplines that will make business systems truly maintenance free—systems based on software that will automatically adapt to change and chaos. These systems will be supported by automated intelligent agents that will, someday, maintain software and respond to environmental change at the speed of thought, a vision we will share with you at the end of this book.

As practitioners, managers, and teachers in the field of information systems, we often talk of change control. Change plays havoc with our plans and products. However, the wealth in the knowledge economy will flow from global excellence, thriving on change and innovation. The only justification for technology will and must be change facilitation, not change control. Are we ready? Read on!

> "Wouldst thou,"—so the helmsman answered,
> "Learn the secret of the sea?
> Only those who brave its dangers
> Comprehend its mystery!"
>
> —Henry Wadsworth Longfellow, *The Galley of Count Arnaldos*

Acknowledgments

We deeply appreciate the effort of Dr. E. C. Subbarao, our teacher, advisor, and professor at the Indian Institute of Technology; his advice in shaping this book was priceless. We thank Jayant Pai and Raghunandan Bhat of Setu Software for their encouragement and enthusiasm for proving the concepts in the book by implementing them in software. We are indebted to Rick Pool, the principal and service line lead for information management optimization in Headstrong for his support and encouragement. We are grateful to Kiran Rao for helping us file and organize the background materials and research papers that contributed to this book, and to our friends and seasoned software executives, V. Srinivasan and Himanshu Mathur for their help, counsel, and resources. We would also like to acknowledge Carol Neighbour, John Dolan, and Margit Schmidt of AIG who were instrumental in sharing their ideas, time, and resources and in helping to prove the concepts and ideas in this book when they first started to take shape. We would like to thank Sarita Rao and Pat Fayad for their continued faith and encouragement.

Prologue

What Is This Book About, and Who Should Read It?

This book is about facilitating change with component technology, but is different from most approaches to the topic. The components in the book are not traditional IT components. Rather, they are shared meanings from which patterns of business knowledge are assembled.

Business meanings, patterns, and rules are the substance of a business process. Without the business layer, technological standards have little meaning. This book establishes a framework for the transfer and reuse of business knowledge in different contexts. This is why we urge architects interested in Service-Oriented Architecture and Business Process Management to read this book.

Computer technology is key to the automation of business processes. It is a central theme and an underlying assumption in this book. Computer programming and technical architecture are tangential to the discussion in this book. However, we urge software architects and technologists to read this book, because the principles and patterns in this book complement the work that has been already been done in developing technology and interfacing standards for information systems. The purpose of this book is not to propose yet another technical standard. The purpose is to describe business intelligence, in component form, which current technical standards must support and be joined to. It is the next step.

What Will the Information Be Used For?

The patterns in this book will address the following business problems:

1. *Agility and adaptability of business processes and systems*: Facilitate designing of agile business processes and flexible systems based on the reusable patterns of information in this book. This will help automate the alignment between business processes and information systems, speed development of systems to support new products and distribution channels, and accelerate process and systems integration when businesses integrate either horizontally or vertically, or reinvent themselves in their product markets.

2. *Integration and coordination of information*: Coordinate integration of information and processes across supply chains, enterprises, and databases. Accelerate the design of Service-Oriented Architecture.

3. *Reduce the time to market new concepts*: Accelerate formulation of functional requirements and process models based on the prefabricated reusable patterns in this book.

4. *Compress the time to develop prototypes:* Develop patterns that can be the basis for early prototypes when iterative prototyping methodologies are used for developing or integrating information systems or business processes.

Ultimately this book is about change. It describes a technology for automating change and the best practices for facilitating it—all in support of the innovation and adaptation necessary for corporations to remain competitive in the diverse and tumultuous business universe of today.

Technology's Broken Promise

Why is change so difficult? That is a question with an easy answer. Each impact has several subsequent impacts, which ricochet through our processes and systems until we are caught in an explosive cascade of change. Business sponsors requesting the change are then faced with a painful choice—either to make the changes at a cost, time, and risk that might be excessive; or to abandon the competitive benefits of innovation because the risk is too high or the change too late.

A recent example was the Y2K problem. It seemed trivial to the layman, but computer technology was such that it may have cost industry as much as $600 billion[1] and a significant part of the world's resource pool of professionals to merely express the year in four instead of in two digits.[2] Many strategic benefits have been difficult to implement for similar reasons. Denial of strategic benefits to consumer and provider alike are so frequent that examples litter the industrial landscape in almost every direction:

- Straight Through Processing and "T+0" settlement in the Financial Securities Industry (i.e., the ability to settle a trade immediately with almost no manual processing);
- Real-time billing for telephone subscribers and personal telephone numbers in the telecommunications industry (i.e., a unique contact phone number that automatically follows an individual regardless of location or geography);
- Timely and reliable order fulfillment and innovative customer service for manufacturers and retailers;
- Risk assessment when providing insurance coverage to complex global clients in the insurance industry.

---

1.   Sources: Gartner Group & Congressional Research Service estimates quoted by Steve C. Yuen, Ph.D., University of Southern Mississippi, and Jo Ann Mitchell, Jones Junior College, at http://dragon.ep.usm.edu/~yuen/present/meca99a/tsld018.htm.

2.   For example, 1/1/2001 instead of 1/1/01. Computer calculations involving dates beyond 1999 had a very high risk of error if the year was not expressed in four digits.

This is only a small slice of such wish lists—strategic innovations and improvements in almost every industry that are deemed too risky or impossible, because changing supporting processes and information systems is deemed too complex.

Despite inventing new technology at a prodigious rate to make change easy (e.g., CASE tools, code generators, structured programming, relational databases, expert systems, object technology, reusable components, and other technological innovations), systems still cannot change fast enough. Why are information systems a bottleneck? Can process reengineering, business innovation, and time to market be accelerated? Why have these technologies not fulfilled their full potential?

The principal reason is that we have not found a way of representing business rules and knowledge in a single place and in such a way that we can change a rule once, and reflect the change wherever it impacts business processes and supporting automation. The rules of business are repeated in different forms and formats, in multiple, tangled ways in several systems at several places. This has been the central problem.

It was not solved in the 1950s, when we replaced the tangled code of machine language with assembly languages, or in the 1960s, when we replaced the spaghetti code of assembly languages with that of third generation languages, such as COBOL and FORTRAN. It was not solved in the 1970s and 1980s, with the introduction of relational databases, expert systems, and CASE tools, nor in the 1990s, when tangled object inheritance became so much of a problem that many advocated making multiple inheritance illegal in tools of the day. *More automation merely tangled business rules further.*

For this reason, the authors asked a different question when starting this research in 1992. What information do we need to model the stimulus response behavior of business processes and the organizations they support in the real world? Further, what is the *natural* real-world structure of information that can represent business knowledge in fully normalized,[3] and hence reusable, form across the universe of diverse global business environments?[4]

Why would this approach work when so many others have failed? It works because it untangles business rules. It untangles business rules even if they were tangled in legacy models and systems. Thus, it allows us to represent business knowledge *once* in a repository of knowledge, from where it can *naturally* manifest itself in different business contexts. Changes made at the right place will automatically impact business systems where they should. It is no surprise that many businessmen and professionals have intuitively felt that business knowledge acquired in one context might often be reused in another. This intuition is a fundamental truth that flows from the natural structure of business knowledge in the real world. We must explicitly recognize this structure, and express it with precision to use it effectively.

---

3. "Normalized" means represented uniquely in a single place once.
4. As the state of the art has matured, it is heartening to see similar patterns being discussed in several areas. See the various papers and reusability projects in the References at the end of the book (especially items Demand and Supply Chains and Standards [4], Knowledge Reuse Projects [116], and the on-line hierarchy browser in [42]). The patterns in this book and the metamodel behind them have certainly withstood the test of time. They support the confluence of these diverse initiatives, despite the passage of the many years since 1992.

Component Reuse—The Genesis

The concept of using reusable components to compress application development time is almost as old as the software industry. Components have evolved from concepts such as copy libraries, common subroutines, or general purpose applications packages, in the early days of batch computing, into reusable GUI, network and data services objects, based on standards such as CORBA and COM, which support distributed, interactive Web and client-server computing.

For historical reasons, software component engineering first focused on the back end of the process engineering value chain. Its first concern was program code and interfaces for communicating data in terms of streams of bits and bytes. The economic impact, however, is usually far larger at the front end of the reengineering value chain—on reusing business knowledge to configure and to innovate business processes, services, and products. Thus, it is not surprising that business had only very limited interest and no involvement in the kind of components that software engineers were interested in. Consequently, the business community's support for the software community's component technology was lukewarm at best. The focus has shifted in step with evolving technology. Now the time is ripe to look at the reuse of knowledge. This territory, long neglected by the software community, is and always has been where the major benefits to business are found. Let us analyze these imperatives.

As business has progressively become reliant on automation, the line between technology and the corporation's key business operations has started to blur. Industry has begun to recognize that the biggest benefit to business will flow from reusing business intelligence embedded in software. Consequently, the software industry has been striving to craft software components to reuse this embedded business intelligence across the supply chain. The intent is to speed business processes, make corporations agile, and to position the business at a competitive advantage.

However, this kind of reuse has remained elusive in spite of over 20 years of industry effort. The reason why the promise was not fulfilled was that industry was not ready to leverage the technology. Processes had not matured, technology was still groping for the right answers, software developers were loath to frontload analysis effort on software projects, and most of all, business sponsorship was weak, since software architecture was not as critical to successful business as it is today.

E- (and M-) commerce has forced cross-enterprise transparency into business processes and driven the need for standards. The market is now ripe for a product offering of software components that will encapsulate and reuse business knowledge to build software designed to facilitate business innovation, speed, and agility—software that must be developed in compressed timeframes.

Scope of This Book

This book focuses on normalizing,[5] encapsulating, and reusing *business* knowledge across multiple industries and business functions. Business knowledge is technology-independent. This knowledge may be embedded in processes that are supported

---

5.   See the note on normalization.

by diverse technologies, and may be automated or manual. Often in large organizations, the same business rules will be expressed in different systems and procedures, on different technology platforms, and in different countries or organizational units. The choice of the technology often depends on the organization's legacy, its local environment, and its infrastructure. Although business knowledge is independent of the technology that implements it, if an organization wants to reuse business knowledge explicitly, it must store this knowledge in an electronic repository. Thus, business knowledge in such a repository is an item of information that is expressed in some physical format and medium, and is an electronic artifact. For this reason, we have called these components of knowledge *Business Knowledge Artifacts* in this book.

Business Knowledge Artifacts complement, but are different from, traditional software components. The companion book shows how Business Knowledge Artifacts relate to software components. A detailed description of the technology wrapped around this core of business knowledge—software, hardware, presentation, and networking issues—is beyond the scope of this book.

Because this book focuses on the rules of business, *Business Knowledge Artifacts* have often been abbreviated to *Knowledge Artifacts* in the material that follows. *Knowledge Artifacts* encapsulate bits of formal business intelligence—meanings that can be stored as reusable components in a repository of business knowledge.

Foundation of Knowledge Reuse: The Three Pillars

Business knowledge is not about files, data flows, formats, screens, or computers. Rather, it is about processes, practices, norms, products, policies, regulations, infrastructure, and people, which are constrained by the physical, regulatory, and ethical contexts in which they function. To recast this knowledge in the form of normalized[6] and reusable capsules of information that can be assembled into configurations of knowledge and innovative ideas, we must first know how knowledge can be normalized. We must also know which parts are reusable, and how to organize people and business practices to leverage these reusable knowledge components. These are the three pillars on which Business Knowledge components must stand. See Figure P.1.

The First Pillar: Metamodel of Business Knowledge

Knowledge only can be reused if it is extracted and stored as a single piece of information in the Knowledge Repository. This information can then be used in as many different contexts as necessary, whenever and wherever it is needed. Additionally, in order to track its impact, we must know the relationship that this piece of information has with other similar bits of knowledge in our repository of business knowledge.

For example, if the exchange rate between the U.S. dollar and British pound changes, it could impact several valuations, such as invoice amounts, credit limits, checks, payment amounts, cash on hand, fixed assets overseas, and so on. In other

6.   Normalization is a structured method of representing information in a nonredundant way. The note on normalization describes it in more detail.

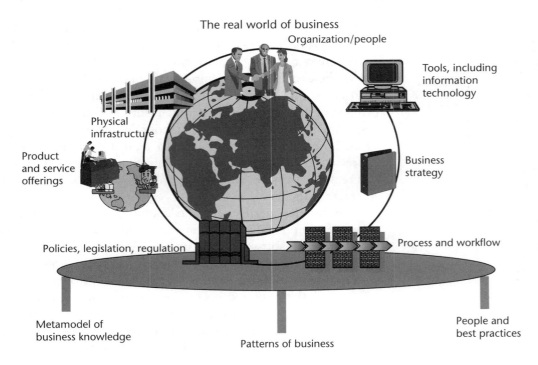

Figure P.1   Reusing business knowledge: the three pillars.

words, we must know the *structure* of information in the real world—that there are interrelated entities, such as processes, resources, work products, units of measure, and so on.

This information about information is called a *metamodel*. The metamodel will provide the scheme for storing business knowledge in a nonoverlapping and nonredundant way. The abstract objects in the metamodel (e.g., process, resource, and unit of measure), and their interrelationships, are containers of nonredundant (normalized) Business Knowledge. Individual Business Knowledge Artifacts would be classified and stored in these buckets provided in the Knowledge Repository.

Specific Knowledge Artifacts can then be extracted from these containers, and assembled into complex business processes and bodies of knowledge around which information systems can be built. The metamodel is the schema of the Knowledge Repository. It is the first pillar on which knowledge reuse stands. Without it, there can be no knowledge components.

The companion book of this series develops the metamodel of business knowledge. Although the metamodel of knowledge is beyond the scope of this book, it lies behind every pattern and ontology of meaning here. They are its polymorphisms.

The Second Pillar: Business Patterns

How many business rules does an enterprise need in order to do business? We know that only a small fraction of business knowledge is explicitly recorded and recognized by most operating businesses. Most business knowledge is implicit. Some are common sense rules that seem foolish to explicitly publish, such as "accept payment

Box 1: Example of the Process Engineering Value Chain

1

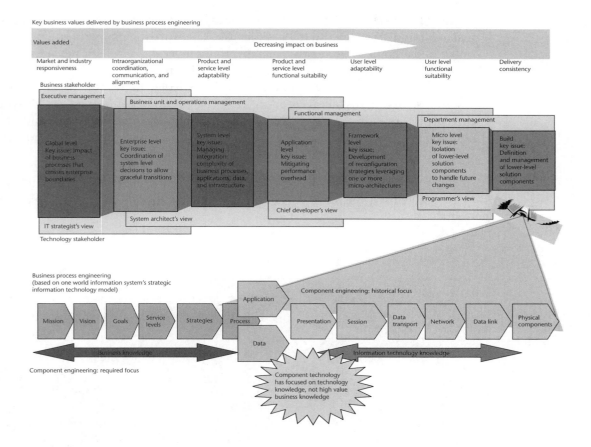

The value chain is derived from Mowbray, T. J., and R. C. Malveau, *CORBA Design Patterns*, New York: John Wiley & Sons, 1997.

"…The supply chain for IT solutions represents the process of technology initiatives, application development, implementation and business use. For example, the supply chain for an ERP system may comprise technology platform selection, systems specifications, systems development, packaging and documentation, implementation, and use in the end user business. The concept of the demand chain, which transfers demand from end users to technology suppliers, is less familiar. To give one example, the demand chain for an ERP may start with business users spotting new opportunities for using the system to support their business. The next link in the chain is the IT department of the user organization looking for potential solutions already in place in the business. In the demand chain of the ERP system, it is the 'missing' process solutions that drive the next stage—a process innovation stage—where new processes and solutions are outlined. The last step in the demand chain is demand for resources and skills needed for using, operating, and developing the ERP system in the user organization over time. . . . What is needed are capabilities to capture an increasing number of business opportunities already in the use … . . the supply chain for IT solutions needs to be managed so that both the current and future applications architecture is scalable, flexible, and modular."

—Jan Holmström and Tiina Tissari,
"IT Value Capture: Creating an Effective Demand-Supply Chain for IT Solutions"

for goods sold," while others might be embedded in the experience or common understanding of the firm's employees, such as "breaking my budget will be a career-limiting move." However, automation has no innate common sense unless it is explicitly built in. Extracting and storing all rules of business, implicit and explicit, for even a small and simple business like a mom-and-pop corner store is not just a daunting task. It is an impossible task. There are too many rules. There can be only one outcome if an analyst attempts to discover *every* rule of business for even the simplest enterprise: *analysis paralysis*. See Figure P.2.

Fortunately there is a solution. The Knowledge Repository is an electronic warehouse that holds an inventory of Knowledge components and facts about how the business operates. Manufacturers and retailers who deal with large and diverse components and product inventories stored in brick and mortar warehouses are familiar with two fundamental laws of inventory management.

1. Only a few kinds of items account for the most frequent movement of inventory. Businesses need the vast majority of other items less frequently.[7]

Rule architecture
-The few universal rules that connect the business of the enterprise

Architecture

Business rules

The few most commonly reused rules

There are too many rules to inventory and common patterns are often lost in this tangled web

Figure P.2   Analysis paralysis: only a few critical rules, reused most often, connect the business of the enterprise, but they are lost in the tangled web of a million rules and details.

7.   Analyses of which items in inventory are needed frequently, and which are needed infrequently, are called ABC analysis. Category A item inventories are the most volatile, and category C are the least volatile.

2. Only a few items (not necessarily those with volatile inventories) are most critical to the business.[8]

Knowledge inventories also follow these laws. Every rule of business need not be extracted and stored before the business can benefit from Knowledge Artifacts. There are only a few critical items of business knowledge that are reused most often. These items can be discovered in common business patterns, which not only orchestrate the internal operations of the enterprise and its many diverse functions, but also connect the enterprise to stake holders across supply and demand chains. This is also the knowledge that is of utmost value to the business, and impacts it maximally! (See Box 1.)

One of the authors was the director of systems architecture for NYNEX, then one of America's largest telecommunications firms. NYNEX was wrestling with the implications of the impending deregulation of the American telecom industry. The author developed information and business architecture for over two decades at leading global corporations, which were in diverse, seemingly unconnected industries—engineering, manufacturing, retail, financial services, insurance, marketing research, advertising, publishing, information services, and others. At another time, when he worked for AIG, a large insurance firm, he identified several fundamental patterns of business that were common to all businesses, regardless of what they produced or where they were located. He found that these common patterns could be applied to the core processes, products, and services of the telecommunications industry as well. Indeed, they even anticipated key changes driven by deregulation, even before users articulated requirements. We will share these fundamental patterns and the frequently reused knowledge artifacts with you in this book.

These patterns are not always obvious to the practitioner, since the practitioner often has to focus too narrowly on a small part of the business. However, as e-commerce and m-commerce begin to shape the business paradigm, it is becoming clear that not only individual corporations, but entire supply chains must compete as coordinated units in order to succeed in the marketplace. Recognizing the critical pieces of frequently used business knowledge that orchestrate not only the business of the enterprise, but also businesses across several enterprises, will be the key to success.

This book will identify these common patterns. The focus can then shift from translating the most critical components of business knowledge into requirements for the design of business processes and information systems, to adding those few components that can truly distinguish the business from its competitors most effectively. This is how Analysis Paralysis can be circumvented. The companion book shows that much of this effort can be automated.

The Third Pillar: People and Best Practices—Managing Change Effectively

Experience has unfailingly demonstrated that any transition is risky. Technology can take quantum leaps, but to effectively utilize new technology, new methods or

---

8. An analysis of how critical items in inventory are to business operations is called 123 analysis. Category 1 items are the most critical to business and category 3 items are the least important.

Figure P.3 Inducting new technology without aligning culture, people, and best practices is risky business!

new processes, organizations, people, skills, and culture must also be realigned. See Figure P.3.

Change cannot be accomplished by quantum jumps when people and organizations are involved. Evolution is key, and the migration path determines risk. The optimal trajectory depends on environmental factors: business drivers, culture, available skills, risk tolerance, and others. This is where organizations usually stumble.

Random or improvised trajectories of change carry a high risk of failure. Change can become chaotic, the credibility of the new technology may erode, and, unless the transition is managed carefully, the organization can even regress to become less capable than before.

Organizations often underestimate the risk of failure. The most common mistake is to try to mitigate risk through staff training or hiring, and acquisition of tools. For this reason, the last part of this book is devoted to managing change.

Although practitioners might find the best practices and themes to implement generic technological change in the last part of this book, that is not the primary purpose of the book. These themes make this book relevant for practitioners who might wish to utilize the technology effectively. They include models for facilitating technological evolution and achieving the level of process maturity that will contribute to effective implementation of the technology proposed here.

How This Book Is Organized

The book is organized into two parts, after an introductory chapter. Part I focuses on shared patterns of business knowledge, and Part II focuses on the best practices to guide technological change. Supplementary materials and references are also available on our Web site.

Reuse of knowledge will flow from the patterns in Part I. Part II has the best practices, priorities, and focus areas needed to leverage and institutionalize this new technology. These have been included because the reusable patterns in this book will change the way we design business processes and develop information systems. Managers who try to transform organizations to leverage new technology usually spread themselves too thin if they do not pick their battles carefully, and more importantly, if they dilute their focus by trying to facilitate everything that needs facilitation. To be successful, they must focus on the most critical issues, which keep changing in step with the organization's readiness to change.[9] Tested and tried reference models to manage technology transformation are described in Part II. Each part stands on its own. You need not read Part I to understand Part II, or vice versa.

To encapsulate business knowledge in common reusable themes, and then to forge components of normalized business information from these themes, we must first understand the concept of knowledge itself—the themes, structures, and abstract information that define knowledge. Only then can we use these structures to describe common components of business knowledge and to automate the design of agile business processes and information systems. Any kind of business knowledge has, as its root, the concept and understanding of Knowledge. Therefore, it is the components in the Metamodel of Knowledge that will be used and reused most often as we forge business knowledge. The companion book, *Creating Agile Business Systems with Reusable Knowledge*, published by Cambridge University Press, describes the Metamodel of Knowledge. This book elaborates on the key components of business knowledge that form the next tier of frequently used themes. It also shares a vision of the future, which the paradigm in this series will eventually lead to. This book is divided into the following chapters.

Preface and Prologue   An introduction to the book: its context, scope, principles, audience, structure, and utility.

PART I

Chapter 1   An introduction to the definition and structure of knowledge, and its reuse in diverse scopes. The purpose of the chapter is to help the reader develop an intuitive understanding of key concepts and semantics without getting lost in technical details. It also serves as an introductory chapter for managers and nontechnical readers who want a broad understanding of the topic.

Chapter 2   The purpose of this chapter is to identify common patterns and the semantics of *business* knowledge, and to demonstrate how these may be configured from components. It demonstrates how business meanings may be derived from other business meanings by adding components, and how these meanings and patterns can be modeled as objects. This chapter consists of four sections.

Section 2.1 describes stock themes, which are reusable subassemblies of business knowledge. It has two parts. The first, Section 2.1.1, describes a business object ontology that demonstrates how adding layers of information may derive business

---

9.   Readers may also see [146, 319, 320].

meanings from one another, whereas the second part, Section 2.1.2, describes a set of universal business interactions between business objects in the ontology, which lead to reusable patterns of business knowledge.

Section 2.2 describes how the stock themes and reusable patterns may be used.

Section 2.3 briefly describes principles for developing work breakdown structures to support this new way of designing systems with reusable patterns of business knowledge.

Section 2.4 describes how business and information systems engineering may be seamlessly integrated and automated by using a shared repository of knowledge. This section also describes the infrastructure that will be required to effectively utilize such a repository.

Chapter 3   This chapter shares a vision of the future with readers. It describes the "Knowledge Machine," a vision of postindustrial business computing that consists of autonomous, self-adapting business models, business processes, and supporting software, all based on a fully automated repository of knowledge configured from components.

PART II

Chapter 4   Chapter 4 and those that follow are for managers who might implement the technology described in this book. This chapter is an introduction to the overall dynamic of change, and how best to manage risk.

Chapter 5   This chapter focuses on the "people" aspect of change, and its risks and solutions.

Chapter 6   Chapter 6 focuses on the process of change and how to govern and institutionalize it, and the evolution of these processes until they are mature enough to harvest the benefits of sharing reusable knowledge.

Epilogue   The epilogue summarizes the benefits of the technology in the book in two scenarios. Using a humorous story, it compares a day in the life of an information systems development manager before and after the technology of automated knowledge components is implemented.

Notes   The notes contain additional technical and background information for the curious or mathematically astute reader. Sometimes they contain suggestions for further reading. They are referenced in the text, and are available on our Web site.

References   This chapter references articles and books [1–337] for those who would like in-depth information or further reading on concepts and ideas that form the basis for those developed in this series of two books.

The other book of the series, *Creating Agile Business Systems with Reusable Knowledge*, published by Cambridge University Press, is the 337th item in the

References. It is referenced in this book as [337]. Auxiliary material is available on our Web site.

Expressing business knowledge in component form and reusing these components draws on a wide variety of areas of active research as well as business experience. The references cover this. We have provided URLs wherever possible to make it easy for readers to access carefully chosen papers and publications on the Web. These URLs are valid at the time of this writing. Most are only a mouse-click away on the Web. However, the Web is forever changing, and we cannot guarantee that these links will always exist.

Boxes   Boxes are embedded within the text of the book. They elaborate on concepts described in the book for readers who might like more detail. These boxes are placed close to the concepts they describe.

PART I

Patterns of Business—Reusable Components of Knowledge

"All was foretold me; naught
Could I foresee;
But I learn'd how the wind would sound
After these things should be."

—Edward Thomas, *The New House*

CHAPTER 1

On Components and the Nature of Reality: Introduction to the Metaworld

This chapter introduces the Metamodel of Knowledge described in the companion book of this series. The intent is to help the reader develop an intuitive understanding of key concepts without getting lost in technical detail. The chapter:

- Describes the emerging need for coordinated business knowledge in software.
- Introduces the concept of normalized knowledge and its configuration from atomic rules or irreducible facts.
- Introduces the concept of behavior, the concept of modeling it, and how knowledge gets replicated in analysis artifacts.
- Introduces fundamental components of the metamodel and their roles in normalizing knowledge:
  - Objects, Relationships, Processes, and Events as repositories for behavior;
  - Domains and their role in measuring, normalizing, storing, and expressing information.
- Introduces the problem of multiple clashing perspectives as a fundamental problem in categorizing real world business information.

Does an arcane discussion on the nature of reality really have a place in a book on information systems? True, the full tapestry of reality in all its richness is better left to philosophers, but we must understand how the real world structures meaning, since meaning is the foundation of information, and knowledge bereft of information is just an empty word. Meaning is the foundation of the metamodel of knowledge.

"And moving thro' the mirror clear
That hangs before her all the year,
Shadows of the world appear.
There she sees the highway near
Winding down to Camelot."

—Lord Tennyson, *The Lady of Shalott*

Even so, why do we, as engineers and practitioners of information systems, need this arcane discussion, when we have built systems, and built them well for over half a century? Why do we need to step into uncharted waters when we have ready experience with tried and tested techniques that have served us well?

Experience is increasingly under pressure from ideation, innovation, and the demands of scope scale and agility as we forge a global economy driven by knowledge (see Figure 1.1). The world we have known is changing, and with the coming of the information age, it will surely change at the speed of thought. Yesterday's paradigms are fading ever more rapidly. Our reach has become global, and our businesses have become bigger and more complex by quantum leaps; technology is making yesterday's impossibility today's imperative.

As we have grown, so have our customers become less forgiving and more fickle. Loyalty can only be bought with performance, and even then, it may be lost as quickly as it was bought. Customers' expectations are high, and standards stringent, yet the scale, scope, and complexity of our systems have grown ever larger. Our employees and partners cannot deliver without automation. E-commerce and m-commerce are here, and even as customers' expectations rise, they interface more with automation than with people.

The methods we have used in the past worked in a smaller, simpler age. Old approaches still hold the line many times, but that line is beginning to fray. More and more, the tried and true are giving way under the demands of scale, scope, and agility that are becoming the keynote of business.

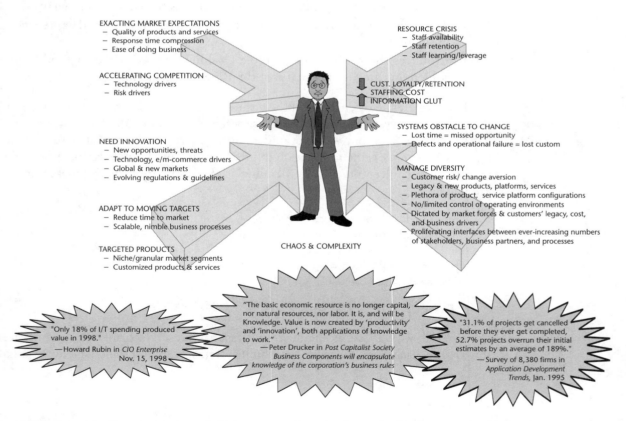

Figure 1.1 Increasingly, past experience is under pressure from the demands of scale, scope, and agility that businesses are placing on systems.

In the Prologue, we described why it has become imperative for business to thrive on change, while systems have become the principal obstacle to the very change that is the lifeblood of business. Businesses pay a price for this. The price is often much more than just the cost of maintaining and revamping systems. Real costs are measured by the cost of opportunities lost or delayed, revenues lost, market shares and competitive standing eroded, goodwill not realized, customers not satisfied, and much more.

Systems are an obstacle to agile and adaptive business practices principally because change has a domino effect on systems. Changes explosively and chaotically ricochet through the system, each impact of which must be managed and resolved before the change can take effect. In many large and complex systems prevalent today, this is not just a difficult task, it is an impossible task. Defects are often discovered and resolved long after applications have gone live and the damage done. We have known situations when, without the supplier's consent or knowledge, savvy customers changed product prices on e-commerce applications. Once a toxic chemical was mislabeled and shipped to the wrong destination because of a defect in a computerized application. This happens because business rules are not normalized, and business knowledge is repeated in multiple ways in several places, all of which should be, but are not always, coordinated.

What is Knowledge and how can we coordinate it? How can we adapt to moving targets as businesses constantly flex and maneuver for competitive advantage? The answer, paradoxically, lies in the real world in which we live, not in computer systems. The natural, or real world, frames all business opportunities, threats, goals, strategies, and operations. All businesses are bound by not only the laws of nations, but also by the immutable laws of nature. Therefore, we must look at the structure of knowledge in the real world, where knowledge is naturally normalized. Knowledge gets fragmented and replicated only when we store information about the real world in our systems, designs, and artifacts.[10] The solution then is to reflect knowledge and business rules in systems as they are in the real world. To do so, we must first understand the nature of reality and the nature of Knowledge.

1.1   The Nature of Knowledge

Knowledge is meaning. It is the meanings of goals, policies, and practices, and how they fit together into a cogent whole. Figure 1.2 shows how this was said has changed, but what was said has not. This meaning has endured the passage of 1,300 years across a sea change of time and a panorama of ages.

Knowledge conveys information about the business environment. Knowledge conveys information about how business goals and guidelines are coordinated with business opportunities and operations. Knowledge conveys information about how the business' products and processes are aligned with business mandates and markets. Knowledge conveys information about breach and recovery—which rules to follow and which to dilute; and what can be safely ignored, and what must be ignored. Knowledge conveys information about how practices and people

10.   See Box 2.

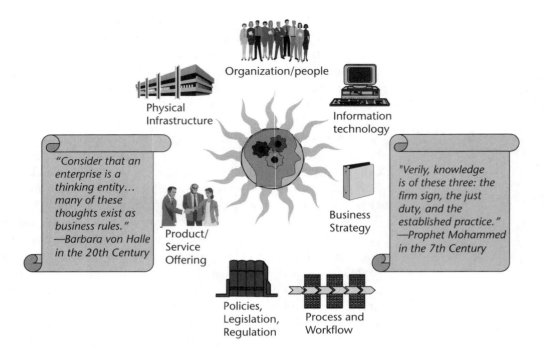

Figure 1.2 Knowledge is the meaning of business practices, rules, goals, and guidelines, and how they fit into an integrated whole.

coordinate resources and requirements. Knowledge is information about customers and competition, about business constraints and configurations.

Thus, knowledge is coordinated information about how rules of business, imposed by man or nature, expressed explicitly or understood implicitly, called policy, common sense, culture, or collective wisdom, can mutually orchestrate the business. Knowledge is how this symphony of information moves business towards its goals, helps it achieve its minor successes and crowning glories, and occasionally creates minor embarrassment, or even catastrophic failure. Yes, knowledge is not only about what to do, how to do it, and when to do it, but also about what not to do, how not to do it, and when not to do it. Thus, knowledge is an orchestra of rules in harmony, guided by meaning and rationale.

Rules are assertions. Knowledge is the configurations of rules and reasons. Rules may be simple or complex, they may stand alone, or they may include several other rules and caveats. Rules carry information about the business. Together, they orchestrate knowledge. Business rules convey the components of information that we can assemble into configurations of knowledge and best practices.

Engineers build complex machinery. Architects build complex facilities. Both build large and complex things from simple parts. They are familiar with techniques that divide and conquer complexity. They know that complex things must be made from simple ones. Small and simple components must be first tested and assembled into subassemblies, which in turn should be retested and assembled into even more complex components. These then might fit into yet larger components, and so on, until the end product is finally assembled.

Business knowledge is also complex and requires the same approach, but there is an added complication. Knowledge is intangible. Unlike buildings, bridges, and machine parts, components of knowledge cannot be seen or felt.

The first step towards forging components of knowledge is understanding which assertions we can divide without losing information and which will lead to loss of meaning or knowledge. If, by breaking an assertion into smaller parts, we lose information that we cannot recover by reassembling the pieces into a "subassembly of knowledge," then we have gone too far. We will call these indivisible rules atomic rules or irreducible facts.[11]

Take, for example, the assertion:

Jenny is a woman who has a son named Michael.

The truth of this statement can be expressed in two smaller and simpler statements without any loss of meaning:

1. Jenny is a woman.
2. Jenny has a son named Michael.

Taken together, they can only, and uniquely, mean that "Jenny is a woman who has a son named Michael." and nothing else. Therefore, "Jenny is a woman who has a son named Michael" is not an atomic (or irreducible) fact. Its meaning can be fully derived from the meanings of two other simpler assertions about Jenny.

Now let us go one step further and try to break the assertion about Jenny into three smaller, and even simpler, assertions.

1. Jenny is a woman.
2. Jenny has a son.
3. A son is named Michael.

At first glance, it might seem that these three assertions together can only mean "Jenny is a woman who has a son named Michael," but they do not—not really. The three bald assertions tell us only three things: (1) Jenny is a woman, (2) she has a son, and (3) somebody's son, not necessarily Jenny's, is named Michael. We have lost information: that Jenny's son's name is Michael. We lost Jenny's son's name when we tried to break "Jenny has a son named Michael" into smaller, simpler components, because that assertion was an irreducible fact or atomic rule.

What do irreducible facts have to do with managing change? Irreducible facts have everything to do with managing change because they are at the root of coordinated requirements. Normalized knowledge will help coordinate requirements in today's complex corporations and cross-company supply chains. Change has a domino effect that radiates chaotically through the system because the same irreducible facts are scattered chaotically, with little control or even awareness, through our software.

---

11. These are called *atomic rules* (Ronald Ross [294]) or *irreducible facts* (G. M. Nijssen in [297]) because they cannot be divided without losing information. Reference [252] has an advanced discussion on coordination of rules.

Knowledge (meaning) is not replicated in the natural world (i.e., it is normalized), whereas in today's information systems, it may be fragmented and replicated. In present-day systems, irreducible facts, the basic building blocks of knowledge, may be replicated and unsynchronized in different applications, in requirements recorded in different forms, in design artifacts, in databases "help" files, and in deliverables, so much so that it is sometimes unrecognizable as the same root knowledge. Therein lies the problem, as we shall see in the two examples that follow.

A customer orders voice mail services from a telephone company. The company adds the service to the customer's record and starts charging the customer. The firm must also reprogram telephone switches to activate the service. The software that instructs the switch does not recognize voice mail services. Now there is not just an unhappy customer who has been billed for services not provided, but also an unhappy phone company that is spending time and incurring the high cost of skilled human resources needed to service an irate customer.

Voice mail is a feature of telephone service is an irreducible fact. You cannot break it into simpler assertions without losing information. Voice mail is a service offering that was recognized by the billing system, but not by the service provisioning system. Knowledge was not normalized, hence requirements were not coordinated in the phone company's systems. That was the root of the problem. (In Chapter 2, we will examine irreducible facts that describe products and services in more detail.)

Let us take a more complex example, where consequences were less serious because customers were not directly impacted, but opportunity costs were incurred. Opportunities for integrating systems in compressed time frames and budgets were lost, and the firm was not even aware that it could have spent less and implemented new service offerings faster.

John was a deliveryman. He worked for "Zippy" Courier Company. Zippy's scheduling system downloaded his delivery route to John's palm computer at the beginning of each workday. Sometimes delivery priorities changed, or Zippy's Command Central, which coordinated deliveries, received information about traffic congestion on parts of John's route. Depending on which deliverymen are where, they reorganized delivery routes and schedules, downloaded changes, alerted their deliverymen by wireless link, alerted their customers to revised timing by telephone, and informed Warehouse Operations of these changes.

Zippy's also had a sophisticated facility in the warehouse for sorting and loading packages onto delivery trucks. Which package was allocated to which truck depended on the final destination of the package and the route of the truck. Sometimes containers or trucks were full before all packages for that route were loaded. These were then loaded on other trucks that might cover similar routes. Warehouse Operations informed Command Central when that happened.

Zippy used two very different systems for two very different applications. Yet both scheduled deliveries, one over roads to geographic addresses, and the other over conveyor belts, picking, packing, and staging systems, to trucks. Both could use multiple routes to deliver their shipments, and in both, routes could sometimes be filled to capacity.

Many scheduling and routing requirements were common between the two systems, but when Zippy improved Command Central's scheduling algorithms,

Warehouse Operations neither knew nor cared, let alone take advantage of the improvements. This was an opportunity cost that was completely hidden from Zippy's Management.

Then Zippy's delivery scheduling system was enhanced to allow customers a facility for special instructions that would facilitate coordinated delivery of two different packages from different pickup points to a common destination. Customers could ask that there be no more than a day's gap in their arrival. Zippy's loading system could have added a new business rule that deferred items must not wait more than a day to be loaded onto a truck that would cover the required delivery address. It was the same atomic rule masquerading as a different requirement for a different system. This was not done, and the new service commitments were harder to satisfy. Consistency and reliability of service suffered while Command Central's operations became more complicated.

The state of the art made it very difficult for Zippy to use the software and design artifacts of one system to change the other. This is true of most firms today. Changes come harder and improvements take longer, at a higher cost than necessary.

The root of both Zippy's and the phone company's problems was not malfunctioning technology. The hardware, software, and networks performed according to design. The problem was uncoordinated requirements. The systems development process did not normalize, or leverage normalized knowledge, to coordinate requirements. Nor did the process seek to save time and development cost through knowledge reuse. Systems professionals could say, with some justification, that the requirements they were given were incomplete, but the bottom line was that the systems failed the customer and the company.

They failed because the firms were too large, and their operations so automated, that coordination of knowledge across the firm was complex. Systems failed because knowledge was not reflected in systems as it was in the real world where meaning is unique, and its expression naturally coordinated at the root. Knowledge, like matter and energy, frames reality and is framed by it. The real world of immutable meaning automatically normalizes knowledge. Thus, the real world becomes the yardstick for success and failure of automation. To reflect knowledge in our artifacts, as it exists in the real world, we must first understand reality, and how reality structures meaning and information. After all, reality frames the artifacts we create.

1.2   Modeling the Real World

"Understand that as the mighty wind, blowing everywhere, rests always in the sky, all created beings rest in Me."

—Translated from the *Bhagvat Gita*, the holy book
of Hinduism by Swami Prabhupada

We will open the discussion on the nature of reality with an extreme and radical assertion: We assert that in the real world there is no such thing as data, and no such thing as process. There is only behavior. Data and Process are mere artifices we have created in order to represent information about the manifest behavior of real world objects.

Having said this, we will ask you to do something so simple that you have probably forgotten how to do it—become a child once more.

What is behavior? You knew that long before you even learned to read—long before you knew of process, data, or normalization—if you hit a sheet of glass, it will shatter. Hit a sheet of metal, it will ring. Hit hard, and it may bend.

Behavior is how an object in the real world responds to a stimulus (or event). Behavior involves events, constraints, rules, location, and shape; but most of all, it involves change, and change involves time. Step back then, to that time long ago, when you knew only about objects you could see, the events that influenced them, and the flow of time, and we will be ready to model reality.

It is important to remember that models are not reality. They only represent reality in a limited scope. The real world is too complex a tapestry to represent fully in all its richness and intricacy. A model represents limited information about reality in a repeatable, consistent, and accurate manner. The scope of the model is circumscribed by the real world behaviors it targets. The reliability and accuracy of the model are circumscribed by the range of error or inconsistency we will tolerate—tolerances in terms of deviations from repeatedly consistent accurate predictions of target behaviors.

Box 2: Example of a Model for Baking a Cookie   2

This model demonstrates:

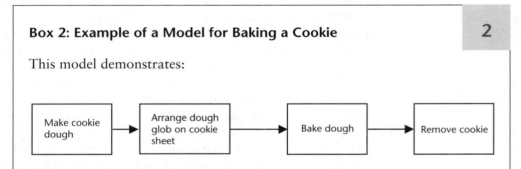

1. How limited a model is compared to reality;
2. How easily knowledge becomes denormalized in artifacts, which must then be coordinated.

The scope of this model is restricted to presenting information about a sequence of a select set of events involved in making cookies. The arrows show a succession of events. The event at the end of an arrowhead cannot occur until the event at the beginning of that arrow has happened. Thus, we cannot bake dough unless we have put a glob of dough on the cookie sheet.

Events like starting the oven, acquiring the cookie dough, and eating the cookie are beyond the scope of this model. The behavior of the dough, such as shaping into globs, hardening under heat, and its color and fragrance are also out of this scope.

The information in the model could also have been expressed in a different syntax. For example, instead of a set of labeled boxes connected with arrows, the sequence and constraints could have been written in English sentences. That would not change the model or its meaning. It would only change the

> syntax, or technique, of expressing information. The information and
> its meaning would be exactly the same in both expressions.
>
> Although the meaning and information are identical in the two
> syntaxes, there are now two artifacts, or deliverables, with the same informa-
> tion, or meaning. To be consistent, the two must be coordinated. This is an
> example of how easily the information and meaning of a single real world phe-
> nomenon can be replicated in our records. If one changes, the other too must
> change. By repeating information in two different artifacts, we have just
> denormalized real world knowledge about baking cookies, and made change
> more complex. We did not even try. It just happened.

2

1.3   Metaworld of Information

> "He is distant in his nearness and near in his distance. He fashions 'how,' so it is not
> said of him 'How?' He determines the where, so it is not said of him 'Where?' He
> sunders 'How' from 'Where,' so He is One—the Everlasting Refuge."
>
> —*Qu'ran*, 112:1-2

To normalize and reflect real-world knowledge in our systems as it is normalized in
the real world, we must understand and model its structure.

1.3.1   Objects, Relationships, Processes, and Events

Let us start by examining the nature of the model in Box 2. We can almost hear you
say that we just contradicted ourselves. We asserted there was no such thing as process in the real world, and almost in the same breath drew processes in Box 2. You
might contend that each box, connected by arrows in the model in Box 2, actually
represents a process. You are absolutely right! However, we are not being inconsistent, and this is why.

We have already seen that objects and their observed behavior manifest reality. In
the real world, objects can, and do, influence each other. The hammer can hit glass
and break it. The dough, the oven, and the cook together bake the dough glob into a
cookie. Buildings are located in geographies. Thus, one or more objects acting in
concert with each other make the real world and orchestrate its behavior. In other
words, objects relate to each other. Some of these relationships, such as baking the
cookie, involve the passage of time, while others, such as the location of the building, are assertions that do not involve time.

These relationships are natural repositories for certain kinds of behaviors of
real world objects acting in concert. Thus, they are also objects in their own right.
For example, we could interrupt and stop "Bake Cookie" before the cookie is fully
baked. This is how Bake Cookie, the object, behaves. Similarly, the same person
may become an employee through an employment relationship with an organization, and a spouse via a marital relationship with another person. In addition to
behaviors common to Persons in general, such as breathing and growing older,

Employees and Spouses can have special behaviors. For example, spouses may get divorced and employees may be promoted.

Processes are artifacts for expressing information about the behavior of those relationships that involve the passage of time (i.e., involve before and after effects). For example, the "Bake Cookie" object in Figure 1.3 captures the information carried by the "Bake Cookie" relationship.

Not only does Bake Cookie relate six objects in the model—"Dough," "Oven," Cookie Sheets new and used, the Cook, and the Cookie—it also sequences them. The object "Bake Cookie" tells us that the objects to the left in Figure 1.3, namely, the Dough, the Oven, a New Cookie Sheet, and the Cook, must precede the existence of objects to the right, namely, the Cookie and the Used Cookie Sheet. Bake Cookie is a process only because it carries information about a temporal sequence. Processes are thus special kinds of relationships that contain sequencing information, in addition to being objects in their own right.

What triggers behavior? What starts a process? We all know that events do.[12] Objects respond to events [166], and their response is behavior. The hammer hit the glass to break it. The hammer strike was an event. Something triggered the bake cookie process. It might have been that the chef asked the cook to start. Thus the chef's request may have been the trigger. In Box 2, the end of the preceding process, Make Cookie Dough, triggered the process, Arrange Dough Gob on Cookie Sheet. These triggers are events.

An event is an occurrence that, unlike a process, may transform nothing. Processes, like events, occur in time, but all processes have a distinct beginning, a finite duration, followed by a distinct end. Events, on the other hand may never end. Processes always make change or seek information. Business process engineers often call the time interval from the beginning to the end of a process its cycle time. A process can even be instantaneous, but it must end. An event may go on forever. For instance, a deep space probe like the Pioneer will climb forever into interstellar

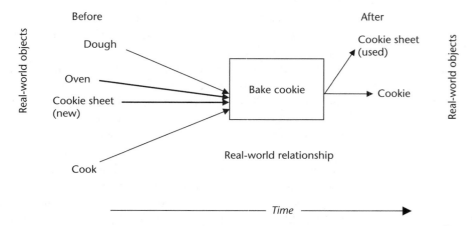

Figure 1.3 Processes specify a special kind of relationship. They carry information on "before and after" effects between objects.

---

12. Objects may sometimes exhibit spontaneous behavior. Spontaneous behavior is not triggered by any obvious external event. For example, stock prices may move at random from minute to minute. Spontaneous changes are also events.

space. A process may thus be considered a special kind of event—one that makes change in a finite time interval. Of course, processes may also be instantaneous, like a blip in time with zero duration. The concept of event subsumes the concept of process, even an instantaneous process. We all know that anything that happens in the real world must take some time, even if the time taken is infinitesimally small. For example, the chef would take a few seconds to vocalize his instruction to start baking cookies. However, for modeling purposes, we can consider that the cook's request is a zero duration occurrence, or in other words, both an event and a process.

Events are important because they trigger actions, processes, and behavior. For example, the cook might hit the stop button on the oven and interrupt the Bake Dough process in Box 2. Hitting the stop button would then be the event that suspended the Bake Dough process. Remember that processes are special kinds of objects. Thus, hitting the stop button was an event that triggered specific behavior of the Bake Dough object. Two key events implicit in the model in Box 2 are the start and the end of a process. It is important to bear in mind that these two events, the start and the end of a process, are implicit, intrinsic, and inalienably associated with the existence of every process. These concepts are discussed in much more detail in *Creating Agile Business Systems with Reusable Knowledge*, published by Cambridge University Press.

1.3.2 Perception and Information, Naturally Speaking: Domains, Units of Measure, and Formats

What is the nature of information manifest in the behavior of reality? What is the relationship between the information intrinsic in reality and its perception through our senses? Is it an exotic, abstruse, and arcane discussion (see Figure 1.4)? Perhaps, but it is critically important to normalizing business rules, as we shall see. The example in Box 2 shows us that meaning must be separated from its expression if we must normalize knowledge.

We need a home for meaning to ensure that business rules that involve meaning are normalized. For this, we must look beyond physical objects and relationships. We must look at how reality structures the information it contains. To do this, we must augment our metamodel to represent additional entities beyond physical

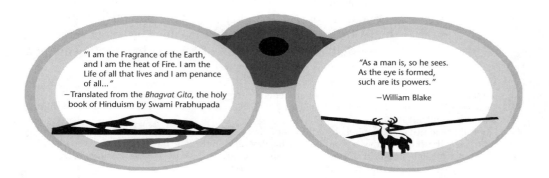

Figure 1.4 How is information naturally manifest in the real world?

objects and relationships. In this section, we will add three new entities to our metamodel: Domain, Unit of Measure (UOM), and Format.

Information exists in the real world, as do matter and energy, but the rules are different. Matter might be more tangible, but no one today will argue that energy is in any way less real or natural than matter is. This was not always true. It took humanity a thousand years to reach that conclusion,[13] and even longer to realize that matter and energy may be expressed in different forms, but cannot be created or destroyed. Information is even more abstract and its laws more complex, but information is no less real than matter or energy. It is only manifested in the behavior of real objects and physical energy.

Unlike matter or energy, meaning is not located at a particular place in space and time. Only its *expression* is.[14] Thus, in the example of Box 2, the same meaning was found in two different artifacts that had no spatial or temporal relationship with each other. Their only relationship was in their shared meaning, or information content.[15] Although meaning in its true sense (and hence the information it conveys) does not occupy space and is immutable in time, it is ironic that we can only know meaning from information expressed and observed in the physical world framed by space, time, and real world objects. A single meaning may have many expressions.[16] Thus, the information stored on printed paper in a filing cabinet, as well as on the hard disk of a computer should be the same; the Spanish and English versions of the owner's manual of your car (should) contain the same information; and the Japanese Prime Minister's speech at the UN should have the same meaning or information as its English translation.[17]

This is a fundamental difference between Information on one hand, and Matter and Energy on the other. The same information can exist at many different places and times, whereas a specific material object, or packet of energy, can exist at only a single location at any given moment in time.[18]

Matter or energy mediates our observation of information. We can only observe the behavior of reality manifested in the behavior of objects located in space and time. This is a very important concept, and we will repeat it again. The information carried by meaning is nonlocal (i.e., it is independent of space and time), whereas specific physical objects like documents, bits of energy, screwdrivers, and people, are local (i.e., they exist in a particular place at any given moment in time). To normalize business rules, it is critical that we understand the natural structures that connect information to its physical expression(s).

What mediates information and its expression in the physical world? There are two meta-objects that do this. One is intangible. It deals with the quantum of information[19] that is intrinsic to the meaning being conveyed, and is closely tied to nature (we shall call it the domain of information, or domain for short), while the other is

---

13. See the note on how the twin concepts of matter and energy were developed.
14. Shannon's Information Theory described in the Notes measures the *quantum* of information. Meanings *structure* information. The two concepts complement each other.
15. Physical phenomena linked purely by information that just *is*, as opposed to information transmitted spatially and temporally by messages, were illustrated by the Aspect Experiments described in the note on messages between objects.
16. This concept can be confusing: In our metamodel, *meaning*, *expression*, and the *quantum of information* are separate objects.
17. See the note on how information relates to physical objects.
18. See the note on the locale of matter and energy.
19. The note on Shannon's information theory discusses the measure of information.

more tangible—it is the format or the physical form of expression. It is easy to recognize the format, and many tools and techniques have done so explicitly. It is much harder to be aware of domain,[20,21] but nature does not care about what we know. Domain just is. If we did not know or care, and combined domain with format,[22] it will come back to haunt us in the form of replicated business rules and inflexible software. Let us see how.

"The curtains seem to part;
A sound is on the stair,
As if at the last . . . I start;
Only the wind is there."

—Bliss Carman, *A Northern Vigil*

A Parable of Jim, Jane, Jugs of Milk, and Robert in the United States of Information

The information content of reality manifests itself to us through the behavior, or properties, of objects we observe. For example, people have birthdays; they age, prefer some colors more than others on their cars, or have a gender that determines certain physical attributes, such as the ability to bear children. Let us take a completely different object, for example, a jug of milk. It stores milk. You can measure the amount of milk in the jug. You can quantify both your age and the volume of milk stored in the jug with numbers that describe their individual magnitudes.

Your intuition tells you that in some sense, the values of both these very dissimilar qualities of very dissimilar objects (i.e., a person's age and the volume of milk stored in a jug) are defined on a domain of information that contains some common behavior; not of the objects themselves, but of the information conveyed "in" (not "by") the act of measurement. That is, each quality can be quantitatively measured. Another example of such a quality shared by disparate objects is temperature. We can measure the temperature of all three: the jug, the milk, and people. Your intuition is right. Let us understand the kind of information, or behavior, that domains naturally normalize by comparing the amount of information intrinsically conveyed by each of these qualities of people and jugs of milk.

Nominal Domains   Let us start with gender. We know that it only conveys that men are different from women, and nothing else. It has no information on how men and women can be arranged in any natural order, nor does gender carry any quantitative information on differences between men and women.

When we store this information on a physical medium, we could choose to arbitrarily represent "male" with a numeric code 1, and "female" with 2. If my friend Robert, a professional and dedicated mad scientist devoted to divining the true nature of things, then claimed that men precede women because the number 1 precedes 2,[23] we would know that Robert's claim is meaningless, because the domain on which gender is naturally defined has no information about sequence.

---

20. See the note on the mathematical theory of categories.
21. Mathematical discussions on generic domains can be found in several mathematical and engineering texts, including [308]. References [232–235] also describe sets, domains, and functions.
22. Many CASE tools and professional publications combine *domain* and format together and call the composition "domain." In this book, we will distinguish between the two. Readers will not be confused if they remember this.
23. This is called "coercive polymorphism." See the notes on polymorphism and the Mathematical Theory of Categories.

This will always be true, regardless of how we physically express or code the information: It is also meaningless to subtract 1 from 2 to find the amount by which men and women differ, or to divide 1 by 2 to find the proportion of difference. The domain just does not have that information. It has nothing to do with how the information is physically expressed. What does not intrinsically exist cannot be expressed; you cannot squeeze blood from a stone.

Domains like this, which contain just enough information to classify objects based on their properties or relationships, are called Nominally Scaled Domains, or Nominal Domains,[24] for short.

Ordinal Domains   Next consider a person's color preference for cars. If the cars are identical in every other way, Jane likes blue cars more than green and red, and cares even less for black cars. She really has no preference between green and red cars, if all else is equal.

She agrees to participate in a consumer survey of preferred colors of cars. First, Jim, the researcher, asks her to rank the four car colors in order of preference, starting with the color she likes most. That is easy: blue first, followed by red and green at par, and black at the end. So far, she has no trouble.

Next, Jim asks her to quantify how much she likes each color by assigning a number to each. Now Jane has a problem. She does not know how to respond. She knows that she should give blue the highest score, followed by an equal score for green and red, and a lower score for black, but what should these scores be? She has no idea. All she knows is that she likes blue more than green and red, that she likes green and red equally, and black least, but cannot quantify her liking. The information is just not there.

The domain on which Jane defines her preference for color of cars intrinsically and naturally contains sequencing, or ranking information, but no information about magnitudes. Should Jim insist, she might quote some numbers, but these numbers will convey no information beyond Jane's ranking of color preferences for cars.[25] It does not matter how Jim codes her color preference: with numbers, letters, colors, or graphic icons.

Domains like this, which have no quantitative information, but do convey enough information to arrange objects in some sequence or order, are called Ordinal Domains.[26]

Note that, because she can rank cars in order of color preference, Jane can automatically group cars into separate groups (e.g., green and red cars would be grouped together; the criterion is her color preference, not the actual color of the car). However, if she just groups, but does not rank, cars in order of color preference, then she is withholding information from Jim. This shows that Ordinal Domains intrinsically carry more information than Nominal Domains.[27] They carry sequencing information as well as, by implication, classification information.

---

24. See *discrete distance* in the note on metric space for more information.
25. See coercive polymorphism in the Notes.
26. Reference [211] has mathematical detail on ordinal measurement.
27. Shannon's information theory in the Notes describes the mathematical measure of information.

Box 3: Objects, Domains, and Formats

3

Domains carry meaning. Formats are how information is physically presented to a person, system, or instrument.[28]

For example, gender may be formatted, with a numeric code such as "1" for "Male" and "2" for "Female," or "M" for "Male" and "F" for "Female." It may be spelled out in written or spoken (where technology supports multimedia) English words—"Male" and "Female," or in another language. It may even be graphic icons or pictures, static or moving, of a man or woman, or any other physical expression. All these are examples of FORMAT, the physical expression(s) of meaning, not meaning itself.

Objects and Domains together convey meaning. Objects frame the context of the meaning conveyed by domains (to be described with more precision later). For example, the meaning of the fact that objects may be female (carry progeny), male (fertilize females to enable them to have offspring), or neuter (neither), is conveyed by the domain alone. A common domain thus normalizes the common meaning and behavior of gender across objects like people, plants, dogs, deer, and other living things. An object, such as a person or an animal, puts this generic behavior into context, giving it a specific meaning[29] for that kind or instance of animal.

Thus, there may be male and female people, parts of flowers, dogs, spiders, cats, and so forth. This conveys the fact that a property, "gender," of a class of objects called "Persons" (or parts of flowers, dogs, spiders, cats, and so forth), maps to the gender domain, with the restriction that only a male or female gender is allowed for an instance of this object. It records an irreducible fact, that people must be either male or female. Similarly, other classes of objects, such as dogs, spiders, parts of flowers, and so forth, would map to the gender domain with the same restriction—an irreducible fact about these objects.

Each earthworm, on the other hand, must be both male and female, because each earthworm may carry and fertilize earthworm eggs.[30] This is also an atomic rule or irreducible fact. Each object thus provides the context of maleness and/or femaleness (or neither), whereas the domain is the bucket for recording the common meaning of maleness, femaleness, or neutrality.

Sometimes more than one property of an object may map to the same domain. Each will represent a distinct irreducible fact needed to represent the real world. For example, the length, breadth, and height of a room all map to the length domain. The domain normalizes the facts that these three properties of room can have the same units of measure, which have the same conversion factors. Thus, they need not be repeated for each property. The same logic

---

28. Called *actor* in the language of object technology, or *observer* in the parlance of physics. Readers interested in more information about actors may refer to books on UML, or the resources in the References. The Universal Modeling Language (UML) is becoming the de facto standard. The Object Management Group and Rational Corporation are strong advocates of UML. See also Rational Corporation's Web resources in the References.
29. See polymorphism in the note on the Mathematical Theory of Categories for more information.
30. See the note on The Question of Gender.

> holds when different properties of very different kinds of objects map to the same domain. For example, people's heights and lengths of rooms both map to the length domain, which provides the common home for their units of measure and conversion rules between units of length.   **3**

Now suppose that Jim, frustrated by Jane's inability to quantify her preferences, assigns some kind of number to her preferences—say, for arguments sake, the rank that Jane assigned to each color (1 to blue, 2 to red and green, and 3 to black).

We know that it would be pure nonsense for Jim to conclude on this basis that Jane likes blue cars three times more than she likes black cars. Nor can Jim conclude that the gap, or difference, in Jane's preference between blue and red cars is equal to the gap between red and black cars. The domain simply does not have this information.

Difference Scaled Domains   Let us consider Jim's and Jane's temperatures next. Jim liked Jane, and asked her to stay for lunch. After lunch, they went to Domain's Metaphysical Diner for a cup of good Colombian coffee. Robert, the mad scientist, happened to be drinking coffee at the next table. Robert was researching the true meaning of temperature, and had a superb collection of thermometers of every kind in his briefcase.

Mr. Domain took great pride in his special coffees, and always served coffee with a separate warm jug of milk for each customer. Jane found that the new waitress had accidentally served her chilled milk in the jug. Robert overheard Jane, and sprang up with missionary zeal to ask if he could address any issues with Jane's and Jim's milk. Mistaking him for the new waiter, Jane graciously accepted.

Robert immediately flung open his briefcase and extracted two high-tech digital thermometers, a scientific calculator, and an elegant notebook. Without further delay, he plunged a thermometer into each jug, did a quick calculation, and declared that Jim's milk was twice as warm as Jane's.

Jenny, the waitress, was piqued, and asked Robert how he knew. "Simple," Robert explained. "Look at the display of each thermometer. Jane's shows 40 degrees Fahrenheit, and Jim's shows 80 degrees Fahrenheit. Eighty is twice as large as 40, and that proves that Jim's milk is twice as hot as Jane's."

"Also," said Robert, to show off his high-tech thermometers and impress Jenny with his erudition, "these thermometers can show you the temperature in either Fahrenheit or Celsius at the touch of a button! Always be sure that you use the same units of measure for both jugs, otherwise you will not be comparing like readings." He hit two identical buttons on the thermometers, and the temperature of Jane's jug of milk read, "4.44 degrees Celsius" and Jim's read "26.67 degrees Celsius."

"Look what you have done now!" Jenny complained. "You made Jim's milk more than six times hotter than Jane's. 26.7 divided by 4.44 is more than 6!"

"I did not," Robert retorted. "I just changed my unit of measurement."

"Sir!" exclaimed Jim. "My temperature is rising as well! We want to drink our coffee in peace. All we need is a fresh jug of warm milk for Jane, or she may use some of mine."

"Impossible!" cried Robert. "Your temperature can only rise if you are sick, or if the mechanism for regulating your temperature cannot cope with the extreme heat of summer! See, my remote sensing thermometer can even sense your temperature from a distance, and it shows that you are holding at a steady 98.4 degrees Fahrenheit."

Fortunately, Mr. Domain arrived just then. "What's the fuss about?" he asked Jenny. Jenny, almost in tears by now, cried, "Robert just made Jim's milk six times warmer than Jane's by measuring its temperature in Celsius rather than Fahrenheit! It was only twice as hot before!"

"Now, ladies and gentlemen, let us be civilized about this," said Mr. Domain, fixing Robert with a specially penetrating glare. "I happen to know all your birthdays. You, Jenny, were born on January 1, 1977. It is now 2001. That makes you twenty-four years old. Your daughter was born on January 1, 1995. That makes her six years old. I can also calculate that there was an eighteen-year gap between the date of your birth and that of your daughter's."

"Now, what would I learn by dividing the date on which you were born by the date on which your daughter was born?" They thought hard about it. No one had an answer.

"Well, there you are," said Mr. Domain triumphantly. "You would learn nothing. It is meaningless to divide one date by another."

"But why?" asked Robert, quite intrigued by Mr. Domain's question.

"Simple, Robert," answered Mr. Domain. "You, of all my guests here, should know. The date domain has no information on ratios because it has no natural zero. The zero hour for the Gregorian calendar (the 'normal' calendar most commonly used in the Western Hemisphere) was arbitrarily set. You can certainly measure the difference between any two dates as I just did. The unit of measurement is your choice—days, years, minutes, hours, seconds, or any other measure of time—but ratios are meaningless. The domain just does not have the information if it has no natural zero. You cannot wring blood from a stone!"

"Ah!" exclaimed Robert, a new light dawning in his eager eyes. "So it is meaningless to take the ratio of temperatures as well! After all, zero degrees Celsius was arbitrarily set at the temperature at which water freezes, as was 32 degrees Fahrenheit."

"That is correct," Mr. Domain replied, addressing both Jenny and Robert, "so it was meaningless to say that Jim's milk is hotter than Jane's by any multiple, be it two, six, or anything else.[31] However, you can say that the difference in temperature is 40 degrees Fahrenheit, or 22.27 degrees Celsius." To make it less embarrassing for Robert, he added, "You were right about the Unit of Measure. When you talk of magnitudes of differences, you must express them in some units of measure, otherwise they are meaningless. There can be a wide choice of units, but you must choose one."

"Domains like this, which convey information on classification, order (or sequence), and the magnitudes of gaps (or differences) between points in sequence, but no information on ratios or proportions, are called Difference Scaled Domains."[32]

---

31. Chapter 4, Section 3, of [337] addresses the information content of ratios. See also the note on the natural zero of temperature and time.
32. Reference [211] describes the mathematical relationship between ordinal and difference scaled measurement.

"All differences in a Difference Scaled Domain must be expressed in at least one, but perhaps many, Unit(s) of Measure. Nominal and Ordinal Domains, on the other hand, need no unit of measure. All they need to express information in the world framed by space and time is Format. Difference Scaled Domains are different. To express information (that already exists in the domain, regardless of whether it was actually expressed in space and time), all Difference Scaled Domains must be associated with at least one, and perhaps many, Units of Measure. Formats must then be linked to each Unit of Measure. I will tell you more about that in a bit."

"I see the truth of that," replied a much more contemplative Robert. "For example, the distance between the door and my table is 10 feet, or 120 inches. The unit of measure I use does not change the actual distance between the door and me, but it certainly changes the number I write down."

"You are right," Mr. Domain replied, "but your question about length takes this discussion to an entirely different level altogether. It should be obvious by now that Difference Scaled Domains are rich in information. They convey enough information not only to classify and sequence objects, but also to measure the magnitude of gaps between objects in a sequence. However, there is another kind of domain that carries even more information. We need to talk about Ratio Scaled Domains."

To Jim and Jane he added, "I did not mean to intrude, and I thank you for being so even-tempered. Robert was right, though. His remote sensing thermometers show that both your temperatures are normal at 98.4 degrees Fahrenheit, and if I may take the liberty of saying so, you are a well-matched pair and very close to each other in the temperature domain. The gap between you is very close to zero."

Ratio Scaled Domains   "What about me?" asked Jenny, quite pleased with the thought of Difference Scaled Domains. "Does that mean no one can say I am four times as old as my daughter?"

"Sorry to disappoint you, Jenny," said Mr. Domain. "Date and age are defined on very different kinds of domains. Age is the gap between the date on which you were born and today's date. It is not a date. Indeed, it is valid to talk about ratios and proportions of gaps between objects measured in Difference Scaled Domains, but the ratios themselves must map to Ratio Scaled Domains. For example, you can say that you are six times as old as your daughter, and Jim will be perfectly right if he says that the difference in temperature between his jug of milk and Jane's was five times the difference in temperature between ice and Jane's jug of milk. That ratio will hold regardless of the units of measure you use to measure the gap, as long as you use the units consistently. Try it for yourself."

Mr. Domain sighed quietly. "What a pity," he thought. "Jim and Jane are so close in the temperature domain, and I wish Jane's jug of milk were closer to Jim's as well.[33] Then none of this commotion would have happened." However, he continued.

"Gaps between objects in a Difference Scaled Domain will always map to a Ratio Scaled Domain, but so do many other things. Almost everything physicists measure, such as mass, length, area, volume, time (in the same sense as age, not

---

33. Box 16 of [337] describes how domains extend conventional concepts of distance. See the note on generalizing distance.

Box 4: Mr. Domain's Calculations   **4**

Robert quickly verified Mr. Domain's calculations.

In Fahrenheit:

Temperature of Jane's milk	= 40 degrees Fahrenheit
Temperature of ice	= 32 degrees Fahrenheit
Difference between temperature of ice and Jane's milk	= 8 degrees Fahrenheit
Temperature of Jim's milk	= 80 degrees Fahrenheit
Temperature of Jane's milk	= 40 degrees Fahrenheit
Difference between temperature of ice and Jane's milk	= 40 degrees Fahrenheit
Ratio of differences	= 40/8 = 5

In Celsius:

Temperature of Jane's milk	= 4.44 degrees Celsius
Temperature of ice	= 0 degrees Celsius
Difference between temperature of Jim's and Jane's milk	= 4.44 degrees Celsius
Temperature of Jim's milk	= 26.67 degrees Celsius
Temperature of Jane's milk	= 4.44 degrees Celsius
Difference between temperature of ice and Jane's milk	= 22.26 degrees Celsius
Ratio of differences	= 22.26/4.44 = 5

(The result of the actual calculation is 5.01, not exactly 5, due to rounding errors. The temperature in Celsius was computed to only two decimal places. Had the temperatures not been rounded, the two ratios would have matched exactly.)

---

date), probability, and so on, and many other things of interest to business, such as money and product or process defect densities, map to Ratio Scaled Domains."

"Of Nominal, Ordinal, Difference Scaled, and Ratio Scaled domains, Ratio Scaled Domains are the richest in information."

"Ratio Scaled Domains convey enough information to classify, sequence, and measure differences as well as ratios between objects that map to them."

"Like Difference Scaled Domains, Ratio Scaled Domains must also have at least one, and perhaps many, Units of Measure. Units of Measure are needed to express information that these domains already have in the world framed by space and time."

"Like my distance from the door!" exclaimed Robert. "It maps to the Length Domain, and I can certainly say that I am twice as far as Jim is from the door, because I am standing 10 feet from the door, while Jim is sitting only 5 feet from the door. Even if I changed my unit of measure to inches, meters, or anything else, the individual numbers might change (although the distance would not), but their ratio must stay the same, as long as I use the same unit to measure both our distances. Now it has all started making sense."

Mr. Domain's Secret   Mr. Domain was beaming happily at Robert. "Now I am almost ready to share my secret with you. It is my secret map of knowledge. It is very old—as old as the universe we live in."

"But first we must pause to take stock of what we know. There are four kinds of domains:"

- "Nominal Domains contain only classification information. They have no information on sequencing, distances, or ratios of properties of objects."

  "In order to physically express this information, it must be physically formatted and recorded on some medium. A single piece of information must be recorded in at least one, and possibly many, formats. For example, a person's gender may be coded as a number (e.g., 1 for 'female' and 2 for 'male') or a letter (e.g., F for 'female' and M for 'male'); a picture of a man for 'Male' and a woman for 'Female,'; a hexadecimal code on magnetic disk that only computers can read; or almost any coding scheme you can think of."

- "Ordinal Domains contain both classification and sequencing information. They have no information on the magnitudes of gaps or ratios of properties of objects."

  "To physically express this information, we only need to choose a physical format and record it on some medium. A single piece of information must be recorded in at least one, and possibly many, formats. Moreover, regardless of format, we can compare which objects are greater or less than others, in terms of properties that map to Ordinal Domains."

- "Difference Scaled Domains let us classify and arrange objects in a natural sequence, and let us measure the magnitude of point-to-point differences in the sequence, but they carry no information on ratios. They have no natural zero."

  "To physically express this information, we not only need at least one physical format, but also a Unit of Measure (UOM). A single piece of information must be recorded in at least one, and perhaps several, units of measure. For example, the ambient temperature may be recorded in Fahrenheit or Celsius, and the date may be expressed in the Gregorian or Islamic calendars."

  "The UOM is not enough by itself to express the information. Each UOM must be expressed in at least one, but possibly several, formats. For example, Fahrenheit may be spelled out as Fahrenheit, or printed as '°F' in different documents, and may be in different fonts or colors. It may even be spoken out aloud, displayed in a graph or icon, or recorded as a binary code on disk for computers to interpret."

- "Ratio Scaled Domains let us classify and arrange objects in a natural sequence, measure the magnitude of differences in properties of objects, and take their ratios. They always have a natural zero."

"Like Difference Scaled Domains, both UOMs and Formats must be specified in order to physically express the information. A single piece of information must be recorded in at least one, and perhaps several, units of measure. For example, lengths of rooms may be recorded in feet, inches, meters, and centimeters; the age of accounts payable may be expressed in months, years, or days; the weight of a wagon may be expressed in kilograms, pounds, and tons; and payments may be recorded in U.S. dollars, British pounds, Japanese yen, and so forth."

"As in Difference Scaled Domains, the UOM is not enough by itself to express the information. Each UOM must be expressed in at least one, but possibly several, formats. For example, the U.S. dollar may be printed as 'USD' or '$' in different documents. 'Feet' may be stored as 'feet' or 'ft,' or as a binary code interpreted only by computers on different media. 'Pound,' the UOM of weight, may be stored as 'pound,' 'lb,' and so forth."

Then, Mr. Domain opened a weathered and ancient book. "Here is my secret map," he said with a twinkle in his eyes. "It is not complete, and I regret I cannot let you into all my secrets just yet, but I promise I will by the time you finish this book. This map is only an introduction to the territory of Domains. It summarizes only what I have just told you. Let me show you how to read it." [The map has been reproduced in Figure 1.5.][34]

"Domains are objects in the Metamodel of Knowledge, as are Units of Measure and Formats. For this reason, we can call them Meta-objects. Not all Meta-objects

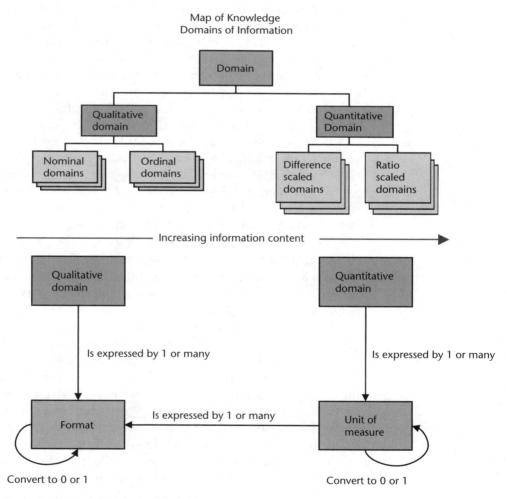

Figure 1.5   (Partial) Metamodel of domain.

34.   Chapter 4 of [337] examines domains and the concept of measurability in more detail.

are shown on this map—not even some you have been introduced to, such as Relationship and Process. [You will find them in Module 5 on our Web site.] The hierarchy at the top of the map classifies different kinds of domains and arranges them in order of intrinsic information content. Chapter 3 of *Creating Agile Business Systems with Reusable Knowledge* shows how these hierarchies help normalize business rules."

"The lower half of the map shows the relationships between various meta-objects; therefore, they are called metarelationships. The meta-objects are rectangles, and the metarelationships are arrows. To understand the rules, you must read along the arrows."

"For example, starting with 'Quantitative Domain,' the full sentence along the arrow reads 'Quantitative Domain is expressed by one or many Unit of Measure.' Note that the lower limit (1) on the occurrence of Unit of Measure shows that each Quantitative Domain must have at least one unit of measure, or else it cannot be expressed at all. Similarly, the next sentence, starting with Unit of Measure reads 'Unit of Measure is expressed by one or many Format.' "

"The arrow that starts from and loops back to Unit of Measure reads, 'Unit of Measure converts to none or at most one Unit of Measure.' This is the meta-object (remember, relationships are objects, too) where conversion rules, such as rules for currency conversion or measurement conversion, reside. This meta-object facilitates storage of the conversion rule in a single place."

"I understand why you have a lower limit of zero—if you had only one UOM, there is nothing else to convert to," interjected Robert. "But why did you restrict the conversion rule to only one other UOM? Cannot yards, for example, be converted to feet by multiplying by 3, or to inches by multiplying by 36? So right there you have Yard, a UOM for length related to two, not one, other UOMs."

"A very perceptive question, Robert," said Mr. Domain. "Of course, you are right, each UOM of a Quantitative Domain can be converted to every other UOM. But remember, the purpose of the metamodel is to avoid redundancy, and you need only one conversion rule per UOM. You could then navigate to any other UOM in the domain via a chain of conversion relationships.[35] One relationship per UOM is all you need. Another would add no information. It would be redundant. I once had a very interesting visitor—I remember his name was Claude Shannon[36]—who helped me understand this."

"It also implies that if you ever create a new UOM for the domain, you have to add just one conversion rule," said Robert excitedly. "You do not need a separate rule for every other UOM in the domain. Boy, isn't that a nice saving! This object (conversion relationship) has both the conversion ratio and the rule that tells you to multiply the value as measured by the source UOM to convert to the target UOM."

"Note also, "said Mr. Domain, "whenever you have two or more UOMs for any given domain, there is automatically and intrinsically a pair of conversion rules that will let you convert one UOM to the other. This is true whether business is currently interested in converting between UOMs or not. It just is, and these rules will apply to any objects that map properties to the domain. For example, the rule for

35. The chain must be *acyclic*, but more on that later.
36. See the note on Measure of Information.

Box 5: Conversion Between UOMs   5

Measurements in any given Difference or Ratio Scaled Domain can be converted from one UOM to another by multiplying by a conversion ratio. If one or more UOM (and conversion ratio) is already in use in a domain and a new UOM is introduced, then we need to introduce only one new conversion ratio to enable us to convert measurements expressed in the new UOM to any, and every, other UOM already in use. We do not need individual ratios for conversion from the new UOM to each of the UOMs already in use. Indeed, we would denormalize knowledge if we specify each ratio individually; each of these ratios can be derived if just one conversion ratio is known.

The following example illustrates these real-world facts. In order to keep the example simple, we have based it on the Length Domain, but the same arguments will apply to UOMs in any Ratio or Difference Scaled Domain.

Let us assume that doctors in different countries decided that they would conduct a survey to find the average height of people. Soon after they started the project, they realized their scales had different units of measure: inches in Inland, feet in Footland, and meters in Metland. They realized they would all have to agree on a single unit of measure to succeed. The conversion rules between inches, feet, and meters are in the following table.

	To		
From	*Inches*	*Feet*	*Meters*
Inches			
Feet	×12		
Meters		×3.2808	

For example, to find the rule for converting from feet to inches in the table above, find "feet" under the "From" column on the extreme left, and then look along the "Feet" row to find the cell under the "Inches" column. That cell contains the rule "× 12," which means multiply by 12 (i.e., to convert feet to inches multiply by 12). Thus, 5 feet = 5 ×12 = 60 inches. Similarly, the rule for converting meters to feet is "multiply by 3.2808." We also know that division is the inverse of multiplication. Thus, the table contains three atomic rules.

We need only these three rules to be able to convert between any units of measure in the table. For example, although the table contains no explicit rule for converting inches to feet, we can derive it by using the rule that division is the inverse of multiplication (e.g., to convert inches to feet, we divide by 12). Similarly, although there is no explicit rule for converting meters to inches, we can derive it from the information in the table. We can convert meters to feet by multiplying by 3.2808, and then multiplying the result by 12 to convert to inches. Had we included the conversion ratio for explicitly converting meters to inches in the table, it would have been redundant, and knowledge would be denormalized.

Had the doctors all used the same UOM, there would have been **5** no need to convert at all, and there would have been no need for conversion rules. (Note that the diagonal cells of the table are all blank.) This is what Robert meant when he said that he understood why the lower limit of the conversion relationship was zero.

The doctors were uncomfortable using UOMs with which they were unfamiliar, and could not agree on which of the three UOMs (inches, feet, or meters) they would use for their project. They finally decided that to be fair to all, they would settle on centimeters, a UOM that none of them used. If we added centimeters to our list of UOMs for length, the conversion rule table would become:

From	To			
	Inches	*Feet*	*Meters*	*Centimeters*
Inches				
Feet	×12			
Meters		×3.2808		
Centimeters			×0.01	

There is only one conversion rule we would add to the table: "Multiply by 0.01 to convert from centimeters to meters." With this single new rule, we could convert centimeters to any of the other units of measure in the table. For example, although there is no explicit rule in the table for converting centimeters to inches, we could multiply centimeters by 0.01 to convert to meters, multiply the result by 3.2808 to convert to feet, and then multiply that result by 12 to convert to inches. We leave it to the reader to try to convert centimeters to the other UOMs in the table. This is an example of what Robert meant when he said that he did not need to add a separate conversion rule for every UOM in the domain each time he added a new UOM to the table—adding a single new conversion rule would be enough.

converting feet to inches will apply to heights of people, dimensions of rooms, lengths of wire, or any other property that maps to the Length Domain."

"So you see," continued Mr. Domain, "even though we have just started, and our metamodel is still rudimentary, some kinds of reusable components are already becoming self-evident." Looking at Jane, who was shaking her head incredulously, he added, "Of course, you might argue that this is all common sense, and it could well be; but bear with me, as the metamodel fills out, many other reusable components will emerge naturally. After all, we are modeling the nature of nature," he added with a smile.

"I can see from the map that much of what we have discussed for UOMs has parallels with formatting issues as well!" exclaimed Robert. "Now I am beginning to see, even if it is still just a glimmer in my eye, how the metamodel of knowledge can help me normalize rules!"

"Now that you can read the map, understanding the verbs in parentheses is easy," said Mr. Domain. "They merely show the relationship in the reverse direction (i.e., read in the direction opposite to the arrow). It is called the inverse relationship,[37] but more on that later."

"One more thing, if I may, before we move on," continued Mr. Domain. "Note that none of these metarelationships involves time. They are not processes. The rules just are. There is no data flow or conversion process in the real world. It is just Knowledge. Later, we will see how these can naturally map to computer implementation and still stay normalized. We will have to link each implementation to a single piece of immutable knowledge that just is."

The Structure of Domains—Perception, Five Senses, and Aliens in the Lost Worlds of Metanesia   Jane was getting a little confused, and felt it was high time she made her presence felt. "Whoa! Hold your horses there for a moment! I really don't understand. What is this fuss about information intrinsic to meaning that exists beyond any spatial or temporal frame? After all, we can only know about the existence of information through our five senses. We know about the behavior of objects that are framed by space and time only because we can see, hear, smell, touch, or feel them. How can we claim something exists when we cannot see, hear, smell, touch, or feel it?"

"Good point, Jane," said Mr. Domain with a delighted smile. "Indeed, you have raised questions that philosophers have long debated.[38] I will have to take you on a tour of my secret zoo in the lost world of Metanesia to explain."

"A word of warning, though," he added a little anxiously. "It is a fantastic journey, but not everyone returns from Metanesia. Moreover, even if they do, they can get somewhat eccentric, like my friend Robert here. Are you sure you want to go?"

"I am not going to be scared off so easily," thought Jane to herself. "Mr. Domain, or whatever he likes to be called, is probably out of touch with reality. I am not going to let him off the hook so easily!" To Mr. Domain, she simply said, "Yes, I am sure I want to go."

"Come, then, and remember that it was your choice!" Jane suddenly plunged into a strange stygian darkness. She could not even see the tip of her nose in the dark. A complete and ominous silence, unlike anything she had ever experienced, enveloped her totally. She felt strangely disembodied. She realized with some trepidation that she was completely cut off from her senses. She could neither see, hear, feel, nor smell. Even the taste of the air she used to breathe was gone. Only the core of her being was left. Gradually, Jane sensed strange presences gathering around her, and as if from very far away, she heard Mr. Domain.

"You are in the presence of a very powerful alien being. It is not like anything you have ever known, or can ever imagine. Its senses are completely different from yours. It does not see, feel, smell, hear, or taste. Yet it knows. Even I do not know how, and it has a Mind. Even I do not understand its thoughts or perceptions. Be extremely cautious."

Jane was beginning to wish she had not accepted the challenge. Oh, wouldn't it have been so much nicer to go back to a warm conversation with Jim, even if her jug

---

37. See the note on the Mathematical Theory of Categories or publications in [252, 253, 308].
38. See the note on Positivism.

of milk was a tad cold! Anyway, here she was. Slowly she felt a thought forming in the fringes of her consciousness. It seemed like a question.

"What are you?"

"I am Jane."

"Do not comprehend response."

"I am human, 5 feet 6 inches tall."

"Do not comprehend response. Explain human. Explain tall."

"Tall is the same as high."

"Do not comprehend response."

She heard Robert's presence replying, "Humans are sets of properties mapped to space."

"Now I don't understand," thought Jane, "but that's okay if we can get out of here."

"Explain Space."

"Boy, whatever this thing is, it must be dumb," thought Jane.

"Careful Jane!"—that seemed to be Mr. Domain.

"Let me try." (Jane was almost sure that it was Robert responding.) "Space has three independent attributes that we call three dimensions. Each is mapped to the same Ratio Scaled Domain that we call length. The three attributes of space are labeled length, breadth, and width. These attributes are uncorrelated."[39]

"Understood!"

"Yes, Robert, as long as you can exchange pure information, any mind, however alien, will have common ground to understand your message. This being senses the world in ways we cannot even begin to fathom, and our senses are equally alien to it. If you talk in terms of things you see, hear, touch, smell, or taste, then it will be confused." Jane was sure that this was from Mr. Domain.

Then she sensed Robert's response. "Understood. However, whatever incomprehensible and unimaginable senses it has, it has to be aware of its environment. That can happen only if it gets information from reality. The same thing is true for us as well. The common structure of information is the only way we can understand it, and it can understand us."

"Oh, get real!" thought Jane.

No sooner was the thought out, when she found herself standing on a sidewalk with Jim, back in the good old United States of Information. Had it all been a dream? Jane was sure that Domain's Metaphysical Diner was somewhere in the neighborhood. She just couldn't see it. She has looked for Mr. Domain's diner ever since. She has never found it. She realizes Mr. Domain is spread so thin. After all, as she understood in a flash just before she found herself on the sidewalk, he is everywhere and every when. You can't really get away from him. Not now. Not ever.

"O World invisible, we view thee,
O world intangible, we touch thee,
O world unknowable, we know thee,
Inapprehensible, we clutch thee!"
—Francis Thompson, *In No Strange Land*

---

39.   Reference [255] defines space mathematically and has succinct descriptions of common spaces of various kinds.

1.4 Meta-Objects, Subtypes, and Inheritance

Meta-objects are objects that structure the meanings of objects. They are the components from which the meaning of Knowledge is configured. Meta-objects help us normalize real world behavior (Nijssen's irreducible facts [297] or Ross' atomic rules [294]). The meta-objects we have discussed thus far are:

- Object (the fundamental meta-object);
- Property;
- Relationship;
- Process;
- Event;
- Domain;
- Unit of Measure (UOM);
- Format.

The kinds of rules each meta-object normalizes are shown in Figure 1.6. Moreover, we have seen that behavior and irreducible facts (or atomic rules) are merely different perspectives of the information content or properties of objects. They are simple in and of themselves, but are the building blocks of knowledge.

An ontology like that in Figure 1.6 arranges objects in a hierarchy of meaning. Objects at a lower level are derived from those higher up by adding information. Thus, Figure 1.6 tells us that the meaning of Process is obtained by combining the meanings of Relationship (an interaction between objects) and Event (the flow of time).[40] The relationships between objects in an ontology are special. They are called subtyping relationships. They convey information from higher to lower levels of the ontology. The lower level object becomes a special kind of higher level object. Thus, Figure 1.6 tells us that Ratio Scaled Domain is a special kind of Domain via the chain of subtyping relationships that lead from Domain to Ratio Scaled Domain via Quantitative Domain.

Thus, we introduce two new meta-objects to our repertoire of meta-objects: the subtyping relationship, and its corollary, the Subtype. They are key concepts, because they help encapsulate and normalize knowledge. Shared behavior is normalized in the supertype object, and automatically shared with subtypes by implication. For example, aging, gender, credit rating, names, Social Security numbers, and so forth, are common to all people. People could be employees, customers, or both. Thus, "Person," the object class, will normalize behavior common to people, such as aging, gender, and so forth, regardless of whether the person is an employee, a customer, or both. Thus, Customer and Employee are subtypes of Person. The subtypes add information that gives them their special meaning. For instance, Employee adds the employment relationship with another person or organization, whereas Customer does the same for the purchasing relationship. This is the information that Employee and Customer normalize. They inherit the rest of their information from Person. This example shows us why inheritance, the subtyping

---

40. Process is a before-and-after interaction, as we have discussed earlier in this chapter. Resources are used to create the products of a process. The resources come before, and the products come after.

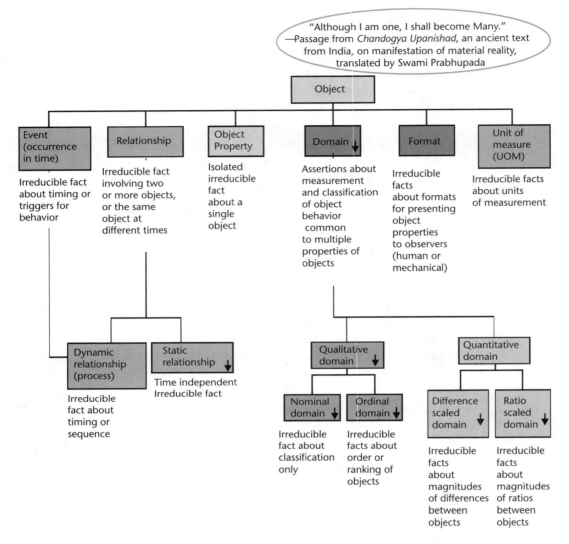

Figure 1.6 Basic meta-object inventory: kinds of rules each meta-object normalizes.

relationship, and subtypes are needed to normalize information, and are therefore critical to the discussion in this book.[41]

Box 6 shows different kinds of information that subtypes may contain to distinguish special behavior of a subset of objects from behavior common to the entire (parent) class.

Readers interested in a more comprehensive discussion of meta-objects and their behavior may refer to *Creating Agile Business Systems with Reusable Knowledge*, published by Cambridge University Press. We will now address how components of knowledge can be configured into rules of business, and how inheritance can automate reuse with an example.

---

41. A relationship may connect several objects; the subtyping relationship is a special kind of relationship. Therefore, a subtype may have multiple parents, a fact inherited from *Relationship*. *Process* in Figure 1.6 is an example of this.

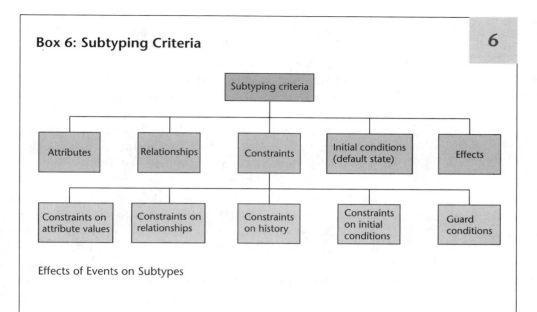

Box 6: Subtyping Criteria   6

Effects of Events on Subtypes

Object instances may respond to events by changing their state. A change of state might make the instance a member of a subclass, or remove it from a subclass. For example, an unemployed person who is hired becomes an employee. Employee is a subtype of Person (see the earlier discussion). Similarly, an employee who is fired skips out of the employee subtype. Thus, individual objects skip in and out of subclasses in response to events (i.e., their roles change). Morphism is the quality of having a form or shape. Polymorphism is the quality of appearing in several apparently different forms. Therefore, subtypes are often called polymorphisms of their supertypes. This term will be used frequently in the chapters that follow (see the note on polymorphism).

A guard condition is a rule that determines whether an event will have an effect on a particular object or not. For example, a request to revise the terms of a sealed agreement is not valid. Thus, the sealed state of the agreement is a guard condition. Thus, guard conditions are just another way of subtyping objects. We could have divided Agreements into those under negotiation and those that are sealed. The revision effect would then be a property (behavior) of only Open Agreements. If the Agreement object were designed thus, then we would not need a separate guard condition on the parent object to check its state.

1.5   Meta-Objects and the Natural Repository of Knowledge

Wisdom, we saw in Section 1.1, is the symphony of collective knowledge that helps to move the firm toward its goals. Knowledge consists of configurations of rules. The most fundamental building block of knowledge, as well as the ultimate repository of information, is the atomic rule—a rule we cannot break into smaller, simpler parts without loss of meaning. The meta-objects of Figure 1.6 are the natural wellspring of atomic rules and the repository of knowledge. They are the home, and basis of real world meaning.

In this section, we will understand how atomic rules are configured into business knowledge, and how reusable components of knowledge naturally emerge from the meta-objects of Figure 1.6. The intent in this introductory chapter is to develop a basic understanding. In *Creating Agile Business Systems with Reusable Knowledge*, these issues are examined in depth.

A configuration of rules is not merely a loose collection of atomic rules. It has structure—atomic rules may also be assembled from other atomic rules. Some atomic rules are reused repeatedly as we polish our business positions with product and process innovation. These reusable rules are our reusable components of knowledge. Sometimes entire structures and configurations may be reused to build specialized domains of knowledge. This is analogous to machinery manufacturers assembling reusable subassemblies from standard (reusable) parts. These reusable subassemblies may in turn be incorporated into multitudes of versions and variations of the end product. Reusability springs from the structures of meta-objects. Therefore, let us understand how the objects in Figure 1.6 are repositories of atomic rules.

Let us start by revisiting the simple example in Box 2. Each process in Box 2 is an object, and they are strung in a chain that shows which process must take precedence over another. These links are relationships, and therefore objects in their own right. These relationships carry irreducible facts about mutual dependencies between processes they connect. Thus, the chain of processes is a structure assembled from atomic rules. It is a very simple configuration of atomic rules.

To understand how atomic rules may be assembled from other atomic rules, and to understand how subassemblies of rules may be reused, let us take another example, which is a simple atomic rule common to many businesses: Organization Ships Product.

The shipment is a relationship between organization and product. It is also an object in its own right (just as all relationships are). The rule Organization Ships Product is shown in Figure 1.7.[42] Read it as you would Figure 1.5; only remember that the arrows (i.e., relationships) are also objects in their own right.

Figure 1.7 illustrates two atomic rules:

1. An organization may make many shipments.
2. Each shipment may contain many products.

This is a simple configuration of knowledge. It is just a set of two atomic rules that are not mutually linked in a structure. The two rules stand on their own.

Now let us examine a scenario that forces change. In the following scenario, as rules of business change, we will add or alter rules, changing the simple configuration above step by step. As we do this, we will understand how knowledge,

---

42. Cardinality and other constraints familiar to advanced business modelers have been deliberately omitted to keep the diagrams simple. The intent of this chapter is not to be technically comprehensive, but to convey the essential concepts. Readers who would like more detail may refer to *Creating Agile Business Systems with Reusable Knowledge*, published by Cambridge University Press.

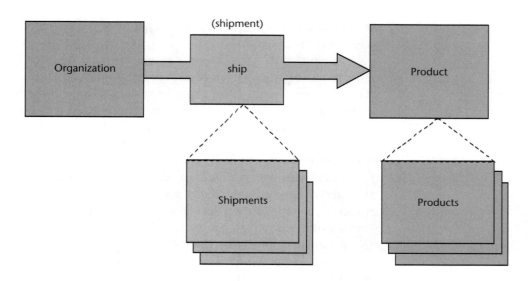

Figure 1.7   A rule, Organization Ships Product, assembled from Objects.

configured in the meta-objects of Figure 1.6, is naturally normalized in the real world. We will step through the process of assembling knowledge from components, one step at a time, as shown in Figure 1.8.

Assume that the firm had negotiated a flat rate per shipment but the contract was about to expire, and that the shipping cost will depend on the gross weight of

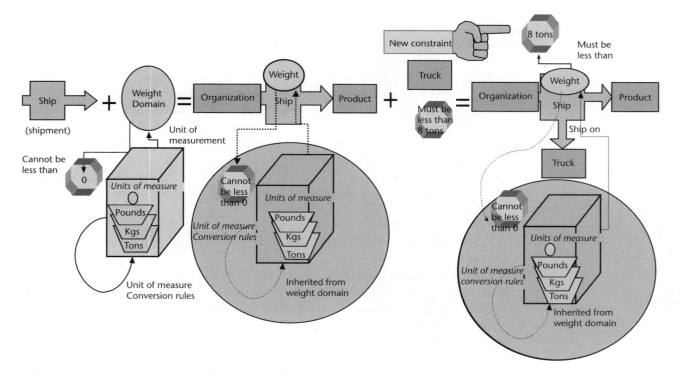

Figure 1.8   Adding components to assemble configurations of rules.

the shipment in the new contract. The scope of the shipping model must expand to include the gross weight.

Assume also that the firm has access to components of knowledge as a part of an inventory of knowledge artifacts that it has already built and stored in a repository. First, we must look for the relevant knowledge in the repository.

We locate the Weight Domain. It is a Ratio Scaled Domain. We understand (from Figure 1.5 and Box 5) that it must be associated with units of measure and conversion rules in the structure shown in Figure 1.5. We also understand that weight can never be a negative number. It is a constraint (i.e., an atomic rule) associated with the domain. (Constraints are also objects; see [337].) Thus, there is a natural structure of irreducible facts associated with the Weight Domain. Assume the artifact in the repository reflects this. This natural structure may then be considered a subassembly of knowledge stored in the repository. Figure 1.8 shows this structure (second structure from the left).

When we assemble Shipment with weight, it implicitly and naturally inherits the entire structure associated with the domain. The units in which shipment weight might be measured, the conversion rules between these units, and the fact that the shipment weight cannot be negative are all irreducible facts that flow from the subassembly. We might choose a preferred, default unit of measure to express the shipment weight when we design the business process. Our default unit of measure might depend on the context. For example, we might prefer kilograms when we deploy the process in the European Union, and tons when we deploy it in the United States. In neither context will the structure change. Indeed, it will be common to both. This is an example of how knowledge is reused.

If the unit weight of the product were also needed, we would reuse the Weight Domain again. We would assemble the product object with the Weight Domain, and inherit the same structures and rules. We would not have to redefine these constraints, units of measure, and conversion rules separately for shipment weight and product weight. If a conversion rule changed, or a new unit of measure was added to the Weight Domain, then it would automatically be available to both shipment weight and product weight, because knowledge was normalized.

In this next step, we will understand how irreducible facts may be reused to build other irreducible facts. Assume that the new contract with the shipping company specifies that all products must be shipped by truck. The atomic rule will read: Organization ships Product by truck.

First, let us test this rule to validate that it is an atomic rule. Let us check to see if we lose information when we break the rule into smaller, simpler pieces.

1. Organization ships Product.
2. Organization ships by truck.

Together, the two rules do not necessarily mean that the product will be shipped by truck. For example, both statements will be true even if the Organization ships other items (e.g., supplies, documents, and so forth) by truck or by air. Therefore, we have lost information by dividing Organization ships Product by truck. It is an atomic rule. We obtained that atomic rule by turning Shipment from a two-way relationship between Organization and Product into a three-way relationship between Organization, Product, and Truck. We have created a new atomic rule from another. It is a special case of the more general atomic rule from which it was derived.[43] This new structure, and how it was assembled from knowledge artifacts in the repository, is illustrated in Figure 1.8.

Now, we have another requirement. We find that trucks cannot carry more than 8 tons (i.e., the gross weight of each shipment by truck must be no more than 8 tons). It is another irreducible fact. This is not a generic constraint attached to the weight domain; rather, it is specific to shipment by truck. Therefore, the constraint is attached to Shipment Weight, a property of Shipment (an object in its own right, as shown in Figure 1.6), and not the Weight Domain. This constraint will not be automatically inherited by weights that are properties of other objects (for example, Product Weight), because it is attached specifically to Shipment Weight, and not to the generic Weight Domain.

The effect of attaching this constraint of 8 tons to Shipment Weight implies that this property of Shipment now has two constraints.

1. Inherited automatically from the Weight Domain, that no weight may be negative.
2. Specific to Shipment weight, that no shipment may exceed 8 tons.

The combined effect of both constraints is to restrict Shipment weight to a range from 0 to 8 tons. The structure on the extreme right of Figure 1.8 shows how these rules have been configured to reflect knowledge about product shipment.

If we reengineered the process to ship by air as well as by truck, then we would again use the structure Organization ships Product in Figure 1.8. However, Airplane would substitute for Truck in the structure on the extreme right of Figure 1.8. The weight limitation might also have to change. This is another example of how knowledge is naturally normalized, and may be reused.

Since the weight limitations imply use of the Weight Domain, all conversion rules also will be automatically inherited from the domain, and will apply to all constraints on weight. In our example, this might facilitate interoperability between European and United States operations.

See also "The Architecture of Knowledge" on our Web site.

1.6   The Problem of Perspective

"Truth fails not; but her outward forms that bear
The longest date melt like frosty rime"

—William Wordsworth, *Mutability*

Can real world objects really anchor reusable components of business knowledge, even as scopes and rules shift? Will subtyping and inheritance truly defeat the dark forces of chaos? Our world is complex, driven by learning, change, opportunity, threats, and competition. To defeat chaos, we must normalize knowledge in the right objects and subtypes. Otherwise, objects will not inherit the behavior they

---

43. The Universal Perspective and the Metamodel of Knowledge have the most frequently used generalized rules, a starting point for reusable components.

must, and might inherit behavior they should not. (We call this inheritance by mistake; see the example in Box 8.) How can we identify the right objects in a shifting, chimerical world? This is the problem of perspective.

As many practitioners know from bitter experience, objects alone cannot normalize and encapsulate reusable knowledge, nor can subtyping and inheritance by themselves defeat the forces of complexity and chaos, because both come up against the problem of perspective. The world is a chimera, and so is our perception of it.[44]

What Is Perspective?   We understand the world around us by experiencing its behavior. We seek its meaning by forming concepts of what behavior is shared by what objects, and what is special to each. These concepts are based on our individual experiences and perceptions. Not only are our experiences and perceptions different, but also two people will never think exactly alike. Therefore our concepts (i.e., generalizations of what is shared and what is special), are naturally different. For example, a physicist might say that a rock thrown by a child and a shell fired from a field gun are similar, because both follow trajectories with similar shapes, under the influence of the same forces (e.g., gravitation and air resistance). On the other hand, a general might say that the shell and field gun are similar, but not the rock, because both the gun and shell are complementary weapons of war that must be issued from his inventory, whereas the rock is a child's toy.

What do differences in perspective mean to objects that try to anchor knowledge? Our concepts of shared behavior are generalizations. They are object classes, sometimes abstract, like the meta-objects we recently discussed. These object classes and subtypes anchor the shared behavior of objects we perceive. Since each one of us generalizes and specializes our perceptions differently, many of our concepts may not match those of others. Objects and relationships are sets of properties based on classification of common behavior of things we experience. Each object may have several features and group several behaviors; hence, we may not agree on object classes and relationships themselves—a fundamental problem on which many software projects have foundered.[45]

Indeed, as scopes shift, new behavior is recognized and old constraints retired. The same individual may change the way he or she classifies common behavior. (His or her perspective changes its state. Did that just happen to you in Box 7?) Object classes become chimerical, and the object model becomes a chimera, which is yet another cause for chaos instead of a firm anchor of reusable knowledge. Almost every data and object modeler has experienced this problem.

We have replaced the domino effect of change ricocheting and rippling through unintentionally replicated and unmanaged knowledge in the system with two other problems (see the examples in Box 8):

---

44. See the note on Multiperspective and Facet Modeling.
45. Some analysts have proposed that we do not try to classify objects intuitively. Instead, they suggest that we mathematically analyze similarities between objects in terms of their properties to group them into object classes and subtypes [283]. While this approach may be useful, it will not guarantee stable object classes. If the scope of the process changes so that some properties under consideration change, the classification scheme may also change. The inclusion or exclusion of behavior may change affinities between object instances, which in turn can change the taxonomy of objects and relationships. This happened because we did not address the root problem; we only mechanized it. Facet Modeling, described in the note on Multiperspective Modeling, is another approach in which *aspects* of an object might be reused. For more information, see [13, 15, 21, 23, 53].

Box 7: Perspective Is an Object   7

Do you see two people in a private conversation or a chalice in the figure above? What you see depends on how you classify the white and black spaces in it—which color is empty and which is solid. Perspective is a point of view. It is also a model. It is the entire structure of interconnected objects that anchor knowledge—classes, aggregations, relationships, constraints, state spaces, domains, effects, and all the other meta-objects in [337], glued to each other in a structure we call knowledge, or more modestly, our perspective of knowledge. It is also an object in its own right—an aggregate object with a structure. Each individual's perspective is an instance of a model. If the model changes in response to new information or an insight, it has changed its state.

Often the changes are minor—a new attribute, a new relationship, an additional effect, or a new subtype. However, sometimes the change can be fundamental. The classification scheme—the objects and relationships themselves—may change.

Consider why the same underlying reality can appear very different from different perspectives. Object instances are things or concepts that have properties. Some properties are shared with one set of things, and other properties with other sets of things. It follows that the same thing might belong to different object classes when perceived from different perspectives. Changing perspectives can change entire classification schemes, which can have a very a profound effect on the model.

Consider what happens when classification schemes change. Object classes are classification schemes based on similar properties of object instances—all properties of instances in a class do not always match. Matching properties are shared, and the others are not. We manage shared properties

7

with the concept of superclass (supertype), and unshared properties with the concept of subclass (subtype). A subclass is meaningless without a superclass; if a superclass disappears, so must all its subclasses. Thus, if entire objects vanish, then they take with them all their relationships, constraints, and subclasses, and their relationships and constraints as well.

Thus, when classification schemes (i.e., taxonomies) change, they can have a domino effect on the entire model, sweeping away entire subclasses, along with myriads of relationships, constraints, partitions, and all other structures that relate objects and subclasses into a consistent and cogent configuration of knowledge. New structures might have to take their place. New and old structures are objects, too. The appearance of the new and the dissolution of the old may impact other structures, which in turn have other impacts. Thus, change can ripple through the entire structure of knowledge until it settles into a new configuration (and the possessor of the change perspective thinks, "Aha—now I understand!"). It is called a paradigm shift—a different model of the world, or a perspective that has changed its state quite radically.

This is why we need the Universal Perspective with its universal object classes and relationships to pin down widely shared ideas about business and reality. The secret of these universal objects[46] that anchor knowledge firmly from every possible perspective is not hidden in some arcane and abstract detail. Rather, it is explicit in the sweeping generalizations that can withstand the incessant pounding of continual change and the immense diversity of creative thought and innovation. The Universal Perspective consists of objects and structures that masquerade as apparently different objects in different perspectives, but are actually different states, roles, and compositions of universal objects. Thus, understanding universal objects and the Universal Perspective help us pin down the essence of universal reality and the unity of all perspectives. All perspectives are states of the Universal Perspective. Paradoxically, the Universal Perspective is changeless, because it underpins change. It is this Universal Perspective we seek to solve the problem of perspective.

1. Inheritance by mistake—wrong behavior was inherited because our object taxonomy was incorrect, or became incorrect when scopes and perspectives changed.
2. Inheritance deficiency—behavior that should have been inherited by an object was not, because the object taxonomy was defective, or became deficient in a new scope and a different perspective.

The example in Box 8 was too simple to be real. It involved only two analysts (you and Jim); three objects (Bill, Payment, and Document); and one subtype (Bill, with two parents, Payment and Document). Even in this simple example, there was ample room for both kinds of mistakes: Inheritance Deficiency and Inheritance by Mistake. In the real world, object instances might share some, but not all, behavior.

---

46. Remember, relationships are objects too.

Box 8: An Example of the Problem of Perspective   8

Consider a bill in an accounts receivable system. You might be justified in considering it to be a request for payment, and hence a state of an object called Payment. You have just generalized two key business concepts: Bill and Payment. The bill is now a subtype of payment, and it inherits various properties of payment, such as currency of payment, the payee and payer, due date, goods and services being paid for, and so forth. You are quite satisfied that you have normalized and reused the behavior of payment, and are certain that other applications will be able to reuse this intelligence. You store it as an artifact in an electronic repository of business components.

In the meantime, your company has expanded its global operations, and has key customers in non-English speaking countries. Speedy international cash flows are critical to growth. Raising electronic bills in the language of the customer is the key to strengthening the relationship with international customers and getting paid on time. The plan is to send bills to customers in the language of their choice, using e-mail. An electronic copy of e-mailed bills will be retained in your employer's database.

The billing system must be enhanced, so that each customer's bills can be formatted in his or her language of choice. Your repository of knowledge artifacts has an object called Document, with special translation behavior attached to it. Jim, a billing analyst, finds your knowledge artifact, called Bill, in the repository classified as a kind of Payment. He is puzzled. "A bill," he thinks to himself, "is not a payment—it is a document we send to customers! I know Documents already have an automatic translation facility attached to them. If I make Bill a subtype of document instead of a kind of payment, then my translation problem will be solved." He proceeds to do just that. To his dismay, bills can now be translated into the customers' languages, but have lost all payment information (e.g., amounts, currency, due dates, and so forth), because Bill is not a subtype of payment any more.

Jim brings the problem to you. You realize at once that it is an Inheritance Deficiency caused by a deficient taxonomy of objects. You look Jim in the eye and sagaciously suggest, "Why not make Bill a subtype of both document and payment? That way we will inherit all the behavior we need." Jim is impressed, thanks you, and does just that. He is quite happy until John, the billing manager, approaches him. John tells Jim that his staff has a problem trying to understand foreign language bills. He wants two copies in the firm's database—one in English, and the other in the customer's language. The Document object is a supertype of Bill, and has copying behavior attached to it. Jim thinks John's request is as good as done. The bill would have automatically inherited this copying behavior from Document.

All hell breaks loose when copies of the bills are made in English. From the perspective of Bills being a request for Payment, duplicate requests for payments are being logged against customers in the firm's accounts receivable system. Customers are understandably upset, and the firm's global position has become vulnerable to competition. This is an example of Inheritance by Mistake, and is just one instance of how the problem of perspective can cause chaos.[47]

8

Worse, any given object instance might share different kinds of behavior with instances of different kinds of objects. Analysis teams may be large, and each analyst may have his or her own unique perspective. How much greater would be the real world risk! Larger teams, more perspectives, more objects, and more multiple inheritances from larger numbers of supertypes all together represent an ideal recipe for chaos!

These issues stem from the problem of categorizing behavior cogently, a need which has been left unresolved for 40 years from the time of the first formal business model. We are still stuck with it.

Does a Universal Perspective Exist?   What is the solution? To group behavior cogently, we must have cogent objects; to get cogent objects, we must solve the problem of perspective; to solve the problem of perspective, we must seek common ground. We know we can seek common ground, because we know individuals perceive the world partly from their own unique point of view, and partly from widely shared ideas generic to the world of business, or imposed by the physical world. Without these shared ideas, each one of us would be forever condemned to our own private universe. We would not understand each other, nor would we be able to work as a team. We know our perspectives can converge quite rapidly when we model simple situations based on these shared ideas. It is much harder when our models are broad in scope and complex in detail. To handle the industrial strength models of today, which span complex corporations and even cross corporate boundaries, we need a more robust anchor. We need a Standard Universal Perspective—a model that will subsume individual perspectives, even as it allows the free play of diversity in support of individuality, innovation, and creativity.

"Without stability or change, Eternal, it has no origin and no end."

—Adapted from *The Gospel of Buddha* by Paul Carus

Does the universal perspective exist? Is it possible to define universal classes that will allow the free play of individual differences and creative thought, or must we be forever chained to the chimera of perspective? Widely shared ideas about business and reality underpin our perceptions, and because of these widely shared ideas, it is possible to define universal classes of objects that encapsulate shared knowledge. It starts with the Metamodel of Knowledge in [337].

These universal object classes anchor knowledge firmly and coherently from every possible business perspective. They create a pattern—a standard perspective that other perspectives can add to, but one which will not have to change to satisfy

47.   See Patterns of Buying and Selling in the Universal Perspective for the answer.

their requirements. Thus, this pattern, like the chassis of a car, is a component that connects standard and custom parts to make the entire unit work. The Universal Perspective grows from it.

Standard parts are the universal object classes in the Universal Perspective. These objects normalize shared ideas. Custom components will inherit this shared wisdom, and will add the special behavior and creative ideas that innovative businesses formulate to prosper and excel, even as the universal pattern of shared ideas in our "chassis" automatically and naturally integrates special behavior with other processes within, and even beyond, the firm.

The metamodel and the Universal Perspective together will defeat the forces of chaos, but there is another practical, and equally important problem that we must overcome to make them one team. It is the tyranny of words.

> "As shadows wait upon the sun
> Vain the ambition of kings.
> To leave a living name behind
> And weave but nets to catch the wind."
>
> —John Webster, *Vanitas Vanitatum*

The Tyranny of Words   What is in a name? Everything! Names are the labels for our concepts, and the means of communicating these concepts to others. Every data administrator knows the tyranny of words, and those that work for large corporations know how intractable it is. Different groups and organizations often need very similar concepts, but call them by different names; different groups also may have the same name for very different concepts. It is a recipe for confusion when organizations merge, or seamlessly integrate business processes and systems. It is also a culture: attempts to standardize names for concepts across organizational borders usually generate more heat than light. A seemingly trivial problem of syntax can take up disproportionate amounts of organizational time and resources.[48]

The Tyranny of Words emerges from the metamodel of knowledge—that the concept is different from its label and the same object may have many names (i.e., name itself is a class of objects that consists of individual instances of name). Different (instances of) names may be preferred in different contexts. The context is the perspective.[49] These concepts are the anchor for the rules in Figure 1.9. (Read it as you did with Figure 1.5.)

In many situations, it might be best not to standardize names. The problem can be quite intractable when deeply entrenched, long-standing interest groups clash over choices of names—there are so many concepts to name in any real business! Consider that battling over names may not only be an exercise in futility—it can

---

48. Recently there has been an interest in standardizing vocabularies across value chains (Module 5, Section 3, on our Web site addresses value chains; see Figure 2.22 of this book). Value Chain Markup Language (VCML) from Vitria Technology, Inc., is one such initiative. VCML defines a value chain as "a network of all of the business partners and transactions in a supply and demand chain from raw materials and subassemblies to the consumer. A value chain spans vertical and horizontal relationships within and across industries. It addresses relationships with all parties participating in designing, manufacturing, financing, marketing, delivering, and supporting a product or service." VCML standardizes vocabularies to facilitate B2B collaboration. VCML models have been published for aerospace, automotive, banking and finance, education, energy, government, healthcare, insurance, petrochemical, retail, telecommunications, and transportation industries. See [65], or visit http://www.vcml.net/.

49. In facet modeling, all properties of an object, not just its name, are said to belong to an *aspect* of the object. Instead of linking a property of an object directly to the object, the aspect is linked to the object. For more information see the note on facet modeling, or [13, 15, 21, 23, 53].

Box 9: Synonyms and Homonyms   9

Different names for the same concept are called synonyms, and a single name for different concepts is a homonym [48].[50]

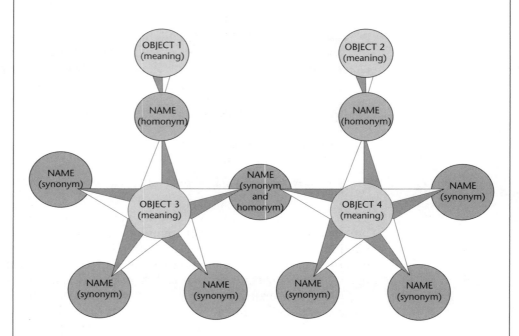

For example, backbone is a network of broadband connections between switches for the telecom industry, and the spinal bone in our backs for the rest of us. It is a homonym. Similarly, SDLC is an abbreviation for Systems Development Life Cycle for the information systems professional, and Synchronous Data Link Control, a kind of data transmission protocol, for a network professional. Thus, SDLC is also a homonym.

A word can be a synonym and a homonym at the same time. For instance, most of us know that an account for a salesperson is a synonym for customer, but to an accountant, it means a category of expense or revenue. Thus, account is both a synonym and a homonym.

Synonyms are common even within the same industry, and even within the same firm. For example, in a major telecommunications company, the operations departments identified central offices[51] for telephone switching facilities

---

50. Synonyms and homonyms are *states* of names. When a single name has a naming relationship with more than one concept, it is a homonym. When a single concept has a naming relationship with more than one name, each name is a synonym. See Figure 1.9.

51. A central office (CO) in the telecommunications industry is a switching center in which telephone trunks and loops are terminated and switched. Some synonyms for central office in the telecommunications industry are telephone exchange, switching center, switching exchange, and even switch.

> with a CLLI code (pronounced "silly" code), whereas commercial departments called the identifier Sensor ID. Senior managers and professionals, including many who had been with the firm for several decades, had no idea that the other half of the firm used a different word for the same concept—a concept that was central to their business.
>
> **9**

bring the entire exercise into question—but also that unfamiliar names might actually sow confusion and become a barrier to creativity. Remember our intent is to make change easier—not harder!

Instead of standardizing names, the group that administers the universal perspective might have its own label or name for each concept (object) that can be the hub around which all its synonyms revolve. See Figure 1.10. It shows three perspectives of two objects with several names each. The Primary names (and objects) at the core are shared, but hidden from all three perspectives. Perspective 1 has one name for object 2, a name that means the same thing to perspective 2 as well, and six synonyms for object 1, one of which is a name for object 2 in perspective 2. Thus, it is a homonym. Perspective 2 has six synonyms for object 2, one of which is a name perspective 1 uses for object 1. Perspective 3 has a name for object 1 that it shares with perspective 1, and another for object 2 that it shares with perspective 2.

The primary name, or Concept ID, can pin down the concept and anchor all its other names and synonyms. In this way, not only can default names be different in different perspectives and still map to the same concept, but users can also see and understand how other groups have named their concepts in the repository of knowledge. These synonyms and other names of an object will be aliases for the object. For clarity, the Concept ID should be crisp, and never be a homonym. The concept is the key to meaning, and we must focus on its meaning.

Thus, if this structure of knowledge is stored in an electronic repository, then each stakeholder need only be aware of names in his or her own perspective. There may be synonyms in a single perspective, too. The homonym between the two objects has a different meaning in each context (perspective), but those who hold

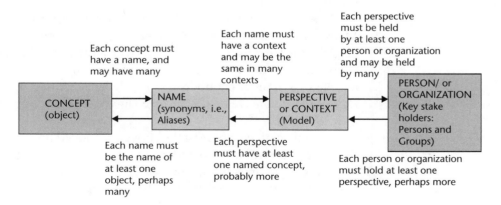

Figure 1.9   Name is an object class linked to perspective.

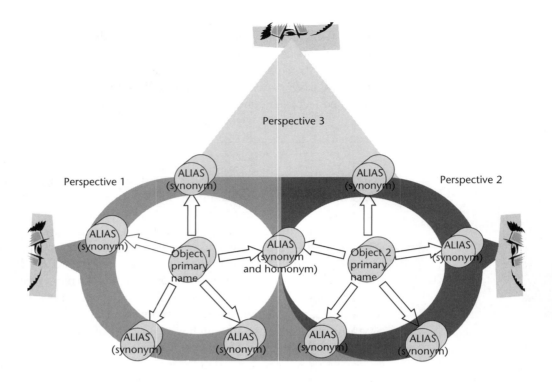

Figure 1.10   Primary Names, Perspectives, and Aliases.

one perspective can be aware that it is a homonym, and will be free (to use the repository) to look up its meaning to others.

The naming structure should be embedded in the Standard Unified Perspective we recently discussed. This "chassis" of shared perspective is a firm anchor for every possible perspective that emerges from the Metamodel of Knowledge in [337]. The Standard Universal Perspective springs from the Metamodel of Knowledge, because that metamodel provides the abstractions that group common behavior and keep knowledge normalized. Thus, to solve the problem of perspective, we will need to understand both the Universal Perspective and the metamodel of knowledge that is its fountainhead.

The intent of this introductory chapter was to give you a "feel" for the Metamodel of Knowledge and some of its key components. The next chapter will describe the Universal Perspective. It will show how business meanings are components configured from other, more elementary meanings. Many of these base meanings lie within the Metamodel of Knowledge. *Creating Agile Business Systems with Reusable Knowledge* by Cambridge University Press elaborates on the Metamodel of Knowledge.

Even if you have not read the above-mentioned book, a healthy dose of common sense is all you will need to understand the Universal Perspective in the next chapter. However, if you must know the rules, laws, assumptions, and abstractions that have shaped the Universal Perspective, then we suggest you read *Creating Agile Business Systems with Reusable Knowledge*.

The Universal Perspective: Scope of Business

> Rama: "When there are countless universes arising and dissolving in the infinite … why do you teach me of their nature?"
> The Sage Vasishta: "In that way you have … gained knowledge of the relationship between a world and its meaning, or the object it denotes … In every atom of this existence are countless universes—who has the power to even count them?"
>
> —*The Yoga Vashishta*, an undated treatise from ancient India

This chapter describes the Standard Universal Perspective. The first part of the chapter describes a hierarchy of business meanings. These meanings are objects. Objects at lower levels of the hierarchy are polymorphisms of the higher-level meanings. These universal polymorphisms normalize shared business rules that connect functions of enterprises, and even complex supply chains, into cogent business models that create and deliver economic value. This chapter then identifies the semantics of universal normalized interactions between these objects. These patterns are expressed in object models.

The chapter concludes by describing how these primal patterns of business information can be used to integrate and engineer business processes and information systems. It also describes how business process engineering may be automated with a shared repository of knowledge, and lists the kind of infrastructure that would be required to utilize such a repository.

The Universal Perspective is a pattern. It is a pattern that underpins our understanding of business—a pattern of information, a scope, and a context. The Universal Perspective is a shared pattern of understanding; therefore, the Universal Perspective is a pattern that connects.

It is not only a shared pattern of understanding that helps businesses communicate, but also a shared pattern that glues together myriad aspects of business and entire supply chains. It is the home of those few, but simple, rules of business that are used most often, and within these rules lie the core values found at the heart of every business. These rules are also those that are the most critical to every business. Indeed, the Universal Perspective creates the very meaning of business.

The Universal Perspective is important because it weaves the enormous diversity of models and perspectives into one harmonious whole. It glues the uncountable expressions of detail and viewpoints into one composition. It is a pattern of unity in diversity. The Universal Perspective subsumes, transcends, and connects individual understanding. It is a pattern of connection, because it is the meeting place where meanings join and melt into their essence. It unites, because it is the essential pattern that weaves diversity into one cogent and coherent whole.

Think of the Universal Perspective as a hub from which all perspectives radiate like the spokes of a wheel. In the timeless stillness of the hub lies the silent confluence of myriad streams of thought. The hub draws them together inexorably, as it weaves these diverse threads into a pattern, a harmony at the heart of the hub, a harmony born of the confluence of meaning.

This hub, a unifying pattern, binds the diverse. Sometimes these diverse perspectives might even be apparent opposites, or even perspectives that clash in noisy conflict, yet the Universal Perspective at the heart of this spinning hub is their fountainhead.

The Universal Perspective is a primal pattern that can bind and hold the similar and diverse alike in harmony, because it seeks their common essence. In doing so, it normalizes those few rules that are used most often in the vast diversity of thoughts and concepts that create businesses and frame their uncountable polymorphisms. Thus, every business concept, old or new, creative or conventional, becomes a polymorphism of this universal pattern.

This chapter will lend substance to the shadowy concepts hidden within the Universal Perspective, and its abstract parent, the Metamodel of Knowledge in [337]. Indeed, together they are the Universal Pattern and the wellspring of meaning.[52]

2.1   Universal Perspective, Universal Pattern

"Up from earth's center through the seventh gate
I rose, and on the throne of saturn sate,
And many knots unravel'd by the road;
But not the knot of human death and fate."

—The Rubaiyat of Omar Khayyam

Widely shared ideas about business and reality underpin our perceptions, and because of these widely shared ideas, it is possible to define universal classes of objects that encapsulate shared knowledge. These universal object classes anchor knowledge firmly and coherently from every possible business perspective.[53] They are a pattern—a standard perspective that other perspectives can add to, but one they will not have to change to satisfy their requirements. It subsumes them all.

---

52. A fundamental premise of the Metamodel of Knowledge is that a single meaning may have several expressions. The equivalence of multitudes of expressions is not always obvious. Moreover, their equivalence may be context sensitive; that is, in a given region of information space, the expressions in question may always yield identical results, but may diverge outside it. Readers interested in more information may refer to [337], the note on lambda calculus, and publications on the topic in the References.

53. Cross-industry process integration and corresponding standards have been driven by the growing realization that competitive advantage lies in positioning the entire supply chain competitively, not just positioning individual suppliers and corporations. Value Chain Markup Language (VCML) is a recent standard that was formulated in support of this need. VCML is an XML-based standard. VCML includes an industry-specific vocabulary of commonly used objects. This vocabulary also includes rules for cross-industry translation of vocabularies. The industries covered thus far have been listed in Chapter 1 under The Tyranny of Words. This list is likely to grow. See also [65] and http://www.vcml.net.

Every model of business is a polymorphism of this universal pattern. The secret of the Universal Perspective lies not in detail, but in generalization. Only the general can withstand the intense pounding of continual change compounded by the diversity of creative thought and innovation.

The Universal Perspective is not the result of business concepts generalized at random. The generalizations in the Universal Perspective are resilient because they are special kinds of generalizations. They flow from the Metamodel of Knowledge, polymorphisms of the normalized knowledge therein.

The Universal Perspective is the entire structure of interconnected objects that anchor knowledge—classes, aggregations, relationships, constraints, state spaces, domains, effects, and all the other meta-objects described in [337], glued to each other in the structure we call knowledge, or more modestly, our perspective of knowledge. It is also an object in its own right—an aggregate object with a structure—an object composition.

Box 10: Aggregation, Composition, Relationship, and Process   10

An aggregate object is a collection of objects. Its internal structure, the nature and existence of associations between its constituents, may or may not be known; all that we need to know is that the aggregate is a collection of objects. When the relationships between objects in a collection are known, it is a composition. A composition is a kind of aggregate—a subtype. An aggregate may be an aggregation either by decree, or based on specific aggregation criteria. For instance, an object class is a special kind of aggregate, based on common features. Relationships may also be compositions, a fact inherited from the generic meta-object we discussed in Chapter 1. For instance, consider the relationships "Person lives in House" and "House located in Town," connected serially create a relationship "Person lives in Town." It is a composition.

Thus, any model is also a composition. Indeed, any network of associations within the model is also a composition. The aggregate object will normalize information that its constituents do not—for example, the number of objects aggregated. Although it might be counterintuitive, an aggregation might even be empty—an aggregation with no members that normalizes the fact that the object count of the collection is nil.[54]

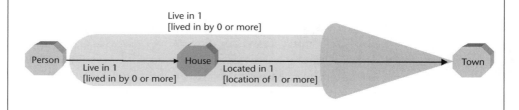

Live in 1
[lived in by 0 or more]

Person — Live in 1 [lived in by 0 or more] → House — Located in 1 [location of 1 or more] → Town

---

54.   See the empty set in Box 19 on our Web site.

10

One kind of derived relationship is also called a transitive relationship. For instance, Person lives in Town is derived from the two relationships in the composition above. A transitive relationship adds no new information, and should be omitted if the composition it was derived from is included. Otherwise, information will be replicated and not normalized. See Module 5, Section 1, on our Web site.

A Relationship may also be derived from another relationship by adding information to the original, and thereby subtyping it. These are called polymorphisms. Thus, a generic "assembly" relationship between machine parts and a machine might assemble parts into a machine. A relationship for assembling cars from car parts will be a polymorphism of the generic Assemble relationship. The assembling of a car is called an inclusion polymorphism of the generic Assemble relationship, because Assemble includes the meaning of assembling cars. See the note on polymorphism, which is also discussed in detail in [337].

A relationship may also loop back to the same object class. For example, a Person may represent Person. These relationships are called recursive relationships. Some recursive relationships (like represent) may be permitted to loop back to the same instance of an object. These are called reflexive relationships. Others (e.g., self help) might have to always loop back to the same instance of the object. These are called idempotent relationships. Some, like Person may be parent of Person, might be barred from looping back to the same instance of the object. These are called irreflexive relationships, as described in Module 5, Section 3, on our Web site.

Figure 116, Module 5, Section 4, and Module 6, Section 1, all on our Web site, show why reflexive relationships are polymorphisms of recursive relationships, idempotent relationships are polymorphisms of reflexive relationships, irreflexive relationships are polymorphisms of idempotent relationships, and nonrecursive relationships are polymorphisms of irreflexive relationships.

A symmetrical relationship is the same as its inverse (e.g., Person is relative of Person; the relationship reads the same in both directions). An asymmetrical relationship must read differently in forward and backward directions; its inverse must be different from it (e.g., the inverse of Person is parent of Person is Person is child of Person; the child cannot be his or her own parent). An antisymmetrical relationship is a recursive relationship that is asymmetrical, except when it loops back to the same object instance (e.g., arithmetic subtraction; the order of subtraction matters, unless a number is being subtracted from itself). Module 5, Section 4, on our Web site, shows that asymmetrical relationships are polymorphisms of symmetrical relationships (e.g., parent of is a polymorphism of relative of), idempotent relationships are polymorphisms of antisymmetrical relationships, and antisymmetrical relationships are polymorphisms of reflexive relationships.

In Chapter 1, we discussed how processes are temporal relationships. A process relates resources with its products. The resources must come before the products. Thus, adding information on the flow of time to any relationship (or composition) turns it into a process. This makes process a polymorphism of relationship. Resources may also be consumed by the process. Consumption of a

10

resource includes any alteration to the resource (i.e., state change). The altered resource is considered a product. Products may also be waste products. Catalysts are resources that are referenced, but not consumed. Shorn of information on resources and products, a process becomes a mere event—an interval in time. A Moment is a time interval of negligible duration.

A process may be the responsibility of a person or organization. There are different kinds of roles a person or organization may play. These include:

- R: The process owner is responsible for the overall quality and relevance of the process;
- A—Authority: The person or organization is responsible for supervising the process, usually a role delegated by "R";
- W—Work: The person or organization who executes the actual process;
- C: The person or organization is consulted in the execution of the process;
- F—facilitator: Usually used in collaborative processes, this person or organization coordinates the smooth running of concurrent engineering or collaborative processes, in which several parties must collaborate concurrently to create work products.

In this book, these ownership roles will be collectively termed "RAWCF" parameters of a process. See detailed discussion in Module 5, Section 3, under Process Ownership, on our Web site.

The knowledge that a set of objects interacts in some unspecified way (i.e., involve each other) is the most basic of relationships. All relationships are polymorphisms of "involve." Relationships have two basic properties: (1) Order, the number of distinct object instances tied into the relationship; and (2) Degree, the number of distinct object classes tied together by the relationship. Relationships of a degree larger than 2 are called "higher degree" relationships, and those of an order greater than 2 are called "higher order" relationships. Relationships may also be constrained in different ways. Constraints (and other added information) create polymorphisms. One constraint is the cardinality constraint—constraints on occurrences of the relationship, or limits (upper, lower, or both) on numbers of source and/or target objects the relationship may link (see the figure in this box).

The existence of a relationship may mandate the existence of another, and vice versa. This is called a mutual inclusion or set equality constraint between relationships. The existence of a relationship might bar the existence of another. This is the property of mutual exclusivity between relationships. The existence of a relationship may mandate the existence of another, but not vice versa. This is a subsetting constraint between relationships—the subset may or may not exist if the superset does, but the superset must exist if the subset exists. These properties flow from constraints on the order and degree of

10

relationships, and have been discussed in detail in Module 5, Section 1, on our Web site. See Figure 74 on our Web site.

Objects also may limit the number of relationships they may have with other objects. The cardinality constraints on relationships are inherited from this feature of the generic meta-object. Constraints may be imposed at both class and instance levels. For example, business rules might dictate that a person, an instance of an object, may participate (a relationship) in only one project (another object) at a time. This is an upper bound on the cardinality ratio of Participate, a relationship between object classes Person and Project. Assume we change the rule. We allow a person to divide his or her time between at most five projects. The upper bound on the cardinality ratio of Participate has become five instead of one.

Along with special projects inside the firm, the individual may spend time with the firm's customers. Then, his or her time must be divided between customer care and internal projects. The total number of feasible relationships that employees may have with projects and customers may then be in question. The model may require that the upper bound limit the total cardinality ratio, rather than the cardinality ratios of relationships between employees and projects, and employees and customers separately.

Thus far, participate, the relationship, has conveyed only nominal information on a person's participation in projects and customer care. At the instance level, it has only told us whether a person is, or is not, associated with a specific project and/or a specific customer. It has not said how much of the resource (person) will be consumed by the project or customer, nor if all projects and customers will consume his (or her) time and effort equally.

The relationship can be more informative than this. For instance, it could tell us that one project might consume twice as much time as another, as might one customer consume twice as much time as another. The time an individual can devote to projects and customers may be limited. Thus, there are two interdependent items of information involved—an individual's capacity to participate in relationships, and the quantum of that capacity depleted by each relationship. The capacity for participation is an attribute of the object and normalized by it, and the capacity consumed is an attribute of each relationship, and is normalized by the relationship. Each relationship between instances of objects may not only convey the fact of association, but also how much of an object's capacity for association with other objects it consumes. Thus, the capacity for association locked up by a relationship may vary by relationship class or by relationship instance. Capacity has been discussed in more detail under Compositions of Relationship in Module 5, Section 1, on our Web site. Size is a polymorphism of capacity. Capacity stems from relationships in general, and Size from the containment relationship discussed in Box 12. It is an inclusion polymorphism of capacity. Size can have different polymorphisms. Each polymorphism of containment is a potential polymorphism of Size. For example, a constraint on how many people can live in a house is a polymorphism of size that stems from the Live in relationship, which in turn, is a polymorphism of containment. The floor space of a house is another polymorphism of size that stems from a containment relationship with the area domain. See Module 4, Section 3, Reusing Knowledge—Building Upon the Old, Rule 2, on our Web site.

10

Occurrence of a relationship also may be enriched with additional information on sequencing and quantitative calculations. For instance, monetary value is related to price and quantity via arithmetic multiplication. This is a quantitative relationship. It carries more information than merely asserting that price, quantity, and monetary value are mutually associated. Adding information to an object creates subtypes. Thus, these are all different ways in which relationships may be subtyped.

Aggregate objects, compositions, relationships, and processes have been described in much more detail in Module 5 on our Web site.

In order to subsume all perspectives and yet capture their common essence, this primal composition cannot be information-rich. It must necessarily be information-sparse. It is timeless in its Spartan sparseness. Therefore, it cannot be a process. It is a static model, but one that can metamorphose into processes, and even supply chains, as Time seeps through the objects it holds.

"Ordinary" occurrence relationships between object classes are among the most information sparse structures in the metamodel of knowledge (see Box 10). Therefore, it is hardly surprising that the Universal Perspective will consist of an object model that glues together generic business objects with exactly these kinds of relationships. These relationships will metamorphose into processes, succession constraints, rule expressions, and even supply chains, in step with the information we add to them.

However, before we can articulate these relationships between objects, we must first identify what these fundamental business objects are. Only then will we be in a position to articulate the common relationships that bind them into timeless truths, a composition at the heart of the Universal Perspective. Thus, the Universal Perspective consists of the Metamodel of Knowledge, fundamental business objects, common of polymorphisms of these objects, and their relationships. Together, they create a pattern. It is this pattern that we call Universal Perspective. In the following sections, we will build the Universal Perspective step by step, one step at a time. Reference [337] describes the Metamodel of Knowledge in detail.

2.1.1 Stock Themes of Business—Polymorphisms of Fundamental Objects

Fundamental business objects are polymorphisms of the inchoate meta-object of Chapter 1. This inchoate object is a pattern of pure information.[55] The objects in Figure 2.1 are the most basic of business meanings, and the root of all themes shared by businesses.

---

55. Reference [337] discusses how the meta-object is a pattern of pure information that asserts the meaning of *All*, which is a mathematical value discussed in Box 51 on our Web site. The mathematical value *Any* is discussed in Module 5, Section 4, on our Web site.

Each object in Figure 2.1 is a polymorphism of the primal object, and will be discussed in this section. Each also may be a resource used by a process. Even events and processes could become resources for processes. Events or processes that trigger processes in a chain are no different from other resources in the before-and-after relationship a process articulates (see Box 10). Thus, predecessor processes and triggering events can be considered to be resources of the processes they trigger. They are "consumed" or "used" by the successor (or triggered) process to produce its products. Similarly, successor processes and events may be considered products produced by predecessors. When one process spawns another, the spawned process is clearly a product of the process(es) that spawned it, either singly or in combination.

Figure 2.2 shows relationships hidden in Figure 2.1, and recognizes that a resource is merely a role of the primal object derived from its relationship with Process. A Resource is any object that is a potential resource of a process. A resource may be used by a process, but does not have to be. Thus, it is a synonym for the primal object of Figure 2.1.[56] The hierarchy between Energy and Physical objects in Figure 2.2 is counterintuitive and will be discussed under Physical Object.

The primary intent of the subtyping hierarchy of Figure 2.1 (and others in this section) is to normalize common features of business in the right objects, and at the right levels. If we can do this, these features will not be endlessly replicated in multitudes of unthinking business objects. Instead, they will be normalized and inherited.

For the most part, these features are business rules and interactions so fundamental that we take them for granted; yet, they are very important because they are so basic. They are so basic that they are endlessly replicated in most business models, yet they connect entire businesses and supply chains. Thus, they are the keys to integration because they are stock themes. They are also the keys used most often,

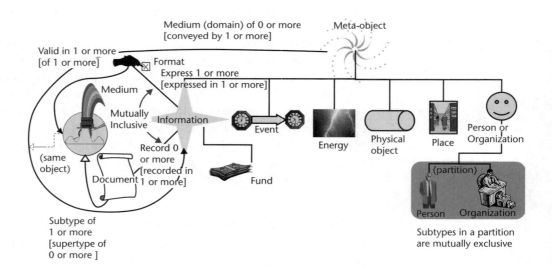

Figure 2.1 Fundamental business objects. See Box 11.

56. The "use" relationship and its cardinality in the Metamodel of Knowledge determines that the term "resource" and "object" have the same meaning. An individual resource may or may not be used by any process. The term "resource" implies that it is a resource because of its potential to be a resource for some undetermined process (see Figure 116 and Module 5, Section 4, on our Web site).

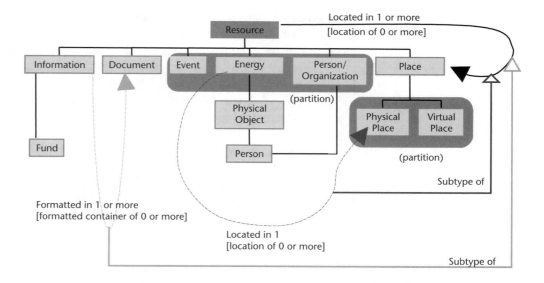

Figure 2.2 Basic polymorphisms of Resource.

masked most often, and hidden in multitudes of polymorphisms. Normalizing these interactions will unmask their polymorphisms. Unmasking their polymorphisms will make business processes agile business systems easy to integrate, and will make information systems flexible. Figure 2.1 and others that follow are templates that will unmask.

The diagrams in this section will be subtyping hierarchies as in Figure 2.1. Inheritance will trickle down from the top of the hierarchy to the bottom; super-types will be on top, and subtypes will be below. Unless they are explicitly shown within the same partition, the subtypes in these diagrams will not be mutually exclu-sive. A specific object instance might simultaneously combine features of several object classes in these hierarchies.

Chapter 1 described how subtypes become polymorphisms of their parents as they combine and inherit their features, and how multiple inheritance can combine features of multiple parents [337]. This is how most business meanings will emerge

---

Box 11: Partitioning Objects   **11**

Object classes may be partitioned into mutually exclusive subtypes.
For instance, the class of Persons may be partitioned into Male Persons and Female Persons. A partition is a meta-object. Subtypes within a partition are mutually exclusive. However, subtypes across partitions need not be. For example, a parent also may be an employee, because the parent/nonparent partition is distinct from the Employee/Nonemployee partition. Chapter 2, Section 3, in [337] describes partitions in detail.

in this section as objects in subtyping hierarchies. The relationships in the Universal Object Model of the next section will give rise to more business meanings. The focus of this section is on universal, frequently used subtypes; the next section will focus on universal relationships between these objects.

For this reason, nonsubtyping relationships have been mostly omitted in the following figures. The few that have been shown have only been depicted because they clarify fundamental meanings, and are sometimes the very basis of the hierarchies we will discuss. These relationships are defining relationships for these polymorphisms. Without these features, there would be no subtype. The subtypes thus described will often normalize the interactions we will cover in subsequent sections. Our subtyping hierarchy starts with the primal meta-object.

Under the primal object we have the following.

Time and Event

An event is a time slot. It captures information on the flow of time, and is a part of the Metamodel of Knowledge in [337] (see Box 10, and comprehensive coverage in [337]). Processes and business events, such as fairs, festivals, exhibitions, and promotions, are polymorphisms obtained by adding business meaning to "Event."

Person/Organization

Person/Organization subsumes the common behavior of people and organizations. A person is an individual human being. An organization is an aggregation, a pattern of people. When it has structure, it is a composition of people. Person/Organization emerges from an artifice—the laws of Man and the conventions of business. In the eyes of the law, and in common business practice, an organization is like a person in many ways. An organization may own assets, owe money, be responsible for tasks, be held legally liable for its actions, be the originator of its ideas, be the repository of expertise and experience above and beyond the expertise and experience of its individual employees, and so forth. Person/Organization is the repository of these features common to both people and organizations. It is an abstraction that normalizes properties shared by both and inherited by each.

Organization is also an abstraction and a polymorphism of Information, but Person is more concrete (and a physical object to boot!). We will discuss the behavior of Person/Organization in more detail in the sections on common polymorphisms of Person/Organization. Any object, including Organization, may be considered to be a manifestation of information, but clearly Person/Organization, Energy, and Event are mutually exclusive manifestations. Figure 2.2 articulates the obvious.

Energy and Physical Objects

A Physical Object occupies physical space, and can only be in one physical place at a time. Contrast this with Information. The same item of information may exist simultaneously at several places (see Box 25). Physical versus abstract state spaces are discussed in detail in the discussion of Pattern in [337]. Box 62 on our Web site has an example of how these differences impact business rules and how change may be automated.

Although the subtyping hierarchy between Energy and Physical Objects has been flattened in Figure 2.1,[57] and both have been shown at the same level, Figure 2.2 shows that one is a polymorphism of the other. This might vex some readers.[58] What does energy have in common with a material object, except that both may be resources used by a process? It has plenty in common. To begin with, both material objects and energy are located in physical space.[59] They share the property that the same item cannot be in more than one location at a time. Other objects, like information and documents, may simultaneously occupy several locations in virtual space. Organizations may even occupy several locations in virtual and physical place simultaneously.

Events too need not be exclusively confined to one physical or virtual location. An event is a time slot; time passes everywhere in physical space. Unless we narrow this generic event down to a specific physical or virtual geography by adding meanings or constraints, and make it a polymorphism, it will occur everywhere simultaneously. Thus, unlike most objects, energy and physical objects are special. They can only be in one (physical) place at any given moment.

Moreover, energy has less structure than a material object. It conveys less information. Energy is a supertype that normalizes the constraint that gives a physical location has exclusive possession of an object. Material objects inherit this constraint from energy. Most physicists are well versed with the equivalence of matter and energy. However, as knowledge engineers, our interest in the subtyping hierarchy is different. It flows from the fact that both matter and energy share the constraint that they must exist in only one physical location at a time—a fact that is inherited by all material objects from Energy, an inheritance also borne out by the laws of physics.

Medium, Document, and Information

A medium of information is a role of the primal object. This role tells us that objects can carry and convey information. Any polymorphisms of the primal object may play this role. Examples abound; they are as much a part of our daily experience as they are prolific.[60] Therefore, being a medium of information is a fact that is articulated and normalized by the primal object itself. The relationship between Information and the primal meta-object in Figure 2.1 tells us that any object can contain and convey information.[61] When it does so, it is a Document. A class of documents is a Medium. It is a special kind of class, as we will see.

Information is recorded in a document, and in a format. That record, the joining of format and information in a medium, creates the document. The document

---

57. See how inheritance hierarchies may be flattened in Box 15.
58. In Figure 2.1, we had "flattened" this hierarchy of physical objects—see Box 15.
59. Chapter 4, Section 1, in [337], under the discussion of Patterns, clarifies the distinction between physical space and other kinds of spaces.
60. Events such as promotions or triggers for actions obviously convey information, as do physical objects, such as books or the stone tablets of yesteryear. Energy constantly pulses information to the television sets in our living rooms. A band of frequencies in the electromagnetic spectrum may not only carry energy, but also may be reserved by a radio station in order to broadcast information. The band is thus both a *medium* for expressing information and a *place* for locating it. Money, or *Funds*, tells us the value of objects that we buy and sell. It is perhaps belaboring the obvious to say that people are sources of information, and organizations hold the collective experience of people, which makes both people and organizations media for storing and transmitting information.
61. Box 12 discusses *Contain*. *Medium of* in Figure 2.1 is a polymorphism of *Contained in* when the contained pattern is a pattern of pure information.

Box 12: Extending UML Composite Aggregation and Physical Location

12

"Location" is always relative. "Locate," a relationship in the Metamodel of Knowledge [337], locates a pattern in state space relative to another. The location of an object is only meaningful in relationship to another; to locate an object in terms of itself conveys no information and is meaningless. Locate is also a symmetrical relationship. The inverse of locate is also locate; the located object also locates the locator. "Contained in" is an asymmetrical polymorphism of "locate" that describes a special kind of relative location, in which one pattern encapsulates another, without necessarily incorporating it. The limits of the encapsulating pattern surround the limits of the enclosed (encapsulated) pattern. "Part of" is a polymorphism of "Contained in" that asserts that an aggregate not only contains another, but also incorporates it as a part. Thus, a room may be considered to be a part of a house, and owning the house will imply owning its parts, but the furniture in the house are not its parts, and owning the house does not imply owning the furniture (e.g., it might be borrowed). The inverse of Part of is the aggregation relationship (Aggregate of). Consists of is a synonym for "Aggregate of." The subtyping relationship is a polymorphism and even more constrained form of "part of," in which an object is incorporated into the class of the containing object and virtually loses its separate identity. For instance, a man is not a part of a person; it is a subtype, because Person (the class) incorporates Man into its meaning. These polymorphisms of "locate" are analyzed in Chapter 5, Sections 2 and 4, and Figure 114, in [337]. Chapter 2, Section 3, in [337], also describes why the existence of a polymorphism is contingent on the existence of the supertype, but not vice versa.

The relationship called "composite aggregation" in UML gives an aggregate object exclusive possession of a part (Box 33 on our Web site). The UML symbol for it is the solid diamond in Figure (c) of Box 33. The UML syntax bars an object in a composite aggregation from being a member of any other aggregation. Note that the "composition of" relationship we discussed in Box 10 is a less constrained form of structured aggregation. "Composition of" tells us that the aggregate is structured. It does not bar membership in multiple aggregations.

We will obtain UML's composite aggregation if we cap the cardinality ratio of the contained in relationship to be at most one. Composite aggregation in UML is thus a configuration of two components—a special relationship (contained in), and a special value constraint attached to its cardinality.

This construct, the composite aggregation of UML, flows from the property that a physical object only may be in one place at a time. It is a subtype of containment used primarily to tie physical parts into physical assemblies, or to make a physical place or object "contain" other physical objects. The metamodel of knowledge makes finer distinctions. It not only distinguishes between structure, and the lack of structure in an aggregation, but also distinguishes membership of a composition (i.e., being a part of an object) from con-

> **12**
>
> tainment of one object in another. Nor does the metamodel bar an object from being a part of several structures simultaneously—not even if both structures depend on it for their very existence and meaning—because the object in question might be a concept or meaning (i.e., a pattern of pure and abstract information). The metamodel must do this because the scope of business knowledge extends beyond gross physical constructs, into structures of information, concepts, and meanings. The power of reason extends beyond the scope of mechanical engineering in the physical world. The metamodel of knowledge extends this power of reason.

need not be a piece of paper. It could be a bit stream of information riding on the wings of radio waves through space. It could be a recorded message we hear, or a holographic image projected in space for us to see. The Document in Figure 2.1 generalizes our everyday concept of document.

It is also common knowledge (and common sense) that every format cannot apply to every medium. For example, sound cannot format a picture, and a paper document does not record sound. The many-to-many relationship between Format and Medium in Figure 2.1 makes room for these kinds of restrictions. The medium-format resolution entity,[62] an object buried within this many-to-many relationship, articulates the fact that a format may have different polymorphisms in different media. Thus, a format for printing images on paper is a polymorphism of the corresponding format for displaying images on the screen of your computer. The bottom line: A Medium is a class of documents that normalizes constraints on its format.

A document can be copied from one medium to another, but it cannot switch media. Each copy may convey exactly the same information, but each is a distinct document in its own right. However, just as it is possible to classify an object in a multitude of ways, it is possible for a document to simultaneously belong to multiple media. For instance, a spoken word, pregnant with information, is a document propagating through Air, its medium. The frequency spectrum is also its medium. Both Air and Spectrum are places for information, because they both normalize constraints on how information may be formatted, and what kinds of symbols are permitted in each medium. The spoken word was a sound constrained by the intersection of constraints imposed by each medium to which it belonged.[63] It was a document that was an instance of two different media. Thus, the class of spoken words is a class of documents with two parents—the frequency spectrum and Air. Both are its media.

A medium, like any class, articulates a potential—the potential of a document to exist. A medium may have no documents—it might lie unused—only a concept and an unrealized potential; or it may have several documents. It is thus a class—an

---

62. Resolution of many-to-many relationships are discussed in Box 24. Details are in Module 5, Section 1, on our Web site. See "Resolving Many-to-Many Relationships" on our Web site.
63. Set intersection is discussed in Box 19 on our Web site.

aggregation—that might even be devoid of members.[64] An instance of a medium is thus an object class that may have no instances, but when it does, these instances will be instances of documents. The bottom line: Medium is a class of documents based on formativeness (formatability). The relationship between Document and Medium in Figure 2.1 is a special polymorphism of the subtyping relationship, and a document will inherit all constraints (such as formatting, information quality, and longevity constraints) that its medium normalizes. Document gives information a place for expression. The medium gives a document its substance and the potential for expression. Document is a subtype that joins two parents (i.e., Medium and Place) into one indivisible whole—a place of expression for information. Formatted information in a document is thus potential realized.

Place, Medium, and Document

The locate relationship (see Box 12) creates the concept of Place. Any resource may be a place. Thus, Place can be either a physical place or a virtual place, such as an electronic bulletin board or a part of the radio frequency spectrum. Located in is a synonym for contained in. It is a polymorphism of locate (see Box 12). When we consider visual patterns, it is appropriate to call the envelopment of one pattern by another "containment," and the relationship between the contained pattern and the enveloping pattern "contained in." However, when we consider the location of a resource such as a meaning conveyed by a medium, convention might consider "located in" a more elegant expression. In either case, they mean the same. Both are the same polymorphism of Locate. We have called it "located in" in Figure 2.2. "Location of," the inverse of "located in," is a synonym for "container of." When a resource is located in another resource, the containing resource becomes the Place of the contained resource. It is an optional role that any resource can play.

Astute readers might ask whether a place can really be empty: Will not a place always contain one resource itself? If this reasonable sounding premise is true, then even a place devoid of other resources cannot ever be truly empty. Consequently, contradicting the assertion in Figure 2.2, the cardinality of Located in can never be nil. The reason for this premise fades away with the quantum of information it conveys—none. A fact must convey information in order to contribute to a model or a component of knowledge. The location of a place within itself fails this test, since it conveys no information. This is why the cardinality of "located in" is the way it is in Figure 2.2.[65]

Thus, while Place is an optional role of Resource, it plays a key role. We all know that places—virtual or physical—are resources we use, buy, and sell. They are the single most important resources at the heart of the entire physical and virtual infrastructure that supports everything that we do. Business is perpetually seeking, jostling, and competing for the right Place, in more than one sense.[66]

A Document is also a kind of Place—a place for Information. However, a document is more than a place. As we recently discussed, a place cannot be a document

---

64. Reference [337] shows how a *Class* is an aggregate object, and may be empty. Thus, the existence of a medium does not require the existence of a document. Medium is a concept based on shared constraints on *Format*.
65. We discuss the irreflexivity of the containment relationship in detail at the end of Module 5, Section 2, on our Web site. See "Location, Containment, and Incorporation" on our Web site.
66. Businesses compete for market space. See the section on markets and market segments in this chapter.

Box 13: Money, Preference, and Economic Value   **13**

Preference and Economic Value (money) are two frequently used business domains, as described in detail under The Information in Domain, Chapter 4, Section 3, in [337]. Preference is an ordinal scaled domain, whereas Economic Value is a ratio scaled domain. Although preferences are usually discrete ranks and economic value is a ratio scaled continuum, economic value and preference are related. Economic Value, being a ratio scaled domain, has more information than preference, an ordinal domain, and may legitimately be considered a subtype of the preference domain (see Box 14). To turn Preference into Economic Value, information on intermediate preferences was added, until the domain became dense enough to be considered a continuum. Information on a nil value (indifference) was also added to the domain to turn Preference into Economic Value. Thus, economic value is really preference information quantified.

Economic Value is also an example of how all ratio scaled domains may not be equally flush with information. The information content of the Economic Value domain lies somewhere between the sparse information of the ordinal preference domain, and the rich certainty of "hard" information inherent in physical ratio scaled domains like mass or length. Economic Value conveys "softer," more uncertain information. Until money was discovered, primitive economies were based on bartering goods and services. They had no unit of measure they could associate with economic value. However, when preference information of large numbers of people was involved in larger communities, information content inherent in the preferences of individuals added up, and the overall preference of the population (an aggregate object) became almost ratio scaled, and monetary exchange evolved. With monetary exchange in place, the near quantitative statistical nature of aggregate preference became evident and firmly established as the domain of money.

As we considered the preferences of large numbers of individuals, the meaning of preference and the meaning of information in the composite, preference information domain "melted" into a single continuum of values. As an increasing number of individuals were considered, the information conveyed by each person's preferences added up,[67] and the relationship between preference and information got denser and denser, until it could be considered a ratio scaled continuum. Thus, we are justified in considering Economic Value as a primary domain that is a subtype of Preference, an ordinal domain. Domains like Economic Value, which were created by adding information to primary domains with less information until they changed into a new kind of domain, are subtypes of the domains from which they grew. See Chapter 4, Section 3, in [337].

Unlike its physical counterparts, the unit of measure of Money is nonstationary (i.e., changes over time). Thus, if you expressed a value, such as

---

67. Readers interested in the mathematics of how individual preferences add up to yield domains richer in information may refer to the discussion on concordance on page 229 in [311].

13

a pay scale, in U.S. dollars 10 years ago, it will not equate to its expression in U.S. dollars today (nations that have experienced hyperinflation know the severity of this problem only too well!). Since the money domain has intrinsically less information than physical domains, such as length or mass, even if you converted 10-year-old dollar values to present-day dollar values, the conversion will intrinsically lack the reliability (certainty of being correct) that, say, converting from feet to inches has.

Rules for converting money from one unit of measure to another conform to the conversion rules for ratio scaled domains (see Chapter 1). Whether we convert one currency to another in terms of their current values, or convert a measure of currency past to the measure of the same currency today, we multiply by a conversion ratio. Converting between currencies is called an exchange rate; converting the same currency between different times is called an index. Each is a conversion ratio, and both change state. Conceptually they are identical. The knowledge is normalized in the money domain, ready to be configured and used when required. Reference [337] has more details.

unless it also formats information. The format might be patterns of energy shimmering in some medium, or patterns of symbols carved onto a rock, but it must be a format and a symbol. Only then will the place be a document. Thus, Formatted in, in Figure 2.2, is a special polymorphism of Contained in in Box 12.[68] Thus, a Document is a special subtype of Place.

Any kind of Place can be considered to be a Document as soon as it contains formatted information. The content of a document is information, and its substance is the substance of its medium; but its format is the hallmark of an individual Document.

Place can have innumerable other polymorphisms. For instance, it can be a physical assembly of parts; then, the assembly is the place for its parts. It also could be abstract information—a meaning that also contains other meanings. For instance, the meaning of Ancestor contains the meaning of Parent, which contains the meanings of Mother and Father. An organization is another kind of abstract place—a place for people, and a place for information. The polymorphisms of Place are too numerous to even attempt to enumerate. Any object, tangible or intangible, can be a Place, and any object located by another is associated with a Place.

Fund

Fund is money in any form, a subtype of Information (see Box 13).[69] Fund and Money are subtly different meanings in this book: like Length and Mass, Money is a domain. Domains have no states. The money domain is therefore stateless, but Fund is not. Fund adds information on states—the quantum of money at a point in

---

68. Figure 114 under "The metamodel of relationship" on our Web site shows how the Metamodel of Knowledge configures the meaning of containment.
69. The information domain is discussed in Box 42 on our Web site.

time—to the stateless money domain. Thus, specific bank balances, budgets, or financial accounts are instances of Fund. The quantum of money in each instance maps to the money domain. Reference [337] has more detail on domains.

From Information, Fund inherits the fact that it may be formatted in documents of different kinds, and conveyed by the same kinds of media as its parent. For example, funds may be recorded in electronic formats and exchanged in virtual space, or recorded on paper currency bills and exchanged physically.[70] Funds are denominated in different currencies that are its respective units of measure. All quantitative values must have units of measure, and may be expressed in multiple units of measure. See Domain in Box 30.

Resource and Its Polymorphisms

Any aggregation, classification, or composition of any of the polymorphisms in Figure 2.2, or any interaction (relationship or constraint[71]) between them, is also a resource, since it also will be a polymorphism of the primal object. Business rules could aggregate resources into groups of mandatory resources or groups that cannot coexist (e.g., products in the marketplace). These resource groups will also be subtypes of Resource; they add information and structure to Resource, the primal meta-object. The implications are profound, but we will defer that discussion to a subsequent section in this chapter.

Mutability of Resources

Liskov's Substitution Principle asserts that a subtype may always be substituted for a supertype in a model without affecting the semantics of the model.[72] Does Liskov's Substitution Principle, applied to the subtyping hierarchy in Figure 2.2, imply that a physical object is a resource mutable with energy, and people are mutable with physical objects? On the surface, the answer is "no." The proposition not only seems counterintuitive, but also incorrect—even ridiculous. However, appearances can be deceptive. Considered literally, the proposition is correct. It only looks ridiculous because we are used to thinking laterally rather than literally, like a computer. To see how, consider what it literally means when we say that a generic physical object is a resource for a process—it means that any physical object will do. There is no requirement that the object be constrained in any way. Indeed, there is a requirement that there be no constraints; not even people are excluded.

Business processes are rarely as generic or abstract. They are more structured, and are usually more specific about the kinds of resources they need to produce specific products. For instance, if a business process requires wood, it cannot do with stone. However, if it truly required only a solid object, either wood or stone would do. We intuitively exclude people when the process calls for material resources. We think in a box. The problem is with us, not Liskov's Substitution Principle.

---

70.   Recognizing that Fund is a polymorphism of Information helped us creatively reengineer the check of Box 62 on our Web site.
71.   A constraint is a kind of relationship. See Module 5, Section 4, on our Web site; a relationship may be a resource.
72.   Liskov's Substitution Principle asserts: "It must be possible to substitute any object instance of a subclass for any object instance of a superclass without affecting the semantics of a program written in terms of the superclass." Although articulated for computer programs, this principle also applies to business meaning. See "The Substitution Principle" in Chapter 2 in [333], and Module 5, Section 1, under "Mutable Perspectives" (on our Web site), Section 3 in the section on process engineering, and the Principle of Parsimony in the Notes.

The process that requires some unspecified form of energy is even less structured. Most business or engineering processes will specify the kind of energy they need (e.g., heat, light, electricity, kinetic energy, and so forth). If the process is so vague that it says any form of energy will do, we could feed it anything, even matter, for matter contains energy. What this process is (literally) telling us is that it requires matter or energy; either item will do. For the same kinds of reasons, we must temper our understanding of mutability when we consider other kinds of subtyping structures, like Fund versus Information or Document versus Place.

When developing models from the patterns in this book, keep the Principle of Parsimony as your guiding principle. The Principle of Parsimony asserts that we specify the minimal amount of information required in a model or process in order to maximize flexibility of resources.[73] *If you do not have to, do not specialize the high-level objects, or add to the patterns in this book. Use them "as-is" as much as possible.*

Business Product Versus the Product of a Process

The same kinds of objects that are resources also can be products of processes. The primal object of Figure 2.1 can just as easily be called Item or Product.[74] However, there is a subtle difference between a business product, which is a proposition positioned for sale in the marketplace, and the product of a process as it is defined in the Metamodel of Knowledge. The difference involves ownership. There may be products of processes that are not owned by any person or organization. For instance, no person or organization is responsible for or holds a title of ownership to a natural process like the condensation of clouds to make rain, nor does anyone own the rain that falls from clouds. Yet rain is a product of condensation, a process. On the other hand, ownership of a product lies at the heart of any proposition positioned for sale in the marketplace. We will call this a business product.

In this chapter, unless we qualify it as the product of a process, the term "product" will mean a business product. Of course, a business product is also a product of a process. The proposition must be produced, but not all items that are produced and owned are meant for sale. Thus, a business product is a subtype of the product of a process, and it is a polymorphism of Resource, based on the usage of this term in this chapter. A corporation could own the rain it creates, if it owns the process for creating rain by seeding clouds.

Ownership of Products and Assets

Ownership lies at the heart of any business. It is a core value. A resource (or product or item) may be owned. The concept of Asset captures this rule and the fundamental value of business. Just as Medium was a role of the primal object obtained from its relationship with Information, and Resource was similarly obtained from its relationship with Event (or Process),[75] Asset is derived from the primal object, because of the ownership relationship it may have with Person/Organization.

---

73. See the note on the Principle of Parsimony. The Principle of Parsimony is also discussed in [337].
74. The product of a process is a polymorphism of the primal object in a different partition from Resource (i.e., a Resource may also simultaneously be a Product). Module 5, Sections 3 and 4, discuss the topic; Figure 116 under "The Metamodel of Relationship" on our Web site shows the *produce* relationship and its cardinality.
75. Process is a subtype of Event and Relationship (Box 10). If an event or relationship is a resource, Process also will be.

Box 14: The Principle of Subtyping by Adding Information | 14

The Principle of subtyping by adding information asserts that adding information to a pattern of information creates a subtype of the pattern. It applies to any pattern of information. Meanings are abstract patterns of information. A constraint on a pattern reduces its degrees of freedom and adds to its information content, thus subtyping it. A condition is also a kind of constraint; it reduces the freedom of a pattern. Therefore, a conditional pattern or concept is a subtype of the unconstrained pattern or concept. Similarly, declaring the contents, components, or internal composition of an object adds information to it. Therefore, it is a subtype of the object that offers no visibility of its parts, contents, or structure (see Boxes 10 and 12). These principles are central to the concepts in this book, and are discussed in detail in Box 43, Module 5, Sections 2 and 4, and Module 6, Section 2, on our Web site. Patterns are discussed in Chapter 4, Section 1, in [337].

Asset, like Resource and Medium, is a role of the primal object, inherited by its polymorphisms.

At one time, every resource in Figure 2.2 could be owned. However, business is now more enlightened; we cannot own people. For this reason, polymorphisms of Asset are almost identical to polymorphisms of Resource; only people are left out. Conversely, Funds are always owned, and hence are always assets.

Thus, Asset is a more constrained pattern than Resource; its degrees of freedom are fewer.[76] Asset is Resource with a restriction—that Person must be excluded. Thus, Asset is a polymorphism of Resource.[77]

Even when ownership is in dispute, the disputed item is an asset—we know that it is owned, although its owner might be "unknown." As the identities of its owners becomes more certain, and the possibilities grow more restricted, the pattern called Asset also becomes more constrained in information space. Thus, based on the principle of subtyping by adding information (see Box 14), an asset with known owners is a polymorphism of the same asset with unknown, or disputed, owners. The only information we need before we can call a resource an asset is that it is owned, even if we do not know by whom. As its owners become clear, the asset becomes a subtype of the bare bones asset of Figure 2.3. Of course, if we know that the resource in question is money (Fund), ownership is always implied.

A business product, as we recently discussed, is an asset that a person or organization positions for sale. Not all items that are owned are positioned for sale. For instance, funds are always assets, but few corporations outside the financial sector call them their principal business products. Similarly, an automobile maker might own stationery for business use. The stationery is an asset, but the firm hardly considers it as an item meant for sale. Of course, if the firm did decide to sell its excess

---

76. Degrees of freedom are discussed in Chapter 4, Section 1, in [337], under Patterns. See also "Mutable Perspectives" on our Web site.
77. Box 43 and Module 6, Section 2, on our Web site describe how constraints carve polymorphisms out of parent objects.

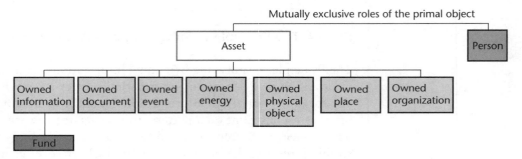

Figure 2.3 Basic polymorphisms of Asset.

stationery, land, or buildings, they would acquire all the characteristics of business products that we will describe later in this chapter. Thus, a business product is a subset of an asset—a subtype based on intent to sell. Figure 2.4 articulates this.

A business product is a polymorphism of Asset in a different partition from those in Figure 2.3. Thus, any of those items (or their aggregations) may be products (and services) that businesses may position in the market place.

Note how even Capacity may also be sold, lent, or used. (We covered Capacity in Box 10.) Capacity is a property of a relationship between objects—an interaction between them. Thus, conforming to the rules we described in our discussion on polymorphisms of Resource, it also may be a resource, and hence, an asset and a business product.

The inheritance hierarchy in Figure 2.3 has been "flattened" to make the figure simple. For instance, we know from our recent discussion that Fund is actually a polymorphism of Asset, because it is a polymorphism of Information. Similarly, we know that a physical object is a polymorphism of Energy. These structures have been simplified and flattened in Figure 2.3. We can flatten a subtyping hierarchy

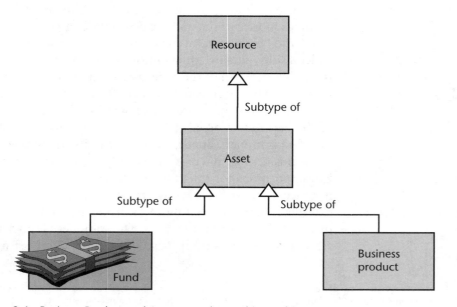

Figure 2.4 Business Product and Asset are polymorphisms of Resource.

because the subtyping relationship is transitive. Two or more subtypes in tandem imply every subtype is also a subtype of the object at the top of the hierarchy.

In the remainder of this chapter, we will often flatten and simplify in order to illustrate, but remember, the complex structures and the multiple levels of inheritance will be hidden within these simplifications (as they were hidden within the simplified objects in Figure 2.1). The simplified diagram is only a view. The electronic repository of knowledge should track and store these hidden structures even if it can present simplified views.

Common Polymorphisms of Event

Figure 2.5 adds information to Event, which is a pure time slot (see Box 10), to derive an ontology of business meanings. The primary intent of the subtyping hierarchy in Figure 2.5 is to normalize features of business events at the right level, so that these features will be inherited by the right polymorphisms of Event.

The hierarchy in Figure 2.5 is not intuitive when we think of manifestations of business events, but it mirrors reality, and has a profound impact on how we can normalize rules to make business processes flexible. Let us understand why, and how we can use it.

Time Period

Time Period is synonymous with Event. An event records occurrences in time. It also records the passage of time. Every event must have a start time and may have an end time.[78] All events are time periods of different kinds, imbued with different

---

Box 15: Flattening Inheritance Hierarchies   15

When we simplify inheritance hierarchies by flattening them, we lose inheritance of information—meanings, constraints, attributes, relationships, and effects—normalized by the objects at intermediate, "flattened" levels (now hidden). These features of hidden objects must now be assigned to visible subtypes of hidden objects. If parents at the top of the hierarchy also are hidden, then their information must be passed to the next level of visible subtypes. As we have seen, this can denormalize and replicate information. For example, the location constraint is replicated when we ignore the subtyping hierarchy between Energy, Physical Object, and Person in Figure 2.2.

When we flatten a subtyping hierarchy, we also lose the kind of automated enumeration of parents described by Rule 5(c) of Box 16. If subtypes are hidden, then we cannot enumerate (or update) populations of parent objects based on cardinalities of and changes in their subtypes. Thus, showing a hierarchy is important in order to determine which polymorphisms will normalize which features and when we must enumerate objects bottom-up.

---

78. Module 5, Section 3, on our Web site describes *Event*.

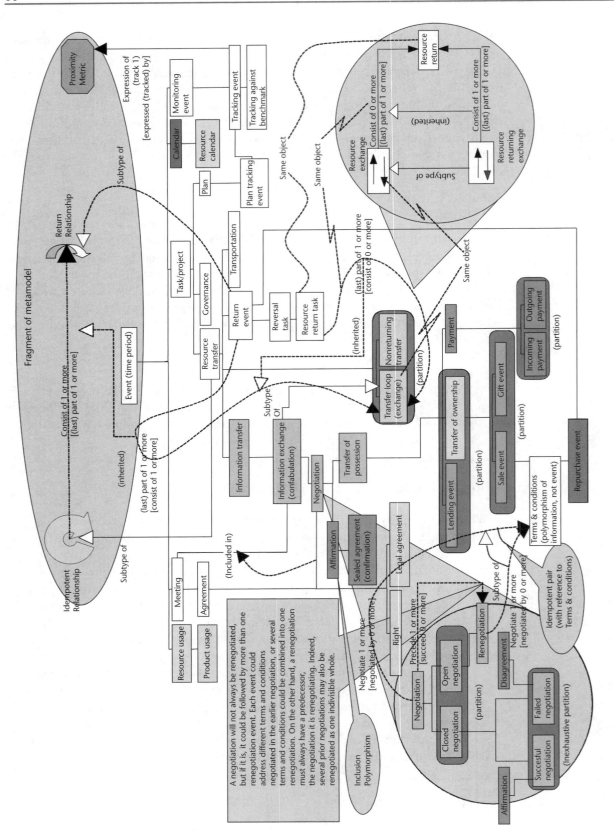

Figure 2.5   Some common business events.

Box 16: Domain Rules Ready Reckoner   16

Domains are discussed in detail in Chapter 4, Section 3, in [337]. The following summarizes the discussion:

Rule 0: Measurability of domains.

a. Nominal domains only carry information on distinctions between values.
b. Ordinal domains rank values in terms of their magnitudes, but contain no information on absolute magnitudes or differences in magnitude between values.
c. Difference scaled domains convey information on the magnitude of differences between values, but no information on a nil value (hence, no information on absolute magnitudes of values).
d. Ratio scaled domains convey information on absolute magnitudes of values. This includes information on a nil magnitude.

Rule 1: Adding meaning to a domain creates a new domain. Meanings added may be new or inherited. If the new domain includes meaning(s) inherited from other domains, then it is a subtype of the domain(s) it was created from, and:

a. The new domain will inherit unit of measure information from its parent domain and add information of its own.
b. If the nil value was included in the new domain and the old parent domain did not have it, the units of measure of the old domain will be inherited with their zeros reset to coincide with the new nil value.

Rule 2: Any multiplication or division operation on values in a ratio scaled domain creates a new ratio scaled domain. Multiplication and division operations may be between values in the same or different domains. Units of measure of the new ratio scaled domain will be expressed in terms of the same operations on units of measure of the domains it was created from, as will conversion ratios between units of measure of the new domain. Thus, units of measure and conversion ratios for the new domain may be derived from its constituent domains (and ultimately its constituent primary domains).

Rule 3: Addition and subtraction operations on values in the same ratio scaled domains map back to a subtype of the same domain. Addition and subtraction are permitted between parent and subtype domains. The subtype domain will inherit all units of measure, conversion, and formatting choices from its parent domain.

Rule 4: Addition and subtraction operations between values in different ratio scaled domains have no meaning if one domain is not a subtype of the other.

Rule 5: Proportions are ratio scaled attributes of aggregate objects that are subtypes of a parent object class. All proportions conform to the following rules:

a. Population: Every aggregate object has a population attribute. The population enumerates its members. Its units of measure are units of enumeration.

b. Sum of a ratio scaled attribute over all instances in a class: Given a ratio scaled attribute of an object instance, corresponding object class(es) will have an attribute that sums up the instance level attribute over all instances of the class. This sum is a class level, not instance level, attribute. Class level totals will automatically be implied by the existence of each instance level ratio scaled attribute, and the units of measure of the class level attribute will be identical to that of the instance level attribute.

c. Sum of class level attributes in a partition:

   i. The sum of populations of individual subtypes in an exhaustive partition will equal the population of the parent object. In a nonexhaustive partition, the sum may be less, but cannot exceed the population of the parent object. The units of measure of the sum will be inherited from the enumeration domain. The subtypes in an exhaustive partition cover all instances of the supertype. For example, the Male/Female partition of Person is (nearly) exhaustive. Subtypes in a nonexhaustive partition do not categorize only some instances of the supertype. For instance, a land/sea partition of vehicles would leave out those that fly.

   ii. Adding to (subtracting from) the population of a subtype will always automatically add to (subtract from) the population of its supertypes, but not necessarily vice versa. The partition may not be exhaustive, and even if it is, we will not know which subtype(s) have increased (or decreased) their population(s) based on increases (or decreases) in the population of supertypes alone.

   iii. The sum of class level attributes (i.e., attributes that are sums of absolute values of corresponding instance level attributes), which are summed across all subtypes in an exhaustive partition, will equal the value of the class level attribute of the parent object. In an inexhaustive partition, the sum may be less, but may not exceed the class level attribute of the corresponding parent object. The units of measure of the sum will be inherited from the domain of the summed attribute.

      Since the partition represents the collection of subtypes in it, the partition normalizes these relationships. They are between the parent and the partition. Each subtype in the partition inherits them.

d. Proportions: The sum of populations of individual subtypes in a partition will equal the population of the parent object in an exhaustive partition, while in a nonexhaustive partition, their sum

16

cannot exceed the population of the parent. The sum of class **16** level attributes, attributes that are sums of absolute values of corresponding instance level attributes, summed across all subtypes in an exhaustive partition, will equal the value of the class level attribute of the partitioned object; in a nonexhaustive partition, their sum cannot exceed the population of the parent. Since the partition represents the collection of subtypes in it, this relationship is between the parent and the partition. Each subtype in the partition inherits it.

The result of a Proportions calculation is independent of the units of measure used to express the divisor (or dividend), provided the divisor and dividend are expressed in the same units of measure. The existence of proportions is automatically implied by the existence of an attribute and partition of an object class.

e. Range: Values in any domain of proportions lie between Nil and Total. The unit of measure of a proportion should assign the nil value to the number zero, and the Total value to a larger number.

f. Sum of proportions: The sum of proportions in an exhaustive partition must equal Total. In nonexhaustive partitions, the sum of proportions cannot exceed Total. The units of measure of the sum of proportions are the same as units of measure of proportions, which is implied by Rule 3.

g. An injunction against arithmetic addition of proportions: Proportions for a given attribute of a subtype in a partition may be meaningfully added. Across partitions, or across different attributes, addition of proportions has no meaning.

Rule 6: Division of one difference scaled value by another is meaningless, and so is multiplication of one difference scaled value by another.

Rule 7: Mutually subtracting pairs of values in a difference or ordinally scaled domains will create a new domain. The new domain is the domain of intervals, or gaps between pairs of values, obtained by attaching a nil value to the original domain. It is a subtype of the domain from which it was created. The units of measure of the domain of gaps will be inherited from the domain from which it was created, as required by Rule 3. If the original domain was:

a. Difference scaled, the new domain of intervals will be ratio scaled.

b. Ordinally scaled, the new domain of intervals will be difference scaled.

Rule 8: Addition of values in the same difference scaled domains is meaningless by itself. It may have meaning in expressions that do not bias the result by changing the arbitrary zero value of a given unit of measure (e.g., by adding, subtracting, or multiplying it multiple times), in which case it maps back to the same domain and the same unit of measure. The entire arithmetic **16** expression must be considered in toto.

Rule 9: Values in the domain of gaps may be meaningfully added to, or subtracted from, values in the domain from which it was generated. The results of the operation will map to the latter domain, in the same units of measure. Addition of values between subtype domains and their parent domains will be meaningful, provided the hypothetical nil value is not distorted. Addition and subtraction operations with values in other domains, with this exception, have no meaning.

Rule 10: A relationship between domains creates a new domain. The relationship may involve a single domain or several domains. The scaling of a domain thus created is:

a. At least the same as the scaling of the participating domain with least information, when all domains thus joined contain sequencing information. We can assume that the new domain is scaled the same as the participating domain with the least information. If the domains were all quantitatively scaled, then the unit of measure of the new domain, a complex value object, will be the arithmetic product of units of measure of domains associated by the Cartesian product.

b. Ordinal, when one or more domains thus joined is ordinally scaled, which is a special case of Rule 10(a) above.

c. Nominal only when all domains thus joined are nominally scaled.

Rule 11: Every domain inherits the following properties from the domain of information.

a. A count of its members is an attribute of every aggregate object, including every domain and object class. It maps to the ratio scaled enumeration domain.

b. Every domain has one or more domain(s) of proximity metrics associated with it. The domain of the proximity metric is a subtype of the domain with which it is associated, and measures the accuracy of values in the domain. Table 2 in [337] describes the scaling of the proximity domain.

c. Every object, including domains and their values, has the ratio scaled attribute of reliability. Values of reliability range from Nil to Total. The reliability domain articulates the consistency of meanings. It maps to the domain of proportions. In a purely deterministic model, reliability may only be Nil or Total.

d. Every object maps to the ratio scaled completeness domain. This domain measures the proportion of information in the object that has been realized. Values of completeness range between Nil and Total. Completion maps to the domain of proportions.

e. Every relationship maps to the ratio scaled validity domain. It is a universal attribute of relationships. Values of validity range from Nil

> to Total. The validity domain articulates the meaningfulness **16**
> of a relationship (rule) between objects. In a purely
> deterministic model, validity is either Nil or Total. Validity
> maps to the domain of proportions.
>   f. Specific relationships with these domains of information may be
>   nominally, ordinally, difference, or ratio scaled, depending on the
>   information content of the relationship.

meanings. This is why Time Period in Figure 2.5 is distinguished from the other events that add meaning to it, and are therefore its polymorphisms.

The sale of time is a common event in business. Indeed, meanings of Asset and Business Product, added to Event, makes it a saleable event. A saleable time period is a subtype of two polymorphisms of Resource—Event (Figure 2.5) and Business Product (Figure 2.4)—in two independent partitions of Resource. Thus, for example, when a staff supplementation agency (a temp agency) sells its employees' time, it is the relationship between Employee and Time Period it is selling. That is a role, a polymorphism of Time Period, and an example of how polymorphisms of the universal perspective mutate into special purpose business objects.

That all the other objects in Figure 2.5 are also events is not always immediately obvious. The facts are subtle because polymorphisms add meaning to their parents, and they can combine meanings of different parents. These added meanings can overwhelm and obfuscate the essential nature of the parent, to the point that we might hardly consider the object an event as we use its polymorphism. Consider an invoice. A business rule might assert that all invoices in excess of $5,000 must be approved for payment by the departmental head. The occurrence of the condition, an invoice in excess of $5,000, is an occurrence in time. It is an event that happens at a Moment in time. A Moment is a time period of no duration, in which start and end times coincide (see Box 10). Thus, the occurrence of the invoice is an event, while its substance is a document.

We must be clear about the aspect of invoice being addressing when we model behavior. An invoice is a request for payment. That is obviously an event. The request for payment in excess of $5,000 is clearly a subtype of this event. Thus, we must distinguish the request, an event, from the document, its physical form, and both must be distinguished from the information in the document. Otherwise, our processes will not be flexible. The following discussion of Payment will make this clear.

Payment

Payment is an event that involves transfer of funds. It also occurs in a Moment, a time interval too short to be of interest to the business. An invoice, as we have seen, has a double meaning. It is a request for payment, an Event, and a document that records that request. Thus, it is could be considered an Event or a Document. In order to normalize knowledge, we must divorce each meaning of Invoice from the other, and consider each separately. Each is a distinct object and component of knowledge.

The occurrence of the request is an event and an item of information. It is information recorded on a document, and indeed, may be recorded on several documents. Invoices are documents, and may be copied (as indeed they were in the example of Box 8). The information that requests payment for an item stands apart from the document it is recorded on. It is unique, and must maintain its identity even if the document that records it is replicated, and indeed, even when the same information is recorded or transmitted in several distinct different documents, formats, or currencies.[79]

To demonstrate the need for this, let us return to the example in Box 8. Had Jim recognized the difference between Information, Event, and Document implied by the invoice, there would have been no confusion about accounts receivable. Duplicate payments would not have been requested of customers, and John's requirement would have been quickly, accurately, and reliably satisfied. Change would have been quick and easy, and the process resilient and automatic. Jim's firm would have leveraged automation to become responsive, innovative, and competitive.

The secret lay in matching the meaning of Invoice against the template in Figure 2.1, and using it to peel back layers of meaning by assigning the information in the invoice to the different generic objects in that figure. The request for payment was an event and an item of information. The event created the information. The template in Figure 2.5 makes this clear.

Subsequent reminders or requests would all point to the same item of information, making it clear that it is the same payment being requested. Each request and reminder is an event. These requests and reminders may be formatted and referred to in different documents, and in different formats and currencies (units of measure), but when two or more documents refer to the same request (or reminder), it must be clear that this is the case. This can only happen if each request or reminder, an event, is uniquely identified and preserves its unique identity. That request, in turn, might refer to the same payment. That also would be clear if the information created by the payment event had a unique identity. This is how the Universal Perspective helps us to normalize information, and to frame flexible processes in flexible contexts. We will return to this example again in the section on buying and selling.

Figure 2.5 shows two mutually exclusive subtypes of Payment—incoming and outgoing payments. These polymorphisms emerge from perspectives of Payment. When considered from a person's or an organization's perspective, Incoming Payment is a payment that a person or organization receives, and Outgoing Payment is a payment that the person or organization pays out. Both are events. Each event will switch polymorphisms, but not its identity, depending on whose point of view we assume.

Meeting

When we think of meetings, a room full of people comes to mind. For some of us, chat rooms and conference calls also might come to mind. However, the object in Figure 2.5 is more than a conventional meeting. It is an exchange that involves two or more persons or organizations. Information is exchanged in meetings. It is a

---

79.   Currency is a unit of measure of *Fund*. See the section on *Fund*.

communication event. It could even be a series of discrete events. If the series stretches to perpetuity, or has no known end, the meeting will be a saga of communication events (see Box 17). Thus, the generic Meeting of Figure 2.5 subsumes and extends our mental image of meetings.

The one resource every meeting must use is people, and there must be at least two or more, otherwise there cannot be a meeting. These people are Parties to the meeting, and they may represent organizations. This will also make the organizations that they represent parties to the meeting. This demonstrates that "party to" (Person may be party to Meeting) and represent (Person represents Organization in Meeting—a ternary relationship[80]) are transitive with respect to each other.

A meeting could, of course, use other resources as well (e.g., space, computers, or telephones), but it must always have two or more participants, and these participants will be persons, who might or might not represent organizations. The occurrence of two or more parties is the central, defining pattern at the heart of Meeting. All polymorphisms of Meeting, including agreements, negotiations, and even disagreement and conflict, will inherit this fact.

Meetings may be sagas. In fact, the concept of meeting extends even beyond sagas of discrete events. For instance, consider an agreement. Agreements always bind two or more parties. Agreements inherit this fact from Meeting; they are polymorphisms of Meeting. Moreover, some agreements have no definitive end. They may be agreements in perpetuity, and hence are sagas. These agreements are not sagas of discrete events, yet they are sagas, and they are also meetings because they bind two or more parties. The parties meet in perpetuity within the agreement. Thus, Meeting in Figure 2.5 is a broader, more general concept than the meeting that comes to mind when most of us think about the word.

However unstructured a meeting is, it always involves two or more parties. Even the most unstructured meetings will crystallize around this central core of meaning. If we mandate that a meeting must end, it will be no longer be a Saga. However, it will still be a polymorphism of the saga it cut short. It will be a polymorphism obtained by adding on information when the meeting will end.[81]

A Meeting may be planned, potential, or actual. Polymorphisms also may be planned, potential, or actual. These states are therefore inherited by Agreement.

Box 17: Sagas **17**

A saga is an event that has no known end. It also might be a series without end of repetitive events. For instance, the series of transportation events for finished goods from a factory is a saga of transportation events. (See also Saga in Box 30.) Module 5 discusses Saga in detail. See Box 55 and Module 5, Section 4, on our Web site.

---

80. A ternary relationship is a relationship between three distinct object classes (Box 10). A transitive relationship is a relationship derived from other relationships. For example, Person live in Town was derived from the two relationships acting in tandem in the composition in Box 10. Module 5 on our Web site discusses relationships in detail.
81. "The Metamodel of Relationship" on our Web site describes how a discrete event crystallizes out of a saga. See Figure 116.

The Agreement in Figure 2.5 subsumes planned, potential, or actually sealed agreements. A potential agreement may be under negotiation. It is a substate of Potential Agreement. Thus, Negotiation is a polymorphism of Agreement that is included in the fact that Information Exchange is a polymorphism of Meeting. Information Exchanges are not Sagas. They must end. So must a Negotiation. This is the information Negotiation contributes to Potential Agreement.

The section on the Netmarket supply chain in Module 5, Section 3, on our Web site, under "Supply Chain Standards," discusses the dynamics of meetings with examples. It discusses structure (see Box 59 in that document), the lack of structure, and how unstructured processes are not necessarily unmanaged processes. Rather, their parameters are determined as they are executed by governing processes, or are determined randomly, without good governance. Naturally, the polymorphisms of Meeting will depend on what its expected work products and resources are. Its work product(s) can be any object in Figure 2.2, or their aggregations, interactions, and polymorphisms. The work product determines the purpose of a process. See Module 5, Section 3, on our Web site. The section on Netmarkets shows how even the purpose of an unstructured meeting may be determined on the spur of the moment, during the meeting. However, all the examples in that section were meetings of finite duration. They had clear beginnings and ends. The generic meeting of Figure 2.5 has even less structure. It could be an indefinite, almost purposeless saga—even a saga without discrete events. This purposeless parent is the concept from which all meetings flow. The parent is important only because its busy and purposeful descendants are the spinning wheels of business.

Resource Transfer

Resource Transfer events transfer resources from one resource to another. They constitute a special kind of relationship between resources. For instance, a transfer event might transfer information from one document to another. Both Document and Information are resources (see Figure 2.2). Information is the resource being transferred, and Document is the resource it is being transferred from and the resource it is being transferred to. Similarly, transferring the possession of an item from one person to another is also a resource transfer. In this case, the receiving and sending resources are persons, and the resource being transferred is some polymorphism of Asset (see Figure 2.3).

Unlike the examples above, resources are not always transferred between similar resources. Some transfers might be between dissimilar resources. For instance, possession of an item may be transferred from a person to an organization. Person and Organization are different kinds of resources. However, any transfer of resources must always involve three resources—the resource being transferred, the resource it is transferred from, and the resource it is transferred to. Resource Transfer is not only an event, but also a three-way relationship between resources. Thus, Resource Transfer is a first order, third degree relationship.[82] Box 10 tells us it is also

---

82. The *Order* and *Degree* of relationships was described in Box 10. See Module 5, Section 1, on our Web site under "Degrees of Combination" for details.

a process—a combination of Event and Relationship. Each normalizes a different aspect of Resource Transfer.

Resource Transfer is a task—it must begin and clearly end. Tasks, unlike sagas, are processes that have distinct ends (see Box 17). The resource transfer event cannot be a saga by itself, but we could have a saga of resource transfer events in a process.

A resource may be transferred, and it may be returned. Both events are resource transfer events. Taken together, they are a composition—a loop that returns to end at the transferring resource (see Figure 2.6). The last leg of the transfer, the return event, might or might not return the same resource, but together the composition is an Exchange. Indeed, both the forward and return legs of an exchange may consist of several subprocesses, which taken together, would loop back to the point of origin.

An exchange is clearly an idempotent relationship (see Box 10).[83] It is perhaps less clear that all transfers are polymorphisms of idempotent relationships. The discussion on polymorphisms of idempotent relationships in Box 10 tell us why (see Box 18 for an example).[84] Figure 2.5 articulates this fact, and demonstrates how

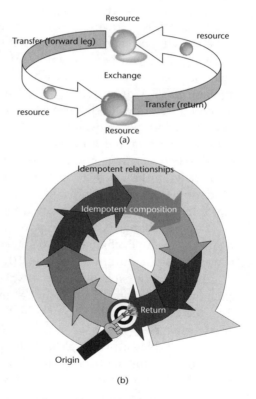

Figure 2.6 An exchange is an idempotent relationship: (a) an exchange is a two-way transfer of resources between resources; and (b) return is an idempotent composition.

83. See also idempotent compositions in Box 61 of the case study on our Web site.
84. Detailed discussions of polymorphisms of idempotent and other relationships are in Module 5, Section 4, and Module 6, Section 1, on our Web site.

abstract universal truths, normalized by the Metamodel of Knowledge in [337], flow into objects of interest to business. Business objects become meaningful polymorphisms of the sparse and spare meta-objects in the Metamodel of Knowledge. Thus is the circle between business and its meaning closed.

Transfer and Exchange are fundamental to the behavior of both the physical world that frames business, and the core values at the heart of business. In this section, we will discuss both. It all flows from the Metamodel of Knowledge. The Metamodel of Knowledge is the fountainhead of the meanings that mesh—mesh like the gears of your car, to create meanings at the heart of every business.

Exchange

An exchange is exactly that—a two-way exchange of resources. An information exchange is a two-way exchange of information. An Exchange is a discrete event. It must begin and end. An exchange can never be a saga, and neither may an information exchange be a saga, but it could be a purposeless confabulation.

This makes Information Exchange a polymorphism with triple parents—Meeting, Information Transfer, and Exchange, as shown in Figure 2.5. Information Exchange is a meeting that always ends, and one that involves communication (an exchange of information).[85] Figure 116, Module 5, Section 4, on our Web site, tells us that a task is a polymorphism of a saga.[86] This hierarchy is hidden in Figure 2.5; the hierarchy in Figure 2.5 has been flattened to avoid clutter (see Box 15). Hence, Exchange also will be a polymorphism of an exchange saga. Thus, an agreement (event), in which parties tell each other that they agree, is a polymorphism of the agreement saga discussed under Meeting. It is included in, and implied by, the subtyping relationship between Meeting and Information Exchange in Figure 2.5 (see inclusion polymorphism in Box 10). Clearly, the subtyping relationship between Meeting and Information Exchange is inherited from the subtyping relationship between Saga and an event of finite duration, shown in the Metamodel of Knowledge in Figure 116 on our Web site. It is yet another example of how the Metamodel of Relationship embraces the Universal Perspective, creating the meaning of business in polymorphisms and configurations without count.

Every exchange is a two-way exchange of resources. Thus, every exchange is a relationship. An exchange is also an event of finite duration. Thus, an exchange is a process of finite duration (see Box 10).

A multiway exchange may always be expressed as a composition of binary exchanges. Of course, if an exchange in the collection depends on other exchanges, then the collection will become a higher order process; that is, the process order is greater than two (see Box 10). For instance, consider a negotiation. In a negotiation, one party tables a proposal, and the other parties respond to it. It is a two-way exchange of information if only two parties are negotiating, and a multiway exchange if several parties are involved.

---

85. *Information Exchange* inherits the fact that at least two (or more) persons or organizations are parties to the event, from *Meeting*; that information is the resource being transferred between these parties, from *Information Transfer*; and that the transfer is a closed loop, an exchange between the parties to the meeting, from *Exchange*. Thus, three patterns, *Meeting, Information Transfer*, and *Exchange*, join as one to create a fourth—*Information Exchange*. It is an example of how meanings in the Universal Perspective engage each other to create new meanings through their polymorphisms, even as they untangle and normalize meanings, rules, and information that are tangled in the everyday world of business.
86. See Saga in Box 10.

The response of each party depends on the responses of the others. Thus, the multiway exchange is also a multiway relationship. The order of this relationship may change in response to events as parties drop in and out of the meeting, but as long as there are two parties to the meeting, the meeting will remain a meeting, and the exchange will remain an exchange. The events that added or removed parties from the meeting may be considered governing processes normalized by Meeting. Meeting normalizes this information because it is Meeting that normalizes the fact that an information exchange must have at least two parties. This is also an example of how the parameters of a relationship need not be cast in stone. Its order, degree, or other features may change in time in response to its governance, or in response to effects of events that impact the Meeting.[87] This example also demonstrates how

---

Box 18: Transfer Versus Exchange—A Difference of Perspective　　**18**

Chains of transfer events that loop back to the same object are expressions of idempotent relationships [see Figure 2.6(b)]. A relationship (and therefore a process) may have several expressions.[88] It follows that the exchange may be implemented in several ways, via different places, intermediaries, processes, and process maps. Each will be a different expression, or implementation, of the same exchange. Moreover, each expression considered as a whole will be a subtype of the expression that it expresses. From this, we can infer that each implementation of an exchange will be its subtype. This subtype tells us how the exchange is implemented, and which intermediaries and processes are used. The supertype captures the fact that all its implementations boil down to the same end result (i.e., the same states and products); in other words, the same exchange. It is common sense embedded in the metamodel of knowledge, and common sense that uses the Universal Perspective as its conduit. Someone or something has to put common sense into dumb automation. The Universal Perspective does.

Even if the exchange is a composition, it must consist of at least one Return, because Exchange is an idempotent relationship. However, an exchange may change into a nonidempotent relationship as we add information to it. See Box 10, and details in Module 6, Section 1, on our Web site. These polymorphisms of Resource Exchange will be nonreturning transfer events. For instance, an organization may move resources from one part to another. The organization is then transferring resources from itself, to itself, which is clearly an idempotent transfer. However, if we discriminate between the two parts of the organization and treat them as different organizations, then the idempotent loop becomes a transfer that is not an exchange, but rather

---

87. Module 5, Section 3, on our Web site, discusses governance of structured and unstructured processes in detail; see "Processes That Gain and Lose Structure" on our Web site.
88. Module 5, Section 1, on our Web site, discusses how aggregates are expressed by their compositions; Box 33, Module 5, Sections 2 and 3, and Chapter 6, Section 2, on our Web site, discuss that a relationship may have many expressions; Module 5, Section 4, and Module 6, Section 2, on our Web site, discuss why each such expression is a subtype of the relationship it expresses.

a straightforward transfer of resources from one entity to another. The information that caused this change was the fact that the organization consisted of distinct and different parts, with the transfer occurring between these parts. Thus, a Transfer, even a nonreturning transfer, is a polymorphism of Idempotent Relationship (as Figure 2.5 shows).

Does this also make Nonreturning Transfer a polymorphism of Exchange? Yes indeed, it does—even though it defies common sense and intuition. Figure 2.5 has flattened and simplified this hierarchy between Exchange and Nonreturning Transfer, to make the hierarchy easier to understand (see Box 15). The example above shows us how we can reconcile these two diametrically opposed perspectives. In Figure 2.5, it is implied by the fact that both looping and nonreturning transfers are polymorphisms of Idempotent Relationship, albeit one level removed. In our example, the idempotent parent normalized the fact that the transfer was from an entity (i.e., an integral whole) to itself, and its nonidempotent polymorphisms normalized the fact that the transfer was between distinct parts of this integral whole.

Whether or not the exchange metamorphoses into an "ordinary," nonidempotent transfer depends on how granular a view of the organization we take; that is, our perspective of it. Even as we break the organization into its parts, we might not have added enough information to distinguish between the parts a particular idempotent transfer has connected. That polymorphism of the exchange will remain an exchange, because the polymorphism of the original idempotent relationship remained an idempotent relationship. Thus, polymorphisms of exchange, and indeed any idempotent relationship, may or may not be idempotent. Module 6, Section 1, on our Web site, describes how these kinds of shifting perspectives flow from the Metamodel of Knowledge. Thus, an electronic repository of knowledge artifacts that recognizes the metamodel will have the capability to resolve these differences in perspective. One will metamorphose into the other, depending on the amount of information available and the level of detail required. The Metamodel of Knowledge in [337] is the ultimate arbiter at the core of the Universal Perspective.

Figure 2.6(b) shows that a Resource Exchange must consist of[89] at least one transfer relationship. It could also consist of several relationships. Transfer relationships are clearly antisymmetrical relationships.[90] They will be asymmetrical unless a resource, such as a person or an organization, transfers another resource back to itself, in which case, the direction of transfer will not matter.

A Return Event is a kind of transfer. It is a subtype of Resource Transfer. Every resource exchange must consist of at least one transfer. However, the reverse is not true. A resource transfer event may not be a part of any exchange relationship; it might be a straightforward transfer of resources that are never returned. If the exchange is a single transfer, the Return Event merges into this

---

89. *Consist of* is discussed briefly in Box 12. The details are in Module 5, Section 2. See "Location, Containment, and Incorporation" on our Web site.
90. See antisymmetry in Box 10.

| sole transfer event (see Box 19). Thus, every Resource Exchange will consist of one transfer event, even if that transfer event is itself. | 18 |

processes inherit governance and other features from their supertypes. Exchange will be governed if Meeting is governed. It is implied.

Every exchange is at least a two-way process; exchanges imply responses or acknowledgements. Thus, an exchange is a chain of resource transfer events that loops back to the originator. It implies that an exchange is idempotent with respect to an originator (see idempotency in Box 10). Idempotent chains are described in Box 61, under the case study on our Web site. The concept of Return is implicit in Exchange. To understand Exchange, we must understand Return. That will be our next step.

Box 19: Exchanges, Returns, and Idempotent Relationships   19

An idempotent ring, or chain of relationships, fused together as an integral whole, will constitute an idempotent relationship.[91] The composition will be asymmetrical if at least one relationship in the composition is asymmetrical. This will be true even when it is not an event or process, and has nothing to do with changes caused by time. When we add time, the relationship becomes an idempotent process that swings around and restores an object to its original state or substate. See Box 61 in the case study on our Web site.

The generic return event of Figure 2.5 is the last leg of the looping composition through state space.[92] A generic return is the leg that ends where the first leg of the composition started. Of course, both legs may be compositions and chains of relationships themselves. See Box 61 in the case study on our Web site. If these chains merge into one loop and lose their individual identities, then the idempotent loop will be a single object, without any known internal structure; the exchange and return will become one. They will merge into the single unbroken idempotent loop, an object that is both an exchange and a return—an exchange with itself, and therefore a return from itself to itself.

A return through state space is the most generic of returns, and an exchange in state space is a composition of paths that collectively loop back to the point of origin, restoring the original state (see Figure 2.6). Polymorphisms of this generic Exchange and Return swing through subspaces that may ignore some features (e.g., axes) of the total space. For example, returning to the same geographical location after a trip, returning a borrowed item to its owner, and restoring stolen property to rightful owners are all polymorphisms of this generic return. Each loop, like the string of places visited on the tour, or the chain of people in possession of an item, is a polymorphism of Exchange. In

---

91. This is discussed in Module 5, Section 2, on our Web site.
92. See State Space and trajectories through it in Chapter 2, Section 2, in [337].

the first example, the traveler on the trip may have started fresh and returned tired. In considering the traveler's state at the end of the round trip, we only considered his or her location in physical space when we called it a closed, idempotent loop; we ignored his or her libido in state space. In the second example, when we considered the chain of people who took possession of the item, we ignored the geographical location of the item. The item may have stayed in the same physical location as it switched owners. Indeed, financial securities are often traded in this manner. The actual certificate remains immobile in the vault of a depository even as its ownership changes. In each example, when we called the chain of resources an idempotent loop, we ignored different aspects and features of the exchange. The exchange in each example was a polymorphism of the generic Exchange of Figure 2.5 (and Figure 2.6). Each polymorphism was idempotent in a different subspace. It was idempotent with respect to one or more features of the resources in the exchange.

An exchange will be idempotent even when it is a barter that does not involve the same item. Then, the loop may not be idempotent with respect to the resource being transferred, but it still will be idempotent with respect to the resources doing the bartering. These resources could be persons, organizations, and even places (or any other resource in Figure 2.2).

The Metamodel of Knowledge in [337] has a return relationship. It captures the meaning of Return in its most generic, nontemporal form. Figure 2.5 shows the fragment of the metamodel that has this relationship. It is an asymmetrical relationship that may or not be temporal. Combined with Event, it becomes a return event. Box 10 demonstrated that a task is a polymorphism of event. A Task, unlike a saga, is a process that has a clear and definite end. Return in this section on events will always mean the Return Event (which is also the Return Task), unless we qualify the term otherwise.

Return and Reversal

The most generic form of return is the asymmetrical form of the idempotent relationship (see Box 10). It lies at the root of every exchange and return, a spare and hidden spirit without business substance; exchanges and returns lend it form.

Returning a resource is common business practice. It could be a borrowed or purchased item being returned, or a return for any other reason. Return is an event and a process. It is a part, and the last leg, of an exchange. It is thus the last leg of an idempotent composition of processes—idempotent chains like those in Box 19 and Figure 2.6. As Figure 2.6 shows, the other legs of the composition are also Transfer events, but a return is special. It is a transfer event that transfers back to the beginning of the loop. It is a subtype and polymorphism of Resource Transfer.

Transportation, Information Transfer, and its subtype Transfer of Possession, are all polymorphisms of Resource Transfer, in partitions that are independent of the partition that has Nonreturning Transfer and Exchange (see Figure 2.5). It follows that the subtyping hierarchy in Figure 2.5 lets Transportation and Transfer of Possession be Nonreturning Transfers that do not loop back to their point of origin.

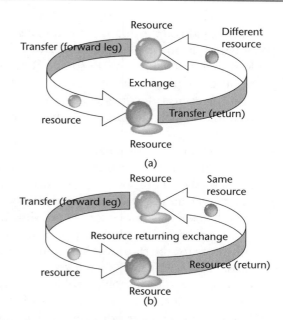

Figure 2.7 A Resource Returning Exchange transfers and returns the same resource: (a) an exchange may, or may not, return the same resource; and (b) a Resource Return returns the same resource.

Neither does the subtyping hierarchy bar Transportation and Transfer of Possession from looping back to the origin.[93] When they do loop back, they are still Transportation or Transfer of Possession events, but they are polymorphisms of Resource Transfer that not only transfer, but also return. Indeed, a transfer event even could be a return event that closes the loop [as in Figure 2.6(b)], and turns a nonreturning transfer into a (Resource) Exchange. The hierarchy in Figure 2.5 provides for every possibility. It does so by following the natural hierarchy of information embedded in generic meanings at the heart of business.

A return event will be the last event in a Resource Exchange, but it need not return the same resource to the point of origin. A different resource might close the exchange [see Figure 2.7(a)]. Thus, a return event must be a part of every exchange, but not every Resource Exchange will have a Resource Return embedded in it. The same event might even complete several exchanges simultaneously. Figures 2.5 and 2.7 articulate this.

A Resource Return constrains a resource exchange, so that the chain (sequence) of events that we collectively call the exchange not only loops back to its originator, but the same resource also comes back to its originator [see Figure 2.7(b)]. A Resource Returning Exchange is thus idempotent with respect to the resource being

93. As we will see later in this section, *Transportation* and *Transfer of Possession* sometimes may be barred from looping back to the origin. For example, we cannot be transported back in time, a time slot that has been used can never be restored, or sometimes the terms of sale may simply bar returns. These kinds of unreturnable resource transfers are more constrained than returnable transfers. It follows from the discussion Box 62 under Product Engineering, and Module 6, Section 2 (both on our Web site), that these constrained, nonreturnable transfers will be polymorphisms (i.e., subtypes) of transfers that do not bar returns. (A thoughtful reader may ask the question: Can a physically unreturnable transfer, such as transportation from the past to the present, be considered a polymorphism of a nonreturnable transfer that merely bars a return to a previous state with a rule that might be relaxed? Hint: Can there be constraints on constraints—on their removal or attachment? Which patterns will be more constrained, with fewer degrees of freedom in information space?)

transferred and the origin of the transfer. Thus, a Resource Returning Exchange is a polymorphism of Resource Exchange. It is implied by the relationship between Resource Exchange and Resource Return (task) in Figure 2.5. The origin of the resource in question also will be a resource, such as a place, a person, an organization, or even a document.[94] The origin can be any resource in Figure 2.2. That resource will be the context of the return. This context will frame the meaning of Return.

A Resource Return may have many polymorphisms. For example, a repurchase is a resource return, as is the return of borrowed resources or the return of shipped items to their point of origin. However, an event cannot always be returned. An event, such as a time slot sold and utilized, cannot be literally returned after it drifts into the past. The moving finger of time passes on, and cannot return.

Another transfer that the parties involved may deem to be equivalent might then substitute for the resource that cannot, or will not, be returned. The "return" of the substitute resource will then reverse the transfer of the unreturnable resource.[95] This kind of reversal is a polymorphism of Return. It adds information on the equivalence of resources (or combinations of resources) with the resource that was transferred in the context of the event that must be reversed. A reversal conveys more information than a generic return. The generic return also transfers resources, but has no information on the equivalence of these resources with respect to any other transfer events; a reversal does. Thus, a reversal is a polymorphism of Return.

A bald resource transfer is a transfer of a resource from one resource to another (or, when the transfer is an exchange, from a resource back to itself). The moment we add business intent to the resource transfer, we make it a polymorphism of the generic resource transfer, because we have added information. The information we have added is business intent. Similarly, a return is the last leg of an idempotent transfer. When we add business intent to this relationship, it becomes a polymorphism of a generic return. The intent often is to compensate for the forward leg of the transfer. Barter, trade, and purchase—the basic values that shape the meaning of business—emerge from this polymorphism of Exchange. The equivalence of resources between the forward and return legs of an exchange exists in a context. That context is compensation in terms of some value (usually the economic value we discussed in Box 13), but the equivalence may be in the context of other values, such as the equivalence of mass, energy, persons, organizations, credentials, and so forth. They all can add business or physical meaning to the equivalence of transfers or reversals.

A reversal must always have a context—the resource transfer event it is reversing, and the resources (products of the event) it is reversing. The reversal may even be ordinally scaled or quantitatively scaled in this context, conveying information on the order of preference and quantum of substitute resources that will do. It is a polymorphism of the generic reversible process in the Metamodel of Knowledge

94. Note that the beginning or end of *any* of the relationships in Figure 2.6(b) might be considered to be the origin of the resource. Similar to the incoming and outgoing payments we discussed, the origin of a resource is a matter of perspective. Resource Exchange is a special kind of relationship between resources—resources *being* transferred, and *transferring resources*; that is, the resources from (or to) which the resource is being transferred. *Origin* is a state of a transferring resource that changes with changing perspective; the *identity* of the resource (instance) does not. This is an example of a change of state that does not involve a process or the flow of time in any way. Instead, it is attached to *Perspective*, and changes when the Perspective does.

95. Module 5, Section 3, discusses process reversibility in detail. See "Processes, Events and Temporal Relationships" on our Web site.

(see Box 30), and will inherit its attributes, such as the efficiency of reversion, repeatability of reversion, and others.

A Resource Return is subject to further constraints. A Resource Return mandates that the resource transferred in a reversal cannot just be any resource, but it must be the same instance of the resource that was transferred in the forward leg.[96] It is a stringent constraint. Thus, a Resource Return is a strictly constrained form, and a polymorphism, of Reversal (see Box 14). Like a reversal, a resource return may convey quantitative information. This behavior is inherited from Reversal, and is a form of inclusion polymorphism (see Box 10).[97] Thus, we may have partial returns, or even reversals that involve returning a larger quantity of the resource than was transferred in the forward leg of the exchange.[98]

Rules of substitution are normalized by reversals. The essential pattern[99] that Reversal normalizes and adds to Return consists of resource equivalence, preference, and quantum, all in the context of the Return event. Thus, polymorphisms of reversal may be ordinal or quantitative rule expressions.[100] For substitute resources in an exchange, these rules tell us the quantity and order of preference of the substitutes. A resource return is a reversal in which the resource that was transferred is also returned. It is a polymorphism.

A generic return does not constrain the resource being returned in any way. It only requires that some resource be returned to the origin of the exchange. It could even be an empty truck returning to a warehouse. However, even a generic return is a constrained pattern that only exists in the context of another transfer; that is, a transfer from the origin [the forward leg of Figure 2.7(a)]. In each context, Return (and Transfer) is a polymorphism that looks different not only because the resource

---

96. A Resource Return mandates that the same *instance* of the resource be returned in an exchange. There are less strict forms of reversion that will be polymorphisms at intermediate levels between Reversal and Resource Return. For instance, the return might merely mandate that the same class, not the same instance, of resource be returned. This is clearly a polymorphism of reversal that is not constrained as much as the Resource Return we have defined in this book. These intermediate levels have not been shown in Figure 2.5. They may be many—indeed, they are too many to show. As we know, any feature, or even any combination of features, may describe a class. For similar reasons, we have not shown ordinal or quantitative polymorphisms of Reversal in Figure 2.5. Box 10 describes quantitative polymorphisms of occurrences. They are polymorphisms in a partition, which is different from the partition that leads to Resource Return. Thus, Resource Return may also convey nominal, ordinal, or quantitative information. These polymorphisms are generic to all relationships, and are implied by the Metamodel of Relationship (Figure 116) on our Web site. All relationships, including reversals and returns, will inherit the hierarchy of rule expressions in the figure, which shows occurrence relationships, Boolean conditions, sequencing rules, difference, and ratio scaled arithmetic expressions in a descending hierarchy of polymorphisms.
97. Inclusion Polymorphism is discussed in detail in Box 21 on our Web site. See also the note on inclusion polymorphism.
98. The parties involved in an exchange *could* agree that a partial return will be adequate to compensate for the earlier transfer. Although it does not restore the resource to its original state, a partial return could reverse the forward leg of the transfer. In terms of the discussion on reversible processes in Module 5, Section 3, on our Web site, the efficiency of the reversion is less than 100%, but it is still a reversion. See Processes, Events and Temporal Relationships on our Web site. The parties in an exchange could also agree that the return of a *larger* quantity than was originally transferred is necessary to compensate for the forward leg of the transfer (e.g., a return with interest added to the principal amount of a loan). In this case, we could say that the efficiency of the reversion (with reference to the discussion on reversibility of processes in Module 5, Section 3, on our Web site) is greater than 100%. Although this formulation of a return might sound unconventional, it is identical to the concept of efficiency of reversions discussed on our Web site. It sounds unusual only because we do not usually frame it in normal business parlance.
99. Chapter 4, Section 1, in [337], discusses Essential Patterns under Patterns. The essence of a pattern gives it meaning and distinguishes the pattern from other patterns. It is tied to the degree of freedom of the pattern to be that pattern. See "Mutable Perspectives" on our Web site.
100. Rule expressions discussed in [337]. See Chapter 3 in [337]; also see Box 43 (in the context of subtyping) and Figure 116 (the Metamodel of Relationship), both on our Web site.

being transferred is different, but also because the originating and the terminal resources are different. Each polymorphism picks a different meaning for each resource from Figure 2.2 (or from polymorphisms of the resources in Figure 2.2).

The possibilities are enormous and too many to count. These polymorphisms are masks that hide the common meaning of Return. In the Universal Perspective, these polymorphisms vanish, and Return stands unmasked in its true scope, an undivided meaning, simplified, and unfragmented.

Among these polymorphisms, Resource Return alone restores the resource to its original (sub)state. A reversal must always reference another transfer of resource event and the resource it is carrying. A Resource Return is a polymorphism of Reversal. Therefore, Resource Return inherits this fact from Reversal. In any kind of reversal, including a Resource Return, the resource being transferred, and the resource being returned, form an idempotent loop, as the origin and destination of the transfer also do, as shown by the Resource Returning Exchange of Figure 2.7(b) (and Figure 2.5). The loop is idempotent in a nominally scaled state space that consists of the identities of the transferring resource, the receiving resource, and the resource being transferred. The axes of the state space that frames the loop are defined by these instance identifiers.[101] The loop may be a composition of transfer events [see Figure 2.6(b)], and each individual transfer might transfer a different resource to the next resource in the chain. As long as the final transfer returns the same resource to its origin, the loop is idempotent with respect to both the resource that was transferred and the origin of the transfer. Both Resource Return and Reversal are patterns of information. Their meanings spring from this abstract pattern in state space.

Indeed, even when it does not return the same resource, any Return will depend on an earlier resource transfer event for its very existence and meaning. Return is a polymorphism of Resource Transfer. Resource Transfer, Return, and polymorphisms of Return, are meanings that flow from patterns of information.

A return is a kind of transfer event, which is a subtype and a polymorphism of an idempotent transfer that may or may not be idempotent (see Boxes 18 and 19).[102] Return is also the final subprocess in an asymmetrical idempotent loop (see Box 10). This gives Return its unique meaning and essence. This is the essential pattern in Return.[103]

Unmasked, Return stands exposed and undisguised—a normalized component of the knowledge machine, ready for use in any of its countless forms. It was the Universal Perspective that unmasked Return. As you forge ahead, remember that Return was but an example of how meanings are forged from the Universal Perspective by the knowledge machine. These meanings are patterns of pure and abstract information that we can use and reuse to forge even more meanings.

Negotiation

Negotiation is a common business event, even more common than the agreements to which they sometimes lead. A Negotiation is clearly a polymorphism of

---

101. State Space is described in Chapter 2, Section 3, in [337]; and patterns in nominally scaled state space are discussed in Chapter 4, Section 1, in [337].
102. Module 5, Section 4, on our Web site, discusses polymorphisms of idempotent relationships in detail. See The metamodel of relationship on our Web site.
103. Chapter 4, Section 1 [337], discusses essential patterns. See "Mutable Perspectives" in Module 5 on our Web site.

Box 20: Returns and Reversible Processes   20

A Return reverses a transfer event, even if it does not reference the resource that the event transferred [see Figure 2.6(a) and Box 19]. Return also depends on that transfer event for its very existence.[104]

The origin of the transfer may be considered a resource (an input) to the process that is the forward leg of the transfer in Figure 2.7(a), as may the resource being transferred (see Boxes 10 and 30). The same origin also may be considered the work product of the return leg of the transfer. Thus, the return leg reverses the forward leg of the transfer. See the discussion on reversibility of processes in Module 5, Section 3, on our Web site; and Box 30 of this book. If the transfer is a Resource Returning Transfer, then the return leg also restores the transferred resource, and hence is a reversal of the forward leg with respect to both the origin and the resource that was transferred. The properties of reversible processes frame the different polymorphisms of Return. See Module 5, Section 3, on our Web site.

Thus, Transfer, Return, and Exchange all have their roots in the Metamodel of Knowledge. They all grow from it. The metamodel is their substance, and they are its expression.

---

information exchange; every negotiation exchanges information. In a negotiation, one party tables a proposal, and the other parties respond to it. Thus, a negotiation is a subtype of Information Exchange, and Information Exchange is a polymorphism of Meeting (as described under Meeting). Thus, negotiations are once-removed polymorphisms of Meeting. Indeed, as we have seen when we discussed Meetings, Negotiation is also a polymorphism of a potential Agreement.

In order to agree, the parties to the potential agreement must negotiate. To negotiate, they must meet, either physically or virtually. They must exchange information, opinions, and proposals. They must also express their agreement and disagreement to each other. In other words, they must communicate.

This communication could even be by snail mail, but it is still communication, and communication involves an exchange. Unlike a saga, an exchange of information is a definitive event. It begins and ends. Although these exchanges may go on forever, creating an unending or indefinite saga of exchanges, we cannot call this train of events an exchange. It is a saga of exchanges. Similarly, Negotiation is a discrete event, but it is conceivable (however improbable it might be) that a train of discrete negotiation events may drag on with no end in sight. This train of events will be a saga of negotiations, which is distinct and different from Negotiation, the discrete event. All negotiations end. They are all exchanges. Negotiation, by itself, can never be a Saga. Its definition prevents it from being a saga. This part of its definition lies in Exchange (resource exchange). As unlikely as it may sound, if we acknowledge that information is a resource, then we must also acknowledge that

---

104. Module 5, Sections 2 and 3, on our Web site, describe existence dependency and the reversibility of processes, respectively.

Negotiation is a subtype and a polymorphism of Resource Exchange (abbreviated to Exchange in Figure 2.5).

No exchange is a saga, and neither can a negotiation be a saga. Each negotiation is a session. Of course, we may divide the session into shorter sessions, depending on how granular our information needs about the negotiation are. Typically, these shorter sessions might be captured in the minutes of the meeting. Every Negotiation, like all other exchanges, must have a clear beginning and a definitive end. It is a fact that *Negotiation* inherits from *Task* through *Resource Transfer* and finally, Exchange.[105] Contrast the position of Negotiation in Figure 2.5 with the position of Agreement. Figure 2.5 clearly articulates that meetings and agreements may be sagas, whereas negotiations must exchange limited information in limited time frames.

Figure 2.5 also shows common states of Negotiation, which as we know, will be subtypes (i.e., polymorphisms) of the event. Negotiations may be closed or open. The mark of a closed negotiation is that it is a process that has ended. An open negotiation is a negotiation in progress.

A negotiation usually closes in one of two states, success or failure. Success implies agreement, and failure implies disagreement. However, it is possible that the negotiation was closed for other reasons. For instance, a party to the negotiation may cease to exist, and the negotiation might be closed without agreement or disagreement. Similarly, external events (e.g., a deadline, an external business event, or some kind of higher order governance) might force a negotiation to end prematurely, without agreement, and without irreconcilable differences. Thus, closure of a negotiation exists in a partition that is independent of agreement or disagreement. It is not only in closed negotiations that parties agree or disagree; they also do so in open, ongoing negotiations. For instance, parties to an ongoing, open negotiation may be in disagreement, and may be discussing ways of narrowing their disagreements, so that they can reach an agreement. Thus, closed negotiations may or may not close in agreement, and open negotiations may or may not be in a state of agreement. Agreement and disagreement are independent of closure of a negotiation. Figure 2.5 articulates this.

Open negotiations may also be renegotiations. Renegotiations are open negotiations related to another negotiation. A renegotiation and the negotiation(s) it is renegotiating are idempotent with respect to terms and conditions. The renegotiation addresses the same terms and conditions as the negotiation(s) it is renegotiating.[106] That negotiation may have been a closed negotiation that was reopened, or it may be a negotiation that was left open and incomplete in a previous session. Thus, Renegotiation is a role of Negotiation that emerges from an asymmetrical, recursive relationship (see Box 10) with another negotiation. The relationship is asymmetrical, because negotiation (and hence renegotiation) is a process. Renegotiation can only negotiate an earlier negotiation. Like any negotiation, a renegotiation may be closed successfully or not.

A successful negotiation is an agreement and an affirmation. It is also a closed negotiation. An unsuccessful negotiation is a negotiation that closes in

---

105. Although individual negotiation events will have definitive ends, it is conceivable (but highly improbable) that a series of discrete negotiations may drag out in an endless saga of discrete events.

106. Module 6, Section 4, on our Web site, discusses idempotent compositions in detail. See The "Metamodel of Relationship" on our Web site.

disagreement. However, an open negotiation also may be in a state of affirmation or disagreement. Thus, affirmation does not always imply a negotiation successfully closed, but a successful negotiation always implies affirmation. Similarly, disagreement does not always imply failure of a negotiation, but a failed negotiation always implies disagreement. It follows that a successful negotiation is a closed negotiation that is also a polymorphism of affirmation. For similar reasons, a failed negotiation is a closed negotiation that is a polymorphism of Disagreement (as Figure 2.5 articulates).[107] As we have seen, failed and successful negotiations do not exhaustively categorize all possible closed negotiations. Negotiations may also be interrupted and closed without ending in either state. These interrupted states, Suspended, and Cancelled, Waiting for event (or latent, which is a subtype of Suspended) shared by all processes and inherited from the metamodel of process, were described under States of an Event, in Module 5, Section 3. Figure 116 on our Web site includes the Metamodel of Process, as an integral part of the Metamodel of Relationship.[108]

Agreement and Confirmation

Consider Agreement. Businesses thrive on agreements, both formal and informal. Some are legal, subject to processes in courts of law, while others may be recorded without any legal standing. Some might even be verbal commitments with no written record. An agreement occurs at a particular time. The occurrence of an agreement is therefore an event. An agreement is valid for a particular period. That period of validity is also an event. Its terms and conditions are information about rights and resources. Thus, terms and conditions are polymorphisms of Information (the object in Figure 2.1), distinct from the event called Agreement. We will return to terms and conditions later in this chapter. In this section, we will focus on the aspect of Agreement that makes it an event.

There must always be two parties to an agreement. There may be more. An agreement inherits this feature from Meeting. Agreement, the class, also inherits the fact that it could be a saga from Meeting (see Saga in Box 17). Although uncommon, some agreements may be valid for an indefinite period, even to perpetuity. Thus, an agreement even could be a saga without discrete events.

A limitation on its duration turns a meeting into a discrete information exchange process. Agreements also will inherit this behavior. Some agreements will be events of finite duration made in meetings of finite duration. Both will be polymorphisms of Agreement.

Some agreements could be sagas, as described under Meeting. A Resource Exchange is also a polymorphism of Saga. Therefore, Information Exchange, its subtype, inherits this fact.[109] A saga may metamorphose into an exchange if it is constrained to clearly and definitively end, but an exchange can only become a saga if we dilute its meaning and make it less specific, and by doing so, remove its definitive end. Thus, even agreements that are definitive exchanges are polymorphisms of those that are sagas. Sagas, as we saw in Box 17 and under Meeting, may or may not be sagas of discrete events.

107. As an exercise for the thoughtful reader, consider the questions: Is coercion a form of affirmation? Would you call it a successful negotiation?

108. Other universal states of events discussed on our Web site are: *Not Started, Started, Finished,* and for events of infinitesimal duration, *Not Occurred* and *Occurred.*

109. *Resource Exchange* has been abbreviated to *Exchange,* and labeled thus in Figure 2.5. Module 5, Section 4, and Figure 116, in "The Metamodel of Relationship" on our Web site, show that processes of finite duration are polymorphisms of Sagas.

Negotiations often lead to agreements, and the affirmation of agreements must be formally accepted before they become binding on the parties concerned. Until the agreement is sealed (confirmed), it does not bind these parties. The formal acceptance, the confirmation of the agreement that binds each party, is also an event. However, unlike the generic agreement (in Figures 2.5 and 2.6), affirmations and confirmations must end. The confirmation binds each party to the terms of the agreement as it ends. The parties agree to agree. They confirm. This is clearly a kind of Exchange, and an agreement. Information Exchange is a kind of Resource Exchange, in which information is being exchanged.

Thus, Affirmation is a subtype of Information Exchange, but one level removed. It is a direct polymorphism of Negotiation. Affirmation affirms concurrence on Terms and Conditions being negotiated, and changes a negotiation into an actual, not just a potential, agreement. Sealing an agreement (i.e., Confirmation in Figure 2.5) is more binding and constraining than its affirmation. It binds the parties in a negotiation to the terms of the Agreement. Thus, confirmation is a subtype of affirmation.[110] Figure 2.5 articulates this.

The example above also shows how objects in the Universal Perspective metamorphose into more specialized, information-rich subordinate business objects, even as they inherit shared meanings from information-sparse parents, and simultaneously normalize the meanings they add. Thus, Negotiation, the resulting Agreement, its affirmation, and confirmation are all states of Information Exchange, their common parent. These events change the state of Terms and Conditions, the information associated with an instance of Negotiation, or Agreement. Perhaps Information Exchange, or simply Exchange, is the better word.

Many agreements are recorded on documents. The document records information, and the agreement (or exchange) event lends a unique identity to this information. The information is the "terms and conditions" of the agreement (or the information exchange) event. Even if the terms and conditions of another agreement (or information exchange) are identical, the terms and conditions of each event will have distinct and different identities. Each will be a distinct instance of term and condition embedded in the relationship, between the event and a subclass of information called terms and conditions. Each has borrowed its distinct identity from the distinct event with which it is associated. The relationship is the class that represents this interaction. The terms and conditions are information. Figure 2.9 shows this.

This information is not only recorded in a document, but the information also may be recorded in several documents. These documents may be copied or reformatted without changing the substance of the agreement (i.e., the information in it), or the occurrence of Agreement. This Agreement is the business event in Figure 2.5. The terms and conditions of the agreement are polymorphisms of the generic entity labeled Information in Figure 2.2, and the documents that record this information (and hence the agreement) are polymorphisms of the generic entity labeled Document in Figure 2.2.

---

110. The pricinples described in detail in [337] tell us that a constraint conveys information; therefore, constraining an object turns it into a subtype. This is reaffirmed by the information on our Web site in Boxes 43 and 62 and Module 6, Section 2. The arguments in Module 6 show that features of objects also may be considered kinds (polymorphisms) of constraints.

The common information in written records of different documents, the documents that record and format this information, and the events that gave them birth, must not be confused with each other. Otherwise, meanings might be replicated and processes made inflexible. We can only ensure this when we distinguish between the polymorphisms of the primal object in Figure 2.1. We must apply these distinctions to the agreement to sift through and separate its mixed meanings, and to give each meaning of Agreement (or Information Exchange) a unique identity. We must distinguish between three versions of the Agreement: its document version; the event and exchange version; and the information version that completes the collection of terms and conditions associated with the exchange. Clearly, terms and conditions may also involve events (e.g., the term of an agreement is an event), but this involvement is different from the relationship we are discussing here.

An agreement valid in a court of law need not always be a written agreement. For instance, some kinds of insurance policies in the United States bind the insurer even before the policy is committed to paper. Some kinds of nuptial agreements in India need only witnesses and not written records. In both cases, the agreement is legally binding on both parties. It suffices that the agreement event can be proven, even if it is not documented. Thus, legal recognition (or lack of it) is independent of whether the agreement is documented or not. They are different partitions of Agreement.

A Right is a term and condition related to an agreement. For example, the right to drive is a term and condition of an agreement between an individual and a Government (i.e., an organization). Even freedom of speech is a term and condition of an agreement made in perpetuity—an agreement between the nation (i.e., an organization) and its individual citizens. Of course, an agreement may simultaneously involve and package several rights into one cohesive Bill of Rights, as the Constitution does. In step with Agreement, rights may be formal or not; written or not; and, of course, some, like the right to use a resource (e.g., a broadcasting medium), may even be sold. We have acknowledged this behavior by acknowledging that information may be an asset. Agreement was an event that sealed the Right to make it an Asset, and Assets may be sold, even if they are pure Information. Of course, Rights that are sold, used, lent, leased, gifted, or revoked[111] must always reference the original agreement that gave them birth.

Thus to normalize knowledge, we must distinguish between the polymorphisms of the primal object articulated in the Universal Perspective we are now unmasking. Objects of interest to business are aggregations and interactions between polymorphisms of the objects in Figure 2.2. Behaviors of these polymorphisms are inextricably tangled in business meanings and concepts. Unless we sift through their behavior and unmask these polymorphisms, it will be hard to normalize behavior. Consequently, the risk and cost of change will continue to be high. The Universal Perspective helps us sift, untangle, and allocate.

Keeping track of conflicting agreements, riders, and modifications can become very complex in large, complex, dispersed, and diverse organizations or supply chains. Separating the substance of an agreement (i.e., its information content), the event that marks the agreement, and its record on a document, are all key to

---

111. Revocation is a polymorphism of Reversal. Module 5, Section 3, on our Web site, discusses *Reversal*. Reversals must always reverse a past instance of a process.

tracking agreements and their consistency. We must sift, untangle, and allocate in order to do this well. The Universal Perspective is the key.

Transfer of Possession and Resource Use

A product or resource may change hands. A sale (or gift) is one polymorphism of this kind of event. The title (ownership) of a product changes hands by mutual consent in a sale (or gift). Thus, Sale and Gift are polymorphisms of this nameless transfer-of-title event, which in turn is a polymorphism of Agreement (the event).[112] When we consider either, we must separate the event that transfers possession from the resource that is transferred, and separate both from the event that transfers the resource.[113] Only then can we frame a flexible business process—one that grows naturally from the universal perspective, normalizing information even as it takes shape.

Indeed, the agreement is only a state of the negotiation that ends in agreement. It may also fail, and the sale would not occur. Even if the negotiation is too trivial or short to be of interest to the business model (e.g., when consumer items are purchased on impulse), negotiation always precedes a sale, and the ultimate agreement that transfers possession will always be a state of Negotiation, a polymorphism. If we are not interested in the negotiation that led to the agreement, then we may always flatten the hierarchy in Figure 2.5. Box 15 gives us the terms of reference for this.

Transfer of ownership is only one polymorphism of transfer of possession. A product or resource might also be lent. Lending and transfer of title are common patterns at the heart of business. Lending and transferring ownership are also mutually exclusive, as Figure 2.5 makes clear. However, note that lending is distinct and different from usage. For instance, a bank may lend you money, but you may not use it. A lender might creatively configure a financial product and charge you only for the part you use. A telephone company does not lend or sell you its network, but will charge you for its use. Thus, the use of a resource also can be a product that a firm may position for sale. It is an event, an occurrence in time, that is being sold. This is why resource use is an event, and Product Use is its saleable polymorphism.

"Lending" and "Use" are meanings often inextricably mixed and consequently confused. To build flexible processes, we must separate and normalize each. Use is

---

112. Figure 2.5 makes clear that *Sale* and *Gift* are mutually exclusive subtypes in a partition of meaning. *Gift* is an event in which ownership is transferred without requiring a barter or exchange of funds. Indeed, both are barred. The giving of a gift must not *depend* on receiving another in exchange, or on paying for it. If this were the case, then it would be a sale. Figure 2.5 shows that both *Sale* and *Gift* inherit the fact that they are agreements from *Negotiation*. Note how the gifting event, which we have called *Gift* in Figure 2.5, is distinct from the resource being gifted, which we could also call Gift. When we consider either Sale or Gift, or even the lending event, we must separate *the event that transfers possession* from *the resource that is transferred*, and both from *the event that transfers the resource*. Each is a distinct and different object, with a distinct business meaning. Each normalizes different kinds of information. Business processes will only be flexible if we isolate each meaning in a different object, so that their interactions are clearly isolated components of knowledge that we can reconfigure at will.

113. *Theft* is an example of a transfer of resources without prior agreement. Even when it is not a theft, and a sale has been executed, the new owner might not get physical possession of the item at the time he or she buys it. Indeed, the new owner could have physical possession *before* the actual sale (e.g., when he or she buys an item already leased to him or her, or when an owner uses an item on a trial basis before confirming the sale). Thus, separating *Transfer of Possession*, a subtype of *Agreement* in Figure 2.5, from transfer of resources, which might occur with or without a supporting agreement, is the right thing to do. The business processes may then support innovative ways of doing business. Corporations will be free to configure different kinds of dependencies between the two kinds of events. The events will be reusable components borrowed from the Universal Perspective. Thus, the Universal Perspective and the Metamodel of Knowledge provide plenty of room for creatively configuring processes to maximize business advantage and to support process innovation.

derived from the defining relationship between a process and its resource (see Box 10). It becomes the Usage event when time is added to the relationship. A lent item, on the other hand, does not have to be used; it only gives the borrower the right to use it. Each meaning may be supported by a different kind of agreement. This agreement is the event in which parties agree to the sale, which is different from the actual event when a resource is actually delivered, which in turn is different from the event in which the resource was actually used. Indeed, it is common sense that a resource does not have to be a business product that has been bought or borrowed in order to be used. Therefore, it is also clear that (Business) product use is a subtype, a polymorphism, of the more generic concept of resource usage. Figure 2.5 articulates this.

Returning or buying back an item is also common business practice. It is an event and a process. It is also a polymorphism of Return in Figure 2.5. The process is the last leg of an idempotent loop (as in Figure 2.6) that restores possession of a product transferred by the first leg of the loop. Repurchase thus restores a past possession relationship between a Person/Organization and a resource. It is therefore also a process. It follows that the repurchase process is idempotent with respect to both Person/Organization, and (possession of) resources transferred.

A repurchase or repossession of borrowed resources must always reference another transfer of possession event. Indeed, it depends on the earlier event for its very existence and meaning. It reverses that event.[114] Some purchases, such as the use of time, may be physically impossible to return. When this happens, an exchange agreed to by all involved parties might compensate for the unreturnable item. This will be a reversal, as well as a return. The hierarchy in Figure 2.5 implies this. Figure 2.5 tells us that a reversal is a kind of return (i.e., a polymorphism).

Repurchasing the product and reversing its sale are two common polymorphisms of the return event. Figure 2.5 shows how a repurchase is a subtype of two parents, a purchasing event and a return event. Because a reversal is a subtype or Return, the relationship in Figure 2.5 also implies that the repurchase might be a reversal or a substitution, unless we specifically bar it. This is another example of the common sense that naturally flows from the Universal Perspective and the metamodel of knowledge that hides within it. Thus, the metamodel anticipates the requirement even before it is articulated by a process engineer!

Indeed, repurchasing agreements, known as REPOs, are when a seller agrees to buy back a security at an agreed upon price in an agreed upon time frame, and are well-known in the financial securities market. Just as a securities trader may buy a security back, a retailer may agree to buy back (or substitute) goods sold within a time frame if a customer is not satisfied, and a bank may agree to buy back a mortgage from its customer. These are examples of how generic objects in the Universal Perspective may be combined with other objects to reuse and unify elements of business process knowledge across the vast diversity of economic activity that defines the global economy of the new millennium.

---

114. Box 61 in the case study on our Web site discusses idempotent processes and state transitions. Box 19 in this book discusses *Return* in the context of idempotent processes. Module 5, Section 2, on our Web site, discusses existence dependency, and Section 3 discusses the reversibility of processes.

Processes across the full spectrum of industries may be assembled from the patterns in this chapter if these patterns are stored in an electronic repository. Software applications also may be assembled from corresponding fragments of prefabricated code and interfaces. Module 5, Section 3, on our Web site, describes how business processes may be automatically expressed in software under "Crossing the Chasm—Business Process to Information Systems." Thus, we need not reinvent the wheel each time we design a process and software to support it. It can reduce time-to-market, and make the business more responsive. Competitive advantage through differentiation and customization can still be obtained by adding special rules to prefabricated code and patterns.[115]

Governance, Monitoring, and Tracking

Monitoring Events may monitor any object, including an event (see Box 30). Governance events may change states of other events.[116] Monitoring events often will be resources used by governance events to monitor states of objects. Based on these enquiries, governance events might change the states of other events.

Unlike governance events, monitoring events by themselves will change no states, except the "observed" state mentioned in Box 30, and discussed in Boxes 54 and 56 on our Web site. Both governance and monitoring events will have uncountable polymorphisms depending on what they govern or monitor. Often they will work in tandem, forming a pattern of monitoring, inquiry, and governance. The pattern may even be a Saga.[117]

Monitoring events may not always be tied to patterns of governance. For instance, regulators and auditors monitor, but do not always govern. They are one of the communities in Box 21, and it is these communities that drive monitoring, governance, and training. Indeed, these events might also be continual, repetitive sagas without end.

Monitoring events often manifest as business tracking events. Tracking events is a kind (subtype) of monitoring event that measures the similarity between two objects in terms of its features. One object in the pair is sometimes the designated benchmark. For example, a controller may track the coordinates of an aircraft against reference coordinates that show where the airplane should be. Tracking events are polymorphisms of the proximity metric, a relationship between a pair of objects. Relationships, we know, become processes when time flows into them as they are joined to Event (see Box 10).

Planning and Tracking

Plan is a state of every object that describes an intent and expectation for the future. That state is set by the planning event. It is a universal process. It also has a universally understood meaning, so we will not elaborate on it.

---

115. Adding special rules and constraints to these prefabricated generic patterns will create custom components, which are polymorphisms of the generic patterns in the repository. See "Supply and Demand Chains" on our Web site. Customization will help us drill down to the core of Figure 96 from its outermost layers. The outermost layers of Figure 96 under "Supply and Demand Chains" hold the Universal Perspective and the Metamodel of Knowledge. The core has the custom components that differentiate the products, services, and processes of the firm from its competition. The generic patterns at the periphery of Figure 96 are abstract, and sometimes are counterintuitive. This makes them difficult to identify. This book will help reduce that risk.
116. Monitoring events were discussed in detail in Module 5, Section 3, and Box 54, on our Web site. Governance events were also discussed in the same section, and in Box 56. See "Processes, Events and Temporal Relationships" on our Web site.
117. Sagas are discussed in Box 17.

Box 21: Polymorphisms by Intent | 21

Many business events are derived by combining the polymorphisms in Figure 2.5 with the goals of the following communities.

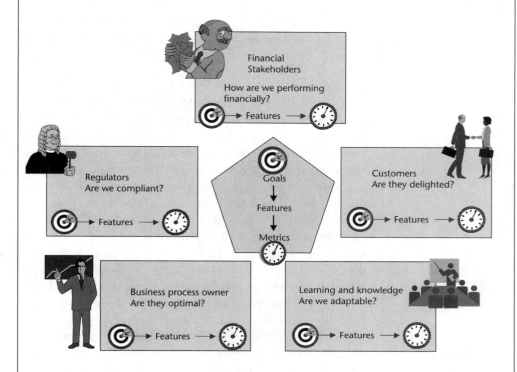

Some events could be of interest to several communities. These events may simultaneously belong to several of the following categories. The following list is by no means exhaustive. It is only indicative of classes of events that are of interest to the communities in the figure above.

- Promotional Events (process owners).
- Delivery Events (polymorphism of the process output event of interest to process owners are detailed in Module 5, Section 3, on our Web site).
- Sourcing Events (polymorphism of process input events of interest to process owners are detailed in Module 5, Section 3, on our Web site).
- Making Events (polymorphism of the transformation event of interest to process owners are detailed in Module 5, Section 3, on our Web site).
- Reconditioning Event (an idempotent process and a polymorphism of the generic making event, of interest to process owners).
- Training Event (of interest to the community of learning and knowledge).

21

- Environment, Health, and Safety Event (of interest to all communities, but of special interest to the regulatory community).
- Accident, Incident, or Exception (a subtype in a different partition that could be combined with any kind of event to show absence of intent, or contingencies). Thus, we could have sourcing accidents, reconditioning incidents, making exceptions, and others. We discussed exception events and defects in Module 5, Section 3, on our Web site, under risk management transforms.

Business intent—the intent of the communities in the figure flows into the lifeless Event of the metamodel from the classes in the list above. Indeed, business events could combine intent, and be polymorphisms of several classes simultaneously. Thus, we could have Environment, Health, and Safety Training events (i.e., processes), Promotional Delivery events, Sourcing Training events, and so forth. These events will be subtypes with multiple parents.

Indeed, business polymorphisms of Event could also combine the classes on this list with those in Figure 2.5. Thus, we may have a Planning process for Reconditioning, a Resource Return event for Sourcing, a Tracking process for Making, a training event for product use, and so forth. Of course, as we have recently seen, events in Figure 2.5 may also combine on their own to produce meaningful polymorphisms, such as Resource Usage Tracking, Resource Return Governance, Exchange Negotiation, and so forth.

Polymorphisms of events (and hence processes) also may flow from the roles they play in nonsubtyping relationships with other events and objects in the Universal Perspective. These polymorphisms will convey meanings that are distinct from those conveyed by the subtyping relationships. For instance, planning a training event is different from training for a planning event. We will discuss these kinds of polymorphisms later in this chapter.

The bottom line is that business events (like other business objects) can be forged from themes in the Universal Perspective and the Metamodel of Knowledge, by combining the stock themes therein to create new and innovative patterns of information that are business themes in and of themselves. A sophisticated knowledge machine could even do so on the fly.

Box 22: Proximity Metric

22

The proximity metric is a measure of similarity between objects. It measures how close a pair of objects is in state space. For example, the difference between budgeted and actual expenditure is a proximity metric. Physical distance is also a measure of similarity—it measures how similar the position of a pair of objects is in physical space. The proximity metric is a component in the metamodel of knowledge. It is discussed in detail in Chapter 4, Section 1, in [337], under patterns, and its metamodel is in Figure 52, and Tables 1 and 2 of that book. See our Web site.

It will suffice to recognize that Plan is an event, which like the others we discussed, also may be recorded on documents, and will convey information. As we did for Invoice and Agreement, we will have to sift through these meanings in order to normalize information. The templates in this chapter will help us do so.

A common pattern associated with a plan is tracking (comparing) it against:

1. Actuals;
2. Changes against a benchmark plan.

Comparison against actuals is a relationship between planned and current states. Infused with temporal information, it can become a tracking process (see the discussion on monitoring processes).

Comparison against a benchmark plan is also a polymorphism of the tracking relationship. It also will become another polymorphism of the tracking process if we add time to it. From Figure 2.5, it is clear that this polymorphism of tracking a plan is included in, and implied by, the fact that tracking a plan is a subtype of the generic tracking relationship. It is the generic relationship to which the proximity metric (see Box 22) is attached. The generic tracking relationship normalizes information on closeness and similarity.

The Track Plan relationship and its polymorphisms are widely and frequently used in business. They are reusable patterns—components of knowledge. The relationship is idempotent with respect to the object instance it tracks. Idempotency was described in Box 10. The tracking process is clearly also a polymorphism of the generic monitoring process. A component of the metamodel of knowledge is mentioned in Box 30, and described in Box 54, Chapter 4, Section 3, in [337].

Calendar

A calendar is a saga of time periods. Relating these time periods to different resources may fill time slots in the calendar. Then it becomes a Resource Calendar—an aggregate object that consists of a collection of time slots. A time period in a resource calendar may have limited capacity for relating to resources of different kinds. Capacity was discussed in Box 10. The calendar tells us which resources are engaged in which relationships, at which times and in which places, and how much room remains in the time slot for additional engagement. Thus, each slot is a role of Event that connects it to Resource and optionally to Place. The time slot in a calendar also conveys information on capacity. When a slot is empty, without information on capacity, it reduces to Time Period. You then get an empty calendar. The empty calendar is actually full—it is full of time slots. A calendar is an aggregate object, full of perhaps even infinite numbers of time slots in an unending saga. It is the time slots (i.e., the events in it) that are empty. The events that constitute the saga may be empty: Empty objects with no relationships except two—their membership in a saga of successive events, and their succession of an immediate predecessor in the saga.

A Calendar is an object. Like other objects, it may be viewed through different prisms, and filtered in different ways, as illustrated by the views in Figure 33, on our Web site. Object instances may be selected for display and displayed in different formats based on different criteria.

Shipment and Transportation

Transportation is a task. It is a process that moves an item. The item(s) moved are resources. Remember that collections of the resources of Figure 2.2 are also resources. They are transported from one place to another. Transportation changes their state by changing their location. Shipment, as it is used in common parlance, often confuses the task with that which is being shipped. We know we cannot permit this. The Universal Perspective must distinguish between the two. Our prior discussion of Invoice, Agreement, and Payment told us why. As we did with Invoice and Agreement, we must separate the task of transportation from that which is being shipped (and thus relocated).

Transportation switches the location relationship in Figure 2.2 (i.e., the containment relationship of Box 12) from one instance of Place to another.[118] Note that a single shipment event may ship a batch of items. Thus, one shipment event could relocate several resources simultaneously A shipment may make multiple drops, and hence relocate different members of the shipment to different places. Each drop is a subprocess, and a part of the shipment.[119] Thus, the products of a shipment may not all be in the same state (location) after they are shipped. Batch processes were discussed in detail in Module 5, Section 3, and Box 57, on our Web site.

The discussion in Box 12 makes clear that transportation could, but need not always, imply that the transported item is either being put inside another resource, or even being incorporated into it as a part integral to the resource that contains it.[120] Consequently, when we think of transportation, it is usually the movement of physical items that comes to mind. However, Transportation in the Universal Perspective is a more generic event. It may involve transportation of information as much as it involves physical shipments. Information may even be transported in virtual space. Thus, Transportation in the Universal Perspective is synonymous with movement of any kind. Shipment of physical items and transmission of messages are its polymorphisms.

Thus, when physical objects are being moved, transportation will switch the containment (location in) relationship of Figure 2.2 from one instance of Place to another. When information is being shipped, the transportation event might only add, not switch, the relationship to a (instance of) Place. Remember that there is no bar against the same information being in several places simultaneously. The transportation event might also delete the relationship without switching it. That also is a kind of Transportation—transportation task to Null Space. Null Space is a region in information space for objects that do not exist. A region within null space is reserved for impossible concepts. It is discussed in Module 5, Section 4, on our Web site. It might not be possible for Physical Objects or Energy to vanish without a trace,[121] but information can.

---

118. Transportation might also switch polymorphisms of containment (such as "part of"; see Box 12), which *automatically* implies switching containment. Module 5, Sections 2 and 4, on our Web site, discuss polymorphisms of containment in more detail. See Location, Containment, and Incorporation, and Figure 114 under the "The Metamodel of Relationship" on our Web site.
119. The *part of* relationship was discussed in Box 12.
120. Module 5, Section 2, on our Web site, discusses the containment of an object in detail. See Location, Containment, and Incorporation, and Figure 116 under "The Metamodel of Relationship" on our Web site.
121. When a physical object or energy is lost, its location is *Unknown*, not *Null*. On the other hand, information may not merely be lost, but it may cease to exist. Then, its location becomes *Null*. A physical object may be destroyed (i.e., change its state and be of no further interest to a process or business), and energy may similarly change its form. In these states, locations may not be important anymore, and

An exchange of messages (i.e., communication) is an idempotent loop that consists of two shipments. The generic Resource Exchange event is also an idempotent loop with respect to at least one participant, in which resources that are not necessarily information are transported (see Figure 2.6). Return is the closing leg of this loop. This kind of idempotent loop, in the context of Transportation, is idempotent with respect to Place (of Figures 2.1 and 2.2). A Return, in the context of transportation, returns to a place. This is a polymorphism of the generic Return event of Figure 2.5. It is a subtype of both Return and Transportation. The Return Transportation event (not shown in Figure 2.5) is included in its generic parents, and emerges only when we create a subtype of Return that is simultaneously a subtype of Transportation. It is yet another example of how polymorphisms hidden within the Universal Perspective stand unmasked when viewed through the prism of the templates in this chapter. The Universal Perspective unmasks itself.

Task

Mathematically, there is little difference between Task and Process (see Box 10). Both use resources to produce products. They would be synonyms if we did not permit sagas (as discussed in Box 17). A task must not only begin, but it must also end; a saga need not. Both are processes.

For instance, Transportation is a task. It is a discrete event with specific beginning and ending times. A single shipment can never be a saga, although we can envision business arrangements that arrange a continual saga of shipments. The saga and the shipment are distinct and different. The saga is a composition, whereas a shipment stands alone.

Conventional English usually considers a task subordinate to a process. In English, a task also might be an action that a person or organization must take. Our definition does not contradict this commonly shared understanding, but it is subtly different. In the Universal Perspective, a generic event or process could be a saga, whereas a task will always end. Sagas, in a system that recognizes discrete change, may consist of discrete tasks, even if these tasks of finite duration are endlessly repeated, or occur without count over an infinite time horizon. In Figure 2.5, calendars, resource use, and monitoring events have not been subordinated to Task, because, as we have seen in prior discussions, they could be sagas. All tasks, and even sagas, may be decomposed into hierarchies of process maps that show increasing levels of detail. Each map will be an expression of the process it details.[122]

Indeed, every event in Figure 2.5 is potentially a polymorphism of Task. It becomes a polymorphism of task at the moment we add the fact that these events use resources and take time to produce the information that is their work product. Thus, an agreement task produces the information in the agreement, the plan event produces the plan, or more accurately information in plan (all the objects in planned

---

set to Unknown. However, there is always the remote possibility that some innovation or process might recycle the unusable object or recover the energy. However, information that is destroyed is not merely made unusable; it can never be recycled or recovered by any process, past or future, because it does not exist any more. Its location becomes null, not unknown.

122. Module 5, Section 2, on our Web site, discusses the containment of an object in another in detail. See "Location, Containment and Incorporation," and Figure 116 under "The Metamodel of Relationship" on our Web site.

states), and so forth. We discussed this earlier in this section, and in more detail in Module 5, Section 3, on our Web site, under "The Essence of a Process and the Goals of Business."

Projects and tasks are indistinguishable in the universal perspective. Each task or project may expand into a process map of interdependent tasks (or projects).[123] Both must begin and end. For us, they are synonyms.

Note how we can create virtually uncountable numbers of meanings by combining the events in Figure 2.5. For instance, a Resource Use Plan is a subtype of Resource Usage and Plan. Figure 2.5 tells us that a plan is a kind of task. Tasks may be decomposed into process maps, expressed as a sequence of parallel and sequential interdependent processes and resources. Thus, implicit in the meaning of Resource Use Plan, a meaning we have assembled from components in the Universal Perspective, is the fact that we can express the plan in terms of a series of planned, interdependent sequences of resource use events. It is knowledge assembled and inherited. Similarly, an Agreement Meeting Plan would be a conjunction of Agreement, Meeting, and Plan. Thus, business objects and business processes flow out of the Universal Perspective in countless polymorphisms, even as the Universal Perspective normalizes knowledge about their meanings and behavior.

Composition and Structure

The concept of structure is fundamental to not only business, but to knowledge itself. In this book, we will call this polymorphism of the primal object Structure. Structure and Composition are identical. In its primal form, a structure only tells us that objects are connected. It is a very basic, information-sparse pattern.[124] We will focus on business polymorphisms of Structure. Figure 2.8 describes this abstraction.

A structure has nodes. It is a structure that connects nodes. It is a structure of nodes. A Node is a role of Resource. A Structure shows connections between resources. A node is a resource thus connected. Although Node and Structure are concepts that depend on each other for their very existence, they are distinct and different. A structure is the sense of their association, and nodes are resources in association. When the two concepts merge, we call it a *Network*.

A network is any association of resources like those in Figure 2.8. It could be a network of people, a telecommunications network (an association of switches, which makes a telecom network a polymorphism of a network of physical objects), a network of roads that connect geographical places, or any other type of network. It might even be the particular route in a network that a particular message takes from its source (a node) to its destination (also a node); or a hierarchical network like an organizational structure or a chart of accounts.

When a structure is a sequenced pattern of association, we call it a Path. A path shows the sequence in which nodes may be traversed. These sequences are not necessarily temporal sequences (e.g., it could be a sequence in space or a roll-up hierarchy of financial accounts[125]). When they are temporal sequences, Path

---

123. Module 5, Section 3, on our Web site, discusses process maps and process decomposition in detail.
124. Chapter 4, Section 1, in [337] and Module 5, Sections 2 and 3, on our Web site, describe how this primal structure crystallizes and changes, in step with information that we add to it.
125. Sequenced patterns have been discussed in detail in Chapter 4, Section 1, in [337].

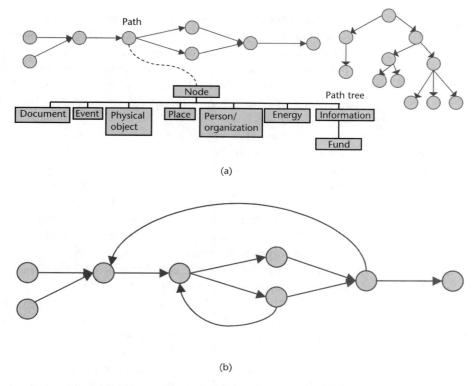

(a)

(b)

Figure 2.8   Structure, Path, and Node: (a) acyclic paths; and (b) cyclic paths.

metamorphoses into a process. Indeed, Path itself is a polymorphism of Structure, because it adds sequencing information to that pattern (see Box 14).

Thus, paths may show links between documents. Paths may be routes that connect places, travel itineraries, charts of accounts, organizational hierarchies, associations between objects, task dependencies in a project, networks of switches and routers in the path of a message, paths of a ray of light, or any other concept that implies structure and sequence. They are all polymorphisms of Structure.[126]

Structures may be tree structures like those in Figure 2.8. In such structures, nodes cannot be traversed in a loop. Accounting hierarchies, decision trees, and organizational structures are examples of Tree. A tree might also be a path if it conveys information on the sequence(s) or direction of traversal. For example, a tree might be a path if it tells us who is subordinate to whom in an organization, or which decisions in a decision tree follow other decisions.

A path might be acyclic or cyclic. Acyclic paths do not loop back. We cannot travel in loops, revisiting the same node several times along acyclic routes. The paths in Figure 2.8(a) are acyclic paths. Although Trees are also acyclic, the rightmost path in Figure 2.8(a) is quite clearly not a Tree.

Trees are polymorphisms of acyclic paths. Simple project plans are often acyclic paths, like the model in the figure in Box 2. The nodes there were events (tasks).

---

126. Note that *Structure* and its polymorphisms address the issues raised in [89] about extending the UML concepts of aggregation to model structured objects. Module 5, Section 2, on our Web site, describes this in more detail.

On the other hand, a reconditioning or rework process may be a cyclic path, in which an item is repeatedly reworked until it is satisfactorily rectified, or failing that, discarded. In Box 18, we demonstrated that acyclic paths may be polymorphisms of their cyclic counterparts, but not vice versa. Thus, inheritance will be from the cyclic to the acyclic polymorphism of the primal object.[127] Clearly, a cyclic path can be a composition of acyclic paths (see Figure 2.6 and Boxes 18 and 19).

Remember that any aggregation of the polymorphisms in Figure 2.8 is also a resource, and may be a node (similar arguments also apply to Asset). Indeed, remember that a composition is a subtype of an aggregate object (see Box 18), and hence so is Network. As we drill down into the nodes of Figure 2.8, each node may resolve itself into collections of objects, or even other Networks, Structures, or Paths, with each a network, structure, or path in its own right. Module 5, Section 2, on our Web site, discusses the rationale for this. Readers interested in a more pristine, mathematical approach may refer to [19].

The following example will demonstrate why Structure is special, and why we need it to normalize knowledge. Consider the insurance industry. Ships and their cargo are often insured against their ports of call. Insurance coverage and prices often depend only on which ports the ship will visit. The sequence does not matter. Thus, insurance costs will depend on Place, not Path or Structure. As we will see later, a place may consist of[128] other places, and the aggregate does not have to be a collection of geographically contiguous places to be considered a Place. On the other hand, the distance the ship must cover, and consequent fuel (and other operating) costs, may depend on the sequence in which the ship calls on different ports. In this case, the cost will depend on Path, not Place. Thus, each normalizes a different item of information. This difference demonstrates the difference between Structure and the lack of it, and tells us why we must have both.

More Polymorphisms of Fundamental Objects

Armed with these fundamental polymorphisms of the primal object, we are now in a position to articulate the next layer of frequently used meanings. Figure 2.9 drills down to this next level.

Note that Figure 2.9 also inserts a level that was hidden in the subtyping hierarchy of Figure 2.5. This hidden level lies between Meeting and Agreement. Collaboration and Conflict have been inserted at this level, above Agreement, but below Meeting. Collaboration and Conflict were objects hidden in the "flattened" hierarchy of Figure 2.5 (see Box 15). Let us start with these two events of critical interest to business.

Collaboration and Conflict

Collaboration is when parties that own or manage processes work towards common goals. Conflict is when they work towards mutually exclusive goals.

---

127. See Box 10. These polymorphisms are discussed in detail in Module 5, Section 4, and Module 6, Section 1, on our Web site. Module 5, Section 4, on our Web site, has various polymorphisms of reflexive relationships.
128. *Consist of* was described in Module 5, Section 2, on our Web site, and discussed with the metamodel of relationships in Module 6, Section 4, on our Web site. See "Location, Containment and Incorporation" on our Web site.

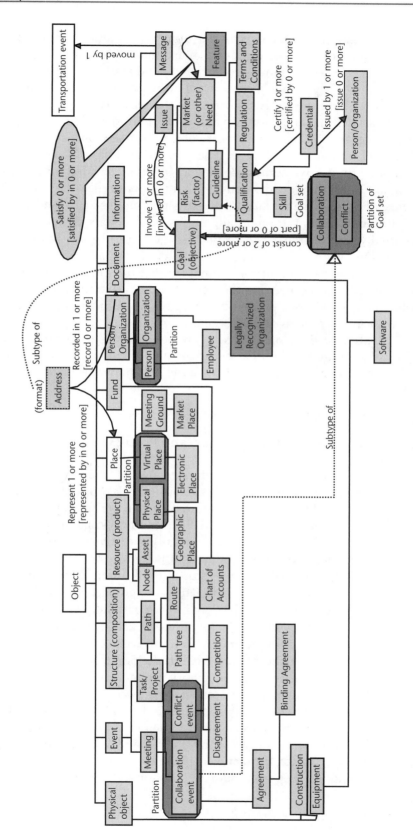

Figure 2.9 More polymorphisms of Fundamental Business Objects.

We know that objects can be parts of an aggregation. They can be parts that are arbitrarily chosen, and even parts that are mutually exclusive. The aggregation only describes a set—an arbitrary collection (see Box 12). Collaboration and conflict are sets of goals. They only become events when we replace goals in the set with processes that have these goals. Figure 2.9 articulates both.

Consider that collaboration and conflict are special kinds of goal sets, and sets are aggregate objects. An aggregate object, by itself, only tells us that it consists of parts. These parts may be parts that are merely allowed to coexist; parts that are mutually supportive because some may be resources used for making others; parts that are in a subtyping hierarchy, so that the occurrence of one mandates the occurrence of others, but not vice versa; parts that must occur together in the aggregate; and even parts that are mutually exclusive. A collaboration is a set of goals that mutually support the existence of other goals (in the set) in one or more of these ways. On the other hand, a conflict is a set of mutually exclusive goals, which may even be in violent and unconditional conflict or competition with each other. We can always replace a goal in the set with a process that has that goal. Then we will obtain a collaborative process, or, if the set is a conflict, we would have turned the conflict into a process and an event.

Goals (and therefore goal sets) are polymorphisms of Information. We obtain the collaboration or conflict event by adding temporal information to the goal. Thus, the collaboration (conflict) event is a polymorphism of the collaboration

---

Box 23: Collaboration, Conflict, and Process   23

Consider the work product of interviewing a candidate with the intent to hire. There are two mutually exclusive work products: an offer letter and a regret letter. Does the fact of mutually exclusive work products make Interview Candidate a conflict? Figure 84 in Module 5 on our Web site has the process map, which shows the two mutually exclusive activities to create the two mutually exclusive work products. Although we are not used to thinking of a job interview as a conflict, if we stop to think about it, then we will see that it is a conflict—not a conflict between the candidate and the interviewer, but between acceptance and rejection (i.e., two mutually exclusive events). Thus, a conflict is always with respect to mutually exclusive products. It only becomes a conflict between people or organizations when each strives to force a process for making a product that will exclude the other. Even a resource conflict can be traced to mutual exclusion of work products of processes that use a shared, but limited, resource. The conflict only occurs when using or engaging a resource to make one work product would not allow it to be used (or engaged) to make another (perhaps in sufficient quantity if the transformation process is a quantitative relationship). Thus, conflict and collaboration are special kinds of sets. In a conflict, the members of the set are mutually exclusive, whereas in collaboration, they are mutually supportive, and may even be mutually inclusive.

23

Thus, collaboration and conflict are stock themes of business determined by mutually inclusive or mutually exclusive goals. The goal of a process and the process itself carry the same essential information.[129] This is why, when we are only interested in whether the aggregation is a collaboration or conflict, a process may be substituted by its goal, or vice versa in the aggregate. If we substitute processes by goals, all we will lose is the temporal information normalized by Process. This information is not always germane to identifying the aggregation as a conflict or collaboration. All we need to know about members of the set is their mutual support or mutual exclusion.

Knowledge about the fact of conflict or collaboration need not imply complete information about process maps and dependencies in the conflict or collaboration. Work products and resources in a conflict or collaboration might not all be known. Indeed, the entire aggregate might not be known. Added information turns a collaboration or conflict into a polymorphism of the collaboration or conflict with less information. See Box 14. Additionally, Box 51, and Module 5, Section 4, on our Web site, as well as Chapter 4, Section 3, in [337], describe why known values are subtypes of the Unknown value.

Note also that subtypes of resources, work products, and processes may substitute their supertypes in a conflict or collaboration. See Liskov's Substitution Principle under Mutability of Resources. It will remain a conflict or collaboration. However, climbing the subtyping hierarchy may resolve conflicts by substituting supertypes for subtypes until a nonconflicting set of resources or work products is arrived at, provided that the process can still satisfy the overall goal (work product) of the aggregate process. Conflict is a polymorphism of exclusion partitions, which are components in the Metamodel of Knowledge discussed in Chapters 2 and 3, in [337]. See also Box 21, Exclusion Partitions, Variation Inheritance, and Polymorphism, on our Web site.

A goal is information. Substituting a goal with a process that has the goal of information turns the aggregate into a process and an event. It is a polymorphism of the timeless collaboration or conflict represented by the set of conflicting or collaborating goals. The goal of a process is also its work product, as discussed in Module 5, Section 3, on our Web site. It could be any polymorphism of Resource in Figure 2.2. Thus, a collaboration or conflict is derived from the objects in Figure 2.2, just as Medium was. It is a set of those objects, with added information—information on mutual exclusion or mutual support borrowed from the Metamodel of Knowledge.

---

129. Module 5, Section 3, on our Web site, under "The Essence of a Process, and the Goals of Business," discusses that the goal of a process is its essence (see "essence" in Box 30). The example of how "assemble car" is derived from "assemble" (see Module 6, Section 2, on our Web site) is a real-life example of this principle. See also the example in Box 56 on our Web site.

(conflict) object, a set of at least two supportive (conflicting) goals. Figure 2.9 articulates this.

We need very little information to call an event a collaboration or a conflict. We do not even need to know what these collaborating or conflicting parts are, nor need we know how many members participate in the event. All we must know is that there are at least two members. If they are mutually supportive in any form (as the resources of a process, or via mandatory or subtyping relationships between themselves), it is a collaboration; if they are mutually exclusive, the aggregate encapsulates a conflict.

What if an aggregate consists of objects that support some members of the aggregate, even as they conflict with other members? The aggregate is then a strategic relationship. A strategic relationship is an aggregation of aggregates. Its parts are collaborating and conflicting aggregates.

In its most generic form, a collaboration is a relationship between two or more objects, in which the relationship between one or more objects also implies or mandates relationships with other objects. On the other hand, a conflict is when a set of relationships is mutually exclusive with other sets of relationships in an interaction. The collaboration and conflict events in Figure 2.9 normalize this commonly understood business meaning of collaboration and conflict, even when it is expressed as conflicts between people or organizations. In this section, we will understand its structure—the abstract pattern of information we call collaboration or conflict between people or organizations.

Only processes have work products, and these work products are its goals. In Box 10, we understood the dimensions of ownership of processes. Only people or organizations may be responsible for processes and have authority over their operation. People and organizations also may play consultative roles. They may or may not actually "work" (operate) the process. It might be completely automated. Even if a process is fully automated, it is very likely that people and organizations will operate the process that operates the automated process, and hence will be considered the operators of the automated process. Working or operating a process is a dimension of process ownership. (See the RAWCF dimensions in Box 10.) Each dimension of process ownership is transitive with others of its kind. This transitivity, discussed in Module 5, Section 3, under "Process Ownership" on our Web site, is the wellspring of the meaning of Delegation. Even if we do not know the specific kind of processes these owners operate or the specific kind of ownership each owner exercises, we still will know that they are collaborators, if we know that the work products of these processes support each other; and we will know that they are in conflict, if we know that their work products must be mutually exclusive.

Thus, collaboration and conflict between people or organizations are aggregations of unknown processes. The only information we must have to call the aggregate "Collaboration" between people or organizations is that the goals of the processes that constitute the collaboration are in harmony. When we call it a conflict, we must know that its goals are mutually exclusive.

We may not even know what these goals and events are. In order to call the aggregate a collaboration or conflict, it suffices to know that their owners either are in harmony or are in conflict, through the goals of the processes they own. Of course, the aggregate might be neither. The goals of its contents could be mutually independent, in which case the owners are neither collaborators nor in conflict with each other. Each has no stake in the outcome of what the other(s) does.

We have seen how agreements and confirmations (binding agreements) are examples of collaboration. Disagreements and competition are examples of conflict. Like any other relationship, a collaboration or conflict may grow into ordinal or even quantitative relationships in step with the fullness of information the event conveys (see Box 10). Thus, we might be in a position to express how intense the collaboration or conflict is. For instance, most of us would agree that a war is a more intense form of conflict than is conveyed by mere competition or disagreement in business. These polymorphisms of collaboration and conflict are naturally implied by the metamodel of relationship. Intensity is a fact inherited from it. We do not have to provide for the meaning of intensity of collaborations or conflicts separately. The Metamodel of Knowledge in [337] automatically implied and created the room for them.[130] They will exist, uninstantiated if need be, but ready to take shape from components in the metamodel of knowledge when required. After all, the Universal Perspective is a polymorphism of the Metamodel of knowledge enriched with business meaning; it inherits everything the metamodel of knowledge implies.

A collaboration may be a process map like the process map in Box 2, with resources and work products added to it.[131] The work products of collaborating processes may be resources used by others in the collaboration to make their products.

Conflict is a topos, a stock theme, in which work products are mutually exclusive, and Collaboration is the topos, in which work products are supportive. Collaboration and conflict are both topoii (see Box 23). Collaboration is the topos from which supply chains emerge (see Figure 2.22).

A topos is a stock theme, and reusable meanings are stock themes. A theme is a pattern of information, and a pattern of information is an object, as described in Module 6, Section 1, on our Web site. The more often a theme is used, the more we are justified in considering it a stock theme and a reusable component in the repository of knowledge. Collaboration is central to all business, and as we enter the new millennium, it is a gathering force. Global supply chains are arguably one of the largest, and most complex, forms of collaboration that span our planet. Collaboration requires at least two participants, and these participants must be people or organizations (or both). Agreements and negotiations are all forms of collaboration in its broadest sense. The opposite of collaboration is conflict. However, there is a nameless pattern that subsumes both. It generalizes both collaboration and conflict to capture their common essence—the interaction between persons, organizations, or both. It even subsumes disagreement. In Figure 2.5, we called it meeting, because this is where information, people, and organizations meet to confer, collaborate, confabulate, and negotiate; and to agree, disagree, compete, and conflict, even conflict violently. A meeting needs a meeting ground. A meeting ground is where people and organizations meet. It is a place, physical or virtual, but a place for meeting, conversing, and exchanging ideas, information, and opinions in cooperation, in conflict, or neither. This book you are reading is not a meeting ground, because we

---

130. Module 5 on our Web site discusses the metamodel of relationship, a part of the metamodel of knowledge, in detail. See our Web site; Figure 116 on the site summarizes the conclusions of those arguments.
131. Module 5, Section 3, on our Web site discusses process maps in detail. Figure 92 on our Web site is an example.

cannot exchange information; it is a one-way flow. Had it been an interactive session on the Web, then the Web would have been our meeting place.

Without the Universal Perspective, meetings are often confused with their meeting grounds because this is where the event and place meet and join meanings. Similarly, without the Universal Perspective, people are often confused with the organizations they work for; with individuals and the roles they play; with events, such as Competition; and with Persons or Organizations that own, manage, or work the event. We need the Universal Perspective. The Universal Perspective makes it easy to untangle, distinguish, and normalize. The Universal Perspective is a prism that separates, clarifies, and unmasks.

Figure 2.9 has some common polymorphisms of collaboration, and some of the milder forms of conflict. They are events, and hence also may be processes. As the scale and complexity of business grows, an organization may be in conflict with another in one context, while in collaboration in another. We cannot capture these strategic roles if the event and the organization are joined as one. We cannot answer strategic questions such as: Which of my competitors are also my collaborators? Which of my suppliers are also my customers and employees? Which suppliers also compete with my business, and which do I have synergies with in the marketplace? Which regulators have vested business interests? The Universal Perspective forces us to distinguish an owner from the process, and a person or organization from an event. It thus helps us support strategic and even unforeseen information needs, even as it normalizes the behavior of the real world of Business Process.

Meeting Grounds, Markets, Marketplaces, and Other Polymorphisms of Place

A meeting ground is a place where resources can be exchanged—any resource. Naturally, every meeting ground must be a Place, but not vice versa. Resources can only be exchanged where they can be contained, but not every place that can contain resources can be the place where those resources can be exchanged. For example, this book is a location and a place for information, but as we recently discussed, it regrettably cannot be our meeting ground. A Place is thus a more general concept than a Meeting Ground, which is therefore a subtype and polymorphism of Place. Figure 2.9 articulates this.

Exchange of resources in a geographical or physical place needs no elaboration. We know information also may be located and exchanged in parts of the electromagnetic spectrum, or on the Web. We sometimes call these "Virtual" places. Indeed, as we have seen in our discussion of Figure 2.2, any venue recognized by any technology, past, present, or future, in which resources can be located (contained), is a Place, and any venue in which resources can be exchanged is a Place of Exchange or Meeting Ground.

We discussed Place early in this chapter, under Figure 2.2,[132] and Meeting Ground was discussed more recently, under Collaboration and Conflict. The partitioning of Place in Figure 2.9 makes clear that a meeting ground may be a physical or virtual place (because a meeting ground lies in a different partition from virtual or physical place). As we have seen earlier, when these Places are classes that also impose formatting constraints, they are instances of Media. Place and its subtypes in

---

132. Place is also described in Box 25 and in the example on automating innovation in Box 62 on our Web site. See also "Mutability and Innovation" on our Web site.

Figure 2.9 are too obvious to merit more elaboration, except to say that they lie at the heart of all exchanges, locations, and transactions, and therefore are clearly central to the business of business.

Marketplace   The business of business crystallizes around a marketplace. A Marketplace is a special kind of Meeting Ground. Rights are exchanged between people and organizations in a marketplace. A Right is information. It is a Term and Condition. The rights exchanged in a marketplace are the rights of ownership and use transferred by the sale, lending, and return events we discussed recently. Thus, a Marketplace is a special kind of place for a special kind of Exchange. It is also the place for forging sales and product use agreements, and a meeting ground for the parties to these agreements. A marketplace is also a place of collaboration, collusion, and conflict—conflict between competitors, and collaboration or collusion between collaborators—including customers and suppliers. Thus, it is a strategic meeting ground for strategic events.[133]

Clearly, the one condition that distinguishes a marketplace from a meeting ground in general, and establishes a marketplace as a polymorphism of meeting ground, are its defining relationships. These relationships, between rights to business products and the owners and the buyers of these products, are what define the agreement and meeting ground for the exchange of rights. An agreement (potential or realized) lies at the heart of the market place. The owner and buyer (potential or actual) are parties to the agreement (or negotiation, when it is not yet an agreement). We will return to this feature of critical interest in Section 2.1.2, when we discuss the universal parameters of marketplaces. For now, it will suffice to understand that a marketplace grows out of a meeting ground; that it is a polymorphism of meeting ground. An agreement, potential or actual, lies at the heart of this meeting ground.

This agreement and its parties frame the universal parameters of Marketplace. This agreement and its parties are clearly the very crux and hub of the pattern that defines the turning wheel of business and the exchanges that spin around it, driving it forward since the business of business began—driving it in a marketplace (see Section 2.1.2).

The Place Within a Medium   A place contains a resource. Therefore, a place can also convey a resource. A Document is a place that conveys or contains information, and a Medium is a class of documents based on formativeness. For example, air is a medium for conveying information in the form of sound, but the specific volume of air that is conveying sound is an instance of a document and an instance of a place. This book is a document, and the class of books is a medium. A radio signal pregnant with information is a document propagating through space, which is its medium. Indeed, the electromagnetic spectrum is also its medium. Both Space and Spectrum are Media because they both normalize constraints on how information may be formatted, and on what kinds of symbols are permitted in each medium. The radio signal we discussed was constrained by the intersection of constraints imposed by each medium to which it belonged.[134] We have seen in our discussion of Figure 2.1 that a Document is a kind of Place. We have also seen that a

---

133. Strategic events were described under *Collaboration and Conflict*.
134. Set intersection is discussed in Box 19 on our Web site.

Medium is a class of documents. Box 25 tells us that a class of places is also a place. It follows that a Medium is also a place. It is a place for information—special information. It is the place, and normalized container, of formatting rules. Thus, a medium is a polymorphism of a Place.

It is easy to confuse a document and place with a medium, since they often have the same name, and are similar concepts. For instance, the word Air was a homonym in the example we recently discussed. Air, the document, was a polymorphism and instance of Place of information called Air. The Place called Air may convey no formatting information. We might only know that it can contain information. Then it is only a place for information. When Air does convey information in symbols that can be sensed, it also becomes a Medium. Thus Air, the Medium, is a polymorphism of Air, the Place. It was easy to confuse the medium with the document and place, not only because they all had the same names, but also because it was compounded by the fact that they had similar (but not exactly the same) meanings. The document was a polymorphism of its medium, which in turn was a polymorphism of a place; the document contained the meaning of the medium within it, and the medium contained the meaning of Place within it. However, the meaning of the document and place were subtly different from each other, and both were different from the medium that carried their name. We must recognize these differences and distinguish between them to normalize information. The Medium normalizes information on formatting constraints and formativeness. Information normalizes the contents of a document, Place normalizes the potential for containment of information (or any other resource), and Document brings information and format together in a Place by expressing it in a form we can sense. In order to normalize meanings across the unending topoii of perspectives and to subsume them, meanings in the Universal Perspective must necessarily be sparse but precise. Much may be left unsaid, but what is said must be extreme in its clarity. It may then be interpreted in only one way because it is not only clear and precise about what it conveys, but also equally clear, and surgically precise about what it leaves out.

Clearly, some documents could even be meeting grounds, depending on their media. Telephone party lines and Web pages that support chat rooms are prime examples. They are also examples of media that go by the same name, but which are distinct classes of information in the Universal Perspective. Formatted information always implies a medium of information, for this is where formatting rules reside and are normalized, but the converse need not always be true. Media can exist without instantiating a single document, and a place can exist without instantiating a single medium, even when it is a place for information. For instance, the meaning of medium contains information—the meaning of Place. It is therefore a place for information, but not a medium of information, because it cannot tell us how we must format the information it contains to give it a tangible form. The Universal Perspective is a fine toothcomb that helps us sift, distinguish, normalize, and unmask meanings. It also helps us engage the meanings that must mesh within the knowledge machine. It engages them with relationships. The polymorphisms that are the focus of this section are expressions of one such relationship—the subtyping relationship. There are also other relationships that we will discuss in Section 2.1.2.

Markets and Market Segments   Indeed, just as Medium classifies documents in the Universal Perspective, Market classifies marketplaces based on one or more parameters [see Box 24, Figure (f)]. When a Market is segmented by Business Products, we call it a Product Market. A Product Market combines the features of markets and products into one state space (see Box 24). The targeting of places in this multidimensional space, whether they are broad regions or narrow niches, is the most fundamental of strategic decisions a business takes; it defines the very nature of the business of a firm.

Box 24 describes how markets, product markets, and their segments shadow the agreement (potential or actual) between buyers, sellers, and rights at the heart of the marketplace. This agreement is a relationship. Every relationship is intrinsically associated with a Borel Object that can classify and categorize it in multiple ways in multiple segments (see Box 24). Product Market is a polymorphism of the generic Borel Object in the Metamodel of Knowledge.

Box 24: Slicing and Dicing Information with Borel Objects   24

Borel Objects are components in the metamodel of Knowledge that support the slicing and dicing of data and pattern analysis. Borel Objects normalize information about groups, patterns, and aggregates. This box summarizes the discussion on resolving many-to-many relationships and Borel Objects, in Module 5, Section 1, on our Web site.

An object has features. These features have values. For instance, the features of a person might be height, weight, and age. A particular person might be 6 feet tall, weigh 150 pounds, and be 34 years old. These values define the state of the person. Thus, its features determine the state space of an object. Each feature is an axis of this space, and each point in the space is a distinct possible state of an instance of the object. Figures (a) and (b) show this.

Thus, regions in the state pace of the object may be used to group instances of the object into subclasses or categories [see Figure (e)]. A relationship is an object. For instance, a retail sale is a relationship between a person, a product, and a retailer. Figures (c) and (d) show this.

The objects it relates determine the state space of a relationship. The axes in Figure (e) represent the object classes that participate in the relationship in Figure (d). Each point on an axis represents an instance identifier of a participating object. Thus, each instance of the relationship in Figure (d) is a point in the state space shown in Figure (e). Regions of the state space in Figure (e) classify the retail sale relationship of Figure (d).

The complete state space represents all possible relationships, regardless of whether or not they exist.[135] Slicing and dicing this state space groups and regroups relationship into different categories (some may be empty

---

135. The entire state space in Figure (e) of Box 24 represents all possible relationships (the conceivable state space of Box 34), regardless of any imposed constraints that might bar some relationships (the lawful state space of Box 34).

24

categories). Each category is also an object, which is identified by a unique instance identifier.

For instance, Figure (e) shows how the state space for "Sale" in Figure (d) may be sliced and diced. Regions may or may not be mutually exclusive. Even disjoint regions can be considered a part of a single collection [see Figure (f)]. These arbitrary collections represent market segments based on what products (or product ranges) were sold to which kinds of customers in which places. These regions need not be three-dimensional volumes. They could be any subspace—lines, surfaces, patterns that may twist and turn, patterns that are bounded, finite, unbounded, or even infinite.[136] For instance, if

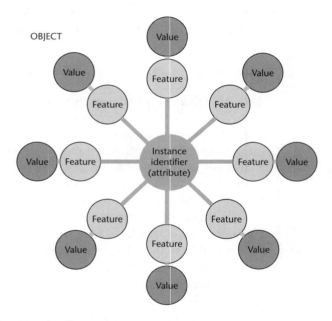

Figure (a) An object has features.

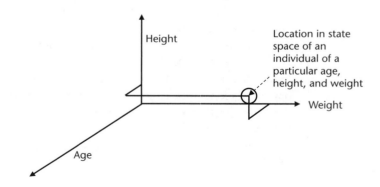

Figure (b) Its features define the state space of an object.

136. The patterns in Figure (e) of Box 24 may be any kind of pattern discussed in Chapter 4, Section 1, in [337].

we only cared about products sold to a specific customer, and were
required to analyze where products were bought, our market segments
would be two-dimensional regions of state space—patterns of points
on a plane. These points will be located in a vertical plane, parallel to the

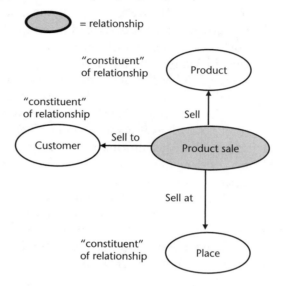

Figure (c) A relationship.

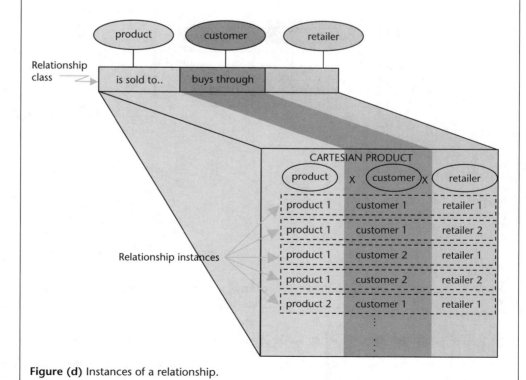

Figure (d) Instances of a relationship.

24

product-place plane of Figure (e). The plane on which these regions are located will intersect the customer axis at the point that represents the customer in question.

On the other hand, if we only cared about products and where they were sold, regardless of customers, we would need a "don't care" value on the customer axis. "Don't Care" will subsume both known values, as well as the Unknown value, as described in Chapter 2, Section 2, in [337]. Assigning this "don't care" value to the customer will be equivalent to reducing the relationship in Figure (d) to a second-degree relationship by eliminating Customer. Degrees and orders of relationships are discussed in Box 10. Module 5, Sections 1 and 4, on our Web site, show that reducing the order of a relationship creates a supertype. Note that "don't care" does not bar the relationship with Customer, nor does it assert its nonexistence, like the null value would. It merely asserts that the information is irrelevant or unavailable.[137] Indeed, Figure (e) makes clear that the existence of the three-dimensional state space implies the existence of its two-dimensional subspaces—the product-place, product-customer, and customer-place planes.[138]

The state spaces segmented in the examples above were nominally scaled. Points in each region (segment) were discrete collections of unrelated objects, with no sense of continuity, no definition of closeness (beyond the fact that each is unique and distinct from others in the region), nor any concept of ordered

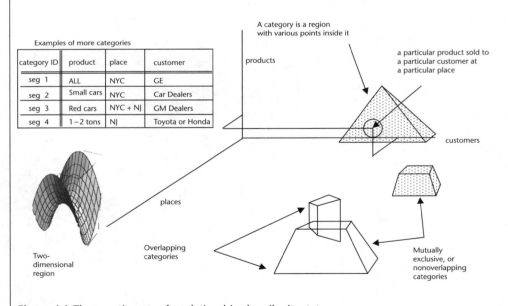

Examples of more categories

category ID	product	place	customer
seg 1	ALL	NYC	GE
seg 2	Small cars	NYC	Car Dealers
seg 3	Red cars	NYC + NJ	GM Dealers
seg 4	1–2 tons	NJ	Toyota or Honda

Figure (e) The constituents of a relationship describe its state space.

137. The "unknown," "don't care," and "all" values are discussed in depth in Chapter 2, Section 2, Box 51, and Chapter 4, Section 3. See Module 5, Section 4, on our Web site.

138 Module 5, Section 1, on our Web site, describes how the metamodel of knowledge infers this under "Slicing and Dicing Associations Between Objects."

24

arrangement within the segment. There were no ranges or intervals between points involved. What if we had to slice and dice ordinal or quantitative state spaces? For instance, market segmentation may depend on the sale price of the product, which is a quantitative attribute of Product Sale. If this happens, Sale Price will be an axis of the state space, which we must segment. Market segments must now consider the set of all possible intervals along ordinal or quantitative dimensions. To make it easier to visualize geometrically, consider a three-dimensional state space in which Product Sale is a binary relationship that only involves Place and Product, two axes of this state space, and the third axis is Sale Price, an attribute of the relationship [see Figure (f)].

Segmentation might get even more complex. What if we wanted to segment sales by the list price of the product, an attribute of, and information normalized by, Product, not Product Sale? The very identity of the relationship, an object, is the conjunction of the identities of the objects it relates, and is dependent on them. Representing each point on an axis by only its instance identifier does not represent the entire information payload of the corresponding object. It ignores the fact that an instance of the object also has a state determined by its features: Each axis unfolds into a state space of its own. In the same way, some of the new axes may also unfold because they are also feature laden. All the axes of the combined state space collectively determine the conceivable state space for segmenting Sale (or for any relationship in general). Thus, the state of the relationship actually includes the information on the states of related objects, which may be used to classify the relationship.[139] The product axis in the state space of the "product sale" relationship would then be limited to only those products that meet the requisite sale price criteria. Thus, this space will be a region and a restriction polymorphism of the conceivable state space of the relationship. See Box 14, and the endnotes on both polymorphism and the Bunge-Wand-Weber model.

The set of all possible intervals also opens the door to a very special object class called the Borel Set. A Borel Set is the set of all possible intervals on an axis of state space, or, when multiple axes are involved, the set of all possible regions in that space. These intervals (regions) may or may not overlap. Each region (delineated or not) in Figure (f) is an instance of a Borel Set for that state space. If we recognize the "Don't Care" value, the Borel Set will include all intervals in state space, as well as intervals in the state spaces of all possible facets (spaces defined by all possible combinations of its axes).

Borel Sets are hard to visualize as a class. An instance of a Borel Set is easier to understand and visualize, at least in one-, two-, and three-dimensional spaces. Every region in space, whatever its shape, size, or extent, is an instance of a Borel Set, as is every collection of regions, whether overlapping or disjoint, finite or infinite, bounded or unbounded, open or closed. Figure (f) has examples.

139. References [283–286] discuss the mathematical concepts that support this kind of unfolding of axes in state space. The state charts in [337] are a technique for representing this kind of rule.

24

When segmentation involves ordinal, difference, or ratio scaled axes, regions will depend on gaps between values, and hence Borel Sets will be involved. When segmentation is in terms of nominally scaled axes, segmentation will involve collections of points in state space of every possible set of combinations of axes. Intervals are also collections of points in state space. We will call the union of these intervals and collections the Borel Object. The Borel Object generalizes the concept of the class of all possible segments, regardless of how the space is scaled, and regardless of whether it has any null values—"holes"—in it. It is the class of segments.

Every relationship automatically implies the existence of its Borel Object. The rules [see the example in Figure (g)] are:

1. The Borel Object of a relationship is also related to the object classes the relationship binds.
2. Relationships between individual object classes and the Borel Object are optional (to support the "all" value we discussed earlier[140]).
3. At least one of these individually optional relationships must exist in order to instantiate a Borel Object. The degree of the combination of relationships between the Borel Object and its constituent object classes must be one or more (see Box 10).

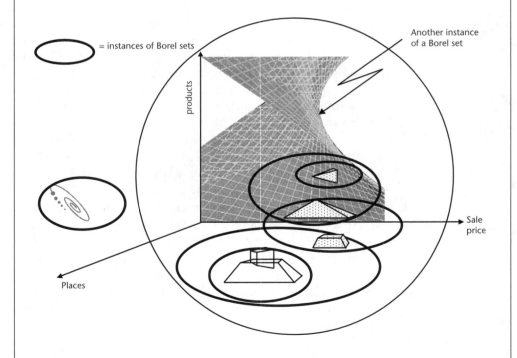

Figure (f) Examples of instances of Borel Objects.

---

140. Chapter 4, Section 3, and of [337], and Box 51, Module 5, Section 4, on our Web site, all discuss the "all" and "any" values in detail.

4. A relationship and its Borel Object have an optional many-to-many association between them.

24

Figure (g) illustrates these rules with an example. In Figure (g), an individual product sale may be simultaneously classified in several ways, and hence may belong to several market segments at the same time. A market segment also may have several sales events. Thus, the relationship between Product Sale and Market Segment (the corresponding Borel Object) is a many-to-many relationship. Note how the many-to-many relationship between Product Sale and Market Segment is resolved by a resolution object, Product Sale in Market Segment, in Figure (g). Product Sale in Market Segment glues a one-to-many relationship to a zero-to-many relationship, to create the optional many-to-many composition. The lower bound is zero because a market segment can be empty (i.e., it might have no sales). This is an example of how the Metamodel of Knowledge can automatically resolve many-to-many relationships by creating a resolution object, and substituting the many-to-many relationship with a composition.

Borel Objects help us to analyze the information content of a relationship class by slicing and dicing it to look for patterns. Borel Objects are containers of analytical patterns that normalize a higher order of nonprocedural knowledge about businesses. The Borel Object is a component in the Metamodel of Knowledge that we use to segment the market by slicing and dicing information that the

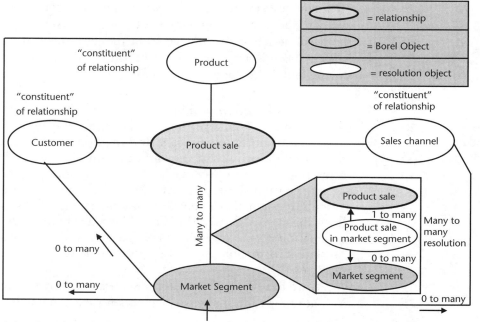

At least one relationship (or combination of relationships) between market segment (a Borel Object) and its constituent objects—product, customer, sales channel—must exist at each moment in time.

Figure (g) Examples of instances of Borel Objects.

24

constituents of a relationship normalize. For instance, we might want to segment the market by list price of product (an attribute of Product), customer revenue (an attribute of Customer), and mean temperature of the place (an attribute of Place), all taken together, and then look for patterns across these segments. To segment the market like this, we will need to consider the entire composition of objects in Figure (c). Since we are interested in combinations of information across constituent objects, we have implicitly recognized that a relationship binds them, and hence implicitly recognized the corresponding Borel Object.

Borel Objects are discussed in detail in Module 5, Section 1, on our Web site, under Collections of objects and the state space of relationships.

Thus, product market segments are regions, or places that may have been carved out of the state space of a product market (see Box 24). Segments thus carved by constraints will be subtypes of the unconstrained category of marketplaces that we call a Product Market, and will inherit the properties of the product market they segment.

A Market is an instance of a Borel Set of a Product Market in which we do not care about the product, but might care about (unsatisfied) market needs in order to design a product (see the Buying and Selling cluster in the patterns of Section 2.1.2). A Market is clearly a supertype of a Product Market, in which a product market inherits the state space of the market (see Box 24), and consequently, a market segment will be a supertype of corresponding product market segments. Thus are Markets, Product Markets, and their segments derived by the Universal Perspective and the Metamodel of Knowledge from the agreement at the heart of Marketplace. Market Need is a polymorphism of Information, which we will discuss under the Buying and Selling pattern in Section 2.1.2).

Places, Events, and Information in Motion   Motion implies change of place. Change implies a change in time. Thus, motion implies a change in place over time—a transportation process. Information in motion is a message. When the transportation or exchange of information like that in Figure 2.6(a) is involved, formatting rules can become rules of translation between the resources exchanging information. Indeed, translation can involve more than mere translation of symbols. It might also involve translation of Units of Measure.[141] When information flows through a network, a knowledge machine might automatically translate information in exchanges across people, resources, and media. Indeed, it could even translate information as it surges from node to node across a network of diverse resources.[142]

As we have seen, all places that contain information can also convey information, but they cannot always be places for exchanging it. For instance, the general

---

141. Chapter 4, Section 2, in [337], discusses translation of formats and units of measure. See also Box 38, Metamodels of Format, Format Conversion, Encryption, and Formatting Constraint; and Box 40, Measure Conversion and Conflicting Subtypes, on our Web site.
142. The arguments in "The Architecture of Knowledge," Module 1, Section 2, on our Web site show that this functionality lies in the interface layer of the four basic layers of the Architecture of Knowledge in Figure 15 on our Web site—Business Rules, Information Logistics, Interface Rules and Technology Rules.

class of places we call Book cannot be a place of exchange, but the places we called Air, Radio Spectrum, or Web page are places of exchange, each with its own formatting rules. A place becomes a document when we join it with Medium. The same formatting rules may apply to many places and documents, but not to all. For instance, both a Web page and paper may contain graphics, but Air can only contain sound. Moreover, a class of paper documents might contain only black and white graphics, although the medium permits color. Further, this class might be a subclass of documents that only contains information on operating vacuum cleaners. This class is clearly a class of documents, but not the class that normalizes formatting rules. It is therefore not a Medium. The key to normalization is to distinguish the Medium from the Place and the Document. The key to business is to turn a meeting ground into a marketplace.

A marketplace exchanges information. Therefore, it also could be a document. Indeed, it often is in cyberspace. A marketplace is a polymorphism of meeting ground. It thus inherits this property. Innovative business often revolves around seeking potential meeting grounds that can also become marketplaces. Technological innovation often revolves around creating the media to support a meeting ground.

A knowledge machine that "knows" this hierarchy of polymorphisms also could seek out innovative meeting grounds to turn into marketplaces, and automatically translate exchanges of information for those who will receive it. The Universal Perspective, joined with the Metamodel of Knowledge, carries within it the power of inference and the seeds of reason. Perhaps someday, it will even have the power to innovate and seek out new patterns of information that grow from the old.

Common Polymorphisms of Structure

Structure is an abstract concept. It is an abstraction borrowed from the Metamodel of Knowledge. We called it Composition in Box 10. We have recently seen how structure only takes a concrete shape when it is joined with a concrete resource. The section on structure demonstrated this with several examples, and discussed polymorphisms of Structure created in this manner. In this section, we will focus only on four widely shared polymorphisms of this kind: a structured task, charts of accounts, Route, and Network. All four are central to the operation of every business.

Networks, Governance, and Organization

Our recent discussion of Structure told us that a Network is a simple, albeit abstract concept. It is a network of associated resources, like a networks of business associates, networks of telephone switches and routers, or networks of roads. The polymorphisms of this simple concept can rapidly become complex and chaotic as we start considering issues of capacity and resources that the network will convey.

To convey, the network must contain. Every node and association in the network may have capacity constraints in the context of each resource it conveys or contains. Capacity constraints (see Box 10) might vary by object instance or object class. It is also clear, from our discussion on capacity in that section, that a node may have capacity constraints that are distinct and different from the capacity constraints of its association (link) with other (or the same) nodes in the network.

Box 25: Common Sense in Metanesia, or the Nature and Composition of Place   25

Places can be made of places. All places have this common characteristic, in addition to the fact that they can contain resources. It implies that aggregations of places are also places. Indeed, each aggregation is also a new and distinct instance of Place (just as a set of instances of an object is also an instance of an object). Places can thus be Borel Objects (see Box 24). Unions and intersections of places are also places.[143] We can have places overlap, and unless the overlapping places are identical, we will obtain a different and distinct Place. Places may be contained in other places (partly or fully), and places may even consist of other places, even when these places are disjoint (i.e., neither adjacent nor connected to each other). Thus, the aggregate will be a place, even if its constituents are unconnected islands. The inverse of aggregation, dividing up a place into segments, will also yield places—each segment will be a place.

Moreover, a Cartesian product of places will also be a place.[144] These will be places of greater dimensionality than the places that were joined by the Cartesian product. "Squishing" a place by reducing its dimensionality is the inverse of taking a Cartesian product of places. There are two ways we may squish a space.

1. We may reduce some of its dimensions to "don't care" values (see Box 24).[145] Common sense tells us that this will generalize the space we squished, and the generalized space will be a (less constrained) supertype of the higher dimensional space (see Box 14).
2. We may constrain some dimensions to fixed values. The same principles tell us this space must be a lower dimensional (more constrained) subtype of the space we squished, or more accurately, sliced into a cross section of some kind. It might even be a curved and contorted cross section like the twisting surface in Figure (f) of Box 24.

These operations also create Places, places we call subspaces of the space we "squished." However, it is clear that each kind of "squished" (or "sliced") subspace is a very different kind of Place. One is a supertype, and the other a subtype, of a place we squished to the extreme, enough to obliterate some dimensions. However, both are places derived from other places. Each place is related to, and located by, the other. Indeed, Box 12 also tells us that the place created by the first operation must also consist of and contain the place from which it was created. Similarly, the place created by the second operation is a part of, and contained in, the place from which it was created. Each of the two

---

143. Unions, intersections, and other set operations are in Box 19 on our Web site.
144. Box 19 on our Web site describes the Cartesian product. The relationship in Figure (d) of Box 24 is an example of a Cartesian product.
145. Box 51 and Module 5, Section 1, under "Collections of Objects and the State Space of Relationships," describe why reducing the dimensions of a state space creates a supertype of the space. See our Web site.

operations above is a polymorphism of "located relative to," the **25** relationship discussed in Box 12. Indeed, a Place is any pattern of places.[146]

The Metamodel of Knowledge can use these rules to define new polymorphisms of Place. Indeed, this is how Place in different perspectives may be derived from the "Place" of the Universal Perspective. A Place is a place if it can satisfy the criteria that it can contain resources. The operations we have discussed are all different ways of locating places in terms of other places. If, for some reason, a resource is barred from a Place derived in this manner, then we call it a Forbidden Place, implying that the ban is a constraint that might be removable. If the place can contain only some resources and not others, then we call it a place of only the resources it may contain. Thus, places also may have contexts. For instance, physical space is no place for an abstract idea, but it is a place for buildings, people, and planets.

Physical space, like state space, also contains itself. Every interval in physical space is also a physical space and a place (a Borel Object; see Box 24). Both physical space and state space are places. However, Physical Space is a very special kind of difference scaled place.[146] It has one characteristic that sets it apart from other kinds of places. Physical objects only may be in one (physical) place at a time. This unique interaction between Physical Object and Physical Place sets them apart from other kinds of objects in other kinds of places. The inverse of this relationship between physical object and physical space also is similarly constrained. Physical space has a finite capacity to hold physical objects. A place completely occupied by a physical object will exclude other physical objects. The notion of physical size and footprint are rooted in this property of the occupancy relationship (interaction) between physical objects and physical space. The occupancy relationship is identical to the containment relationship of Box 12 that leads to the concept of capacity and size, which we discussed in Box 10.

Just as a physical place may hold more than one physical object until its capacity to hold is exhausted, so too may a physical object occupy many places until its capacity to occupy is exhausted. The footprint of a physical object is a place. That place contains other places within it. All these places—the entire Borel Set of places within its footprint—are occupied by the physical object, and vice versa. Borel Sets were discussed in Box 24. The one constraint that must hold is that these places must be mutually adjacent. No other physical object (uncontained by the object in question) may occupy this space, and neither may the same physical object occupy any other place. This is what we mean when we say that a physical object is constrained to one place that has exclusive claim to it. Strictly speaking, the object is occupying an infinite number of places, but they are all instances of Borel Sets of

---

146. Chapter 4, Section 1, in [337], describes the architecture of Pattern. "A place is any pattern of places" may be mathematically articulated as "Place, the class, is idempotent with respect to any operations that locate places (i.e., we start with Place and end with Place as we sweep around the relationship implied by the operation)."

its footprint (or volume), and are all parts of the one primary place that the object is considered to occupy. (Part of is stricter than contained in—see Box 12.) In considering parts of the place that a physical object occupies, we divided the physical place into an infinite number of overlapping and disjoint regions. We could do the same to the physical object, and in that sense, a physical place also may be said to contain infinitely many, possibly overlapping, parts of a physical object. However, they all make a single object, because they are all notional parts of it. Thus, we come to a crucial question about the nature of physical occupancy. Which occupies which—does the physical object fill the space it occupies, or can the space be said to fill the physical object to give it substance? It is impossible to say. Both mean the same. They mutually locate each other; each fills the other to make it exist in itself.

The (complete) occupancy relationship is similarly constrained in both directions. Occupancy only becomes asymmetrical when it is partial—when the entire object occupies less than the entire space, or vice versa. If the object occupies less than the entire place in question, then the place locates the object, but the object cannot locate the complete place, and vice versa. Occupancy then turns into containment. Otherwise, the object and place merely locate each other, and location is a symmetrical relationship. On the other hand, "Contained in" is asymmetrical. The occupancy relationship between Physical Object and the complete Physical Place that it occupies is thus a symmetrical polymorphism of locate that has not yet blossomed into containment. Symmetry of relationships was discussed in Box 10.

Indeed, the entire notion of adjacent places emerges from the concept of patterns of association.[147] Location and containment are polymorphisms of that abstraction in the Metamodel of Knowledge. Physical Place is a pattern of association of the places it holds. Similarly, Time is a polymorphism of the sequenced pattern of association.[148] Unlike Time, physical space is an unsequenced pattern of association between places, a pattern that is sufficiently dense to become difference scaled.[149] Thus, physical space is a polymorphism of the generic Place in Figure 2.2, albeit a very severely constrained Place.

25

Remember also that there is no bar on idempotent associations. Idempotent relationships are described in Box 10.

---

147. Earlier in this chapter, Medium and Document, Energy and Physical Objects, and Box 12 discuss different kinds of physical and nonphysical spaces. Chapter 4, Section 1, in [337], discusses physical and nonphysical space in the section on patterns.
148. Chapter 4, Section 1, in [337], discusses patterns of association under the architecture of patterns.
149. In mathematical terms, difference scaled spaces are dense [208], and distances between places in such a difference scaled space is totally ordered [213]. See Value Difference functions in [211] for a more mathematical elaboration of the theory behind difference scaled spaces. Chapter 4, Section 3, in [337], discusses the concept of continuity in terms of the density of information in a domain under The Information in Domain. The discussion on density of information in Box 45 on our Web site adds to this discussion in [337]. A continuum of distances, such as those in ratio and difference scaled spaces, is said to be mathematically *dense*. More precisely and pedantically speaking, an ordered set of values is said to be mathematically dense when there are infinite numbers of values between two distinct values of a set, regardless of how close the two values are to each other. See the density of partial order in [208] for a more rigorously precise mathematical description of density of a place that consists of places; [208] also discusses the mathematics of dense sets. The smallest dense, unbounded totally ordered class, is the class of rational numbers [220], and the largest is the class of surreal numbers. See [213, 231]. For more mathematical detail on the continuum of magnitudes, see [204, 216].

At one extreme, every node and association may utilize a different proportion of its capacity to convey different instances of a resource. Moreover, capacities of each node and association may depend on the capacities of other nodes and associations, or even on their histories (including its own). At the other extreme, the capacity utilized by all objects being conveyed by the network might be the same, and at the very extreme, that capacity might be null (i.e., the network has no capacity constraints) for any object that traverses it.

The network is more than an aggregate object. It is a composition, a subtype of an aggregation (see Box 10). A network also consists of networks, as we saw in the section on Structure. The aggregation that is a network may normalize rules about how resources traversing the network will be routed—along which networks that are parts of the overall composite. These rules can address and resolve capacity conflicts between resources that traverse the network. For instance, a message traversing the Web might be broken up and each piece routed differently before it is assembled at its destination. Similarly, a network of individuals may delegate work dynamically, depending on how busy each person is.[150] Indeed, the network itself may be a dynamic object: shifting, evolving, and changing continually in response to its governance, its environment, and its load; adding, dropping, and altering its nodes and associations; and extending, shrinking, and changing its capacity and state as it continually responds to events external and internal. Needless to say, without careful governance, a complex network could easily become chaotic.[151]

All Petrinets are temporal networks (see the endnote on Petrinets). A wireless network of cells and telephones is a network, as is a network of individuals seeking work, or a network of relationships between objects, temporal or not. A Network is a universally useful concept, a glue that connects, and a route that conveys. Its polymorphisms are without count. When it conveys, it is also a Place. When it conveys in a direction, the network becomes a Route. Thus, a Route is a network with information on direction added. A Route is a key polymorphism of Network. Naturally, networks are needed to support transportation and exchanges. Indeed, without networks, there can be neither meeting ground, nor transportation, nor conveyance.

Aggregating resources is the first step in organizing them. Giving the aggregate a structure is the next step. Structure is a polymorphism of aggregation (see Box 10). Structure is a meaning. Things (e.g., compositions, objects, or processes) can be more or less structured. Things become more structured as we add information to them.[152] Structures with information added are polymorphisms of those to which they add information (see Box 14). As we add information to an aggregation of objects, creating a structure, we increase its organization. The quantum of its organization increases in step with the information we add to it. Thus, a process that creates a structure or an aggregate is a process of organization and governance. A process that restructures also reorganizes as it governs.

Networks and aggregate objects organize their members (i.e., nodes). A Network is a network of resources (i.e., a subtype with two parents—Resource and

---

150. Module 5, Section 3, on our Web site discusses this example in "Processes That Gain or Lose Structure." It demonstrates the meaning of unstructured processes and shows how the Metamodel of Knowledge can configure well-managed but unstructured processes that can be more responsive than rigidly structured processes.
151. See [292, 293, 312, 323]. See also [72–74, 83] for more information on chaos.
152. Module 5 on our Web site discusses in depth the parameters, partitions, and polymorphisms of different kinds of *Structure*.

Structure). Networks have no information on the directions of associations between their nodes. (Network was omitted in Figure 2.9 to reduce clutter). The nodes of a network may all belong to the same class of objects, or they may belong to different classes. We will call networks of nodes of the same class homogeneous networks, and networks of nodes of different classes, heterogeneous networks.

> Most homogenous structures (or aggregations) that consist of the basic objects in Figure 2.1 are organized (or aggregated) forms of the resources they organize; that is, the network (or aggregation) belongs to the same object class as its nodes. Structures inherit this property from the aggregation (see Box 10). Thus, a network (or aggregation) of energy is (organized/aggregated) energy; a network of physical objects is an (organized/aggregated) physical object; a network of information is (organized/aggregated) information; a network of events is an (organized) event; a network of documents is an (organized) document; a network of organizations is an organization; and a network of places is an (organized) place. Each organized/aggregated object is an instance of an object class with two parents, Structure and the class of its nodes.[153] An aggregation of Persons is "people." A network of persons is also people, but it is also known as an "organization" or "organizational unit." The English language makes this exception; it is more discriminating when dealing with structures made of persons. Thus, networks of persons are organizations of persons, which is different from Person. It is the exception among the objects in Figure 2.1. Unless we qualify the term otherwise, Organization or Organizational Unit in this book will mean organizations of people or organizations of organizations of people.

The concept of organized people, places, and other resources brings us to the nature of routes and distribution channels, both of which are critical components of supply chains that are the lifeblood of business.[154]

Route and Distribution Channel   A Route is a polymorphism of Path and Resource. We saw this in the section on Structure. This is because every resource also can be a Place. Place, as we have just seen, is a role of Resource (see Figure 2.2).[155] A Route is a route through places, and hence through resources. We have no information on what will be conveyed on this route. We only know that a route exists because resources may be locations of resources, and some locations may be directly accessed from others, whereas other locations may not be (see Box 26).[156] A

---

153. Mathematically speaking, we can say that the class of a homogenous aggregation of high-level (information-poor) objects is idempotent with respect to the class of its nodes. This property of idempotency of homogenous aggregations with respect to its class of its nodes is inherited by *Homogenous Structure*, and extends beyond the objects in Figure 2.1. For instance, this property of networks will hold for all objects, except Legal Entity in Figure 2.10; it will hold for polymorphisms of *Information* and *Physical Object* in Figure 2.9, and for polymorphisms of *Negotiation, Plan, Monitoring Event,* and *Calendar* in Figure 2.5. As we descend the subtyping hierarchy, polymorphisms of this idempotent relationship will open out into nonidempotent polymorphisms, as discussed in Box 10. Thus, a collection of tables is not a table, nor is a collection of soccer balls a soccer ball.

154. Module 5, Section 3, in [337], discusses supply chains. See *Supply and Demand Chains,* and Box 59 on our Web site.

155. *Place* is a polymorphism of Resource created by the *Locate* relationship (see Box 12). Places that do not contain other resources are empty (*Contain* is a polymorphism of *Locate*). *Route* not only adds information on connectivity to Place, but also adds information on the directions of associations between places. Therefore, *Route* is a polymorphism of Place and Path.

156. Chapter 4, section 1, in [337], Patterns Of Sequenced Versus Unsequenced Association, discusses the connectedness of location in detail.

> ## Box 26: Connections and the Concept of Neighborhood   26
>
> The concept of a neighborhood, or neighboring points in a region, does not hold in all kinds of spaces. For instance, a nominally scaled space has no information on which points are closer to which other points. It only conveys that each point is distinct and different. Thus, there is no concept of neighborhood in a nominally scaled space. A difference or ratio scaled space could be considered an infinitely dense network of an infinite number of infinitely connected nodes that make a neighborhood. Chapter 4, Section 1, in [337], discusses this in more detail, with examples, in the section on patterns. A space is also a place where things can exist—a place of containment, location, and conveyance. It might seem strange, but a space in which the concept of neighborhood stands is a polymorphism of a network, and a space in which there is no neighborhood is a polymorphism of an unstructured aggregation. Both are components in the Metamodel of Knowledge described in [337]. The Universal Perspective is derived from this abstract knowledge.

Route is a pattern of association between resources that are also places. The nodes on a Route are always Places. Therefore, a Route is also a Place—it is a polymorphism of Path and Place. The added information is not only that the meanings of Place and Network are joined in Route, but also that the directions of associations between places in a route are known. This information is inherited from Path. Thus, a Route is an inclusion polymorphism of Network. Box 10 describes inclusion polymorphism.

The route may be a chain of people or organizations in a supply chain that is distributing and delivering products and services to customers. It then becomes a Distribution Channel (see Figure 2.10). Distribution Channel is a key polymorphism of Route, and is of great importance to business. Distribution Channel is the thread that stitches partners in a supply chain into a collaborative process. The people and organizations between the first and last nodes of a distribution channel are Intermediaries, a polymorphism of Person/Organization in Figure 2.10.

Nodes on a route need not necessarily be people or organizations in order to mediate between the beginning and end of a path. The route also could be a geographical route—a route for transportation, transshipment, and travel of physical objects. A route could be the route that information takes through a set of virtual places to reach a destination—a route in the information logistics layer of Figure 15 in [337], on our Web site. It could be a roadmap of the kinds of energy that will convey information from source to destination, or a path through a set of physical containers that will deliver jewelry to a vault for safekeeping. The Route in Figures 2.9 and 2.10 is a generic route. It subsumes all routes, telling us only that Path and Resource have joined to create a Route. A Path is an abstraction that only lends a

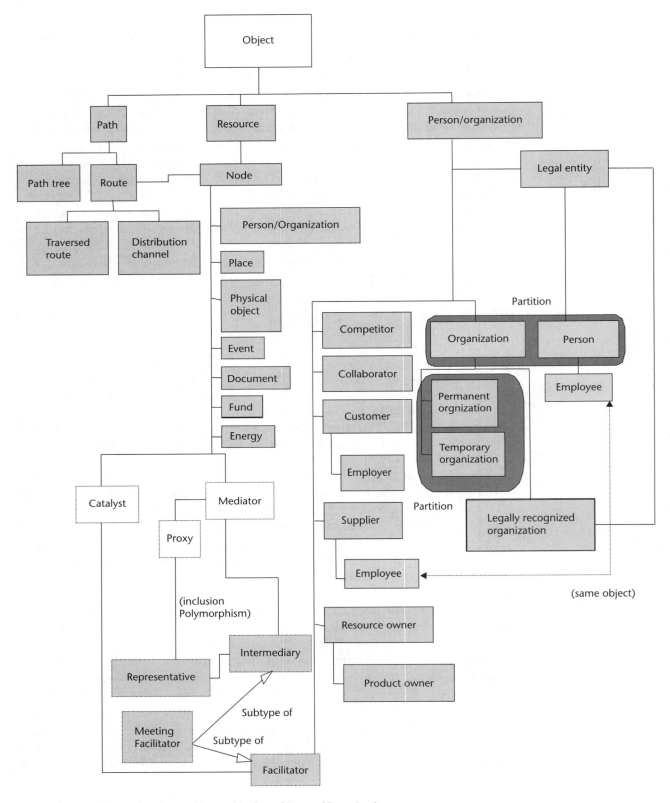

Figure 2.10   Additional polymorphisms of Path and Person/Organization.

sense of direction to Structure.[157] Route is concrete. It tells us that resources constitute the nodes of a Path. Polymorphisms of Route will tell us what these resources are. Clearly, Route subsumes, captures, and contains the common essence of polymorphisms without count.

From Figure 2.8, it is clear that a path may consist of other paths. Any route through the networks in Figure 2.8 is a path. Thus, the path actually taken by a resource being conveyed on a route is a Part of the potential path (i.e., route) that it is permitted to take. The Part of relationship was discussed in Box 12. The actual route traversed, as opposed to the route(s) available in a path, is also a key polymorphism of Route that has frequent interest to business. It is often tracked against a baseline. That baseline could be a planned route, or the set of available routes. All three—the actual route, the available routes, and the planned routes—are resources frequently used by polymorphisms of the tracking processes in Figure 2.5. As we have discussed earlier, tracking and governance go hand in hand.

Charts of Accounts   Clearly, with reference to the discussion of Path and Tree in the section on Structure, a chart of accounts is a tree-structured path. It is a tree, because each account directly rolls up into only one other (although several accounts might roll up into a common parent that summarizes them);[158] and it is a path, because the roll-up hierarchy has a direction. Clearly, the accounts in the hierarchy are polymorphisms of Fund. Thus, a chart of accounts is a structure that is a polymorphism with two parents, Path Tree and Fund. Note also how the hierarchy in Figure 2.9 has been flattened. The tree in question is also a polymorphism of Route, and Fund is a polymorphism of Resource. Had it been shown in this manner in Figure 2.9, the hierarchy would have been deeper and more complete. However, in the interest of clarity, it has been flattened (see Box 15).

Organizational Structure   Organizational Structure has been omitted in Figures 2.9 and 2.10, because it is very similar to Chart of Accounts. It is a polymorphism of Path Tree and Person/Organization. There are several polymorphisms of this basic tree structure that are often of interest to business, such as reporting structures, ownership structures, and others. We will discuss organizational structure in more detail in the section on polymorphisms of people and organizations, and when we discuss relationships and rules of engagement between the objects in this section. These interactions are also stock themes of business.

Structured Task   Structured Task needs little further elaboration. Process maps are polymorphisms of Path and Task.[159] In unstructured tasks, dependencies, ownership, resources, products, and other parameters of tasks are determined at

---

157. *Structure* is the abstract pattern of association discussed in Chapter 4, Section 1, in [337]. *Route* adds to Structure by telling us that the pattern is a pattern of association of *resources*. Thus, *Route* is a polymorphism of an abstract pattern that resides in the Metamodel of Knowledge. *Path* is the abstract pattern of *sequenced* association of Chapter 4, Section 1, in [337]. Indeed, every theme and concept we deal with in the real world blossoms from the abstraction that we have called the Metamodel of Knowledge (details in [337]; see also Box 30). They blossom as polymorphisms, or grow out of interactions between objects therein.
158. If the accounting hierarchy is not a tree, and a node is associated with multiple higher level nodes, then we might have to apportion the quantities we roll up by some rule of allocation. Allocation is discussed in Chapter 3, Section 2, in [337].
159. Box 2 has an example of a process map, but it omits detail on resources and products of processes. See Figure 92 on our Web site. Module 5, Section 3, on our Web site, discusses process maps and process decomposition in detail.

execution time. See "Supply Chain Standards" and Box 59 on our Web site. Figure 2.9 reiterates that the restructuring of process maps and structured tasks are not normalized by Task or Process, but by Structure. For instance, the effect of a restructuring event will restructure a Structure or Path. Changes in direction will be normalized by Path and changes in connection by Structure. This behavior will be common to the restructuring of process maps, organizations, routes, charts of accounts, task or resource dependencies in a project plan, or any other structure. The effect resides in Structure, and is automatically inherited by, and shared with, every kind of Structure, including Task.

Indeed, the same computer code could be used to restructure tasks, organizations, routes, accounting hierarchies, process maps, and other structures in different software applications specifically targeted for each kind of structure. This demonstrates how Structure, as well as its behavior, is a reusable component of knowledge that can be borrowed from the Universal Perspective, and is also an example of how normalized knowledge can save cost, time, and effort.

In Section 2.1.2 we will discuss in more detail Task, the theme and pattern of information, in terms of its relationships with business objects, people, and organizations.

Mediation and Proxy   Mediators mediate between nodes of a Structure. They could be transshipment nodes between the source and destination, nodes in the Network, and roles of resources in a resource transfer within a Network. The resource being transferred or shipped through the network could be any resource in Figure 2.2—rights, agreements, business products, or anything else. The transferring and receiving nodes in the network also may be any polymorphism of Resource, including Person/Organization. The nodes between the source and destination are Mediators, and people or organizations that play this role in a network of Person/Organizations will be Intermediaries. Thus, Intermediary is a polymorphism of Mediator.

The distinction between Intermediaries and inanimate Mediators becomes important when conflict of interest issues must be resolved in a network of Person/Organizations, in which an Intermediary may represent one or both parties in a Meeting. This is also a stock theme, a Topos if you will, which we will discuss later in this chapter, in the section on common roles of people and organizations.

Note that mediation does not always imply a process or the flow of time. Any asymmetrical relationship implies a directional interaction. For instance, representation of one object by another is a nontemporal flow of information, and a polymorphism of Mediator.[160]

A Proxy is a special kind of Mediator. Inherent in the concept of one object standing in as a proxy for another is the fact that an object may not only mediate between resources, but that it also could be a resource or symbol that represents a resource when it is "sought" by another in an interaction. This kind of representative is also known as an Agent.[161] Seen in this manner, it is clear that representation implies an in-between node in a directional structure (i.e., a Path). Figure 2.10 has

---

160. Box 36 on our Web site discusses representation and its polymorphisms, some of which are also in Box 38.
161. *Expression*, an object, is identical to *Expressed by*, its defining relationship; the information conveyed (and hence meaning) is identical. See Module 6, Section 2, on our Web site and teh note on functional programming.

this polymorphism of Resource. A node in this role will be a Proxy. We will discuss this role in the context of people and organizations later in this section. It is a special role. A human Proxy is a Representative; so is an organization in this role.

Symbols express information through the formatting relationship. It is a polymorphism of "represent." The role of being a mediator is also a polymorphism of "represent." It is a role that attempts to manage conflicts of interest or resolve differences in expressions, such as protocols, languages, and so forth. Indeed, the Formatting relationship is also a polymorphism of mediation. The diversity of its application illustrates how the Universal Perspective unites seemingly unrelated meanings in concise generalizations—generalizations that are not always intuitive until they are articulated.

Objects in the Universal Perspective are unifying patterns that articulate the essence of common concepts. They are essential patterns of information, and are the seeds from which everyday meanings grow and flow. These objects are like broad oceans into which rivers of meanings flow, to lose their individuality, even as they preserve their essence. Thus, these Universal Objects are the ultimate integrators of concepts, processes, objects, data, and even databases, a topic on which we will elaborate in Section 2.1.2.

Common Polymorphisms of Information

Information is arguably the most abstract object that we have described in this book. Its polymorphisms are impossible to exhaustively enumerate. Indeed, information is so abstract a concept, that it was more than two thousand years, from the time Thales of Miletus formally recognized the concept of matter in ancient Greece, to the time Claude Shannon of Bell Laboratories gave the concept of information equal status. See the endnote on the topic. Indeed, it may even be argued that we sense the physical world only through the information conveyed to us by our senses, and hence the physical world itself is merely a polymorphism of information. (See the parable of Metanesia in Chapter 1.[162]) However, such debates are better left to philosophers and scientists. We will only focus on those few, but sufficiently generic, polymorphisms of abstract information that are stock themes used and reused all the time in the world of business. They are meanings and patterns of pure information that represent only information.

Business is built on information, or more appropriately, on the communication and exchange of information. Therefore, it is perhaps most appropriate to start our discussion with Message, the stock theme at the heart of all communication.

Message   A message is information in transit. It is information that is currently being acted on by the transportation process we recently discussed. A message is thus a role of information—a subtype and a polymorphism. Information might be in transit in physical or virtual space. Accordingly, a radio broadcast is a message, as is the information recorded on a paper document being hand carried by a courier, or news in electronic transit from one Web page to another. Note that, unlike physical objects being transferred, delivery of a message does not imply removal of the information from its source.

162. Chapter 4, Section 1, in [337], expands on this theme, under "Five Fundamental Formats."

Box 27: Issue Management—A Stock Theme and Common Polymorphism of Meeting and Negotiation   27

Issues may be interrelated. The resolution or closure of an issue also may resolve or close several other issues, or it might take the resolution or closure of several issues to resolve a single issue. In other words, issues may involve each other through (optional) many-to-many relationships.[163] Often, one person or organization will "own" the issue. That person or organization should usually be the party that tabled the issue, even though the primary coordinator who will track and coordinate its resolution and closure could be a different party. Several parties may have to coordinate with each other to resolve the issue, but it should not be considered resolved or closed unless its "owner" agrees that the issue is resolved or closed. The dimensions of ownership of an issue are identical to those of any process. These "RAWCF" dimensions (see Box 10) are inherited from the metamodel.

Resolution of an issue involves governance. The primary processes are processes for tabling and coordinating issues, processes that will analyze issues to determine what work products will resolve the issue, and who will own those intermediate steps that use or produce these work products (in terms of "RAWCF" dimensions). The issue management process is a common polymorphism of Meeting. Issue resolution is a common polymorphism of Negotiation.

The process of resolving an issue is a common event and shared theme of business. It is a coordination and communication mechanism that glues together business. Its polymorphisms can be the source of several states of Issue between the time when it is opened, resolved (or declared irresolvable or redundant), and closed. Note that reopened is also another universal state of Issue that we must recognize.

Issue resolution is not only a common theme of business, but is also an example of a stock theme that is an unstructured process, because work products, resources, resolution processes, and ownership can change from instance to instance of issues, and may be decided "on the fly" at execution time.[164]

Goals, Features, Issues, and Risks   A goal is a purpose. Every business has a purpose. Goals were discussed under collaboration and conflict. It was clear that a goal is information about the work product of a process. It is a polymorphism of Information, and the purpose of a Guideline. In this book, we will not distinguish a goal from an objective.

---

163. An issue may (optionally) involve several issues, and each involved issue may also involve several issues. Box 24 discusses many-to-many relationships. Figure (g) of Box 24 shows a many-to-many composition.

164. Module 5, Section 3, discusses unstructured process. See also Box 59 and "Processes That Gain or Lose Structure," both on our Web site.

Issues are associated with goals. An issue is perhaps the most generic item of information businesses manage. An issue is information about a goal. It could be any information about the goal—the risks associated with the goal, an elaboration of the goal, information on guidelines, regulations, resources, processes, or anything else. Issues must usually be tracked, acted upon, resolved, and closed. Sometimes, they also might be marked irresolvable or redundant, and closed. These are all states of Issue. Note that an issue might not always be closed on resolution, or on the determination of irresolvability or redundancy. Closure, resolution, and redundancy are independent states of Issue.

A risk is a special kind of issue; it is the risk associated with a goal. Therefore, Risk is a polymorphism of Issue (see Figure 2.9). It is common practice to resolve Risk into different kinds (polymorphisms) of risks that flow from different risk factors. These risk factors can be traced back to risks that stem from resources, or uncertainties that stem from uncertain information about resources.[165]

Requirements, Needs, and Product Markets   A Need is a requirement of some kind. For instance, a process may require specific kinds of resources, or customers may require specific kinds of products and services. A Need is information. Like Risk, it also is a special kind of issue. Market Need is a special subtype of Need, and usually an issue of paramount importance to a business and its goals. A business can only thrive if it satisfies the needs of its marketplace. A Market Need is always associated with one or more market segments, each of which in turn may have several market needs (see Figure 2.18). Needs are satisfied by features. Features are characteristics of the resources of Figure 2.2 (hence, also characteristics of Business Products). Market Needs flow from one or more of the five communities in Box 21. Hidden in the relationship between Products and Markets, and mediated by Need, lies an object of utmost importance to business. It is arguably the single most strategic object we will encounter in business: Product Market.

In a product market, features map to market needs, and vice versa. This many-to-many relationship is optional, because it is possible that there may be features that satisfy no needs, and conversely, there may be unsatisfied needs.[166] It might even be that removal of a feature satisfies a need. See Box 62 on our Web site. Market Need is a special kind of Stakeholder Need. It is a polymorphism in which the stakeholders of Box 21 is a customer, or a market segment based on aggregations of customers, potential or actual.

Guidelines and Regulation   A guideline is information that guides. The concept scarcely needs elaboration, and has many polymorphisms. Policies, standards, rules, regulations, and instructions are all guidelines. An unadorned goal, without process or resource, is perhaps the simplest of guidelines. A generic guideline is an information-sparse relationship between resources. It only tells us that unknown numbers of unknown resources are mutually involved with each other, towards some unknown goal. In order to call a pattern of information a guideline,

---

165. Chapter 4, Section 3, in [337], discusses the relationship between risk and information quality.
166. The satisfaction of market need and its relationship to product and process reengineering are discussed in detail in Module 5, Section 3, on our Web site. See "Product Reengineering and the Mutability of Compositions," on our Web site. See also the discussion under the buying and selling cluster in Section 2.1.2 in this book.

all we need to know is that one resource, perhaps the only resource in the relationship, must be a goal. Thus, a Guideline adds information to Goal, and reduces to a Goal as we leach it of information. Therefore, Guideline is a polymorphism of Goal.

A guideline is also an issue, because every guideline involves some goal or purpose. However, it is an issue that is marginally more structured than the generic issue we recently discussed. A guideline guides; an issue may not. Therefore, a guideline adds information to an issue, and its degrees of freedom are fewer (see Box 30). This is why Guideline is a subtype of both Goal and Issue in Figure 2.9.

This generic guideline crystallizes into a concrete instance of a guideline or rule as we make its components more specific by adding information to them. For instance, the template, on which the terms and conditions of an insurance policy is based, is a guideline. Similarly, the checklists of processes needed to implement and institutionalize change in Part II of this book are also guidelines, because they are tied to goals.

Guidelines may be mandatory or merely desirable. A mandatory guideline is a Regulation. Mandatory and desirable guidelines are mutually exclusive polymorphisms of Guideline. As we add information to the composition of information we call Guideline, it could tell us how desirable its goals are. The guideline will descend through the hierarchy of quantitative relationships in Box 10, in step with the information we add. At the nominal level, it might tell us whether the guideline only offers guidance, or if compliance is mandatory. As we proceed deeper and lower into the subtyping hierarchy of Guideline, we will gain information on priorities, desirability, and ultimately even quantified indicators of desirability, importance, or enforcement. The metamodel of Relationship on our Web site shows this in Figure 116. Guideline is an inclusion polymorphism of the hierarchy in that figure.

When we add temporal information to a relationship, it turns into a process (see Box 10). It follows that adding temporal information to a guideline will turn it into a governing process. Governing processes can resolve conflicts by prioritizing goals.

Terms and Conditions   Terms and Conditions is a role of Guideline usually associated with agreements. However, it is a relationship with a Person or Organization that normalizes and distinguishes Terms and Conditions from generic guidelines or standing instructions (e.g., those in technical manuals). Terms and Conditions not only binds resources to one or more goals (like guidelines do), but also describes who will be bound by them. Terms and Conditions must always apply to the party it either binds or proposes to bind. Moreover, the Term of a Condition tells us how long the party(s) will be bound, and hence is a polymorphism of Event. A Condition, a relationship between the resources of Figure 2.2, must always be valid[167] for a Term, even if that term has no end, and binds parties in perpetuity.

For instance, the template on which the terms and conditions of an insurance policy is based, turns from Guideline into Terms and Conditions at the moment we

---

167. Chapter 3, Section 2, in [337], describes how validity is a pattern of information, represented by inclusion and exclusion sets. These sets determine what is permitted, what must exist/occur, and what cannot be. This is different from the term in Box 30 in this book, yet related to it. Validity of measurement describes what items may or may not be measured to obtain an item of information.

fill in the blanks on the template (a form) to insure a specific item for a specific person or organization. Similarly, the change management checklists in Part II of this book will turn from guidelines to terms and conditions when specific managers in specific organizations agree to implement them or give them the status of a proposal under consideration.

Qualifications, Skills, and Credentials   A qualification is information that provides the basis for confidence or belief towards some kind of capability or functionality. A qualification always qualifies a resource, which also may be a product (see the discussion on Figure 2.2). For instance, a person becomes a carpenter when he or she obtains the qualification by learning carpentry. An aircraft being manufactured is qualified to fly after it acquires this capability at the end of the manufacturing process. A home becomes qualified as a living place when certified by a building inspection.

Qualification is pure information. When a competent authority (a person or organization) accredits the information, it becomes Credential. For instance, an aircraft may be qualified to fly, but obtains the credential to do so after a competent authority certifies it as flightworthy. Similarly, a building may qualify as a living place at some point in its construction, but is accredited as such only after the town issues a Certificate of Occupancy—a credential. Credentials even may be issued jointly. Consider a check. It becomes an instrument for payment when signed. Some checks might need multiple signatures before they become payable. Several people or organizations issue the credential for the check that certifies the belief that it will be paid. The credential is then the aggregation of individual signatures.[168]

Can a resource without the requisite capability be accredited? It should not be, but it can certainly happen in real life. Exceptions are a component in the Metamodel of Knowledge, as discussed in Module 5, Section 3, under "The Risk Management Transform in Crossing the Chasm," on our Web site. When this happens, the resource must be considered accredited and qualified, however mistaken this qualification might be, and even if the resource does not actually have the requisite features to justify the qualification. Why? The opening phrase of this section tells us why: "A qualification is information that provides the basis for confidence or belief." Even if the information is untrue, the resource is qualified at the moment we link it with a qualification—a belief.[169]

The qualification of that feature expresses a belief, whereas the Possession of that feature expresses a fact. The two relationships are distinct and different. For instance, a check may bounce, even after its signatories have certified it.[170]

---

168. A credential is actually pure information. For instance, the credential for a check is the authorization to pay by its signatory; the actual signature is only the format of this authorization (i.e., a symbol and a token). The authorization may be formatted in several ways, for example, a voice instruction backed by a password, a biometric authentication (such as a voice print or a retina scan), or an electronic signature.

169. Mandating a relationship between the resource in question and the feature being qualified, contingent on the resource-qualification relationship, can represent the validity (i.e., the truthfulness) of the qualification. Module 5, Section 1, on our Web site, discusses mutually inclusive and subset relationships. A subset relationship is contingent on another relationship, but not vice versa. The subset may or may not exist if the superset does, but the superset must exist if the subset exists.

170. We would attach a subsetting or mutual inclusion constraint between the two relationships (i.e., possession of the qualification and possession of the feature), to ensure that the qualification will be accurate, but as described in Module 5, Section 3, on our Web site, constraints can always be violated, and beliefs belied. In the real, uncertain world we live in, exceptions occur.

Box 28: Qualification Versus Credential—Patterns of Meaning   28

A credential only qualifies another qualification. Note also that there is no bar on a credential certifying another credential. Both the accredited qualification and the accrediting qualification can be credentials. A Qualification may qualify any resource. Therefore, Credential is a more restricted form of qualification than (the generic) Qualification. Credential has fewer degrees of freedom, and more information content, than Qualification. This makes Credential a subtype and polymorphism of Qualification (see Box 14).

Thus, even an unearned qualification is a qualification. It might even be a certified, albeit undeserved, qualification. A qualification becomes a credential when the accrediting person or organization confirms the qualification. It still remains a mere belief, not inviolate truth. Thus, an accredited or certified qualification is a role of qualification—when the belief is linked to the accrediting authority via the certification relationship in Figure 2.9. That relationship is the credential. It is a polymorphism of Information. A credential might reduce risk, but cannot be a substitute for untarnished reality.

Usually, the credential is recorded on at least one document. However, the fact of accreditation is the credential, not the document(s) on which it is recorded. We know that we can only normalize knowledge if we distinguish information from the documents that record it. Credential is a relationship and an object. Indeed, a qualification may carry more than one credential. A Credential is also a qualification. It is a qualification of a qualification, a polymorphism of Qualification. Figure 2.9 articulates this.

A Skill is a special kind of qualification. Unlike Qualification, which might apply to any resource of Figure 2.2, a skill qualifies only people or organizations for particular kinds of tasks. It is a more restricted pattern of information than a generic qualification. It follows that Skill is a polymorphism of Qualification. Figure 2.9 shows this.

Sometimes, in common parlance, we distinguish skill from (work) experience. "Skill" is a term applied to specialized tasks, such as carpentry or football, whereas the term "Experience" is often reserved for more complex, softer tasks, such as management of a business or formulation of strategy. However, in this book, we make no such distinction. The term Skill, as it is used in this book, can qualify a person or organization for any task.

Qualification mediates between Resource and Capability. Thus, it is a relationship between the two objects. Skill mediates between a Person/Organization and Task. It is a polymorphism of Qualification. Like all relationships, both may convey ordinal or quantitative information, and it may be possible to rank or quantify skill or qualification levels. It is a fact inherited from the Metamodel of Knowledge in [337], and a fact intrinsic in the Metamodel of Relationship in Figure 116 on our Web site and is summarized in Box 10 of this book.

Place Versus Address   An address is a polymorphism of the Locate relationship of Box 12. A Place is a location, and an address locates it. The Place could be a physical location or a virtual location. An address is only information that points to it. However, an address is not an abstract meaning like the other polymorphisms of Information we discussed. An address is concrete and formatted information instantiated in a document. Address, the class, normalizes the rules for formatting this information, whereas an instance of an address is the formatted information on locating a place. Thus, address is a polymorphism of two parents—Format and Locate. Figure 2.16 shows this.

We also could call an address a subtype of two parents—Medium and Locate. Address is a subtype of a special kind of Medium. A Medium tells us what formats are permitted. It categorizes the substance of a document in terms of formativeness. The format of an address, on the other hand, offers no leeway (i.e., no degrees of freedom) in the way the address must be formatted. There are no alternatives, because every alternative format becomes a different address. This is why an address has been billed as the subtype of Format, not Medium, and this is also why it is a subtype of Format and Locate. One parent is a rule on how information will be represented by symbols, and the other is the relationship that gives rise to the concept of Place.

Address and Place are distinct and different objects. A place may have many distinct and very different addresses. For instance, a mailing address is formatted differently from the abbreviated address in a telephone directory. Sometimes the postal address of a place may put it in one town, whereas the municipal address may put it in another. The Place will stay the same, but its postal and municipal services may be provided from different towns, and they will address the same place differently. The post office might use street, house number, town, and zip code to locate a place, whereas a town might use block and lot numbers. Similar examples of diversity of formats of location abound in virtual space as well. The wellspring of this diversity is not only the multiplicity of potential formats for a single meaning,[171] but, perhaps at a more fundamental level, it bubbles out of the cardinality of the Locate relationship of Box 12. A Place may be located from multiple points of reference.[172]

Thus, Address is formatted information on location—a symbol. It is neither the location, nor the meaning of that location; it is not Place. It is information, and a stock theme of business, but not information that strictly is a business meaning. Place is that meaning. Address only formats and represents that meaning. Thus, Address is a component useful in the design of interfaces used by various actors, human or mechanical. Indeed, the same Place could have as many addresses as an application has interfaces.[173]

An address format is a standard. Standard is a polymorphism of Guideline, and different addressing conventions are classes of symbols and standards for formatting information on locations of places. Figure 2.9 articulates this role of Address

---

171. The fact that a single meaning may have many expressions is central to the metamodel of knowledge. It is discussed in Box 33, and Module 6, Section 2, both on our Web site. The fact that information may have many formats is a polymorphism of this central fact, as discussed in Chapter 4, Section 1, in [337].
172. The cardinality and subtypes of Locate are discussed in detail in Module 5, Sections 2 and 4, and in Figure 114, on our Web site.
173. *Address*, like *Format*, belongs to the interface layer in the Architecture of Knowledge, described in "The Architecture of Knowledge" (see Figure 15) on our Web site, and in Chapter 4, Section 2, in [337].

Box 29: Elaboration and Exception   **29**

Elaborating on exceptions and exclusions constrains a meaning. Constraints forge subtypes of the meanings they constrain. Constraints are information (see Box 14). Thus, elaborating on exceptions or exclusions also creates polymorphism of meanings that are elaborated. For instance, a negotiation for any car except a Yugo is a subtype of a negotiation for cars in general.

Sometimes elaboration also could appear to reduce information by elaborating on the fact that a meaning is a generalized form of another. For instance, we might assert that a Transfer of Ownership is like a Sale, and subsumes it, but also includes other kinds of transfers of ownership. When this happens, we are not elaborating on the item that we are generalizing. Rather, we are elaborating on the generalization (i.e., Transfer of Ownership in this case), and describing one or more of its polymorphisms (i.e., Sale and other unspecified kinds of transfers of ownership that are not Sale, in this case). Thus, elaboration always subtypes the concept elaborated.

Format, the class, which is distinct from Address, a symbol and instance of the class. Indeed, in that sense, a medium is also a container of formatting guidelines; but these are usually guidelines mandated by nature or technology, not convention. On the other hand, address formats are usually standards driven by convention and common understanding. This is what makes Address a stock theme.

Elaboration Interpretation and Shifting Perspectives   We often elaborate, and always interpret, when we communicate. Both are stock themes. When information is added to information, we have elaborated on it; when we clarify it, we interpret it, perhaps in a new context.

Elaboration involves reducing the freedom of the meaning, a pattern of information, by restricting it in some way.[174] Thus, we could elaborate on the meaning of a meeting by saying that it is a negotiation for the sale of a car. Common sense clearly tells us that we have added information to Meeting and made it more specific by elaborating on it, so that it has become a polymorphism of the generic concept of Meeting in Figure 2.5. On the other hand, we could elaborate on Meeting, to explain that we mean that it is the general Meeting of Figure 2.5, and not one of its polymorphisms. That is also information added. We have implicitly added information and identified the existence of its polymorphisms. Thus, we have created implicit subtypes.

Although subtyping may sometimes be subtle, with a bare modicum of information added, elaboration will turn a meaning into a subtype by adding information. Sometimes, we may not even be aware that we are subtyping a bare meaning by elaborating on it, because we meant it to be that specific subtype in any case, and are just making sure that it is interpreted correctly when we describe it.

---

174. Chapter 4, Section 1, in [337], discusses degrees of freedom, under the Architecture of Patterns.

Interpretation maps the equivalence of meanings between objects. It is another polymorphism of Locate (see Box 12). To elaborate on this assertion, interpretation is the mapping of relative locations of identical information in information space. Thus, what is an incoming payment for a vendor might be an outgoing payment for the customer. It is the same information and the same payment seen from two different perspectives. When we locate information relative to another pattern of information, we are also interpreting one in terms of another. For instance, in Figure 2.5, we interpreted a sale event in terms of transfer of ownership, because we located the meaning of Sale within the meaning of Transfer of Ownership. Thus, interpretation is the mapping of meanings between objects—meanings that are patterns of information in information space. When we add temporal information to the mapping relationship, it becomes a process of interpretation.

When we infuse time into the elaboration relationship that adds information to information, then it becomes the Process of Elaboration. The process of interpretation is asymmetrical, as all processes are, because of the one-way, asymmetric flow of time.[175] Interpretation in its most generic form is always a symmetrical relationship, because if one object is interpreted in terms of another, the reverse is also true. Relative location is a symmetrical relationship (see Box 12). However, polymorphisms of locate may be asymmetrical, and could subtype the objects interpreted (see Boxes 11 and 13). The subtyping relationship is also a polymorphism of locate.[176]

Generalization and Specialization are both asymmetrical polymorphisms of Interpretation. Both locate a shared meaning across objects. Elaboration also specializes a meaning by adding to it. Thus, Elaboration is a polymorphism of Specialization, and therefore is a polymorphism of Interpretation, once removed. Translation involves mapping of shared meanings, and is a polymorphism of Interpretation.[177]

When one meaning firmly locates another in a bijective (i.e., one-to-one) relationship,[178] then the translation is symmetrical. On the other hand, if the translation only locates a rough meaning that contains the meaning being translated, then the translation is asymmetrical. Containment establishes the boundaries of a pattern, but may not locate it precisely. It only establishes that the pattern lies somewhere inside the boundary. Containment is an asymmetrical polymorphism of locate (see Box 12).[179] For instance, a mother may be called a parent, but not vice versa. A man might be called a "male," but all males are not necessarily human. If the meanings roughly but not completely, overlap, then the reliability and validity of the translation must be considered. Reliability, Validity, and the interpretation of meaning are important concepts in changing Perspectives.[180] For example, the context of a model

---

175. The impact of adding time to relationships in order to create processes was discussed in detail in Module 5, Section 3. See "Processes, Events and Temporal Relationships" on our Web site.
176. See the subtypes of "locate" in Figure 114 on our Web site.
177. Chapter 4 in [337] discusses translation of formats, units of measure, and languages.
178. Bijective (on-to-one), injective (one-to-many), and surjective (many-to-one) relationships are discussed in Module 5 on our Web site. See also the note on the Mathematical Theory of Categories.
179. Module 5, Section 2, under Location, Containment and Incorporation, and Section 4, discuss the containment of one pattern by another. See our Web site, and Figure 114, therein.
180. Reliability and Validity are components in the Metamodel of Knowledge, discussed in detail in Chapter 4 in [337], under "Information Quality." Interpretation and translation of meanings discussed under "Meanings That Represent Meanings" at the end of Chapter 4, Section 3, in [337]. See also Box 36 on our Web site.

might be restricted to only humans, but if we changed scope to include all living creatures, then we may need to review the validity of all expressions that refer to "male."

Shifting of perspective involves mapping meanings from objects in one Perspective to objects in another. Mappings between objects may be one-to-one, one-to-many, many-to-one, or many-to-many (see Box 24). Many-to-Many mappings between object classes in different perspectives may sometimes be ambiguous at the instance level. Multiple interpretations may seem equally valid, and it may not always be clear where an instance of an object may be located, especially if the footprint of each object only partially overlaps the footprint of the other. Seasoned analysts are familiar with these issues. For instance, "Peace" shares a common meaning (i.e., absence of conflict) across most languages, but nuances are different. For example, in the languages of Northern India, the word that translates most accurately into the English word Peace is "shanti." "Shanti" also mixes absence of conflict with ideas of harmony, tranquility, and the spirit of universal unity of all creation.[181]

The mappings from the stock themes of the Universal Perspective to every other perspective only will be one-to-one, one-to-many, and many-to-one. This is how the Universal Perspective becomes the hub that draws other perspectives together, binding each into an interpretation that flows from the hub. Object classes of subordinate perspectives will either be sundered as they map to the stock themes of the Universal Perspective because they are compositions of meanings (e.g., the concept of an Invoice may be sundered to map to Document, a Payment Event, and Information); or they will be polymorphisms of the broad but precise generalizations that constitute the Universal Perspective.

Throughout this book, we have specialized, generalized, elaborated, translated, and shifted perspectives. In other words, we also have interpreted. It is a familiar theme in this book, and a stock theme of business. Shifting of Perspective is the cornerstone of all creativity and innovation in the world of business. It is therefore also a topos that is the key to survival in an age of surging change and global business, driven by knowledge and information.

Common Polymorphisms of Physical Object: Construction, Equipment, and Software   Thus far, our polymorphisms have been abstract meanings. Physical objects are more tangible. They are also fixed or mobile. Constructions, such as bridges, buildings, tunnels, and goalposts on playing fields, are usually fixed in place, whereas cars, soccer balls, and cordless phones move around—sometimes too fast for comfort. We will call an immobile physical object Construction. Some readers might call it a misnomer. Cordless phones and cars are also constructed (i.e., made from raw materials), but as long as we know what the term means in this book, it will suffice to understand the theme it represents.

Lest readers be tempted to cast objects irrevocably into the category of mobile and immobile objects, a word of caution is also worthwhile here. Bridges are quite clearly "constructions," yet the London Bridge now sits on the deserts of Arizona. It was moved from London to the United States when it was sold. Who said bridges

---

181. The problem of perspective is discussed in detail in Chapter 2, Section 4; Chapter 4, Section 3, under "Measurement of Meaning—A Paradox of Perspectives"; and Box 49, all in [337].

could not move? For these kinds of reasons, it would be prudent to call Constructions objects that are usually immobile.[182]

Constructions are central to many processes and functions that play supportive roles. Naturally, they can also be considered Places. Constructions are resources of special interest to business, and often incorporate special behavior, such as environmental and climate control, management of facilities, use of utilities, such as power and water, and so forth. A construction is often a key facility for business, and a significant contributor to the fixed costs and overheads of business.

Equipment is also a facilitator and a Physical Object. It is any tangible tool. Equipment may be mobile or not. Construction and Equipment are subtypes in different partitions of Physical Object. For instance, a blast furnace in a steel plant is Equipment, and an immobile Construction. Equipment is used to transform or change the state of something, or to elicit information from something. Vehicles, pens, computers, diskettes, pressure gauges, thermometers, scissors, and hammers are all examples of Equipment.

A physical object has no intrinsic property that turns it into Equipment. It only becomes Equipment when we use it as such. A rock was just a rock, until someone in the Stone Age used it as a tool. It then became Equipment. Equipment is a role of physical object created by users of tools, and derived from its use. Anything can be turned into equipment if we are creative enough to do it. Equipment is a polymorphism of physical object, which flows from the mind of man and the power of reason when it turns a physical object into a tool with a purpose.[183]

It is perhaps less clear that Software is also Equipment. Software is a tool. It can change the state of information, or even physical objects, when it controls machinery. Software can certainly elicit information, report, and measure. It satisfies all requisite criteria to qualify it as Equipment. The only criterion in doubt might be the criterion that Equipment be a tangible physical object. Software satisfies this, too. Software is not abstract meaning. It is formatted and coded information, symbols recorded on a physical medium, such as a magnetic or optical disk. Even when the symbols are transmitted through space in the form of radiant energy, they are messages coded in patterns of energy, and as we have seen earlier in this chapter, a tangible object is a polymorphism of energy. The code is always recorded as symbols in a document, even if that document is energy. When the code is used to transform, make, or inquire, then it is recorded on a physical and tangible medium. It is a Document. The code cannot be abstract information devoid of form, format, language, and medium.

However, central to the concept of Software is the fact that the code is a meaningful pattern of symbols. The code conveys instructions. Instructions are pure information, a polymorphism of Regulation. It might sound strange that software is a kind of Regulation, until we consider that software always regulates something—a machine, a robot, or perhaps only the computer or telephone on your desk. An item of software is a set of instructions. This set of instructions determines the purpose, functionality, and class of equipment of which an individual copy of

---

182. A point to ponder for the thoughtful reader: Would you consider soap, shampoo, candy, or other consumer goods "equipment"? Soap can change the state of a resource by making it cleaner, or perhaps only soapy. Candy can change the state of a person who eats it, by giving him or her physical pleasure. What about a pet rock? How far can we take the argument within the bounds of reason?
183. Box 11 in [337] discusses how the Metamodel of Knowledge interprets these so-called "constants."

the software is an instance. The actual instructions instantiated in symbols on a document instantiate the item of equipment that is also an individual copy of software in question.

If the code is replicated in many documents, then each document may be considered an item of equipment and an instance of Software. Each may be maintained, serviced, and used separately. Each is a separate instance of the same class of equipment. Figure 2.9 makes clear that Software has two parents—Equipment and Document. Software combines Equipment and Document into one inseparable polymorphism, a tool we have labeled Software.

Common Polymorphisms of Person/Organization   An organization is an aggregation of people. Naturally, it even may be an aggregation of other organizations, because those organizations are also aggregations of people. An aggregate may be an empty aggregate, and so too may organizations. There could be empty organizations without any members; that is, an aggregate object without members that only holds the meaning of an aggregation of people or organizations. For instance, we might conceive of a task force to address an issue. Before we determine its members, the task force is an empty organization. See Box 10. Module 5, Sections 2 and 4, on our Web site discuss aggregation and structure in detail.

Communities, the residents on a street, a family, or a corporation are all examples of organizations. A network of people and/or organizations is a structured organization. Organizations also may be amorphous collections of people or other organizations, such as clubs or communities. Organizations could be structured, like a corporation or a distribution channel. In Box 10, we discussed how a structured composition is a polymorphism of an amorphous aggregate. A structured organization is also a polymorphism of an unstructured organization.

As we have seen, a hierarchy is a special kind of structure. A hierarchically structured organization is a common subtype and polymorphism of a structured organization. Corporations, governments, and armies are all examples of hierarchical organizations. It is a common business pattern that we will discuss in Section 2.1.2.

The concept of an aggregate infuses the concept of some kind of organization into a collection, and a structure amplifies on it. Implicit in Person/Organization is the concept of an organization of people or organizations of other Person/Organizations—even organizations that are empty. Figure 2.10 articulates some of its polymorphisms.

An aggregation of persons is Organization. Therefore, the logic of mathematics dictates that an Organization is a polymorphism of Person, as discussed earlier in this chapter under Common Polymorphisms of Structure. However, the English language makes a sharp distinction between Organization, a collection of persons, and Person, an individual human being. To be consistent with common usage in English, we must distinguish person from organization, and distinguish both from the theme that subsumes the meanings of persons and organizations. The convention makes "Person" special. It bars polymorphisms of the locate relationship (see Figure 2.1 and Box 12) from looping back recursively to Person [see Figure 2.13(c)]. Thus, a Person cannot contain another Person.[184] This constraint implies that a Person cannot be contained in, be part of, consist of, or be aggregate of Person.

Contained in is the inverse of contain, Part of is a polymorphism of Contained in, and consist of is the inverse of Part of and a synonym for aggregate of (see Box 12). If Contained is barred, the logic of mathematics also will bar Contained in, Part of, Consist of, aggregate of, and Subtype of (see Box 12). This is why Person is a theme that is distinct from Organization or Person/Organization in the Universal Perspective.[185] This is also how the Metamodel of Knowledge lends the Universal Perspective the power of Reason.

We will call the theme that subsumes the shared behavior of persons and organizations Person/Organization. Person/Organization is the supertype of both Person and Organization. Many polymorphisms of Person/Organization are neither people nor organizations, but roles that people and organizations share in their interactions with events and other objects. These roles normalize the shared behavior of people and organizations. We turn to Legal Entity first. It is a fundamental theme of business and a key role shared by people and organizations.

Legal Entity   All people are legal entities. Any person may be recognized as a party to a legal dispute, event, or right in the eyes of the law. It is convention, and a broadly accepted practice, that makes it a stock theme and a common role of Person.

The law also treats some kinds of organizations in the same way. This is why the role subsumes both people and organizations. However, not all organizations are valid parties in the eyes of the law. Usually corporations and registered businesses, such as partnerships, recognized charities, registered political, educational or religious groups, and others, are treated like people in many legal processes and events.

However, the meaning of Organization is much broader. Organizations also subsume groups that have no legal standing or recognition in Law. For instance, task forces, departments, project teams, a coffee clutch in the office, an informal community of interest, and others, are all organizations. Thus, all people are Legal Entities, and so are some but not all organizations. Figure 2.10 articulates this artifice of Law.

Temporary Versus Permanent Organization   People have a limited life, and so do organizations, especially those deemed Temporary, such as project teams and task forces. A Permanent Organization is an organization with no known end (much like a Saga), whereas a temporary organization has a scheduled end, or at least is known to have one, and is not required to exist indefinitely. A temporary organization is usually an organization established to manage an event with a known end, such as a task or a project. Without the Universal Perspective, the task and the organization are sometimes confused. For instance, a government investigation, and the Special Prosecutor's organization set up to conduct the investigation, are sometimes treated as one entity. The Universal Perspective forces

---

184. Unless we consider an unborn child a person.
185. Mathematically, a *Person* is a constrained form of *Person/Organization* in which a person cannot be an aggregate, and *Organization* is a form of *Person/Organization* that is an aggregation of persons (even if it is an empty set or a set with a single member). Module 5, Section 2, on our Web site, discusses aggregation. It also discusses how a constraint adds information, and how constraining an object class subtypes it. Thus, Person and Organization are subtypes of Person/Organization—an abstract but logical mathematical proof of the obvious that would satisfy the monster of Metanesia in Chapter 1!

us to distinguish between the organization, a resource that is responsible for the task, and the event, which is the task itself.

Distinction adds to clarity and normalizes behavior. For instance, when an insured project starts failing, exceeds its allotted time, or breaks the bank, the insurer might have the right to take it over. This right must specify what they will control and own—the event and process, the project team, the work product(s), or all of them.

Facilitator Versus Intermediary   We have recently seen that a mediator is an intermediate node, between the beginning and the end of a path, and an Intermediary is a Person/Organization that plays this role in a network of people and organizations. For instance, a distributor is an intermediary and a Mediator for business products in a supply chain, because the person or organization in this role is an intermediate node in a supply chain between the maker and the consumer of the product. In other words, a Distributor facilitates getting the product to its destination. An Intermediary (as well as a Mediator) might even add value to a product (e.g., a service or other features) on the way to its destination. For instance, a Value Added Reseller (VAR) is an Intermediary, as is a plain distributor or reseller. On the other hand, a facilitator makes no changes to the resource being conveyed.

An intermediary may or may not be a catalyst. For instance, if an intermediary adds value to a product by guaranteeing it, he or she (or it) is bound by a guaranty. It is a change of state for both the Intermediary, and the resource being guaranteed. In this case, the Intermediary is not a catalyst, because the process has changed not only the product, but also the state of the mediator. On the other hand, if the intermediary merely plays the role of a consultant or a manager of the process, he/she/it will emerge unchanged, and therefore may be considered a catalyst and a facilitator (see Resources and Work Products in Box 10).[186] A facilitator will always be a catalyst.[187]

We need not always have complete information on structure to call a person or organization the intermediary or facilitator of a process or event. Even unstructured events could have facilitators and intermediaries. Sometimes the structure of an event might unfold as it occurs, and even before it occurs, so we might know that the structure will have roles for people who mediate its occurrence or facilitate its results. Indeed, we may have created and assigned those roles ourselves. Thus, a facilitated workshop has a facilitator, and an arbitration has an arbitrator. An agreement may be reached with the help of facilitators, as in the historic Camp David agreement between Israel and Egypt that changed the complexion of the Middle East. The government of the United States, an organization (and a Legal Entity—see Figure 2.10), facilitated the agreement. Intermediaries who facilitate the end results of a process, like the binding of parties by an agreement, are its Facilitators. When they also provide warranties, guarantees, or other commitments, they are Intermediaries. They do this for the principal parties to, and the owners of, the event.

---

186. "Resources and Work Products" are discussed in detail in Module 5, Section 3, on our Web site.
187. The facilitation (F) role was also discussed under process ownership in Box 10.

An Intermediary mediates a Meeting (i.e., the generic Meeting we discussed earlier in this section). There must be at least two parties to an event between whom the intermediary is mediating. On the other hand, a Facilitator need not facilitate an event or a transfer of resources between people or organizations. A Facilitator is a catalyst for any process or event. For instance, each process owner-ship role discussed in Box 10 was a polymorphism of Facilitator. Thus, the Facilita-tor of a process is a Person/Organization in the role of a catalyst. On the other hand, an Intermediary is a resource that may or may not change state in the generic Meeting we discussed earlier. Only some polymorphisms of facilitators also will be intermediaries—only those who facilitate meetings (see Figure 2.10). The two roles are independent polymorphisms in different partitions of Network. An Intermedi-ary is an intermediate node in a network of Person/Organizations, whereas a Facili-tator is a Person/Organization that is also a catalyst in a network of any kinds of resources.

Meeting and Person/Organization normalize the optional role of Intermediary, whereas Event and Person/Organization normalize the optional role of Facilitator. The role is optional because not all processes will have owners or facilitators (see the examples in our discussion of Figure 2.2). Naturally, these features will be inher-ited from Person/Organization and Meeting (or Event) by all their polymorphisms, which is a topic we will discuss in Section 2.1.2.

Supplier and Employee; Customer and Employer   A supplier agrees to furnish a resource. Suppliers are people or organizations that agree to supply resources. An agreement (potential or actual, formal or informal) lies behind this role and relationship (potential or actual, formal or informal), and the signing of the agreement seals this relationship. The relationship and the agreement are one indivisible object—they are the same. Note the distinction between a party that agrees to furnish a resource it owns, as opposed to a party that actually furnishes the resource. A transporter might actually furnish the resource physically, but is not considered the Supplier of the Universal Perspective, whereas the owner is considered a supplier because he or she agrees to furnish it. The transfer of possession agreement is the key to this role. It is the same transfer of possession agreement we had discussed earlier in this chapter. This difference between a supplier and furnisher of resources is one more example of the need for surgical precision of meanings in the Universal Perspective, as opposed to the need for infinite detail that drives business. Detail does not always imply precision and clarity. On the other hand, precision and clarity need only a few crisp facts, not a lot of detail. The Universal Perspective demands precision and clarity, not detail. It needs crisp and universal facts.

An employment agreement is a polymorphism of the generic agreement that transforms a Person/Organization into a supplier. Persons bound in this manner are Employees. Only people may be employees, not organizations. On the other hand, organizations may be owned, and people may not. An employee agrees to provide his or her employer a slot of personal time in an Exchange, for a prescribed purpose, included in the Terms and Conditions (informal and official) of the employment agreement. This is the central theme around which polymorphisms of Employment crystallize.

However, the distinction between an individual supplier and an employee is fine and sometimes fuzzy, as even the Internal Revenue Service and many contractors will testify. We will not attempt to cast it in stone in the Universal Perspective, except to say that an Employment is a stock theme and a polymorphism of the more generic role of Supplier of resources, in which the (potential or actual) Employee agrees to (potentially or actually) trade a slot of personal time in an exchange with the Employer. The Employee must be a Person, whereas the Employer may be a Person or Organization. The dividing line between a Person who is a Supplier of Personal Time, and a person who is an Employee, may shift from Place to Place (and even time to time, and Perspective to Perspective). A shift in either direction will be the work product of a Universal Process of Interpretation (or Reinterpretation).

Interpretation is a process that changes Perspective. It shifts between polymorphisms, aggregations, and compositions. We will return to Interpretation in Section 2.1.2.

A Customer is the purchaser (actual or potential) of a product or service. An Employer is a polymorphism of Customer, just as Employee was a polymorphism of Supplier. The Employer and Employee are parties at the opposite ends of the Employment relationship, just as Customer and Supplier are the principal parties at the opposite ends of the transfer of possession agreement. We have discussed both relationships, and will refrain from belaboring the obvious, except to say that both are universal themes with innumerable variations and polymorphisms. However, the Customer, Supplier, and Employment roles in the Universal Perspective capture their common essence.

Resource or Business Product Owner   A resource owner has the title to a resource. It is a different and distinct role from managing, controlling, or keeping it. For instance, a minor may own a bank account, but a guardian may operate it. A firm may manage and operate another firm by contractual agreement, without owning it. A financial security may be owned by a person, but the depository may keep it in trust. These are only a few examples that demonstrate that the fact of ownership does not imply the fact of control or management. The two are independent roles of Person/Organization.

Clearly, regardless of who manages it, only the owner of a resource can sell it. However, intermediaries also may furnish a resource or facilitate its sale, and thus be considered mediators in the supply of the resource, even though they may not own it. Thus, a managing or controlling organization, including those with powers of attorney, can be intermediaries in the Transfer of Possession event we discussed earlier.

Business Product Ownership is clearly a subtype and polymorphism of Resource Ownership, as the discussion of Figures 2.3 and 2.4 make clear. It follows that this relationship will inherit the facts and behaviors of Resource Ownership that we just discussed.

Competitor, Collaborator, and Representative   Competitors and collaborators are parties to the competition and collaboration events we discussed earlier. An event always furnishes the context of collaboration or conflict. Thus, the same person or organization may be a collaborator in one context, and a competitor (or worse) in another. The relationship between parties joined in this manner, mediated by both conflict and collaboration events, is a strategic relationship. A strategic relationship, as we have discussed, is an aggregate object—an aggregation of collaborative and conflicting relationships. It is also a Topos, a stock theme, gaining momentum in an exceedingly complex and broad world of global commerce, backed by enormously complex and vast supply chains with global footprints.

Regulations and policies for managing strategic relationships may change between different footprints of the same enterprise or supply chain. Regulations and policies may lay down the law about which conflicting and collaborative roles may be allowed to coexist and which may not, and under what conditions. The Universal Perspective furnishes the framework for attaching these constraints. These attachments might vary by footprint, even as they share the common essence of the strategic relationship.

Representation of one party by another is a special form of mediation.[188] Intermediary automatically inherits the role (see Figure 2.10). It implies that some intermediaries are intermediaries because they represent others in a structure or trade. The role may or may not carry a special baggage of constraints with it. For example, a realtor is an intermediary who might represent both parties in a sale, whereas an attorney is barred from representing both parties in a conflict. Moreover, rules may change from nation to nation, or even from state to state within a nation. When people or organizations represent collaborators, competitors, or those in more serious conflict, the rules of mutual inclusion, mutual exclusion, and subsetting of relationships between them may become complex (see Box 10).[189] The Metamodel of Knowledge in [337] gives us the components that will help us shape these interactions in the Universal Perspective to match the requirements of the stakeholders in Box 21. Specific business rules may vary in different footprints, but barring the same party from playing multiple roles in a strategic relationship (especially that of representing different parties in different roles in one or more footprints) is also a stock theme of business, and is a polymorphism of the role of representative.

The Power of Attorney is a legally recognized polymorphism of Represent that lets one person or organization represent another almost like a borrowed identity, albeit in a limited context. It is a common and powerful kind of legally binding representation that is also a frequent stock theme subsumed under the Represent relationship.

Table 2.1 summarizes the principal polymorphisms that we have discussed thus far in this section.

---

188. Box 36 in [337] discusses representation. See our Web site. Representation is a polymorphism of Mediation; it restricts mediation to actually standing in for the object being represented.

189. Module 5, Section 1, on our Web site, discusses mutual inclusion, exclusion, and subsetting of relationships. See Figure 74 on our Web site.

Table 2.1   Summary of Stock Themes

THEME (OBJECT)	DEFINITION	TYPICAL POLYMORPHISMS	TOKEN FEATURES
INFORMATION	Knowledge or intelligence about a concept or meaning	Market Need Message Risk Factor	Validity Accuracy Reliability Amount
ENERGY (A medium of information that normalizes the fact of physical location; a bridge between information space and physical space)	The capacity for performing physical work	Heat Light Kinetic Energy of an object in motion Gravitational Energy of an object lifted against the force of gravity	Quantum Form (kind of energy) Physical Location
PHYSICAL OBJECT (Polymorphism of Energy)	A tangible object detectable by our hysical senses or instruments	Vehicle Equipment	Weight Volume Physical Shape Physical Footprint (Polymorphism of Physical Location)
CONSTRUCTION (Subtype of Physical Object and Place)	An immobile construction used to support or service business activities	Building Room Living unit Bridge Tunnel Factory Parking lot	Floor space Geographical Location (Polymorphism of Physical Location)
EQUIPMENT (Subtype of Physical Object)	A tangible tool	Machine Vehicle Software	Function Usage
SOFTWARE (Subtype of Document and Equipment)	Program code to elicit specific responses from equipment	Switching software Numerically controlled machine program Computer program/operating system	Medium (inherited from Document) Language (inherited from Document) Function (inherited from Equipment) Usage (inherited from Equipment) Instruction (inherited from Regulation via Document)

Table 2.1   (Continued)

THEME (OBJECT)	DEFINITION	TYPICAL POLYMORPHISMS	TOKEN FEATURES
PERSON/ ORGANIZATION	Any individual or organization that has an invested interest, stake, or business dealing with the enterprise	Collaborator Competitor Applicant Beneficiary Broker/Distributor Payer Payee Customer Vendor Participant Legal entity	Date of birth/creation or appointment in role
PERSON (Subtype of Person/Organization and Physical Object)	A Human being	Employee Spouse Male Person Female Person Child	Gender
ORGANIZATION (Subtype of Person/Organization)	An association of people, which could be an empty association	Joint Venture Controlled Organization Bank Clearing House Industry Evaluation Organization Task Force Project Team Department Community	Organizational Charter Mission (An organization might be controlled and operated by one or more persons who are its members and have a common mission, purpose, and responsibility.)
TRANSPORTATION (A sequential composition of one or more Resource Transfer events; a subtype of Resource Transfer)	Movement from one place to another with possible multiple drops	Transportation of cargo Transportation of passengers in a vehicle Movement of a frame from one Web Page to another Conveying a message Movement of mail Transfer of an individual from one organization to another	Pick-up points (polymorphism of Source) Drop-off points (polymorphism of Destination) Resource (object) being moved (inherited from Resource Transfer)
CONSIGNMENT (A possible aggregation of one or more resources; polymorphism of Resource)	A resource that is picked up from one place and dropped off at another on a conveyance	Mail addressed to an individual or organization Road consignment to a particular place Air consignment E-mail to an individual Payload with a single target Passenger in a vehicle	Consigned quantity Mode of transportation

Table 2.1   (Continued)

THEME (OBJECT)	DEFINITION	TYPICAL POLYMORPHISMS	TOKEN FEATURES
SHIPMENT (An aggregation of one or more consignments)	A particular cargo that is sent from one place to another on a conveyance; Each consignment in the shipment may be dropped off (and picked up) at a different destination (or source).	Mail in the mail van Road shipment with several drop-off points Air shipment E-mail broadcast to several individuals Network transmission Payload with multiple targets Group of passengers being transported by a vehicle	Shipment quantity Consignments in the shipment
RESOURCE TRANSFER (A polymorphism of Task)	The transfer of resources between resources	Delivery of mail The process for feeding resources to a mechanism that will transform them Output process from a machine after it has worked on the resource fed to it Transportation of passengers from one airport to another	Source Destination Resource (object) being moved
MESSAGE (Polymorphism of Information and Shipment)	Information or signal in transit between nodes	Radio broadcast Memo or letter E-mail message Telephone conversation	Source (inherited from Shipment) Destination (inherited from Shipment) Content (inherited from Shipment; in this case the content may only be some subtype of Information)
EXCHANGE (A polymorphism of Task)	Swap; to transfer a resource, and to receive a resource in return	A barter The exchange of goods for funds in a sale	Resource(s) Exchanged Objects exchanging resources Place of exchange
MEETING GROUND (A polymorphism of Place)	A place of exchange	Marketplace A telephone network Internet chat room Fair Shop Mall	Object Classes involved in an actual or potential exchange Contents of a Meeting Ground (inherited from Place)
RETURN (A polymorphism of Idempotent Relationship, a kind of Structure; included in the Metamodel of Knowledge, as shown in Figure 2.5)	To go back to the same place; the last leg of an idempotent composition	Return from a trip Return of a borrowed item Reversion to a rank or level in a hierarchy	Place or position returned from Place or position returned to
RETURN EVENT (A polymorphism of Resource Transfer, a kind of Task, and Return, which is a kind of Structure; the event has no information on what it is returning, or the equivalence of places being returned to or resources being returned)	An event that takes back to a place.	A return trip, the leg of a journey that returns an individual to his or her starting point The event or process that restores a borrowed item to its owner The process that reverts an individual to a rank or level he or she held previously in an organizational hierarchy	Place or position returned from (inherited from Return) Place or position returned to (inherited from Return) Start Time (inherited from Event via Task) End Time (inherited from Task)

Table 2.1   (Continued)

THEME (OBJECT)	DEFINITION	TYPICAL POLYMORPHISMS	TOKEN FEATURES
REVERSAL (Polymorphism of Return Event)	A return to a condition deemed equivalent to its former condition	The event or process that restores a borrowed item or an item of equal value to its owner The process that reverts an individual to a rank or level equivalent to one he or she held previously in an organizational hierarchy	Substituted item(s); (Could be an aggregation) Substitute item(s); (Could be an aggregation) Place or position returned from (inherited from Return Event) The place that is its equivalent (the equivalent could also be the same place) Place or position returned to (inherited from Return Event) The place that is its equivalent (the equivalent could also be the same place) Start Time (inherited from Event via Task) End Time (inherited from Task)
RESOURCE RETURN TASK (A polymorphism of Reversal, in which no substitutions are permitted)	To take back a resource from which it came	Return of a person from a business trip to the exact point the journey from which it started Return of a borrowed book to the library from which it was borrowed Reversion of an individual to the same rank or level he or she had held previously in a hierarchy	Place or position returned from (inherited from Return); substitutions barred Place or position returned to (inherited from Return); substitutions barred Resources being returned (e.g., Book, Person); substitutions barred
NEGOTIATION (A polymorphism of Agreement and Information Exchange, a kind of Resource Exchange in which the item exchanged is pure information)	A meeting in which attempts are made to reach an agreement through discussion and/or compromise	Negotiating a sale Negotiating the settlement of a conflict Negotiating a collaboration	Start Time (inherited from Event) End Time (inherited from Task) Negotiating Parties (inherited from Meeting) Purpose of Negotiation (Proposed) Terms and Conditions (Inherited from Agreement)
RENEGOTIATION (A polymorphism of Negotiation)	A negotiation that references a prior negotiation and its terms and conditions	Renegotiating the terms of collaboration	Prior Negotiation Terms and Conditions under renegotiation
MEETING (A kind of Event)	A gathering of two or more people or organizations for a time period	A Christmas party A conference A joint product design event An interview	Start Time (inherited from Event) Person/Organizations meeting (must be at least two, may be more)
EVENT	Something that takes place in a time slot; a significant occurrence in a time slot or a moment in time; a happening in a time slot	Phone call Accident Payment Customer Order	Start time End time (optional)

Table 2.1   (Continued)

THEME (OBJECT)	DEFINITION	TYPICAL POLYMORPHISMS	TOKEN FEATURES
PROJECT, TASK (Subtype of two parents: Event and Path)	A clearly defined piece of work that consumes or references resources to create or alter resources or their relationships; usually the responsibility of a person or organization	Project Litigation Negotiation Service Call	Responsibility Resources Cost
CALENDAR (A sequential composition of Events; also a polymorphism of Event)	A sequence of time slots	Gregorian Calendar Jewish Calendar Meeting calendar Holiday schedule Production schedule	Start time (inherited from Event) Time slots
RESOURCE CALENDAR (Subtype of Calendar)	A set of relationships between event(s) and resource(s)	Maintenance schedule Financial calendar Meeting calendar, holiday schedule Production schedule	Capacity booked Capacity left Capacity used
DOCUMENT	A collection of information formatted in a medium	Form Letter Recording Check	Medium Language
MEDIUM	A class of places that imposes constraints on formativeness or format	The electromagnetic spectrum Paper Air	Formatting Rules Permitted Formats Impermissible Formats
AGREEMENT (A subtype of Meeting)	An arrangement that is negotiated or accepted by two or more parties to a meeting	A sale Insurance policy Warranty Marriage	Terms and Conditions Parties State (Potential, Planned, Being Negotiated, Affirmed, Bound, and so forth)
AFFIRMATION (A subtype and state of Negotiation)	An event that asserts the concurrence of the parties in a Negotiation to the terms under discussion	An exchange in which the parties to the sale concur on its terms and conditions	Start Time (inherited from Event) End Time (inherited from Task) Terms and Conditions concurred upon (a subset and select state of all terms and conditions being negotiated; Terms and Conditions are inherited from Agreement via Negotiation)
RETRACTION (A polymorphism of Negotiation and Reversion; see Box 30)	The reversion of an affirmation or proposal	Retraction of intent to buy a home	Proposed terms and conditions retracted
CONFIRMATION (A subtype of Affirmation; a state)	An event that binds parties to the terms of an agreement	A sale event	Parties bound Terms of conditions they are bound to within the agreement
REVOCATION (A polymorphism of Retraction)	An event that reverts a confirmed agreement to an unconfirmed state	Revocation of a treaty between nations	The confirmed agreement being revoked

Table 2.1   (Continued)

THEME (OBJECT)	DEFINITION	TYPICAL POLYMORPHISMS	TOKEN FEATURES
TRANSFER OF POSSESSION (A subtype of Negotiation—a task. A transfer of possession may be under negotiation, a successful negotiation such as a confirmed/affirmed agreement, or even a failed negotiation that did not end in agreement.)	An agreement or negotiation to transfer ownership, or permit use of a product (including services)	Sale Lease Rental Gifting	Price Start Time (Inherited from Event) End Time (Inherited from Task. The duration of the event is often negligible; Start Time and End Time might coincide and be subsumed by Time of Occurrence; both Start Time and End Time are polymorphisms of Time of Occurrence.) Terms and Conditions (Inherited from Negotiation)
LEGAL AGREEMENT (Subtype of Agreement)	An arrangement that is recognized by law	Credit card agreement	Covering law
PLACE	An object that contains, locates, or conveys information, energy, events, material objects, organizations, or people Contiguous or disconnected location(s) where information, energy, events or physical objects, organizations, or people may be found	Internet bulletin board Part of electromagnetic spectrum Country, city, zone Contour Ports of call State Space Pattern	Coordinates Web URL (Universal Resource Locator or Web page address) Address Contents
PHYSICAL PLACE (Subtype of Place)	Contiguous (or disconnected) location(s) within boundaries or points in physical space, where physical objects or energy may be located	Continent Location of a bridge Ports of call The surface of a ball The floor space inside a room Interplanetary or interstellar space	Physical Area Perimeter Physical Length Volume Zoning Time zone Zip code Surface area Latitude (for Geographical Place only) Longitude (for Geographical Place only) CPFR's Global Location Number (GLN), described under "Supply and Demand Chains," on our Web site CPFR's Duns plus 4 code
VIRTUAL PLACE (Subtype of Place)	A nonphysical object that contains information	Web page Frequency spectrum	Contents (only information, formatted or not) Location
ADDRESS (Subtype of Format and Location)	Formatted information for locating a place.	Mailing Label Telephone Directory Address Postal address, e-mail address Grid locations on a map	Location (inherited from Locate) Line number Text, style Language Map coordinates

Table 2.1 (Continued)

THEME (OBJECT)	DEFINITION	TYPICAL POLYMORPHISMS	TOKEN FEATURES
FORMAT (Polymorphism of Proxy; a symbol that is a proxy for Information)	A symbol that may be sensed	Printed letters Sound An image Odor Tactile symbols like Braille codes	Form or shape of the symbol Physical or relative location of the symbol Composition of the symbol
RESOURCE (Role of Information, Document, Physical Object, Place, Person, Organization, Event, Fund [or their interrelationships and aggregations])	Real world objects or concepts that may be altered, consumed, referenced, or created by tasks or processes	Work product Byproduct Node Consumable Catalyst Facilitator	Description Relationship with Task or Place in a structure
RESOURCE OWNERSHIP (Relationship between an asset and the Person/Organization who owns it)	The fact of owning a resource as a property	Property ownership Ownership of a baseball team Ownership of a television show Ownership of a right, such as a copyright or patent	Owning Person/ Organization (Asset Owner) Owned Asset Proportion Owned
FEATURE	An object property or constraint	Product feature Insurance coverage/exclusion offerings Telecommunication USOC codes Equipment capabilities	Color Capacity Speed Boundary
FEATURE GROUP	A set of features	Set of services that go with a purchased product	Features in the group Relationship with requirements Relationship with goals Relationship with Product Market
STRUCTURE	A set of associations	Topology of a telecommunications network Topology of a trestle Topology of a trellis Topology of linkages between Web pages	Linked Objects Capacity of Link between objects
NODE (Polymorphism of Resource)	A resource associated with itself, or another resource in a structure	LAN node Telephone switch Place on Travel Itinerary Start or end of task in project Position in organizational chart Account in chart of accounts	Associated Node Capacity
NETWORK (Subtype of two parents: Structure and Node	An association of resources	A telecommunications network A trellis A set of linked documents or Web pages A network of people who exchange information A network of roads, linking geographical places and facilities	Capacity Footprint

Table 2.1   (Continued)

THEME (OBJECT)	DEFINITION	TYPICAL POLYMORPHISMS	TOKEN FEATURES
TREE STRUCTURE (Subtype of Structure)	A branching topology without closed loops, which may be traversed in at least one direction without converging on the same node along two different associations, and has at least one node that cannot be traversed forward [termination node(s)], and at least one other that cannot be traversed backwards [starting node(s)]	A hub with spokes The topology of a hierarchical communications network	Position in a hierarchy
PATH (Subtype of Structure)	The continuous series of positions that are assumed in any motion or progression	Directional topology of a flight plan	Predecessor node Successor node Direction Directional capacity
ACYCLIC PATH (Subtype of Path)	A path without loops; a path that cannot loop back to a node if it is always traversed in one direction; a path in which any given node may be traversed at most once when the path is negotiated in a single direction (although the path may converge on the same node along two or more different associations)	The directional topology of a network of rivers and tributaries, possibly flowing around islands A radio broadcast The topology of a one-way communications network of repeater stations The directional topology of a supply chain that forbids return of goods	Longest distance from a starting node in terms of the largest possible number of nodes that must be traversed to reach it Longest distance to an ending node in terms of the largest possible number of nodes that must be traversed to reach it
PATH TREE (Subtype of Path and Tree Structure)	A directional Tree Structure	Organizational Hierarchy Reporting Structure in which an individual must report to only one other	Level number Subordinate Roles Supervisor
ORGANIZATIONAL STRUCTURE (An inclusion polymorphism of Path Tree)	A path tree in which the nodes are people or organizations	Management hierarchy Hierarchy of supervisory roles	Level in organizational hierarchy
ROUTE (A subtype of two parents: Path and Node)	A sequence of points visited	A network of rivers and tributaries, possibly flowing around islands Travel Itinerary Routing of materials in the standard operating procedure for manufacturing an item Route plan Supply Chain	Sequence number Resource ID
MEDIATOR (A polymorphism of Node)	A resource that connects resources in a Structure	Reseller Router in a network Power distributor	Connected Nodes Terms of Mediation

Table 2.1   (Continued)

THEME (OBJECT)	DEFINITION	TYPICAL POLYMORPHISMS	TOKEN FEATURES
PROXY (A polymorphism of Mediator)	A resource that represents another resource in a structure	Agent Distributor Format Encrypted message A map Floor plan A photograph A scale model	Item Represented (inherited from Mediator) Terms of representation (constraints, scale, and so forth; polymorphism of Terms of Mediation) Resource represented to (inherited from Mediator)
INTERMEDIARY (An inclusion polymorphism of Mediator)	A person or organization in the role of a mediator between other people or organizations	Value Added Reseller	Persons or organizations mediated
REPRESENTATIVE (An inclusion polymorphism of Proxy)	A person or organization in the role of a proxy	Person/Organization with the Power of Attorney for another Spokesperson Congressman	Resource represented (inherited from Proxy) Context of representation (Polymorphism of Terms of Representation)
ASSET (Role of Information, Document, Physical Object [Construction, Equipment, and so forth], Organization, Event [Agreements, Projects, and so forth], Place [land, electromagnetic frequencies, and so forth], Fund)	A tangible or intangible item of value owned by a person or organization; an owned resource	Construction Network Element Facility Right Product Accounts Receivable	Ownership Proportion of ownership Type of ownership Value
BUSINESS PRODUCT (Subtype of Asset)	Assets positioned in markets to define the corporation's business; those assets that will be sold, rented, or offered in the normal course of business to generate income	Product—Service Offering Service Planned product Withdrawn product	List Price Purpose Market positioning (Intended Product-Market)
BUSINESS PRODUCT OWNERSHIP (An inclusion polymorphism of Resource Ownership)	The fact of ownership of a right, resource, service, or product positioned for sale lease, lending, or use in the marketplace, in order to trade it for other resources	Joint ownership of a property meant for sale Ownership of Shares	Owner Owned Product
GOAL/PURPOSE (Polymorphism of Information)	An intention, an aim or objective	The objective of a business plan The intended destination of a journey	The objects (such as a person, organization, or process) that have the goal
COLLABORATION	A set of mutually supportive goals	A supply chain Intermediate work products used to produce a final product that meets a goal The set of processes that are intermediate steps in meeting a goal or satisfying a need	Membership of the collaborative aggregation
CONFLICT	A set of mutually exclusive goals	Competition War A case in a court of law	Conflicting goals or processes

Table 2.1   (Continued)

THEME (OBJECT)	DEFINITION	TYPICAL POLYMORPHISMS	TOKEN FEATURES
STRATEGIC AGGREGATION OF GOALS	An aggregation of conflicting and collaborating goals	A set of competitive targets, along with the goal of collaborating with a competitor to promote common interests of the industry	Goals in the aggregation, and the fact of their mutual support or mutual exclusion
COLLABORATOR (A role of a person or organization relative to another person or rganization)	Persons or organizations assigned mutually supportive objectives	Owners of processes in a supply chain	Membership of a collaboration
COMPETITOR (A role of a person or organization relative to another person or organization)	Persons or organizations assigned mutually exclusive, competing objectives	Opponent Rival	Participation in competition Person/Organizations who are competitors
STRATEGIC PERSON/ ORGANIZATION (A role of a person or organization relative to another person or organization)	Persons or organizations assigned mutually exclusive and mutually supportive objectives	A person or organization in a strategic relationship that includes both competitive and collaborative goals	Other members of the strategic relationship Their interests and goals
SUPPLIER/VENDOR (A polymorphism of Person/Organization)	A person or organization that owns a right or resource and is a potential or actual conceder of ownership in an actual or potential transfer of possession event	Supplier of components for the manufacture of a car Real Estate developer Car distributor Internet Services Provider Temp Agency	Resource owned The vendor's business products
EMPLOYEE (A polymorphism of Supplier and Person)	A person bound to an organization by an employment agreement to furnish personal time to the employing organization	Manager of a department Sales representative	Salary Frequency of payment Work Hours
CUSTOMER (A polymorphism of Person/Organization)	A person or organization that is the transferee of an actual or potential Transfer of Possession Event	Shopper Person or organization that buys resources from another in order to manufacture its products A client	The relationship to the potential or actual transfer of possession event that casts a person or organization in the role of a customer Requirements
EMPLOYER (A polymorphism of Customer)	A person or organization that hires an Employee	A corporation Government	The employment relationship with one or more employees
ISSUE (A polymorphism of Information)	A subject of concern; information related to the achievement of one or more goals	Nonavailability of requirements for a project Shortage or excessive resources Lack of coordination Delays in schedule Deviation from plan	Goals involved Priority States Open Closed resolved Unresolved Irresolvable Reopened

Table 2.1   (Continued)

THEME (OBJECT)	DEFINITION	TYPICAL POLYMORPHISMS	TOKEN FEATURES
RISK (A polymorphism of Issue)	A hazard	Risk of loss Risk of fire Risk of unforeseen exceptions	Goal involved Probability
REQUIREMENT (A polymorphism of Issue)	An articulated need	Market need	Level of satisfaction Validity (inherited from Information) Accuracy (inherited from Information) Reliability (inherited from information) Priority (inherited from Issue)
GUIDELINE (Polymorphism of Issue)	A course or method of action based on specified conditions to guide or determine decisions	Regulation Supplier Guidelines Underwriting Guidelines Policy Instructions	Authority Purpose or goal State indicators: Proposed Planned Filed Approved Rejected Endorsed Unendorsed Violated (normalized by the relationship between an Event and the Guideline)
TERMS AND CONDITIONS (Subtype of Guideline)	A guideline associated with a Negotiation or Agreement that establishes and (potentially or actually) binds a party to a set of constraints on resources and their relationships	Right Terms and Conditions of Sale Terms and Conditions of Use Terms and Conditions of Employment Credit card terms and conditions Insurance terms and conditions Settlement terms and conditions Order terms and conditions	Relationship with one or more Resources, Parties and Negotiations, or Agreements
REGULATION (Subtype of Guideline)	A mandatory rule	Stock Trading Regulation Mandatory instructions	State indicators: Enforced Unenforced
QUALIFICATION (Subtype of Information)	Information that provides the basis for confidence or belief	Skill Experience Permission	Relationship with qualified resource
SKILL (Subtype of Qualification)	Qualification of a person that provides the basis for confidence or belief for executing a task	Languages known Technical ability	Relationship with Person/Organization and task type
CREDENTIAL (Subtype of Qualification)	Qualification issued by a person or organization that is the basis of entitlement to rights or privileges or the basis for confidence, belief, or credit	Degree License Certification Authentication Permit	Permission Expiry date/time Exceptions, Exemptions and Limitations Issuing Authority Owner or certified resource

Table 2.1   (Continued)

THEME (OBJECT)	DEFINITION	TYPICAL POLYMORPHISMS	TOKEN FEATURES
MARKET (A Borel Object defined on the transfer of Possession relationship)	A class of Marketplaces which may or may not consider business products as a classification parameter	The Generation-X market Baby boomers market Health care market Stock market Futures market Auction Residential Real Estate Market on the West Coast The mainland China market	Characteristics of objects involved in the transfer of possession event
PRODUCT MARKET (Polymorphism of Market)	A market that includes characteristics of products and services traded in it	Market for soap among teenagers Market for pharmaceutical products Market for two-wheeled vehicles in China	Characteristics of products exchanged in the market
MARKETPLACE (A polymorphism of Meeting Ground)	An actual or potential meeting ground where Transfer of Possession agreements may occur	A 7-11 store Auction Web site Telemarketing call A mall The stock exchange	Classes of buyers, sellers, and business products traded
MARKET SEGMENT (A Borel Object defined on product transfer/usage agreement)	A category of actual or potential product transfer/usage agreements	Line of Business Class of potential Customers Class of products A geographical footprint Class of customers, for a class of products in a geographical footprint	Potential value Profitability Boundaries or limits on values or ranges of parameters of the market that define the market segment

MARKET NEED (Subtype of Information)	Intelligence about requirements of a market segment	Preferences
		Product use
			Relationship between issues, problems, and requirements
			Preferred features
			States of Market Need
			  Satisfied
			  Unsatisfied

PAYMENT (Subtype of Event)	Actual or potential transfer of money from one fund to another	Incoming Outgoing payment	Amount Currency Payer Payee
PAYMENT INSTRUMENT (Subtype of Asset)	An asset that is actually or potentially transferred to make payment	Funds Property	Value
PLAN (A subtype of Goal)	An intended state with or without intended processes and state transitions to achieve the goal	Delivery Schedule Strategic Plan Sales targets Estimated production Maintenance schedule	A planned state State transitions from current to planned state Processes with or without the process map to achieve the goal

Table 2.1   (Continued)

THEME (OBJECT)	DEFINITION	TYPICAL POLYMORPHISMS	TOKEN FEATURES
BASELINE (A subtype of Resource)	A reference state that is used as a basis for comparison	The first agreed-upon project plan Standard Reference item	Baseline status for a resource Items it is a baseline for
TRACKING PROCESS (A polymorphism of Process)	A process in which the state of one object is compared with the states of others	Deviation from flight plan	Quantum of difference between Baseline and state(s) of tracked object(s)
ELABORATION (A polymorphism of the subtyping relationship)	Furnishing of detail about an object or meaning previously described in less detail	Description of the meaning of a word Explanation	Elaborated item
INTERPRETATION (A polymorphism of Location of information)	An ascription of a particular meaning	Interpretation of a law Interpretation of a meaning in a context (for example, "time flies" might mean that time moves swiftly, or that flies must be timed in some activity performed by them)	Context of interpretation
GENERALIZATION (A polymorphism of Interpretation)	The common aspect shared across several specific aspects	Generalization of a solution to address several classes of problems Generic concept A class of products	Classes subsumed Exhaustivity Exceptions
SPECIALIZATION (A polymorphism of Interpretation and the inverse of Generalization)	An adaptation of a broader concept to a particular niche	Customizing a service to fit the needs of a specific customer	Nonstandard components or custom patterns not shared with other members of the class
CHANGING PERSPECTIVE (Polymorphism of Interpretation)	Mapping meanings from one Perspective to another	Incoming Payment to Outgoing Payment Owner to Person/ Organization Invoice to Payment, Document, and Information	Object correspondence Accuracy (inherited from Information) Validity (inherited from Information)

The Universal Perspective is a polymorphism of the Metamodel of Knowledge. The meanings in Table 1 are all derived from components of that Metamodel. The Metamodel of Knowledge [337] is configured from broader, more generic meanings than the Universal (Business) Perspective; hence, its components are used more frequently than the objects and patterns in this chapter. Box 30 summarizes select components in the Metamodel of Knowledge, and provides references to where each is described in [337]. The polymorphisms and components in Box 30 are abstract and not always intuitive. We advise those who would like more clarity, or are uncomfortable with the assertions in Box 30, to read [337].

The focus of Table 2.1 and this section was on polymorphisms of the fundamental object. It let us peel back and normalize meanings layer by layer. Polymorphisms are created by the subtyping relationship. Next, we will focus on the interactions that these polymorphisms normalize. The key to normalizing the behavior of objects and

Box 30: Selected Components from the Metamodel of Knowledge in [337]

(References in this box are to chapters, sections, and figures in [337], unless a different context is specifically mentioned.)

- Pattern (Chapter 4, Section 1). This is the root of the Metamodel of Knowledge. All its components are polymorphisms of Pattern. An object instance is also a kind of pattern—a meaningful pattern, as described in Module 6 and Figure 31 on our Web site.
- Essence (of a pattern) is the information that gives the pattern its identity and distinguishes it from other similar patterns. It is closely tied to the freedom the pattern has to be that pattern. The meaning of "essential" is derived from "essence," and the meaning of "freedom" is derived from the degrees of freedom of a pattern, as described in Chapter 4, Section 1, under Pattern.
- Meaning: Meanings are polymorphism Patterns (Chapter 4, Section 1). They are patterns of abstract information. Meanings include the meaning of a rule, as opposed to its expression, as described in Box 33, and ModuleChapter 6, Figure 117, on our Web site. Indeed, this is the inchoate universal object. Polymorphisms of Meaning carve object instances and object classes from the primal meta-object, as described in Module 5, Section 4, and Module 6, Sections 1 and 2, on our Web site.
- Meta-object: A generic and inchoate instance of an object. All objects are subtypes of this primal object.
- Name, and its subtypes, Synonym, Homonym, Alias, and Concept ID.
- Object Class: A subtype of an aggregate object. A list is also a different subtype of an aggregate object in this partition.
- Object Partition: A criterion for dividing an object class into mutually exclusive subtypes. A partition may be exhaustive (i.e., the subtypes in the partition collectively cover all possible members of the partitioned class), or inexhaustive (i.e., the subtypes do not cover all possible members of the partitioned class). See Chapter 2, Section 3, Object Partitions and Role Modeling.
- Object Instance (Chapter 2, Section 1).
- Object Property: Attributes, relationships, effects of events, and constraints associated with the object (see Box 10). It is also described formally in Module 6, Section 2; see Figure 117 on our Web site.
- Value encapsulates the concept of existence and measurability. It may convey distinctness, an ordered sequence, a magnitude, the absence of magnitude (the Nil Value), Infinite magnitude, the absence of meaning (the Null Value), the concept of "All," "any," and "Unknown." See Chapter 2, Section 3, and Chapter 4, Section 3, of [337]; also see our Web site.
- Number: Number is an expression of Quantitative Value, and therefore a subtype of both Expression and Quantitative Value (see Chapter 4, Section 2).

Note also that Format is a kind of expression of Value in symbolic form (see Chapter 4, Section 1). This makes Format a subtype with two parents, Value and Symbol. The relationship Expression of /Express is a polymorphism of the subtyping relationship, as described in Module 5, Section 4, on our Web site.

30

- Attribute: A kind of object property that is also a subtype of Domain. It is a relationship between an object class and a subtype of a domain that consists of a single value at any given time; see Module 3, Section 2.

- Aggregate object: A collection (see Module 5, Section 2, on our Web site). A composition is a structured aggregate. See Box 10 of this book.

- Relationship is an interaction. It is a polymorphism of a List, which in turn is a polymorphism of Aggregate Object. See Module 5, Section 4, and Figures 31 and 116, on our Web site.

- Transitive relationship: When one set of relationships implies another, the implied relationship is transitive with respect to the others (see Box 10 of this book). In a transitive triad of relationships, any two relationships in the triad imply the third. See Module 5, Sections 1 and 3, on our Web site.

- Intransitive relationship: When a composition of relationships disallows the existence of another relationship. See Module 5, Section 1.

- Subtyping relationship (a kind of relationship). See Incorporation in this box.

- Polymorphism (synonym for subtype). See Box 21; Chapter 3, Section 2; Chapter 4, Section 3; Module 5, Section 4, on our Web site; and Module 6.

- Subtype and Supertype, both subtypes of Object Class (in the same, exhaustive partition).

- Idempotent relationship: See Box 10 of this book.

- Recursive relationship: See Box 10 of this book.

- Location, containment, part of: See Box 12 of this book.

- Event: A time interval, which is introduced in Chapter 1, Section 2, and described in more detail in Module 5, Section 3, on our Web site.

- Process (a subtype of two parents—event and relationship). See Module 5, Section 3, and Processes, Events and Temporal Relationships, on our Web site. Processes use resources to produce products (see Box 10 of this book). Process inherits the features of Relationship and Event, such as the cycle time. Combined with temporal information from Event, the features inherited from Relationship acquire new characteristics: temporal succession; productivity; reversibility; temporal mutability (the time dependence of mutability between objects); temporal order (how far back into history a process reaches to articulate rules about a change of state at present); temporal degree (repeatability and concurrency); and, for idempotent relationships, the number of times a process loops back to the same product, or reuses the same resource; and so forth. A Reporting Process changes the state of an object from Unknown to a known value. An Inquiry changes the state of an object from

Unknown to Observed. It may or may not change other features that **30** constitute the overall state of the object.

- Effect is a kind (subtype) of process that changes the state of a single object. It is not always a business process, but effects always map directly to computer systems processes. See Chapter 2, Section 2, under Events, Effects, and Actions, and Module 5, Section 3, under "Transforming Business Processes into Effects of Events," in "Crossing the Chasm," on our Web site. See also Figure 109. An effect is also a subtype of Object Property in the same partition as Attribute.

- Saga: A process with no definite end, which is also a supertype of a process with a definite end. An endless saga is a polymorphism of Saga, in which it is definitely known that the process will not end. An Endless Saga is also a polymorphism of Saga. See Module 5, Sections 3 and 4; and Figure 116, on our Web site.

- Perspective is a classification scheme. It is expressed in a network of objects and relationships. It is also a Composition. See Chapter 5, Section 1, under Compositions of Relationships on our Web site. Compositions are also subtypes of relationships. A Composition is also a synonym for Expression. Therefore, Perspective is the same as Composition, which is a subtype of Relationship. See Module 5, Sections 1 and 4, and Module 6, Section 2, on our Web site.

- Universal Perspective is a subtype of Perspective.

- State, State Space, Trajectory in State Space and Set of Possible Trajectories in State Space, all subtypes of Aggregate Object. The last two are also Compositions. A composition is a subtype of aggregate object. See Module 5, Section 2 on our Web site. Thus, Trajectory in State Space and Set of Possible Trajectories in State Space are actually subtypes of Composition, and therefore a subtype of Aggregate Object, once removed.

- (Generic) Constraint: A generic Constraint is a generalized Meaning, synonymous with Object Property. See Module 6 on our Web site. Rule Constraint and Value Constraint (see Chapter 3, Section 3.2) are special subtypes of this generic constraint.

- Domain: A domain is a class of values, as introduced in Chapter 1, Section 3.2, and detailed in Chapter 4, Section 3. The class may contain finite or infinite numbers of distinct values and lends its members a common meaning, such as "length." The meaning of Qualitative measurement is encapsulated in nominal and ordinal domains. Nominal domains only distinguish between values, and Ordinal domains add information on sequences. The meaning of Quantitative measurement is encapsulated in difference and ratio scaled domains. Difference scaled domains add information on magnitudes, and Ratio scaled domains add information on ratios, and adds the concept of nil magnitude. The Metamodel of Knowledge infers that quantitative values must be expressed in units of measure, of which it may have several. See Chapter 4, Section 2.

30

Domains are arranged in a subtyping hierarchy shown in Figures 67 and 68 on our Web site. The most elementary business and physical meanings start with Primary domains: Enumeration (ratio scaled), Mass (ratio scaled), Physical separation (ratio scaled), Date/Time Lapse (difference scaled—includes date and time of occurrence), Electric Charge (ratio scaled), Overall Information Content (ratio scaled), and Preference (ordinal). Secondary domains are derived from primary domains as polymorphisms, or from relationships between domains. A few frequently used secondary domains discussed in [337] are Domains of Information Quality (Validity, that we are measuring the right thing; Reliability, that the measurement is always consistent; Completeness and Accuracy, that the measurement is unbiased); Economic Value Added (Ratio-scaled polymorphism of Preference); various domains of proportions; various domains of change/growth; and Gender. The cardinality of a domain is a measure of its size, which might be infinite. A dense domain has an infinite number of values between any ordered pair of values (e.g., a difference scaled domain like temperature, or a ratio scaled domain like mass).

- Precision (Chapter 4, Section 1) is a synonym for Accuracy, and Exhaustiveness is a synonym for Completeness. Note that less precise and less complete patterns convey less information than their more precise or more complete counterparts. Therefore, the more precise or more complete pattern is a subtype of its less precise or less complete counterpart.

- Format (introduced in Chapter 1, Section 3.2, and detailed in Chapter 4, Section 1).

- Unit of Measure (introduced in Chapter 1, Section 3.2, and detailed in Chapter 4, Section 2).

- Purpose or goal (see Module 5, Section 3, on our Web site).

- Resource (see Module 5, Section 3, on our Web site).

- Product (see Module 5, Section 3, on our Web site).

- Feature: Any property of an object, such as an attribute, relationship, effect, or constraint. See object Property, Box 10, on our Web site. Module 5, Section 3, and Module 6, Section 3, on our Web site, expand on the description of Feature/Object property in Box 10 and Figure 32.

- Process Owner. Various kinds (subtypes) are described in Module 5, Section 3, and Process Ownership on our Web site. See also Box 10 of this book.

- Cardinality (the "size" of a class). See Enumeration Domain, in Chapter 4, Section 3. Cardinality is a supertype of Enumeration.

- Capacity: A kind of cardinality constraint. See Chapter 5, Section 1, and Box 10 of this book.

- Size: A polymorphism of Capacity. See Module 5, Section 4, on our Web site, and Box 10 of this book.

- Resource Life: A temporal polymorphism of Capacity. When time is added to the meaning of capacity, the capacity to engage with objects will change over time. When the capacity decreases, we might conceive of an "unknown" process that has engaged the capacity of an object. The "unknown" process starts "consuming" it, or diminishing its capacity for engagement. If the decline is precipitous at a particular point in time after the resource is created, that interval may be considered the life of the object. Resource Consumption is a polymorphism of Resource Life, in which the capacity of a resource to engage is diminished over time by a known process. If a process changes the state of a resource, then it is considered consumed, and the changed resource is a Product. It could be a work product, a waste product, or a byproduct. See Module 5, Section 3, on our Web site.

30

- Cycle time: The time interval from the start to the end of a process. Cycle time is a subtype of Event. See Module 5, Section 3, on our Web site.
- Moment: An event of nil duration in Module 5, Section 3, and hence a subtype of event. See Module 5, Section 4, on our Web site.
- Beginning and ending moments of an event (both are subtypes of Moment).
- Activity (and other) costs (Module 5, Section 3, on our Web site).
- Array (Chapter 4, Section 1).
- Borel Object: A generalization of the concept of Array, useful for categorization and segmentation of objects and state spaces, such as a power set of values, or an infinitely large power set of ranges. See Module 5, Section 1 on our Web site.
- View (see Chapter 2, Section 5).
- Symbols (see Module 5, Section 1, on our Web site).
- Language (see Chapter 4, Section 1).
- Proximity Metric: Measures of similarity. May also be a measure of distance. See Chapter 4, Section 1. See also the note on generalizing the concept of distance in this book.
- Tracking Process: A process obtained by infusing temporal information into the proximity metric. It is a polymorphism of the proximity metric and Event.
- Extent (see Chapter 4, Section 1).
- (Degree of) Freedom (see Chapter 4, Section 1).
- Inclusion and Exclusion sets (mutually exclusive subtypes of Partition). See Figure 39 under "Constraints on Nominal Attributes," on our Web site).
- Value Sets: A collection of values at a point in time (Figure 40, Chapter 3, Section 2).
- Bounds (see Chapter 3, Section 2).
- Ranges: Ranges are subtypes of twin parents—Sequenced Pattern and Value Set. See Chapter 3, Section 2.
- Delimiters (see Chapter 4, Section 1).
- The expression of a rule (see Box 33 and Figure 117, on our Web site). A meaning may have many expressions. Each expression is a perspective of that meaning. Therefore, Expression and Perspective are identical. Expression is the result of Express (Expression of and Express are synonyms; their inverse

30

is Expressed By).[190] Express is a polymorphism of the subtyping relationship (as is "instance of"). See Module 5, Section 4, on our Web site.

- Instance of: A different polymorphism of the subtyping relationship in the same partition as Express. See Module 5, Section 4, on our Web site.
- Representation: A polymorphism of expression. See Chapter 4, Section 1.
- Temporal succession: Sequence in time; a supertype of Process and subtype of relative location. See Module 5, Sections 2, 3, and 4, on our Web site.
- Rule Constraint: A rule that constrains a nominal, ordinal, or ratio scaled Value; a kind of Constraint. See Chapter 3, Section 2.
- Assemble, a polymorphism of Process and the Part of relationship. See Module 5, Section 4, on our Web site. Assemble emerged from a process that made an item a part of an aggregate in step with the flow of time. Similarly, disassembly cuts the relationship between an aggregate and its parts, so that the part does not remain a part of the aggregate after disassembly has occurred. Thus, Disassemble is also a process, but it is a polymorphism of the Exclude relationship (near the top of Figure 116 on our Web site). Polymorphisms of Disassemble will tell us how an aggregate is picked apart (e.g., explosively, all at once, or in steps, or perhaps even one item at a time).
- Pick: A polymorphism of Process and the instance of relationship. See Chapter 5, Section 4. Pick, the polymorphism, also may have subordinate polymorphisms. For instance, one polymorphism may pick a single item out of a collection or assembly of items, whereas another might pick a class of similar items out of that collection of parts, and yet another polymorphism could pick a batch of similar or dissimilar parts out of the collection.
- Consist of: The inverse of Part of and a subtype of Locate. See Module 5, Sections 2 and 4, and Figures 114 and 116 on our Web site.
- Incorporation: A subtype of Consist of, wherein the object loses its identity as a member of a separate class of objects. It becomes a subtype.
- Composed of: A subtype of Consist of. See Module 5, Section 2. In Figure 116, on our Web site, its inverse has been labeled component of.
- List of: A subtype of Consist of. See Module 5, Section 4, and Figure 116 on our Web site.
- Contain: A supertype of Consist of, and a subtype of Locate. See Module 5, Sections 2 and 4, and Figures 114 and 116 on our Web site.
- Location (locate) and Origin. See Module 5, Sections 2 and 4, and Figures 114 and 116 on our Web site.
- Value Constraints: A kind (subtype) of Rule Constraint, in which specific values are permitted or excluded. See Box 28 on our Web site, and Chapter 3, Section 2.

190. *Expression*, an object, is identical to *Expressed By*, its defining relationship; the information conveyed (and hence meaning) is identical. See Chapter 6, Section 2, in [337], and the note on functional programming.

30

- Joint Constraints: When a value is constrained by an interaction between multiple objects. Joint Constraint is a polymorphism of Value Constraint. It is a relationship of a higher order, with more information in its Rule Expression and meaning. See Chapter 3, Section 2.

- Magnitude Constraints: Restricts the magnitude of a difference or ratio scaled value. Based on the principle of adding information, a magnitude constraint is a polymorphism of Value Constraint. Joint Constraints and Magnitude Constraints are subtypes in different, independent partitions of Value Constraint, so a constraint could simultaneously be both (see Chapter 3, Section 2).

- Truncation slices a pattern into a part. Truncate relates an object to its truncation. A truncated pattern conveys less information than the pattern that was truncated. It is therefore a supertype of the original pattern, and the inverse of Truncate is a polymorphism of the subtyping relationship (see Chapter 4, Section 1).

- Transformation, Input, and Output Processes (subtypes of Process): Transformation processes use resources to create products. Input processes convey resources to transformation processes, and output processes convey products from transformation processes (see "Input and Output Processes" on our Web site). They are all polymorphisms of Process, and every business process consists of all three, input, transformation, and output process, assembled in tandem (see Module 5, Section 3, on our Web site and Chapter 4, Section 3).

- Use: The defining relationship between a process and its resources. The input process is a polymorphism of "Use"—Module 5, Sections 3 and 4. See also Figure 2.16 of this book.

- Exception Process (polymorphism of Process): Processes triggered when constraints are violated. Exception processes are polymorphisms of Process in a different partition from input and output processes. Thus, there may be exception processes for inputs, outputs, and transformations. See Module 5, Section 3, under the "Risk Management Transform" under "Crossing the Chasm" on our Web site. The Web site also discusses exception management patterns in that section.

- Supply Chains (polymorphisms of Process). See "Supply and Demand Chains," on our Web site.

- Mutability: Substitutability of one object by another (see Module 5, Section 1, on our Web site).

- Symmetry (see Module 5, Section 1, on our Web site). Note that processes cannot be symmetric; they incorporate information on the flow of time, which is asymmetrical.

- Reversibility and Reversion (of processes). See Module 5, Section 3, on our Web site. Reversion is a process that is the inverse of another process—it restores the original states of all involved objects (i.e., undoes the effects of the reversed process).

- Efficiency and Productivity (of processes). See Module 5, Section 3, on our Web site.

30

- Load balancing of processes. See Module 5, Section 3, on our Web site.

- Observation, Inquiry and Reporting: Processes that are polymorphisms of a generic "inquiry" process, which changes the state of the object queried/observed to "queried/observed," and may or may not change it in other ways. See Module 5, Section 3, Box 54.

- Governance and nonstationarity (Applies to constraints, patterns and processes). Nonstationarity is the property in which features and parameters change over time; governance sets parameters and features. Governing processes are processes that set parameters of processes. See Chapter 3, Section 2; Chapter 4, Section 1; and Module 5, Section 3, on our Web site. Governance processes often depend on tracking and exception processes to govern, which is another commonly used theme in business.

effects of events is to normalize interactions between objects. These interactions flow from relationships, and lead to even more polymorphisms of objects, based on the relationships they have with other objects, or even recursively with themselves. Therefore, we will turn next to patterns of objects and relationships.

Events have effects on objects. These effects cut, switch, stitch, and manipulate relationships. Effects of events on objects are features of objects. They encapsulate the temporal behavior of the object and are derived from business processes.[191] Normalizing relationships with the right polymorphisms will not only normalize features, but also the effects and the processes from which they flow. In other words, it will normalize shared behavior. This shared behavior is a shared component of business knowledge that seeps into business processes and information systems through polymorphisms, flowing through their structures, infusing them with shared knowledge, and integrating and engaging via relationships. We will now focus on these relationships that engage the universal polymorphisms we discussed, and thus weave the Universal Perspective, a seminal pattern that lends itself to the world of business, and in doing so, also lends it shared meaning. This is the purpose of Section 2.1.2.

2.1.2 Stock Themes of Business—Relationships and Rules of Engagement

The purpose of polymorphism was to peel back, normalize, and sunder meanings. The purpose of structure is to synthesize and engage meanings. Relationships engage; they are the seeds from which processes and supply chains grow.[192] The

---

191. Effects may be directly translated into computer systems processes. Chapter 2, Section 2, in [337], discusses effects under *Events, Effects, and Actions*; and Module 5, Section 3, on our Web site, discusses effects under "Transforming Business Processes into Effects of Events." See "Crossing the Chasm" on our Web site.
192. See Module 5, Section 3, on our Web site, for the topics: "Processes, Events and Temporal Relationships," "Supply and Demand Chains, and Input and Output Processes."

purpose of this section is to synthesize normalized meanings by engaging the universal polymorphisms of Section 2.1.1 into common patterns of business information.

The Universal Perspective is a vast network of interrelated generic concepts in a web of relationships. It is impossible to grasp the complete pattern all at once. This section is therefore divided into many parts. In each, we will analyze a cluster of objects and relationships. These clusters are not isolated compositions. Each pattern is a fragment of the Universal Perspective; they are partial views of a single grand composition. Each figure in this section is a small window into the whole. The other patterns are not missing. They are merely hidden from view to help us focus on one aspect of the Universal Perspective at a time. In the following figures, subtypes are often shown inside supertypes. The intent is to make the relationships between subtypes and supertypes visually clear.

Before we analyze business meanings, values, and patterns of exchange and excellence, we must analyze the basic concepts in which the physical world frames business patterns. We will start with Physical Location.

Stock Themes—The Physical Location Cluster

Physical limitations on places in space and time are fundamental. Figure 2.11(a) articulates polymorphisms of time as a place, and Figure 2.11(b) does the same for physical place. Both figures articulate common sense, and that is perhaps why each is replicated in countless systems and processes. Given an automated reasoning repository of knowledge artifacts, each would be identified as a single rule, naturally inherited, and implied in a myriad of models as needed.

Each location relationship in Figure 2.11 is inherited from, and implied by, the location relationship in Figure 2.2. Each location is its polymorphism derived from the irreducible fact that objects may locate other objects (see Box 12). When several objects locate a single place, the relative locations must be mutually consistent if the objects also locate each other (for instance, in a triangulation; see the endnote on generalized distance). This is automatically implied by the transitivity of Locate, and a sophisticated repository would validate consistency of location, and raise exceptions where necessary. If it is known that the accuracy, validity, or reliability of one of these clashing locate relationships is better than the others, then the repository might even automatically override relationships of doubtful (information) quality. See information quality in Box 30; details are in Chapter 4, Section 3, in [337].

Each location relationship is symmetrical, but implies the potential existence of many asymmetrical polymorphisms in Box 12, such as being contained in, being a part of, or being a subtype of the other. Moreover, Event will have additional polymorphisms of temporal location, such as succession, timings and several other properties of mutual dependence between events (see Box 30). They all flow from the fact that each object may be a Place, and that an Event is a place in time (i.e., a time slot). Place normalizes location and its nontemporal polymorphisms, while Event normalizes their temporal polymorphisms. Indeed, the polymorphisms of locate (see Box 30) are all transitive relationships, and hence a place being a location is contingent on another object locating it. Thus, contingent on is also a polymorphism of locate. Physical objects, physical places, and events inherit the nontemporal polymorphisms of location from the primal object.

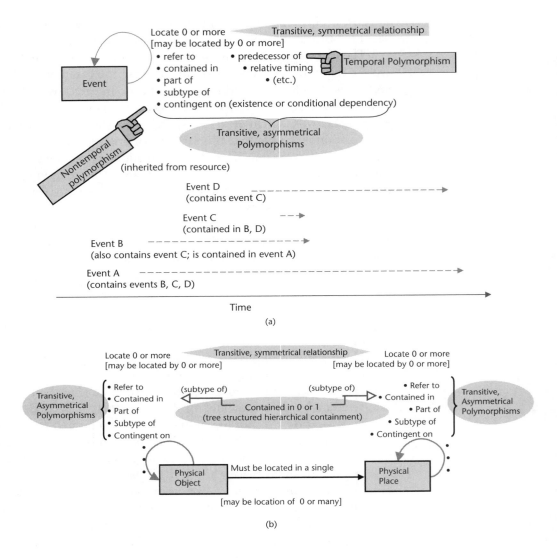

Figure 2.11   Some common physical polymorphisms of Place: (a) the place of Event; and (b) the location of Physical Object.

The Bills of materials structure, in which an instance of an item only may be contained in one other item at a time, is a polymorphism of Contains (e.g., a part in a subassembly or a subassembly in a machine).

The Metamodel of Knowledge tells us that any object (even object classes) may be classified, and each class also will be an instance of an object (see Chapter 2, Section 1, in [337]). It implies that a class of physical objects (e.g., a kind of machine or subassembly) may not only consist of other kinds of physical objects, as Figure 2.11 explicitly articulates. Each such (type of) part also may implicitly be a part of several other types of machines and subassemblies, which also may be considered parts of yet other parts, and so forth. Of course, we are free to bar this by exception. We may attach a rule to a class of parts that makes that kind of part exclusive to a specific kind of assembly. Thus, instead of replicating the structures in Figure 2.11(b) for every item that consists of parts, we only need to articulate the exceptions. These exceptions may be articulated by attaching the exclusivity rule to some kinds of object classes. The Metamodel of Knowledge and the power of reason that resides within it will imply the rest.

Note how located by and its polymorphisms, Contained in, Part of, and Subtype of, are reusable components from the Metamodel of Knowledge that we have reused in radically different contexts in Figure 2.11. It is an example of how a component of knowledge—even common sense—may be automatically applied to different objects via the structures of meaning we discussed in Section 2.1.2. Those structures also told us that the relationship between Physical Object and Physical Place is an inherited relationship—inherited and derived from the relationship between Energy and Physical Place (see Figure 2.2). It is a polymorphism of the generic locate relationship of Box 12.[193] This polymorphism gives a place exclusive possession of an object (see Box 25). The moment that we declare an item a physical object, the repository will infer that it must be in only one, exclusive place, and that its footprint may include only places that are a part of that exclusive place. It is all a matter of common sense and a modicum of automated intelligence.

Common Polymorphisms of Path

We have discussed polymorphisms of networks and paths in Section 2.1.1. Figure 2.12 shows some frequent manifestations of Path. The paths in Figure 2.12 are not an exhaustive list of possible paths. The purpose of Figure 2.12 is to accelerate requirements analysis by establishing that these objects will automatically inherit the shared behavior of Path (such as restructuring, as discussed in Section 2.1.1), which we may then define once, in only one place.

Distribution Channels, for example, are often chains of people or organizations in the supply chain for a resource being delivered to a user or consumer. However, as Figure 2.12 shows, not all distribution channels will consist of people or organizations. Paths through nodes of automation, documents, and media of different kinds also may be considered to be distribution channels.

Note that there is no bar on the same person, organization, or resource participating in different distribution channels simultaneously. The same resource could be a node on different paths. Its position relative to other nodes might be different in different paths. It is the topology that counts, and each topology, a distinct Path, will be a different and distinct distribution channel—even if some nodes are shared between different distribution channels, and even if individual nodes are the same, but their sequence is different on different paths. This structure also lets us measure and compare the efficacy of different routes to determine which arrangement might be preferred. It is the key to process improvement.

A route is a path through places, and when these places are geographies, the route becomes a geographical route, like a flight path or a travel itinerary (see Figure 2.12). Task dependencies are also routes through events. Again, Figure 2.12 is a

---

193. Module 5, Sections 2 and 4, on our Web site, discuss how polymorphisms of locate are derived. See "The Metamodel of Relationship," Figures 114 and 116, on our Web site.

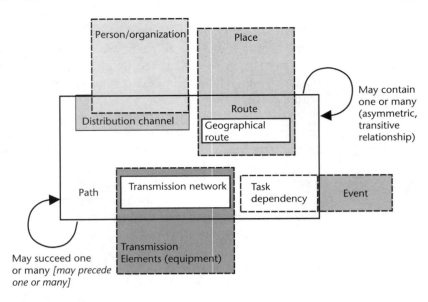

Figure 2.12   Some Common Paths.

reminder that we may subsume process maps and task dependencies into the generic concept of route, and that these polymorphisms will inherit the shared behavior of all routes. Thus, we may replace painstaking replication of behavior and computer code for each kind of path, by automated inheritance based on the shared nature and behavior of Path. Indeed, the Principle of Parsimony and Liskov's substitution principle tell us that we should not subtype Path or Network unless we are adding information they do not normalize. See Mutability of Resources in Section 2.1.1, and the note on the Principle of Parsimony. To align with business terms, we can always create synonyms. See The Tyranny of Words in Chapter 1.

Networks that transmit energy, materials, or information through routers, switches, and other equipment are also polymorphisms of Path. Figure 2.12 shows that networks may contain (and by implication, also consist of, or be subtypes of) other networks. Networks may be divided into parts that succeed each other along a route (as shown in Section 2.1.1), and the governing process could dynamically rearrange the succession relationship, restructuring the network as resources flow (and routed) through it. It does not matter what kind of network it is. This behavior is shared, and automatically inherited, from the Universal Perspective. All effects that change a topology are normalized by Structure, and those that change the topology of a directional structure are normalized by Path.[194] Structure and Path give us the room that we need to be flexible under the pressure of change, and innovative in the face of competition.

Person/Organization

Person/Organization encapsulates the shared behavior of people and organizations (see Section 2.1.1). A significant part of this shared behavior lies in the melding of

---

194. See Box 30. Module 5 on our Web site discusses in detail the properties of temporal and nontemporal structures.

people and organizations into hierarchical tree structures of the kind we discussed under Path. Figure 2.13 lists several significant and frequent polymorphisms of these hierarchies of people and organizations. In Section 2.1.1, we discussed how organizations are aggregate objects with or without internal structure. In this section, we will focus on hierarchically structured organizations.

Figure 2.13(a) articulates common relationships that Person/Organizations have with each other. Usually, these relationships form hierarchies of Person/Organizations. These hierarchies are independent irreducible facts, unless they are merged, separated, or joined via mutual inclusion, mutual exclusion, or subsetting constraints.

For instance, a hierarchy of legal entities may be useful from a legal or management viewpoint, but the hierarchy itself might not be a legal entity unless it is

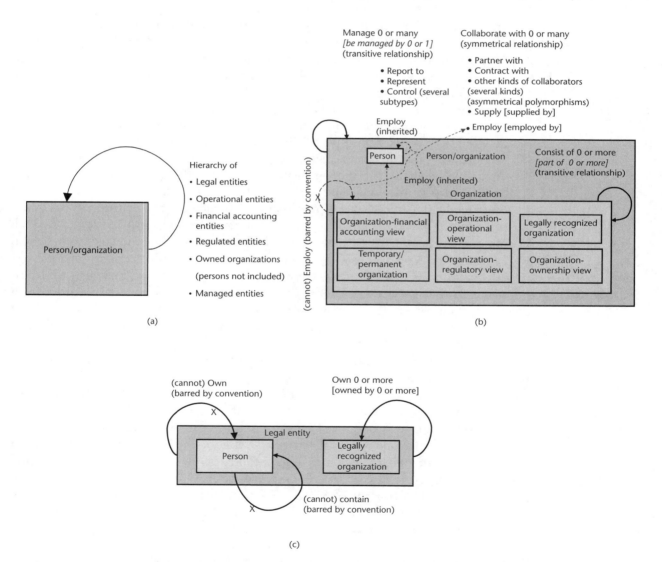

Figure 2.13   Common hierarchical relationships between Persons and Organization: (a) common hierarchies of Person/Organizations; (b) common polymorphisms of organizational hierarchies; and (c) legal entity normalizes ownership.

explicitly incorporated as one. For instance, a hierarchy of holding companies may be a legal entity in and of itself, constituted of other legal entities. On the other hand, a hierarchy of legal entities, such as subsidiaries and joint ventures, also may be organized in a reporting structure for internal management purposes. This hierarchy may have no legal standing as an entity in the eyes of the law.

Thus, managers of organizations, especially organizations that are large, complex, autonomous, and global, may have to consider several simultaneous viewpoints to manage, orchestrate, and harmonize different aspects of their organizational units. Each view may be a different hierarchy of associations (or path through) nodes constituted of the same organizational units. At the lowest level, these units could be roles played by individual employees. The most frequently used hierarchies have been shown in Figure 2.13.

Let us start by divorcing ownership from control. Ownership does not always imply control. For instance, an insurance firm in the United States might manage an insurance firm in Korea for a fee, without actually owning any shares in it. Although it is difficult to conceive, it is not impossible that the reverse also may happen—that an owner of a firm might abdicate any right to control a firm he or she owns, possibly by legal agreement. Thus, hierarchies of ownership and management control may be different and independent—unless, of course, we mandate that owners also manage, by imposing a mutual inclusion or subsetting constraint between the two relationships (see Box 10). This is often the case.

Similarly, for financial accounting purposes, the firm might be organized in one hierarchy, whereas for management accounting, the configuration of departments and organizational units may be different. For example, some operational units might not follow the formal reporting structures of departments and their sub units. Take the case of a firm that organizes itself into customer-focused, multidepartmental teams that draw on resources and individuals from several departments. A team consisting of a team leader and members of customer service, information systems, and engineering departments might be members of a customer-focused service team for a product that must be engineered to order for a strategic customer. The team is an organizational unit that might follow a different functional or operational reporting hierarchy from the administrative or departmental hierarchy of the firm.

In the same way, information, such as performance measurements and various costs, might have to be rolled up, or presented in different drill-down hierarchies to regulators of different kinds. These hierarchies need not always follow the administrative or financial accounting structures of the enterprise.

Even if a firm is organized into a multiplicity of structures for different purposes, the correspondence of the lowest-level nodes between these structures must be clear and unambiguous. Otherwise, the integrity of organizational data and performance metrics will be at risk. In other words, every structure must clearly map to every other. The concept of Structure automatically creates these maps between structures. At the lowest level, it is individual roles that are being organized by the hierarchy. Each hierarchy is a different Path, but each hierarchy is a path that consists of the same nodes. It is these nodes that naturally ensure that each path can map to every other; that is, they are all views of the same enterprise seen from different perspectives.

The problem of mapping between views becomes more complex when organizations are restructured. In order to compare prerestructuring performance with postrestructuring performance, it is important that past and future measurements of the same measures (e.g., revenues, costs, and customer satisfaction) be sourced and summarized from the same nodes of the organization after restructuring as it was before restructuring.

This is easier said than done, because the reorganization changes which organizational units are considered parts of which other organizational units (i.e., associations between nodes change). This kind of change invalidates comparisons of performance measures (such as cost, income, revenues, sales, and so forth), between the unrestructured and restructured versions of the organization. However, like can be compared with like if we can map the correspondence of nodes between the old and new structures.

These maps naturally exist when we restructure associations between the same organizational units. In this kind of restructuring event, some organizational units are detached from others, while others are attached to each other, to create new groups and hierarchies. Therefore, we may map nodes in one structure to corresponding nodes in the other at the lowest level. Processes and information systems only have to recognize this information in order to leverage it. As a part of the restructuring, if nodes are not merely associated and dissociated from each other, but are deleted or added to the enterprise as a whole, then the contributions of these additions and deletions also will be clear. They will be contributions (negative or positive) from sources that are truly new to the structure. The following real-life experience demonstrates that corporations only can ignore this aspect of the Universal Perspective at their peril.

In the final decades of the twentieth century, a large telecommunications company went through a period of turbulence and continual restructuring, in its transition from closely protected to intensely competitive markets. Organizational units were continually attached to and detached from each other, as the corporation attempted to flex in response to its new, and rapidly evolving, environment. The firm's old information systems imposed a rigid financial accounting hierarchy that recognized no past states of hierarchies. The charts of accounts admitted no possibility that innovative management might require different windows into the same organization. This made it increasingly difficult to compare past and present performance, in terms of costs, effectiveness, revenues, and income. The firm changed its accounting structure to make it more flexible. It took the firm several years to make the change, at a significant cost.

The new accounting systems, built on old assumptions, recognized that some kinds of overlapping organizational hierarchies might coexist, but set these in stone. It did not admit the possibility of new and innovative hierarchies to match new ways of focusing on customers. Neither did the new software admit that structures might need continual realignment, nor that each kind of structure may have a history of alignments. Even after the new charts of accounts were deployed (at a very significant cost and effort), it often was impossible to gauge the efficacy of reorganizations, or to draw lessons learned, because it was virtually impossible to compare like with like after restructuring and realigning organizational units. Eventually, the firm had to resort to draconian and drastic measures to survive. In the turbulence of the new millennium, agility is the key to survival, and old assumptions must give way to the tumult of change. The lesson learned was that in order to be agile, processes and information systems must recognize the polymorphisms and multiple views articulated in Figure 2.13.

Normalization is the key to flexibility. Figure 2.13(b) resolves hierarchical views of organizations into those common to Person/Organization, versus those normalized separately by Person and Organization. Person/Organization normalizes several kinds (polymorphisms) of management hierarchies. It also normalizes the various kinds of collaborative structures listed in Figure 2.13(b). Person and Organization separately normalize the relationships shown specifically against each. These relationships were discussed in detail in this section and in Section 2.1.1.

Clearly, only organizations may consist of other organizations. People cannot consist of people, nor can people consist of organizations! This is why the "consist of" relationship in Figure 2.13(b) loops back on Organization alone. As we have seen in Section 2.1.1, employment is a special polymorphism of the supplier relationship. People or organizations may employ individuals, but cannot strictly employ another organization. They may of course purchase time or services from another organization, but that contract is, strictly speaking, not an employment contract.

Similarly, a person or organization may not literally own a person. Figure 2.13(c) makes this clear. We also discussed it under Figure 2.3. The constraint against doing so is the same component of knowledge, articulated in both Figures 2.3 and 2.13. Ownership is a legal concept established by Man, not nature. It is encapsulated and normalized by the concept of the Legal Entity we discussed in Section 2.1.1. The bar against ownership of people is also a legal concept, forged by Man in recent, more enlightened times. Legal Entity normalizes ownership (with Asset; see Section 2.1.1), because, strictly speaking, only legal entities may own assets.

It might surprise some readers that barring a relationship is also a polymorphism of the relationship it denies. For instance, in Figure 2.13, denial of the employment relationship is as much a polymorphism of employment as are its inherited forms. Constraints add information, and hence create polymorphisms, of that which they constrain. See Module 6, Section 2, on our Web site. Barring a relationship constrains its existence. Knowing it cannot exist is different from asserting that we do not know if it may exist. Thus, asserting something cannot exist is tantamount to creating a new polymorphism for it. It is a form of the Unaffecting Inheritance. See Box 21 in [337], or the note on polymorphism.

Box 21 in [337] describes the risks of inappropriate unaffecting inheritance. The unaffecting inheritance in Figure 2.13(b) springs from a somewhat arbitrary distinction between an employee and a supplier of time and services that is not considered to be an employee. It is a pattern by decree. This is its justification.

The bar against ownership of individuals is also a decree that aligns business practice with ethics. The packaging of goods and services into business products are also patterns by decree, as are the terms and conditions of agreements that involve the resource groups we discussed in Section 2.1.1. In the same way, information is always information about a resource group. We will review this in more detail in our discussion of documents and information in this section. These resource groups may be arbitrary patterns, like the tax code, hammered out in compromises with different special interests. These kinds of patterns may consist of arbitrary exclusions, inclusions, and exceptions designed to navigate a narrow path that may be ideal for no stakeholder, but will be acceptable to all of them. Unaffecting inheritance may be appropriate in such situations. The patterns of this chapter are the basis for determining when unaffecting inheritance will facilitate, not hinder, agility. Thus, the patterns in this chapter are also the basis for determining when unaffecting inheritance should be used.

Ownership may be partial, and even of different kinds. For instance, a person or organization may own only a share, or a proportion, of an asset, such as another organization. Moreover, ownership may be differentiated by the kind of shares owned. Examples include common stock, preferred shares, nominal shares (nominal or notional share prices are sometimes used to compute the economic value added by a business unit that might not be a legal entity), and so forth. The concept of Asset in Figure 2.4 is embedded and hidden in the ownership relationship of Figure 2.13(c). The recursive relationship in Figure 2.13(c) summarizes one polymorphism of Asset—the asset that is an owned organization.

The role of Supplier involves transfer of ownership of some resource (see Section 2.1.1). Thus, the simple recursive Supplier relationship in Figure 2.13(a) summarizes a complex high order relationship hidden within it. That relationship not only involves buyers and sellers, but also products and services supplied. We will return to this relationship later in this section. It is a seminal relationship from which supply chains and many other items grow.

Regardless of how we organize or own, we may have multiple windows into an organizational structure, each a perspective as discussed in Figure 2.13(a). Figure 2.13(b) also shows this. They are needed to understand and manage the conflicting goals and strategic interactions that commonly occur in large organizations.

Shipment, Transportation, and Place

A shipment is a resource(s) in transit. It always must be located on a route. We discussed shipments, transportation, and routes in Section 2.1.1. We know that a shipment may contain or consist of other shipments, and that parts of the shipment may be consigned to different destinations. A consignment is a special part of a shipment. It is the part of the shipment that is picked up at a single node, and must be delivered to a single destination (node) at one time as one unit. The consignment is the basic building block of Shipment.

Naturally, a consignment must traverse a route that is a part of the route that the aggregate shipment traverses. If the shipment consists of a single consignment, then the route of the shipment and the consignment will be identical (i.e., the part will equal the whole). A Route, as we know, may contain or consist of other routes. We discussed this in Section 2.1.1. These are facts inherited from the primal object (see Figure 2.1 and Box 12). Similar rules also will hold true for the other objects in Figure 2.14. For example, messages might contain or locate messages, resources may do the same for resources, places may do so for places, and so forth. These facts have been hidden in Figure 2.14 to reduce clutter, but remember that they are there,

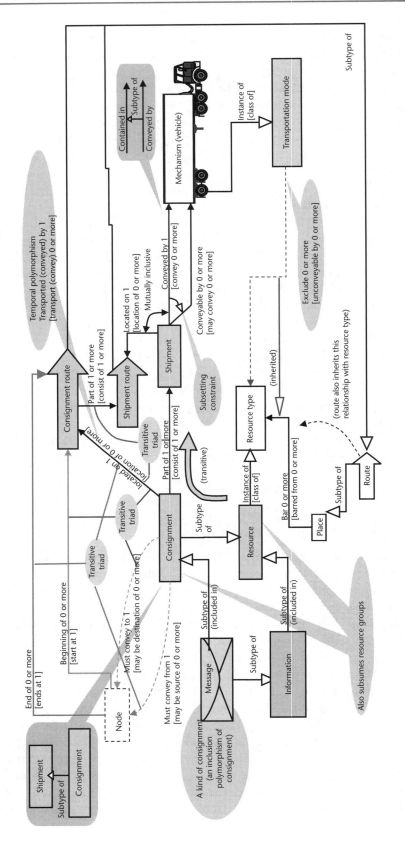

Figure 2.14 Common relationships—the Shipment and Transportation cluster.

casting their shadow from the Metamodel of Knowledge into the Universal Perspective. Business processes can ignore these patterns of containment and consistency only at their own peril. They exist, timeless and immutable, normalized within the Universal Perspective.

Shipping Routes and Transportation

A route is a place. It is a place that consists of its nodes. The location of a consignment on a route is always expressed in terms of the node in which it is located at any given point in time. Thus, the precision with which a route may locate a consignment depends on the density of nodes that constitute the route. If the node density reaches a point at which the route may be considered a continuum of nodes, as Box 25 describes, then the consignment theoretically may be located with infinite precision—for example, in physical space. The relationship that locates a consignment at a particular node is an inclusion polymorphism of the location relationship in Figure 2.14, which locates the consignment in the route. This is in turn is an inclusion polymorphism of the location relationship in Figure 2.2, which is identical to the location relationship in Figure 2.1.

Since a Route is defined in terms of its nodes, the relationship between the Consignment and Node is implied by the relationship between Node and Route. The fact that a consignment is located on a route tells us that it also must be located on a node in that route. The three kinds of relationships (between consignment and Route, Route and Node, and Node and consignment) thus form a transitive triad (see Box 10). In order to normalize information, one of the three must be dropped in each triad because the other two will always imply it. Figure 2.14 articulates this. Similarly, the fact that the route taken by a consignment is a part of the overall route of the shipment is implied by the fact that the consignment is a part of the shipment.

If we add temporal information to located on, then it becomes the transportation event. It tells us that the nodes must be visited in a time sequence, and might even tell us when each node was actually visited, and/or when the consignment (or its shipment) was scheduled to be there.

All routes start and end at nodes. This is inherent in the structure and definition of Route. It implies that consignments must start and end at the same nodes as the route. The consignment route identifies these starting and ending nodes. The source and destination of a Consignment is an implied, not explicit, fact. The Route that contains the consignment implies it. Thus, Route normalizes this information. Indeed, the very identity of the route depends on the nodes that form its path.

Resources in Transit

A consignment is a Resource (or Resource Group) in transit (actually or potentially) on a Route. A Resource Group, as we have seen in our discussion of Figure 2.2, is a subtype of Resource. When you review Figure 2.14, remember that Resource also subsumes the concept of Resource Group. The consignment is transported on its Route, as a part of a Shipment, by some mechanism (e.g., a vehicle). Figure 2.14 articulates this. Thus, Consignment is a role of Resource defined by its relationships with Route, and through Shipment with Shipment Mechanism. Different resources may be bound together into a single consignment, which in turn may be grouped into a Shipment. If the consignment is a consignment of information, then it simultaneously may be a part of several "shipments." Then, the consignment is merely a Resource Group in (potential or actual) transit. A shipping manifest is the Document that records this information.

Naturally, if a consignment consists of different resources, and a shipment consists of consignments, then the shipment also will consist of the collective resources of all the consignments that constitute it. Figure 2.14 articulates that the relationship between Resource and Shipment is implied by (transitive with) the relationship between Resource and Consignment, and the relationship between Consignment and Shipment.

Constraints, Capacity, and Special Instructions

Not all mechanisms may convey all shipments. For example, it might be hard to fit a shipment of trucks into a car, or regulations might bar highly inflammable and unstable chemicals from aircraft. Hazardous materials may be barred from a construction such as a tunnel or a building, or even from a geographical Place. This kind of fact that bars a resource from a place (or, conversely, insists on its inclusion) is normalized by constraints on Place. Mode of Transportation and Route inherit this relationship (see Figure 2.14). Remember that a node on a Route is a Place, and a Route through a Place is a special polymorphism of that Place. See the discussion on polymorphisms of structure in Section 2.1.1. Thus, if a resource is barred from a place that is also a node on a Route, a shipment that contains that resource also will be barred from that route. It will be an inherited fact. For instance, the Lincoln Tunnel across the Hudson River connects New Jersey to New York City. There is a list of hazardous materials that cannot be transported through there. Therefore, trucks carrying materials in this list cannot be routed through the Lincoln Tunnel. The Route inherits this constraint from its Node. It is an inferred fact, because the Metamodel of Knowledge, at the heart of the Universal Perspective, holds within it the power of reason.

Conveyance is a polymorphism of containment, which is a polymorphism of location (see Box 12), which, in turn, articulates the fact of transportation within the container (see Figure 2.14).

Naturally, only that which is conveyable by the shipping mechanism (e.g., a truck) may be conveyed by it. The subsetting constraint between the two relationships between a shipment and its shipping mechanism in Figure 2.14 articulates this. The subsetting constraint was discussed Box 10. Violations should trigger an exception process (see Box 30), a fact automatically inherited from the Metamodel of Knowledge and implied by the power of reason that resides in it. A knowledge machine would know this, just as a human analyst should know this.

Naturally, a mechanism will have a capacity, and (its relationship with) shipment will engage this capacity. We discussed the capacity in Box 10. The conveyability of a shipment might depend on its capacity requirements. Thus, it also may be a relationship derived from the quantum of capacity it must engage (a fact hidden in Figure 2.14 to avoid clutter). This is also a fact that a knowledge machine

---

195. The shipment mechanism is not the only object that may have a constrained carrying capacity; routes also may impose capacity constraints on the shipment and its conveyance mechanism. Capacity constraints on Routes were discussed in Section 2.1.1.

may infer from the Metamodel of Knowledge.[195] The Metamodel of Knowledge lends the Universal Perspective the power of reason.

A consignment, as we recently discussed, is a polymorphism of a Resource. It might be a Resource Group. Consignment inherits the relationships between Resource and Resource Group explicitly articulated in Figure 2.15. Those relationships tell us that a consignment might aggregate many resources. There is no bar against the shipment consisting of consignments from different parties who might share the vehicle (or the shipping mechanism) to realize economies of scale.

As evident from the inclusion/exclusion relationship inherited from Resource Group, there may be complex rules about what kinds of resources may be combined together in a shipment. For example, heavy steel girders may be barred from a shipment of fragile crystal glasses. Although hidden in Figure 2.14 to avoid clutter, these relationships are articulated in Figure 2.15. Figure 2.14 tells us that these relationships will be inherited by Consignment and Shipment, since both are polymorphisms of Resource. Indeed, there may be special instructions about which consignments may or may not be included in which shipments. The optional include/exclude

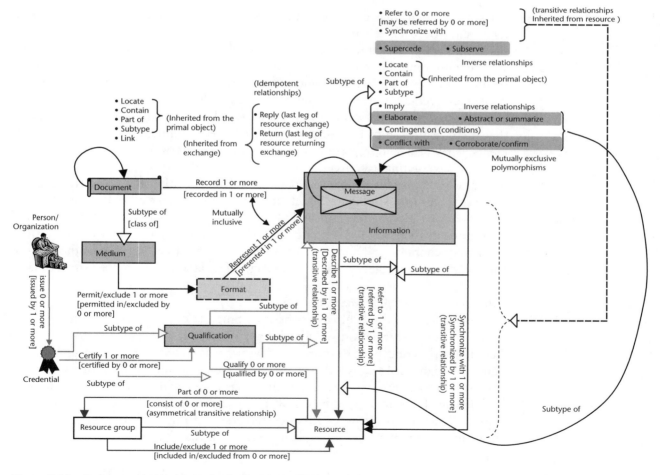

Figure 2.15 Common relationships—the Document and Information cluster.

relationship between Consignment and Shipment is similar to that between Resource and Resource Group in Figure 2.15. It is inherited from Resource.

Building and Breaking Shipments

Consignments may switch shipments, as shipments are broken, reorganized, and rerouted in a network. This process emerges when we add temporal information to the "Part of" relationship between Consignment and Shipment (see Box 30).

The shipment also might consist of multiple consignments, with different sources (pick-up nodes) and destinations (drop-off nodes) on the route. We discussed this in Section 2.1.1. A consignment is a special kind of Shipment—one with a single origin and destination. Thus, a consignment is a more restricted pattern than a shipment. This makes Consignment a subtype of Shipment (see Box 14). Figure 2.14 shows this in an inset. The "Part of" relationship between Consignment and Shipment is distinct and different from the subtyping relationship in the inset. The subtyping relationship admits that Consignment is a special kind of shipment—one with a single pick-up point and a single destination. That consignment may constitute a part of the whole shipment. This last assertion is merely a special case of the fact that a shipment may be made of shipments that are considered to be its parts. We have discussed this in Section 2.1.1 and in the discussion of Figure 2.14. A shipment that consists of a single consignment may be considered a shipment made of just one part.

Combining consignments into shipments that will fit the capacity of a shipping vehicle with a minimum of wasted space can be complex. Complex rules and constraints may be required. Shipments, and even consignments, may be broken, pooled, and rebuilt at transshipment points along the shipping route. This is an area of specialized mathematical research in logistics. For us, it will suffice to understand that these relationships lead to processes that break shipments, including consignments. They also lead to processes that build shipments and consignments by pooling and aggregating resources. Processes that pool and aggregate resources are temporal polymorphisms of the "Include/Exclude" relationship between Resource and Resource Group in Figure 2.15.[196] It all boils down to the capacity of an instance or class of the shipping mechanism in Figure 2.14, with respect to different kinds of consignments that may be combined into shipments. Like any other object, a shipment may contain (or be a part of) other shipments (see Box 12). Although not explicitly shown in Figure 2.14, it is a universal fact inherited from the primal object.

Consigning and Shipping Messages

A consignment need not always consist of tangible objects (see Section 2.1.1). It could be pure information, in which case we call it a message. Information is included in the concept of Resource, and Message is included in the concept of Consignment. Figure 2.14 shows this. Thus, the vehicle that ships the consignment need not always be a truck, a plane, or machines that we normally associate with the concept of Vehicle. It might also be the Web, the postal service, a telecommunications network, a broadcasting network, or even carrier pigeons. The concept of the mechanism for transporting resources is more general than our everyday concept of a

---

196. Reference [313] and other publications on operations research discuss rules for building, breaking, and optimizing shipments.

vehicle or a mode of transport. The mechanism and transportation mode in Figure 2.14 subsumes our everyday concepts of physical vehicles and modes of transport, and extend beyond them, to include any mechanism that can move information, or any kind of resource along any kind of Route, physical or virtual.

A node in a network is a place. Any resource may be a place (see Section 2.1.1).[197] A place is a state of a resource in which it locates another; it is a subtype (see Figure 2.2). Place therefore inherits this recursive locate relationship on Resource, along with its polymorphisms—"contained in," "part of," and "subtype of" (described in Box 12). An address is formatted information on location (see Section 2.1.1). Figure 2.16 articulates this cluster of relationships. Therefore, nodes also may have addresses, and each node may even have several addresses. However, its identity as a place will be unique. This place could be a virtual or physical place.

Indeed, places are only located relative to other places (see Box 12). A resource or a place may change its location in relation to places that locate it. This is the generic process of movement. If the destination of a consignment is a resource, and the resource moves in the virtual or physical space that locates it, then the network will still convey the consignment (or message) to the resource to which it was addressed, not the place(s) that locates the resource. This is a very important concept. It implies that we must specify sources and destinations on a route in terms of the resource between which we wish to move the consignment, and not between the places that contain (or locate) these resources.

Location is a transitive relationship (see Box 10).[198] If we follow the rule above, then the places that contain (or locate) the source and destination nodes (and the in-between nodes) will be naturally inferred by the transportation process. If the source of a consignment moves before the consignment is picked up, or if the destination moves in virtual or physical space while the consignment is in transit, then the transportation process will naturally track the movement and pick up the consignment from the right place, and deliver it to the right Place—its target Resource on the Route, regardless of where it is located in space. In an increasingly mobile world of rapid and continual change, where processes must flex rapidly and continually as they respond to the churn and tide new instructions, changed expectations, and new information, this kind of flexibility in routing and delivery can be key to success, satisfaction, and even survival of a business.

Thus, for example, if an individual has a unique address, then a worldwide network will track down and deliver the message to the individual, wherever he or she logs on to the network. On the other hand, if the destination is a notebook computer with a unique address [it could be an Internet Protocol (IP) address], then the message will be delivered to the notebook, regardless of its geographical location, or who signs on to the computer. The message goes where we say it must, and the intended destination must be the intended resource, not the container that might convey the message, because resources may shed containers in the flux of a world built on mobility and responsiveness.

Like any other object, a Message may consist of other messages. It may have an internal structure. This structure even may be a temporal structure that involves

<hr>

197. Module 5, Sections 2 and 4, on our Web site, describe in detail how resources are places. See Figure 114 on our Web site.
198. Module 5, Section 4, on our Web site, discusses the transitivity of *locate*.

timing and sequence. Each component of a message may follow a different route, and on arrival at the common destination(s), the information on its structure will automatically ensure that the aggregate message preserves its integrity. This behavior is inherited from the generic structured object (see Box 10). The message will not be just data, but also information on its structure.[199] The Metamodel of Knowledge demands consistency of all that grows from it.

The same information also may travel along multiple routes (see Section 2.1.1). Indeed, the same information even may move from the same source to the same destination, touching the same nodes, but perhaps in a different sequence. Each sequence will be considered a different route, since each is a different path. The information in transit on a given route is "Message." Message resolves the many-to-many relationship between the information conveyed and the routes on which the information is conveyed (at a given time).[200] Indeed, we all know that different messages may even convey the same information. It is common sense. The Universal Perspective is common sense, formally structured and normalized in a model of reality.

Document and Information

The cluster of relationships that surround Information and Document in the Universal Perspective will be the topic of this section.

Information must always be recorded on a document. What we do not know is not information. We discussed the relationship between Information, Document, and Medium in Section 2.1.1 (see Figure 2.1). Our focus in this section will be the relationships in Figure 2.15.

The list of relationships in Figure 2.15 is by no means complete. It cannot be, since the real world is much too rich a tapestry to exhaustively model in the bland diagrams of this book. However, we can abstract its essence. The relationships in Figure 2.15 frequently extract the essence of complex patterns of information, which are the essential patterns relevant to business models. In Section 2.1.1, we have seen how the recording relationship between Document and Information is an inclusion polymorphism (see Box 10) of locate that applies to Information.

In Figure 2.15, Refer to is a special asymmetrical relationship. Only Information may refer to an object. In common parlance, a document referring to an object really means is that the formatted information in the document refers to an object, perhaps even another document. Similarly, when we say an object refers to another (e.g., when a doctor refers a patient to another doctor), what we really mean is that the object refers to information about another object. Reference is transitive between the referring object and the object to which it is referred, via the relationship each has with the Information to which they refer. In the example of the doctor, the referring doctor did not really "send" or "move" the patient to another doctor. He or she only gave the patient information about the other doctor (i.e., a guideline) that suggested that the patient visit the other doctor. That is why it was a reference. Reference is a universal relationship that connects a resource to information.

---

199. Internet telephony is based on this principle. Chapter 49 of [334] describes its physical implementation.
200. Box 24 discusses resolution of many-to-many relationships.
201. The recursive reference relationships in Figure 2.15 are inclusion polymorphisms of the reference relationship between objects and information in general.

Information is also a resource. Thus, the recursive reference relationship on Information in Figure 2.15 is inherited from resources in general.[201]

All relationships in the Universal Perspective are either inherited from the Metamodel of Knowledge, or are polymorphisms of those inherited relationships. Reference to information about an object is inherited. Relationships may be conditional (see Box 10; details are in Module 5 on our Web site). This fact is inherited by all relationships including references to information, a fact normalized by the metarelationship between meta-objects in the Metamodel of Knowledge.[202] Based on Box 14, conditional reference is a polymorphism of unconditional reference. It is a kind of description and elaboration. Figure 2.15 articulates this.

Locate, and many of its polymorphisms, are also common to all objects, and are inherited by both Document and Information. In Figure 2.15, we have "flattened" this hierarchy of polymorphisms, because we have already discussed this hierarchy. Locate and some of its common polymorphisms are relationships normalized by the primal object and inherited by both Document and Information in Figure 2.15.

Implication firmly embeds a meaning—a pattern of information—in another meaning, to create a subtype or a mutual inclusion constraint (see Section 2.1.1 under Elaboration Interpretation and Shifting Perspectives).[203] If the entire set is being divided, and its smaller parts are all considered subsets of the whole, as shown in Box 19 on our Web site, then mutual inclusion becomes a special case of the existence of a subset implying the existence of the superset.[204] If all parts of the divided set are mutually inclusive, then we will get back the set we divided into parts. Implication is thus a polymorphism of the subtyping relationship. The existence of a subtype implies the existence of the supertype, but not vice versa. A relationship also may be implied by a composition (see Box 10). The composition has a larger information payload, elaborates on the implied relationship, and as a whole, is a subtype of the implied relationship. Only meanings imply meanings. Meanings are patterns of pure information, as described in Module 6, Section 2, on our Web site; hence, only information may imply information. Therefore, implication is an inclusion polymorphism of the subtyping relationship (see Box 10).

We also know that information about an object may supersede other information.[205] Supercession only applies to information. Section 2.1.1 also discussed elaboration, interpretation, conflict, and collaboration; each (object) applies only to Information. Thus, only information in a document, not the document itself, can qualify, imply, elaborate, corroborate, conflict, interpret, or supersede.

Describe is a polymorphism of Refer to. A description always is a description of some object, which it therefore refers to. A qualification is a kind of description—a belief about a resource. We discussed the Qualification-Credential cluster in Section 2.1.1. Figure 2.15 makes these relationships explicit. It is clear that the certification relationship between Credential and Qualification in Figure 2.15 is transitive with the Qualify relationship between Qualification and Resource.[206] Thus, we also may

---

202. Figure 116 describes the "Metamodel of Relationship" on our Web site.
203. Module 6, Section 4, discusses an example on our Web site.
204. Mutual inclusion is a special case of the subsetting operation, one in which we consider not only *proper subsets*, but also the entire set being subtyped as a subset. Subsets, both proper and improper, are described in Box 19 on our Web site.
205. Information superseding information is the basis for *Unaffecting Inheritance* in Box 21 on our Web site. See the note on kinds of inheritance.
206. Transitivity was discussed in Boxes 10 and 30.

say that a credential certifies a resource. It is implied by the Certify and Qualify relationships in Figure 2.15. Common sense is the power of reason embedded in the Universal Perspective—that one fact can be inferred from others.

Elaboration is also a kind of description that adds information. It is therefore a polymorphism of the subtyping relationship (see Box 14). We know that elaboration adds information by describing an object. Therefore, Elaboration is also a polymorphism of Description. The meaning of elaboration is included in the meaning of description. Elaboration is a meaning that also creates subtypes of what it describes. Elaboration is thus a subtype with two parents, Description, and the subtyping relationship itself. Figure 2.15 articulates this.

Abstract is the inverse of Elaborate. One summarizes, and the other details. Thus, Abstract implies the existence of Elaborate, and vice versa, which make them inverse relationships.

Some readers might consider elaboration and abstraction to be mutually exclusive relationships. This is not correct. Elaboration actually implies the existence of its inverse. Elaborate must elaborate on something. Thus, the less detailed form of the elaborated object is implied by the very fact of elaboration. Elaboration and abstraction are inverses, not mutually exclusive relationships or objects.

Unlike Abstraction and Elaboration, Collaboration and Conflict are mutually exclusive objects (see Section 1.1). However, both add information on mutual support or mutual exclusion. Corroborate is a polymorphism of Collaborate that only applies to pure information. It is a relationship between two items of information that signals confirmation of the validity of one with respect to the other (see Validity in Box 30).

Mutual inclusion and subtyping (collectively, a collaboration; see Section 2.1.1) and conflict (mutual exclusion) are different kinds of constrained relationships (see Box 10). Box 14 describes how constraints lead to subtypes. Thus, conflict and corroboration not only elaborate on a reference or description, but they also subtype what they describe by adding information on constraints. Both are polymorphisms of Elaboration.

One meaning may be contingent on another, and subject to various conditions. It is clear that making a meaning contingent on others is a polymorphism of elaboration. When we make a meaning conditional on other meanings, we impose constraints on it. When we qualify an object, we add information on what we believe it can or cannot do. Both are polymorphisms of elaboration.

Information refers to objects, even if they are other items of information. Formatted information in a document also may do the same. It is a fact inherited from Information. A Document is different. It might surprise some readers and defy intuition, but the fact is that a document does not refer to information, and cannot refer to another document. The document records information, and the information in it may refer to other objects, even other documents or other items of information, but the document does not normalize this fact. The information in it does.

On the other hand, documents may link to other documents. Linkages between documents belong to the interface layer in the Architecture of Knowledge, as shown in Figure 15 on our Web site. Linkage navigates between documents. It is a physical implementation of Path, in which the nodes are all documents of different kinds. Thus, this linkage is a polymorphism that is a kind of format, and a physical expression of abstract information. Abstract information may only refer, and be a node in an abstract Structure. Linkage and hypertext may mirror this structure, but they are only formats and physical implementations of abstract references between abstract items of information. A linkage is a symbol that triggers a transportation process between documents. The symbol formats and represents a reference. Chapter 4, Section 1, in [337], discusses symbols and formats in detail. This is why linkage has not been shown as a relationship that can associate pure information with pure information in Figure 2.15.

Represent, Encrypt, and Decode are also missing from Figure 2.15. They are relationships inherited from the Metamodel of Knowledge and impinge on information. They are hidden in Figure 2.15 to reduce clutter. Encrypt and Decode are polymorphisms of Represent (see Box 30). Boxes 36 and 38, on our Web site, and Chapter 4 discuss Represent, Encrypt, and Decode in the context of information and Document. Encryption of meaning is discussed in Chapter 4, in [337], at the end of Section 3. Encrypt and Decode belong to the interface layers of the Architecture of Knowledge described under "The Architecture of Knowledge" on our Web site.

Information is always information about a resource. It could be a single resource or a conjunction of resources. Resources may be bundled together, based on complex rules mandating or excluding resources from the bundle. The presence or absence of a resource in the bundle may depend on the presence or absence of other resources (e.g., fire insurance may be bundled with theft insurance for a car). Box 14 articulates why a resource group is a subtype of resource. Mandatory inclusion or exclusion of resources in a group restricts membership of the group. A restricted group has fewer degrees of freedom than an unrestricted group. Therefore, a group that restricts membership is a subtype of a group that does not. The inclusion or exclusion constraint, the relationship between Resource and Resource Group in Figure 2.15, adds this information to the Part of relationship in that figure. Thus, Resource Group is a subtype of Resource, and therefore a resource with an identity of its own—a recursion on Resource, and a subassembly of parts that is also a part. Thus, Resource Groups will automatically inherit the relationship that asserts that Information will always refer to one or more resources.

The inclusion and exclusion constraints discussed thus far have been occurrence constraints. Occurrence constraints are nominally scaled relationships. The Metamodel of Knowledge in [337] asserts that Ordinal, Difference, and Ratio Scaled interactions are polymorphisms of nominally scaled (occurrence) relationships (see Box 10 and Domain in Box 30). The Universal Perspective inherits this information from the Metamodel of Knowledge. Thus, the nominally scaled exclusion and inclusion constraints in Figure 2.15 between Resource and Resource Group are the thread around which richer ordinal, difference scaled, and ratio scaled rules can crystallize. Thus, the inclusion and exclusion relationships in Figure 2.15 could metamorphose into rules about the quantity of one resource that may or may not be bundled with the quantity of another in a resource group. For instance, $1 million life insurance might be bundled with $500,000 disability insurance. Product and process innovation depends on these concepts in the Metamodel of Knowledge, as we will see under the Buying and Selling Cluster.[207]

The idempotent relationships on Message are manifestations of exchanges and returns, which we discussed in Section 2.1.1. Reply is a polymorphism of the returning leg of a Resource Exchange that applies only to information. Return is identical to the Return event we discussed in Section 2.1.1.

The structure that relates resource groups and resources in Figure 2.15 is common sense, but its implications are as profound as they are varied, as the following examples make clear.

Consider lessons learned—a key, and universally addressed issue in almost every walk of business and beyond. It is information about conjunctions of resources—their outcomes, dependencies, interactions, and risks. Resource Group normalizes this information. Consider regulations. Guidelines and regulations also address objects and their interactions. Resource Group normalizes this kind of information as well. For instance, an accounting regulation requires that the cost of failed or abandoned projects be written off in the quarter that the project was abandoned (see GAAP Rule SOP 98-1 of the AICPA).[208] The rule is information about a resource group: that is, the cost of the abandoned project, a polymorphism of Fund; the quarter the project was abandoned, a polymorphism of Event; the abandoned project, a polymorphism of a task in a cancelled state; and the write-off, also a polymorphism of Fund. If we add temporal information to this resource group, then it will become the write-off process that supports the regulation. Clearly, GAAP Rule SOP 98-1 is a higher order relationship and a ratio scaled rule expression (see Box 10). Furthermore, a resource group is a polymorphism of the "high degree" relationship (see Box 10) in the metamodel of knowledge. We will return to resource groups when we discuss features of products later in Section 2.1.2.

The relationships in Figure 2.15 are useful for auditors who might need to track references, elaborations, and governance. They are also useful in multilingual or multimedia environments, when consistency and corroboration of several documents must be tracked and timed, and conflicts resolved, or when information in different documents must be synchronized.

The Part of and Synchronize relationships in Figure 2.15 together constitute multimedia environments. Multimedia presentations (e.g., an audiovisual presentation) may be considered compound documents, which consist of other documents, like a sound track and a video, each a document in its own right, and a part of the multimedia show. Moreover, the two parts must be synchronized. Thus, both "consist of" and "synchronize" collaborate to produce the multimedia presentation from its parts.

---

207. Module 5, Section 3, on our Web site, discusses how process resilience, product, and process innovation depend on the Metamodel of Knowledge. See also the case study, Box 62, "Mutability and Innovation," "Processes That Gain or Lose Structure," and "Product Reengineering," and "The Mutability of Compositions," all on our Web site.
208. GAAP is an acronym for Generally Accepted Accounting Practices, which is a set of accounting principles accepted by Certified Public Accountants (CPAs) in the United States. SOP is an acronym for Statements of Positions, which are established accounting guidelines within the GAAP framework. AICPA is an acronym for the American Institute of Certified Public Accountants.

The presentation and its parts are all documents. Synchronization is a question of timing. Therefore, it is also a process (see Box 10). Clearly, synchronization requires that each document that is part of the multimedia presentation refer to the other documents that are part of the presentation, so that the composition as a whole can proceed in lock step. Thus, synchronization is a temporal polymorphism of Refer to. It is a meaning manifested when we infuse the flow of time into the meaning of reference.

Synchronization also may be time delayed or forward looking. It might synchronize states of different objects at different points in time with each other. For example, stock prices published on your computer might be delayed twenty minutes, unless you are a paid subscriber to the publishing service. The same object also might track a state with reference to its own past or expected future states (such as planned states). We discussed the tracking process in Section 2.1.1. It is also a polymorphism of the reference relationship.

Thus, the relationships in Figure 2.15 are the roots of several diverse but key polymorphisms and processes of interest to all businesses. The structures in Figure 2.15 normalize the information content and the behavior of each.

Tasks, Projects, Processes, and Risks

A project is a temporary endeavor undertaken to create a unique product or service [61]. In the Universal Perspective, Task and Project are synonyms. In our discussion of Business Products (versus the products of processes) in Section 2.1.1, we saw that natural processes are not always owned (in RAWCF terms; see RAWCF in Box 10). Thus, a generic process may or may not be owned. It could be an unowned and purposeless natural process, or a purposeful human endeavor. A task or project is the purposeful endeavor that is always owned, initiated, and controlled by people or organizations.

A task is a subtype and polymorphism of the generic metaprocess in the Metamodel of Knowledge. The generic metaprocess also subsumes natural, unowned processes. Tasks use resources and produce products (see Box 10), at least one of which is the objective of the task (see Box 23).[209] People and organizations that facilitate or execute the task are also its resources. We discussed the "RAWCF" relationships between tasks and Person/Organization in Box 10. The "RAWCF" relationships are special polymorphisms of the Use relationship between tasks and resources. Use is normalized by Process and Resource.[210] Person/Organization normalizes the "RAWCF" polymorphisms of Use.[211] Figure 2.16 shows the "R" and "W" dimensions. We know that these relationships, which are inclusion polymorphisms of "Use" between Person and Task, are mandatory for every task.

Delegation

When an organization has "RAWCF" roles in a task, it must delegate these roles to individuals who will be accountable to the delegating organization. Individuals also

---

209. Module 5, Sections 3 and 4, on our Web site, exhaustively discuss tasks and processes.
210. Figure 116 on our Web site normalizes "use."
211. "Use" is the defining relationship between a process and its resources, inherited from the Metamodel of Relationship (in the Metamodel of Knowledge). See Module 5, Sections 3 and 4, and Figure 116 on our Web site.

may delegate these roles to other individuals or other Representatives (see Section 2.1.1).[212] The "RAWCF" roles of a Person/Organization are transitive with corresponding "RAWCF" roles of accountable individuals.[213] Figure 2.16 articulates this fact, where the "R" role is shown with a dashed line between Person/Organization and Task. It is equally true for the other "RAWCF" roles. This kind of transitivity is also an automated pathway for common sense and inference. It is a pathway that surges out of the junction where the Universal Perspective engages the Metamodel of Knowledge. Indeed, delegation is a polymorphism of the recursive management relationship of Figure 2.13 that we recently discussed. All views of the Universal Perspective are connected—they are parts of the whole.

Resource Use and Resource Management
A person or an organization always uses a resource through a task. When the task is hidden, or its information content is irrelevant to our purpose, we summarize the use of resources by attributing it directly to a person or organization. The task that connects the resource to the person or organization is then buried in the Use relationship between the Person/Organization and Resource (shown with a dashed line in Figure 2.16). In other words, this summarized form of Use, which connects a Resource to a Person/Organization (the user) directly, is transitive with the task's usage of the resource, and the task's "RAWCF" relationship with Person/Organization. Showing all three will replicate information. Figure 2.16 articulates this. Similar arguments also apply to products of processes, which are also subsumed by Resource. See the definition of Resource in Section 2.1.1.

The use of a resource is an event, and all tasks are events (see Box 10). Events also may be resources, and like any other resource, an event may be a business product positioned for sale in the marketplace. For instance, a telecommunications company does not usually sell its telecommunications network; rather, it sells the use of it. This use is derived from an event that is a task for the customer. The task of making a call, from the firm's perspective, is irrelevant; only the use of its resources matters.[214]

Just as a Person/Organization's use of resources was derived from the task that uses those resources, the "RAWCF" roles a Person/Organization plays in the context of a task also translate to management of resources and products in the ambit of the task. However, when resources (or products) used by several tasks move through supply chains, responsibility for a resource shifts in step with the responsibility for the task that is using it. Therefore, a separate and independent overall management responsibility is sometimes justified for resources that must be shared. This management relationship between Person/Organization and the managed resource subsumes and overrides local management of resources in a task. Figure 2.16 shows this relationship. Indeed, the recursive management relationship on

212. Box 36 in [337] discusses representation. See also our Web site.
213. The accountability relationship between *Person* and *Person/Organization* in Figure 2.16, the dashed lined responsibility relationship between *Person/Organization* and *Task/Project*, and the responsibility relationship between *Person* and *Task/Project* are a transitive triad. Transitive triads were discussed in Box 30. We could substitute responsibility for any of the other "RAWCF" dimensions (Box 10), and it would still be a transitive triad. Any relationship in the triad may be inferred from the other two. This is another example of the power of inference embedded in the Universal Perspective.
214. The use of resources might be summed over several usage events for billing, analysis, or other purposes. Rule 3 in Box 16 shows why this kind of summarized event is also an event. The Metamodel of Knowledge can infer this from rules about domains.

Person/Organizations in Figures 2.13 and 2.16 are polymorphisms of this relationship. Person/Organizations are also resources, and inherit this relationship, whereby they may be managed by people or by organizations. Infused with time, the relationship becomes a governing process.

To use a resource, the resource and the task must meet. In other words, both must reside in the same place. This place may be physical or virtual, but it must be their meeting place. The product also is produced in the neighborhood of the task. To avoid clutter, Figure 2.16 leaves out the crucial fact that resource use is idempotent (see Box 10) with respect to the place of a resource and the task that uses it. The precision with which the task and resource must be colocated is the field of the task. It is a feature of Use.

The Input Process closes the gap between a task and its resources, whereas the Output Process conveys the products of a task to their destinations. The task is the seminal object from which supply chains grow, and its input and output processes are the seminal parts from which sourcing and delivery processes within a supply chain grow.[215]

Qualification and Risk

We discussed qualification of resources in Section 2.1.1. A qualification is information about a resource or resource group. A resource group is also a kind of resource; see the recent discussion on information and documents. Figure 2.16 articulates this. A qualification always qualifies a resource in the context of a task (or a class of tasks). Figure 2.16 makes this explicit.

A task is also a polymorphism of a resource, inherited from Event (see Box 10). Thus, a task also may be qualified in the context of another. The Metamodel of Knowledge implies this. Similarly, a person or organization in an "RAWCF" role is a resource that might have to be qualified for a task. The relationship between Qualification and Resource in Figure 2.16 implies this. Skills, experience, and credentials are all polymorphisms of qualifications, which might be needed by people and organizations in the context of a task they must manage, execute, or otherwise facilitate.

Thus, the skills that will qualify individuals to perform "RAWCF" roles in a task are polymorphisms of the relationship that optionally qualifies a class of resources for a class of tasks in Figure 2.16. Although they are implied, these inherited relationships clarify and articulate the discussion in this section, as shown in Figure 2.16. They are all subsumed and normalized by the generic relationship between Task, Resource, and Qualification.

This relationship between Task, Resource, and Qualification is the seminal relationship from which quality assurance and risk management processes emerge. It is clear that the qualification in question might qualify resources and products of the task, or the task itself, each in the context of the other. The risk associated with the task also may be partitioned into components. Each object (and relationship) in Figure 2.16 can potentially contribute to the total risk involved.

---

215. Input and output processes are components of the Metamodel of Knowledge. Module 5, Section 3, discusses them in detail, under "Process Maps," "Supply Chains," and "Business Process Engineering," and "Crossing the Chasm—Business Process to Information Systems." Module 5, Section 3, discusses Supply Chains. See these items on our Web site.

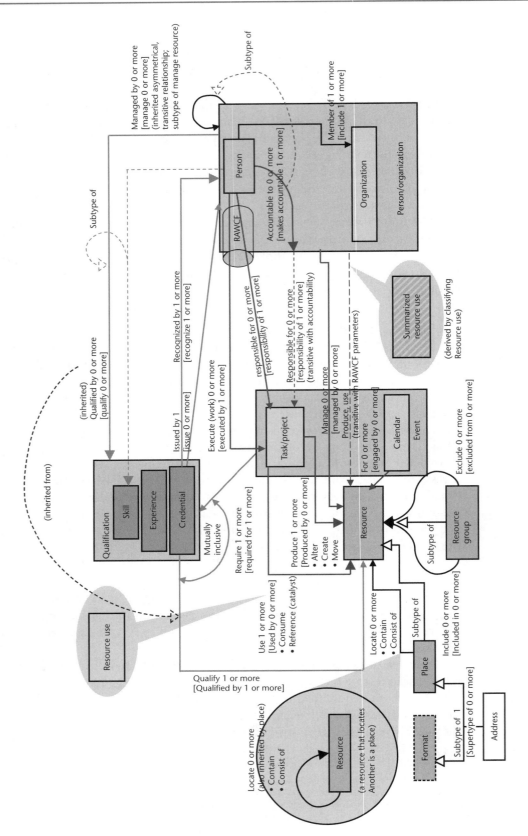

Figure 2.16   Common relationships—the Task-Resource Cluster.

We also know that Risk may be partitioned into different kinds of generic risks described by the domains of information quality, such as Enumeration, Validity, Accuracy, Reliability, and Exhaustivity (completeness) (see Box 30, and Rule 11 in Box 16). Each of these domains measures a different kind of risk.

Task is a polymorphism of Process in the Metamodel of Knowledge. Every feature of Process is a potential source of information, and consequently a source of risk in terms of its validity, reliability, and accuracy. Some features of processes are in Boxes 30 and 10; features of processes are exhaustively listed in Module 5 on our Web site. Each kind of risk may lead to quality assurance criteria for tasks, resources, and products. The exhaustivity of our coverage of constraints on these features is also subject to risk. Thus, Enumeration, Validity, Accuracy, Reliability, and Exhaustivity of the features of processes, and of the contribution of each object in Figure 2.16, may all contribute to overall risk.

Thus, the objects in Figure 2.16, the dimensions of information quality (validity, reliability, accuracy, and exhaustivity), and features of processes, are all dimensions of risk. Each is an axis in a multidimensional array[216] for the (qualitative or quantitative) measurement and classification of risk. In this array, risk analysis may be made as granular or as gross as required. This is the universal risk assessment framework at the heart of the universal themes of risk management that follow.

The Project Management Body of Knowledge (PMBOK) [61] partitions risk as follows.

- Performance Risk: Performance of resources, such as unproven technology, unrealistic goals, and changes in standards or benchmarks. At the most granular level, performance risk stems from features of processes, such as cycle times, resource engagement capacities, and others, described in Module 5 on our Web site.
- Governance (Management) Risk: Quality of governance processes, such as those that stem from resource allocations and management quality.
- Organizational Risk: Risk of conflicting priorities, goals, and resources.
- External Risk: Environmental risks, such as changes in regulatory, legal, and political environments; the weather; natural disasters; or other kinds of force majeure that cannot be governed.

Risks must be managed and addressed. The model of Tasks and resources in Figure 2.16 and the components we discussed in Section 2.1.1 are a basis for identifying and managing sources of risk. Management of the process that manages risk is also a governing process and a task on its own, with its own subprocesses, resources, and work products. The PMBOK identifies the following subprocesses that, taken together, comprise the process that governs the Risk Management process.

- Risk Management Planning addresses how risk management tasks will be approached and planned.

216. Chapter 4, Section 1, in [337], discusses the configuring of arrays from components in the Metamodel of Knowledge.

- Risk Identification addresses identification of risks that must be considered.
- Risk Analysis addresses assessment of the qualitative or quantitative impact of risks on project goals and consequences.
- Risk Response Planning creates tasks and techniques to reduce the threats posed by identified risks.
- Risk Monitoring and Control monitors the execution and tracking processes for risk management tasks.

These are the common and universal themes for managing risk. We discussed the universal processes for tracking, monitoring, and governance in Section 2.1.1. These risk management processes are their polymorphisms. Readers interested in more information about these themes may refer to [61] in the References.

Agreement and Ownership

Agreements and ownership are the basic building blocks of business. Figure 2.17 shows both from the Universal Perspective. We have discussed each object in Section 2.1.1.

We have seen how meetings, negotiations, agreements, and disagreements are all polymorphisms of Event, whereas the associated Terms and Conditions agreed to, disagreed upon, or under negotiation, are all polymorphisms of Information. Thus, Meetings, Negotiations, Agreements, and Disagreements inherit the properties of relationships and processes, such as being contingent on, succeeding, preceding, or including other events, and so forth.[217] These events also could be meetings, agreements, disagreements, or negotiations. Indeed, as we have seen in Section 2.1.1, they are all states of Negotiation. On the other hand, Terms and Conditions will inherit the relationships in Figure 2.15 from Information. Thus, strictly speaking, it is not true that an agreement supersedes, implies, qualifies, or conflicts with another. It is the terms and conditions of one agreement that supersedes, implies, qualifies, or conflicts with those of another. The Agreement itself is only an event that occurs. It cannot, strictly speaking, supersede, imply, qualify, or corroborate another event, but its terms and conditions may supersede, imply, qualify, or corroborate the terms and conditions of another event (temporarily or permanently). Of course, if an event truly conflicts with another event, because a mutually exclusive pair of events has occurred in spite of the rule that asserts that they must not, then it means that an exception has occurred. It is a violation of rules, and should trigger an exception process (see Box 30). This kind of exception is different from the conflicting information we discussed in Section 2.1.1. The conflict between agreements, technically speaking, is not an exception pertinent to the agreement event; rather, it is a conflict between the information with which the agreement is associated.

Information normalized by the event, such as the time of its occurrence, its participants,[218] and its place(s) of occurrence, also may be recorded in a document. Remember that the meeting even may be a discussion by mail, spread over dispersed participants. Its place is then an aggregation of the places that contain its

---

217. Boxes 10, 23, and 30 discuss a few key features of processes. Module 5 on our Web site has the complete list.
218. *Meeting* normalizes the participants of an event. Figure 2.17 shows this.

participants. We discussed this kind of aggregate place in Section 2.1.1, and in this section under Shipment and Transportation. Thus, the record in the document may join all three—information on terms and conditions, the time, and the place of the event. Indeed, documented agreements, disagreements, negotiations, and minutes of meetings often do so. Of course, the place only can be recorded in terms of its address in a document. We discussed this relationship in Section 2.1.1. The record of the agreement is thus a polymorphism of the record of a meeting. Figure 2.17 articulates this pattern.

In Section 2.1.1, we have also seen how negotiations, agreements, and disagreements inherit their relationships with participants from meetings. We have also seen in Section 2.1.1 that a structure or aggregation of people and/or organizations is an organization. Mediators emerge from structures of this kind. The fact that some participants in a meeting optionally may be mediators is inherited from Structure. Naturally, every negotiation, agreement, or disagreement also must have at least two principal participants who are not mediators. This fact is also implied by Structure. The mediators and representatives in a structure must naturally mediate between at least two nodes (see Section 1.1). Even if we do not know the precise structure that changes a participant into a mediator, the fact that a person or organization is playing this role will suffice to distinguish a mediator or representative from the principals in an agreement, a negotiation, or a disagreement.

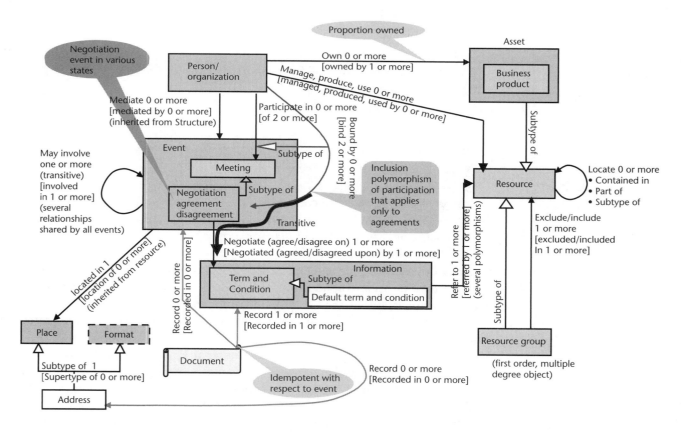

Figure 2.17 Common Relationships—the Meeting and Agreement cluster.

Figure 2.17 articulates that the binding of participants by the agreement is a state of the relationship between Meeting and its participants. It is this state that distinguishes the agreement from other states of Meeting. This relationship is transitive with respect to the terms and conditions of the agreement. Thus, we can say that the binding of the agreement binds its parties to its terms and conditions.

Information is always information about resources. We discussed this in Figure 2.15. Terms and Conditions are special polymorphisms of Information. We discussed this in Section 2.1.1. Thus, terms and conditions are always terms and conditions about resources. Terms and Conditions may be infinitely varied, but a few common patterns are worth mentioning. Many business agreements are associated with goals, and the terms and conditions include these goals, statements of work, and scope of the agreement. Agreements like these are often based on the following patterns, their combinations, and variations.

- Fixed Price Contracts (equality constraints on the quantum of Funds involved in the Terms and Conditions of the agreement)
  - Cost not to exceed a given amount (upper bound on the quantum of Funds involved in the Terms and Conditions of the agreement)
- Fixed Time Contracts (equality constraints on the duration of the Event involved in the Terms and Conditions of the agreement)
  - Duration not to exceed a given amount (upper bound on the duration of the Event involved in the Terms and Conditions of the agreement)
- Reimbursable Cost Contract
  - Limits on reimbursed costs
  - Limits above which cost will be reimbursed (a cost deductible)
- Time and Materials Contract
- Incentive contracts
  - Cost incentives
  - Schedule incentives
  - Volume or quantum of business incentives
  - Shared risk and reward contracts (e.g., lawyer's fees that are contingent on winning a reimbursement in a court of law)
  - Contracts that stipulate collateral resources to compensate for exceptions, contingencies, or reduced levels of performance

Like any other object, the agreement may be an aggregate of other agreements, each with its own terms and conditions. The features above may be attached to the aggregate agreement, rather than to individual members of the aggregate. Thus, a number of individual agreements may be packaged together into a cogent integrated agreement.

Riders to a master agreement are also common patterns that temporarily or permanently supersede terms and conditions of the master agreement These riders are also agreements with their own terms and conditions. The structures in Figures 2.17 and 2.15 provide a framework for agreements like these as well. Terms and Conditions inherit the (optional) supercession relationship shared by all Information in

Figure 2.15. This is another way in which agreements may be integrated. Change management also fits into this framework.

Sometimes agreements are based on a "boilerplate," which is a template in which blanks are filled in and clauses added or deleted as the agreement is customized for each situation. For instance, insurance coverages are usually boilerplates in which costs and prices are filled in as a person or organization is bound to its terms and conditions. Similarly, many corporations have templates for contracts with suppliers and customers. Your credit card agreement is an example. Where do these templates fit into the model in Figure 2.17?

Objects may have initial (default) states.[219] Terms and Conditions are objects. The boilerplate is their initial state. Terms and conditions are also polymorphisms of Information. This initial state is also therefore pure information. Information must be formatted in at least one document (see Figure 2.15). The default state therefore must be documented in some format, electronic or otherwise. These documents are physical manifestations of the boilerplate. The initial state of an object might have unknown values (see Value in Box 30). Usually, unknown default values are blank spaces that must be filled in within these "boilerplate" documents.

The null value articulates absence of meaning. Therefore, null valued features should be absent on these boilerplate documents. However, sometimes the same document may be a shared interface for several subtypes (variations) of a common theme. Then, it might be expedient to represent with blanks those values that might be null for some, but not all, subtypes. Sometimes the defining features in these documents also may be blank. For example, in a boilerplate for the terms and conditions of an insurance agreement, the linkage to the agreement event (e.g., date, time, and parties) may be intentionally left blank, because this is the facility that will help an operator tie the terms and conditions to the agreement. The design, format, expression, and the security of these documents are business process automation issues. These documents reside in the interface layer of "The Architecture of Knowledge" on our Web site; see Figure 15). We will therefore not stray farther into this. The main thrust of this book is the topmost business theme layer of the architecture of knowledge, whereas boilerplates are the link between pure meaning and business process automation (or the lack of it).

Thus, the shared and universal patterns of information encapsulated in all business agreements are normalized in the pattern of Figure 2.17. When we model agreements of different kinds, it will often suffice if we structure them as we have structured Figure 2.17, then add special features and constraints to it. However, one kind of agreement is very special, and merits explicit recognition of its own special features. This is the agreement that transfers the right to use or own a resource. Remember that an Asset is a state of Resource. It encapsulates and normalizes the fact of ownership. Agreements about ownership and use of assets are the hub around which all business revolves.[220] We discussed it in Section 2.1.1. We will now elaborate on it.

---

219. Chapter 2, Section 2, in [337], discusses default and initial states.
220. Under Figure 2.16, we discussed how the use, production, and management of resources by a person or organization are derived from the relationships of these objects with Task. These relationships in Figure 2.17 are transitive, with corresponding relationships with *Task* in Figure 2.16 (as discussed earlier).

Buying, Selling, and Forging of Products

In Section 2.1.1, we saw why we must distinguish the physical transfer of resources from the transfer of rights (e.g., the ownership or the right to use a resource). One right relates to information. Its transfer may be a part of the terms and conditions of a Negotiation or agreement, which we know is a state of Negotiation (see Section 2.1.1). Since agreements and disagreements also were states of the Negotiation in Figure 2.5, this generalized Negotiation of Figure 2.5 has been abbreviated to "Negotiation/Agreement," or "NAG," in Figure 2.18.

The Right to a Product

Not all rights involve use or ownership of products. Indeed, not even all rights about products involve their ownership or use. For instance, a patent is a right to produce a product. A contract may give a distributor the right to distribute a product, without necessarily ceding ownership to the distributor, or giving the distributor the right to use the product being distributed. The transfer of ownership or the right to use a resource is a special right. It is also the right at the heart of all commerce. We know from Section 2.1.1 that a resource thus positioned in the marketplace is a business product.

The use of a resource is an event. This event also could be a business product, even when the resource being used is not. For instance, a telecommunications network may not be up for sale or lease, even if its use is. The sale or lease of a resource, or the sale of its use, is a special case—a polymorphism—of an event that transfers rights between the parties to a meeting. Figure 2.18 shows this.

The generic transfer of rights event in Figure 2.18 was hidden in Figure 2.5. The transfer of a right is always negotiated. It cannot happen unless the transferor and transferee, respectively, agree to divest and accept a right. Thus, the transfer of a right is a polymorphism of Negotiation hidden between Negotiation and Transfer of Possession in the hierarchy of Figure 2.5. Figure 2.18 reveals this hidden hierarchy.

Of course, it is always possible that the right may be vested in a person or organization, without the vesting person/organization losing it in the process. Information is right, after all, and may be vested in several persons or organizations simultaneously. We discussed the transportation of information between places in Section 2.1.1 and this section. A person or organization vested with a right can be considered a location of that right.

Figure 2.18 reduces clutter by not explicitly showing the rights to a product. It is embedded and hidden in the many-to-many relationship between Product Rights Transfer and Business Product in Figure 2.18. Figure (g) of Box 24 shows how many-to-many relationships embed and hide objects. Figure 2.18 also hides the generic terms and conditions shown in Figure 2.17. Instead, it shows some common resources that these terms and conditions involve when the possession of, or the right of use of, a resource or product is vested in a party to an agreement. The terms and conditions of such agreements usually involve the terms of payment, the terms of shipment, and naturally, the product in question.

Payment in Exchange for Rights

Remember that when goods and services are exchanged in payment, it is a form of Exchange (see Section 2.1.1 on the Exchange event). Figure 2.14 makes clear that

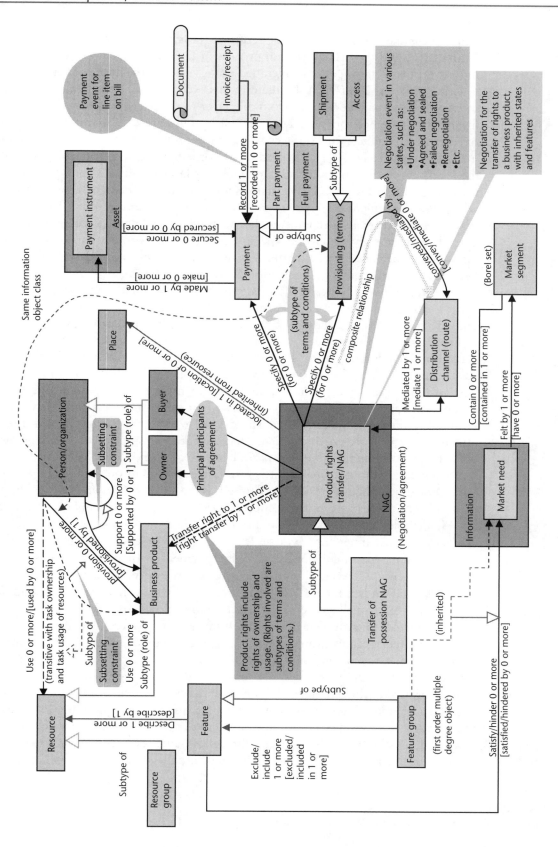

Figure 2.18   Common relationships—the Buying and Selling cluster.

Shipment is the bridge between the terms of transfer of the product (or service) in Figure 2.18, and the transportation process in Figure 2.14. The constraints on the mode of transportation may be included in these terms; the mode of transportation is a kind of Place. The return shipment in this exchange is a shipment of funds. Payment also must transport funds from the payer to the payee. Fund is a form of pure information (see Section 1.1). Thus, the pattern in Figure 2.14 covers the terms of payment for products and services sold. Payment assumes some kind of payment instrument, such as cash, check, credit card, or letter of credit. We will discuss Payment and its terms under Patterns of Funding later in this section. The mode of transportation in Figure 2.14 normalizes information on the kind of mechanism by which the instrument of payment will be shipped. Naturally, not all instruments may be shipped by all mechanisms. For instance, paper currency cannot be transported electronically in virtual space, but electronic expressions of Fund may. Figure 2.14 articulates this pattern as well. It is subsumed in the relationship between Resource and Transportation Mode in that figure.

The relationship between the mode of transportation and the payment instrument is similar to that between Format and Medium (see Medium in Section 2.1.1 and Table 2.1). Just as Medium may exclude some kinds of Format, some modes of transportation may exclude some instruments of payment. These rules might be forged by law, convention (e.g., some telephone service providers will not accept cash sent by mail), or forged by nature (e.g., the bar against transportation of paper currency in virtual space). Constraints forged by nature are inherited from the constraint that bars some resources from certain modes of transportation. They are also immutable and inflexible, and set in stone. On the other hand, constraints forged by law or convention are polymorphisms that are not set in stone. They could be candidates for process improvement. Box 62 has an example on our Web site.

Since the quantum of payment is ratio scaled information, a unit of measure is automatically implied (see Box 30). This unit is the currency shown in which the payment must be made (see Fund in Section 2.1.1).[221] The framework in Figures 2.18 and 2.17 is flexible. The terms and conditions of sale may or may not leave open the currency and instrument of payment. It may or may not leave open the timing of the payment. It may or may not synchronize payment with delivery and shipment. Indeed, the terms and conditions may involve any resource. It is a potential inherited from Information (see Figure 2.15). The flexibility with which terms and conditions may be crafted, as well as their infinite variability, flows from this potential.

The payment instrument is an asset. It must be a resource owned by somebody (i.e., a person or organization).[222] Assets also may be used to secure, or guarantee, a payment. Thus, when you check into a hotel room, your credit card may be used to secure your payment, even if it is not charged at that time, and even if you later pay by cash or use another credit card. Indeed, the asset that secures a payment need not even be a payment instrument. For instance, a house that you own (i.e., an asset) might secure your monthly mortgage payment to the lender for the money you borrowed to buy the house. Similarly, your assets may secure your repayment of the money you borrowed to send your children to college. The relationship between

---

221. Chapter 4, Sections 2 and 3, in [337], discuss money.
222. Assets normalize the fact of resource ownership. Assets were discussed in Section 2.1, under Figure 2.3.

Asset and Payment in Figure 2.18 articulates and generalizes these kinds of relationships. The meaning of Collateral emerges from this relationship. It is a role of Asset.

An invoice records a request for payment. In other words, it records in a document a payment in a requested state. Similarly, a receipt is a document that records a payment in a paid-up state. Both are records of payments in different states. We could generalize both concepts and subsume them into a general nameless document that records the state of Payment. This document may switch between polymorphisms in step with the state of the payment it records. Thus, a paper check may be a payment instrument that also becomes a receipt after the bank endorses it. Indeed, checks, invoices, receipts, and other records of the payment event in different states are merely manifestations of this general, nameless document.

A payment, like any other object, may be aggregated. Thus, the payment against an invoice or receipt may aggregate payments for several items. Each payment also may be a partial payment. These partitions of Payment are compositions embedded and hidden in the relationship between a Payment and its documentation in Figure 2.18.[223]

Sometimes, we may not have the information that links a payment to individual line items. Then, all we can do is link it to the amount of the invoice or receipt. Sometimes even this may not be possible. We may have received payment that is not even explicitly linked to an invoice. Then, all we can do is to apply it to the payer's account as a whole. If the payer is unknown, the payer's account also will be Unknown. Information we receive afterwards, or standing instructions that are part of the terms and conditions, may help us allocate these gross amounts with more accuracy. Similarly, payments made by different payment instruments, and in different currencies, also may be rolled up into aggregates. The three partitions of the payment event—partial or full payment, payment instrument, and payment record—are independent of each other. This independence, and the ability it gives us to slice and dice partial or full payments as we apply them to the items for which they are paid, lays the groundwork for being responsive to customer needs in a global, multicurrency, and yet integrated environment. It gives us this agility by being equally flexible in recording and measuring the financial impact of payments in different currencies, with different levels of accuracy on multiple aspects of a complex business. It is a topic we will hold in abeyance until we discuss patterns of funding later in this chapter.

Provisioning the Product

We have recently discussed why Transfer of Rights is a Negotiation and therefore an Exchange. An exchange of information needs a route. When the exchange also envisions moving the product or service to make it accessible to a user (who may or may not be the buyer), it also must be conveyed on a route. This route need not be the same as the route for exchange of information in the negotiation, but it is still a Route, and a Distribution Channel. Figures 2.18 and 2.14 articulate these facts. Indeed, the transfer of possession event in Figure 2.18 may (optionally) include in its terms and conditions, information about the route by which the product or service

---

223. Recognizing that *Payment* is linked to its documentation in this way would have saved Jim and John of Box 8 much trouble, as they tailored their business processes to fit changes in their business environment. Recognizing the Universal Perspective would have helped them to be responsive, rapid, flexible, and *correct*, all at the same time, and all the first time around.

will be conveyed to the user. Thus, it is linked to a distribution channel transitively through Shipment. It follows that the Market Segment in Figure 2.18 will have two potential dimensions in terms of distribution channels—those used to communicate while negotiating or sealing the negotiation, and those used to physically ship the business product to its users. See the discussion in Box 24 to understand how Market Segment is derived from the rights transfer event in Figure 2.18.

Indeed, a shipment might aggregate many products, sometimes from different parties who might share the same vehicle (or the shipping mechanism) in order to realize economies of scale. It might consist of multiple consignments with different destinations (nodes) on the route. There may be complex rules about what kinds of products may be combined in a shipment, and what routes are permitted for which products. We discussed these rules with Figure 2.14. They have been hidden in Figure 2.18 to minimize clutter.

Provisioning does not always imply conveyance of resources on a physical route; it is a more general concept. The intent of provisioning is to give the user access to the purchased products and services. Access also might involve setting up the user on the system. For example, a firm might sell settlement and trading services for financial securities. It also might provide the software for trading and settling securities. Customers who subscribe to the firm will receive the software to enable them to connect with the firm's database of securities up for sale. However, customers also must be activated and registered in the firm's customer database before they are allowed to trade. Thus, to access the service, customers must be activated (in the computer system), and users must receive the physical shipment of software. They are subprocesses that, in conjunction, give the user access to the purchased service. Thus, the provisioning and conveyance composite of Figure 2.18 is more generic than conventional concepts of shipment, transportation, and distribution of physical goods. It is a supertype that subsumes physical transportation and more. Figure 2.18 makes this clear.

Indeed, any Planned Amount may be partitioned in many different ways. Estimation is a frequently used polymorphism of the planning process. Estimated Amount is a generic polymorphism of Planned Amount. Expectation is a kind (polymorphism) of Estimation. Thus, Expected Amount is a polymorphism of Estimated Amount. For instance, a fund might accumulate payments made by checks that have not yet cleared, because the amount is expected when the checks clear. The fund is then a fund of pooled Expected Amounts. Estimated Fund Amounts, like budgeted, pledged, forecasted, and expected funds, are all polymorphisms of their generic parent, the generic Planned Amount.

A product cannot be used unless it is provided, although the converse is not true. A product may be provided, but may not always be used. This is articulated by the subsetting constraint between business product use and business product provisioning in Figure 2.18. Indeed, the provisioning of the product is a special case, a polymorphism, of the generic provisioning of a resource that permits its use. The use of a resource, as we saw in our discussion of Figure 2.16, is through one or more tasks. The use of a resource by a task is contingent on the input process (see Box 30).

The input process provisions a resource for use by a task, and the use of the resource is contingent on it. The provisioning relationship in Figure 2.18 is a special case, applicable to a resource that is a business product, and one in which task information may or may not be missing. Similarly, the Task(s) were "unknown" in the derived and summarized "use" relationship in Figure 2.16.

Figure 2.18 also articulates the fact that a person or organization may support another. It is a form of collaboration, as discussed in Section 2.1.1. That support may be in the context of a product. The support person or organization may support a product for another person or organization; indeed, the relationship does not preclude self–support, it is reflexive on Person/Organization.[224] This support relationship between Person/Organization and Business Product is a polymorphism of the more general Manage relationship between Person/Organization and Resource in Figure 2.16.

The Market and Its Demand Chain

Features of products are inherited from Resource (see feature in Box 30).[225] Like the resource groups of Figure 2.15, features may form feature groups. Thus, the color of a car is its feature, and so are its financing options, some of which, for instance, might be only offered with a burglar alarm, another optional feature of the car. Inclusion or exclusion of features in a group restricts membership of the group. It tells us what features may or may not be bundled together in the product. A restricted group has fewer degrees of freedom than an unrestricted group (see Box 30). A group that restricts membership is therefore a subtype of the group that does not (see Box 14). On this basis, Feature Group is a subtype of Feature, and therefore a feature with an identity of its own. Feature Group will inherit all features of feature in Figure 2.18, and from the Metamodel of Knowledge in [337].

Features of products and services should satisfy one or more Market Needs that flow from the goals of the communities in Box 21. Naturally, a business product should have features that make it useful to one or more of those communities (a dictum often followed in the breach, as lessons learned from failed products show). However, some stakeholder needs may be insatiable, or unsatiated—there may be no features that address them. Conversely, a feature may have little value; it may satisfy no stakeholder need. It will then be a candidate for reengineering or a target of obliteration. The many-to-many relationship between Feature and Stakeholder Need also implies that many features may address a single need, and some features therefore may be redundant. Those also could be targets of product reengineering. Optionality of the many-to-many relationship between features and market needs in Figure 2.18 flows from features that address no market need on one hand, and market needs not addressed by any feature on the other.

Sometimes, a feature may be of worse than marginal value. It might be a hindrance and cause dissatisfaction. Removing the feature then will increase the value

---

224. If the person/organization supports the product for all organizations, then the "value" of the organization in the relationship will be "Don't Care." See "Value" in Box 30. Box 51 on our Web site has more detail.
225. Module 5, Section 3, discusses *Feature* under product reengineering. Also see Module 6, Section 2, Box 62, and Figure 107, all on our Web site.

of the product to the constituency it serves. For instance, constraining a check to be a paper document can increase handling costs and delay payment, as it is physically transported from payer to payee, whereas an electronic payment might be faster and cost less to process. Features like these are also candidates for reengineering and innovation.[226] Often the challenge in process and product design is to balance the needs of the communities in Box 21. Features that satisfy one community or group of communities might be a hindrance to one or more of the other communities.

A Market Segment shares these needs and satisfactions. The NAG object in Figure 2.18 is a higher order relationship, an associative object that is the basis for this market segment. Box 24 shows that Market Segment is a Borel Object. Box 24 discusses how every association implies a corresponding Borel Object. It describes the laws that connect these Borel Objects to the associations from which they were derived. A market segment is a polymorphism of a Borel Object. It is also a core concept at the heart of the Demand Chain, and the foundation of useful innovation. It is a concept used and reused all the time in business, and a component of knowledge that resides in the Universal Perspective—a component that grows from the Borel Object in the Metamodel of Knowledge.

Forging and Positioning Products

In information space, a product or resource is the collection of its features.[227] The products of Figure 2.18 could be individual services, such as an insurance policy; individual physical items, such as a car; packages of several services or physical items bound into a product; or even services packaged with tangible physical items, such as a car with a warranty and 24/7 customer service, or a computer with information on upgrades or new features, membership of chat rooms or communities of interest, and so forth.

Forging a resource (and therefore its polymorphism, the business product) involves forging its features and tying them to a single object. Of course, we may also do this by combining and packaging resources into a composite object. Add temporal information to this relationship in Figure 2.18, and it becomes the Make process. Make is not necessarily restricted to the production of a single feature; it may produce many. Conversely, there may be different processes that can all produce the same feature. This is why the relationship between a Feature and Process is many-to-many in the figure. It tells us that there may be many different ways of producing the same feature. See details in Module 5, Section 3, on our Web site, under supply chains. See also the SCOR supply chain model on our Web site.

Turning a resource into a product involves positioning it in the marketplace as a desirable product with a proposition—a resource that helps satisfy a Market Need. It amounts to attaching the right qualifications and credentials to the resource to create the right beliefs, which should be aligned with its features and satisfactions, in target market segments (a state of Market Segment). We discussed qualifications and belief in Section 2.1.1. The processes that change a resource into a business product consist of processes that change the state of a market segment to a target segment; change the state of a resource to a business product; obtain the necessary credentials; and create the requisite qualifications and beliefs, which are all a part of

---

226. Box 62 on our Web site discusses *Feature* in more detail, with an example of product reengineering.
227. Module 6, Section 2, on our Web site discusses the metamodel of *feature*.

the demand chain. The demand chain analyzes customer needs, designs products and services to satisfy those needs, and positions the product in the market (see Figure 2.22).

Several processes might be involved, such as market and consumer research that leads to product designs, user communications, product positioning, and others. The features of the sale event (the NAG in Figure 2.18) address the basic features that constitute the state space of a market. Market research and industry experience can enhance these features and elaborate on them. Market research gathers data about the marketplace and can identify the dimensions, beliefs, attitudes, concerns, and habits that influence consumer or buyer behavior. Product engineering parameters also may be added to the list. These parameters and features define the dimensions of the state space that constitutes the market. Regions of the state space may be carved into segments, depending on the homogeneity of needs, and the cohesiveness of patterns in this state space. Simple intuition and common sense, or complex techniques and pattern recognition methods, may be employed.[228] The state space of markets was discussed in Section 2.1.1 (see Markets and Market Segments, Boxes 24 and 25).

Positioning a product also may involve special promotions, events, and a host of other processes. They are details that have been hidden in Figure 2.18. They would all link to the NAG, and thereby provide the grist for more dimensions of market space and market segments (see Box 24). Thus, for example, we might measure the impact of specific kinds of promotions on specific kinds of products, or we could measure the cost of promotions versus their impact on revenues by geographical footprint, and so forth. The possibilities are enormous and varied, but they are all framed by the pattern in Figure 2.18.

Integrating the Supply Chain
Taken together, buying, selling, delivering, and forging products translates to "Supply Chain" (see Module 5 and "Supply Chain Standards" on our Web site).[229] Supply chains are polymorphisms of Figure 2.18. The flow of time, added to the relationship between Resource Group and Resource, corresponds to the Make process at the heart of supply chains. The flow of time, added to the relationship between Feature Group and Feature, bundles features that may or may not be offered together, or may mutually interact or have synergies that also are features of the resource. Business Product inherits these properties from Resource (see Figure 2.18).

Giving the user (or customer) access to the product as stipulated by the terms and conditions of NAG amounts to delivering the product. It becomes the delivery process when we add information on cycle times and temporal sequences to this relationship. See how the Universal Perspective generalizes the meaning of "delivery" under Provisioning the Product. Sourcing processes are polymorphisms of the generic input process in the Metamodel of Knowledge, delivery processes are

---

228. Chapter 4, Section 1, in [337], addresses the architecture of patterns and pattern recognition.
229. Chapter 5, Section 2, in [337], describes supply chains. See "Supply and Demand Chains" on our Web site. The SCOR supply chain under Supply Chain Standard describes polymorphisms of processes for sourcing resources, making, and distributing products. See also the discussion under Figure 107 on our Web site.

polymorphisms of the generic output process, and Make is a polymorphism of the generic transformation process in Box 30.

Figure 2.18 tells us that resources may be combined into resource groups. When different firms are responsible for different resources in a resource group (e.g., services, warranties, physical items with engineered features), which are then joined into a cogent package offered in the marketplace as an integrated business product, then we get complex and dynamic supply chains. Rosettanet and the Netmarket supply chain models are examples, described under "Supply and Demand Chains" on our Web site. All supply chains flow from the Universal Perspective, which is their common home and the immutable anchor for things dynamic and things that must flex. This section has made that clear.

Fund and Payment

Business is about creating value. Funds measure value. Funds are central to the business of business. Our focus now will shift to funds and payments. A Fund may be a pool of money. Pools of money are also known as Financial Accounts. Financial Accounts classify Fund by purpose, product, place, and other features. Payments are also funds. They are funds in motion. Payments are often the last leg of an exchange.

Payments and Receipts

Money is pure information about economic value (see Fund at the beginning of this chapter). Pure information only can be manifest when it is associated with a physical token. See details in Chapter 4 in [337]. See also Box 38 on our Web site. The exchange of value needs a token—a symbol to be manifest in the physical world. This token is the Payment Instrument of Figure 2.19. It might be a check, paper currency, gold, or any other widely accepted medium of exchange. To be accepted, it must be qualified as such. People and organizations must believe that it will be honored, and will actually transfer economic value (funds). Figure 2.19 articulates this. This belief is usually anchored by some kind of credential. For instance, banks guarantee letters of credit, credit or debit cards and demand drafts, and the federal government guarantees the money it prints, and so forth. An ordinary check, of course, is not certified by anyone but its signatory(ies).

An exchange may be barter. We discussed exchanges in Section 2.1.1. When the exchange is underpinned by a token that conveys compensation for goods or services transferred, it is an instrument of payment. Payment may be an outgoing or incoming payment. Incoming payments are sometimes called Receipts. However, as we have seen, the payment event is distinct from Receipt, the document. This distinction must be maintained at all times in the Universal Perspective. This classification of payment into outgoing and incoming payments is based purely on the perspective of the payer and payee. If we switch perspectives, the incoming payment will become an outgoing payment, and vice versa. We discussed this in Section 2.1.1. For this reason, when payments are accumulated in pooled funds, incoming payments are balanced by a contrafund that reflects the same payment from the perspective of an outgoing payment. Figure 2.20 shows that it is a special case, a polymorphism of the pattern in Figure 2.19, that accumulates payments in pooled funds, also known as Financial Accounts. It is a common accounting principle dubbed "double-entry bookkeeping."[230]

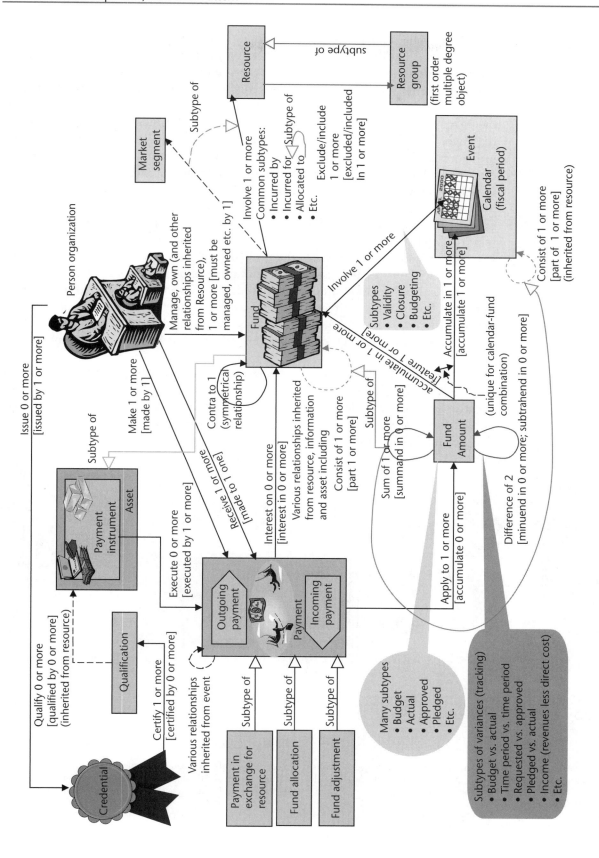

Figure 2.19   Patterns of funding.

Thus, when a payment is applied to, and accumulated in, an accounting fund that conforms to Generally Accepted Accounting Practices (GAAP), it also must be applied to the contrafund. Figure 2.19 does not show this graphically in order to minimize clutter, but Figure 2.20 shows this rule. The pooling of payments in funds in Figure 2.19 is a generic practice that need not always conform to the GAAP. Payments may be pooled in funds to informally monitor business activities. This is why the lower bound of the generic relationship that applies Payments to Fund Amounts in Figure 2.19 has been shown as one (i.e., a payment must be posted into at least one fund). However, if it is a financial accounting transaction that conforms to GAAP, this lower bound will be two. The transaction will post the expense or revenue payment to a pair of contrafunds. Figure 2.20 makes this explicit. This kind of application of a payment to fund amount is a special polymorphism of the generic relationship in Figure 2.19. It is a financial accounting relationship, which becomes a transaction and a process when the flow of time is also considered. We will return to it when we consider processes for accruing expenses and revenues later in this section. Note also that different books of accounts are sometimes needed for different purposes. For instance, different roll-up hierarchies may be attached to each view of Organization in Figure 2.13(b). Then, the same payment may be posted in different pairs of contrafunds—each pair a different partition of Fund, in a different book of account.

Allocation of value in terms of costs, revenues, or other kinds of funds, also could be considered kinds of payments.[231] Allocated value is a subtype of Payment, because it is an attribution of economic value that transfers value from one class of pooled funds to another. It is a kind of payment that is independent of payments that spring from the direct commercial exchange of goods or services. The two

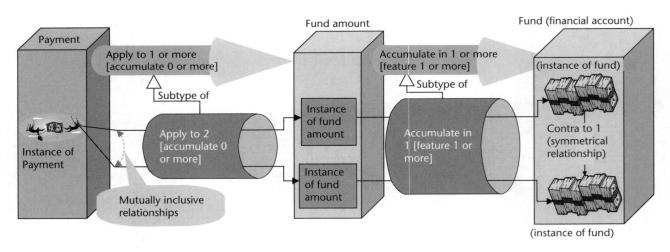

Figure 2.20   Double-entry bookkeeping.

230. The GAAP, which is an acronym for Generally Accepted Accounting Practices, a set of accounting principles accepted by Certified Public Accountants (CPAs) in the United States, has more detailed rules, but those are beyond the scope of this book. Interested readers may refer to [134, 137–139, 142], and the links therein, or to several publications on accounting practices freely available in the marketplace, for more information.
231. Module 5, Section 3, on our Web site, discusses allocation under "Added Value" and "Activity Cost."

kinds of payments are different partitions of the generic payment event of Figure 2.19, just as is partitioning Payment into incoming and outgoing payments. Similarly, adjustments are payments that correct perceived inaccuracies in a pool of funds. For instance, corrections to compensate for incorrect or cancelled transactions, reversals, write-offs, and the like are often accounted for by adjusting the pooled value in an accounting Fund. Note that some payments may have negative amounts, such as downward adjustments for returned goods, write-offs, and so forth.[232] Figure 2.19 shows each of these common classes of Payment. They are all funds in motion between classes of Funds. Each is featured by the quantum of funds being transferred between classes of pooled and summarized funds.[233]

Hierarchies of Funds

A Fund is pure information on economic value. Funds may consist of other funds. It is a fact inherited from Resource. Funds may be pooled in hierarchies of funds that roll up and summarize the net economic value of their constituent funds. A fund, like any resource, may simultaneously belong to several hierarchies (see Box 11).

A fund is described by its purpose and its features. These features may be relationships with people, business products, goals, and so forth. For instance, a fund might carry information on who (which person or organization) incurred the expense (or earned the revenue), what it was for, why it was incurred, and so forth. The fund might be a budget (i.e., a polymorphism of Plan and Fund), actual expenditure (or revenue), and so forth. These are all different states or classes of funds. Figure 2.19 has a few typical examples. The quantum of a fund is evaluated in terms of its amount. The amount of a fund, unlike the money domain it maps to, is an object with states. For instance, a line item in a budget is an instance of a fund with an amount for every budgeted period. Each time slice is a fund, which is an instance of the class represented by the line item. The line item in turn is an instance of the category(ies) it rolls up into. These temporal instances also may be considered the planned state of the fund at those times. Each is a time slice.[234] The time slice (technically called a fiscal period in financial accounting terminology) and the category together uniquely identify the amount. Figure 2.19 shows this.

Date-Time is a difference scaled domain (see Box 30, under Domain), and time periods are ratio scaled differences between times. Chapter 4, Section 3, in [337], discusses how the Metamodel of Knowledge "knows" this. See "Metamodel of Domain" on our Web site. A time slice may be a part of another, just as a class of funds may be a part of another, inherited from Resource [see Figure 2.11(a)]. For instance, a line item in a budget may have an annual amount earmarked for the purpose. The line item also may have monthly amounts earmarked for the same purpose. Naturally, the monthly amounts must roll up into the annual amount, because a month is a part of the time period we call a year. Figure 2.19 shows this. The summation of fund amounts may be by time period, or by class of fund.[235] Rules 5(b) and 5(c) of Box 16 make clear that we cannot sum across partitions, and that we may only sum amounts of subtypes (or instances) in the same partition. Otherwise, we

---

232. Readers interested in more information about accounting adjustments may consult [136].
233. Transferring funds between people or organizations also changes the classification of the fund in terms of its possession (or management). Thus, payments between people and organizations also may be considered transfers of funds between different classes of funds.
234. Chapter 2, Section 2, in [337], describes how object instances are time sliced into states. See Figure 22 on our Web site.

could end up by accumulating the same amount multiple times in a summation (as evident from Figure 2.21). Thus, these rules, normalized by domains, ensure that amounts in different roll-up hierarchies stay consistent with each other. Furthermore, these rules ensure consistency between roll-up hierarchies by class of Fund, or by time period for a given instance of fund, or by a combination of both.

The summing of individual amounts in a hierarchy of funds is a polymorphism of the fact that funds may consist of other funds. Box 31 tells us why, and Figure 2.19 articulates this fact, inherited from the logic of ratio scaled domains and polymorphisms of the fact that one object may be a part or an instance of another.

Differences between amounts also are a polymorphism often used to track the similarities of fund amounts, or to compare intent with reality. Figure 2.19 shows this, but leaves out the fact that differences are subtypes in a different partition of the same objects as sums. This structure was hidden in Figure 2.19 to avoid clutter.

Patterns of Allocation
Funds may be allocated to other funds in any arbitrary way, provided that the constraints imposed by the rules in Box 16 are followed, and that incoming payments are balanced by a contrafund that reflects the same payment from the perspective of an outgoing payment. It is a common accounting principle dubbed "double entry bookkeeping," which we discussed under payments.

Most allocation methods involve either dividing the amount to be allocated equally between the funds to which it is being allocated (e.g., by allocating a fixed amount to each fund, or by dividing a fixed amount equally between accounts), or prorating the allocation in proportion to some ratio. The ratio may be set arbitrarily or calculated. Calculated ratios are based on features of object classes, such as population (e.g., numbers of widgets sold), amounts (e.g., fund amounts), and so forth. These ratios are often based on enumeration of object instances and the

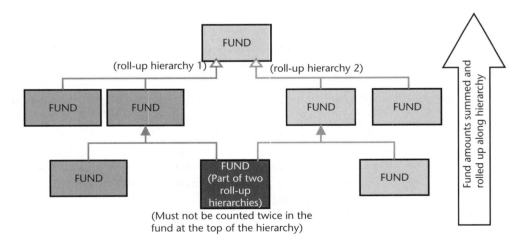

Figure 2.21 A Fund may belong to several roll-up hierarchies simultaneously.

235. The complete set of parts, taken together, expresses the whole, and hence, collectively, the aggregate is a subtype of the whole (Box 14). Rules 3 and 4 of Box 16, in conjunction with this fact in Box 14, enable the Metamodel of Knowledge in [337] to "know" that a complete set of ratio scaled values that constitute a whole may be rolled into the whole by summing them up. See Box 31.

Box 31: The Paradox of Sums and Differences

A summarized fund is a stock theme—a topos. To many readers, it will seem that the pooled fund, which sums the amounts it pools from its constituent funds, is a supertype of the funds that it pools, because it contains less information than its constituents. The constituents are the details that elaborate on the pooled summary. Reality contradicts this. The pooled fund is the subtype, and its constituents are its multiple parents. To understand why, we must understand that a sum has no independent existence; that is, it is derived from its summands. Therefore, we cannot consider the sum in isolation. We also must consider its relationship with its summands. A subtype is a polymorphism of a part (see Box 12). The domain of sums is a subtype of the domain that it summed because each sum also implies, through its inverse, all the quantities that were summed to produce it (Chapter 4, Section 3, in [337], on ratio scaled domains). The topos of sums carries this information within it. The automated systems we implement often ignore this information. Without it, we cannot drill down to see the constituents of a sum. Figure A makes this clear. The topos of sums carries information on its constituent amounts as well as the meaning of arithmetic summation. It has more information than the domains that were summed. The sum is the subtype. Thus, the subtyping relationship in Figure 2.19, which asserts that the summation of amounts is a subtype of the relationship that makes funds consist of other funds, is consistent with Box 12, which asserts that a subtyping relationship is a polymorphism of the Part of relationship. Summation is included in that rule. It is an inclusion polymorphism that occurs when ratio scaled information is involved.

Sums and Differences convey more information than their constituent amounts.

The topos of differences is similar to the topos of sums. Rule 3 of Box 16 tells us this.[236] Chapter 4, Section 3, in [337], on ratio scaled domains tells us why. We discussed the tracking process in Section 2.1.1. The difference

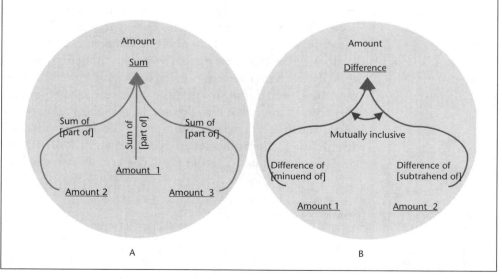

A   B

31

between amounts is a subtype, a polymorphism of the generic proximity metric of Figure 2.5. Differences between fund amounts are also fund amounts, but these funds are now tracking funds, such as objects used to measure deviations from budgeted amounts, or growth/shrinkage of like amounts between time periods, and so forth. Indeed, items such as income and profit also are a polymorphism of funds that track. For instance, income tracks revenues against direct cost, and Profit tracks Income against total cost. Figure 2.19 asserts this with examples. Figure B in this box shows the corresponding instance level structure. It is clear from Figure B that the topos of differences carries within it the drill-down capabilities to show how these differences were derived, just as the topos of sums had drill-down capabilities to show the constituents of each sum. These kinds of derived funds also can lead to objects that use other kinds of tracking metrics, like percentage growth or proportionate differences that map to the domains of growth (see Chapter 4, Section 3, in [337]). Performance measures recommended by GAAP are in [140–142].[237] These facts, along with drill-down and analytical capabilities, are common to objects that have ratio scaled attributes, and are normalized in the corresponding domains of sums, differences, and growth.[238]

proportionate populations of subtypes in the class, or on the proportionate value of some class level attribute of the subtype (e.g., sales volumes) compared to that of the overall class. For instance, the cost of heating a building might be allocated to individual departments in the ratio of the floor space they occupy. In this case, the object class is Construction (see the section on polymorphisms of physical objects in Section 2.1.1), and the feature in question is floor space. The subtypes of this object class are the parts of the construction occupied by different departments. Rule 5 of Box 16 frames the rules for computing these kinds of allocation ratios in a consistent, nonoverlapping way [see especially Rules 5(f) and 5(g)].

These rules protect against multiple overlapping allocations of the same amount. However, in some cases, the same expense may be allocated, or the same revenue recognized, multiple times when the performance of people or organizations is being measured. For instance, if multiple departments are involved in winning a new customer, management might determine that corporate synergies will be best promoted if each department is given full credit for entire revenue stream from the new customer, even if it means that the same revenue is counted multiple times. Contrast this with an approach that divides the revenue stream between departments in some ratio, and does not permit overlapping allocations and double counting of revenues. Overlapping allocations focus more on metrics for motivating and governing teams, and less on accounting accuracy. They are, strictly speaking, not accurate measures

---

236. Differences, or gaps, between amounts are framed by Rules 3, 7, 8, and 9 of Box 16.
237. Performance measures recommended by GAAP are in [140–142].
238. Quotients are rates. For example, the ratio of last year's sales to this year's, the ratio of prices last year to those this year, and growth rates in terms of percentages. They all map to the domain of quotients. The domain of gaps is ratio scaled for ratio and difference scaled domains. *Quotients of domains of gaps with other ratio scaled domains measure rates of change* and are domains of growth. Note that domains of change/growth do not always mean growth or change over time. (Details are in Chapter 4, Section 3, in [337].)

of Fund Amount, and overlapping revenues must not be included when the revenues generated by each department are rolled up into the firm's total revenues. Otherwise, the same revenues will be counted several times. Our focus here is on Fund and its representation, not on methods for motivating staff. Fund is the ambit and scope of the pattern in Figure 2.19.

Common Subtypes and States of Funds

Funds always reference some resource or purpose. The characteristics of resource(s) involved are one basis for classifying funds. Figure 2.19 has a few common polymorphisms of how funds may involve resources. Polymorphisms of the involvement relationship between funds and resources are another basis for classifying funds. The resource involved may be a market segment. Market segments were discussed in Section 2.1.1, Box 24, and under patterns of buying and selling. From those discussions, it is clear that Market segments are Borel Objects. For the same reasons, aggregations of resources also may be Borel Objects. Thus, the pattern in Figure 2.19 involves Borel Objects. The Borel Objects give us an enormous amount of flexibility in measuring the financial impact, or in earmarking funds, for market segments and resource groups sliced and diced in different ways to facilitate management accounting and business analysis. For instance, revenues, budgets, and profitability may be analyzed by customer, by geography, by product or service characteristics, by promotional events and their characteristics, by products and services packaged together in different geographies, and so forth.

The relationship a Fund has with a resource or resource group, despite the enormous flexibility implied by this relationship, is merely one way of partitioning Fund. We also may partition funds based on the states or subtypes of Fund Amount. These partitions are independent of the partitions based on the relationship between Resource and Fund.

For instance, we recently discussed how a fund amount might be in a planned state. This is usually a Budget Amount, and the fund is then a Budget. As opposed to being a planned amount, the amount may have been incurred. It is then an Actual Amount. Budgets and Actuals may be in an Approved, Disapproved, or Pending Approval state. These are subtypes in a different and independent partition of Fund Amount, based on an approval process. Sometimes an amount may be pledged, but not actually paid into a fund yet. This is another common polymorphism of Planned Fund Amount. A Pledged Amount may be independent of Budget Amount. Pledged Amount and Budget Amount are subtypes in two different and independent partitions of Planned Fund Amount.

The composite process in Figure 2.18 provides the product or service to the user in the sense that the user gets access to the agreed-upon rights when the process culminates. Access does not always imply physical transportation of physical objects. For instance, you get access to an e-mail service when your account is activated. This process delivers the service to you. Shipping a product is only one method of delivering it. Bear this in mind when you use the Universal Perspective.

Figure 2.18 provides the leeway for the actual provisioning method from being different from that in the terms and conditions of the "NAG." Although the information content of the provisioning relationship between Person/Organization and

Business Product is identical to that of the provisioning object attached to the rights transfer event at the class level, the two of them need not be the same instance of the class. Figure 2.18 reiterates this.

We also may classify fund amounts based on the kinds of payments they accrue, and characteristics of those payments. Thus, there may be funds that accumulate or net allocated amounts, adjustments, direct costs, revenues, interest, and so forth.

Fund amounts also may be subtyped based on their relationship with Payment. For instance, funds may be marked open or closed. Payments may be accumulated in open funds, but not in closed funds. A fund amount may be flagged as unavailable for payout (e.g., outgoing payment), but open for accumulating incoming payments (e.g., checks pending clearance). A fund amount also may also lapse; that is, become unavailable or for all transactions (except perhaps the transfer and disposition of any residual amount). The availability of a fund amount to accept incoming payments is in a different partition from its ability to make outgoing payments. Of course, a fund may be termed "frozen" if it is rendered inoperative in both partitions.

A Fund, like any resource, may be a Baseline. Baselines are reference objects used by tracking processes. Tracking processes compare characteristics of that which they track against a reference object called the Baseline. They measure deviations in terms of a Proximity Metric. We discussed this in Section 2.1.1. The Baseline is a subtype in a different and independent partition from those we discussed above. For instance, different versions of a budget may be compared against a baseline budget. Similarly, Actuals may be tracked against a budget, in which case the budget is playing the role of the baseline.

A financial account (fund) may be deemed to start (i.e., be declared valid) from a given time, or may be within a time slot. The lapsing of a fund is one aspect of this kind of behavior. A fund deemed valid emerges into a valid state, and a lapsed fund becomes an invalid fund after it lapses. Like all states, the state of a fund or fund amount may occur only in certain time slots, or from certain times. Thus, the closure, lapsing, availability of, and other states of funds and fund amounts may be tied to a calendar of events. Figure 2.19 articulates this. This is a polymorphism of resource life discussed in Module 5 on our Web site.

The polymorphisms of Fund that we have discussed in this section are by no means exhaustive. They are the polymorphisms that we find most frequently. Fund is a fundamental polymorphism of the primal object that is of utmost importance to business. It belongs to the Universal Perspective, from which all perspectives flow. Each perspective or accounting model may have special rules, states, features, and polymorphisms of Fund, but they all will flow from the pattern in Figure 2.19.

Accrual, Deferral, and Interest on Funds

We know that some funds, like our savings accounts, earn interest, and that many of us pay interest on funds we have borrowed, like the mortgage loans on our homes. Both incoming and outgoing payments could be interest payments. Interest payments are a special polymorphism of Payment. Interest payments are special because they involve both a fund amount and the flow of time. It follows that the accrual of interest is a process (see Box 10). The relationship between Payment and Fund in Figure 2.19 is thus a process. The flow of time is hidden within it.

This relationship is actually a third-order relationship. It also involves the Fund Amount. That leg of the relationship has been hidden in Figure 2.19 in order to minimize clutter. The interest rate is also embedded and hidden within this relationship in Figure 2.19. It is a common pattern that most of us know well. The relationship in Figure 2.19 is a process and a ratio scaled rule (see Box 10). The interest may be compounded, so that each interest payment is the product of the interest rate and the amount accumulated in Fund amount at the time. It also could be simple interest, in which the interest payment is based only on the initial state of the fund. Both are polymorphisms of the generic relationship in Figure 2.19. Both polymorphisms are ratio scaled rules used and reused in many contexts, across several perspectives. The Universal Perspective is their home.

Sometimes funds and payments also might be insured, which is a fact inherited from Resource. Any resource may be insured against contingencies or perils. The contingency is an event. Insurance premiums also have similar features—time dependency, as well as possible dependency on the fund amount as it ebbs and flows in time. Insurance payments also may involve perceived risk. Frequently, the rules for calculating interest are reused to compute insurance payments, with interest rates inflated to account for risk. Indeed, these kinds of rules may be used to compute expected returns of projects and proposals (e.g., Internal Rate of Return and Present or Future Value calculations).[239] They are all polymorphisms of the same rule expressions that reside in the Universal Perspective, and each specialty area may reuse and tailor these rules to fit their requirement for information quality. The domains of information quality are in Box 30. They all are derived from the Universal Perspective.

Infusing the relationship between Payment and Fund Amount in Figure 2.19 with temporal information also leads to new polymorphisms of the process by which payments are applied to pooled Funds. These generic accounting processes are called Accrual Basis Accounting and Cash Basis Accounting. In the remainder of this section, we will discuss these two polymorphisms that are universally accepted by GAAP.

In accrual basis accounting, revenues are recognized when they are earned and either realized or considered realizable. Revenues are considered to have been earned when products are delivered or services provided, and they are considered to have been realized when the corresponding payment is received. Revenues are considered realizable when it is reasonable to expect that products or services provided will be paid for in the future. Expenses are accrued (recognized) in the period in which related revenues are recognized. In contrast, in cash basis accounting, revenues are recognized only when the incoming payment is received, and expenses are recognized only when outgoing payments are made.

Products and services may be prepaid (in part or in full), or payment might follow their provisioning. When we consider the flow of time, considerations of timing and synchronization create significant differences between the two accounting methods. When accrual basis accounting is used, revenues and expenses may be

239. Exhaustively listing all possible polymorphisms and inverses of rule expressions that support compound or simple interest/growth are out of scope. References [61, 310, 314] and several other publications on finance, pricing, and evaluation available in the marketplace have more details. A short presentation at http://www.swlearning.com/accounting/wolk/ppt/08.ppt summarizes issues related to financial return and risk.

accrued before payments are received (or made) because a product or service has been provided, and the payment is deemed realizable, although not yet realized. Similarly, for prepaid items, revenue and expense recognition may be deferred until the product or service is provided. On the other hand, when cash basis accounting is used, revenues will be recognized whenever the payment is received, and expenses will be accrued whenever a payment is made, regardless of when the corresponding products or services are provided.[240] These differences in timing may lead to significant differences in time-sensitive interest and insurance payments. Readers interested in more detail may refer to [135]. Thus, the infusion of time and temporal dependency into the application relationship between Payment and Fund Amount in Figure 2.19 leads to different polymorphisms of the financial accounting process.

Like the relationships in Figure 2.19, any relationship in the Universal Perspective infused with temporal information will lead us to a universal process. Having understood the universal object model in Sections 2.1.1 and 2.1.2, our focus must necessarily shift to its implications in terms of these universal processes.

Universal Processes and the Birth of Supply Chains

Universal processes emerge from the Universal Perspective, just as the Universal Perspective emerges from the Metamodel of Knowledge. Each object, relationship, and rule in the Universal Perspective leads to a universal process, as does every object, relationship, and rule of the Metamodel of Knowledge in [337]. Each event in the Universal Perspective is a Universal Process. We discussed how events lead to processes in Box 10. We discussed some of these under polymorphisms of Event in Section 2.1.1.

Every object must be created (or recognized/identified). The creation (or recognition/identification) of each object is also a universal process that can have several manifestations (polymorphisms). Each relationship in the Universal Perspective and the Metamodel of Knowledge also will become a process if it is infused with time. Each may have different polymorphisms in step with the information we add, and the features we attach (see Boxes 10, 14, and 21). All these processes are Universal Processes. The Universal Perspective and the Metamodel of Knowledge are the seminal patterns from which Universal Processes emerge. These processes are the components from which supply and demand chains are built.

A supply chain is a succession of interlinked activities, resources, and intermediate products needed to create and deliver products and services to consumers or end users. Several enterprises (also known as supply chain partners) may be responsible for different processes, resources, and intermediate products linked by the supply chain. Supply chains tie suppliers, producers, distributors, retailers, financers, warrantors, and others together into a process focused on bringing value to the end user of the product or service. Therefore, although the customer at the end of the supply chain is the end user, customers at other points in a supply chain might not

---

240. In terms of the *Exchange* event we discussed in Section 2.1.1, in accrual basis accounting we have a choice of accruing payments in corresponding Fund Amounts, either when the first leg of the exchange occurs, or when the exchange is complete. On the other hand, in cash basis accounting, we apply payments to requisite pooled funds whenever they occur, regardless of any exchanges in which they might participate.

be end users. For instance, customers of a confectionary manufacturer may be distributors or retailers, whereas the end users of a confectionary manufacturer are their customers.

An integrated supply chain has two parts (see Figure 2.22). The upper half is a chain of processes that add value to the product or service in order to generate customer demand, whereas the lower half focuses on making and delivering products and services to customers.

The upper half of the integrated supply chain addresses the satisfaction of customer needs that creates the demand for products and services. It is called a Demand Chain. The Demand Chain is where new products, services, and business propositions are developed based on market needs. Customers' needs, market segments, and product-service use is analyzed to create new product-service propositions and specifications. The demand chain is where providers of products and services awaken to new opportunity, embrace their vision of business, articulate missions, state their objectives, assert their intent in product markets of their choice, and articulate product-service requirements, specifications, and designs.

The lower half of the integrated supply chain produces and delivers products and services that were conceived and designed in the upper half. Sourcing and staging of resources, production, and delivery of products happens here. "Delivery" might involve physical transportation, or merely giving users access to services, software, or information (see Provisioning the Product, under Figure 2.18). The Demand Chain creates demand and the Supply Chain fulfils it.

Figure 2.22 An example of a supply chain.

We have seen how Make, Sell, and Deliver emerged from the pattern in Figure 2.18. Infusing temporal information into the Use relationship in Figure 2.18 will turn it into the Use process. Indeed, the pattern in Figure 2.16 does so via Task. Analyze is the aggregation of processes that identify instances of Market Need and Market Segment, as well as relationships between them (see Figure 2.18). The Awaken/Envision process in Figure 2.22 is the communication of this need to the right resources. It is a polymorphism of the pattern for conveying information in Figure 2.14, and the trigger for the next process in the cycle. Design/Improve maps to processes that identify features (including Feature Groups), and links them to Market Need (see Figure 2.18). Elaborating on the relationship between Feature and Market Need in Figure 2.18 will describe how a feature satisfies a Market Need, and will be a polymorphism of the relationship in Figure 2.18. Elaboration was discussed in Section 2.1.1. If some of this information involves temporal sequences, tasks, or timings, then the relationship metamorphoses into the process by which features satisfy needs.

Under Figure 2.18, we also discussed how the sourcing process flows from the concept of an Input Process. Figure 2.14 articulates some of the logistics involved. Processes that identify suppliers and forge supply agreements also may be embedded and hidden within the input process. These processes are polymorphisms of processes that identify tasks and resources in Figure 2.16, identify owners and mediators in Figure 2.18, and describe the forging of the agreement therein (see Figure 2.17). Temporal sequences, constraints, contingencies, process owners, and the structures of process maps might change between different supply chain standards. Each is designed to serve different markets, market needs, and constituencies,[241] but each is assembled from components in the Metamodel of Knowledge and the Universal Perspective (see Sections 2.1.1 and 2.1.2), albeit configured differently for their different constituencies. They all flow from the Universal Perspective and the Metamodel of Knowledge, which is its source.

"What is the substance, whereof are you made,
That millions of strange shadows on you tend?
Since every one hath, every one a shade,
And you, but one, can every shadow lend."

— William Shakespeare, *Sonnets* LIII

2.2 The Universal Perspective—Its Use and Abuse

We need the Universal Perspective because it integrates. It is the ultimate integrator because it unmasks universal meanings—meanings shared, used, and reused at the heart of business—and the shared understanding that drives it. Thus, it is the ultimate tool for integration of perspectives, processes, and systems. Its propensity to integrate leads to uses as varied as they are diverse.

---

241. Module 5, Section 3, on our Web site, discusses supply chain standards. See also "Supply and Demand Chains" on our Web site. As an exercise, you might try mapping the processes in each supply chain standard to processes, resources, and patterns derived from the Universal Perspective. It will help you understand how each standard is a polymorphism of the Universal Perspective.

2.2.1   Integrated Applications

The Universal Perspective normalizes business rules, which can help integrate business applications.

For instance, consider the constraints on location of resources that we discussed under Figure 2.14. Should a new regulation bar some kinds of materials from a geographical footprint, transportation routes would instantly recognize the constraint, and ensure consignments that consist of barred resources are not shipped to or through those places. Attempts to do so will lead to exceptions and the exception processes (see Box 30). Simultaneously, inventory control applications will recognize that inventories of banned resources cannot be stored in those geographical footprints. Exceptions will flag any banned resources in affected footprints, and will not be resolved until exception processes resolve these violations. Manufacturing applications also will recognize that banned resources cannot be made in the footprints from which they are barred, and violations will lead to exception events, addressed by exception processes.

2.2.2   Agile Systems and Processes

Normalized business rules lead to flexible systems that can adapt quickly under the pressure and turmoil of change. The example we just discussed showed us how. The change, made at the right place, can radiate through the business system, impacting what it must impact, and letting be what it must not be impacted.

The challenge is to build systems and automated business processes that are so agile that they will respond to business changes and innovations by automatically adapting.[242] In this book, we call these self-adapting systems "Knowledge Machines," to be discussed in Chapter 3.

2.2.3   Reusable Components and Validation of Business Processes

The Universal Perspective normalizes shared meanings. This leads to reusability. Thus, in the discussion in Section 2.2.1, an exclusion constraint between a Resource and a Place was a component and a pattern of information reused across logistical, inventory management, and manufacturing applications. This was an example of how the same components can fit very diverse business processes.

Reusable components of business knowledge flow from both the Metamodel of Knowledge and the Universal Perspective. The Universal Perspective is a polymorphism of the Metamodel of Knowledge. The Metamodel of Knowledge has the broadest, and hence the most widely used, components of knowledge. The most widely shared intelligence in the Metamodel resides in Domains (see Box 30); they are everywhere. The rules enforced by domains (see Box 16) validate the consistency of information. For instance, Rules 5(b and c) of Box 16 imposed the injunction against double counting funds (see Section 2.1.2 under Hierarchies of Funds). Other examples of how rules that flow from the Metamodel of Knowledge might be

---

242. A recent branch of mathematics called pi-calculus lays the theoretical foundation for automating the development of information systems from business process specifications. See [161]; the note on pi-calculus; [75–77]; publications in the section on agile processes and adaptive software in the References; as well as the discussion in Module 5, Section 3, "Crossing the Chasm—Business Process to Information System" (available on our Web site), also address automatic adaptation.

applied are: Rule 5(d) in Box 16 would flag inconsistent allocations that do not add up to 100 percent; Rule 8 would raise an exception when difference scaled values are summed to produce a meaningless quantity; and violations on lower bounds of Length and Mass domains would flag exceptions when negative lengths or masses occur (see Chapter 1, Section 5). Consider another set of complex rules that also may be automatically applied in diverse contexts. A bill of materials identifies parts in a subassembly, which also might be subassemblies of parts or of other subassemblies. The Metamodel of Knowledge would automatically flag an exception if any subassembly or part was already deemed (directly or indirectly) to be a part of the first, because Contained in is irreflexive (i.e., a polymorphism of the generic irreflexive relationship), although it is transitive with respect to itself (e.g., a subassembly that contains another subassembly also will automatically contain the parts of subassemblies in it). An irreflexive relationship is a polymorphism of a reflexive relationship. A composition adds information, therefore a composition of irreflexive relationships cannot be reflexive or idempotent. Part of is a polymorphism of Contained in (see Box 12), and inherits this property. See Box 10, and details in Module 5, Section 4, on our Web site. This behavior also would apply to other transitive compositions of irreflexive relationships like "ancestor of," which assert that a person may be an ancestor of another.

The Universal Perspective would add more business-specific rules. For instance, the presence of banned resources in a prohibited locale would raise exceptions, regardless of whether the locale is a vehicle, a mode of transportation, a route, a building, a tunnel, a Web site, or a part of the frequency spectrum (see Section 2.2.1). The Metamodel of Knowledge also has shared patterns for recognizing and resolving exceptions, which the Universal Perspective inherits. See Box 30, and details in Module 5, Section 3, under "Crossing the Chasm" on our Web site, "When rules are violated." Thus, the Metamodel of Knowledge and the Universal Perspective are instrumental in identifying common themes, including exceptions.

2.2.4 Alignment of Information Systems with Business Process

The Universal Perspective can help align information systems applications with business processes. This is because a universally shared business information architecture flows from the patterns in Section 2.1. Object, data, and process models all may be derived from those patterns. For instance, we have seen how supply chain integration is automatically supported by the information architecture in Section 2.1. Module 5, Section 3, on our Web site, under "Crossing the Chasm," has several examples of how information systems may be reduced to expressions of business processes and derived from them.

2.2.5 Enterprise Resource Planning and Supply Chain Management

The Universal Perspective can help vendors of Enterprise Resource Planning (ERP) and Supply Chain Management (SCM) systems, by providing a ready template that they can elaborate, customize, and build on, as they develop integrated information architectures supported by integrated data, object, and process models. Indeed, for these reasons, the Universal Perspective can help any developer of integrated systems, by providing a shared information architecture that will help integrate business processes and business systems, as in the example of resources barred by regulations from prohibited places that we discussed in Section 2.2.1.

2.2.6   Evaluation and Customization of Business Software

The Universal Perspective can be a test bed that helps users of systems or software products to identify gaps in the functionality of applications that they are evaluating. Constraints imposed too high in the hierarchy of polymorphisms or in the patterns in Section 2.1 may impose restrictions that are not shared universally. Missing structures also will imply missing business functionality.

For instance, between Figures 2.15 and 2.16, if we had attached the qualification relationship between Qualification and Resource to Person instead of to Resource, then we would deny the fact that resources (e.g., elevators) might have to be qualified, and may need credentials, before they are deemed fit for use. On the other hand, if we had attached the mandatory "record" relationship between Payment and Invoice in Figure 2.18 to Document instead, then it would imply that every document must record a payment—a patently false, and needlessly restrictive, assertion.

Note that the emphasis is on shared business functionality across multiple scopes. This is the most common business functionality, and therefore the functionality that integrates business. These functions are often those that profoundly impact the critical success factors of a business (see Box 1).

However, the Universal Perspective has limitations. For instance, it does not provide a style guide for user interface in terms of display windows or point and click functions, because the Interface layer in the Architecture of Knowledge is beyond its scope (see Figure 15 on our Web site). The Universal Perspective also might miss out on detailed, custom-built functions that are not commonly shared business practices. However, it does provide a framework for customization. Customization often involves imposing custom constraints in limited scopes, or creating special context-sensitive polymorphisms of the objects and structures in the Universal Perspective.

2.2.7   Customization Facility

We recently discussed how agility flows from the Universal Perspective. Easy customization is the hallmark of agility and adaptability. The Principle of Parsimony (see the endnote) should be a key to determining what patterns and polymorphisms need customization. New polymorphisms of objects or patterns in the Universal Perspective and the Metamodel of Knowledge should not be configured, unless customization is needed in order to normalize added features that cannot be normalized by the Metamodel of Knowledge or the Universal Perspective. This will optimize the resilience of processes, objects, and patterns (Liskov's Substitution Principle—see Mutability of Resources in Section 2.1.1, under Resource and its Polymorphisms).

Adding constraints and features (e.g., attributes, relationships, effects, compositions, elaborations, states, and so forth) to the "prefabricated objects" in Section 2.1 will create custom polymorphisms. These will inherit the shared features and behaviors of the original object and will add the special custom behaviors and features required in limited scopes (see examples in Box 21). For instance, if we turned the relationship between "buyer" and the rights transfer event in Figure 2.18 into a process by adding "event" to it (see Box 10), and if we constrained the repetition to two or more (a temporal polymorphism of cardinality—see Box 30), then we would create a polymorphism of "buyer" called "repeat customer."

Shared, universal behavior will not need to be rediscovered and renormalized each time custom processes or systems are required. This kind of "prefabricated normalization" in "prefabricated objects" and "prefabricated models" (see the patterns in Section 2.1 and the Metamodel of Knowledge) also will minimize the unintended impacts of customized features on other objects through the "rule tangling" mentioned in the prologue. Thus, the Universal Perspective can facilitate customization by facilitating adaptable and agile models.

2.2.8 Information Architecture

The Universal Perspective is information architecture, packaged; that is, a generalized template for normalizing shared data and features of objects. Customizing these patterns to fit a given scope or enterprise will suffice to define an information architecture (see Section 2.2.7). The Principle of Parsimony admonishes us to elaborate and add the minimum information required. Frequently, customization only will involve adding context-sensitive object names. For example, Business Product might become "Insurance Policy" in the insurance industry, or "Building" in the construction industry (see Box 9, and Figures 1.9 and 1.10). When this is not enough, the methods in Section 2.2.7 will be needed to elaborate on the Universal Perspective to fit a given scope. The metamodel [337] encapsulates the rules of elaboration. The tenet is that information may be added to the universal perspective in step with new learning to satisfy new requirements. The Universal Perspective is resilient and can adapt business processes and facilitate the automation of information systems [337].

Our discussion of supply chains at the end of Section 2.1 articulated how every object in the Universal Perspective signals the existence of a generic process that must make it. For instance, Coverage is a feature of an insurance policy. In most jurisdictions, innovative forms of insurance coverage must be conceived (proposed by the insurer) and filed for approval by a regulatory (government) organization, before it can be offered to customers. Each step establishes a state for a conceived insurance coverage. It elaborates on the condition of, and adds information to, the coverage that was conceived. It flows from a process. This process that elaborates on states of coverage is a fragment of a process map (i.e., a composition) that created this coverage. The overall process it elaborated on is a polymorphism of the generic process that created the product Feature of Figure 2.18. This is an example of how the patterns and relationships in the Universal Perspective are that can be detailed, and sometimes elaborated on, by compositions (see Box 10).

2.2.9 Database Integration and Data Normalization

The Universal Perspective provides a noncontext-sensitive template for normalizing shared features, including attributes of objects. As such, changes in data structures will be more stable than they can be with conventional methods that normalize data based on breaking up repeating groups. When new data must be included, or some kinds of data eliminated, repeating groups may change, and so may data structures based on normalizing repeated groups. Structures derived in this manner are unstable under the pressures of change (see the examples in the note on normalization). Changes in data structure cascade through information systems. It has unintended side effects, and requires changes in the very structure of the system and its underlying computer code. Current systems cannot adapt easily to changes of this kind. It is a fundamental source of conflict between business and the information systems built to support the business. Seasoned analysts and data administrators have often experienced this conflict.

Businesses face intense competitive pressure from the global economy, driven by new ideas and technology. They must flex, change, and innovate in order to survive and succeed, whereas the stability of its data structure is critical to the information system. The patterns and inheritance hierarchies in the Universal Perspective can complement and stabilize the hierarchies and objects obtained from normalizing data based on eliminating repeating groups.[243] This extends not just to data, but also to all features of business objects—relationships, constraints, and effects. Stable data (or object) structures not only will help stabilize the database, but also will simplify maintenance of the systems that use the database, which can make information systems more responsive to changing business requirements.

Typically, this would involve making the Universal Perspective the broker and translator of legacy models. It would mean mapping objects in a legacy data (or object) model to the patterns in the Universal Perspective. That map might split a legacy object in order to normalize behavior (e.g., the way Invoice was mapped to Event, Document, and Information in Section 2.1), or it might merge them by generalizing multiple objects and subsuming them into an object (or relationship) in the Universal Perspective. For example, Customer and Supplier might both be merged into Person/Organization. See the Principle of Parsimony in Section 2.1.1, under Mutability of Resources, and the note. This kind of merging also might introduce new capabilities into databases, such as the ability to answer the question: Which of my customers are also my suppliers? It also could lead to capabilities like the ability to compute net payments owed to these suppliers, which might simplify payment and realization processes with key customers and suppliers.

2.2.10 Integration of Legacy Systems

Normalization of data, behavior, and business rules can provide a hub that will be a road map for integrating legacy databases or applications. The recent discussion hightlights that mapping legacy data structures, constraints, and behavior to the Universal Perspective can turn it into a broker and interpreter between legacy applications. It can be the hub around which an integrated legacy spins.

2.2.11 Causal Analysis and Knowledge Management

In Section 2.1.2 and Box 31 (under patterns of funding), we saw how the Universal Perspective and the Metamodel of Knowledge provide the framework for drilling

---

243. Normalization of data by eliminating repeating groups has been described in the note and [305].

down from summary information. This is one kind of causal analysis. For instance, the publisher of a magazine in an integrated supply chain that includes the printer could drill down from overall publishing cost to printing cost, and then drill further from printing cost to find that the lacquering of printed pages to give them the requisite glossy finish contributes a disproportionate amount to overall printing cost. He or she might then determine that the glossy finish is not commercially viable.

Section 2.2.3 had other kinds of causal analysis. Forward and backward causal chains also support causal analysis. They are components of the Metamodel of Knowledge. Forward chaining is a form of causal analysis in which cause and effect are tracked along chains of associations, which are expressions of rules, to project or assess the end result and the impact of each rule. Rules are polymorphisms of relationships (see Box 10). Backward chaining tracks a result back to root causes along the inverses of rules. Forward and backward causal chains are polymorphisms of Path (Section 2.1.1).

Pattern recognition is another form of causal analysis. Chapter 4, Section 1, in [337], describes the universal features of Pattern. The freedom of the pattern (i.e., how different it may be, in terms of which features, before it is considered a distinctly different pattern) is the key to pattern recognition.

The dimensions of information quality in the Metamodel of Knowledge (see Box 30) frame the quality of pattern recognition, judgments of causality, and other assessments. For example, instances of the Market Segment in Figure 2.18 may be based on how the quantum or frequency of purchases tracks the (values of) features of the rights transfer event in that figure. For instance, the market may be segmented by the combination of business product (e.g., class of books), order amount (e.g., payment), and distribution channel (e.g., retail outlets and Web sites), if it is shown that these variables impact buying frequency most significantly.

2.2.12 Improved and Integrated Business Process Engineering (CAPE) and Systems Engineering (CASE) Tools

The Metamodel of Knowledge carries within it functional requirements and specifications for automated tools that can support the modeling of business processes as well as object and data models [337] (also see Modules 5 through 7 on our Web site). It normalizes rules about the encapsulation, normalization, and synthesis of Knowledge. Components in the metamodel seamlessly translate patterns into business processes, behavior, data, and information systems. Information systems become expressions of patterns of business knowledge and business processes. A process designer could use an automated tool based on the Metamodel of Knowledge to design a business process, and test and tune it to meet functional and performance requirements, with simulations and the power of inference already resident in the Metamodel of Knowledge. The tool could then automatically create matching information systems, with exception management processes and capacity plans matched to anticipated business volumes. Reference [337] and the modules on our Web site have the details.[244]

---

244. The automation of information systems development from business process specifications also has been addressed in [161].

The patterns and objects in Section 2.1 are "prefabricated" business objects and events (processes), forged from the Metamodel of Knowledge, which may be elaborated on by applying the laws articulated by the Metamodel (see the examples in Section 2.2).[245] The patterns in Section 2.2 would add value to the integrated CAPE-CASE tool, by providing prefabricated templates as starting points for process or systems design.

These "prefabricated" objects from Section 2.1 will support many common requirements even before users articulate them. For instance, telecommunications companies had traditionally provided telephone services directly to their customers. The customer's telephone number identified him or her. If the customer moved, the telephone number had to change. This made it difficult to track a customer's history, which could have helped the business in many ways. The pattern in Figure 2.18 clearly distinguishes the provisioning of a business product from its buyer. It tells us that the customer number and the telephone number should be distinct and different. Provisioning connects the customer to the telephone number through the agreement. The customer number then may also be used to track a customer's history, behavior, and movement. The patterns in Figures 2.17 and 2.18 also tell us that the selling of telecommunications services through intermediaries is an option. Indeed, when deregulation of the industry introduced competition, business processes were reengineered to support the sale of service through intermediaries. Thus, the pattern in Figure 2.18 anticipated requirements and facilitated innovation.

2.2.13   Business Modeling Standards and Language Design

The themes in Section 2.1 are standard themes, shared and reused all the time. Developers of integration, communications, and cross enterprise business standards, such as XML, BPML [63], standard ontologies, and Knowledge Reuse projects will find them useful (see References). Supply chain and enterprise integration frameworks flow naturally from the patterns, objects, and abstractions in the shared themes of Section 2.1 and the Metamodel of Knowledge.

Designers of business modeling languages, such as UML or BPML (for process modeling), could use the Metamodel of Knowledge to scope, encapsulate, and normalize requirements of business modeling languages and standards. The Universal Perspective, in Section 2.1, can augment these languages and standards with prefabricated "standard and generic" objects and patterns that can be customized to fit specific requirements. The metamodel describes the rules and operations for customizing and combining the objects in this book.

2.2.14   Prototyping and Continuous Improvement

The Universal Perspective is a generic business model. It can be the basis for an integrated prototype information system and business process model. The events and relationships in it describe universal business processes and relationships, and provide navigation paths between objects of different kinds. For instance, if we

---

245. Reference [337] describes in detail the Metamodel of Knowledge.

picked a consignment in Figure 2.14, we could track its route plan and the shipments of which it will be a part. From the Shipment, we can track conveyance vehicle(s) that will be used, and so forth. Alternatively, if we start with a transportation event, we could track the consignments it carries, and what their destinations would be.

Each object and relationship may be attached to views, windows, and other kinds of interfaces that provide query and navigation facilities between objects. The level of detail may be customized to fit the requirements by using the techniques discussed in Section 2.1 and this section and [337]. Features and polymorphisms may be added, and relationships and objects may be expanded into compositions and aggregates that can normalize and hold the requisite information. (Processes are a kind of relationship—see Box 10.[246])

The initial prototype would use the Universal Perspective augmented by the Metamodel as a starting point for object behaviors, features, business rules, and navigation. The Metamodel would contribute behaviors of different kinds of domains and other objects in it, and would provide the facility for customizing and elaborating initial prototype based on the Universal Perspective. See Section 2.1 for examples of object elaborations. Thus, the design of business processes, information systems, and the specification of user requirements need not start from scratch each time a process is developed, a system integrated, or software developed. Instead, they would start with the information in the Universal Perspective. This would accelerate development and reduce resource requirements.

Each industry and firm has its own special terms, rules, and nomenclature. The prototype could provide a facility that lets each user look at the prototype in his or her nomenclature, without losing the integrity of meanings across the organization or supply chain (see Box 9 and Figures 1.9 and 1.10).

2.2.15 Software Product Design

The resilience, adaptability, broad reusability, and customizability of the objects and patterns in the Universal Perspective will be valuable for software developers, including vendors of software products. Implementation of packaged products, especially those that require cross-departmental or cross-organizational integration, often requires customization. If vendors of packaged software use these patterns, then their products will be resilient and easily customizable. The pattern in Figure 2.18 is resilient. It will facilitate development of new products and services or upgrading the functionality of current software products for newer releases. For the same reasons, the Universal Perspective also will facilitate creation and maintenance of custom software developed in-house.

The Universal Perspective also will facilitate the development of adaptable software to support nonsoftware product, service, and process innovations. It will be relatively easy to add new product/service features or to reconfigure the structures of a product in the model in Figure 2.18. Thus, software that reflects this pattern in its internal design will be easy to reconfigure in support of new or changed products and services.

---

246. Chapter 2, Section 5, in [337], discusses attaching views to objects. See "Windows into Objects" and Figure 33 on our Web site. Module 5, Sections 1, 2, and 4, on our Web site, discuss customizing levels of detail to fit the requirements.

Thus, the Universal Perspective and the Principle of Parsimony will facilitate the design of resilient, adaptable, and tightly coupled business processes supported by agile and tightly integrated software.

2.3 Work Breakdown Structure

The Work Breakdown Structure of a systems development methodology is a process map. It describes the process for building business models and information systems. The Metamodel of Knowledge and the Universal Perspective, on the other hand, tell us what information we must gather to formulate business requirements. They do not tell us how to gather it. There may be many ways of gathering and storing this information. A detailed work breakdown structure is beyond the scope of this book. The intent of this section is to articulate how current approaches could flex to leverage the Universal Perspective.

Regardless of what process is used to articulate business requirements and develop systems, shared functional requirements and business rules are embedded in the Universal Perspective. The work breakdown structure will not have to elicit them again. Rather, it should accelerate the process by mining and using these rules and requirements as is, or by adding and building upon them.

Thus, the primary difference with conventional Work Breakdown Structures will be the use and configuration of shared components from an inventory, and the application of the Principle of Parsimony (see the note) to determine what may be used as is, and what must be customized, derived, or configured.

The approach also will address the derivation and customization of components required in limited scopes, functions, product lines, or geographies. The methodology will address the hierarchy of local repositories of shared knowledge and processes for managing, deploying, synchronizing, and exchanging components that are shared in different scopes. The work breakdown structure would distinguish between tasks that determine quantitative attributes (mapped to domains, which apply over all footprints) from tasks that determine units of measure in each footprint, and those that associate context-dependent or technology-sensitive accuracy and format requirements with these quantities.

The work breakdown structure will recognize that the Universal Perspective supports diversity by extracting the common essence of diverse meanings and nomenclatures. It will apply the Principle of Parsimony to reduce and control object proliferation and chaotic denormalization of behavior. It will thereby manage chaos in the midst of complexity. However, despite their resilience and support of diversity, the Universal Perspective and the Metamodel of Knowledge have important limitations. Their scope is limited to business meanings; and they do not address the styles of interfaces, the technology, and the logistics of storing, staging, transporting, displaying, or capturing information. However, they do address the issues that matter most to business. The value chain of Box 1 is front-loaded, and the resilience of the Universal Perspective will support innovation, improvement, change, responsiveness, business alignment, and the creation of business value.

Styles of interfaces, the technology, and the logistics of storing, staging, transporting, displaying, or capturing information may be added from the numerous models and standards already available. This has been focus of many conventional approaches in relation to component technology. The Universal Perspective and the Metamodel of Knowledge complement them.

The Universal Perspective will lend itself to both "waterfall" and iterative prototyping methodologies, such as the Rational Unified Process and Extreme Programming (see the section on Software Process in the References). The Principle of Parsimony will support lean approaches to business process design. Indeed, an iterative prototyping approach could start with the prototype in Section 2.2.15. The work breakdown structure might identify choke points in the business process and hone in on clearing those. It might gather volume information (e.g., data, defects, and transactions) at choke points to build a capacity plan that links computer and network capacity to business process load.

Automated processes and electronic repositories of Knowledge Artifacts are not absolutely essential for using and benefiting from the Universal Perspective, but automation would help leverage it far more effectively. Without automation, it will be difficult to track and elaborate on the enormous amounts of complex information we must store, analyze, mine, reuse, and elaborate on. An electronic repository of reusable knowledge artifacts will lie at the heart of any automated process. We will call this the Repository of Shared Knowledge.

2.4 The Repository of Shared Knowledge

The Metamodel of Knowledge and the patterns of Section 2.1 will lie at the heart of this repository of shared knowledge. However, by themselves, these patterns have little value. Their value is derived from facilitating agility and integration of diverse business processes and information systems. Prerequisites for effective use of the Universal Perspective (which includes the Metamodel of Knowledge) are the ability to easily find, format, view, manage, combine, configure, and customize patterns and objects in it to match business requirements. The scope and the functionality of the repository of knowledge artifacts in Figure 2.23 are derived from these requirements.

The same objects may be reused in different configurations and polymorphisms (e.g., those in Box 21 and Section 2.2). Configuring constraints, features, patterns, and polymorphisms from these objects will carve new meanings.[247] Therefore, the repository of knowledge artifacts will need a configuration management facility. The Metamodel of Knowledge carries within it the operations and specifications that can carve new objects (meanings) from those that are provided within the repository. Therefore, the Metamodel of Knowledge will lie at the heart of the repository, surrounded by facilities for finding, accessing, configuring, and customizing these objects.

In Section 2.2, we discussed how every combination of features and constraints imposed on an object results in a polymorphism with the potential for a different name. For instance, a Person/Organization in Figure 2.18 becomes a "Buyer" when tied to the Product Rights Transfer event in that role. This buyer also may be called

---

247. Reference [337] shows that the more we constrain a meaning, the greater its information content. See Boxes 43 and 62 on our Web site.

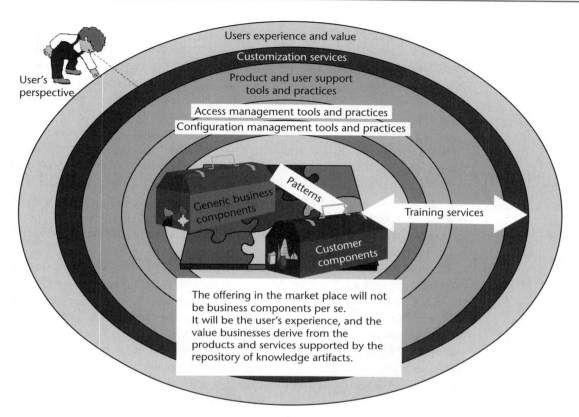

Figure 2.23   The Repository of Knowledge.

the "customer" or the "consumer" of the product in question. This is why the repository must provide a facility to impute and manage context and industry sensitive homonyms and synonyms for each object, its polymorphisms, and generalizations. Figures 1.9 and 1.10 and Box 9 describe the model for this. It belongs to the configuration management layer in Figure 2.23.

In order to use shared patterns and objects, users of the repository must be able to find and review them (i.e., the repository must be searchable). Each object, pattern, and combination of assembled configurations and objects must be easy to identify, access, review, understand, and use. The repository must therefore provide the tools to facilitate this, along with requisite services and training. These tools and services will mine and present patterns at the heart of the repository through the configuration layer. The configuration management facility will respond to requests passed to it through the access management layer in Figure 2.23. It will present requisite objects, patterns, and configurations of information to the access management layer. The access management layer will manage security, format this information, and present it to users in easily understood forms. The configuration management facility even may be context-sensitive as it interprets these requests for access to patterns at the heart of the repository. With the tools and services within these layers, users will be able to find reusable patterns, configure business models, design business processes, and automate the creation of information systems to support them.

The patterns at the core of Figure 2.23, and the layers around them, may comprise a packaged software product that automates the storage and manipulation of Knowledge Artifacts. To leverage this repository effectively, we will need a set of best practices for searching, configuring, and customizing the patterns in the repository. These best practices will be an integral part of each corresponding layer of Figure 2.23.

These products and practices must be managed and supported. Support involves version management; defect monitoring; repair and reconditioning; continuing improvement; planning, release, and distribution of new releases; and a host of other functions and services. The repository is a business product. It must be managed as all business products are managed. This will require support services, as well as the requisite tools and infrastructure to support these services. These tools, infrastructure, and product support services belong to the product and user support layer of Figure 2.23.

Competitive strength flows from differentiation of products and services from those of competitors. Customization supports this need. Customizing the objects at the heart of the repository will create new components. Each custom component will be a polymorphism of its generic parent. New constraints, new features, and new information will carve specialized new meanings. We have seen several examples throughout this book. The Customization Services layer in Figure 2.23 addresses this. Note that customization of the repository as a software product, as well as the policy that permits or bars it, resides within the Product Support layer, not the customization layer of Figure 2.23. The customization layer customizes the information content of the repository.

As we customize, constrain, add detail, and fit patterns into narrower scopes, we will obtain repositories valid only in limited contexts (see Figure 2.24). These "localized" repositories necessarily must work in tandem with the generic objects stored in repositories of broader scope. For instance, "Subrogator" is a role of Person/Organization in the insurance industry, in which the subrogator represents the claimant in recovering the insurance claim amount. Thus, it would reside in a repository that supports insurance functions. Indeed, as the repository and its use evolve in the organization, new polymorphisms and reusable patterns will be discovered. Configuration management practices will determine which of these patterns may be shared on a broader basis, and must therefore be "promoted" to higher-level repositories that support broader contexts. For instance, can a generalization of the "subrogator" role also apply to recovering amounts due outside of the claims area, or even in other industries? If so, under what names? Remember that the same object may be known by different names in different industries and organizations (see Box 9). Does the Principle of Parsimony justify distinguishing an insurance subrogator from the generalized role of "agent," "representative," "intermediary," or "proxy"?

Thus, applications may be created by combining, configuring, and customizing components from a repertoire of generic components, and then reused in several contexts, augmented by a repertoire of specialized components used in special contexts. Configuration management practices must continually review, allocate, adjust, and even retire these components and best practices that capture the collective knowledge of the organization and its operation. Figure 2.24 illustrates this architecture. The Architecture of Knowledge on our Web site elaborates on each layer in Figure 2.24.

Together, the layers in Figure 2.23 turn the abstract patterns at the heart of the repository into agile and adaptable business models, business processes, and integrated information systems that respond rapidly to user requirements in the tumult of business. The patterns in this book only can be translated into user experience and measurable benefits if the products and services in the layers of Figure 2.23 support them.

The extent of automation may vary. As we automate the repository more, our systems will become increasingly agile. At some point, we will cross a threshold, and the repository will transmute into the knowledge machine. In the Knowledge Machine, fully automated work breakdown structures will automatically reconfigure software and business processes as the knowledge machine responds to changes in the business environment, its rules, and its requirements. It is a vision for the future.

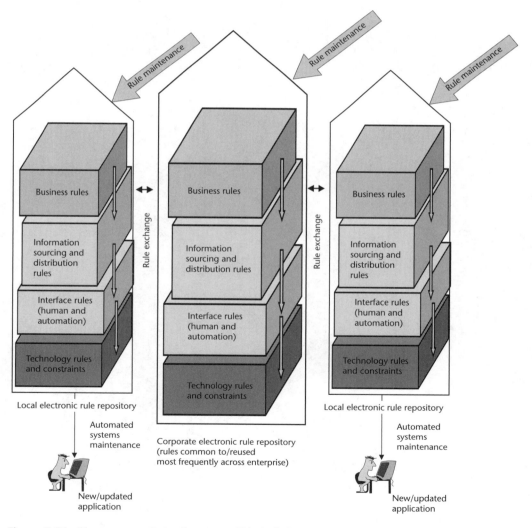

Figure 2.24   The new paradigm of automated knowledge.

CHAPTER 3

The Knowledge Machine: A Vision of the Future

"For I dipt into the future, far as human eye could see,
Saw the vision of the world, and all the wonder that would be;
Saw the heavens fill with commerce, argosies of magic sails,
Pilots of the purple twilight, dropping down with costly bales ..."

—Lord Tennyson, *Locksley Hall*, 1842

This chapter describes the kind of autonomous, self-adapting business models, business processes, and supporting software that can flow from a fully automated repository of Knowledge Artifacts. It discusses the functions, features, and characteristics required of these ultimate systems. It is a vision of business automation in the postindustrial age.

The Knowledge Machine is automatic and adaptive. Its currency is business meaning. The Knowledge Machine adapts to changing rules by configuring the meanings in its repository to match new requirements with new behavior and new polyorphisms. It creates new meanings from old in response to new rules and requirements. It seeks and changes its goals in response to changes in its environment; goals are also meanings.[248]

Meanings can be forged from meanings. We have seen how we can carve, constrain, sculpt, and join meanings, which are normalized patterns of abstract information, to create even more meanings. The Metamodel of Knowledge forged the rules, and the Universal Perspective was the conduit for substance. Together, they create the abstract pattern at the heart of the Knowledge Machine.

Thus, components of the Knowledge Machine can be made by the Knowledge Machine from its own components, and may be assembled by the same components. These components are meanings (i.e., patterns of abstract information) which not only create the ever-expanding ensemble of knowledge, but also forge its growing and numberless components as the ensemble expands. Box 21 has a few examples. It is a saga of a growing ensemble in information space that contains within it the meaning of Growth, and indeed the meaning of Saga itself.

However, the Knowledge Machine does not exist. It is only a vision—the paradigm at the end of a fully automated repository of Meaning, created from Knowledge Artifacts.

Long ago, the currency of computing machinery was hardware. Long before present-day computers made their debut, the logic within patterns of information

---

248. Module 5, Section 3, describes how the Metamodel of Knowledge transforms goals into processes aligned with goals. See "The Essence of a Process and the Goals of Business" and Box 56 on our Web site.

(i.e., the logic and data) was implemented directly with hardware in unit record machines, punched card sorters, timers, cams, levers, and switches. Today, the currency of computing is software—a mutable code that runs less mutable hardware. The hardware still exists and implements the behavior programmed into the software that operates it, but it is the software with which we interface. The currency of the knowledge machine is one more step removed. It consists of mutable meanings, intentions, and abstractions. In the Knowledge Machine, concepts must be expressed in code if they are to be stored in a repository and realized in an automated process. It is the concept and the meaning, not the software code, that will provide the window to its environment and the interface with its users. Just as software operates the hardware that implements it, the abstract concepts in the knowledge machine will be implemented in software, but the currency of the knowledge machine will not be coded software. The currency will be mutable meanings—the mutable knowledge that will operate and write mutable software to express itself.

Box 32: Adaptation of Knowledge   **32**

We have seen how meanings assimilate new information and transform themselves into richer meanings derived from the old. We have seen how new processes, structures, and patterns of information grow from the old. In Chapter 2, we have seen how the Universal Perspective is a seminal pattern, and the seed from which new structures, patterns, and practices can grow and adapt, in step with added information, new features, and constraints of different kinds.

The Universal Perspective is a pattern that underpins our understanding of business. It is a pattern of information, a scope, and a context. The Universal Perspective is a shared pattern of understanding; therefore, the Universal Perspective is a pattern that connects. It is also a pattern that adapts as it integrates. The Universal Perspective and the Metamodel of Knowledge will be the patterns that will drive the heart of the Knowledge Machine, the fountainhead of self-adaptive business processes and self-adaptive, autonomous software.

The Universal Perspective underpins a dynamic architecture—one that can change in step with new information and new requirements. It is an architecture that can carve new polymorphisms from older components in response to change. It is the architecture of business, its rules, and processes. The architecture itself can be dynamic, changing in response to governing processes that continually monitor, change, and alter. Indeed, governing processes also may be governed and changed by higher order governance, which in turn is subject to even higher order governance, ad infinitum (see Box 30). In the ultimate Knowledge Machine, governance of governance becomes dynamic. It monitors, changes, and learns from experience, spawning new processes of new orders of governance. This kind of architecture will support a new order of dynamism, and this order will separate the logic of governance from the logic of execution. Each level and order of governance will be distinct from that

32

which it governs. The Metamodel of Knowledge mandates this. See Module 5, Section 3, on our Web site.

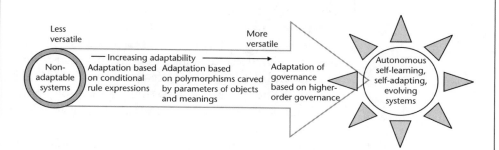

Evolution of the Knowledge Machine. ("System" subsumes business models and processes.)

Thus, the Knowledge Machine must support dynamic architectures and adaptation. In the Knowledge Machine, the concept of dynamic architecture and adaptation will not be confined to the top layer of the Architecture of Knowledge (see Figure 17 on our Web site), but will permeate every layer, adapting and optimizing interfaces and information logistics for new or different actors, and optimizing performance for new and different technological platforms.[249]

An adaptable system is a kind (subtype) of a self-adaptive system. In adaptable systems, actors outside the system provide governance and change the behavior of the system. Self-adaptive systems are more autonomous. A self-adaptive system governs its own adaptations, and automatically changes its behavior in response to changes in its environment. For instance, if human workers reconfigure components and customize processes in Figure 2.24, then it will be an adaptable system. On the other hand, if automated governance provided by the system does so in response to changed requirements, then it will be self-adaptive behavior. The Knowledge Machine is self-adaptive.

Self-adaptive systems are a subclass of Adaptable systems. A self-adaptive system is also adaptable. An external agent also may reconfigure, customize, and improve a self-adaptive system. Adaptation also may be partitioned into closed and open adaptive behavior. The behavior of a closed (dynamic) system and its repertoire of adaptations are set when it is built, whereas the behavior of open (dynamic) systems continually evolves after it is built, and has room for adaptations that were not anticipated a priori. The Knowledge Machine is an open dynamic system.

---

249. References [160, 162, 163] discuss the engineering of dynamic architectures and adaptation contracts.

32

Adaptive systems associate configurations with regions of state space. Moving from one region to another triggers reconfiguration. These regions may be regions within the conceivable state space of the system, its environment, or a space that subsumes both (i.e., a space within which each is a subspace). Governance processes may reshape these regions and the configurations associated with each, in step with changing goals or new learning. Governance processes may add new dimensions and new axes to this conceivable state space, even as they constrain, sculpt, and reshape its regions and the lawful state spaces within each.[250] The Knowledge Machine will be self-adaptive, self–governing, and autonomous.

Thus, governing processes within the Knowledge Machine must address:

- Adaptation events: Triggers, conditions, and occurrence, both internal and environmental.
- Open and closed adaptations: Open adaptation opens the possibility of learning from a repertoire of best-of-breed adaptations from a collection of agents in the environment of the self-adaptive system. As we have seen, the Knowledge Machine will not only be self-adaptive, but also open-adaptive.
- Autonomy of adaptation: The kinds and extent of autonomy, and how much the environment and external actors will guide adaptations and adaptability. For instance, at the low end of the spectrum of autonomy, external agents might govern and customize the adaptable system. At an intermediate level of autonomy, external agents (e.g., human users or intelligent agents) might sign off on changes suggested by the autonomous system. At the high end of the autonomous spectrum, the autonomous system may adapt its behavior on its own, without external approval, coordinate and signal these changes in its state to its users, stakeholders, and the agents that interface with it.
- Effectiveness and the value of adaptations.
- Frequency of adaptation, performance monitoring, and tracking: The mix of processes that periodically and routinely poll and monitor governed processes, as opposed to exceptions, demands, and alerts issued by these governed processes to the processes that control them. Indeed, in some situations, rapid and continual changes in behavior may be disruptive for its users and other actors with which the system might interface.
- The information that will be monitored (the features of metaprocesses, metarelationships, and meta-objects in the Metamodel of Knowledge), the accuracy, reliability, validity, and timeliness of the values thus monitored (see Box 30).
- The planning, tracking, coordination, deployment, implementation, and validation of adaptations, including consistency and reliability checking

250. When new actors and partitions are added to its environment, or new behaviors and features are created within the business system, the degrees of freedom of conceivable adaptations will increase, and so will the dimensionality of the state space within which adaptations are conceived.

32

(and testing),[251] and exception and contingency planning (see Box 30). Details are in Module 5, Section 3, in "Crossing the Chasm," under the risk management transform on our Web site. Ideally, the Knowledge Machine will be open to requests for tuning or rolling back adaptations in response to requests from perturbed actors (and users), if any.

- The Knowledge Machine also should pinpoint sources of these perturbations and requests, and record and analyze them, in order to update and adapt its adaptation strategy.
- Planning, tracking, and monitoring are universal processes, which lead to corresponding universal states of objects (see Chapter 2, Section 2.1). It follows that these processes (and states) will also apply to every order of governance, planning, tracking, and monitoring. The functions of the Knowledge Machine flow from the Universal Perspective and the Metamodel of Knowledge, which also anchor its continually mutating and evolving architecture.

Indeed, as the Knowledge Machine adapts to its environment, and perhaps even adapts its environment in step with its goals, the Principle of Parsimony and the mutability that flows from it will be its guiding light, framed by the Universal Perspective and its polymorphisms.

In the Knowledge Machine, the layers of Figure 2.23 are fully automated. They configure and customize in response to the requirements of the environment. The process in Figure 2.24 also is automated. The Knowledge Machine shares and customizes meanings, and tunes its behavior to fit a context. That context may or may not be constant. It is a parameter and an input that can evolve and change, and the Knowledge Machine will change its responses in lock step.

To quote the Defense Advanced Research Projects Agency (DARPA): "Self-adaptive software evaluates its own behavior and changes behavior when the evaluation indicates that it is not accomplishing what the software is intended to do, or when better functionality or performance is possible." Indeed, in the context of the Knowledge Machine, it is not just software to which we must attribute these qualities, but to the business process itself, integrated with the software. The software is merely a facilitator and an expression of the process, which can be automatically derived from the process itself. See Module 5, Section 3, under "Crossing the Chasm," on our Web site.

DARPA elaborates on this concept by asserting that it "seeks a new basis for making software adaptive, that doesn't require specific adaptive techniques, such as neural networks or genetic programming, but instead relies on software informed about its mission and about its construction and behavior. This implies that the software has multiple ways of accomplishing its purpose and has enough knowledge of its construction to make effective changes at runtime. Such software should

---

251. The Universal Perspective and the Metamodel of Knowledge provide a broad and generic guideline for consistency checking across different adaptations of the architecture of an adaptive system.

include functionality for evaluating its behavior and performance, as well as the ability to replan and reconfigure its operations in order to improve its operation. Self-adaptive software should also include a set of components for each major function, along with descriptions of the components, so that components of systems can be selected and scheduled at runtime in response to the evaluators. It also requires the ability to . . . generate some of this code from specifications." In other words, DARPA is asking for the Knowledge Machine.[252]

There are four unstated assumptions we have carried forward from the Industrial Era into the Information Age, which belie the Knowledge Machine:

- All requirements of the product are known and articulated before it is built.
- All uses of the product are known and articulated before it is designed.
- The product cannot be easily reconfigured or changed after it has been built.
- The product will degrade with time or use, and must be continually maintained and refurbished.

None of these assumptions holds when the product in question is information. These assumptions bear the stamp of the lessons learned from the Industrial Era, when overwhelming numbers of products were physical ones. These practices, which worked well for designing and manufacturing the physical products of the Industrial Age, strongly influenced knowledge management, information systems, and software development in the twentieth century.

In sharp contrast with the mass-produced physical products of industrial machinery and its rigid processes, the use and benefits of knowledge are often unpredictable, immeasurable and ill-defined. Software and business processes do not degrade. Instead, the environment changes, and renders them obsolete. Despite the widespread use of the term "systems (or software) maintenance," we do not, strictly speaking, maintain software or business processes as we would do with a physical product. Instead, we upgrade and evolve them to meet the needs of a changing environment. The New Age needs a new paradigm—the paradigm of adaptability, agility, innovation, and blinding speed. The Knowledge Machine is this machine, dedicated to the new gods of change, speed, and responsiveness.

Flexible processes must recognize, accept, and continually discover new information, and feed it back to make course corrections and tailor the product appropriately. Flexibility, response to change, and enabling the creative process are paramount in the Age of Knowledge. Collaboration, continual improvement, and organic growth in response to change will be the buzzwords of the twenty-first century. Live processes, backed by enabling software, and not just by documentation of specifications, will measure progress. The focus will shift from building and deploying software, to building and managing a responsive process. The creation of software and information systems will be automated. In other words, the Knowledge

252. DARPA intends to apply this technology (self-adaptive systems) for automatic target recognition, signal and image processing, image understanding, planning, scheduling, and robotics. See http://msrc.wvu.edu/nsf_epscor/cluster_research/arpa_baa98_1.html.

Machine will write its own software. It will program and reprogram itself in response to change.[253]

Flowing from the first three assumptions of the Industrial Age is the assumption that construction is significantly more expensive than design, and the cost of construction mistakes rooted in incorrect design can be enormous. Therefore, conventional wisdom tells us that it is worth determining requirements exhaustively, and designing thoroughly, before building the product. These assumptions held for the software of the twentieth century because construction and design of software were labor-intensive. As we have seen, design and construction can be automated. When this happens, the reasons for these assumptions will vanish like mist in the heat of a new day and the light of a new sun. In the new age, autonomous processes will continually "hunt" for requirements and utilization, continually adjusting products, and optimizing themselves in step with changing needs.

Customization, configuration, and reconfiguration will leverage commonality to produce processes and information products with unprecedented resilience and agility.[254] Feedback loops in every layer of the architecture of the Knowledge Machine will optimize performance and autonomy by "tweaking" products and processes in response to changes in the environment.[255] The Knowledge Machine even may be the root cause of its own change. It may change its environment, and then respond to the changes it has wrought by changing itself.

The Knowledge Machine can respond in this manner only if its components have governance ports to govern, monitor, and reconfigure their performance. The governing, tracking, and monitoring processes we discussed (see Chapter 2, Section 2.1) will be an integral part of the performance-optimized components of the Knowledge Machine. Indeed, in the Knowledge Machine, it is a governing process that will build and configure these components from the patterns within the repository. The interlocking pieces of software that constitute these components will soon be beyond the comprehension of most humans—even developers of information systems. Only automation will be able to manage the vast amounts of information that will reside in the repository and the complex interactions that will weave through them. This Knowledge Machine, customizing, managing, and configuring the meanings sleeping within its repository, will be as far removed from our present-day computers as our computers are from the Roman abacus. Then, at last, the Age of Knowledge will have truly arrived.

253. Howard Smith and Peter Fingar have elaborated on shifting the focus of systems engineering to business rules, and automating any consequential software development. See [161, 335]. Pi-calculus lends mathematical precision to these concepts. See the note on pi-calculus [75–77].
254. Reference [164] presents a succinct overview of the state of the art of adaptive, goal-seeking software.
255. See Figure 17 on our Web site.

PART II

The Book of Change

"The time has come," the Walrus said,
"To talk of many things:
Of shoes—and ships—and sealing wax—
Of cabbages—and kings—
And why the sea is boiling hot—
and whether pigs have wings."

—Lewis Carroll, *Through the Looking-Glass and What Alice Found There*, 1872

CHAPTER 4

On the Nature of Change and Winged Pigs

Can pigs really have wings? Don't be too surprised if you find winged pigs when you are making fundamental changes. See Figure 4.1. Try the following experiment the next time you use Microsoft Word. Open a new document and type "= rand(200,99)" (the text within the quotes, not the quotes themselves, with no spaces between characters), hit enter and wait three seconds. Surprised?

As managers of real organizations of real people in the real world, we all know that the only constancy in change is surprise. "Expect the unexpected" is a wise maxim for those who are brave enough to risk the turbulence and chaos that change involves. We must survive in order to succeed. Change is like surgery. It is undertaken to cure, but it is always risky. Change gone wrong can kill individuals' careers in the corporations for which they work, and even kill the corporations being changed. This could happen because of faulty vision, defective business practices, or mismatched technology, but the greatest risk lies in the emotional storm change unleashes. It can kill careers and corporations. We might be dead right, but we will not benefit, nor will the organizations for which we work, if we are dead.

To implement the technology in this book, you must enter uncharted waters and make change. Change is fraught with risk. Managing risk was therefore too

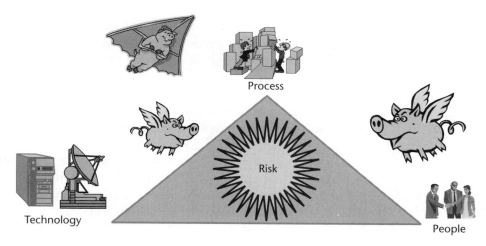

Figure 4.1 Managing change involves balancing people, process, technology, and winged pigs.

important a topic to ignore. This part of the book will provide a road map for managing risk—actually, two complementary road maps:

- The process, or *best practices map*, to help to chart your course;
- The emotional parameters, or *people map*, to help you take each step on the course you have charted.

Together, these maps will help you manage the risk of change.

4.1 The Technology Dimension

New methods, processes, tools, and techniques will be required to support the approach in this book. You must realign your organization around these new processes. The journey into uncharted waters is arduous, and the risk of getting lost high. For this reason, the road maps in this part of the book provide points where you can pause to take stock at every evolutionary step.

Experience shows that organizations cannot change by quantum leap and still survive. The experiment with Microsoft Word was a harmless demonstration of a technological glitch—a risk. The risk could have been much greater, but risk is unavoidable when you abandon the old to reach for excellence. In this new age of knowledge and unrelenting competition, the risk of stagnation is far worse than the trials of blazing new trails. This makes it even more important to manage risk judiciously, and change skillfully.

Organizational and process risks far outweigh the risk of new technology. Even if we ignore the risk of technological failure, and consider only changes to the process, the risk involved in aligning people, perceptions, attitudes, and organizational culture to embrace the new process dwarfs any risk inherent in the process itself. This is the reef on which the ship of change most often founders, and when it does, emotions rise to the boiling point and the sea gets boiling hot.

The full risk of change is not just a sum of risks involved in changing people's attitudes, organizational processes, and technology. Each risk compounds the others. See Figure 4.2. Trying to change all three simultaneously is usually a recipe for disaster. Yet, more and more, technical innovations are driving changes in processes and people. The safest strategy often is to change people through the process, making only the changes that we must in technology and tools. As much as possible, adapt the techniques to the tools that people know, and with which they are comfortable. As much as possible, try to keep the same look and feel for the techniques you use. For instance, if people understand UML,[256] format reusable components as UML diagrams. If they have traditionally used PDM,[257] use PDM to show process flows. Add necessary notations or standards to capture, manually if need be, the information these techniques might not support. Only when the process and the people are ready can new tools and techniques be introduced, absorbed, and used

---

256. UML is an acronym for the Universal Modeling Language, a set of techniques and diagramming convention used to analyze, design, develop, and deploy information systems. See the discussion in Box 22 in [337] and on our Web site.

257. PDM is an acronym for the Precedence Diagramming Method, a process mapping technique discussed on our Web site. See Figure 87 on our Web site.

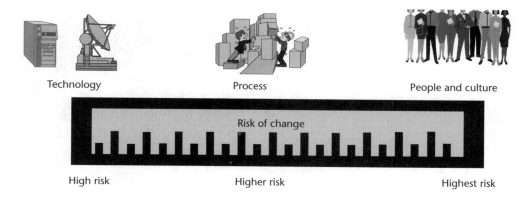

Figure 4.2 Technological change and sources of risk.

effectively to optimally benefit the business. Before that, they may actually compound the confusion and increase the risk.

In Chapter 6, we will discuss the critical levels of organizational and process maturity needed to implement and absorb the tools and the technology of Knowledge Artifacts. However, regardless of the elegance and sophistication of these Knowledge Artifacts, improved quality and increased agility for a business only will flow if (business) systems engineers understand and utilize these artifacts. This must be followed by their acceptance of artifacts and the support infrastructure, which will include supporting services, methodologies, and tools. For this, we must change both processes and people.

Figure 4.3(a) articulates this principle of change, highlighting that both improved quality and acceptance of the solution are prerequisites for a tangible and positive effect of new technology on the business.

Figure 4.3(b) tells us that the quality of solutions delivered to a customer will depend on the ability of the process or information system built with the knowledge artifacts to:

- Perform or support requisite tasks (Functionality);

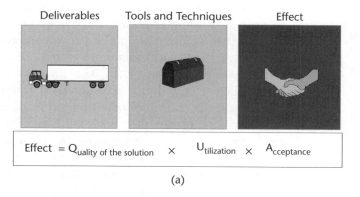

(a)

Figure 4.3 Realizing the benefits of quality, agility, and resilience: (a) success is not begotten by quality alone, but it requires *acceptance* and *utilization* of a solution; and (b) perception of quality, agility, and value.

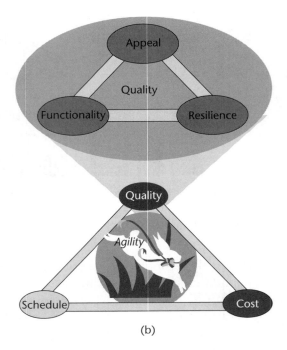

(b)

Figure 4.3   (Continued.)

- Adapt to changing requirements or innovative usage (Resilience);
- Satisfy quantitative and qualitative performance expectations (Appeal).

The agility of the business process or information system will be measured by its ability to provide high quality business solutions in reduced time frames, and at reduced cost. To achieve these goals, the right processes must support the right engineers and designers of business processes and systems.

4.2   The Process Dimension

In Chapter 2, we have seen that the right process for leveraging Knowledge Artifacts requires an automated repository. Process engineers and information systems architects will use a combination of processes and techniques, augmented by substantive knowledge assets encapsulated in components stored in the repository, to rapidly leverage quality at low cost. The low cost and rapid leverage will flow from repeated reuse of widely shared universal patterns of knowledge. The intent will be to amortize the one-time cost of building and setting up these knowledge assets in the repository against their repeated use. There also will be repeating operational and maintenance cost components, but these will be much smaller. The more often they are used, the more the initial cost will be justified and spread over each use. To do this, the process must combine industry knowledge with solution components, as articulated in Figure 4.4.

Reuse requires a measure of standardization, consistency of use, and mechanization of the process for building processes and information systems. This kind of

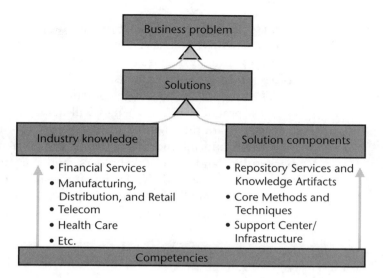

Figure 4.4 The development process must combine industry knowledge with solution components.

standardization demands a high level of technological prowess and process maturity in the organizations charged with building business processes and software.

Effective and economical reuse of knowledge artifacts in these organizations can only occur if multiple projects and initiatives reuse the same artifacts, which are repositories of shared knowledge. Few organizations have this capability at present, and the large majority is far removed from this level of process maturity and technological sophistication. Chapter 6 addresses the issue. It provides a staged, evolutionary road map that sketches the path from a state of chaos and ad hoc fire drills, through well-managed processes, to a level of process maturity where the organization is capable of continually anticipating its needs and reinventing itself. It then can improve its processes in step with the needs of its evolving environment.

In terms of the road map in Chapter 6, to utilize the technology of knowledge artifacts effectively, an organization must be at the third or higher level of process maturity. At this level, processes are well understood, standardized, and consistent throughout business engineering and information systems development groups. For most present-day organizations, this is a clarion call for fundamental change.

The risk of basing the map of change on the experience of one person alone, or even the collective wisdom of several wise men, is too high. It is too risky, even if they all have impeccable credentials. The model of organizational evolution presented later in Chapter 6 is based on the lessons learned by organizations in four continents across the globe. The Capability Maturity Model® (CMM®) is the basis of our best practices road map.

The CMM® focuses on Process. The Software Engineering Institute (SEI) developed the CMM®. The SEI collected best practices and lessons learned by a very large cross section of organizations over several years. The CMM® is a tested, tried-and-true set of best practices that have succeeded across a broad spectrum of information technology organizations in a very wide variety of circumstances, business environments, and cultures. It is used as a reference model throughout the world to improve performance, quality, and productivity of software organizations. That is why this book has embraced it as the reference model that will help an organization gradually acquire the capabilities needed to leverage and nurture the technology of Knowledge Artifacts.

The CMM® consists of key practices. These are common themes of governance and best practices. These themes will help organizations evolve and mature their processes. With the CMM®, organizations may evolve their processes in step with their needs and internal strengths. They can match the evolving demands of the marketplace and their stakeholders, and rise to the challenges thrown by their competitors. The CMM® is dynamic—it is designed to keep organizations in motion—continually evolving, improving, and excelling as they rise to meet rapidly evolving strategic challenges in their environments.

4.3   The People Dimension—The Emotional Dynamic of Change

However, the implementation of each key CMM® process can be a mini-change on its own, and any change can cause turbulence in a corporation—political, emotional, and technological. Even more than the CMM®, this is the primary risk you must successfully navigate to make change. The root of this turbulence stems from the emotions it unleashes among those impacted by change. This dynamic is even more intense, if the organization grew to a position of leadership based on its past successes; then sank into secure somnolence as it rested on its laurels; and now must be jolted out of smug, self-satisfied stagnation, due to competition or fundamental changes in its business environment that are looming large.

Experience has shown that the cycle of emotions, from the initiation of change to its conclusion (successful or not), follows a predictable path. It is this cycle we will examine first, and it is this cycle we must learn to navigate, because your success as a change maker depends on it. The cycle will repeat itself for each key process and phase of the CMM®, and, indeed, for whatever process you favor, if you choose not to follow the CMM®.

This is why, even before we consider the CMM®, we must examine the emotional dynamics of change. After all, that is the first, and worst, rock on which one can founder. It is critical to chart a course around this obstacle as one steps through the CMM®. That will be the focus of the next chapter.

4.4   Why Change?

"Companies are able to jump and stay ahead by implementing changes faster than the competition."

— Judith Hurwitz, *a recognized authority on business rules*

Change is risky business, and must be made judiciously. It must be sponsored to mitigate even larger threats looming on the horizon or to seize strategic opportunities. In this age of intense competition and rapid innovation, these threats are an increasing phenomenon. Opportunities and threats will force the pace even if we do not. Survival and success in the New Age will increasingly belong to the makers, not the followers, of change. One must be the first to see and grasp opportunity from the confluence of process, technology, and above all, innovation, in order to prosper and sometimes even to survive.

Business engineering holds the key. Organizations that offer business process engineering services could start becoming implementers of business transformation through focused entry points. They should be an integral part of the team that leads business transformation. They must support business transformation and process improvement with high quality information systems and services, at low cost and in tight time frames. Figure 4.5 tells us that the managers of business and systems engineering organizations should consider a mix of strategies as they strive toward this goal. Knowledge Artifacts are but one component of this strategy, but they are a powerful component. Used appropriately, they can lend business processes and information systems resilience, high quality, responsiveness, agility, and competitive strength. Knowledge Artifacts will automate the development of business processes and supporting information systems of the future. The process will become less and less labor intensive. Perhaps, as the Age of Knowledge unfolds, business engineers will leverage the technology of knowledge to lead the charge towards the nimble, innovative, and competitive automated businesses of the future.

Figure 4.5   Reach for both quality *and* economy by automating knowledge.

CHAPTER 5

Managing Emotions Unleashed by Change

The focus of this chapter is on managing the emotions unleashed by change. Change will only succeed if there is a healthy dissatisfaction with the status quo. Let us assume that you have decided to make fundamental changes to the way you operate, and the way you develop your processes and information systems. It is process, governance, and goals that must change, but people also must commit to them, implement them, and execute the change. See Figure 5.1. Herein lies your primary risk. Without people, change will not happen, and change makes people anxious. It might also make them curious or hopeful. When it does not, it will make them angry, fearful, apathetic, despondent, or frustrated. The primary focus of any change initiative must be on people, and must be vested in people. Only then will change be fruitful. Figure 5.2 recommends communication, clarification, commitment, and participation at every step of the journey, from conception to fruition of change. It is a road map that cannot emphasize this aspect of change more. Its message is to focus on people, every step along your way. Make them hopeful, curious, committed, inspired, and excited.

Communication must focus on creating commitment and implementing change. This is easier said than done. Jeanie Duck in [320] has identified four common sequential steps, from the time the decision to change is taken, to the point of

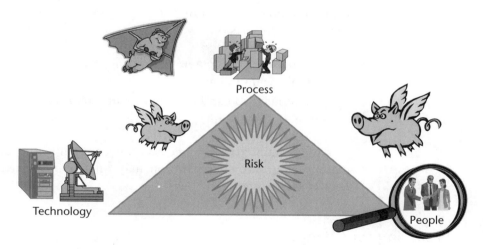

Figure 5.1 People make change. Focus on people.

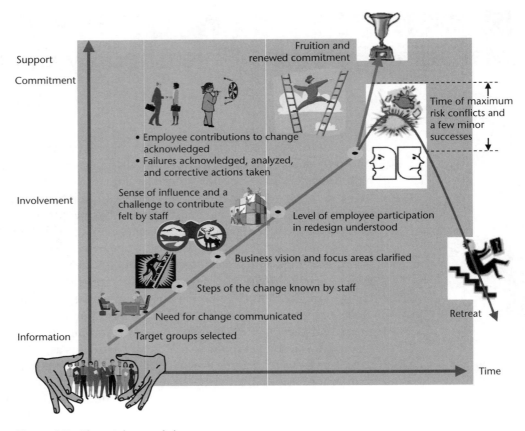

Figure 5.2 The road map of change.

fruition or abandonment of change.[258] Jeanie Duck's model envisions a change trajectory that consists of:

- Preparation and planning for change;
- Implementation and cut over;
- Determination and postimplementation review;
- Fruition (or Failure).

Adequate preparation and accurate communication are the keys and the foundations of Fruition. Preparation may only be neglected at grave risk, but it is neglected too often.

5.1 Preparing for Change

As you prepare for change, you must have:

---

258. Reference [320] envisions five phases on a "change curve," which includes a "stagnation" phase prior to preparation. Stagnation occurs before the organization realizes that it must change, and before the decision to change is taken. It is the cause for change. In this chapter, we have omitted the stagnation phase, because we have assumed that the cycle of change starts with the decision to change. Readers will find more detail on the change curve in [320], a very readable book richly illustrated with many real-life examples.

- A vision of where you want to be after the change is complete.
- A sound and clear change strategy for getting there, and a passionate belief in it. The strategy should include:
  - The rationale for the change;
  - The scope, purpose, and specific objectives of the change;
  - The current and proposed business model, and the migration strategy;
  - Business footprints and changes therein;
  - Critical products, services, and capabilities, both current and planned;
  - Critical values that will be shared by the organization, and their rationale;
  - Deployment strategy: implementation, piloting and replication strategy, organizational test beds, and risk management strategies.
- A high-level, time-bound change plan for the initiative. This plan must address:
  - The high-level, generic processes and information systems involved, including key processes, technologies, and information systems;
  - Resource requirements, allocations, and the resource plan;
  - Division of responsibility for these processes (the roles, not necessarily individuals at this point), and any contingency plans;
  - Required facilities, support, and locations;
  - Organizational structure, compensation, and incentive plans;
  - Size, skills, qualifications, and capabilities required of the work force (current and planned), and the plan for achieving this;
  - Deliverables and measures of success, including methods of assessing success (i.e., how the measurements will be made, both qualitative and quantitative);
  - Deployment plan: target groups, business footprints, deployment schedule, key events and milestones.
- Acute sensitivity to emotional issues and the willingness to address them.
- A leadership team that will champion the change. This must be a senior management team. It is this team that will articulate the vision, purpose, and rationale for change; formulate the change strategy; develop the change plan; sponsor it; and foster, lead and manage the change (see Figure 5.3).

Naturally, each element in the plan and strategy should mesh and be synergistic with the others, but most of all, the leaders must be aligned. There must be unflinching commitment within the team that will lead and champion the change before it is implemented. This is critical. It is also the single largest source of the single largest risk.

Not everybody will have an appetite for change. Dissension and lack of alignment within the leadership team will quickly percolate through the organization. It will lead to dissension within the organization, turf battles, power struggles and resistance to change, jockeying for position, low morale, loss of productivity, and loss of faith in the organization's leaders. Other undesirable side effects will follow. Naturally, there must be consequences for those who resist or cannot see the vision. However, if the vision is not sharp, or if its articulation is not clear, then it will be hard to gain commitment. People cannot support what they cannot understand. The clearer the strategy is, and the easier it is to understand, the easier it will be to

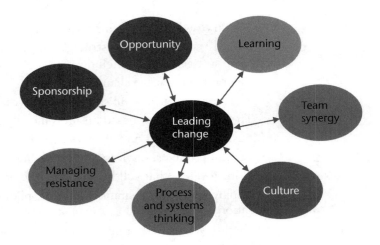

Figure 5.3 Leaders of change must foster, balance, integrate, and manage several leadership themes.

resolve issues within and without the leadership team, and to foster alignment. Radical change demands deep, firm, and even passionate, commitment from the organization's leadership team.

This commitment, passion, and enthusiasm must filter into, and permeate, the organization. Indeed, even before the plan is ready, it will help smooth the change if the planning process is clear and transparent. It will help even more if it welcomes contributions from those who might be impacted, and is supported by processes to elicit feedback. Web-based discussion forums, lunch meetings, telecommunication-based public question-and-answer sessions, frequently asked questions (FAQ) boards with answers, suggestion boxes, and a plethora of other mechanisms could support a policy of transparency. The champions of change might even consider setting up a mechanism to respond to suggestions, describe what alternatives were considered, and explain why they were accepted or rejected. Participation will help secure commitment, and adding optimism to anxiety will foster hope, and hope will foster anticipation as well as curiosity.

Hope is the key to commitment. Hope can inspire, excite, and ignite change. It can sow an eagerness to contribute to the organization's future. It can make people commit. Openness, transparency, and the chance to have an input will foster hope and participation. It will reduce cynicism, disbelief, and annoyance. However, participation also will distract, and distraction reduces productivity. On the other hand, even if the plans were formulated in secrecy, and the processes were opaque, rumors would abound, and the resulting distraction, accompanied by anxiety, fear, jockeying for position, rejection of change, and sabotage might be even greater. Productivity might suffer more.

The plan must be reasonable. If the plan does not provide enough time or resources, then stress levels will increase. The goals will not be realizable. People will burn out, or credibility will suffer. The stress of change will be compounded to intolerable levels. People will lose hope, and with it, their feelings of anticipation and excitement. They will spin their wheels unproductively. The initiative will lose steam, and the leaders will lose their credibility.

Even if the vision is clear, the plan sound, and the organization caring, there always will be doubters, along with individuals at every level of enthusiasm. Given the corrosive impact of uncertainty and anxiety about personal adequacy (or the lack of it), and uncertainty about career and individual prospects within a changed organization, it is imperative that preparation for change be done expeditiously. Yet preparation must do diligence to the change strategy and plan; otherwise, the same issues and turf battles will surface with far more impact when the change is underway, and with redoubled intensity. There must be adequate time to prepare for change, but only enough to prepare well.

Rushing to implement change without adequate planning and preparation can break the initiative. If this happens, the technology, change initiatives, and management in general will lose credibility. Cynicism will increase, and future initiatives will be much harder to implement. The time allotted for planning and preparation must be judiciously balanced to navigate between these two rocks that can make or break the change.

Large corporations, especially global corporations, and supply chains can encapsulate multiple business philosophies, values, and national cultures in their diverse parts and departments. When the vision is well articulated, the goals clear, and the planning process open, responsive, and well understood, this diversity of cultures and business philosophies need not be hurdles. Instead, diversity can be cause for synergy, creativity, and innovation. How cultural diversity will impact the process of change depends largely on how it is managed. Figure 5.4 articulates how cultural diversity, when managed correctly, will foster trust, respect, and creativity; but managed incorrectly, it will degenerate into a downward spiral of conflict fired by mistrust.

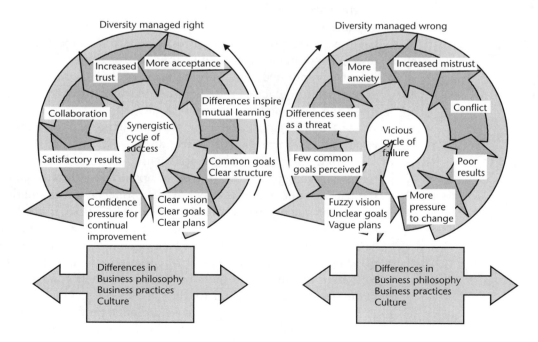

Figure 5.4 The cycle of managed versus mismanaged cultural diversity.

People prefer clear, motivating, realizable goals. Without a clear vision, it will be difficult to inspire and easy to confuse. There will be little to communicate, and it will be even harder to consistently and credibly address the concerns of the workforce, especially as the lines of communication lengthen and extend through layers of management. Without understanding the plan, the workforce cannot do the right things expeditiously, let alone do things right. The plan must be clear, and it must be detailed. Above all, the plan must be discussed and agreed upon. Leaders must be well briefed and prepared to answer, in depth, employees' questions and concerns.

5.2   Implementing Change

The plan rolls out and starts deploying. Real people fill roles. New structures and processes cut in. The emotions that had their genesis in the preparation phase intensify. People start operating in new ways, and under new structures and business models. Some people become confused. Confusion leads to frustration, annoyance, anger, and feelings of inadequacy. People become apathetic or resentful. The situation becomes volatile and unstable. It needs even more management attention. The leadership team cannot afford to prepare the ground and abdicate responsibility for implementation. It must stay focused on implementing the change, supporting people, and resolving problems. Only then will it mitigate the negative aspects of implementation, foster recognition, and address the causes of confusion, apathy, resentment, and inadequacy, in order to provide relief and inspire excitement.

One major cause of stress during the implementation phase is that it demands a lot from individuals. Stress will increase even more if individuals have little control on the nature of these demands. Compounding the stress, and raising it to even higher levels, is the fact that these individuals may be in highly visible positions, being watched carefully. The stress can become unbearable if they also worry that they may not have the requisite knowledge or ability to meet expectations. For these reasons, communication and resolution of issues, concerns, and problems acquires even greater urgency as the organization starts transforming itself. Communication must now be joined by support systems. Only with formal implementation support systems and organizational support mechanisms will implementation problems, issues, and concerns be adequately addressed.

Communication during implementation must address a much broader scope than just telling people what to do or how to do it. It must continue to explain why. It must continue to address how the decision was made, and the issues considered. It must continue to seek feedback, and correct course, if need be. Implementation is hard work, and people tend to burrow into their own work, teams, and projects. Therefore, communication must seek to connect people to the rest of the organization via regular updates and status reports. It will help individuals to feel connected to the larger cause, help them to understand their contribution, and, above all, to maintain their commitment to, the hard work of change.

If individuals do not agree with or understand the new rationale, then they will not change their beliefs and assumptions. The commitment that flows from conviction and understanding is essential to making change succeed. However, even with the best efforts and the most responsive implementation processes, there will always be naysayers and saboteurs of change. Therefore, there must be consequences for individuals who consistently violate the agreed-upon rules, or who abandon the change altogether.

Conversely, even small successes and tangible deliverables merit recognition and celebration. Major successes, such as delivery of high quality, agile, and resilient processes or software, in compressed time frames and at lower cost, might have to wait for fruition of the change initiative. However, to prevent people from burning out, it is essential to keep up the morale, momentum, and excitement of change, even as it is being implemented. Therefore, even small successes and deliverables are worth recognizing, commending, and even celebrating.

5.3   Determination—A Fork in the Road: Fruition or Failure?

Only after the change is implemented, absorbed, and integrated will its real impact be clear. At this point, the change must begin to take root. Otherwise, it will wilt, and may die on the vine. Management cannot afford to declare victory, and shift their attention elsewhere. The leadership team must now nurse the change so that it takes root. Support and communication must continue, but may change in their tenor. It is a new and different phase, postimplementation, which will make or break the change and the vision that spawned it.

The results of the change should now start becoming evident, but people are exhausted. It is still a period of review, experimentation, interpretation, improvement, and fine-tuning. The new way is implemented, but is not yet an old habit. People will get tired of spending energy to think and rethink their daily work and ordinary day-to-day tasks. If they see signs of success, they will maintain their hope and momentum in spite of their exhaustion and discomfort. Otherwise, they will give up, or only will go through the motions, while hoping and waiting for the inevitable retreat.

Sometimes when implementation is poor, corporations will not even review the change. Instead, they will let it die a quiet death. The firm will retreat, and the change will quietly fail. Sometimes, the sponsors even may resort to "declaring victory," and then retreating quietly. Determination is the time of maximum risk. It can draw defeat from the jaws of victory (see Figure 5.2).

Postimplementation, the change becomes reality. It changes people's work lives. They will feel both the direct and indirect effects of change. They will know that it is no passing cloud. It is how they will have to live and act in their new roles, under new rules, and with new or different responsibilities. There will be some discomfort, some conflict, and some negativity. Even if a part of the change does not sit well, it can call the entire initiative into question. If support, attention, and communication cease, or become tenuous, then the change will not take root, and it will be the beginning of the end. Management must continue to nurture the change by continuing the program of communication and support. They must keep communicating, supporting, and resolving issues, concerns, and problems as the change takes hold.

The leaders of change also should make the time to formally and informally connect with people at all levels, in order to get unfiltered feedback. The leaders must not neglect mutual communication between themselves. They must ensure that the changes they have fostered reinforce each other, coordinate, and mesh. They may tire of repeating the same messages ad nauseam, but, at this stage, repetition will be necessary to reinforce even familiar messages. In other words, the leaders must continue to pay attention, or the change will fail.

Measures, metrics, and missed targets cannot merely be interesting information. They must be cause for course corrections or recovery plans. Leaders must continue to penalize those who abandon the process, or the agreed-upon rules. People also must be made aware of how their actions can affect the metrics, and can ricochet through the initiative. At this time, what people truly believe, as opposed to what they say they believe, will become clear. When the values articulated in the plan are in conflict with business expediency or old instincts, believers will align their actions with the new values, whereas nonbelievers will not. Actions, especially difficult actions, aligned with values, will build trust, confidence, and momentum. On the other hand, the actions of unbelievers will speak for them. Their actions will not align with the new values, and because noncompliance will erode trust, will reduce the momentum of change. Since this will disillusion the others, it cannot be permitted.

The leadership can only shift its attention away from the change initiative prematurely at great peril to the program they are leading. Given the amount of hard work and stress people have suffered to make it happen, failure at this point will fuel an intense feeling of futility, and morale will plummet like a rock. Cynicism will set in, and the credibility of the leadership will be at stake. To manage the risk of failure, problems and concerns must continue to be addressed honestly and openly. Negative events, setbacks, and failures must be acknowledged and addressed frankly. It will raise, not lower, morale, and will nurture the change until its roots strengthen enough to let it survive on its own.

As the roots of change slowly strengthen, people will truly begin to understand and appreciate their present place in the new order. They will think about their future prospects. They will consider what the change will mean to their careers. They will reevaluate their capabilities, their trust in the leadership, their personal and professional rewards and losses, and their compensation. Many people will have been impacted profoundly for the better or for the worse. They will consider the benefits of sticking with the change, versus jumping ship to a new job. Some will question the vision, others will question the goals, and some, even if they concur with the vision and goals, will question the business model, the strategy, or the plan. Some may even back away from their own recommendations.

If key people start leaving en masse, then the hemorrhage can feed on itself, encouraging others to leave. Recruiting the requisite talent also can become painfully difficult if the change is cause for insurrection or an exodus of employees. The change then will falter. However, backing off at this point can be disastrous. Management will lose credibility and respect. Those who worked hard at change will feel marginalized. With their efforts wasted, morale will plunge. The leadership must not let this come to pass. It will pin the firm and its leaders into a no-win situation. Mass exodus or insurrection must be forestalled. Communication, management, and addressing of employee concerns on time can forestall it. Communication and support systems must alert management to these possibilities, and arrest the downward spiral well before problems reach this fever pitch. Like any other activity, even small successes will provide the key.

People need and want to be associated with success. In this phase, one should put the spotlight on achievements, to foster hope and to keep up the momentum painfully built. Assimilate and spread the learning that stems from both successes and failures. As always, honesty, openness, and the willingness to address concerns and manage conflict, backed by even a few successes, will win friends and build support. It will take the organization forward to fruition and away from failure. Intellectual and operational commitment was obtained during preparation and implementation. Now is the time for emotional commitment to the change. Emotions, both negative and positive, will peak in this phase. The postimplementation phase will determine the success, or the abject failure of change. The leadership must stay deeply involved to make it happen. Only then will we have a change that lasts.

5.4   Fruition and Continuing Improvement

At last, the change takes root. The real and tangible benefits envisioned during preparation are evident. Everybody recognizes them. The plan has borne fruit. Fruition is the time to reflect and learn from the experience. It is a time for celebration, a time of recognition and euphoria, a time for rest and success—but only for a little while. It is also the time to prepare for the next cycle of change. If the lessons of implementation and determination have been well assimilated, then change will be easier the next time around. The model of staged evolution in Chapter 6 has these rest stops until its final destination. It ends in an organization mature enough to constantly anticipate its environment, and to adapt to it just in time.

The model in Chapter 6 fosters evolution in discrete stages. Fruition of each level of organizational capability in that model sets the stage, and is the launching pad for the next. If the trust, unity, and camaraderie that have percolated through the organization at the fruition of a stage are cemented before launching the next cycle of change, then evolution will become progressively easier. Rewards and recognition should be equally shared, and relationships strengthened and consolidated. The organizational capabilities and positive attitudes that were painfully acquired should be institutionalized, so that they do not fade away with the passage of time. These hard-won strengths will be critical for winning the next stage, and bringing it to fruition rapidly and successfully. They will be invaluable assets when the stresses of change must be managed once again.

Faith in the management team, and the trust placed in them, would be at an all-time high at fruition. Management should capitalize on this confidence to institutionalize and nurture the newly acquired "soft" capabilities forged on the anvil of change. These capabilities will include the skills of self-observation and course correction, the positive attitudes to idea of change, and the feelings of confidence bolstered by a "can-do" culture energized by camaraderie. Consolidating and preserving these soft assets should be the new focus of the leadership team.

Management could reinforce and institutionalize these assets by awarding performance bonuses, establishing new incentives and compensation plans, and creating and giving awards tied to accomplishment of goals. The leaders may establish schemes and career tracks to motivate the workforce to strive towards even greater success the next time around. The champions born of the last cycle could become the new leaders, trainers, and mentors for the next. Fresh blood can help build future leaders and shore up those who are tired of the turmoil of change. Some may be reluctant to change the changes they wrought. The next time around, it will be easier, because everybody will be better prepared after assimilating the emotional lessons of the changes just made.

The leadership team may be tempted to prolong the time it basks in the glow of success before taking up the next challenge, but like the preparation phase, if they tarry too long, then the glow will fade, stagnation will set in, and the next steps may become harder. The staged evolutionary model in the next chapter will discourage the transformation of old innovations into sacred cows without good reason. They will drive a culture that discourages stagnation, encourages constant examination, and stays abreast of a rapidly evolving environment. However, management must stay involved, listening, communicating, and examining. They must set the pace, and like preparation, the cycle of change must be paced correctly. The organization must navigate between fatigue and the glow of past success. If the pace is too slow, hard-won emotional assets may fade, and stagnation will replace evolution. If it is too fast, the organization may be too tired to continue. Individuals may balk at plunging into the intense turmoil of change again, and may not rise to the challenge. Chaos and retreat may prevail over evolution.

Changes rarely can be made in one leap, but must be negotiated in small steps. It is extremely risky for a large organization to change all at once. It is much safer to change its parts one at a time, profiting from lessons learned at each step, and building the core of expertise and experience needed to lead the entire organization through fundamental changes. Usually, visionary leaders who are willing to take judicious risks to earn commensurate benefits lead the parts that are the first to embrace change. When the change involves new technology, the technology enthusiasts must support the leaders. They must, as one team, be the engines that ignite change. Their first focus necessarily must be on the benefits and features of the new technology that will act as force multipliers to magnify their business leverage. However, as we will see next, this focus must change, as change gathers momentum and starts spreading through a large organization (or an industry).

Those who are the first to embrace change and bring it to fruition in an organization also will be the leaders who would spread the change to its other parts. They usually will be risktakers. However, most people are risk-averse. They will seek mitigation of risk and the comfort of reassurance more than the glitter of new technology. The organizations that changed first must provide this support for risktakers. It means emphasis now must shift from technology to unstinting support and handholding of those who seek to change. It means setting up support mechanisms, such as help desks, call centers, deputation of experts, and so forth. This aspect of change is often overlooked, and many new ideas or new products have come to fruition in universities or isolated corporate and industrial islands, only to wither and die there. It is difficult to bring change to fruition, but it is even harder to spread it and make it the norm.

Successful, but isolated changes only can become the new norm if the first few organizations that were instrumental in making the change now switch their focus from new technology (the benefits of which they have already demonstrated, and are the living proof of) to risk mitigation, reassurance, support, and leadership for those who wish to follow them. Of course, there are some who will not change even if hell freezes over, but most will follow a demonstrably good idea if they are supported and their risks mitigated.[259] In the age of constant learning and rapid innovation, the cycle of change has less and less room for those who seek the comfort of stasis.

The cycle of change is slowly tightening. It is beginning to spin ever faster. The postindustrial knowledge economy, driven by rapid dissemination of knowledge, innovation, new learning, and technology, is driving the pace. The optimal gap between fruition of change and the next cycle is reducing. The line between basking in the sunshine of success and stagnating in the laurels of the past is beginning to blur. Anticipation is beginning to replace reaction. Processes and plans that cannot adapt even as they are being prepared and implemented run the grave risk of becoming obsolete even before they can bear fruit. Less often can organizations shoot at stationary targets. More often, the vehicles of change must track and home in on moving targets even after the change initiative has been launched. The desired state of the organization may change even as the program of change is underway. The age of change is upon us. The process of change must flex accordingly. Continual improvement is the ultimate goal of the Capability Maturity Model®, which is the topic of the next chapter.

---

259. Reference [321] has more information for readers interested in spreading proven but new technology.

CHAPTER 6

Governance of Change

6.1 Developing and Keeping Organizational Capability

The last chapter was about managing the emotions unleashed by change. This chapter will be about the processes that govern change and drive its evolution. Change is difficult, both emotionally and operationally. It is even harder to keep changing. People like stability. Change sows insecurity and discomfort. It also sows risk. However, learning drives the knowledge economy. It demands that we keep changing. It requires, on the pain of extinction, that the constancy of stability be replaced by the constancy of change and rapid evolution. This is a kind of constancy, in which the search for opportunity, and the response to change, is constant. As shown in Figure 6.1, change requires new systems and processes that will stabilize the capability to constantly learn, change, improve, invent, and evolve. To do this, the organization must develop a kind of emotional and operational resilience that is rare in most present-day organizations. For most organizations, it is hard to change, and even harder to institutionalize change. We must have a process that will help us do so.

This is why this chapter will be about the processes that govern change and drive its evolution. Our model of evolution and governance will be based on the Capability Maturity Model® (CMM®). We discussed the reasons for this in Chapter 4. The CMM® is a tested and tried road map for acquiring technological capability by evolving into it. It will help us evolve to the state where we can effectively

Figure 6.1 The focus of this chapter will be processes for governing change. Institutionalize them.

use Knowledge Artifacts to build and deploy robust and resilient business processes and information systems. More and more, the New Age demands unprecedented resilience and agility of our businesses, our operations, and our information systems. Knowledge Artifacts support the technology of resilience. To use and evolve them effectively, we also must institutionalize the values, and foster the culture of resilience agility and responsiveness. We must learn to turn on a dime before, and better than, our competition.

Most organizations find this difficult, and the larger the organization is, the harder it is to change. Henry Ford once said that customers could have any color car they wanted, as long as it was black. The Industrial Age put its faith in stability and mass production. It is this legacy that we must change, but we cannot change our paradigms in one grand, quantum jump. We must evolve, step by measured step, towards a business paradigm that replaces the value of stability with the value of change; the constancy of operation with the constancy of resilience and responsiveness; and the stability of unchanging information systems with the constancy of agile, resilient, responsive, and robust information systems.

Evolution is risky. We have seen that it is also painful. If it is risky, painful, and random, then the risk of chaos will turn to certainty. Chaotic change will erode the credibility of new technology. The organization may actually regress, lose what little resilience it had, and become more cynical and even less capable than before. We must therefore direct our evolution. The CMM® is a model of directed, measured evolution.

The CMM® will help us evolve towards the goals we discussed in five measured steps (see Figure 6.2). The goals and capabilities at each step are carefully selected to prepare for the next. For most present day organizations seeking to replace the legacy of the past with a culture that values change, innovation, resilience, and responsiveness, there are too many battles to be fought. When organizations attempt to turn the legacy of the Industrial Age into the whirling chimera of the age of agility they find it impossible to do everything that can be done. There is simply too much to do. The CMM® will help select the right battles at each step along the way. It will maximize the positive impact appropriate for *that* level of organizational capability. It will help you time and choose your most critical battles, so that you can eventually win them all.

Even if the new practices are better than the old, we have seen that we will need deep commitment and constant nurturing to make them survive. They must not be a flash in the corporate pan, otherwise the effort would be wasted, and the next steps would be impossible. The CMM® will help one to install the processes which, when done well, will govern and institutionalize the best practices you would have painfully built at each step. The CMM® helps to nurture and maintain commitment at every step.

Organizations and business environments are as diverse as they are many. One size cannot fit all. There are multiple paths to success. The best depends on environmental factors, such as business drivers, culture, available skills, risk tolerance, and other characteristics of the organization. The CMM® recognizes this. It maps a broad and flexible, but proven, path that allows for environmental and cultural differences between the vast diversity of organizations.

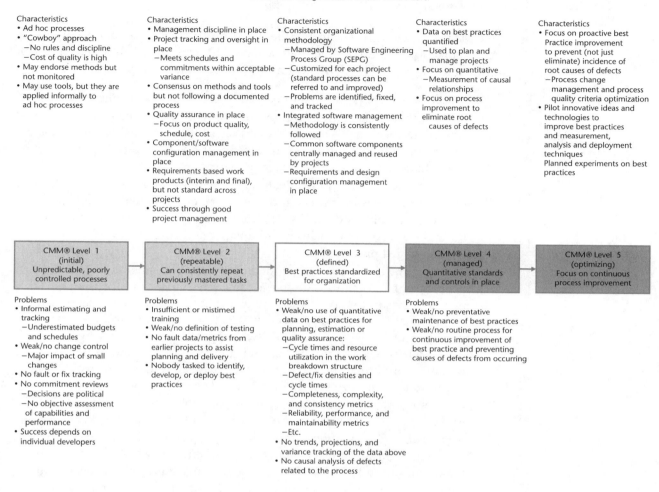

Characteristics of organizations at each CMM® Level

Characteristics
- Ad hoc processes
- "Cowboy" approach
  - No rules and discipline
  - Cost of quality is high
- May endorse methods but not monitored
- May use tools, but they are applied informally to ad hoc processes

Characteristics
- Management discipline in place
- Project tracking and oversight in place
  - Meets schedules and commitments within acceptable variance
- Consensus on methods and tools but not following a documented process
- Quality assurance in place
  - Focus on product quality, schedule, cost
- Component/software configuration management in place
- Requirements based work products (interim and final), but not standard across projects
- Success through good project management

Characteristics
- Consistent organizational methodology
  - Managed by Software Engineering Process Group (SEPG)
  - Customized for each project (standard processes can be referred to and improved)
  - Problems are identified, fixed, and tracked
- Integrated software management
  - Methodology is consistently followed
  - Common software components centrally managed and reused by projects
  - Requirements and design configuration management in place

Characteristics
- Data on best practices quantified
  - Used to plan and manage projects
- Focus on quantitative
  - Measurement of causal relationships
- Focus on process improvement to eliminate root causes of defects

Characteristics
- Focus on proactive best Practice improvement to prevent (not just eliminate) incidence of root causes of defects
  - Process change management and process quality criteria optimization
- Pilot innovative ideas and technologies to improve best practices and measurement, analysis and deployment techniques
  Planned experiments on best practices

| CMM® Level 1 (initial) Unpredictable, poorly controlled processes | CMM® Level 2 (repeatable) Can consistently repeat previously mastered tasks | CMM® Level 3 (defined) Best practices standardized for organization | CMM® Level 4 (managed) Quantitative standards and controls in place | CMM® Level 5 (optimizing) Focus on continuous process improvement |

Problems
- Informal estimating and tracking
  - Underestimated budgets and schedules
- Weak/no change control
  - Major impact of small changes
- No fault or fix tracking
- No commitment reviews
  - Decisions are political
  - No objective assessment of capabilities and performance
- Success depends on individual developers

Problems
- Insufficient or mistimed training
- Weak/no definition of testing
- No fault data/metrics from earlier projects to assist planning and delivery
- Nobody tasked to identify, develop, or deploy best practices

Problems
- Weak/no use of quantitative data on best practices for planning, estimation or quality assurance:
  - Cycle times and resource utilization in the work breakdown structure
  - Defect/fix densities and cycle times
  - Completeness, complexity, and consistency metrics
  - Reliability, performance, and maintainability metrics
  - Etc.
- No trends, projections, and variance tracking of the data above
- No causal analysis of defects related to the process

Problems
- Weak/no preventative maintenance of best practices
- Weak/no routine process for continuous improvement of best practice and preventing causes of defects from occurring

The organization must be at least CMM® Level 3 before it can effectively implement and utilize reusable components

Figure 6.2   Characteristics of organizations at each level of process maturity.

To be broadly applicable, the themes prescribed by the CMM® necessarily must be broad; that is, the CMM® must be generic.[260] The CMM® provides the space that most organizations need to fit it to their own custom environments. Yet the CMM® is unambiguously sharp, crystal clear, and brutally specific about what must be done at each step to gradually evolve towards a culture that thrives on change and basks in the glow of constant improvement. The structure of the CMM® will make this clear.

260. Liskov's Substitution Principle and the Principle of Parsimony discussed in Chapter 2, Section 2.1, demonstrate how generic themes support mutability and creativity. Liskov's Substitution Principle discussed in more detail in Module 5, Sections 1 and 3, under "Mutable Perspectives," and under process engineering is on our Web site.

6.2   Structure of the CMM®

The CMM® envisions five sequential levels of process maturity that progressively lend organizations the capabilities they will need to foster an institutional culture of continual technological improvement and resilience. They are:

1. *Initial state:* Processes are unpredictable and poorly controlled.

   It is not that organizations cannot function and deliver products and services in this state;[261] it is only that they cannot be consistent in terms of the effort required, and are more dependent on characteristics of individuals than on consistency of processes.

   Excellence is not impossible, even in the initial state. It can be achieved through the "heroic efforts" and hard work of individual employees. However, quality and consistency are better served if normal efforts of normal employees can deliver both quality and consistency with well-managed processes.

   Given the chaotic nature of the initial state, focusing on improving the processes of an organization in this state pays more than focusing on improving its technology. Technology cannot be effectively leveraged if processes are weak, and conversely, selection and use of technology will be haphazard unless robust processes support them. This is why the CMM® first seeks to rationalize and stabilize the processes of the organization. It does not seek major initiatives to induct new technology, nor does it emphasize standardization and sharing of processes or technology across projects and groups. To evolve to Level 2, CMM® looks for consistently repeatable results within a group or project team.

2. *Repeatable:* The capability to consistently repeat previously mastered tasks with consistent results and consistent effort has been reached, but the organization has no standard processes. Each group or project team uses its own processes, but each has the capability to consistently get the same results from the same processes within acceptable limits. The CMM® now shifts its attention to evolving to the next level, by culling the best of breed from each group to create organization-wide process standards. If Knowledge Artifacts are being used by even a few projects, then they may be harvested as the organization prepares for its Level 3 assessment.

3. *Defined:* Standardized and consistent best practices are the norm now. This is the least required by the effective use of Knowledge Artifacts. We discussed this aspect in Chapter 4. By institutionalizing shared best practices across projects and processes, it prepares the organization for their measurement and maintenance. If the use of Knowledge Artifacts was harvested from Level 2, then it will be a part of the shared standard at this point.

4. *Managed:* Consistent quantitative standards and management controls are in place. They are aligned with business goals and business processes. It

---

261. Sometimes Level 1 organizations may even endorse methods, but rarely will they monitor them, or verify compliance.

may be a cliché, but it is also true that what cannot be measured cannot be managed. By focusing on measurement and corrective action, this step prepares the organization for continual improvement and preventive maintenance of its processes. It is the launching pad to Level 5, which is the state of the organization in which the culture of optimization and the use of Knowledge Artifacts can properly thrive.

5. *Optimizing:* Focus on continual improvement and adaptation of processes, and anticipation of change in "preventive maintenance" mode, now comes into their own. The organization will thrive on the continuing challenge of remaining resilient, responsive, and "state-of-the-art," under the intense pressures of a rapidly evolving business environment. Knowledge Artifacts will thrive.

The vast majority of organizations are at Level 1, a state with weak controls and inconsistent governance. They must evolve from Level 1 to a state where governance is so sophisticated that change may be welcomed, and even institutionalized, without cutting a swath of chaos through the organization. It is a daunting task. It only can be done in measured steps. No step may be skipped. Figure 6.2 charts the evolution from Level 1 to 5. It articulates the typical characteristics of organizations at each level, and the problems that will spur the organization onto the next level in its search for comfort under the constant drumbeat of improvement, both institutionalized and continual.

The CMM® is a model for improving and evolving software development capabilities. With Knowledge Artifacts, the line between software and business process becomes hazy. It might even vanish. The software may become a seamless expression of the process. The CMM® consists of generic themes. They are equally applicable to software and to business process design projects. In the sections that follow, we have adapted the CMM® to reflect this seamless unity between software and the business process that it supports. The term "business system," sometimes abbreviated to simply "system," reflects this unified meaning.

In CMM® lexicon, the adjective "Key" is used to describe items that will contribute most to the intent of that level. Each level has specific focus areas, called Key Process Areas (KPAs). These KPAs identify which battles must be fought to reach the level. The others can wait. Each KPA has specific goals that describe results, not actions. Each KPA consists of multiple activities. Activities are processes for achieving the goals of that KPA. Each goal may be served by several activities, and conversely, an activity may serve several goals. The KPA is satisfied only when all of its activities are *properly* completed. The adjective "properly" is the operative word here. Each activity has specific performance criteria. These criteria are called Key Practices.

Moreover, business processes are almost never infinitely reliable and consistent. Sometimes they will fail, or be cause for anomalies. The results they produce may be beyond the pale of the acceptable. Monitoring, governance, and tracking of processes are a prerequisite for consistency. We have discussed this in Part I. The CMM® focuses on governance and control. It also prescribes processes for higher order governance that will institutionalize governance. Thus, we end with well governed institutional processes at the conclusion of each level of process maturity. These create the stable base that facilitates evolution to the next level.

The risk of change gradually shrinks as the organization matures and steps up through levels of capability. See Figure 6.3. No level may be skipped. Each is a ski-jump for the next. Moreover, at each level, the organization must not merely prepare to propel itself to the next level, but it must keep working on retaining the capabilities it had acquired earlier. Otherwise, it may slip back. There are processes at each level that will institutionalize and maintain these gains. At each level, the CMM® not only identifies immediate goals and key processes for achieving them, but also seeks:

- *Commitment* to perform: The CMM® focuses on Management commitment, and identifies key practices and criteria for commitment at each level.
- *Ability* to perform: The CMM® focuses on key practices, ensuring that adequate resources, such as time and money, are available, and enabling conditions are met.
- *Performance measurement and analysis:* The CMM® identifies the key practices and the performance criteria, ensuring that all stakeholders transparently and accurately know the status of prescribed activities. It facilitates clear and accurate communication.

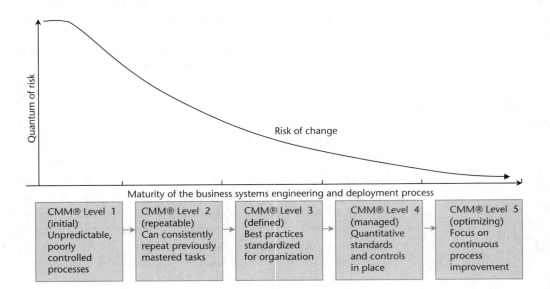

Figure 6.3 The risks of change gradually shrink as the organization matures.

• *Verification* of implementation: The CMM® describes the management reviews, key verification practices, and verification criteria that will keep the initiative on track.

Thus, the CMM® drives and institutionalizes change through commitment, ability, measurement, and verification. In CMM® lexicon, these four items are collectively called the *Common Features* of CMM® levels. Figure 6.4 shows the overall structure of the CMM®.

Figure 6.5 shows, level by CMM® level, the issues on which management must focus. These are the CMM® KPAs at each level. The goals of each KPA, and the activities that support those goals, are shown in Figures 6.6 through 6.28.[262] Broken-lined arrows in these figures associate activities with the goals they directly support. Note that these goals, activities, and KPAs do not operate in isolation—they reinforce each other. When activities are not associated with specific

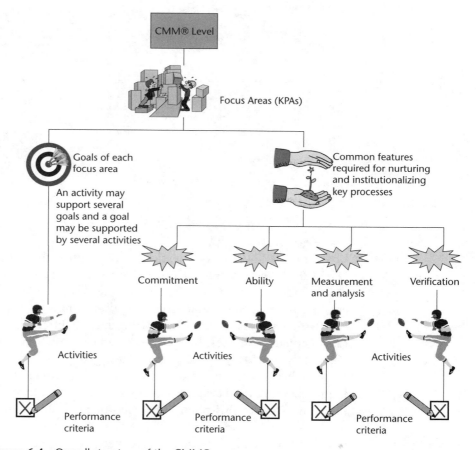

Figure 6.4   Overall structure of the CMM®.

---

262. In CMM® lexicon, a "product" is an item delivered to the end user or customer, whereas "work product" includes both CMM® "products" and intermediate work products in the supply chain. The terms in Figures 6.6 through 6.28 conform to these meanings. Bear in mind also that the term "Upper Management" in our adaptation of the CMM® is a synonym for "Senior Management" in CMM® version 1.1. "Upper Managers" have general responsibility for the operation of the firm, more than project level responsibilities. References [146, 147, 319] detail the CMM®.

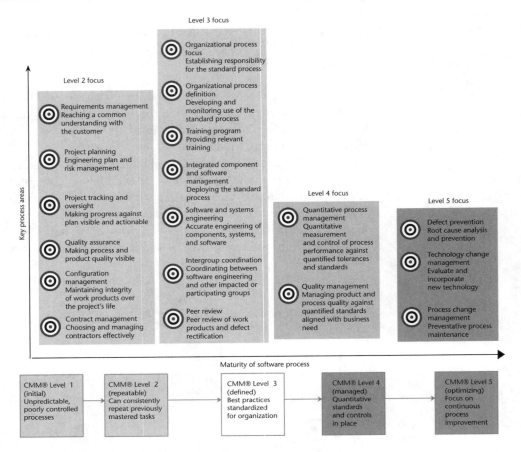

Figure 6.5 Focus Areas for Management.

goals in Figures 6.6 through 6.28, it means that these activities generically impact all of the goals of the KPA.

For most Level 1 organizations, streamlining the management of requirements brings the biggest benefits. Knowledge artifacts encapsulate the rules and functional requirements shared most often across businesses and information systems. Knowledge Artifacts help the analysis of requirements.

If the patterns in Parts I and II initiate requirement captures and requirement management processes, then they could help streamline them, although this is not absolutely necessary at this point. A few groups or projects might start using these patterns in some fragmented or rudimentary form as the organization starts preparing for Level 2. However, expect no major benefits from Knowledge Artifacts over other methods at this point. The need of the hour is good, coordinated management. Any process that manages requirements will have a major impact with or without Knowledge Artifacts. Moreover, we will need a consistent process before we can improve on it by introducing Knowledge Artifacts.

Once we have the consistent, if fragmented, processes that will establish a Level 2 capability, then we can consider introducing Knowledge Artifacts. If even a few Level 2 groups or projects use Knowledge Artifacts, then they may be harvested at Level 3. Even if these processes use Knowledge Artifacts in a rudimentary or fragmented form for the management of requirements at Level 2, then these processes can be improved and harvested as the organization prepares for its Level 3 assessment. If the use of Knowledge Artifacts was harvested from Level 2, then they will be a part of the shared standard at Level 3, which may then be refined at Level 4, and eventually be optimized to thrive at Level 5.

Figure 6.5 tells us that risks are front-loaded in the CMM®. The largest risks, and the hardest and largest number of battles, must be fought early in the journey. After the organization climbs past Level 2, the path becomes smoother, and evolution becomes easier. There are fewer battles and less risk. The culture of change will begin to take root, and institutionalized experience will pave the cow path.

To qualify at a level, the organization must meet *all* the requirements of that level. However, different parts of large or widely-spread-out organizations may be at different levels of maturity. Indeed, each also may be at different points of the emotional curve we discussed in Chapter 5. Some may vacillate back and forth between the different emotional states we described in Chapter 5 as they evolve. This is normal and expected. However, on occasion, when the change has not been managed effectively, the organization even may slip back. This will be unacceptable, and must not happen.

On the other hand, shooting for a CMM® level does not mean that an enlightened organization should give up the higher level activities that it may have already institutionalized. Many activities are enlightened common sense, as we will see later in this chapter. An organization (or its enlightened parts) might routinely conduct some of the activities mandated at higher CMM® levels. However, unless it meets all the criteria demanded by the higher CMM® level, the organization (or the part of the organization) cannot qualify at that level. Conducting activities mandated by higher levels may smooth the process of evolution, and make it less painful. Every KPA, and to some extent every activity, will be cause for cycling through the emotional states described in Chapter 5. Change of any kind can be emotionally stressful.

The following sections will describe, level by CMM® level, the goals, activities, and performance criteria for each KPA in Figure 6.5. They include the activities that will institutionalize, nurture, and stabilize the change at each level. The figures in these sections also may be used as process templates and dashboards to steer the organization through painful evolution. If some of these figures are busy, it is because they substitute for, and convey several hundred pages of, textual information on the CMM®. Change is painful, but it also can be exhilarating.

6.3   CMM® Level 2: Consistent Repeatability—KPAs, Goals, and Activities

The set of business requirements is the reason for the creation and the existence of a business system and its supporting software. Consistency in managing requirements necessarily must be the first prerequisite for consistent business and systems software development processes. It is naturally the most important KPA at Level 2.

Inconsistency also flows from poor planning and ill-managed risks. Consistent project planning and oversight are necessary preconditions for consistent delivery of business systems and supporting software. Figure 6.6 confirms this.

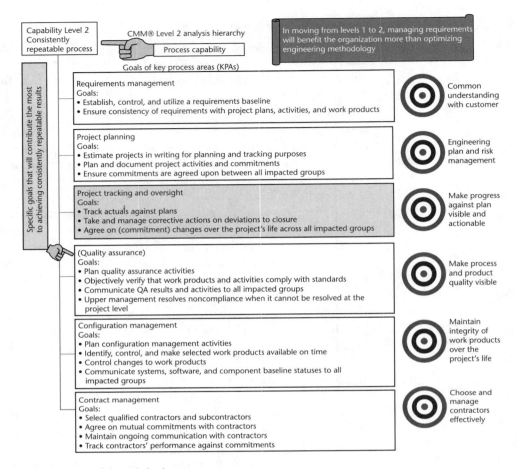

Figure 6.6 Level 2 goals by key process area.

At Level 1, Quality Assurance (QA) activities usually are not integrated into the project plan. Quality Assurance is required to ensure consistent performance and consistent course corrections. Without consistent quality, there can be no consistently reliable process. Figure 6.6 also tells us so.

If the wrong versions or incorrect components are deployed or combined, then the system will not perform reliably. Consistent delivery and performance of business systems and software requires consistent configuration management (abbreviated to "SCM" or just "CM" in the figures that follow). It should be no surprise that the CMM® focuses on configuration management processes at Level 2. The CMM® requires a configuration management board called the SCCB to oversee and coordinate components and releases across all impacted parties in the project team. The actual configuration and repository administration is the responsibility of a separate group. The SCCB oversees the activities of this group. For small and simple projects, repository administration even may be a part time responsibility of a team member. Figure 6.11 has more detail.

Inconsistent management of contractors, their activities, and products also will lead to inconsistent components and inconsistent performance. Reliable contract and contractor management necessarily must be a Level 2 KPA.

In short, Level 2 is about consistently managing the processes that matter most to consistently reliable performance. Figure 6.6 describes the goals of each Level 2 Key Process Area. Figures 6.7 through 6.12 describe how these goals, activities, and acceptance criteria mesh and reinforce each other. Each activity in Figures 6.7 through 6.12 has been linked to the goal that it supports. A few activities in these figures imply their own acceptance criteria, which therefore have not been explicitly elaborated. The figures are annotated and self-explanatory. They need little further elaboration. Together, they describe the processes required to move from the chaos of Level 1 to the consistently reliable performance of Level 2.

Given the chaotic and inconsistent nature of Level 1, the transition to Level 2 emphasizes management and process more than technology. This focus is reflected in the kind of training that the CMM® envisions at Level 2. The focus is on planning, estimating (see Figure 6.8), and managing (see Figure 6.9), more than on the tools and technology of computerized systems. Indeed, the CMM® recognizes that leaders are often promoted to positions of management based on their technical skills and past technical performance. The CMM® tells us that we must shore this up with equal, if not greater, emphasis on the enlightened management of people, processes, and resources. Only then will consistent performance be possible.

The emphasis on written and formal procedures in transitioning from Level 1 to 2 appears at first to be somewhat onerous and ridden with red tape. The transition from Level 1 to 2 often meets resistance on this count. However, documented communications, plans, and policies are needed to institutionalize and institute lasting change amid the chaos of Level 1. They are tangible and lasting tools for clearly communicating and coordinating with consistency, and are symbols of management commitment.

Written communication is needed because inconsistency often goes hand-in-hand with informal, unwritten communication and inconsistent interpretation. Formal documents will make communication tangible and puts it on record, along with the clarifications, changes, commitments, risks, and disagreements that will occur from time to time, so that processes become consistent before we cull and collect the best practices from them at Level 3. It is worth investing the effort to formally foster consistency.

Depending on their size, complexity, and situation, organizations will determine how elaborate each activity (and corresponding work products) in the following figures must be. They will be customized to fit, and the activities always need not be as onerous as they seem. The activities and their acceptance criteria in the following figures are not just institutionalized business sense—they are institutionalized common sense.

Although the CMM® does not demand it, experience shows that automation will facilitate the process, especially configuration management. However, regardless of how it is done, clear communication is the single most important issue in successfully making it to Level 2. We have discussed this in Chapter 5.

The requirement for estimating resource and schedule requirements from work products (see Figure 6.8) also meets resistance when the organization is moving from Level 1 to 2. At Level 1, estimates and changes are often pushed through based on "political muscle" or wishful thinking. The result is that projects are often late and over budget. Although estimates conformed to the wishes of important

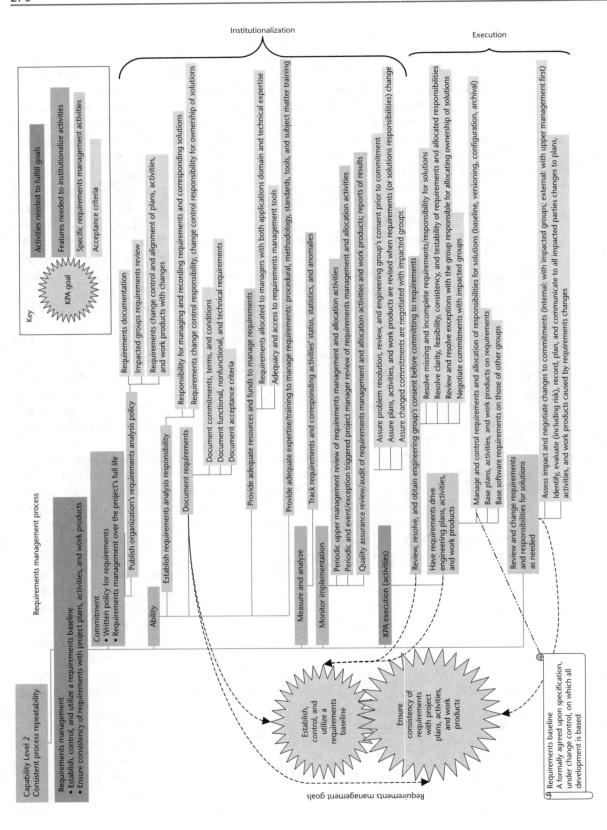

Figure 6.7 Support for Requirements Management goals: activities and key practices.

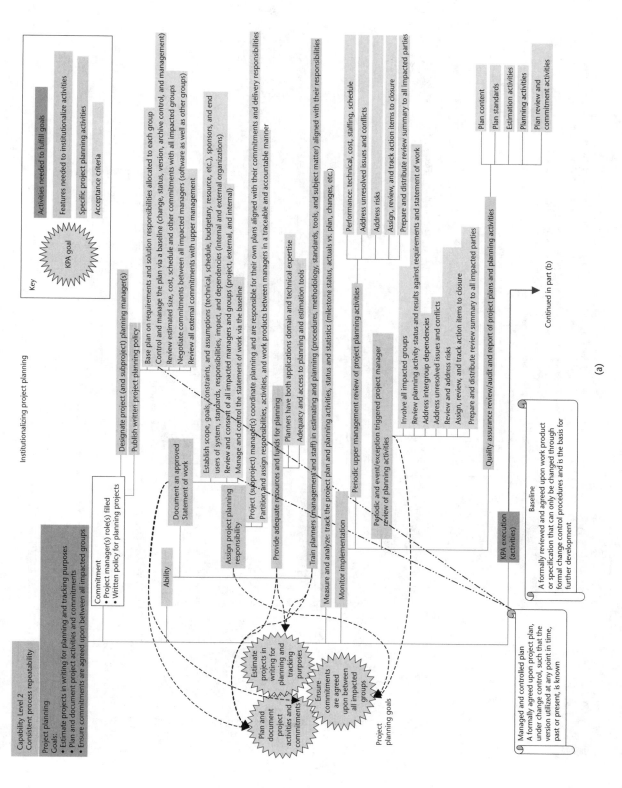

Figure 6.8 Support for Project Planning goals; activities and key practices.

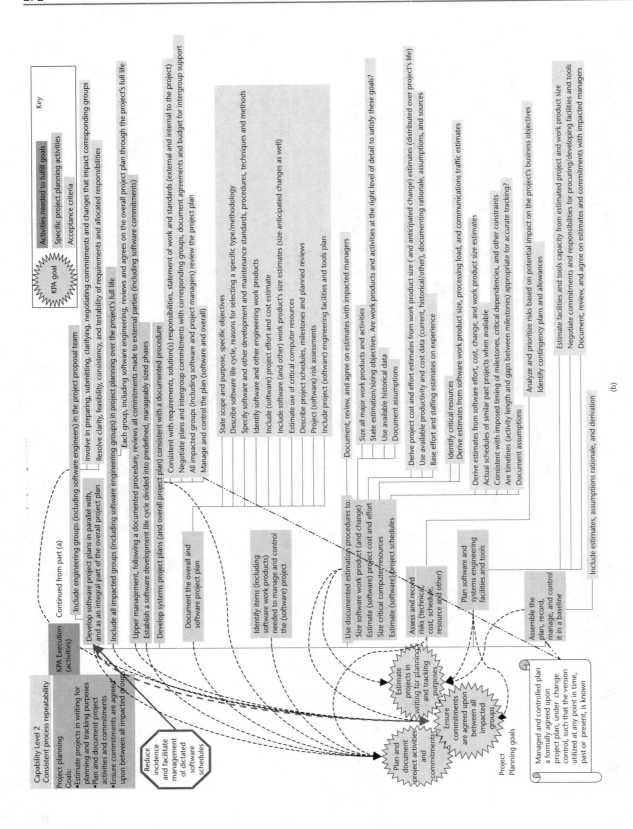

Figure 6.8 (Continued.)

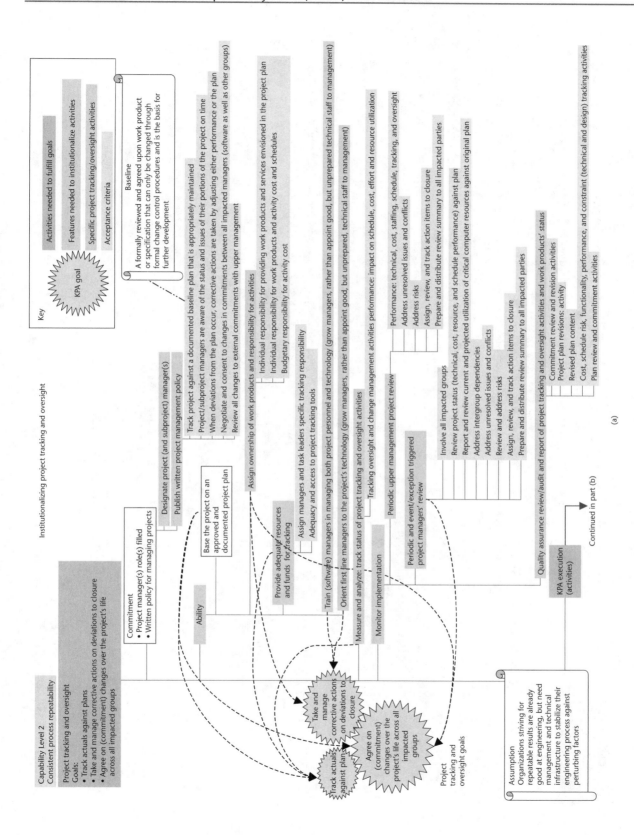

Figure 6.9 Support for Project Tracking and Oversight goals: activities and key practices.

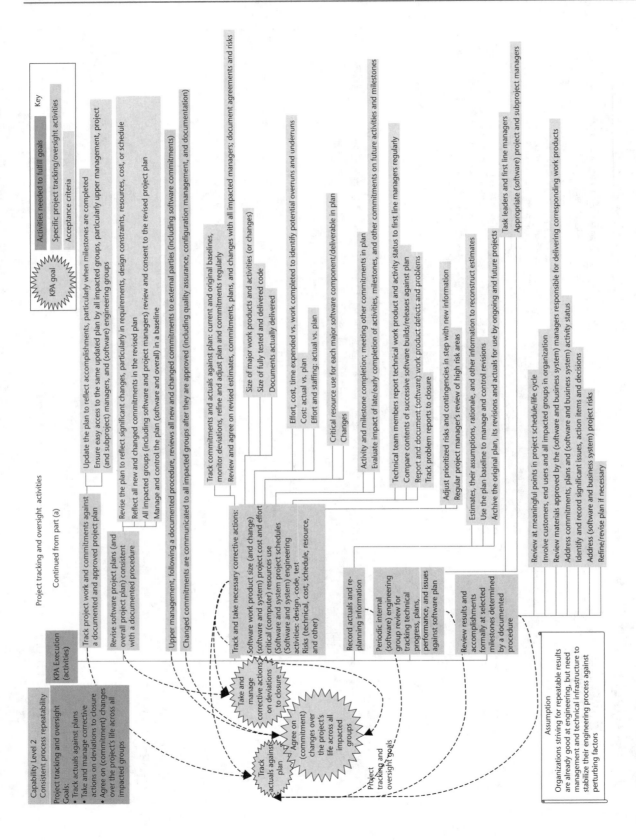

Figure 6.9 (Continued.)

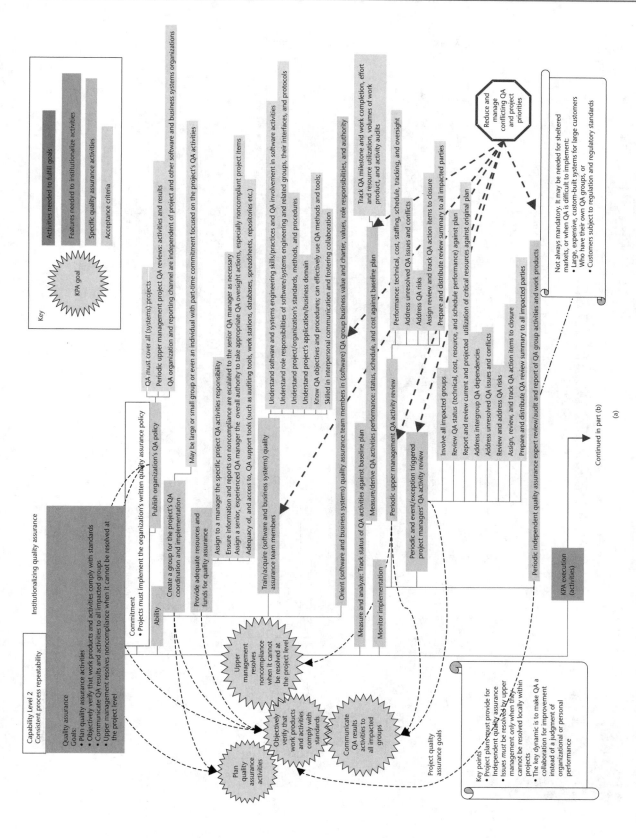

Figure 6.10 Support for Quality Assurance goals: activities and key practices.

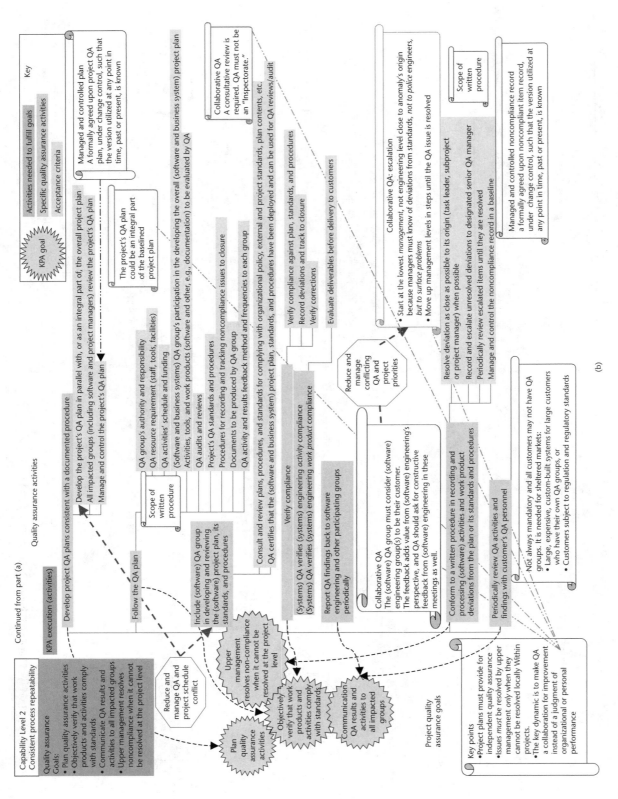

Figure 6.10 (Continued.)

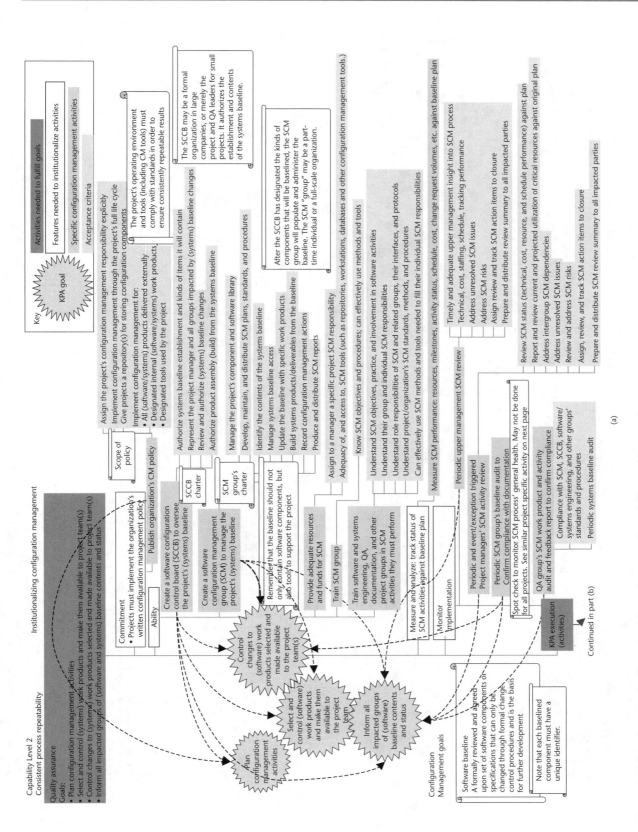

Figure 6.11   Support for Configuration Management goals: activities and key practices.

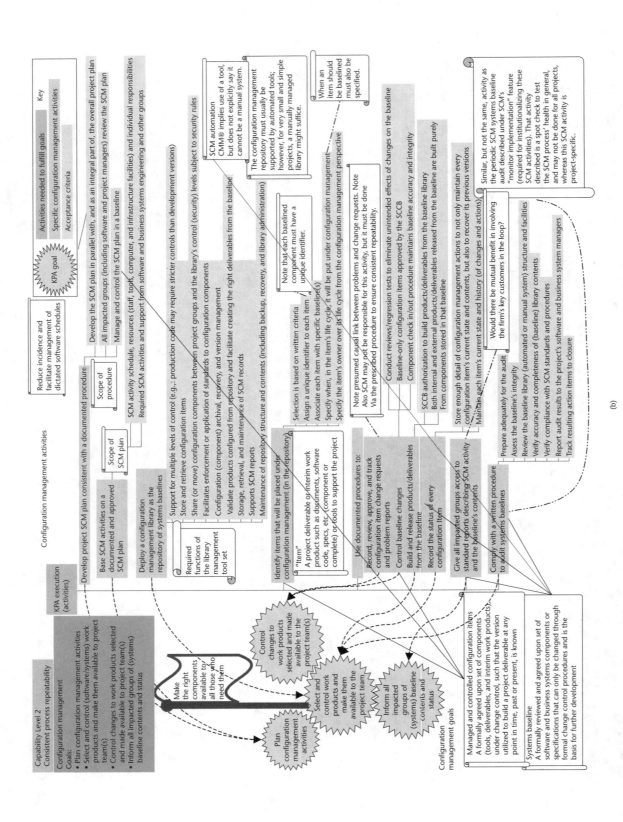

Figure 6.11 (Continued.)

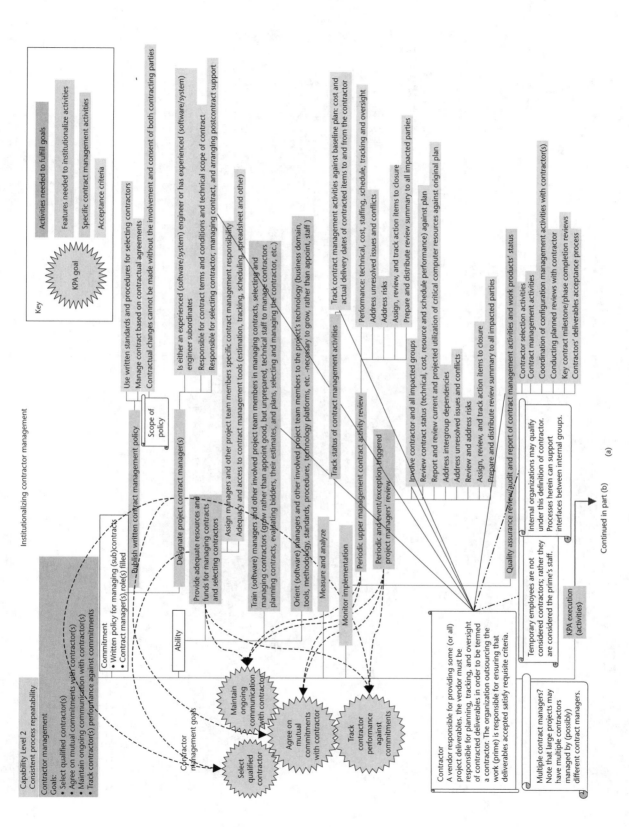

Figure 6.12 Support for Contractor Management goals: activities and key practices.

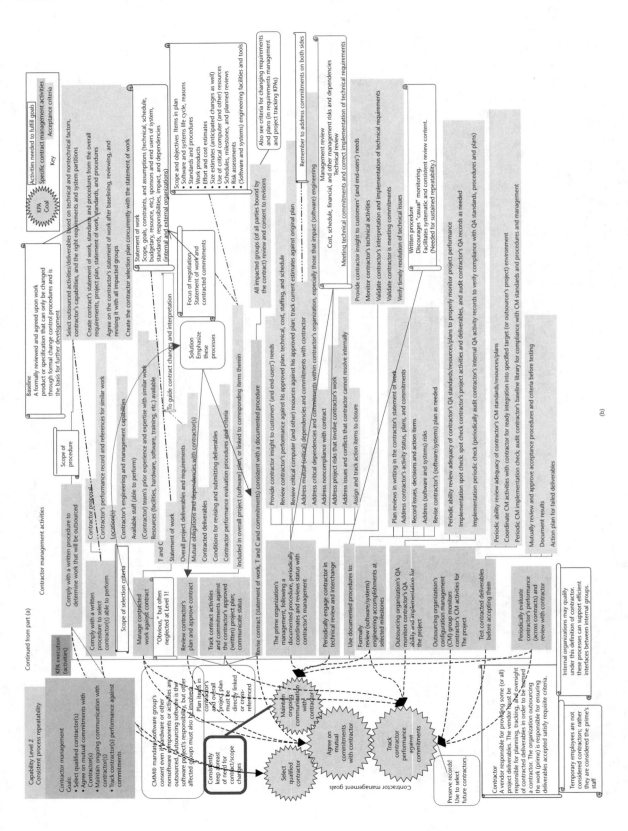

Figure 6.12 (Continued.)

stakeholders at inception, the products nevertheless were delivered late, and were sometimes defective.

Even when projects are finished on time, this mode of operation causes enormous stress in the organization, and quality can suffer. At Level 2, the requirements are that schedules and resource requirements be negotiated, based on concrete work products, and not dictated by vacuous wishes. This will be even more true when changes are considered (see Figure 6.9). Transitioning to this mode of estimation may be stressful, but no more so than the collective and cumulative stress that the organization already faces from missed schedules and budgets. Moreover, stresses will reduce as the transition nears completion. All stakeholders will be winners in processes that finish projects on time, within budget, and with few surprises.

6.4   CMM® Level 3: Standardized Best Practices Deployed and in Use—KPAs, Goals, and Activities

At Level 2, the organization has processes that perform consistently. However, they are not integrated, and are often fragmented. The need of the hour is to cull the organization's best practices from its fragmented parts and standardize the whole, in order to share the common experience, so that the entire organization can benefit from it. This is in what the CMM® calls the Organization's standard process. The Organization's standard process integrates the best practices culled, collected, and improved from Level 2. Note that it is possible for an organization to have more than one standard; different standard processes may support different assumptions or environments.

Someone has to build, own, and maintain the standard process(es). The CMM® calls this group the *Software Engineering Process Group* (SEPG). Of course, if Knowledge Artifacts are involved, then the standard process will not be for software alone. Rather, it will integrate the software process with the process for engineering business processes. We will call this integrated process the "business systems process," or "systems process" for short. If the intent is to deploy and standardize the use of Knowledge Artifacts, then the SEPG will own the business systems process.

At this time, management must necessarily shift focus to standardizing best practices across the organization. Only then can businesses reap the benefits of organization-wide use of best practices. The CMM® calls this "Organization Process Focus"—the focus on collecting and transferring process improvements and best practices across projects throughout the organization. It is a Level 3 KPA (see Figure 6.13), and the SEPG is the organizational engine for it. The SEPG coordinates the sharing of best practices across the organization. It does so with the Process Repository.

The Process Repository is the storehouse of the organization's collective experience in building, coordinating, and governing business systems development projects. This information must not only be organized and deployed throughout the organization, but also must be easily accessible by individuals. The Process Repository facilitates this. The Process Repository includes and expands on the Repository of Knowledge in Figure 2.23. Figure 6.14 shows its contents.

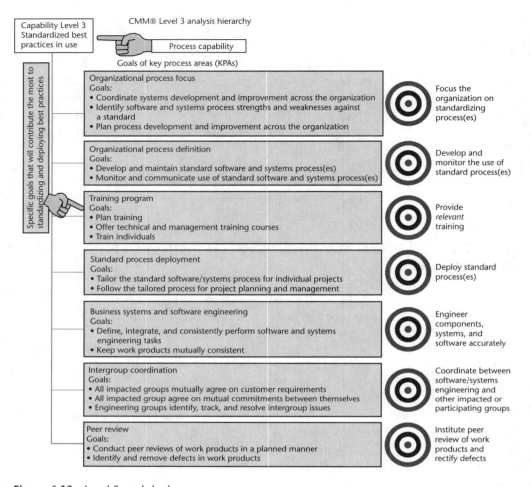

Figure 6.13 Level 3 goals by key process area.

The process repository contains all of the work products of Level 2 processes, enhanced and augmented by Level 3 key practices, as well as the work products unique to Level 3. It contains the standard process(es), as well as their project level customizations.

The process repository does not mandate the use of the Knowledge Artifacts of Parts I and II of this book. They are not absolutely essential for standardizing the business systems *development* processes, but the process repository and the practices at Level 3 are necessary for leveraging Knowledge Artifacts. We discussed the reasons earlier in this chapter. Knowledge Artifacts will optimize the benefits of the reuse and sharing of *business process knowledge*.

When Knowledge Artifacts are used, the objects, patterns, and rules in this book (and [337]) will be reusable components that the standard process(es) will repeatedly leverage as it weaves them into business systems. These Knowledge Artifacts may be customized to produce industry-, enterprise-, and even project-specific components, as articulated in Chapter 2 (see Figure 6.14). Customization guidelines (i.e., the activity called "Create and Maintain the Process Assets repository" in Figure 6.16) should require that customization of knowledge artifacts be done by

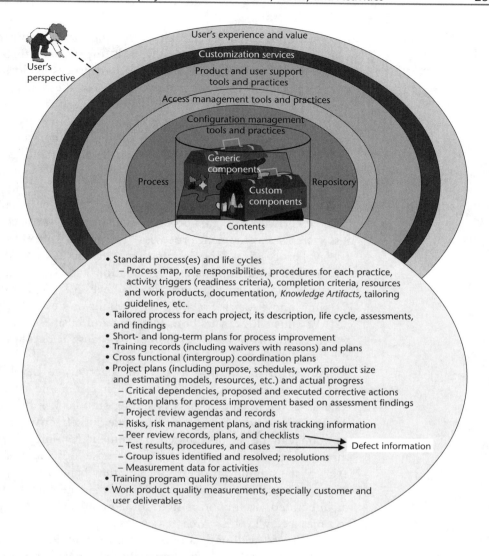

User's perspective

User's experience and value

Customization services

Product and user support tools and practices

Access management tools and practices

Configuration management tools and practices

Generic components

Process

Custom components

Repository

Contents

- Standard process(es) and life cycles
  - Process map, role responsibilities, procedures for each practice, activity triggers (readiness criteria), completion criteria, resources and work products, documentation, *Knowledge Artifacts*, tailoring guidelines, etc.
- Tailored process for each project, its description, life cycle, assessments, and findings
- Short- and long-term plans for process improvement
- Training records (including waivers with reasons) and plans
- Cross functional (intergroup) coordination plans
- Project plans (including purpose, schedules, work product size and estimating models, resources, etc.) and actual progress
  - Critical dependencies, proposed and executed corrective actions
  - Action plans for process improvement based on assessment findings
  - Project review agendas and records
  - Risks, risk management plans, and risk tracking information
  - Peer review records, plans, and checklists ⎫
  - Test results, procedures, and cases ⎬——→ Defect information
  - Group issues identified and resolved; resolutions
  - Measurement data for activities
- Training program quality measurements
- Work product quality measurements, especially customer and user deliverables

Figure 6.14   The Level 3 process repository.

attaching constraints (which are also components) to those objects.[263] This will preserve the integrity of the Universal Perspective, and the reusability of the artifacts that flow from it, across multiple scopes and applications. The figures in this chapter describe Level 3 processes that populate and leverage the repository of Figure 6.14. The repository is a key asset and a resource for processes at Level 3 and beyond.

The flip side of "Organization Process Focus" is "Organization Process Definition." This includes the creation and maintenance of the organization's standard processes, its software and systems development methodologies, plans, procedures, and training materials. It also involves collecting process history, in terms of performance, quality, cost, size, and other parameters, which will form the basis for quantitative standards. Although these standards will be developed in Level 4, an

263. Module 6 of our Web site, and Chapter 3 of [337] discuss how features flow from constraints.

organization still will be capable of looking forward towards the standards that it wishes to consolidate and quantify, as it forges ahead through Level 3.

Instituting organization-wide standard processes does not mean that one size will fit all. Rather, it means that standard processes will be reference models, just as was the Universal Perspective. Individual projects may tailor a standard process to fit their specific situations and environments. Standard processes must help, not hinder. They must leverage shared learning and common patterns, and not needlessly restrict the process best suited for the project and its staff. This can only happen if the users of the organization's standard processes not only understand them, but also understand how to use and customize them. Therefore, Level 3 also calls for focusing on *relevant* training.

The CMM® calls this process of customizing project level software and business systems development processes "Integrated Software Management." The project level process involves planning, tracking, and management of projects, based on *managed* customization of an organization-wide standard methodology, and sharing the lessons learned from it. It is a Level 3 KPA that complements the Project Planning and Project Tracking KPAs built at Level 2. In our adaptation of the CMM®, this KPA covers both software and business process engineering. We will call it *Standard Process Deployment*, because it deploys the standard process to individual projects.

Although training was a recognized activity in Level 2, it could sometimes be mistimed or suboptimal. Now, we must refine and optimize it. At Level 3, the systems development process is stable, standard, repeatable, and under control. Organization-wide changes can be made and effectively coordinated. The training program can be a coordinated instrument for integrating changes and process improvements. Indeed, it must be, otherwise individual projects will not be able to leverage the standard process, nor will they benefit from it. The benefits of organization-wide standards will flow only if management focuses on making training an integrated, well-coordinated, and organization-wide program. Training thus becomes a Key Process Area at Level 3.

Shifting to well-understood, organization-wide standards, which also will be systematically used and systematically shared, calls for peer reviews and coordination between groups. These also must be areas of management focus. Hence, they are also Level 3 key process areas. Figure 6.13 tells us this.

All this is in support of better business systems and software engineering. With the chaotic and inconsistent processes of Level 2 streamlined and made consistent, we can at last focus on better engineering. With processes being well-managed, good systems engineering starts paying higher dividends to the business, and becomes the key to better business systems. The engineering of software and business systems, based on organization-wide best practices and a standard methodology, is the bottom line at Level 3. The work product of the process is a business system. Therefore, the process is called Business Systems and Software Engineering in our adaptation of the CMM®.[264] It is a KPA in Figure 6.13. Figure 6.13 also emphasizes the fact that when Knowledge Artifacts are involved, this KPA will

---

264. The CMM®, with its exclusive focus on software development, calls this KPA "Software Product Engineering." References [146, 319] have more information. Reference [147] has the more recent versions of staged and continuing improvement CMM® models published by the Soaftware Engineering Institute (see Chapter 4).

cover the engineering (or the incorporation, if these components are available "off-the-shelf") of the components that we discussed in Part I. Figure 6.19 elaborates on these concepts, to tell us that there is more to good business systems engineering than writing good program code.

Like the goals and processes at Level 2, the goals and processes at Level 3 are interdependent, and must mesh with each other. Figures 6.15 through 6.21 describe the processes that build and use the process repository in support of the goals articulated in Figure 6.13. The figures show how these processes all work together. Like the figures that described Level 2 processes, the figures for Level 3 are annotated, and require little further elaboration.

6.5   CMM® Level 4: Quantitative Standards and Controls in Place—KPAs, Goals, and Activities

The real focus of Level 4 is quality assurance; that is, the quality of business systems and software development activities and work products must stay within quantitatively measured tolerances.[265] Thus, there are two prime foci—process quality and product quality. Each is a KPA in Figure 6.22.[266]

Level 3 set the stage for this. Processes, practices, and work products were standardized and continually assessed. A robust databank was built in the Process Repository (see Figure 6.14). With this accumulated information, we can start establishing quantitative standards and tolerances at Level 4, which will then become the springboard to Level 5. Level 5 will focus on the preemption of problems, preventive maintenance of the process, and its continuing improvement. Before we can do this, we must set realistic expectations. This is the primary thrust at Level 4. At Level 4, we focus on the establishment of the ranges within which we expect our standard processes and work products will perform. We do this from the performance histories we collected in our process repository at Level 3.

At Level 4, the thrust is to address the special causes that perturb process quality and that of its work products, and to plan for and control them, based on quantified metrics. It means that these metrics and tolerances must be formulated and tracked. Just as the standard process had to be tailored to fit individual projects at Level 3, the performance standards of the standard process (and its work products) must be tailored to fit each individual project. This practice is a natural next step, an evolutionary outgrowth from the best practices that were institutionalized in the *Standard Process Deployment* KPA of Level 3.

Each project can use these tolerances to quantitatively estimate its expected performance —the ranges within which performance norms for its processes and products should lie. The CMM® calls this "Process Capability." These expectations are derived from the norms for standard processes, after accounting for the deviations from the standard, and the customizations sanctioned for individual projects. The

---

265. Tolerances are Knowledge Artifacts derived from the Metamodel of Knowledge. See Chapter 4, Section 3, under Information Quality, in [337].

266. The CMM® calls the KPA that focuses on product quality *Software Quality Management*. With knowledge artifacts, the boundary between software and business process becomes less sharp, and given the right tools, it can even vanish. Our adaptation of the CMM® takes this into account. We call this KPA *Quantitative Product Quality Management* in our adaptation, because that is what it really is. The product in question may be software, the business process, or an intermediate work product of the process that produces them.

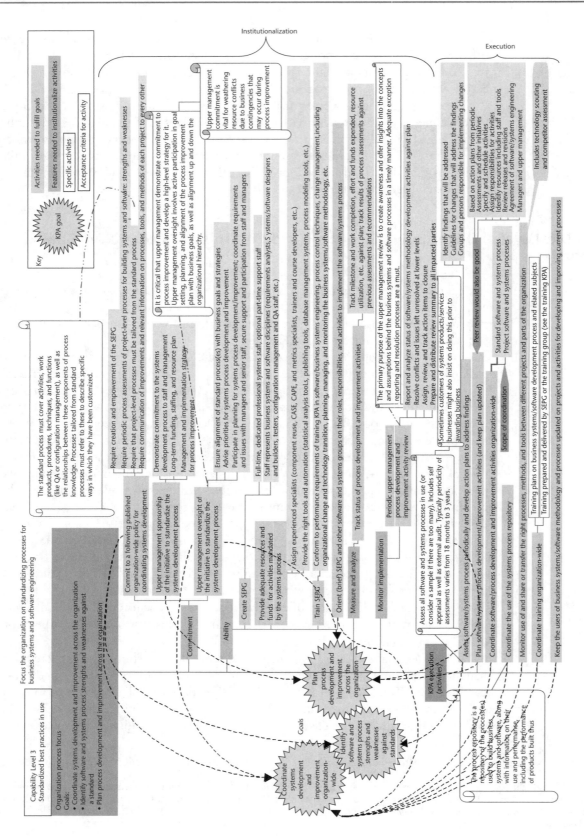

Figure 6.15 Support for Organization Process Focus goals: activities and key practices.

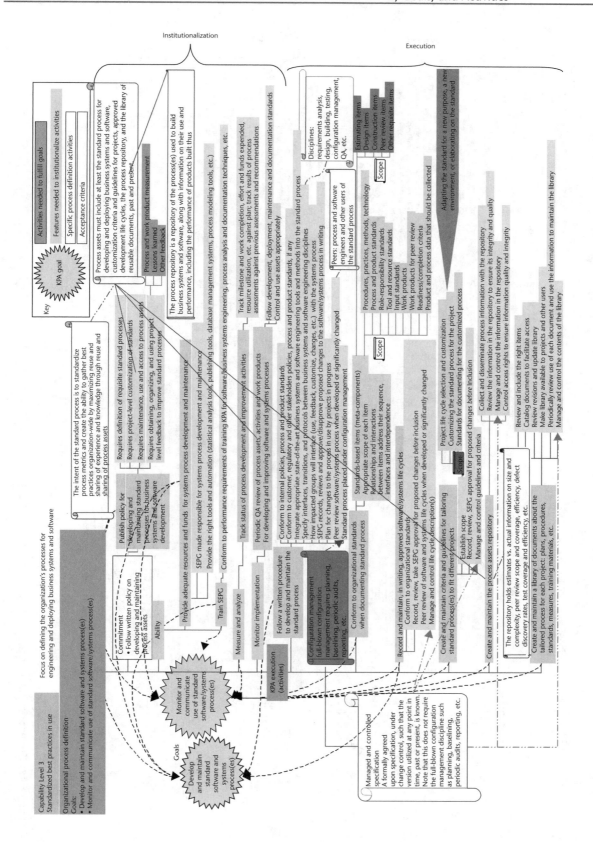

Figure 6.16 Support for Organization Process Definition goals: activities and key practices.

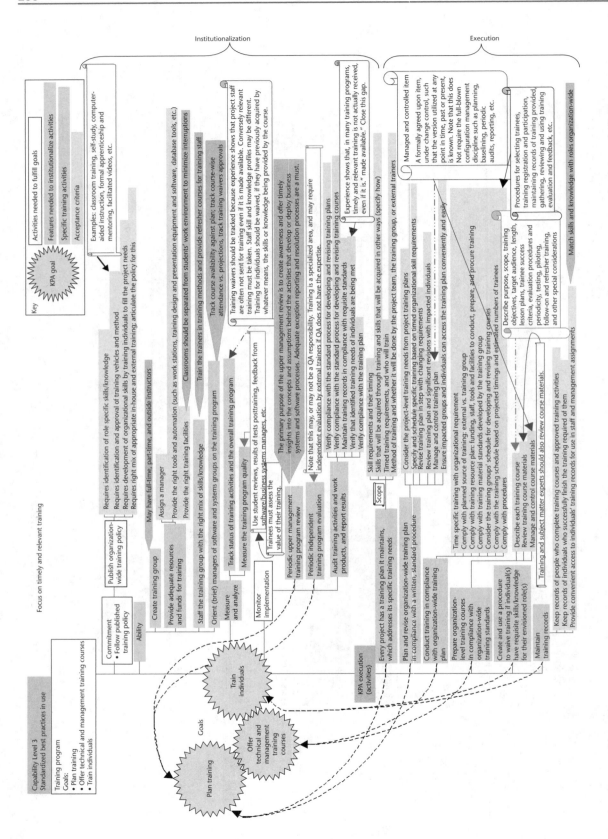

Figure 6.17 Support for Training goals: activities and key practices.

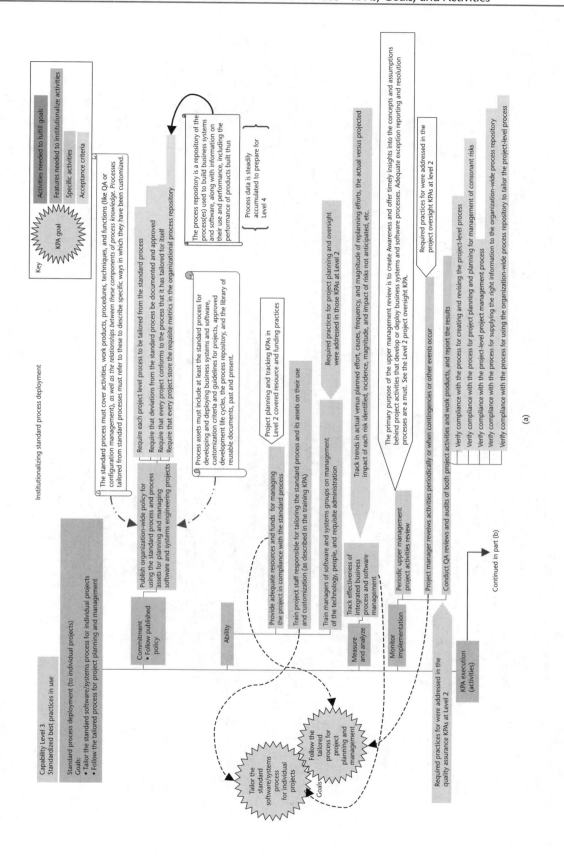

Figure 6.18 Support for deploying standard processes: goals, activities, and key practices.

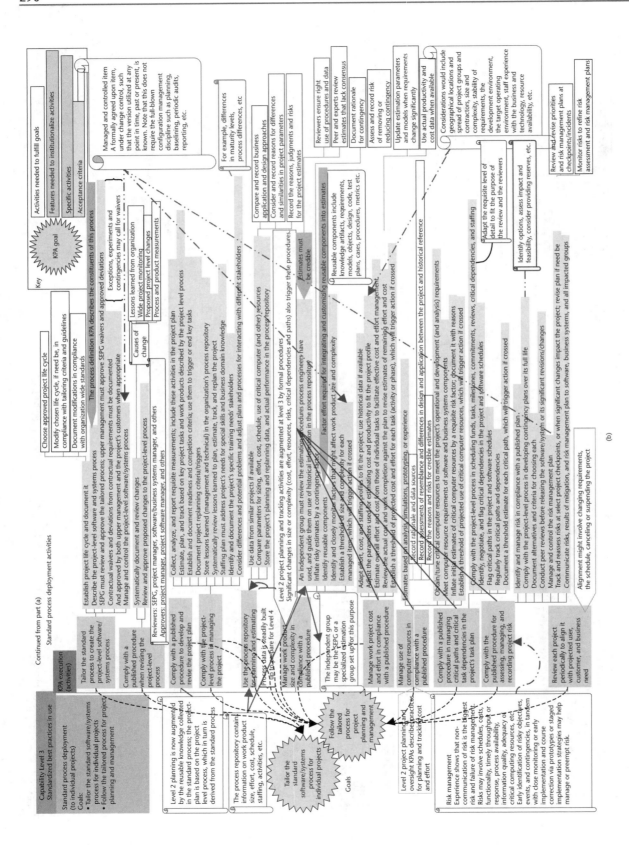

Figure 6.18 (Continued.)

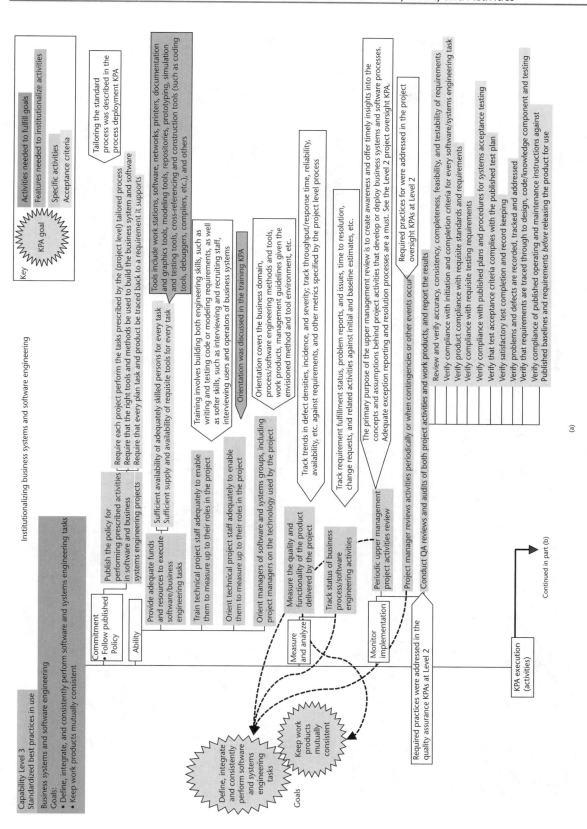

Figure 6.19 Engineering of business systems: goals, activities, and key practices.

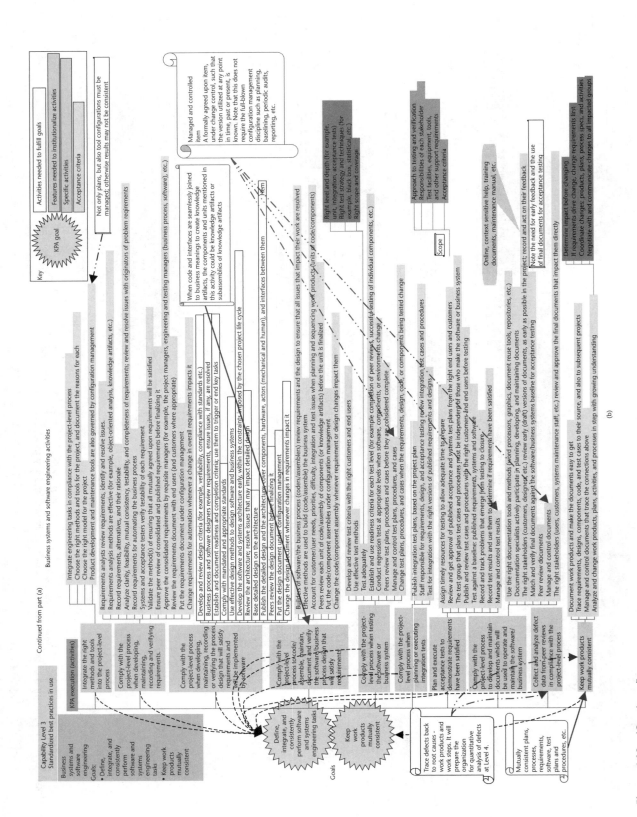

Figure 6.19 (Continued).

Figure 6.20   Coordination between stakeholders and engineering groups: goals, activities, and key practices.

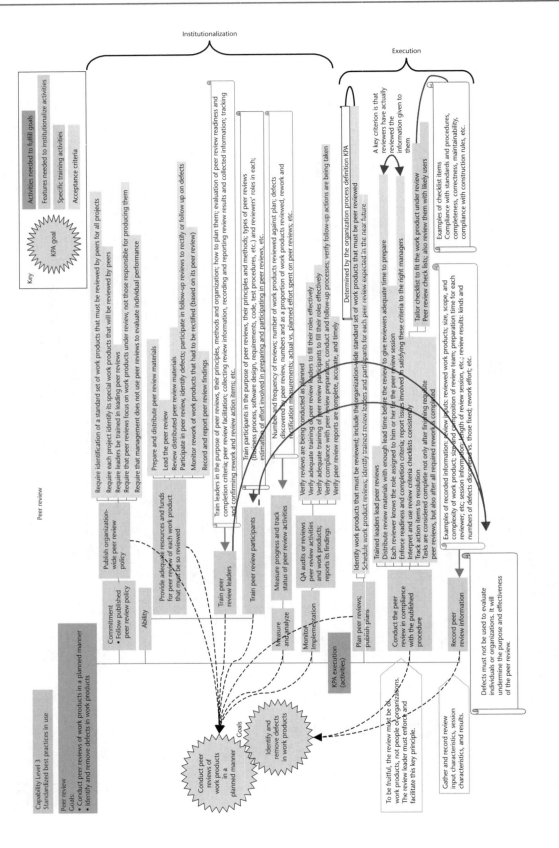

Figure 6.21 Peer review goals, activities, and key practices.

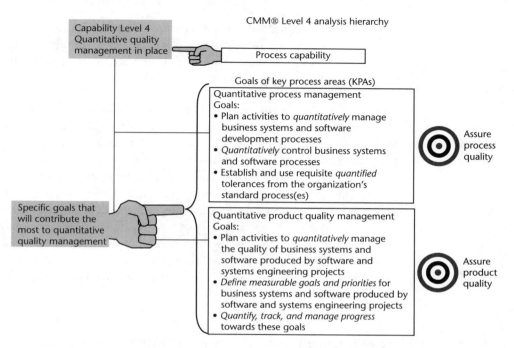

Figure 6.22 Level 4 goals by key process area.

main aim at Level 4 is to build robust cause-and-effect models for process and work product performance for the process that develops business systems and software. In doing so, we can make the Level 4 process adaptive. It can respond to change and make near real-time course corrections.

The following figures describe how Level 4 activities support the KPAs in Figure 6.22. Note how the Level 4 baseline not only describes measurement points, but also real-time control points in the process. The process repository established in Level 3 gets commensurately richer at Level 4. It includes the following information that was missing at Level 3.

- The Level 3 project plan is enriched with governing tasks to home in on requisitely quantified work product quality.
- Process measurement information augments other process and task information.
- Project baselines are enhanced with process control parameters and tolerances.
- Project goals are enriched with quantified information on work product quality, in terms of features of objects. "Object" includes the processes and tasks we discussed in Chapter 2.
- Work products carry information about actually measured, quantified product quality.
- The process repository now includes historical records of work product and process quality.

• The standard process is enriched with quantitative information on standard tolerances of key characteristics (features) of work products, and the performance of key tasks and processes, in terms of the features of processes described in Chapter 2.[267]

A Level 4 organization must focus almost exclusively on quality measurement and control. The strong Level 4 focus on quality does not mean that organizations at lower levels should not also focus on quality. Indeed, as we have seen, the quality focus starts at Level 2. However, it does mean that Level 4 organizations will benefit the most from a robust and *quantitative* focus on the quality and performance of processes and work products. This quality focus will also enable the organization to take the next evolutionary step up to Level 5. At Level 5, the organization will perpetually strive to improve quality by unceasingly realigning work products, processes, and technology with rapidly evolving business and technological environments. Like the figures that described the best practices for Levels 1 and 2, the best practices for Level 4 are annotated in Figures 6.23 and 6.24, and need little additional elaboration.

6.6   CMM® Level 5: Continuous Process Improvement in Place—KPAs, Goals, and Activities

Processes change resources into products. They are the agents of change. They also may change other processes (see governing processes in Chapter 2). Evolution and change are processes. They are processes that change institutions and institutionalized processes. The governance of evolution is the primary focus of Level 5.

At Level 4, we developed processes that would give us continuous feedback on the quantitative performances of our products and processes. Level 4 gave us robust mechanisms for cause-and-effect analyses. The next logical step is to use this feedback to start improving our processes and products, even anticipating and preempting defects and problems *before* they occur. In other words, at Level 5 we can institute higher order governance that institutionalizes the very process of evolution and change. A Level 5 firm is not a victim of evolution; instead, it anticipates and directs evolution.

The CMM® recognizes two kinds of evolution—evolving technology and evolving processes. To be effective, each must mesh with the other, evolving in lock step. Each is a Level 5 KPA in Figure 6.25.

Any change, however well directed, and even when it is anticipated, involves risk. The peer reviews started at Level 3 evolve into robust defect prevention practices at Level 5. Defect prevention is needed to keep directed evolution on track. It is also a Level 5 KPA (see Figure 6.25).

It is not that organizations at lower CMM® levels do not, or cannot, change. Indeed, in the Age of Knowledge, they often have to change, since they are driven by the imperative to compete and conform to evolving regulations, even as they strive to compete effectively. Those organizations that cannot change will perish in the New Age. Most seasoned practitioners have experienced the pangs of change, the

---

267. Module 5 on our Web site describes in detail features shared by all processes.

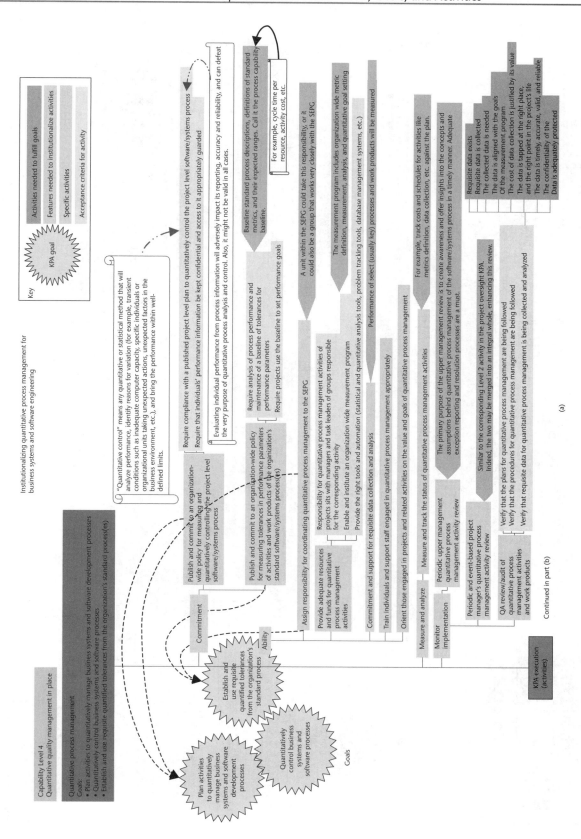

Figure 6.23   Support for Quantitative Management of Process Quality: goals, activities, and key practices.

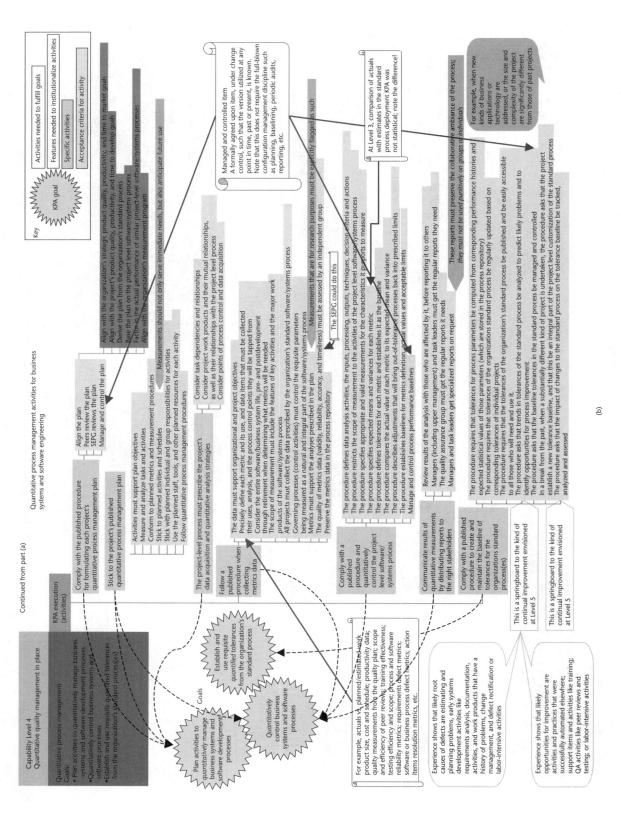

Figure 6.23 (Continued.)

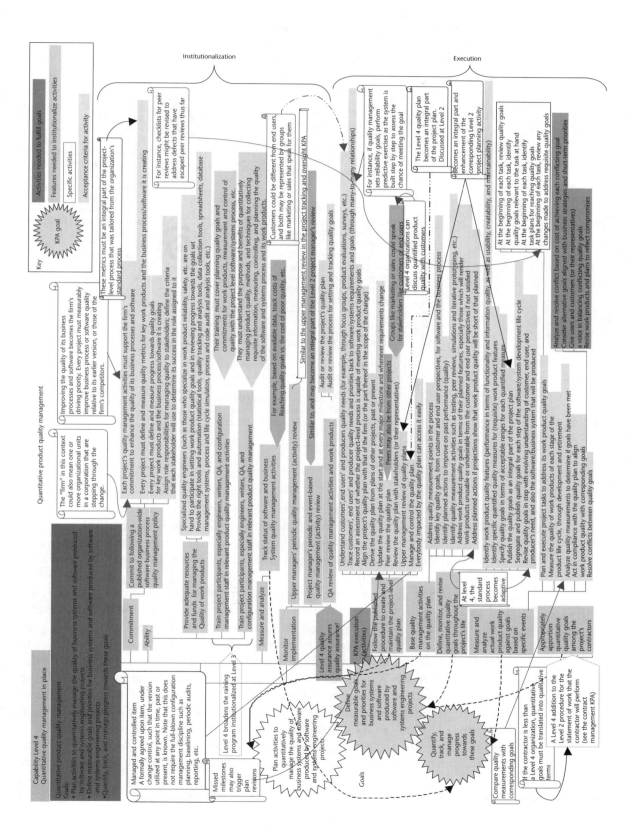

Figure 6.24   Support for Quantitative Management of Product Quality: goals, activities, and key practices.

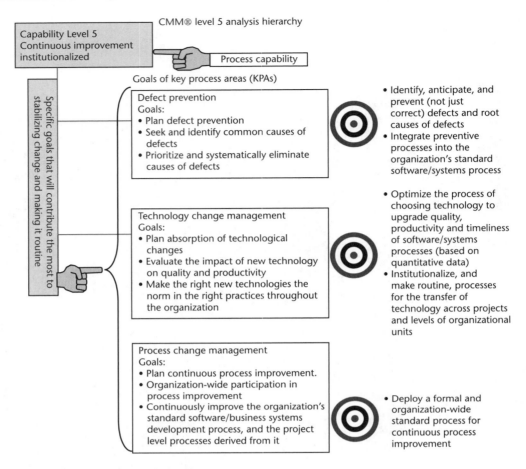

Figure 6.25   Level 5 goals by key process area.

glow of success, or the frustration of failure in organizations at every level of the CMM®. However, at Level 5, change becomes institutionalized, relatively painless, and, if such a thing can ever be said of change, it becomes routine. The risk of change is reduced, and is balanced against the risk of *failing* to change. Institutionalized change becomes the norm.

At Level 5, a stable and well-controlled process will continue to consistently produce effective work products even as it is changing, because the focus at Level 5 is on *anticipating and preventing*, not just correcting, defects. The Level 4 peer reviews, the Level 4 analyses of the impacts of proposed changes, as well as the Level 4 trends in tolerances that predict problems and scout for opportunity (in the Quantitative Process Management KPA), are together the kernels from which the best practices of Level 5 sprout and grow. They change the way we make change, institutionalizing the process of change itself. Level 5 ensures that repose will not be the destiny of Man,[268] or the destiny of organizations and the people who run them.

At Level 5 we take preventive, not just corrective, actions. Consequently, the process repository at Level 5 must be enhanced to support and institutionalize this

268. Oliver Holmes, Jr. (1841–1935), a prominent American jurist and associate justice of the U.S. Supreme Court, said in a speech in 1897, "Certainty generally is illusion, and repose is not the destiny of man."

continuous striving for process improvement, complemented by the unceasing search for new opportunity. This requires that the following additional items become integral to the process repository at Level 5, enhancing and adding to its contents from earlier levels (see Figure 6.24 and Section 6.4):

- Quality, Productivity, and Time-to-Market information;
- Standard Process Improvement Proposals;
- Standard Process Improvement Plans;
- Standard Process Improvement Actions;
- Technology Selection Criteria;
- Technology Assessments;
- Technology cost benefit analysis;
- Technology change plans;
- Pilot Project Plans;
- Pilot Project Results;
- Root causes of defects;
- Preventive actions;
- Defect Prevention recommendations;
- Defect prevention action items;
- Project level defect prevention data;
- Defect prevention Experiments and Results;
- Status of activities for Defect Prevention, Technology Change Management, Process Improvement, and Standard Process Change Management.

The following figures describe the Level 5 activities and best practices that build and use these contents of the process repository. Like the earlier figures in this chapter that described the activities and best practices of prior CMM® levels, Figures 6.26 through 6.28 for Level 5 are annotated and require little further elaboration.

6.7   Gaps and Red Tape in the CMM®

Even a cursory inspection of Figures 6.6 through 6.28 tells us that implementing the CMM® will not be a trivial task. Worse still, it seems that the task will be needlessly onerous, burdened as it is by vast amounts of documentation and red tape. This was true when the CMM® first entered the public domain in 1991. Fortunately, automation can help reduce the burden. For instance, the CMM® requires that we record and measure the time taken for individual tasks, and thereby arrive at quantified expectations of cycle times and variances in these (see Levels 3 and 4). Most projects have time sheets that log the time individuals have worked on the tasks allotted to them. Automating the time sheet and integrating it with the process repository will automate data collection, and simplify the process of measurement. Much of the other (apparent) red tape comes from CMM®'s insistence on getting all impacted parties to agree on actions, and then documenting the actions. This is normally good business practice, and most well-run businesses record the minutes

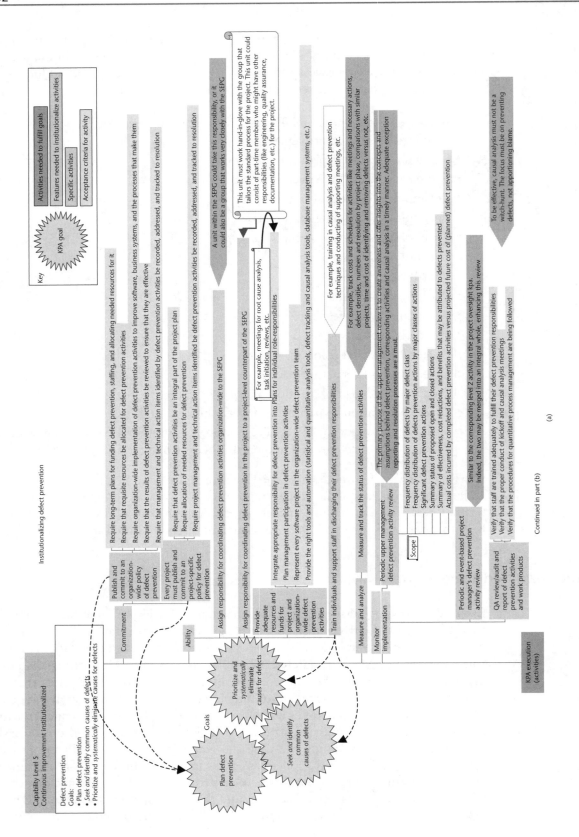

Figure 6.26 Defect Prevention: goals, activities, and key practices.

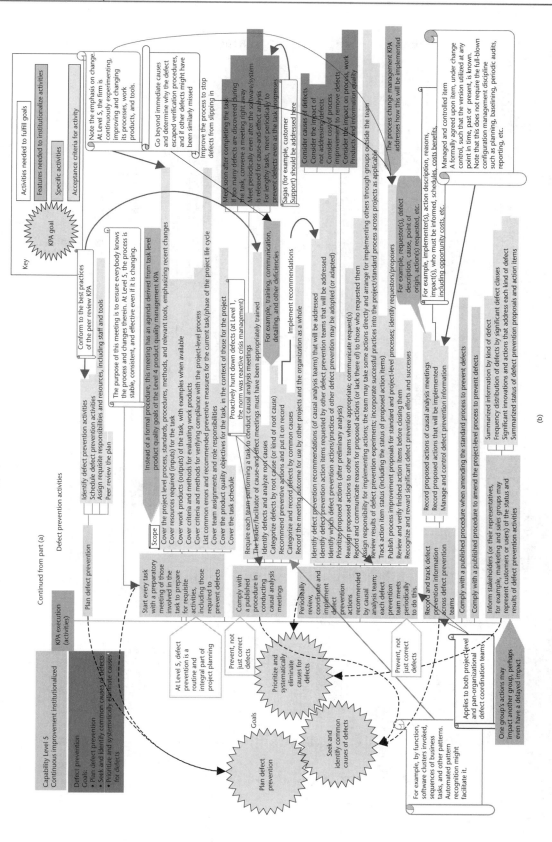

Figure 6.26 (Continued.)

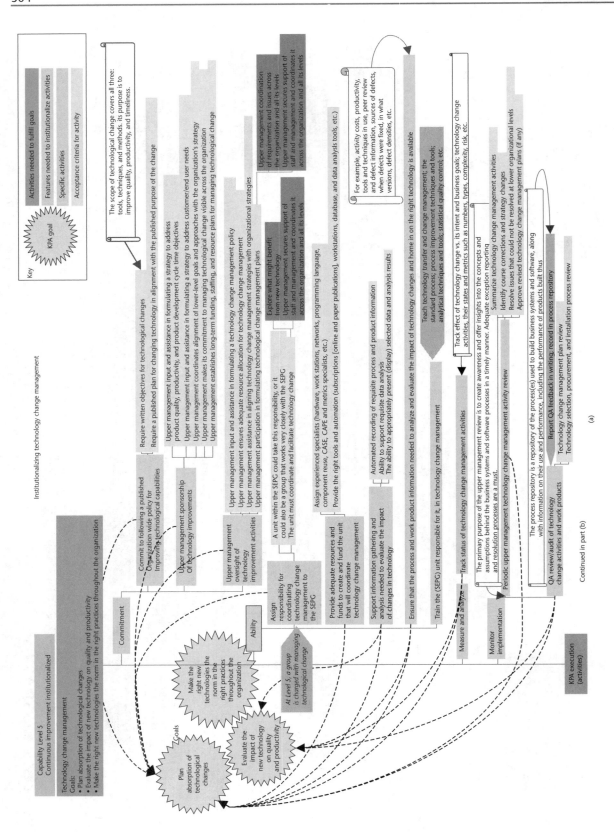

Figure 6.27 Managing Changing Technology: goals, activities, and key practices.

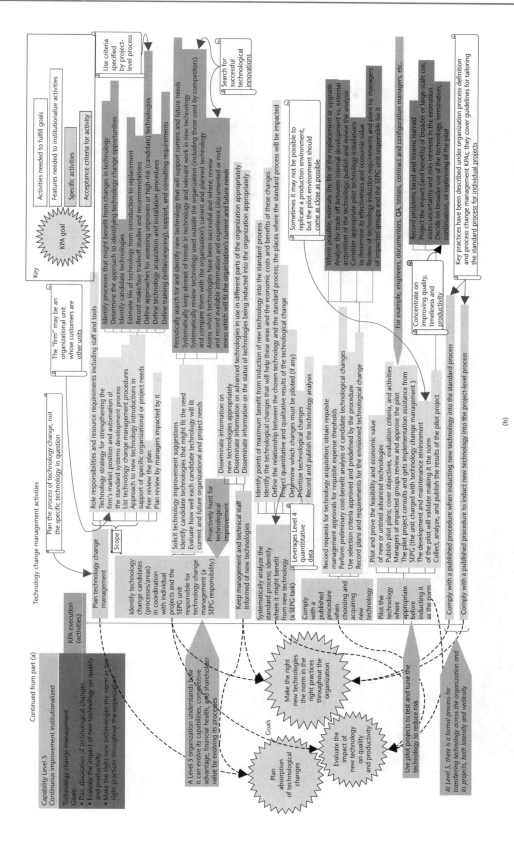

Figure 6.27   (Continued.)

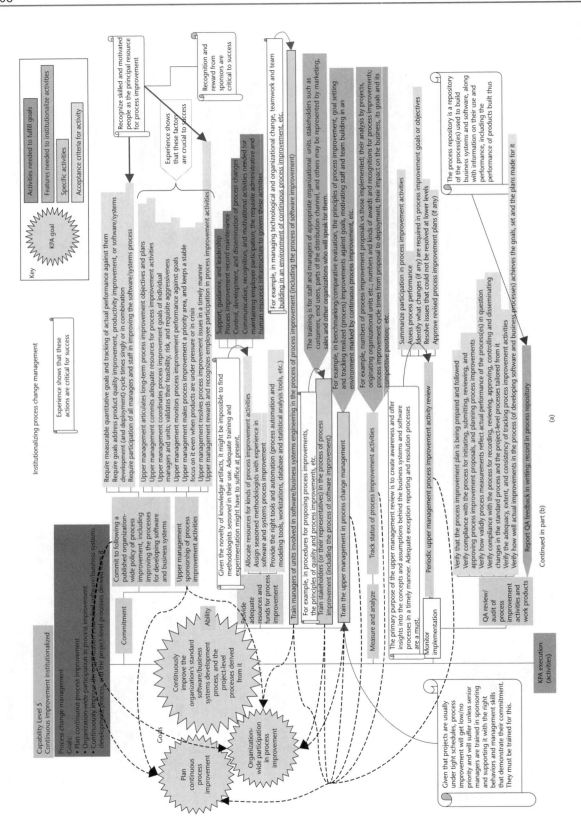

Figure 6.28 Managing Changing Processes: goals, activities, and key practices.

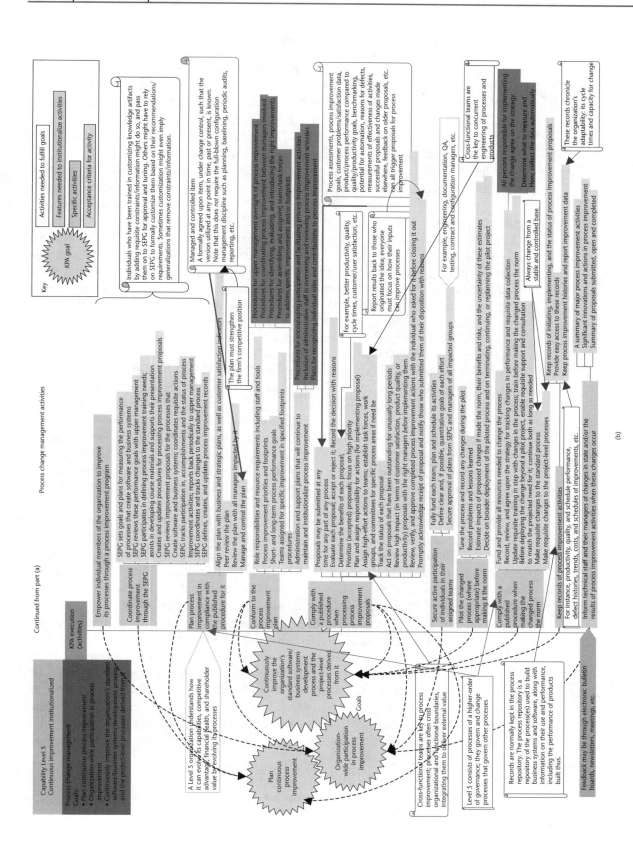

Figure 6.28   (Continued.)

of important meetings. Automation can help us associate these minutes, requirements, and assigned actions with the right items in the process repository, so that they are easy to access, and easy to navigate from the right places. Today, there are several vendors that provide the automation that will cut red tape and ease the burden of implementing the CMM®.[269] With automated help, much of the documentation that the CMM® asks for (e.g., written and published policies, plans, procedures, reviews, and records of actions) does not need to be excessively complex or voluminous, unless of course, the organization chooses to make it so.

The CMM® is proven and stable, yet it is not perfect. There are gaps in it—common themes and issues that it does not address adequately. Like the processes it strives to change, the CMM® also must continually improve, evolve, address changes in its environment, be driven by new learning, and continually close new gaps even as they open. This will be the focus of the rest of this section.

The CMM®, forged for the U.S. Department of Defense, entered the public domain in 1991. The definition of its five levels of process maturity has been stable since the late 1980s, and its core of key processes and best practices has changed very little since 1991. CMM® Version 1.1, released in 1993, made only minor revisions to the version released in 1991. Readers interested in more detail may refer to [146, 148]. This chapter has adapted CMM® Version 1.1. It is a stable, proven version; most important of all, experience shows that it works in all industries and cultures across the world. However, the unadapted CMM® limits its scope to software development only. With Knowledge Artifacts, the distinction between business process and software not only becomes hazy, but with the right kind of automation, it can even disappear. Therefore, in our adaptation of the CMM®, we have expanded the scope of best practices to include the business system. However, this adaptation of the CMM® does not assume that development of software *will* be completely automated. It leaves open the possibility that most probably it will not be. Therefore, the practices in Figures 6.6 through 6.28 address both software and business systems.

The CMM® is strong in addressing processes that develop custom solutions, but weak in explicitly addressing processes that focus on solutions that can be bought off-the-shelf and subsequently customized or integrated into the firm's overall business process. Standards help communication and interoperability. Standards may be implemented with standard components bought off-the-shelf (e.g., software, processes, interfacing standards, protocols, and procedures).

The right standards will simplify, shorten, remove process redundancy, and give each partner in a value chain visibility into the processes and information of the other. Partners in a value chain may be supply chain partners, internal organizational units, or business functions that must be coordinated to produce value. On the other hand, competitive advantage stems from differentiation of products, services, processes, and customers'/stakeholders' beliefs about the firm, its values, and products. Therefore, a delicate balance must be struck between competitive strength (through customized differentiation) and interoperability through standardization.

---

269. For instance, CITIL, a software subsidiary of Citibank, Pragma Systems, based in Fairfax, Virginia, and other vendors have products for automating CMM® implementation. As the CMM® gains broad acceptance worldwide, it is a rapidly burgeoning business opportunity for vendors of process software.

The Metamodel of Knowledge is a standard that can foster integration of the custom with standards that foster sharing, lean thinking, and communication.

In the past, the availability of off-the-shelf generic components was either

---

"Supply and Demand Chains," on our Web site, discusses how custom and standard components may collaborate, and how the Metamodel of Knowledge orchestrates both to foster innovation and interoperability. The principal challenge in leveraging standards while fostering differentiation and innovation is in striking the right balance between the shared and the unique, as we saw in Chapter 2. If this division is defective, then insistence on the standard will get in the way of innovation, responsiveness, and lean processes. The intent of the Universal Perspective and the Metamodel of Knowledge is to make it easier to separate the shared, and to identify the unique. As we have seen in this book, the shared is often abstract, and is not always intuitive. Determining the optimal balance between standardization and custom solutions is therefore fraught with risk. The Universal Perspective will mitigate this risk. See Figure 96, and the discussion under it, in "Supply and Demand Chains" on our Web site.

---

sparse or nonexistent. This gap in the CMM® was therefore not a major issue. The business-technology environment has changed, and the change is accelerating. Leveraging off-the-shelf solutions is beginning to pay steadily increasing dividends. It increases the effectiveness of businesses even as it reduces time to change. Our adaptation of the CMM® addresses this issue. In Figures 6.6 through 6.28, we have expanded the community involved in selecting best practices from the community of software engineers, to the community of all stakeholders, such as customers, end users, distributors and retailers of products (or their internal spokespersons), the marketing and sales departments, and so forth. Indeed, more and more, the process of producing business systems will resemble the SCOR Level 2 supply chain model, in which products are made to stock, engineered to order, or configured to order from components in stock, and then shipped to customers or users (see Figure 101 under "Supply and Demand Chains" on our Web site).

Much present-day software is manufactured, packaged, and delivered like an industrial product. It might be packed and physically shipped (e.g., on a compact disk), or delivered electronically through the Web. The CMM® does not explicitly address best practices for handling, storing, packing, delivering, and installing software, or activating customers and users, and then servicing them for the life of the product. Neither does the CMM® address continuing maintenance, security, and possibly automated product upgrades through the Web. However, the processes and practices of the CMM® are generic enough to subsume and accommodate these practices. It is important that those involved in designing or tailoring the standard process and procedures at Levels 3, 4, and 5 bear these factors in mind. Best practices would be developed in individual projects at Level 2, and then will be swept into the standard process at Level 3.

With its large administrative overhead, emphasis on formal and written communication, recordkeeping, and potential for red tape, the CMM® also has been criticized as being geared only towards large corporations. In smaller firms (or smaller parts of large firms), communication and coordination can be much simpler, and it might seem that several practices of the CMM® will be too burdensome. However, good communication and recordkeeping are the keys to consistent operations that consistently produce work products (and services) of similar quality, even if the people involved change. The CMM® does not ask that records be complex, or procedures onerous. In a compact organization, possibly operating in a single (or compact) geography in which communication and coordination are simple, the procedures and records required by the CMM® can be commensurately simple. The right kind of automation in support of the CMM® can reduce the administrative overhead even further.

6.7.1   Continuously Improving and Adapting the CMM®

The CMM® must adapt to change just as the process of evolution that it governs must. Version 1.1 has enjoyed a record period of stability for a product that thrives in an age of rapid-fire evolution and constant improvement. However, at the turn of the century, a new version of CMM® called CMMI® was released. CMMI® (for CMM Integrated) addresses the gaps we recently discussed.

- Links management and engineering activities to business objectives in more detail than the CMM®, and requires alignment between project and organizational objectives.
- CMMI® expands the scope of, and visibility into, product life cycles and engineering activities to better align products and services with customer expectations, and reduce the risk of mismatches more than CMM® does.
- CMMI® absorbs and integrates more lessons learned from best practices (e.g., measurement, risk management, and supplier management).
- CMMI® explicitly supports concurrent engineering and moving targets. CMMI® has absorbed the Integrated Product Development Capability Maturity Model®.
- CMMI® implements more robust high-maturity practices than the CMM®. In the mid-1990s, more than three-quarters of organizations were at Level 1, barely 15% were at Level 2, less than one in 10 at Level 3, and the number of organizations at Levels 4 and 5 could be counted on the fingers of one hand. As organizations have climbed the ladder of process maturity over the years, CMMI® has absorbed and integrated the lessons learned into its high-maturity best practices.
- CMMI® addresses additional functions and practices critical to products and services.
- CMMI® is better aligned with the International Standards Organization's (ISO) quality standards.
- CMMI® is customizable. Just as the standard process described by the CMM® has tailoring criteria and guidelines so that individual projects may customize the process to fit specific needs, the CMMI® has tailoring

guidelines that let users customize it to fit specific functions, industries, or products.

CMMI® absorbs into itself, and integrates several models of evolution that address specific contexts (e.g., software acquisition, systems engineering, product development, and so forth). It has a total of 22 key process areas, as opposed to the 18 of CMM® Version 1.1; 70 goals for these areas, as opposed to the 52 goals of CMM® Version 1.1; and 417 activities, as opposed to the 316 of CMM® Version 1.1.

CMMI® adds a Measurement and Analysis KPA at Level 2. At Level 3, CMMI® recognizes that managing risk is a KPA by itself, and maps Integrated Software Management of CMM® Version 1.1 into new Risk Management and Integrated Project Management KPAs. The Integrated Project Management KPA of CMMI® also subsumes the Intergroup Coordination KPA of CMM®. Moreover, CMMI® breaks the Software Engineering KPA of CMM® into Requirements Development,[270] Technical Solution, Product Integration, Validation, and Verification KPAs. Verification also subsumes the Peer reviews of CMM®. Moreover, CMMI® adds a Decision Analysis and Resolution KPA to Level 3.

CMMI® reorganizes CMM® Level 4 practices into Organizational Process Performance (performance of the Standard Process) and Quantitative Project Management KPAs. At Level 5, Causal Analysis and Resolution in CMMI® subsumes the Defect Prevention of CMM®, and a new KPA that focuses on innovation and its deployment (appropriately called Organizational Innovation and Deployment) subsumes both Technology Change Management and Process Change Management, tightly integrating each with the other.

CMMI® has shown an early promise of broad acceptance in the market. It addresses the integration of business processes with software products, which is precisely where Knowledge Artifacts fit.[271] Version 1.1, released in 2002, included two years of lessons learned, and is expected to be stable.[272] In contrast, the CMM® is older, and experience in its use is commensurately richer. This is why this book adapts the CMM® to support seamless integration of business process and software engineering with Knowledge Artifacts. CMM® or CMMI® will prepare the organization to make effective use of standards, and the Universal Perspective is a standard set of business rules.

Knowledge Artifacts will only thrive and be used effectively when change is critical to the goals of the organization, its success, and survival. Effective management of change, supported by a culture of adaptability, resilience, and continuous improvement, is the crux. The CMM® has demonstrated that it can address these

---

270. CMMI® asks us to focus on not just managing requirements, but on actually defining them via the Requirements Development KPA. The CMM® subsumed this into its focus on engineering. Many practitioners will agree that this is a prerequisite for high-quality information systems aligned with business goals. Knowledge artifacts contain prefabricated common requirements, usually those that are absolutely essential to orchestrating the business, and integrating its major functions or supply chains. Thus, CMMI® and Knowledge Artifacts are strongly synergistic and mutually supportive.

271. Knowledge Artifacts go beyond mere integration and alignment of business process with software. They address the synthesis of knowledge and its expression through systems and software. It is the next step.

272. Reference [150] not only provides an overview of CMMI® and its early adopters, but it also describes their experience of CMMI®.

crucial needs effectively. It is not the only way (perhaps not even the best way), but it is a proven approach. It works, and will address the heart of the problem.[273]

6.7.2   Alternatives to the CMM®

The CMM® is not the only framework for guided evolution of processes. Several alternatives, such as Trillium (from Canada), SPICE, and others, exist and have been successfully used. However, each has limitations and niches of excellence.[274] Thus, those who must lead change have a wide choice of models and best practices to choose from. They might even prefer to rely on custom models based on their own experience. It will be a long haul for most firms before they can institutionalize agility, continuous adaptation, and process improvement; and most of all, before they can ensure that the quality of their work products will be consistently preserved, even as processes change and goals shift. A proven, widely used framework like CMM® or CMMI® will reduce that risk.

6.8   Chief Information Officer, Chief Knowledge Officer, or Chief Process Officer?

The chief information officer (CIO) of a corporation is responsible for its automated information systems. It was not always so. Four decades ago, there was no CIO. Five decades ago, there were few automated information systems.

Until the role of the CIO gelled, managers responsible for various operations were also responsible for their local information system, either manual or automated. The role of the CIO evolved from the corporate need to orchestrate its operations through integrated and timely high quality information. Information Technology provided the opportunity. Information turned into a corporate asset, and information systems became the utility that piped this asset to the business, helping it scale up, increase productivity, and operate far more efficiently than before. Local islands of information melted into the corporate information utility that orchestrated the whole. Someone had to own this process and operate this utility. The CIO was born.

Today, the CIO's organization constantly develops new information systems, while retiring or modifying the older systems, to address information quality and alignment. The information systems department is responsible for improving the alignment between automated information systems, business processes, and evolving business requirements. It is the CIO's responsibility to ensure that this happens.

---

273. Models of change evolve as much as the very change they seek to foster. CMMI® promises to be better than the CMM®, and is better aligned with Knowledge Artifacts. The right balance between risk and payoff will change from situation to situation. Like the change CMM® (and CMMI®) address, we can always change our model of change in step with new learning. The risk must justify it, and risk reduces in step with experience.

274. References [148, 149, 151, 319] succinctly describe and compare different process maturity and capability models. A presentation by Sterling Software in Impacts 2000, the 15th Annual SEI Symposium, at http://www.omahaspin.org/slide/200101CMMI.pdf, also lists several niche alternatives to the CMM®, and compares them to an early version of CMMI®. Tantara, Inc., a business consulting firm that specializes in software practices, the improvement of process effectiveness, and software product/service potential, also discusses the relationships between various process improvement and quality models at http://www.tantara.ab.ca/a_isorel.htm (and the links provided therein).

The Information Age is upon us. In this new age, corporations are caught in the pincer of rapid technological progress and intense competition. They are hammered by frenetic innovation. Businesses must struggle to stay abreast, succeed, and survive, by being more innovative and customer-focused than their competitors. In this, they are aided by technology, and by an educated, well-trained workforce that they can empower to make the right decisions. Businesses must address the escalating expectations of their customers. They can be nimble enough to do this if they empower the workforce to make the right decisions at the point of contact—the place where the organization meets its environment and delivers value.

To do this right, business not only must do things right, but also do the right things. Nimble, ever-changing processes must support the workforce, the supply chain, and the customers of the business. It is not just software that must be maintained and continually developed and retired. Processes must continually change, be altered, developed, tested, maintained, and retired. In other words, business processes now need maintenance, just as software once did, and still does. Rapid-fire innovation of processes is a key to survival, as much as rapid-fire innovation of products and software.

New learning and innovation are rapidly expanding the horizons of knowledge. New knowledge is driving the knowledge economy. Knowledge Artifacts seamlessly integrate knowledge (e.g., business rules, products, and processes) with information systems. Information systems become expressions of automated business knowledge. Business knowledge can be bound so tightly to its automated expression that the boundary between the information system and the business process could vanish.[275] Does this mean that the CIO must now become the chief process or chief knowledge officer (i.e., the keeper and guardian of corporate knowledge)? Does it mean that we will have automated Knowledge and Business Process utilities that will help businesses constantly turn on a dime to satisfy their customers, supply chain partners, and stakeholders (see Box 21)?

Someone has to own, maintain, and run this Knowledge and Business Process utility, and ensure the timeliness, relevance, and quality of its outputs. The office of the CIO must evolve to take charge. This office will seamlessly integrate automated information systems with automated technology and automated business processes, all derived from the repository of corporate business knowledge, the management of which will also be automated. The Age of Change requires us to change and to be driven by new knowledge!

6.9   The Journey's End

We must respond to change. The speed and agility of our response will be the keys to power in the New Age (see Figure 6.29). Knowledge Artifacts—engineered patterns of information that normalize business meanings—will help us become agile and speedy. At Level 5, we will not only react to change, but will truly anticipate and respond to it. We will seek to lead and shape, not just to correct and fit. In this

275. Figures 16 and 17 under "The Architecture of Knowledge," on our Web site, describe the distinction between business rules, information systems, and business process automation. Module 5, Section 3, describes how programming and developing automation for business systems may be automated. See "Crossing the Chasm" on our Web site.

Figure 6.29 Agility and speed will be the basis of power in the marketplace.

chapter, we have seen how we can acquire this capability. Evolution is the key, but it cannot be random; it must be directed evolution. At Level 5, we will thrive on change. We will be agile and resilient businesses, thriving on innovation facilitated by automation, and continually configuring, synthesizing, and reconfiguring the meaning of business.[276]

Chapter 3 gave us a glimpse of the road that we will travel when Level 5 capability meets Knowledge Artifacts in an automated process repository of the future. It showed us the journey's end, a world in which the chief knowledge officer, perhaps assisted by his subordinates, the chief process officer and the chief technology officer, preside over the corporate Knowledge utility. This utility will be an autonomous, self-adapting, self-governing system for building similar business systems. Both will be powered by knowledge and meaning. They will respond to the environment by flexing, changing, and seeking the goals they must. Someday this might happen. Its time has not yet come, and even when it does, it will still not be the journey's end, because, in Eliot's words from *The Four Quartets*, "To make an End is to make a Beginning. The End is where we start from."[277]

What we call the end is often a beginning. This book has ended. We trust it will herald a new beginning.

> "We shall not cease from exploration
> And the end of all our exploring
> Will be to arrive where we started
> And know the place for the first time,
> Through the unknown, remembered gate.
>
> —T. S. Eliot, *Little Gidding*

276. Figure 1.7 has an example of how business processes may be configured from meanings.
277. T. S. Eliot (1888–1965) was one of the first modern poets. "To make an End is to make a Beginning. The End is where we start from," is quote from "Little Gidding," a poem he composed in 1942. "Little Gidding" is a part of a set of related poems known as *The Four Quartets* by T. S. Eliot, composed from 1935 to 1942.

Epilogue

"The moment of the rose and the moment of the yew-tree
Are of equal duration ...
For history is a pattern
Of timeless moments."

—T. S. Eliot, *Little Gidding*

Visions Past and Future

Scenario 2003

On June 13, 2003, I met Allwys Preshurd of Insure Anything Anytime Inc. in his office. Allwys and I had known each other for many years, and he wanted to show me a typical day in his work life. I had confessed to him that I just love to watch people at work, and that I do have the ability to literally become a fly on the wall. Moreover, as a fly, I am very quiet and quite unassuming—unless, of course, I spot a flyswatter. Allwys had said that he would find it quite amusing to see me sitting quietly on his wall for a change, and I was welcome to come and see him at work the next day.

Allwys had a tough job—just the kind he wanted me to experience. He thought it might be a sobering experience. He was a director of information systems at Insure Anything Anytime, better known as IAA. IAA is a global insurance giant with revenues in excess of $50 billion. Many of IAA's large customers also are large global firms with complex arrangements, which include subsidiaries and joint ventures spread out across the globe. Their business and regulatory environments are as diverse as their geographical footprints. Under the new initiative to better manage IAA's global risk, the intent was to centrally manage and integrate key corporate information systems, such as those for risk management, underwriting, and financial accounting. This was Allwys' charge.

Moreover, Bigguns Grandsons, the chairman of the board, had said that the ability to be the first with the right products for the right customers, and sold through the right channels, was imperative to the firm's survival, because smaller, more agile companies had started nibbling at IAA's traditional share of the business. This made Allwys' job even harder. He was asked to meet impossible, nay insane, delivery and development schedules to support the new products his colleagues wanted to bring to market in record time.

Horrid Cutlass, the president and CEO of IAA's auto insurance subsidiary, spurred by Hurrid Cutloss, the CFO, had recently declared a new policy. Insurance products would be consolidated, and those that were making losses, or were judged to be high-risk, would be dropped. Only low-risk drivers would be insured. Drivers under 25, and drivers of new sports cars, were judged to be high-risk. The new rules asked that they be dropped, and that all insurance products exclude them in the future. It was critical to Allwys and IAA business managers that new business systems to support the new rules be delivered under very tight deadlines.

As I sat on the wall quietly in the midst of these tight deadlines, resisting the strange urge to make loud buzzing noises, Ina Rush, the country manager of The Republic of Karmania, rushed in. Ina told Allwys Preshurd that in Karmania, any driver under 20, driving any sports car, new or old, or driving any new car of any type was too risky to insure. Moreover, Karmanians were impatient customers, and competition for low-risk drivers was stiff in Karmania. Ina's sales force would visit customers at home and at work, and generate insurance proposals on their new notebook computers. Further, armed with the high quality and timely loss information available in Karmania, they would offer to bind good customers to the proposed insurance policy on the spot. Ina insisted that the delivery schedule for the system must remain unchanged if IAA was to retain its envisioned competitive advantage.

Allwys was just recovering from a sinking feeling in the stomach when his phone rang. It was Presson Rushmore, the business manager for the Federation of Trustlandia. Presson had changed the business policy for his country. Presson wanted invoices to be sent to drivers based on verbal agreements, even before their policies were mailed. Moreover, Presson wanted the payment made in advance for drivers who were a high credit risk. Allwys was currently doing some rush work for Presson. Presson wanted these changes included, but insisted that the old deadline remain in place. After some argument, he reluctantly agreed to extend the delivery schedule for the system by only one week. Allwys knew that without divine intervention, he could not meet the schedule, but try telling Presson that!

As Allwys was trying to come to terms with this, his computer chimed. It told him he had urgent mail. The message was from Parriand Thrust, the business head of Gondola, a new market for IAA. The Gondolans had just changed their laws to force the company to accept a threshold number of high-risk drivers. Parriand Thrust had decided that not only would car dealers in Gondola be allowed to sell some insurance products on a commission basis, but also that the company would package its insurance products with optional warranties for its slow boats, a Gondolan favorite. Parriand ended his message by saying that he could not extend delivery schedules beyond a month, since he feared that competition would steal a march on him.

Allwys arranged a teleconference to sort out priorities. As Allwys negotiated for additional time, Presson Rushmore and Parriand Thrust (who were also competing with each other internally) said that they might have to engage local outside resources to do the development work. Only a year ago, President Horrid Cutlass was pressuring the CIO, Allwys' boss, who had been hired into the position, for not being flexible enough to support the firm's "be there first" policy. He was unhappy about the situation. The new CIO had a reputation for bringing in his own management team from the outside.

Allwys' Dilemma

Allwys Preshurd needed to respond rapidly to innovative products, services, and changing regulations, with high-quality applications that must be successfully deployed overseas. Otherwise, his position in IAA may be in jeopardy.

In order to do this, he needed to reference and classify large numbers of business rules at a moment's notice, and accurately assess the impact of changes on project deadlines, systems specifications and code. He needed to minimize impact by leveraging the specifications (including models), code, and test stubs already in place, and rapidly updating or adding additional business rules. Allwys' inability to do this efficiently is costing the company market share and revenues, and was jeopardizing his career in IAA.

Scenario 2015

Being a fly makes me sleepy, especially when I am not even allowed to buzz around. I fell asleep and had a strange dream. Allwys tells me I sleep and dream too much anyway. I dreamed that I was a fly on the wall of a spanking new office. The calendar read June 27, 2015. It was a hot and sticky summer day outside—just what any self-respecting fly would dream of. As I was getting ready to fly out of the window, I noticed that it was hermetically sealed, and that a new man sat at a spanking new desk.

I soon learned his name was Hed Teclov. I gathered that he had Allwys' job in 2015, and that IAA had evolved into a CMMI® Level 5 company. Over the years, it had successfully integrated Knowledge Artifacts into a highly automated and autonomous Level 5 process repository.

After his conversation with the business manager for The Republic of Karmania, Teclov pointed and shot at the "Auto Insurance" icon on his strange-looking compact holographic desktop computer, and selected "business rules." He drilled down through "client" and "insurable client" icons to "insurable client vehicles" with a touch of the mouse. He confirmed to the business manager that the corporate policy insisted that the clients be at least 25 years old for new sports cars, and that since his standards were actually stricter than the corporate standard, it would be easy to do. He invited the manager to confirm the requirement by reviewing a quick prototype.

The business rule was keyed into the rule engine, resident on an IAA rule server. Corresponding specifications and a prototype were created automatically. The business managers reviewed the prototype and requested a few alterations to the GUI, which were made within the hour. Project schedules were not impacted.

Similar scenarios were played out for Trustlandia and Gondola. While prototyping for Trustlandia, there was some discussion of how the terms of the verbal agreement with customers would be recorded and confirmed. Teclov suggested that a voice recording of phone or "across-the-table" conversation be stored in the system, pending confirmation. The artifacts in the process repository could give renditions in any language in different scripts. The suggestion was accepted based on the prototype. Teclov also suggested that individual salespersons download the credit rating of prospects from a central server whenever an update was available (the system would automatically check for it), in order to determine terms of payment. This was demonstrated in the prototype. The business manager pulled his chair closer, and asked, "How much would this cost?" After some discussion, the business manager thought that he might not have the local infrastructure to support this in all offices worldwide, and would defer his decision, pending further analysis of his local infrastructure in some of his newer markets. The boot, I thought to myself, is on the other foot in 2015!

Analysts working for Teclov met with subject matter experts in Gondola to identify rules for combining boat warranties with car insurance. They added these rules to the "auto insurance product" category for Gondola, and developed a proof-of-concept underwriting system that could be cloned to run on dealers' PCs. A server at IAA would track high-risk drivers insured under the new regulation, and a link to dealers' systems to enforce a rule that stops insuring high-risk drivers once IAA's quota is reached. Teclov and the country manager agreed to scale up the prototype, and turn it into a production system.

The country managers wrote to Teclov, congratulating him on being responsive to their pressing needs. The president of IAA recognized that the chief knowledge officer was doing business in a new and more responsive way than before. The chief knowledge officer congratulated Teclov, and told him he was being promoted.

The dream also had a surprise in store for me. The chief knowledge officer was none other than my old friend Allwys! He was only slightly grayer at the temples. I immediately flew off the wall to head out of the window, forgetting that it was sealed. A nasty crack on the head woke me up. My dream ended. Allwys was standing over me in an obviously bad mood, holding a humongous flyswatter.

Notes

Normalization

Normalization is a structured method of representing information in a non-r edundant way. The opposite of normalization is denormalization. Designers sometimes denormalize information to optimize computer performance.

The objective of normalization is to simplify change. Since normalized information is not duplicated redundantly in a system, changing it at its source automatically makes the change effective wherever it impacts the system [297, 304]. See also "Data Normalization—A Primer," by Jeffrey K. Tyzzer, http://www.prestwood. com/community/database/info/normalize.asp.

In the 1960s, there were rapid advances in database technology. It was natural that industry first focused on data, as opposed to more generic business rule normalizations. In 1970, Dr. E. F. Codd, a researcher at IBM, published a seminal paper, "A Relational Model for Large Shared Databanks," in *Communications of the ACM*. This paper introduced data normalization. It was called "normalization," because President Nixon was normalizing relations with China at the time. Since then, many prominent researchers have made significant contributions to data normalization and the relational model.

Most popular database management systems are relational, and follow Codd's model closely. A relational database is a collection of two-dimensional tables consisting of rows and columns. The tables, rows, and columns are called relations, attributes, and tuples. The name for a relational database model is derived from the term relation for a table.

In normalizing data, redundancies of data are progressively eliminated, and tables decomposed into smaller and smaller relations as follows.

1. *First Normal Form*: A relation is said to be in First Normal Form if it describes a single entity and it contains no repeating groups of data attributes.

    For example, an order table with a stream of several concatenated line items is not in First Normal Form. To normalize it, line items would have to be moved to a separate line item table and associated with the order, via an order number common to both tables.

2. *Second Normal Form*: A relation is said to be in Second Normal Form if in addition to the First Normal Form criteria, all attributes are dependent

on the full primary key. That is, the value of each attribute can be determined only if we know the value of the full primary key of the table, and not just a part of the key.

For example, if the vendor code is incorporated into the order number, and each line item in a purchase order repeats the vendor's code, name, and address, then it is not in second normal form. The vendor code would have to be separated from the order number in the line item table, and the vendor name and address would have to move to a vendor table with vendor code as its primary key, to reduce the relation to Second Normal Form.

3. *Third Normal Form*: A relation is in Third Normal Form if, in addition to Second Normal Form, all nonkey attributes are completely independent of each other. That is, each attribute is a function of the key, the whole key, and nothing but the key.

For example, assuming that the vendor has only one mailing address, if the vendor address in the vendor table had both the full and abbreviated names of the state, then it would not be in Third Normal Form. The name of the state then could be derived from either the vendor code or state abbreviation. To reduce it to Third Normal Form, the full name of the state would have to move to a state name table, where the primary key would be its abbreviated name.

4. *Fourth Normal Form*: A table is in Fourth Normal Form if, in addition to Third Normal Form, it has, at most, one many-to-one or one-to-many relationship.

For example, if the vendor table has information on items the vendor may supply, and vendors supply several items, and also includes the URL of his home page, of which there also may be several for each vendor, then the table would not be in Fourth Normal Form. The vendor-URL combo and vendor-item combo would have to be removed to different tables to reduce it to Fourth Normal Form.

5. *Fifth Normal Form*: A table is in Fifth Normal Form if, in addition to Fourth Normal Form, it has no cyclic dependencies.

For example, suppose each vendor has a head office; each head office has a CEO, which implies each vendor has a CEO; and each vendor is assigned an internal credit rating, depending on these three items: the vendor's S&P rating, the location (country) of the head office, and the name of the CEO. If the CEO's identity is included in either the vendor table or the head-office table, then it is implied in the other. To be in Fifth Normal Form, the key of the internal credit rating table would have to be a composite of only two of the three items: S&P rating, head-office, and CEO.

The process of normalization generally breaks a table into many independent tables. While a fully normalized database can yield very flexible models, it might perform very inefficiently on computer systems. Database designers then reintroduce redundancy, but in a strictly controlled form, so that the impact of change can be readily traced and controlled. This process, the opposite of normalization, is called *denormalization*.

Codd developed the algebra of data normalization, and much subsequent progress has been made in normalizing *data*. Codd's algebra and associated data normalization theory do not address *business meaning*. They only address the structure of two-dimensional tables, and how data can be stored nonredundantly in these rows and columns.

Ideally, it should be possible to store any information (e.g., data, business rules, or knowledge) in a single place in a nonredundant way, so that if it changes, the change can automatically become effective wherever it impacts business processes and supporting automation. This book and its companion book describe the basis for this concept. The Metamodel of Knowledge and the Universal Perspective normalize not only data, but *business rules*, in general.

Messages Between Objects

In information systems parlance, objects are said to pass messages to each other. Similarly Petrinets, SPREM, and other process algebras, model sequencing and conditional branching of processes by pretending processes are passing tokens to each other. See Process Algebras and Techniques in the References for more detail. These are undoubtedly useful in some contexts, but we must not lose sight of the fact that they are mere *artifices* to try to force the behavior of the real world into the same mold as computer network, software, and hardware systems. *Real world behavior just is. The rules are merely assertions about reality.* Objects, relationships, and other components of our metamodel are merely natural expressions of reality. *Passing messages in the real world is a different issue, distinct from assertions about sequences and relationships that just are.*

On a more arcane level, a set of experiments called the "Aspect experiments" has become a cornerstone of modern physics. These experiments were performed between 1981 and 1982 by Alain Aspect, Philipp Grangier, Gerard Roger, and Jean Dalibard, at the Institut d'Optique Theoretique et Appliquee, Orsay, France.

The results surprised and shocked many physicists by demonstrating that physically separate objects can, and do, influence each other without passing messages or signals of any kind between them. The scientifically inclined reader will find more information on this experiment in *The Meaning of Quantum Theory*, by Jim Baggot, pp. 131–156, published by Oxford University Press in 1992; and in *The Conscious Universe*, by Menas Kafatos and Robert Nadeau, pp. 9, 71–72, and 165, published by Springer-Verlag in 1990.

History of How the Concepts of Matter and Energy Were Developed

Thales of Miletus (638–548 B.C.), a Greek philosopher, developed the theory of matter based upon water. Antoine Laurent Lavoisier (1743–1794), a French chemist, was the author of the first version of the law of conservation of matter in 1787.

The curious reader can find more information in an article in *The Internet Encyclopedia of Philosophy* by Patricia O'Grady, the Flinders University of South Australia, Adelaide, Australia, http://www.iep.utm.edu/t/thales.htm.

Starting in the 1650s, it took over 150 years to develop the concept of energy. Huygens (in the 1650s) was the first. He stated that energy is a measure of the ability of a physical system to do work, and can be measured (in *ergs*). He added that energy, unlike matter, has no size or shape, nor does energy occupy space or have inertia. Julius Robert von Mayer (1814–1878), a German physicist, and James Joule shared the credit for the discovery of the universal law of conservation of energy, in 1842 and 1843, respectively.

Shannon's hallmark paper on information content was published in 1948, almost 300 years after Huygens. That paper did to information theory what Huygens did to the concept of energy. We have dedicated a separate endnote to Shannon's paper, "A Mathematical Theory of Communication," for the curious reader.

How Information Is Related to Physical Objects

Other less obvious examples of different expressions of the same information in the real world may be found in the physical sciences as well. We take for granted that a single physical law can govern the behavior of several physical objects. The law is a single piece of information. The objects that express it may be many.

For example, the formula for the gravitational attraction between two material objects states that the attractive force is proportional to the product of their individual masses, divided by the square of the distance between the two objects. It is a single piece of information expressed individually by every possible pair of material objects in the universe. This does not make the *information* conveyed by this formula any less real than the matter contained separately in each object, or the energy contained in the gravitational field between each pair of objects.

Indeed, we only can sense physical objects because of their *information content*—the information that they convey to us directly through our five senses, or indirectly via our instruments and sensors to one or more of our five senses.

Locale of Matter and Energy

We have ignored quantum effects in making the statement that matter and energy are localized. Quantum mechanics is hardly germane to phenomena of interest to business, and in any case, the scope of this book is limited to purely deterministic behavior.

There are several excellent books on quantum phenomena such as: *The Meaning of Quantum Theory*, by Jim Baggot, published by the Oxford University Press in 1992; *The Nature of Space and Time*, by Stephen Hawking and Roger Penrose, published by Princeton University Press in 1996; and *Quantum Mechanics and Experience*, by David Albert, published by Harvard University Press in 1992.

Measure of Information: Shannon's Information Theory

Claude Shannon of Bell Laboratories published his landmark paper, "A Mathematical Theory of Communication," in 1948. His theory involved communication theory, statistics, and probability theory.

In Shannon's theory, information is a measure of surprise based on uncertainty. Shannon's theory does not deal with meaning and its implications in terms of information, which is the focus of the book. Shannon's model of information measures the *expression* of information, observed either in a message or a system.

To quote verbatim, Shannon says that uncertainty is the average *"surprisal for the infinite string of symbols produced by a device."*

Shannon's theory implies that the less the content of the message, and the less the result actually observed were expected, the more the information content of teh observation will be. The unit of measure of information is called *bit*. If a system has an even chance, or probability, of being in one of *M* possible states, or a message has *M* possible values, all of which are equiprobable, then the amount of information in that system or message is given by the following formula:

Amount of Information = $\log_2(M)$

where *M* is the number of possible states or values.

When the chances of outcomes are uneven, the amount of information is computed by:

$$H = -\sum_{i=1}^{M} \left[P_i \mathrm{Log}_2 \left(P_i \right) \right]$$

where *H* is the amount of information and P_i is the probability of the *i*th of *M* possible outcomes.

One of the most prominent mathematicians of the twentieth century, A. N. Kolmogorov, showed that Shannon's measures of information are consistent with the increasing amounts of information conveyed by nominal, ordinal, difference scaled, and ratio scaled domains, respectively.

For example, in the parable about Jim, Jane, and Robert in Chapter 1, how much information does a person's gender convey? Assume that it is equally likely that a person may be a man or woman. Since there are only two possibilities (*M* = 2 in the formula), Shannon's formula would yield:

Amount of information = $\log_2(2)$ = 1 bit of information

Let us compare the information content of gender, defined on a nominal domain, with the information content of color preference, which is defined on an ordinal domain. To make the calculation simple, assume that Jim asks Jane to consider only red and green; that is, he asks, between green and red cars, which would Jane prefer, if all else were equal. Until she actually tells him, Jim has to assume that all answers are equally likely. The possibilities are:

1. Jane likes red cars more than green cars.
2. She likes both equally.
3. She likes green cars more than red cars.

Since there are three equally likely answers, Shannon's formula says:

Amount of Information in Jane's answer to Jim = $\log_2(3)$ = 1.585 bits of information

This is more than the amount of information conveyed by gender.

It demonstrates that the quantum of information conveyed by Jane's preference for car color is more than that conveyed by the knowledge of her gender. The reason this happened was because color preference mapped to an ordinal domain, whereas gender mapped to a nominal domain. Thus, ordinal domains are richer in information. This conclusion is consistent with our metamodel of knowledge.

Shannon's theory is tangential to the metamodel of knowledge in this book. Shannon's theory focuses more on the fundamental laws of data compression and transmission. My focus is on discovering the natural structure that will help us *normalize knowledge*, not measure information expressed by messages or observations. However, the two perspectives are mutually consistent.

The *Information Theory Primer*, by Thomas D. Schneider, though written for molecular biologists, is a lucid introductory document that can explain information theory to any mathematically inclined reader. The publication may be found at http://www-lecb.ncifcrf.gov/~toms/paper/primer/latex/index.html

Lecture notes from "A Short Course in Information Theory," a set of eight lectures on information theory, by David J. C. MacKay of Cavendish Laboratory, Cambridge, Great Britain, January 1995, has links to Tom Schnieder's primer, as well as to other relevant publications. The publication may be found at http://wol.ra.phy.cam.ac.uk/pub/mackay/info-theory/course.html.

Advanced material may be found in the paper, *Entropy and Information Theory*, by Robert Gray of Information Systems Laboratory, Stanford University, published by Springer-Verlag in 1990. The publication may also be found at http://ee.stanford.edu/~gray/it.pdf.

In "Fifty Years of Shannon Theory," by Sergio Verdu, Fellow, IEEE, published in *IEEE Transactions on Information Theory*, Vol. 44, No. 6, October 1998, the author details Shannon's work and its extension by other researchers. Verdu describes how the theory also applies to diverse fields of knowledge beyond just data compression and transmission. The publication may also be found at http://www.ehb.itu.edu.tr/~devrim/shannon.pdf.

Mathematical Theory of Categories (or Types): Domains, Functions, Groups, Functors, and Morphisms

Categories are among the most basic structures in mathematics created to describe natural transformations, according to Saunders McLane, one of the creators of the theory of Categories. The theory of Categories is the theoretical foundation of the techniques in this book. It is also the underpinning of various popular process algebras and theoretical work on Information Systems.

A category is a set of objects and mappings between categories, called *morphisms* (see the definitions of category and morphism later in this Note). The fundamental axiom of the theory of categories is that everything happens between and within categories.

A complete of transformations on rules, which does note alter the original rules after the full set of transforms have been applied, is called a *Group*. The item subject to transformation may be anything at all (e.g., objects, rules, numbers, relationships, attributes, state spaces, and so forth). Mathematically, a group is a category with one object, in which all morphisms are isomorphisms (i.e., the set of transformations leaves the rules unchanged). For a more rigorous definition of a group and more information, see:

Group:
http://www.math.niu.edu/~beachy/abstract_algebra/study_guide/31.html

Isomorphism:
http://www.math.niu.edu/~beachy/abstract_algebra/study_guide/34.html or Isomorphism from Wikipedia at http://www.wikipedia.com/wiki/isomorphism. "An isomorphism is a bijection from one set of a mathematical object to the set of another mathematical object, such that the structures defined upon these sets in these objects, such as orderings and operations, are preserved."
Order isomorphism from Wikipedia: http://www.wikipedia.com/wiki/order+isomorphism. Useful for ordinally scaled values: An order isomorphism is an isomorphism between a pair of partially ordered sets that preserves the order of elements in each set when the elements of one are mapped to the other.

Each group is characterized by mathematical rules that do not care about *what* is being changed, just as mathematical operators, such as addition, subtraction, multiplication, and division, do not care about what is being added, subtracted, multiplied, or divided. These transformations are called *morphisms*. This generalization is why group theory and category theory are so useful in analyzing of the laws governing sets and their relationships. This also makes group theory and category theory powerful tools for deriving and analyzing the properties of meta-objects, and a robust theoretical foundation for the metamodel of knowledge.

For the mathematically inclined reader, some key concepts in category theory are:

A *category* is a collection of objects, and a collection of *morphisms* (shown by "arrows" in the following material), such that:

1. Each morphism f has a "typing" on a pair of objects A, B, written $f: A \rightarrow B$. This is read "f is a morphism from A to B." A is the "source" or "domain" of f, and B is its "target" or "codomain." (See the mathematical root of relationships, in Box 33.)
2. There is a partial function on morphisms called composition, represented by an infix ring symbol, o. We may form the "composite" $g \circ f: A \rightarrow C$, if we have $g: B \rightarrow C$ and $f: A \rightarrow B$

(the mathematical root of process decomposition and traversal of relationships in object models).

3. This composition is associative: h o (g o f) = (h o g) o f
   (the mathematical root of transitive relationships).

4. Each object A has an identity morphism id_A:A→A associated with it. This is the identity under composition, shown by the equations id_B o f = f = f o id_A
   (the mathematical root of reflexive relationships).

Sometimes the composition ring is omitted. The use of capitals for objects and lowercase letters for morphisms is common but not universal. Variables that refer to categories themselves are usually written in a script font.

Morphisms between a pair of objects need not form a set, to avoid Russell's paradox, described at the end of this note. An example of a category is the collection of sets where the objects are sets and the morphisms are functions. The mathematical foundations of the relationships and conjunctions described in this book are based on the following kinds of morphisms:

- *2-morphisms* are morphisms between morphisms, *3-morphisms* are morphisms between 2-morphisms, and so on, to *n-morphisms*. Categories with n-morphisms are called *n-categories*. These kinds of morphisms are the basis for rules, like policies, that govern or regulate other rules.

- *Isomorphism*: An isomorphism is a *bijection* (see *bijection* later in this Note) from one set of mathematical objects to another set of mathematical objects, such that the structures defined on these sets in terms of its member objects (e.g., orderings and operations) are preserved.

- *Homomorphism*: A homomorphism (sometimes simply called a morphism) from one object to another of the *same kind*, is a mapping that preserves all relevant mathematical structures.

A *domain* in the theory of functions is the set of argument values for which a function is defined. A *codomain* is the set of values or type containing all possible results of a function. The codomain of a function f of type D→ C is C. A function's image is a subset of its codomain.

Mathematically sophisticated readers interested in more information on sets and functions also may refer to [166–168, 232–235, 308], as well as to some of the other publications listed under "Set Theory" in the References.

The *image* (or range) of a function is the set of values obtained by applying the function to all elements of its domain. So, if f : D→ C, then the set f(D) = { f(d) | d in D } is the image of D under f. The image is a subset of C, the codomain.

A *function* is a relationship that maps an object from one set (its domain) to one, and only one member (its image) in a target set (*range*). A function is a special kind of *morphism*. The precise mathematical definition of a function is:

If D and C are sets (the domain and codomain), then a function f from D to C, normally written "f : D→ C" is a subset of D × C, such that:

1. For each d in D, there exists some c in C, such that (d, c) is an element of f. That is, the function is defined for every element of D.

2. For each d in D, c1 and c2 in C, if both (d, c1) and (d, c2) are elements of f, then c1 = c2. That is, the function is uniquely defined for every element of D.

Inverse of a Function

Given a function, $f : D \rightarrow C$, then a function $g : C \rightarrow D$ is called a left inverse for f, if for all d in D, g (f d) = d; and a right inverse for f, if for all c in C, f (g c) = c; and an inverse, if both conditions hold. Only an *injection*, in which no two different inputs give the same output unlike a many-to-one relationship, has a left inverse. Only a *surjection*, in which every element of the codomain maps to an element of the function's domain, has a right inverse. Only a *bijection*, in which there is exactly one element of the domain that maps to each element of the codomain, has inverses. The inverse of a function "f" is often written as f^{-1} (the mathematical root of cardinality ratios and inverse relationships between objects).

A mathematical *morphism* is a member of a class of mappings between two objects (e.g., X and Y) of a category.

Map is a function over lists. Map applies its first argument to each element of its second argument (a list) to create the list of results.

Functors are a generalization of "*map*," the function. The type operator here takes a type T and returns type "list of T." It is a subtle difference from the map function, which takes a function and applies it individually to each element of a list, but does not return a single item called *List*, which might *contain* a list of individual items (the mathematical root of relationships and aggregations).

A *functor* F is an operator on types. It is also considered to be a polymorphic operator on functions with the type $F : (a \rightarrow b) \rightarrow (F\ a \rightarrow F\ b)$.

Ring

A ring is a commutative group (R, E), together with a second binary operation Ω, such that for all *a*, *b*, and *c* in *R*:

$$a\ \Omega\ (b\ \Omega\ c) = (a\ \Omega\ b)\ \Omega\ c$$
$$a\ \Omega\ (b\ \Omega\ c) = (a\ \Omega\ b)\ \Omega\ (a\ \Omega\ c)$$
$$(a\ \Omega\ b)\ \Omega\ c = (a\ \Omega\ c)\ \Omega\ (b\ \Omega\ c)$$

such that there exists a multiplicative identity, or unity (i.e., an element like the number 1) for the set of numbers, such that for all *a* in *R*:

$$a\ \Omega\ 1 = 1\ \Omega\ a = a$$

Sometimes groups without the multiplicative identity are also called rings. When this happens, the term "unitary ring" is used for rings that have the multiplicative identity as well.

In other words, a ring is a mathematical system of a set *R* of elements and two binary operations, such that the first operation is commutative, and the second operation is associative and distributes over the first (see commutative operators; associative operators; distributive operators).

A commutative ring is one in which the commutative law holds for both operations. Examples of commutative rings are the sets of real numbers (including integers).

Commutative Operators

A binary operation combines two items via some operation. The binary operation is commutative if changing the order of the items will not affect the result of the operation. For example, when we add two numbers, the order in which we add the numbers does not matter. Therefore, addition is commutative. Not all operations are commutative (e.g., subtraction and division are not). For example, 4 divided by 2 is 2, whereas 2 divided by 4 is 0.5.

Associative Operations

An operation that combines three items, two at a time, is associative when the initial pairing is of the items does not matter to the result of the operation. For example, addition is associative, because $(a + b) + c = a + (b + c)$, but division is not associative, because $(a \div b) \div c \neq a \div (b \div c)$. When an operation is associative, the parentheses, which indicate which quantities must be combined, may be omitted without affecting the results.

Distributive Operations

Given any two operations, Ω and E, then Ω is *left distributive* over E, if $a \, \Omega \, (b \, E \, c) = (a \, \Omega \, b) \, E \, (a \, \Omega \, c)$ for all possible choices of a, b, and c, and *right distributive* over E, if $(a \, \Omega \, b) \, E \, c = (a \times c) \, \Omega \, (b \, E \, c)$ for all possible choices of a, b, and c.

For example, multiplication is right distributive over addition, because $a \times (b + c) = (a \times b) + (a \times c)$.

Polymorphism

The concept was first articulated by Christopher Strachey in 1967 and developed by Hindley and Milner. It is a concept in which context-specific behavior is normalized by generalizing and subtyping relationships. For example, the concept of length may apply to both words and rooms. The exact meaning of length depends on whether the object in question is a word or a room. That object is a parameter of length that fixes its meaning and properties more precisely than does the generic concept of length. For instance, the length of a word is the number of letters in it, which only can be an integer, whereas the length of a room may be any real number.

Infix Rings and Infix Notation

In infix notation, the functions are shown between their operands, such as in "1 + 2." A partial function on morphisms, called composition, is shown by an infix ring symbol, o. We may create a "composite" g o f: A→ C, if we have g:B→C, and f:A→B.

Box 33: Kinds of Polymorphism   33

Polymorphism describes the common behavior of objects of different classes. There are two kinds of polymorphism, each of which may be further subdivided into two major categories [90, 91, 239].

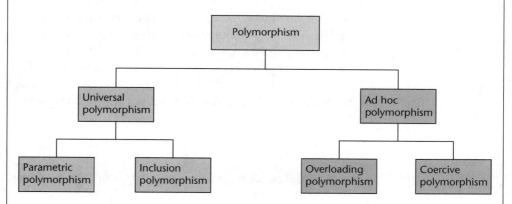

Universal, or *"true," polymorphism* refers to a uniform type structure in which polymorphic behavior exists over an infinite number of types that have a common feature. Parametric and inclusion polymorphisms are examples of universal polymorphism, a central concept in this book.

Parametric polymorphism is an abstraction that operates uniformly across different types. This is the common behavior that flows from domains and their mutual relationships. For example, the age of different kinds of objects, such as people, documents, or ideas, may be computed by the following formula. Overloading and coercion are examples of ad hoc polymorphism.

Age = Current Time – Time of Creation

Current time and time of creation are the two parameters that are needed by the "Age" function, hence the term *Parametric* polymorphism.

Inclusion polymorphism is the kind of polymorphism where subtypes inherit behavior. For example, Persons may speak, which means both male and female persons may speak.

Ad hoc polymorphism is an artificial construct over a finite number of possibly unrelated types. It usually flows from a somewhat unnatural and ad hoc assignment of behavior or names to objects. Overloading and coercion are examples of ad hoc polymorphism.

Overloading is the ability to use the same syntax for objects of different types; for example, "+" for addition of complex numbers and integers, "length to compute the length of a room," or a character string. Parametric polymorphism allows the same object code for a function to handle arguments of many types but overloading only reuses syntax (name for the function), and requires different code to handle different types. The function name is really a homonym (two different meanings with the same label) in an overloaded polymorphism.

33

Coercive polymorphism occurs when an object instance is arbitrarily (and perhaps unnaturally) declared to belong to some subtype for a function. For example, special characters are assigned a sort sequence, just as numbers are, even though they do not have any natural sequence in which they must be arranged. Coercion also occurs when values in a nominal domain are arbitrarily assigned an order or magnitude; when differences or ratios between values in an ordinal domain are arbitrarily assigned a magnitude; or ratios of values in any but ratio scaled domains are compared.

In *object-oriented programming*, coercive polymorphism is a term used to describe variables that may refer at runtime to objects of different classes.

A partial function is a function that is not defined for all arguments of its input type. For example,

$$f(x) = 1/x, \text{ if } x \neq 0$$

Russell's Paradox and the Axiom of Regularity

This is a logical contradiction in set theory that was discovered by the British mathematician and philosopher Bertrand Russell (1872–1970). Russell's paradox is based on the question: If R is the set of all sets that don't contain themselves, then does *R* contain itself? If it does, then it doesn't, and vice versa. Type theory restricts sets to contain only elements of a single type (e.g., integers or sets of integers), and no type is allowed to refer to itself; thus, no set can contain itself. This is called the *Axiom of Regularity* of the *Axiom of Foundation*.

Formally, the Axiom asserts that for every set *S*, there is an element in it that is disjoint from *S*. Thus, no set can belong to itself.

Natural Zeros for Temperature and Time (Date)

Long after Celsius and Fahrenheit became the established units of measure for temperature, physicists discovered the natural zero for temperature. More recently, cosmologists have arrived at a natural zero for date, as well. However, these are hardly relevant to our discussion of a metamodel for *business* rules, or the truth of the fact that there are domains of information that convey information on differences, or gaps between objects mapped to the domain, but do not have any information on ratios.

Readers curious about the natural zero of the date domain may refer to any publication on modern cosmology. Some books by famous physicists, who dilute the dose of mathematics, are:

- *A Brief History of Time*, by Stephen Hawking, published by Bantam Books;
- *The Nature of Space and Time*, by Stephen Hawking and Roger Penrose, published by Princeton University Press;
- *The Inflationary Universe*, by Alan H. Guth, published by Addison-Wesley;
- *Principles of Physical Cosmology*, by P. J. E. Peebles, published by Princeton University Press;
- *The Elegant Universe*, by Brian Greene, published by W. W. Norton and Co.;
- *The Whole Shebang*, by Timothy Ferris, published by Simon & Schuster;
- *Before the Beginning*, by Martin Rees, published by Addison-Wesley.

Readers curious about the natural zero of temperature may refer to the many publications on thermodynamics or low temperature physics. You can also find brief explanations in the glossaries of a few books we have listed as references for the natural zero of time:

- *A Brief History of Time* (under "Absolute Zero");
- *The Whole Shebang* (under "Kelvin");
- *The Elegant Universe* (under "Absolute Zero").

Positivism

Positivism is a philosophy. The principle at the heart of Positivism is that concepts exist only as observable "quantities," which implies that any issues about the nature or source of real-world phenomena should be eliminated. This debate is tangential to this book, and we do not need to be overly concerned about it. Our focus is on developing a metamodel that will facilitate normalization of knowledge—a very real and tangible outcome for information systems.

Definition of the State Machine

Mathematically, a state machine is a six-tuple described by inputs, outputs, and internal states.

State Machine = (I, O, S, T, E, S_0)
where:
I = set of input events
O = set of output events
S = set of states

T is a function that maps I and S to O; that is, the outputs that will result from inputs applied to the system, given its internal state. In other words: $O = T(I \times S)$. T is the *transfer function* or *transform* of the black box when the state machine is described with the black box technique.

E is a function that maps I and S to S; that is, the state of the system *after* inputs applied to the system in its current state. In other words, $S_{next} = E(I \times S_{current})$, where

$S_{current}$ is the current state, and S_{next} is the state immediately after applying the set of input events I to a state machine in state $S_{current}$. In the metamodel of knowledge, E is the set of effects of events in set I that change the state of an object.

S_0 is the set of possible initial states. Naturally, $S_0 \subseteq S$.

S could be a set with an infinite number of members. When S is a finite set, the six-tuple describes a *finite state machine*, also called *finite state automata*.

The Question of Gender

Gender is a complex domain, rich with meaning. It is much richer than many of us may think. The following excerpts and references show how the meaning of gender expands and flexes in step with our biological knowledge of living species.

General Discussion on Gender, from http://pages.ripco.net/~barbarian/archive_08NOV00.html. "How many genders are there in the animal world? . . . There are hermaphroditic species, female-only species, and some sea creatures that have a third or fourth gender . . . Those species that have asexual reproduction could provide at least a couple more (if you include amoebas and whatnot).

". . . We have . . . male, female, and hermaphrodite, but there are two known variations of hermaphrodites—those that can reproduce with themselves, and those that must mate with another of its own species to procreate. Do we count this as one sex or two?

"Add to this a number of species that sometimes exhibit 'intersexual' characteristics, and we start to blur the distinction even more. Intersexual animals combine male and female organs without being hermaphroditic. A very significant example of this was the discovery . . . of . . . 'masculinized females' in wild bears. These bears have the internal reproductive anatomy of a female, combined with portions of the external genitalia of a male, including a 'penis-like' organ. . . . They are able to reproduce and give birth to cubs successfully.

"There are also many species that have transsexual sexes—the individuals actually change sex as a regular part of their life cycle. This might be caused by environmental factors, reaching a certain age or size, or it may occur spontaneously.

"Most of these are just variations on 'male and female,' but for a real fun example, you have to take a look at the striped parrot fish. The fish have five genders, based on biological sex, genetic origin, and 'color phase.' . . . These three designations combine to create five genders: (1) Genetic female: born female, each of these initial-phase fish will become male and change color; (2) Initial-phase transsexual male: born female, these become male before they assume their terminal-phase color; (3) Terminal-phase transsexual males: born female, they become male and change color at the same time; (4) Initial-phase genetic male: born male, most change color, but don't change sex; and (5) Terminal-phase genetic male: born male, they start out as initial-phase males and change color, but not sex, at a young age.

"So, depending on how you want to count, we've got anywhere from four to nine, maybe ten, natural genders or sexes. It really depends on what criteria you are using to differentiate them."

Earthworm Gender, Earthworms are hermaphrodites, which means that each worm is both male and female. It has both sex organs. Each worm has two receptacles for sperm. However, two worms must mate to produce offspring. The two worms mate with their heads pointing in opposite directions. The sperm is released into grooves in the skin of the earthworm, which turns into tubes and conveys the sperm. After the sperm has passed between the two mating worms, they separate. Then several eggs from the oviducts and sperm from the receptacles are fertilized inside a capsule.

Fish Gender, by Aaron Rice, Department of Biology, Davidson College, North Carolina, http://www.bio.davidson.edu/Courses/anphys/1999/Rice/Rice.htm.

"Of the vertebrates in the animal kingdom, sex determination is usually a fixed characteristic in terms of life history. Interestingly, there are a few organisms for whom sex is a plastic condition, often determined by a combination of internal and external signals.... The majority of reef fish change sex at some point throughout their life. In fact, reef fish that remain as the same sex for their lifespan (gonochoristic) are in the minority. There are many different patterns for sex change. Some species will begin life as males and switch to females (protandry), and others switch from female to male (protogyny). Further still, some will change sex in both directions, and others will be both sexes at the same time. Sex change therefore becomes quite fascinating from several different perspectives."

The University of Michigan, Museum of Zoology, Animal Diversity Web article, by Erin Wayman, http://animaldiversity.ummz.umich.edu/accounts/cirrhilabrus/c._exquisitus$narrative.html.

"Found from East Africa to the Tuamotu Islands, north towards Japan, and in the Great Barrier Reef of Australia, the Exquisite Wrasse is an extremely interesting fish . . . because of its ability to change sex midlife. . . . Females attain the ability to change sex during their lifetime. When the female changes sex, her coloring and markings change into that of the male."

Plant Gender, from an article by Rachel Clark, published on Earthsky.com in 2000.

"Most flowering plants have ... 'perfect flowers'—each flower contains both male and female parts. That means ... an insect, bird, or moth ... can easily pick up and deposit pollen in the same visit.... Some plants don't rely on animal pollinators. Many desert plants use the wind instead. They often have separate male and female flowers—which means they may end up pollinating themselves—and not getting the genetic benefits of mating with other plants.... But there's a desert shrub that's solved this problem in a remarkable way. Within a population of the shrub, known as Zuckia brandegei, half the plants open with male flowers first, and half open with female flowers first. Then a few weeks later, they switch. Male and female flowers shrivel up, and a new flower of the opposite sex emerges. Because of this unusual adaptation, these wind-pollinated shrubs are able to reliably 'outcross,' or mate with other flowers."

Species with a Single Gender, from *Lizards Without Dads,* by Maryalice Yakutchik, Copyright © 2000 Discovery Communications, Inc.

"... The New Mexico whiptail . . . mere slip of a lizard living in the southwestern United States embodies one of the greatest mysteries of nature: The 6-inch-long creature clones itself, regularly and naturally.

"A single female New Mexico whiptail, all by herself, quite efficiently and handily, produces entire populations of lizards without Dads: Offspring that are genetically identical to her in every detail (except for very rare mutations). All are ... healthy females.... This bizarre method of reproduction is known as parthenogenesis.... when a female's eggs require no fertilization, and its offspring are exact and complete genetic duplicates of the mother.... The fact that parthenogenesis happens among vertebrates is a startling, and recent, discovery.

"The parthenogenetic New Mexico whiptail ... came into being when two lizards of different whiptail species somehow met and ... mated.... Genetic evidence indicates that this species' original mother was a western whiptail that lived in the desert, and that its father was a grassland-dwelling little striped whiptail.... Their offspring, like most hybrids, were sterile, except for at least one female, which ... was parthenogenetic.... Today, we know that parthenogenetic lizards occur in diverse parts of the world."

The Bunge-Wand-Weber Model

The Bunge-Wand-Weber (BWW) model was developed from 1990 to 1996, and is based on a rigorous mathematical foundation. Both the BWW model and the theory of categories (described in another endnote) seek to unify the means of describing an abstract and a natural reality. The BWW model is primarily a concept and an instrument for testing the accuracy, redundancy, and completeness of Information Systems methodologies.

The BWW model can check methodologies not only to ensure that they provide *all* constructs (see [12] for BWW ontological constructs) needed to represent the behavior of information systems (*completeness* of the methodology), but also to discover if any constructs overlap. That is, the same concept and behavior might be represented with different or redundant syntax (i.e., *redundancy*, called *over specification* in the BWW model of the methodology). The intent of this endnote is to give to curious readers who do not care for mathematics a basic understanding of the core concepts in BWW, based on [21].

According to the BWW model, the real world consists of things that have properties. Some properties may be common to two or more things, which show the relationships between things. A set of things may form a system (see the examples in Chapter 1, Section 1.5). These things are called components of a system. A system is itself a composite thing that may also be a component of a still larger system (see Box 11). This is the part-of relationship over things. The properties of a composite may be hereditary or emergent. A hereditary property is one that belongs to a component, while an emergent property does not; it belongs to the system, an aggregate thing.

According to the BWW model, a class is a set of things that have a particular set of properties. Things, properties, systems, and classes are some of the metaconstructs in the BWW model. Things and properties are fundamental, while classes and systems are derived items in the BWW model.

Things and properties are the only fundamental metaconstructs of the BWW model that support static structure. "State," "Transformation," and "Stable state"

Box 34: BWW Model Test Criteria   34

A methodology is *incomplete* (i.e., has construct deficit in BWW terms), unless it has at least one construct for each BWW ontology construct.

- The methodology's *clarity* (in BWW terms) is measured by:
- *Construct Overload*: If there is more than one way of specifying a BWW ontological construct, then the methodology is considered to suffer from *construct overload* that detracts from *clarity*.
- *Construct Redundancy*: If there is more than one methodology construct specifying the same BWW ontological construct, then the methodology is considered to suffer from *construct redundancy* that detracts from *clarity*.
- *Construct Excess*: If there are constructs that do not map to BWW ontological constructs, then the methodology is considered to suffer from *construct excess* that detracts from *clarity*.

BWW model constructs are listed in the following figure. Refer to the BWW model references for a detailed explanation of each.

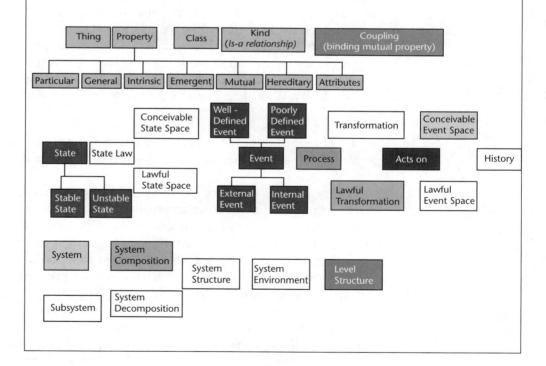

support dynamic (time-dependent) behavior. Hence, systems and classes are derived from, and only from, things and properties. Therefore, things and properties are the basic static building blocks of the real world. Consequentially, the BWW model assumes that systems and classes exist in the real world.

This implies that systems should be represented as validly and completely as possible, and that all analysis methods should systematically support examination of relationships within and between each metaconstruct.

Multiperspective Modeling and Facet Modeling

This discussion is based on the research published in [15]. Every seasoned analyst and business systems professional has tasted the bitter fruits of multiple perspectives. Indeed, we might not be very far from the truth if we say that many a project has foundered because of differences in professional opinions of the *correct model*, given the same requirements. This has often been cause for friction and intense professional disagreement in large project teams. Let us understand why this happens.

This happens because of the problem of multiple perspectives. The basic assumption of multiperspective modeling is that analyses involve several stakeholders, who may be future users and business and IT managers, as well as the analysts themselves. Stakeholders have different experiences, backgrounds, values, and beliefs that shape their perspectives of the problem domain. Consequently, they may have very different perspectives of the problem, business processes, and requirements for information systems. Typically, different individuals have different perspectives, see different things, and structure the world differently depending on their interests, background, education, and culture. Individual stakeholders also will play different roles in different contexts at different times, making even individual perspectives situation-dependent and subject to change.

What do perspectives consist of? The real world consists of things with properties (see the BWW model). Therefore, a perspective can shape the real world by limiting:

1. The set of things in the problem domain that is part of the perspective;
2. The set of properties of these things that is part of the perspective.

A perspective is therefore an excerpt of the problem domain. It has a profound effect on how that excerpt is conceptualized. The BWW model defines a class as a set of things that possess a particular set of properties, and a perspective extracts only a subset of properties of each thing. Therefore, it follows that the same thing may belong to different classes when perceived from different perspectives.

Each perspective focuses on different sets of properties. Mutual properties correspond to relationships between things. Therefore, different perspectives of the same things may correspond to different relationships between these things. Therefore, when perceived from different perspectives, the problem domain seems to consist of different systems of things, classes, and properties.

We, as observers, are a part of the reality that we observe. Thus, it is not possible to regard observation of reality as distinct from the reality being observed. Therefore, from the facet modeling point of view, perspective and conception are as important as things and properties in the problem domain.

Is it possible to define universal classes (as implied by the BWW model), or must we be chained to the chimera of perspective? Individuals perceive the world partly from their own unique point of view and partly from widely shared ideas either generic to the world of business or imposed by the physical world. Because of these widely shared ideas, it *is* possible to define universal business classes as we have done in this book.

Four metaconstructs are essential to multiple perspectives modeling. These ideas are:

1. *Things:* This is the elementary unit of the BWW model. The real world is made up of things. A composite thing may be made up of other things.
2. *Properties:* Things have properties. Properties are intrinsic, mutual (i.e., shared in relationships), emergent (i.e., emerge when things are assembled, such as the movement of a car when its parts have been assembled into a complete car), or hereditary (i.e., acquired through inheritance).
3. *Conceptions:* Conceptions emerge when things are perceived from a perspective. Conceptions have a subset of the properties of the underlying thing.
4. *Perspectives:* Perspectives are stakeholders' views of the problem domain, in a given context, at a moment in time. A perspective consists of a set of conceptions with properties and class definitions.

Object-oriented methodologies do not explicitly recognize perspective as a fundamental meta-object, and rarely support specific representations of perspectives. On the other hand, Facet modeling supports multiple perspectives when requirements are formulated.

Facet modeling considers that the problem domain consists of phenomena (similar to "things" in the BWW model), properties, aspects, (similar to "conceptions" in the BWW model), and perspectives.

- Items represent phenomena. Items are durable categories, instances, and aggregations; but not events, because events are not durable.
- Facets of items represent aspects of phenomena.
- Primitive subfacets represent properties of aspects. Properties are perceived only from an aspect; hence, they belong to the aspect, not directly to the item. Sometimes the same property may emerge from two or more aspects. This is key to reuse across aspects.
- Perspectives are views extracted from the facet model.

Generalizing the Concept of Distance—Metric Spaces and Metrics

The closeness between objects in our three-dimensional world is easy to understand in terms of distance. The concept of distance can be mathematically generalized to the concept of a *metric* [266, 309], which measures similarities of positions in *metric spaces* [265, 266]. The three-dimensional space we live in is only one kind of metric space, and distance along a straight line is only one kind of metric. State Space is also a kind of a metric space. Mathematically, metrics and metric spaces are defined as follows. The function "d" is like distance.

A metric on a set X is a real valued function d on X x X, which satisfies all of the following [305]:

1. Positivity: $d(x, x) = 0$, but $d(x, y) > 0$, if x is distinct from y (i.e., two positions are identical if they are at the same place, but different if the distance between them is not "nil").
2. Symmetry: $d(x, y) = d(y, x)$ [i.e., the metric (distance) between any two points is the same regardless of which of the two from which it is measured].
3. The triangle inequality: $d(x, y)$ is at most $d(x, z) + d(z, y)$ for every z. The "direct metric" between two points cannot exceed the metric via a third point. The direct metric is like the length of a straight line in our space.

A set X with a metric on it is called a metric space. The state space can be a *discrete metric space* [267] when the attributes of an object are nominally scaled.

A discrete metric, D, is:

$$D(x, x) = 0$$
$$D(x, y) = 1 \text{ if } x \neq y$$

The discrete metric tells us that there is no difference between two or more objects in the same state, and that two or more objects in different states are different, but has no information on the *quantum* of differences between them.

Pseudometric spaces are those in which $d(x, y) = 0$, for some x, y pairs, even if x and y are different. That is, two positions are identical not only if they are at the same place, but sometimes even if they are different. The property of mutability of aggregations springs from this. However, in this book, if one component of an aggregation is replaced by another, then we consider the aggregation to have changed state. Thus, in our metamodel of knowledge, we assume state spaces are metric spaces, never pseudometric.

Semimetric spaces are those that do not satisfy the triangle inequality. This might happen, for instance, when the cycle time of a business process that makes a direct state transition is more than the sum of cycle times of processes that pass through intermediate states. For example, a process in a warehouse, in which the position of a crate is changed by laboriously dragging it over an uneven surface might take longer than another process, in which the crate is loaded onto a trolley that is routed through several other locations, before it deposits the crate at the intended location.

Mathematically inclined readers may refer to the References for publications listed in the section on *Spaces and Their Properties*. Reference [266] has an apt definition of various kinds of spaces, and [268, 269] have mathematical, but succinct, descriptions of how the concept of distance can be generalized.

Hilbert spaces are an interesting offshoot of metric space used for modeling state spaces of stochastic systems. However, this book deals with discrete *deterministic* systems and the issue is moot. They are difficult to visualize as analogs of the two-dimensional planes we experience or the three-dimensional space in which we live—or even the higher dimensional state spaces we have discussed in this book. Each axis of a Hilbert space is a complex number.

Information can be arranged in Hilbert space so that each complex coordinate represents the probability of a given state. Each axis represents *possible* mutually exclusive behavior (i.e., mutually exclusive from the behavior represented by other axes). Hilbert space can have infinite dimensions, but it is not a space like those with which we are familiar in geometry. Each dimension of Hilbert space represents a state of *potential* existence of a system. All possible states, even those that are mutually exclusive, coexist and add up *before* it is observed.

Each object in an unknown state is a complicated pattern in infinite-dimensional Hilbert space. The object is not fully defined. Each object can have its own Hilbert space. When many objects interact, or for an aggregate object, the Hilbert space of the aggregate is the product of individual Hilbert spaces of its components. Components lose their identity in this entangled state, and may be thought of as being in all possible states all the time (with different probabilities).

In our metamodel, querying the state of a system cannot change its state. However, Hilbert spaces can represent states of stochastic (nondeterministic) systems where this is not the case. Such systems do occur in real life. For example, the reliability of key production systems was negatively impacted after a major layoff in a large corporation. Subsequently, line management was asked to report back on specific performance metrics in their data centers. This query alone was cause for major performance improvement. However, in real life, these effects are difficult to predict or measure, and many seasoned managers will agree that performance can improve even when such effects are ignored in formal models. Often, this is best left to managers' "gut feelings." We can safely ignore Hilbert spaces in this book. Those interested in more information may see [283–286].

Kinds of Inheritance

Figure N.1 shows the principal ways inheritance is used [328]. Bertrand Meyer, the creator of the object-oriented language Eiffel and the president of ISE, first described this scheme. Meyer's scheme is based on several practical considerations related to the state of the art in software, as well as the fact that those involved in modeling and programming may not be perfect in what they know and what they do. Remember that polymorphism (described in a separate endnote) is also an inheritance mechanism. The inheritances in Meyer's taxonomy emerge naturally from the Metamodel of Knowledge, and need not be explicitly classified in this manner. The metamodel unifies these concepts, and these distinctions might only clutter and confuse the metamodel.

- *Model Inheritance:* When an item is related to another with an *is-a* relationship.
- *Variation Inheritance:* When an object class is described by identifying their *differences* from another object class. Variation Inheritance may apply to Model or Software Inheritance, described as follows.
- *Software Inheritance:* Inheritance used to express pure software issues, rather than external "real-world" issues that the software is modeling.

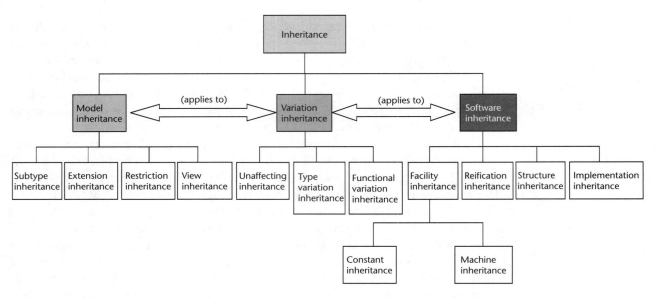

Figure N.1   Kinds of inheritance.

Model Inheritance

Inheritance is described in terms of set partitioning and shared facets of state space in Box 20. That description covers all of the following kinds of inheritance, and provides a naturally unified view of inheritance that renders this taxonomy almost irrelevant. Inheritance naturally emerges from the principles in Box 20, and although Meyer's taxonomy is not wrong, and might be useful from a programming language perspective, there seems to be little need for it in the naturally unified, real world perspective.

- *Subtype Inheritance* is when mutually exclusive subtypes inherit the behavior of a class of objects. In Box 20, we understood that this must naturally happen, because subtypes *must* exist in the state space of their supertypes, and hence share their attributes and effects.

- *Extension Inheritance* is when a subtype has additional attributes and effects; that is, its state space is an extension of the state space of the supertype into additional dimensions. In Box 20, we understood that this must naturally happen, because supertypes must share attributes and/or effects with their subtypes. The subtype will inherit these shared properties.

- *View Inheritance* is when an object instance may exist in two or more subtypes (in different partitions) simultaneously. Naturally, the object will share properties of the supertype when this happens, and will have all special properties and restrictions of each subtype, as described in Box 20.

- *Restriction Inheritance* is when a subclass is created by restricting the state space of an object class by constraining the values of its attributes or behavior (via guard conditions). Remember that constraints add information and subtypes are created by increasing the information content (i.e., adding meaning to supertypes). Naturally, the region shares the state space of the superclass, because it exists within it.

Variation Inheritance

Reuse of knowledge implies that we gather common components and *add* to them, rather than *modify* them. A variation created by excluding or overruling some properties implies that a reusable component with common properties might have been overlooked. From a practical point of view, as Meyer points out, Variation Inheritance might be expedient, even if not theoretically perfect. For example, it might be expedient to assume that all birds fly, and then declare exceptions for specific nonflying birds, such as ostrich, penguins, and so forth. This also may be addressed by assigning different default values to different subtypes.

- *Unaffecting Inheritance* is when subtypes are described by *excluding* specific behaviors of their superclasses. Unlike Extension Inheritance, no *new* properties may be added to the subtype; only some properties of the supertype may be *excluded*.

  The supertype in this case may be considered a collection (set) of objects obtained from the set union of its subtypes. Theoretically, these subtypes may or may not have properties in common, although they usually do have common properties. This difference with other "normal" supertypes is the basis for generalization—set union rather than commonality of facets of state space. Note that excluding behavior is the same as declaring one or more attributes "null." "Null" signifies "no meaning."

  Unaffecting inheritance flows from exclusion partitions. When we define a subtype in terms of what it is *not*, we may specify what properties it does *not* inherit from the supertype.

  For example, constraints on a subtype may be more restrictive than those on the supertype. The subtype may be confined to a region *inside* the lawful state space of the supertype. The set of lawful states of the subtype, is a *proper subset* of the set of lawful states of the supertype (see Box 19 for the meaning of proper subset). Thus, it may not violate the constraints that it inherited from the supertype, but may be denied some state transitions, in order to keep it within the region that defines *its* state space. Unaffecting inheritance and exclusion partitions can be convenient constructs for normalizing knowledge under these conditions.

  Meyer [328] assigns unaffecting caused by constraints like these to *Restriction Inheritance*. However, it might be more appropriate to say that restriction and unaffecting inheritance converge under these conditions.

- *Type Variation Inheritance* is when one or more states require recognition of additional behavior(s). "State" is defined in Box 10, where we discussed the reasons that this book would make no distinction between state indicators, type indicators, and attributes. For example, male persons do not bear children, whereas female persons do. It boils down to applying extensional inheritance in a restricted region of the state space of an object.

- *Functional Variation Inheritance* is when the subclass overrules some behavior(s) of the superclass. It boils down to combining "unaffecting" with Extension Inheritance. The comments related to Unaffecting Inheritance apply here as well.

Software Inheritance

- *Facility Inheritance* is when the supertype is an arbitrary collection of properties, from which other object classes may inherit properties. Reusable properties should naturally flow from the object classes in the Universal Perspective and the Metamodel of Knowledge. These supertypes might be some composition of real world objects, tailored to optimize performance on specific software platforms. Perhaps the business model just did not do due diligence, and designers find reusable facets on the fly, and decide to use them in the interests of expediency.
  - *Constant Inheritance* is when subtypes inherit attributes from the supertype.
  - *Machine Inheritance* is when subtypes inherit effects from the supertype.
- *Reification Inheritance* is the actual structure that implements a concept, or is an intermediate step towards making it concrete. "Reification" means to make something abstract into a material thing. For example, tables might implement Entity-Relationship data models in relational databases.
- *Structure Inheritance* usually applies to mathematical properties, or to domains that might inherit properties because they are subtypes of other domains. For example, the set of integers is naturally ratio scaled, because it inherits properties from ratio scaled domains (see Domains in Chapter 1).
- *Implementation Inheritance* is when a software object inherits properties from a concept in order to implement it in software.

Lungfish

Lungfish are amphibious fish. They inhabited most of the world from 345 to 395 million years ago. Currently, there are six known species of lungfish. All lungfish breathe with both gills and lungs—gills for water and lungs for air. They live in swamps and small rivers in West and South Africa, South America, and Australia. African and South American lungfish burrow into soft mud, and breath through their mouths when water dries up. The African lungfish may survive up to 4 years outside water. The Australian lungfish can be as much as 7 feet long and weigh over 100 pounds. It has been seen walking on dry land on its fins, much like a like a seal walks with its flippers. For more information, see http://www.oregonzoo.org/Cards/Rainforest/lungfish.african.htm.

Refactoring

Object-oriented software is usually not reusable when it is first written. Systems designers experience problems as they try to reuse code written for one application in another application. Reusable software emerges after several modifications have been made in step with attempts to reuse code for new applications.

These modifications not only involve writing new code, but also changing existing code. The changes must be *behavior-preserving*, in order to preserve the behavior required by applications that already use this reusable code. The behavior-preserving manipulations that change the design of the reusable code are called *refactoring*. The process is also called "refactoring."

Refactoring keeps software well-structured under the pressure of change. It focuses on changing the internal structure of software to make it easy to understand and modify without changing its functionality. *Refactoring* does not alter behavior. Instead, it redistributes and reorganizes behavior among components of the system. If properly done, this can increase the reusability of components.

Changes usually follow certain patterns. Effects, relationships, attributes, and constraints are moved from one class to another. Classes may be broken into smaller components or subclasses, so that one part can be changed independently of another part. Sometimes classes are generalized into a common superclass, which is usually followed by migrating common functionality up into the new superclass. Reusable components emerge from trial and error, but modification becomes easier and easier as components becomes progressively more reusable.

Done manually, refactoring is time-consuming, resource-intensive, and error-prone. Only from this painful experience do reusable components gradually emerge. The intent of the patterns and metamodel in this book is to reduce the pain and increase the speed of refactoring by rapidly reducing the side effects of modifying code between design iterations. Automated refactoring tools like *refactory* can assist.

See Chapter 2 of [329] for more information on refactoring and when to use it. The University of Illinois has a research project on developing automation to facilitate refactoring, which too is a good source of additional information, *Refactory*, an automated refactoring tool, was developed by Don Roberts, John Brant, and Ralph Johnson there. See http://st-www.cs.uiuc.edu/users/brant/Refactory/.

How Attributes Emerge from Domains

In an abstract sense, an attribute might be thought of as an overlap between the domain, with shared properties, and an object, with specific properties, in the metaworld. See the discussion on set intersection, in Box 19 on our Web site. Each distinct intersection of the object with a domain gives birth to an attribute of the object. Sometimes the same object and domain may have several distinct intersections. Each will be an attribute that maps to the same domain. For example, a box is an object with length, width, and height. Each is an attribute that maps to the length domain. This is because our three-dimensional space, which the box encloses and in which it exists, has three distinct intersections with the length domain in the metaworld.

In general, each axis of an object's state space is an intersection of the object with an abstract domain—an irreducible fact that a distinct property exists. Thus, the dimensionality of an object's state space is the number of times the object intersects a domain in the metauniverse.

Lambda Calculus

Lambda calculus, developed by Alonzo Church in the 1930s, is also written as λ-calculus. It is a formal mathematical system for expressing relationships between functions, expressions, and values. Each is considered a type of mathematical object that exists on its own. Relationships between these objects are expressed in λ-*expressions*, which is the object at the heart of λ-calculus.

The power and convenience of λ-calculus springs from the concept at its core, which is that functions, values, and λ-expressions can all be arguments of λ-expressions; and when λ-expressions are evaluated, results may also be λ-expressions, functions, or values. Thus, expressions might operate on other expressions, or be defined in terms of other expressions (and objects), like a logical daisy chain or a string of beads on a necklace.

This makes λ-calculus a sound theoretical foundation for the metamodel of knowledge. λ-calculus is a powerful tool for generalizing and abstracting concepts related to meaning and expression. The essential equivalence of business rules, constraints, relationships, and objects all spring from the ability of λ-calculus to express all of these as arguments of λ-expressions, and the fact that λ-expressions, in turn, also can be arguments of λ-expressions. Readers interested in λ-calculus may refer to the several publications listed in the References on the topic. Automation implements λ-calculus with Functional Programming (see the endnote on functional programming).

The *Church-Rosser theorem* and *Normal Form* (of λ-expressions) in λ-calculus address the issue of equivalence of λ-expressions; that is, the same meaning may be expressed differently, which is a concept at the heart of our metamodel of meaning. Interested readers may refer to the endnote on the Church-Rosser theorem, or to the several publications on the topic listed in the References.

Church-Rosser Theorem and Normal Forms

The Church-Rosser theorem, discovered by Alonzo Church and J. Barkley Rosser, proves that a Rule Meaning has no more than one normal form, and this normal form is the value of a λ-expression (see λ-calculus in [240–242, 250]). The Church-Rosser theorem asserts that equivalent rule expressions all may be reduced to the same normal form if it exists. However, there can be λ-expressions that cannot be reduced to a normal form.

Strategies for reducing rule expressions to their normal forms, and hence, showing the equivalence of expressions with the same meaning, come in two basic types.

1. Applicative Order Reduction;
2. Normal Order Reduction.

Applicative order reduction is similar to the "bottom-up" approach in systems analysis. It is less (computing) resource-intensive, but may not always be successful in finding the normal form, even if one exists. Normal Order Reduction, on the other hand, is more like the "top-down" approach. It uses more computing resources, but it guarantees that it will find the normal form if it exists. Of course, not all λ-expressions have normal forms.

Gluing Objects Together

Objects are glued to each other with operators. This is why we need the theory of categories and Rings to create configurations of components (see the endnote on the theory of categories). There may be different kinds of operators. Let us call one of them "E." Consider what it means when two objects are joined with the "E" operator. For brevity, let us call one object A, the second one B, and the result of the junction C. Then we could say:

C = A E B

Like the arithmetic plus operator, if one of the objects (e.g., A) has a null value (equivalent to the arithmetic 0), then the result of the junction (i.e., object C) will be identical to object B. The arithmetic "+" is a special case or instance of "E"; that is,

B = null E B

Like the arithmetic plus operator, "E" could be commutative (i.e., A E B = B E A in the example). In other words, the order in which two objects (or object classes) are joined are not important. Think of the operation as though we were putting the objects in a box. Only the *contents* of the "box" give the box its properties. Thus, only the contents of the box are important in terms of its behavior, not the order in which items are arranged inside the box. Indeed, from our perspective, the order of arrangement does not *exist*, because A E B = B E A.

Similarly, we could define a commutative operator Ω, for which an arithmetic multiplication like rule will hold. Indeed, the arithmetic multiplication is a special case or instance of "E":

null Ω B = null

This operator is at the heart of the mutual existence dependency between objects. For example, the conjunction between object instance and the instance identifier in the metamodel is one such operation. The object instance will not exist if the instance identifier is null [see Box 24, Figure (a)]. The relationship between Document and Format is another such conjunction (see Figure 2.1).

All operations might not be commutative (see the endnote on the theory of categories). Let ϑ be such an operator. Then, unlike the arithmetic plus operator, A ϑ B ? B ϑ A. The order in which two objects (or object classes) are joined might yield different and distinct objects (or object classes) with different properties. The *Parent Of* relationship is an example of such an operation. Noncommutative operators between objects are like the division operation in arithmetic, in which switching the divisor with the dividend would result in a different quotient. This is the basis of the asymmetrical relationship in the Metamodel of Knowledge.

"Glue" objects that join two or more propositions into a compound proposition are called *connectives*. Connectives may be monadic, like the negation operator (i.e., they operate on only one object), dyadic (i.e., they operate on two objects at a time), triadic (i.e., they operate on three objects at a time), and so forth, up to p-adic connectives that glue "p" objects together at a time.

Functional Programming

Functional programming is based on λ-calculus. Unlike traditional languages, functional programming languages do not have assignment statements, iterative loops, or variables. Instead, functional programming focuses on evaluating functions (see Box 33) that might have values, rule expressions, and mathematical functions as arguments, and return functions and/or values as results. Functions that take functions as arguments, and return functions as results, are called higher-order functions. Functional programming often depends on recursion. For example, a functional programming call to a function, which has itself as its argument, may be computed without multiple calls.

Some functional programming languages are Haskell, Scheme, ML, and LISP. Haskell is an area of intense research, and several variants, including some that involve parallel distributed computing, have been developed. Interested readers may visit http://www.haskell.org/ for more information.

Dimensions of Color

Colorimetrics is the science of measuring color. The physics of color is well established—its identity in terms of the wavelength of light in the electromagnetic spectrum, and its intensity as a function of this wavelength. The subjective sensation of color, however, is more difficult to describe and quantify. There are several systems for classifying color, of which Maxwell's color triangle theory is one. Maxwell's color triangle describes the subjective sensation of color in three dimensions: hue, saturation, and brightness.

Brightness is the "luminousness" of a color—a sensation that correlates with the amount, or intensity, of light that a color object reflects back to the eye compared with a similar white object. The hue of a color correlates with its position in the electromagnetic spectrum. It tells us what kind of color it is in terms of the primary colors —red, blue, and green. It even tells us about their mixtures, two at a time. For example, shades of magenta will correlate to a mix of red and blue in different proportions. However, Maxwell's color triangle (see Figure N.2) tells us about mixtures of *all three* primary colors, and consequently, it conveys information on hue, as well as its "richness," or saturation.

Colors at the periphery of Maxwell's triangle are fully saturated. They are not made "paler" with any shade of white. Colors at the three corners of the triangle are the three "pure," fully saturated, primary colors—red, blue, and green. In the middle, it is an equal mixture of all three primary colors, which is pure white. Along its edges, they are fully saturated mixtures of two colors. A point on the edge has pro-

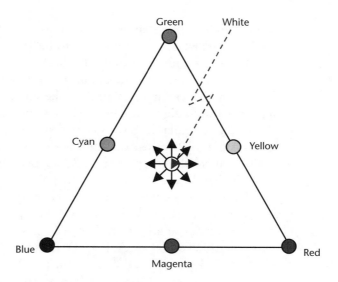

Figure N.2 Maxwell's color triangle.

portionately more or less of a primary color, depending on its distance to the corners on that edge, but none of the primary color of the corner opposite it; hence, no shade of "whiteness." As the point moves into the triangle, it starts mixing the third primary color—that of the corner opposite it. The closer the point is to the opposite corner of the triangle, the (proportionately) more of the third color it has. Thus, it gets "paler," (i.e., less saturated and more "whitish") as it approaches the middle, and "richer" and more "colorful" as it approaches an edge.

Maxwell's triangle is a simplified tool for standardizing colors. It must be modified to accurately represent all the colors it claims to represent. However, its modifications retain the three fundamental attributes of color—hue, saturation, and brightness.

The Commission Internationale de L'Eclairge (CIE) oversaw the first international agreement on mathematical treatment of color in 1931, at a meeting held in the United Kingdom. They started with the Maxwell Triangle as their basis, and modified it in various ways to reconcile various approaches to measuring color. The Munsell system is another widely accepted standard for colorimetry, first developed in the United States. It also has three attributes, and the Munsell system can be mapped to the Maxwell triangle and its modifications, although the mapping is complex.

Readers interested in more information and modification of the Maxwell triangle may refer to [324]. Even with these modifications, it is hard to factor in phenomena, such as Simultaneous Color Contrast, by which the same color looks different against different backgrounds.

Number Systems and Radix

Many readers are familiar with binary, octal, decimal, and even hexadecimal numbering systems. The decimal system is our normal numbering system with 10 digits,

0 through 9. The system is based on powers of 10. It uses 10 different numeric digits, hence its base, or *radix* is said to be 10.

There are only two digits in the binary system, 0 and 1. Thus, the order of counting becomes 0 (the same number as 0 in the decimal system), 1 (the same number as 1 in the decimal system), 10 (the same number as 2 in the decimal system; we have run out of digits, and hence have done exactly what we did when we ran out of the 10 digits available in the decimal system), 11 (the same number as 3 in the decimal system), 100 (the same number as 4 in the decimal system), 101, 110, 111, 1000…. It is based on powers of 2 (i.e., uses only two different numeric digits). The radix is therefore 2.

The octal system is based on 8. Therefore, starting from 0, its order of counting becomes 0, 1, 2, 3, 4, 5, 6, 7,10, 11, 12,….

The hexadecimal system has 16 digits, six more than the decimal system. The extra digits beyond 9 are A, B, C, D, E, and F. Thus, numbers, starting from 0 are:

0, 1, 2, 3, 4, 5, 6, 7, 8, 9, A (same as 10 in the decimal system), B (same as 11 in the decimal system), C (same as 12 in the decimal system), D (same as 13 in the decimal system), E (same as 14 in the decimal system), F (same as 15 in the decimal system), 10 (same as 16 in the decimal system), 11 (same as 17 in the decimal system), 12 (same as 18 in the decimal system), 13 (same as 19 in the decimal system), 14 (same as 20 in the decimal system), 15 (same as 21 in the decimal system), 16 (same as 22 in the decimal system), 17 (same as 23 in the decimal system), 1A (same as 24 in the decimal system), 1B (same as 25 in the decimal system), 1C (same as 26 in the decimal system), 1D (same as 27 in the decimal system), 1E (same as 28 in the decimal system), 1D (same as 29 in the decimal system), 1E (same as 30 in the decimal system), 1F (same as 31 in the decimal system), 20 (same as 32 in the decimal system)….

There is no bar against a number system with any radix. The binary system is useful in computer technology when dealing with hardware, and has found its way into software via that route. The octal and hexadecimal systems condense the binary format, and are the basis for standards that had their roots in how we thought about the internal hardware and memory of a computer. Thus, they acquired the halo of "tradition" and seals of approval as "accepted conventions" for formatting information stored in automated systems.

Ordered Sets and Sequences

A *well-ordered* set of symbols has a lower bound. A ranking scheme that starts with 1 is an example of a well-ordered set. The set of section and chapter numbers in this book is another example of a well-ordered set. On the other hand, consider the set of integers. If we allow negative as well as positive integers in our set, then it will be an unbounded set of integers that are naturally sequenced from lower to higher magnitudes. This is an example of a *totally-ordered* set. The only requirement for a totally-ordered set is that it be possible to position every member of the set in a sequence. *Mapping ordinal values to a totally-ordered set of numbers suffices to convey the information in them.* Naturally, all well-ordered sets are also totally ordered but not necessarily vice versa.

Pi-Calculus

Pi-calculus is a formal mathematical language that describes multiple interacting concurrent processes. A feature called "mobility" in pi-calculus recognizes that a network of interdependent events may dynamically reconfigure its topology in step with interactions between events. Pi-calculus was developed in the late 1980s by Robin Milner as a formal language for the simulation and analysis of complex interacting processes.

Pi-calculus includes the following:

- A syntax to specify the behavior and interactions between processes;
- A set of "laws of congruence" to determine the equivalence of syntactically different expressions;
- A set of "reduction rules" to determine the timing and nature of the interaction in terms of: (1) a repertoire of states; (2) an initial state; (3) a set of transitions that describe a starting state, an action, and a postaction state; and (4) a set of accepting states.

Pi-calculus can address both deterministic and nondeterministic interactions. Along with issues of timing, state transitions, and guard conditions, pi-calculus addresses the location and migration of processes from one place to another. The concept of *Place* in pi-calculus is an extension of the concept of a purely geographical place (see Chapter 2 of this book). Readers interested in the mathematics of pi-calculus will find more information in [75–77].

Petrinets

A Petrinet is a process modeling technique. It is a graphical technique that models interdependent networks of processes. Carl Petri at the Technische Universität Darmstadt in Germany developed the technique. The concept was presented in his dissertation, *Kommunikation mit Automaten*, submitted in 1962 to the Faculty of Mathematics and Physics.

Petrinets implement concepts such as cardinality and event conjunctions, with the artifice of passing "tokens" to successor processes that enable the execution of these successors. The successor begins only after its predecessors have provided all tokens it requires as follows.

Think of a Petrinet as a network (see Figure 2.8). Each node in a Petrinet is an event, called a *transition*, and each connection between them is a succession relationship, called an *arc*. Arcs are conduits for *tokens*. Each token tells successors at the end of an arc about the state of the event at the beginning of the arc (i.e., whether it has occurred or not). *Places* associated with transitions hold incoming and outgoing tokens. Think of the area within a node in Figure 2.8 as a "place." A window of opportunity for a latent process is represented by allowing places to hold a token for only a limited period of time, while the transition waits to complete its collection of requisite tokens that will trigger it.

Thus, a Petrinet consists of *places*, *transitions* (activities), and *arcs* (dependencies) that connect *transitions*. *Input arcs* convey tokens from *places* to *transitions*, whereas *output arcs* convey tokens from a *transition* to *places*. Places may contain *tokens*. They may also be empty. The number and type of tokens in each *place* determines the state of the Petrinet. Transitions cause state changes. They can only fire (occur) if all preconditions are satisfied (i.e., they are *enabled*). A transition is enabled when enough tokens have been collected in its input places. When a transition fires, it removes tokens from its input places, and may add some to its output places. The cardinality of each arc determines how many tokens are added or removed. Firing delays also may be associated with each transition. Figure N.3 is an example of a simple Petrinet.

Petrinets may have several other kinds of transitions (e.g., stochastic transitions of different kinds with different chances of occurring), and several kinds of arcs (e.g., arcs that convey tokens that *prevent* a transition).

Petrinets that associate data with tokens (i.e., assign values to tokens) are called color petrinets. Color petrinets are especially well suited for capturing rules about time delays, guard conditions, and event conjunctions. Sometimes input tokens are complete but are not output to new places. When this happens, output conditions and output values (i.e., the token's values) are shown as box numbers of token data inside the input place for each output place. This is called an output set place (OSP). CO petrinets are color Petrinets with OSP. For instance, a business rule that forbids

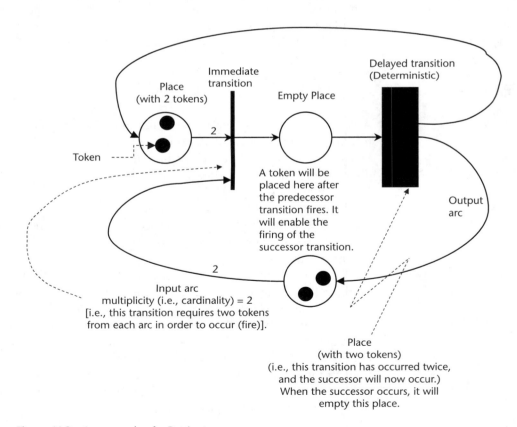

Figure N.3 An example of a Petrinet.

assembly of parts unless all parts are complete may be represented with a CO Petrinet. Readers interested in more information on Petrinets may refer to [69–74, 78]. Section 2.5 of [72] has an especially succinct description of various features and extensions to the basic technique.

The Law of Minimal Specification and the Principle of Parsimony

The law of minimal specification is a version of Occam's Razor, a principle formulated in the fourteenth century by philosopher William of Ockham (1284–1347). It asserts that that only the minimum assumptions needed, and no more, must be made (sometimes also called the *Principle of Parsimony*).

The Principle of Parsimony requires the elimination of concepts, variables, or constructs that are not really needed to model (or explain) a phenomenon. This simplifies the model, and reduces the risk of inconsistencies, ambiguities, and redundancies within or without the model. In other words, Occam's Razor asks that we generalize as much as possible, provided we do not generalize essential patterns away. Chapter 4, Section 1, in [337], discusses essential patterns.

The Principle of Parsimony is especially important for universal models such as those in this book, because their domains are complex. Without the Principle of Parsimony, the chances of arriving at a manageable model are very slim. The principle is a guiding star in the shadowy domains of extreme abstraction, where few other guideposts exist.

In its original form, Occam asserted, "Pluralitas non est ponenda sine necessitas." Translated into English, it reads, "Plurality should not be posited without necessity." In other words, "Keep it simple." Simplicity can have different interpretations in different situations. This is why Occam's Razor can be interpreted in several ways. In this book, we have interpreted it as admonishing the maximum level of generalization, without compromising on patterns essential information; or in our words, the *Essential Features* of the model.

In ancient Greece, Aristotle also formulated this principle. His version asserts, "Entities must not be multiplied beyond what is necessary." Occam's and Aristotle's principles will be as valid in the futuristic Knowledge Machine of Chapter 3 as they were in the philosophical debates of ancient Greece three millennia ago.

References

Papers

Intelligent Agents

[1] Nissen, M., professor of systems management, Naval Postgraduate School (NPS); Course BA248D: Telecommunications and Distributed Processing: Intelligent Agents: A Technology and Business Application Analysis, November 30, 1995.

[2] Shen, W., and D. H. Norrie, Division of Manufacturing Engineering, The University of Calgary, "Agent-Based Systems for Intelligent Manufacturing: A State-of-the-Art Survey," *Knowledge and Information Systems*, Vol. 1, No. 2, 1999, pp. 129–156.

[3] Cetus Team, "Distributed Objects and Components: Mobile Agents," March 17, 2001, Copyright © 1996–2000, at http://www.cetus-links.org/oo_mobile_agents.html. Cetus team members are listed at http://www.cetus-links.org/team.html.

Business Process (Re)engineering and E-Commerce

[4] de Vries, B., J. P. van Leeuwen, and H. H. Achten, Eindhoven University of Technology, the Netherlands, "Design Studio of the Future," 1997, http://www.ds.arch.tue.nl/Research/publications/bauke/CIBW78_97.htm. (Describes structures of Physical Object, Feature, Activity, and application of virtual reality to engineering design.)

[5] Standing, C., School of Management Information Systems, Edith Cowan University, Joondalup, Western Australia, "Managing and Developing Internet Commerce Systems with ICDM," *Proceedings of 10th Australasian Conference in Information Systems*, 1999, http://www.vuw.ac.nz/acis99/Papers/PaperStanding-048.pdf. (Gives perspective of the full BPR process—Strategic planning through process design and rollout. Focuses on differences between business processes in a traditional versus collaborative e-commerce environment.)

[6] Kettinger, W. J., J. T. C. Teng, and S. Guha, "Business Process Change: A Study of Methodologies, Techniques, and Tools," *MISQ Archivist*, March 1997, Appendices 4 and 5, http://129.252.51.247/bpr/aa-4.htm. (May have to access the paper from the *MISQ Archivist* site at http://www.misq.org/archivist/home.html.) Appendices 4 and 5 have an alphabetical list of major Business Process Reengineering techniques and tools with brief descriptions.

[7] QPR Software, "Activity Based Costing and Management," http://www.qpronline.com/abc/activity_based_intro.html. (May have to access from http://www.qpronline.com.)

[8] U.S. Department of Defense, "Framework for Managing Process Improvement," December 15, 1994.

[9] Gottesdiener, E., president, EBG Consulting, Inc., "OO Methodologies: Process and Product Patterns," © EBG Consulting, Inc., SIGS Publications. All Rights Reserved. Published in *Component Strategies*, November 1998, Vol. 1, No. 5, http://www.ebgconsulting.com/OOmethodsArticleCSmag.html.

[10] van der Vegte, W., assistant professor, Delft University of Technology, "Reflections on artifact related process modeling," *EDIProd Conference*, October 14, 2000, Dychow, Poland, http://www.ediprod.uz.zgora.pl/files/ediprod2000.html, http://dutoce.io.tudelft.nl/%7Ewilfred/WFvdVegte-EDIProd2000.htm, http://www.sdpsnet.org/journals/vol6-2/vegte1.pdf, and http://dutoce.io.tudelft.nl/~wilfred/. (Summarizes and assesses different Process Modeling techniques and a process classification scheme.)

Ontologies and Component Reuse Projects

[11] Vasconcelos, J., Department of Computer Science, University of York, U.K., and Multimedia Resource Center, University of Fernando Pessoa, Portugal, C. Kimble, Department of Computer Science, University of York, U.K., F. Gouveia, Multimedia Resource Center, University of Fernando Pessoa, Portugal, and D. Kudenko, Department of Computer Science, University of York, U.K., "A Group Memory System for Corporate Knowledge Management: An Ontological Approach," September 2000, http://www-users.cs.york.ac.uk/~kimble/research/ECKM-2000-paper.pdf.

[12] Green, P., Department of Commerce, University of Queensland, Australia, and M. Roseman, School of Information Systems, Queensland Institute of Technology, Australia, "Ontological Analysis of Integrated Process Modeling: Some Initial Insights," *Proceedings of the Australian Conference on Information Systems (ACIS 2000)*, Brisbane, Australia, December 6–8, 2000. (Evaluates ARIS against BWW criteria.)

[13] Rosemann, M., Queensland University of Technology, School of Information Systems, and P. Green, University of Queensland, Department of Commerce, "Enhancing the Process of Ontological Analysis—The 'Who Cares' Dimension," *Proceedings of the Information Systems Foundations Workshop on Ontology, Semiotics and Practice*, 1999, http://www.comp.mq.edu.au/isf99/Rosemann.htm. (Discusses the BWW model applied to facets and information systems analysis and design.)

Knowledge Reuse Algebras and Test Beds for Techniques

[14] Dampney, C. N. G., and M. S. J. Johnson, Department of Computing, Macquarie University, "An Information Theory Formalization and the BWW Ontology," *Proceedings of the Information Systems Foundations Workshop: Ontology, Semiotics and Practice*, 1999, http://www.comp.mq.edu.au/isf99/DampneyJohnson.htm. [Describes the Bunge Wand Weber (BWW) Framework—Rigorous algebra for testing the completeness of techniques/ontologies concerning Business Rule expression.]

[15] Opdahl, A. L., and B. Henderson-Sellers, School of Computing Sciences, University of Technology, Sydney, "Evaluating and Improving OO Modeling Languages Using the BWW-Model," *Proceedings of the Information Systems Foundations Workshop: Ontology, Semiotics and Practice*, 1999, http://www.comp.mq.edu.au/isf99/Opdahl.htm. [Describes the Bunge Wand Weber (BWW) Framework—Rigorous algebra for testing the completeness of techniques/ontologies concerning the Business Rule expression.]

[16] Winskel, G., and M. Nielsen, Computer Science Department, Aarhus University, Denmark, "Categories in Concurrency," 1997. See abstract at http://www.brics.dk/upd/EP/97/WN_CC/EP-97-WN_CC.bib and https://booktrade.cambridge.org/catalogue.asp?isbn=0521580579. (Describes a comprehensive process algebra based on Category Theory and Functors.)

[17] Rowe, D., and J. Leaney, Computer Systems Engineering, School of Electrical Engineering, University of Technology, Sydney, "Evaluating Evolvability of Computer Based Systems Architectures—An Ontological Approach," *IEEE International Conference on Engineering of Computer-Based Systems (ECBS Workshop 1997)*, 1997, http://csdl2.computer.org/persagen/DLAbsToc.jsp?resourcePath=/dl/proceedings/&toc=comp/proceedings/ecbs/1997/7889/00/7889toc.xml&DOI=10.1109/ECBS.1997.581903. (Applies BWW to systems evolution trajectories and architecture.)

[18] Mylopoulos, J., University of Toronto, "Information Modeling in the Time of Revolution," *Information Systems*, Vol. 23, No. 3–4, June 1998. (Compares various well-known Reuse, Modeling, and Knowledge Representation algebras.)

[19] van Zyl, J., and D. Corbett, School of Computer and Information Science, University of South Australia, "Framework for Comparing Methods for Using or Reusing Multiple Ontologies in an Application," *Proceedings of the 8th International Conference on Conceptual Structures*, Darmstadt, Germany, August 2000. (Lists and compares several major Ontology and Reuse projects/frameworks.)

[20] Nulden, U., Department of Informatics, Göteborg University, Sweden, "The Why, What, and How of Reuse in Software Development," *20th Information Systems Research Seminar*, Scandinavia, Hankø, Norway, 1997, http://staff.cs.utu.fi/IRIS/y/1997.htm. (Translates the set-theoretic BWW framework to a more easily understood metamodel, and compares various modeling algebras in terms of BWW criteria. Evaluates the BWW framework itself.)

[21] Opdahl, A. L., Department of Information Science, University of Bergen, "A Comparison of Four Families of Multi-Perspective Problem Analysis Methods," 1998. (Analyzes the nature of multiple perspectives in BWW ontology for information systems and identifies principal differences between structured analysis, object-oriented analysis, faceted analysis, and viewpoints-based analysis.)

[22] Wand, Y., Management Information Systems, Faculty of Commerce and Business Administration, The University of British Columbia, Canada, and R. Y. Wang, Sloan School of Management, Massachusetts Institute of Technology, Cambridge, MA, "Business: Anchoring Data Quality Dimensions in Ontological Foundations," http://web.mit.edu/tdqm/www/papers/94/94-03.html. (Analyzes various modeling techniques in terms of their ability to satisfy information quality requirements.)

[23] Opdahl, A. L., associate professor, Department of Information Science, University of Bergen, "Towards a Faceted Modeling Language," *Proceedings of the Fifth European Conference on Information Systems*, 1997.

[24] National Committee for Information Technology Standards, Technical Committee H7: Object Model Features Matrix (document number X3H7-93-007v12b), May 25, 1997. (Describes the Object Management Group core metamodel, and compares it with various other metamodels and standards, such as Eiffel and CORBA.)

Knowledge Reuse Projects

[25] Kingston, J., AIAI, University of Edinburgh, "Merging Top Level Ontologies for Scientific Knowledge Management" (ref EDI-INF-RR-0171), *Proceedings of the AAAI Workshop on Ontologies and the Semantic Web, AAAI-02 Conference*, Edmonton, Canada, July 29, 2002, http://www.inf.ed.ac.uk/publications/report/0171.html. (Lists, describes, and compares various major Knowledge Reuse and Ontology projects.)

[26] EU information technologies programme Esprit and Marexpo Transeuropean Information Dissemination on Maritime Industry Related on ICT Projects: List of several key Domain Specific and Cross Industry Software Component Reuse Projects, with links to each, at http://marexpo.balport.com/Project-Navigator/project_navigator.htm and http://marexpo.balport.com/Project-Navigator/matrix12.htm.

[27] Clark, P., Boeing, Knowledge Systems Research Group, The University of Texas, Austin, Computer Sciences Department, "Some Ongoing KBS/Ontology Projects and Groups," http://www.cs.utexas.edu/users/mfkb/RKF/related.html.

[28] Institute of Applied Informatics and Formal Description Methods, University of Karlsruhe, "Ontology Projects," http://www.aifb.uni-karlsruhe.de/Projekte/english.

[29] Artificial Intelligence Laboratory, Vrije universiteit Brussel, Brussels, Belgium, "COMMET and KREST Knowledge Reusability and Configurability Projects," http://arti.vub.ac.be/www/krest/information/commet-krest.html.

[30] Enterprise Integration Laboratory, University of Toronto, "TOVE (TOronto Virtual Enterprise) Knowledge Reuse project," http://www.eil.utoronto.ca/comsen.html.

[31] Enterprise Integration Laboratory, University of Toronto, Toronto, Canada, "TOVE Ontologies," http://www.eil.utoronto.ca/tove/toveont.html.

[32] KACTUS Reusable Knowledge Modeling, 1995, http://www.swi.psy.uva.nl/projects/Kactus.

[33] Espirit Program of the Commission of the European Communities Project 8145, Cap Gemini Innovation (January 1994–September 1995), Integral Solutions Limited (September 1995–September 1996), CAP Programator, DELOS S.p.A, FINCANTIERI, IBERDROLA, LABEIN, Lloyd's Register, RPK Universität Karlsruhe, STATOIL, SINTEF Automatic Control, University of Amsterdam, "Modeling Knowledge About Complex Technical Systems for Multiple Use (KACTUS)," several papers, http://hcs.science.uva.nl/projects/Kactus/Papers.html.

[34] Project.Net, San Diego, CA: PROJECTXML™, http://www.project.net/scripts/SaISAPI.dll/website/products/ProjectXML.jsp.

[35] The One World Information System (OWIS) General Enterprise Management (GEM), Engineering, and Improvement Framework, http://one-world-is.com/rer/owis/emeif.htm.

[36] Rational Corporation: Rational Requirements Framework, Net Market Edition, 2000.

[37] Cox, S., Dublin Core Metadata Initiative, "DCMI Box Encoding Scheme: Specification of the Spatial Limits of a Place, and Methods for Encoding This in a Text String," July 28, 2000, http://dublincore.org/documents/2000/07/28/dcmi-box/.

[38] Cox, S., Dublin Core Metadata Initiative, "DCMI Period Encoding Scheme: Specification of the Limits of a Time Interval, and Methods for Encoding This in a Text String," July 28, 2000.

[39] Cox, S., Dublin Core Metadata Initiative, "DCMI Point Encoding Scheme: A Point Location in Space, and Methods for Encoding This in a Text String," July 28, 2000, http://dublincore.org/documents/2000/07/28/dcmi-point/.

[40] Menzies, T., Department of Artificial Intelligence, University of New South Wales, *KBS Methodologies: KADS and Others*, Technical Report TR95-28, Department of Software Development, Monash University, 1995.

[41] University of Amsterdam, ESPRIT Program, "KADS: A Development Methodology for Knowledge-Based Systems," http://www.mdx.ac.uk/www/ai/samples/ke/53-kads.htm.

[42] Martin, P., University of Adelaide (Australia)—Computer Sciences Department, "KADS Top-Level Ontology of Concept Types and Relations Types," http://meganesia.int.gu.edu.au/~phmartin/WebKB/kb/topLevelOntology.html, http://meganesia.int.gu.edu.au/~phmartin/WebKB/interface/hierarchyBrowser.html?objectKind=concept+type&top=Thing&relation=Subtype&minDepth=0&openNodes=Entity+Situation+Spatial_entity+Information_entity, http://meganesia.int.gu.edu.au/~phmartin/WebKB/interface/hierarchyBrowser.html?objectKind=relation+type&top=BinaryRel&relation=Subtype&minDepth=0&openNodes=BinaryRel_from_a_situation+BinaryRel_from_a_Process.

[43] Schreiber, A. T., et al., "Knowledge Engineering and Management: The Common KADS Methodology," http://www.commonkads.uva.nl/frameset-commonkads.html and http://www.commonkads.uva.nl/frameset-commonkads.html.

[44] O'Hara, K., Artificial Intelligence Group, University of Nottingham, U.K., "A Representation of KADS-I Interpretation Models Using a Decompositional Approach," *Proceedings of 3rd KADS Meeting*, 1993, http://eprints.ecs.soton.ac.uk/4164/.

[45] Kingston, J., Artificial Intelligence Applications Institute, University of Edinburgh, "Common KADS: Overview of Knowledge Engineering Methods," http://www.aiai.ed.ac.uk/~jkk/kadspubs.html.

[46] Laresgoiti, I., and A. Bernaras, LABEIN, Spain, A. Anjewierden, A. Th. Schreiber, and B. J. Wielinga, University of Amsterdam, Department of Social Science Informatics, the Netherlands, and J. Corera, IBERDROLA, Spain, "Ontologies as Vehicles for Reuse: A Mini-Experiment," 1996, http://ksi.cpsc.ucalgary.ca/KAW/KAW96/laresgoiti/k.html.

[47] American National Standard (dpANS): Knowledge Interchange Format (KIF) draft of proposed American National Standard (dpANS) NCITS.T2/98-004, "A Framework for Com-

paring Methods for Using or Reusing Multiple Ontologies in an Application," 1998, http://logic.stanford.edu/kif/dpans.html.

[48] Rational Corporation, "Rational Reusable Asset Specification." Major contributors: Grady Booch, Catapulse, CTO; Peter Eeles, Rational, RSO U.K.; Luan Doan-Minh, Rational, SSO U.S.; Kelli Houston, Rational, A&AF senior architecture specialist; Ivar Jacobson, Rational, VP of business engineering; Wojtek Kozaczynski, Rational, director of A&AF; Philippe Kruchten, Rational fellow; Grant Larsen, Catapulse, senior architecture specialist; Jon Lawrence, Rational, A&AF product manager; Davyd Norris, Rational Software, RSO Australia; Jim Rumbaugh, Rational fellow; Bran Selic, Rational, methodologist; and Jim Thario, Rational, A&AF senior software engineer.

Unified Modeling Language (UML)

[49] Lee, M., Project Technology, Inc., "Object Oriented Analysis in the Real World," 1992.

[50] Rational Software Corporation, "UML Quick Reference for Rational Rose," 2001; includes UML General Purpose Concepts, UML Class Diagram, UML Class Diagram Relationships, UML Collaboration Diagram, UML Component Diagrams, UML Class Visibility Notation, UML State Transition Diagrams, UML Sequence Diagram. See links, at http://www.rational.com/uml/resources/quick/index.jsp.

Extended Modeling Language (XML)

[51] World Wide Web Consortium (W3C), "XML Information Set W3C Working Draft," March 16, 2001, and "XML Information Set, Second Edition," W3C Recommendation, February 4, 2004, http://www.w3.org/TR/xml-infoset/#infoitem.element.

[52] World Wide Web Consortium (W3C), "XML Schema Part 1: Structures, W3C Candidate Recommendation," *World Wide Web Consortium*, October 24, 2000, http://www.w3.org/TR/xmlschema-1/.

[53] World Wide Web Consortium, Massachusetts Institute of Technology, Institut National de Recherche en Informatique et en Automatique, Keio University, "XML Schema Part 0: Primer W3C Proposed Recommendation," March 16, 2000; D. C. Fallside, (ed.), IBM, http://www.w3.org/TR/2001/PR-xmlschema-0-20010316/primer.html. [Copyright World Wide Web Consortium (Massachusetts Institute of Technology, Institut National de Recherche en Informatique et en Automatique, Keio University). All rights reserved.]

[54] Object Management Group (OMG), "XML Core Metamodel," http://www.omg.org-cgi-bin-docad-01-02-03.txt and ftp://ftp.omg.org/pub/docs/ad/01-02-03.txt.

[55] World Wide Web Consortium (W3C), "Extensible Markup Language (XML) 1.0 (Second Edition)," Copyright © 2000, W3C® (MIT, INRIA, Keio), all rights reserved, and "Extensible Markup Language (XML) 1.0 (Third Edition)," W3C Recommendation, February 4, 2004, http://www.w3.org/TR/REC-xml.

Process/Task/Schedule Management and Models

[56] Veryard Projects, "Process Management Workflow, Workload, Work Control," (© 1995–2001), http://www.users.globalnet.co.uk/~rxv/sebpc/workflow.htm.

[57] Tanuan, M. C., software engineering manager of Waterloo EAServer QA, eBusiness Division, Sybase, Inc., "An Introduction to Workflow and Business Process Modeling," http://se.uwaterloo.ca/~mctanuan/cs645/IntroBPMWF.htm.

[58] Jernigan, S. R., M.S.E., and K. S. Barber, The University of Texas at Austin, "Distributed Search Method for Scheduling Flow Through a Factory Floor," 1996, http://www-lips.ece.utexas.edu/~stevej/papers/thesis/masters.html.

[59] Various practitioners and academics, "Diverse Manufacturing Process Summaries of Refereed Conference Papers," *ICME 2000, 8th International Conference on Manufacturing Engineering in Sydney*, August 27–30, 2000. See http://www.unisa.edu.au/ame/pubs/2000.asp.

[60] Jernigan, S. R., S. Ramaswamy, and K. S. Barber, The Laboratory for Intelligent Processes and Systems, The Department of Electrical and Computer Engineering, The University of Texas at Austin, "A Distributed Search and Simulation Method for Job Flow Scheduling," November 30, 1995, http://www-lips.ece.utexas.edu/~stevej/papers/simulation/simulation.html.

[61] Project Management Institute (PMI), "A Guide to Project Management Body of Knowledge: PMBOK Guide," 2000 Edition, http://www.pmi.org/info/default.asp.

[62] Sauer, J., and L. Jain, *Intelligent Techniques in Industry, Knowledge-Based Scheduling Techniques in Industry*, Boca Raton, FL: CRC Press, 1998, http://www-is.informatik.uni-oldenburg.de/~sauer/paper/scheduling.html.

Process Algebras and Techniques

[63] Arkin, A., Intalio, Inc., from the Business Process Management Initiative (BPMI) Consortium: "Business Process Markup Language (BPML) Working Draft 0.4," March 8, 2001, http://www.bpmi.org. ["Business Process Modeling Language (BPML) is a metalanguage for the modeling of business processes, just as XML is a metalanguage for the modeling of business data. BPML provides a . . . model for collaborative and transactional business processes based on a . . . finite-state machine."]

[64] Vitria Technology, Inc., "Executive Overview: Value Chain Markup Language™—VCML™: A Collaborative E-Business Vocabulary," Copyright © 2001. (Vitria home page, http://www.vitria.com.)

[65] Vitria Technology, Inc., "Downloads: Value Chain Markup Language™—VCML™: A Collaborative E-Business Vocabulary," Copyright © 2001. (Lists transactions in different industries—indicator of functions that are similar and different across industries. Visitors may download sample schemas and documentation.)

[66] Cowie, A. J., School of Computer and Information Science, University of South Australia, "The Modeling of Temporal Properties in a Process Algebra Framework," 1999, http://www.cis.unisa.edu.au/~cisajc/thesis.pdf. (Describes, for the mathematically inclined reader, a comprehensive review of process algebras, their meaning, operation, utilization, and properties.)

[67] Pandalai, D., Honeywell Technology Center, Honeywell Inc., Minneapolis, MN, and L. Holloway, Center for Robotics and Manufacturing Systems, University of Kentucky, Lexington, KY, "Template Languages for Fault Monitoring of Concurrent and Non-Concurrent Discrete Event Processes," March 1997. (Describes an algebra that deals with the rules of single and multiple interleaved instances of identical concurrent processes.)

[68] Alur, R., and D. Dill, Computer Science Department, Stanford University, CA, "A Theory of Timed Automata," 1994. (Abstract available at http://www.cis.upenn.edu/~alur/Icalp90.html and http://citeseer.ist.psu.edu/alur94theory.html.)

[69] Zimmermann, A., Dr.-Ing., research assistant, Technische Universität Berlin, Faculty of Electrical Engineering and Computer Science, Real-Time Systems, and Robotics, Performance Evaluation Group, "Petri Nets," http://pdv.cs.tu-berlin.de/~azi/petri.html#pnresearch.

[70] Shinshu University, Japan, "Graph Theory: Color Petrinet," http://markun.cs.shinshu-u.ac.jp/learn/graph/cn7/colorPetrinet.html.

[71] Shinshu University, Japan, "Graph Theory: CO Petrinet (Color Petrinets with OSP)," http://markun.cs.shinshu-u.ac.jp/learn/graph/cn7/coPetrinet.html.

[72] Ramaswamy, S., Ph.D., University of Southwestern Louisiana, "Hierarchical Time-Extended Petri Nets (H-EPNs) for Integrated Control and Diagnostics of Multilevel

Systems," 1994. (For the mathematically inclined reader, this is an excellent dissertation on the properties of processes, as expressed by petrinets.)

[73] Garg, V. K., University of California, Berkeley, CA, and M. T. Raghunath, University of Texas, Austin, TX, "Concurrent Regular Expressions and Their Relationship to Petri Nets," 1992, http://citeseer.ist.psu.edu/garg92concurrent.html. (Describes, for mathematically inclined readers only, a flexible way of specifying concurrent processes. Deals also with interleaving, interleaving closure, synchronous composition, and renaming of processes.)

[74] Ramchandani, C., Timed Petri nets, Technical Report 120, Project MAC, Massachusetts Institute Technology, *A Study of Asynchronous Concurrent Systems*, February 1974. (This is an old but interesting paper. Project MAC was one of the first visionary attempts to program common sense in the form of business rules into automation. MAC was an acronym for "Man and Computer.")

[75] Nestmann, U., assistant professor, Programming Methods Laboratory, Institute of Core Computing Science, School of Computer and Communication Sciences, Swiss Institute of Technology Lausanne, "Calculi for Mobile Processes." (Lists a set of links to research papers on Pi-Calculus. You may need permission from LAMP Programming Methods Laboratory, Institute of Core Computing Science, School of Computer and Communication Sciences, Swiss Institute of Technology, Lausanne, http://lamp.epfl.ch, to access the site.)

[76] Lumpe, M., University of Berne, Germany, "A Pi-Calculus Based Approach to Software Composition, an Inaugural Dissertation," January 21, 1999, http://www.iam.unibe.ch/~scg/Archive/PhD/lumpe-phd.pdf.

[77] Wischik, L., University of Bologna, "New Directions in Implementing Pi-Calculus," August 30, 2002, http://www.newcastle.research.ec.org/cabernet/workshops/radicals/2002/Papers/Bertinoro/18.pdf. (Describes a succinct, mathematical description of pi-calculus.)

[78] Courtiat, J. -P., et al., LAAS-CNRS, France and Ecole Mohamedia d'Ingénieurs, Rabat, Morocco, Experience with RT-LOTOS, a Temporal Extension of the LOTOS Formal Description Technique in Computer Communications 23, 2000, pp. 1104–1123, http://www.laas.fr/~courtiat/PAPERS/ComCom00.pdf. (Describes Real-Time LOTOS Process Algebra.)

[79] Harel, D., "On Visual Formalisms," *Communications of the ACM*, May 1988, Vol. 31, No. 5, pp. 521–523, 527. (Describes an algebra to simplify state representations in real world finite state automata.)

[80] Davis, A. M., "A Comparison of Techniques for the Specification of External System Behavior," *Communications of the ACM*, Vol. 31, No. 9, September 1988, p. 1105.

[81] Harel D., and A. Pnueli, "On Development of Reactive Systems," Department of Applied Mathematics, The Weizmann Institute of Science, Rehovot, Israel, 1985, pp. 8–10.

[82] Harel, D., "On Visual Formalisms," *Communications of the ACM*, Vol. 31, No. 5, May 1988, p. 519.

[83] Jones III, R. L., Langley Research Center, VA, NASA Technical Paper 3491, "Design Tool for Multiprocessor Scheduling and Evaluation of Iterative Data Flow Algorithms," August 1998, http://www.iis.sinica.edu.tw/JISE/2000/200005_07.pdf. (Although this paper focuses on distributed computer capacity and process efficiency, several concepts are also germane to real world, distributed business processes.)

[84] Bandinelli, S., A. Fuggetta, and S. Grigolli, "Process Modeling in-the-Large with SLANG," *Proceedings of the Second International Conference on the Software Process*, 1993. (Deals with evolution of large process models and high-level petrinets.)

[85] Pitstick, M. E., and W. L. Garrison, Path Research Report UCB-ITS-PRR-91-7, Institute for Transportation Studies, University of California, Berkeley, *Restructuring the Automobile Highway System for Lean Vehicles: The Scaled Precedence Activity Network (SPAN) Approach*, April 1991. (Describes SPAN Process diagrams.)

[86] Neumann, K., and W. G. Schneider, in Dokumenteserver der Universitätsbibliothek Karlsruhe (describes GERT concepts), *Heuristic Algorithms for Job Shop Scheduling Prob-*

lems with Stochastic Precedence Constraints, Technical Report, 1997. (Describes GERT concepts, http://www.ubka.uni-karlsruhe.de/cgi-bin/psview?document=/1997/wiwi/6&search=/1997/wiwi/6.).

[87] Liang, B.-S., and F.-J. Wang, Institute of Computer Science and Information Engineering, National Chiao Tung University, Taiwan, and J.-N. Chen, Samar Electronics Corporation Ltd, Taiwan, "A Project Model for Software Development," *Journal of Science and Engineering*, No. 16, 2000, pp. 423–446, http://www.iis.sinica.edu.tw/JISE/2000/200005_07.pdf. (Describes SPREM Process Algebra.)

[88] *Workshop on Design of Algorithms*, Module 17 Design Algorithms Channel: "A Matrix Calculus for the Analysis and Generation of Binary Relations Generalizations and Applications, Part 1," Dresden, 1996, http://marvin.sn.schule.de/~inftreff/modul17/task17_e.htm.

[89] Forsbak, O., University of Oslo, Department of Informatics, "A Critical Review of Aggregation in Object Models, and a Proposal for New Aggregation Concepts in UM," 2000. (This is a thesis that is a comprehensive and comprehendible treatise on different kinds of object aggregations, as well as their real world implications.)

[90] Rogers, W. P., senior engineering manager and application architect, Lutris Technologies, "Reveal the Magic Behind Subtype Polymorphism," *Java World*, April 2001, http://www.javaworld.com/javaworld/jw-04-2001/jw-0413-polymorph_p.html.

[91] Allen, E., Ph.D. graduate student, Programming Language Technology Group, Rice University, "Behold the Power of Parametric Polymorphism," *Java World*, February 2000, http://www.javaworld.com/javaworld/jw-02-2000/jw-02-jsr_p.html.

[92] Armstrong, R. et al., "Towards a Common Component Architecture for High-Performance Scientific Computing," *CCA Forum*, 1999.

[93] Booch, G., Rational Software Corp., M. Christerson, Rational Software Corp., M. Fuchs, Commerce One Inc., and J. Koistinen, Commerce One Inc., "UML for XML Schema Mapping Specification," *UML Resource Center*, December 8, 1999.

[94] Rumbaugh, J., *Collection of Papers on OMT, Objects, and Patterns*, OMT Papers, September 1995.

[95] Aiken, P. H., "IBM: Reverse Engineering of Data," 1998, http://www.research.ibm.com/journal/sj/372/aiken.txt.

Demand and Supply Chains and Standards

[96] Hakanson, B., Executive Director Supply Chain Council (SCC), "Supply Chain Management: Where Today's Businesses Compete," December 2, 1997, http://www.ascet.com/documents.asp?d_ID=228. (Presents Supply Chain meaning and process overview.)

[97] Kenneth Kmack Associates, "Gaps in Common Knowledge Between Professions," August 2000. (Provides an analysis of gaps between standard business process models and initiatives such as SCOR, CFPR, ARIS, XML, and others.)

[98] Stewart, G., "Supply Chain Operations Reference Model (SCOR): The First Cross Industry Framework for Integrated Supply Chain Management," Logistics Information Management, Vol. 10, No. 2, 1997, pp. 62–67.

[99] QPR Software, "SCOR Supply Chain Model from the Supply-Chain Council" (May have to access this publication via http://www.qpronline.com/.)

[100] American National Standards Institute (ANSI), and Instrumentation, Systems, and Automation Society (ISA): ANSI/ISA-95.00.01-2000: S95 Standard, May 2001, http://www.pera.net/Standards/Stds_S95.html.

[101] Brandl, D., director, Enterprise Initiative Sequencia Corporation, NC: "A Tutorial on the SP95 Enterprise/Control Integration Standard."

[102] Unger, K., EnteGreat Inc., "Integrate ERP with Control Systems Using the S95 Model," Mountain Systems Inc., *Mountain Systems Conference*, May 13–17, 2002, http://www.entegreat.com/eg_downloads_presentations_mountainsystems2002.htm.

(Describes an overview of S95 standard and its object model. May have to access the site via http://www.entegreat.com.)

[103] Manufacturing Enterprise Solutions Association International, Pittsburgh, PA, "Controls Definition & MES to Controls Data Flow Possibilities," MESA International White Paper Number 3, © MESA International, Pittsburgh, PA, http://www.mesa.org.

[104] Sawyer, P., PES Associates, "CAPE Tools for the Design and Operation of Batch Processes," *CAPE-21 Conference on Computer Aided Process Engineering Tools and Techniques for the 21st Century*, August 13, 2001. (Information on CAPE-21 is at http://cape-21.ucl.org.uk/ and http://cape-alliance.ucl.org.uk/.)

[105] Johnson, B. A., managing partner for strategy, research, and thought leadership, Cross Financial Services Solutions Group, Accenture Corp., "Fault Lines in CRM: New E-Commerce Business Models and Channel Integration Challenges," White Paper, January 15, 1999, http://www.crmproject.com/documents.asp?d_ID=706.

[106] Sheth, J., professor of marketing, Goizueta Business School, and R. Sisodia, trustee professor of marketing, Bentley College, Waltham MA, "Marketing's Final Frontier—The Automation of Consumption," 2000, http://www.jagsheth.net/pubs_articlesbytype.html and http://www.crmproject.com/documents.asp?grID=187&d_ID=709.

[107] Turan, O., Department of Industrial and Systems Engineering, Virginia Tech, "Introduction to Supply Chain Management," 2000.

[108] QPR Software, "Introduction to Supply Chain Management," 2001, http://www.qpronline.com/supplychainmanagement/supplychain_intro.html.

[109] Cyber M@rketing Services, "Demand Chain Management: New Strategies for E-Business," © IMA 1998, 1999, 2000. Cyber M@rketing Services, Teaneck, NJ, may be found at http://www.elsnet.org/orgs/1697.html. Information Management Associates, Inc. (IMA), Irvine, CA, may be found at http://www.elsnet.org/orgs/0770.html.

[110] Holmström, J., and T. Tissari, The ECOMLOG Research Program, Department of Industrial Engineering and Management, Helsinki University of Technology, "IT Value Capture: Creating an Effective Demand-Supply Chain for IT Solutions," *Logistics Research Network (LRN) 5th Annual Conference*, Cardiff, U.K., September 2000. The paper may be accessed at http://www.tuta.hut.fi/logistics/publications.html. (Describes the Information Technology Value Chain.)

[111] REM Associates of Princeton, Inc., "Supply Chain Move Over, It's Time for Demand Chain," March 2000, © 1999, 2000.

[112] Noller, J., project consultant, Renaissance Worldwide, "Integrating the Demand Chain and the Supply Chain: Technology and Trends," June 1999, http://www.afsmi.org/journal/jun99/jun-003.htm. Please register at register at: http://www.afsmi.org/ to access this site. ["There is an inherent difference between enterprise resource planning (ERP) systems and customer management systems. ERP systems measure financial transactions. Customer management systems measure customer contact events. However, to maximize the demand-chain value, processes and events need to be defined and systems implemented to reduce the demand cycle time."]

[113] Holmström, J., et al., McKinsey & Co., "The Other End of the Supply Chain," *McKinsey Quarterly*, 2000, No. 1, pp. 62–71.

[114] Michel, R., Manufacturing Systems, "Why Best Practices Make Perfect: CFAR and SCOR Initiatives Aim to Improve Supply Chain Operations," *Manufacturing Business Technology*, 1997. The paper can be accessed online by registering at http://www.mbtmag.com/Default.asp. (Access this publication via http://www.manufacturingsystems.com/.)

[115] Fleisch, E., and H. Osterle, Institute of Information Management, University of St. Gallen, Switzerland, "A Process Oriented Approach to Business Networking," *Virtual Organization Net*, Vol. 2, No. 2, 2000. Access at http://verdi.unisg.ch/org/iwi/iwi_pub.nsf/wwwPublRecentEng/9A080ADF5173DC38C1256FC600471E98. (Maps supply and demand chain models to collaborative business networking models.)

[116] Crowston, K., School of Business Administration, The University of Michigan, MI, "A Taxonomy of Organizational Dependencies and Coordination Mechanisms," MIT Sloan Center for Coordination Science (http://ccs.mit.edu/), May 1999, http://ccs.mit.edu/papers/CCSWP174.html. (Describes task and resource coordination models.)

[117] Milowski, R. A., XML architect, and R. Waldin, senior XML engineer, Lexica LLC, "iLingo—The Language of Insurance e-Business," 1999, http://xml.coverpages.org/ilingowhitepaper19991218.html. (Describes the Insurance Supply Chain).

[118] Scheer, A. W., Instutut Fur Wirtschaftinformatik der universitat des saarlander, "ARIS Business Process Model," http://www.iwi.uni-sb.de/teaching/ARIS/aris-i/aris-e-i/index.htm and http://www.iwi.uni-sb.de/teaching/ARIS/aris-i/aris-e-i/.

[119] Lee, H. L., and C. Billington, "Managing Supply Chain Inventory: Pitfalls and Opportunities," *Sloan Management Review*, Vol. 33, Issue 3, Spring 1992, p. 65.

[120] Alt, R., E. Fleissch, and H. Osterle, Institute of Information Management, University of St. Gallen, Switzerland, "Electronic Commerce and Supply Chain Management at ETA Fabriques d' Ebauches SA," 2000. (Maps the Complementary Relationship between the intensively collaborative processes that support Electronic Commerce and traditional Supply Chain process models, such as SCOR.)

[121] Voluntary Interindustry Commerce Standards (VICS) Association, "The CPFR Process Model," http://www.cpfr.org/ProcessModel.html and http://www.cpfr.org/Images/5.htm.

[122] Voluntary Interindustry Commerce Standards (VICS) Association, "The CPFR Data Model," 2002, http://www.cpfr.org/Images/AppendixH.HTM or http://havinghadlunch.com:8080/tamikin/GLS/matter/CPFR_Tabs_061802.pdf (also see links to current papers at http://www.vics.org/committees/cpfr/).

[123] VICS, "Corporate Values: A Shift Toward Collaboration," Collaborative Practices Research Initiative Sponsored by the Neeley Supply and Value Chain Center, Texas Christian University, November 15, 2004, http://www.vics.org/committees/cpfr/academic_papers/academic_papers.

[124] VICS, "Process and Results Metrics: Measuring the Success of a Process-Driven Value Chain," http://www.cpfr.org/Process-Results%20.html. See also http://havinghadlunch.com:8080/tamikin/GLS/matter/CPFR_Tabs_061802.pdf.

[125] VICS, "VICS CPFR XML Messaging Model standard," draft dated January 17, 2001, for public comment, http://www.cpfr.org/XMLMessageModel.doc.

[126] VICS, "ICS/CPFR IDEF0 Format Model," June 2002, http://www.cpfr.org/AppendixI.html. See also http://havinghadlunch.com:8080/tamikin/ GLS/matter/CPFR_Tabs_061802.pdf.

[127] Rosettanet Consortium, subsidiary of the Uniform Code Council, Inc., (UCC), Rosettanet Standards, http://www.rosettanet.org/rosettanet/Rooms/DisplayPages/LayoutInitial?container=com.webbridge.entity.Entity%5BOID%5B5F6606C8AD2BD411841F00C04F689339%5D%5D&expanded=com.webbridge.entity.Entity%5BOID%5B5F6606C8AD2BD411841F00C04F689339%5D%5D. (May have to access the site via http://www.rosettanet.org.)

[128] Rosettanet Consortium, subsidiary of the Uniform Code Council, Inc., (UCC), Rosettanet PIP Directory, http://www.rosettanet.org/rosettanet/Rooms/DisplayPages/LayoutInitial?Container=com.webbridge.entity.Entity%5BOID%5B9A6EEA233C5CD411843C00C04F689339%5D%5D. (PIP is an acronym for Partner Interface Processes. The site has a list of standard rosettanet PIPs—transactions exchanged by trading partners in a supply chain. May have to access the site via http://www.rosettanet.org.)

[129] Rosettanet Consortium, subsidiary of the Uniform Code Council, Inc., (UCC), Rosettanet PIPs, http://www.rosettanet.org/rosettanet/Rooms/DisplayPages/LayoutInitial?Container=com.webbridge.entity.Entity%5BOID%5B279B86B8022CD411841F00C04F689339%5D%5D. (PIP is an acronym for Partner Interface Processes. The site classifies rosettanet PIPs—transactions exchanged by trading partners in a supply chain. May have to access the site via http://www.rosettanet.org.)

[130] Rosettanet Consortium, subsidiary of the Uniform Code Council, Inc., (UCC), Rosettanet Fundamental Business Data Entities, http://www.rosettanet.org/rosettanet/Rooms/Display Pages/LayoutInitial?Container=com.webridge.entity.Entity%5BOID%5B07C504EE1A96 D411BD89009027E33DD8%5D%5D. (May have to access the site via http://www. rosettanet.org.)

[131] Rosettanet Consortium, subsidiary of the Uniform Code Council, Inc., (UCC), Rosettanet Business Data Entities, http://www.rosettanet.org/rosettanet/Rooms/DisplayPages/Layout Initial?Container=com.webridge.entity.Entity%5BOID%5BF7C104EE1A96D411BD890 09027E33DD8%5D%5D. (May have to access the site via http://www.rosettanet.org.)

[132] Rosettanet Consortium, subsidiary of the Uniform Code Council, Inc., (UCC), Rosettanet Business Properties, http://www.rosettanet.org/rosettanet/Rooms/DisplayPages/Layout Initial?Container=com.webridge.entity.Entity%5BOID%5B62C104EE1A96D411BD890 09027E33DD8%5D%5D. (May have to access the site via http://www.rosettanet.org.)

[133] Sprott, D., *Open Market Components: A CBDi Forum Report*, January 2000, http://www.componentsource.com/services/cbdiopen_market.asp. (Analyzes the market and emerging supply chain standards in terms of how components must be defined.)

Financial Accounting

[134] AccountingSTUDY.com[SM], "Accounting Study Guide, 1999–2002," © http:// accountinginfo.com/study/index.html. (Succinctly describes the key principles used in financial accounting.)

[135] AccountingSTUDY.com[SM], "Accrual Basis Versus Cash Basis Accounting, © 1999–2002," http://accountinginfo.com/study/accrual-01.htm. (Succinctly describes accrual and cash basis accounting, with examples.)

[136] AccountingSTUDY.com[SM], "Introduction to Adjusting Journal Entries, 1999–2002," http://accountinginfo.com/study/aje-01.htm. (Describes reasons for accounting adjustment transactions, with examples.)

[137] Wikipedia, "U.S. Generally Accepted Accounting Principles," http://en.wikipedia.org/ wiki/U.S._generally_accepted_accounting_principles. (Briefly describes Generally Accepted Accounting Principles and related standards.)

[138] AccountingSTUDY.com[SM], "FASB Statements," © by Financial Accounting Standards Board. ARB, "APB Opinions," © by the American Institute of Certified Public Accountants, Inc. (All Rights Reserved), Generally Accepted Accounting Principles in the United States Index, © 1999–2002, http://cpaclass.com/gaap/ gaap-us-01a.htm. (Provides a comprehensive source of U.S. GAAP information.)

[139] BookkeepersList.com Consortium, BookkeepersList.com, © 1999–2003, http:// bookkeeperlist.com/gaap.shtml. (Succinctly describes the principles that guide financial accounting practices.)

[140] CPAClass.com, "Ratios for Financial Statement Analysis Web Site, Financial Ratios: Summary," © 1999–2002, http://cpaclass.com/fsa/ratio-01a.htm. (Succinctly defines key ratios used for financial analysis and evaluation.)

[141] CPAClass.com, "Ratios for Financial Statement Analysis Web Site, Financial Ratios: Index," © 1999–2002, http://cpaclass.com/fsa/ratio-01.htm. (Lists common ratios used for financial analysis.)

[142] CPAClass.com, *Annual Report Project Resources*, © 1999–2001, http:// www.cpaclass.com/arp/. (Provides a comprehensive source of information related to developing a corporate annual report.)

Software Process

[143] Chappell, D., Chappell & Associates, "The Next Wave: Component Software Enters the Mainstream," April 1997, http://www.mc.edu/campus/users/gwiggins/syllabi/csc320/papers/dynamic-3.html.

[144] Kruchten, P., Rational Software Corp., Canada, "The 4+1 View Model of Architecture," *IEEE Software*, Vol. 12, No. 6, November 1995, pp. 42–50.

[145] Perry, D. E., and A. L. Wolf, "Foundations for the Study of Software Architecture," *ACM Software Eng. Notes,* October 1992, pp. 40–52.

[146] Capability Maturity Model® for Software (Version 1.1) Publication TR 25, from Software Engineering Institute (SEI).

[147] Carnegie Mellon University, CMMI® Models, Copyright 2002, http://www.sei.cmu.edu/cmmi/models/models.html. (May have to access the site through http://www.sei.cmu.edu/cmmi/.)

[148] Paulk, M., Carnegie Mellon University, "A History of the Capability Maturity Model® for Software," http://www.dfw-asee.org/archive/cmm-history.pdf. (Describes how the CMM® was sponsored, how it evolved, the other models it absorbed in the process, and its continuing evolution. Access the site through http://www.sei.cmu.edu/cmmi/.)

[149] Carnegie Mellon University, "Concept of Operations for the CMMI®," Copyright 2002, http://www.sei.cmu.edu/cmmi/background/conops.html. (Provides background and introduction to the Capability Maturity Model Integration® project. May have to access the site through http://www.sei.cmu.edu/cmmi/.)

[150] Rassa, B., Raytheon Corporation, and C. Chittister, Software Engineering Institute, © 2002, Carnegie Mellon University, "State of the CMMI®: Improving Processes for Better Products," http://www.raytheon.com/feature/stellent/groups/public/documents/legacy_site/cms01_042355.pdf.

[151] Sheard, S. A., Software Productivity Consortium, "The Frameworks Quagmire: A Brief Look," http://www.software.org/quagmire/frampapr/frampapr.html. (Briefly describes several quality and process maturity frameworks and standards, and their relationships with each other.)

[152] Bandinelli, S., A. Fugetta, and S. Ghezzi, "Software Processes as Real Time Systems: A Case Study Using High Level Petri Nets," *Proceedings of the International Phoenix Conference on Computers and Communications*, Phoenix, AZ, April 1992, pp. 231–242.

[153] Succi, G., University of Calgary, Canada, and L. Benedicenti, P. Predonzani, and T. Vernazza, University Di Genova, Italy, "Standardizing the Reuse of Software Processes," *StandardView*, Vol. 5, No. 2, June 1997, pp. 74–83, http://portal.acm.org/citation.cfm?id=260564. (Develops a model for reuse of processes, and contains some excellent references to other research in the area.)

User Interface Standards

[154] Microsoft Corporation, Microsoft Inductive User Interface Guidelines, 2001.

[155] World Wide Web Consortium (W3C), CSS2 Specification, Cascading Style Sheets, Level 2 W3C Recommendation, May 12, 1998, http://www.w3.org/TR/REC-CSS2/.

Agile Processes and Adaptive Software

[156] Norvig, P., and D. Cohn, Harlequin Inc., "Adaptive Software," http://www.norvig.com/adapaper-pcai.html.

[157] Meade, L. M., Automation & Robotics Research Institute's Enterprise Engineering Program, the University of Texas, "Agile Process Design," http://arri.uta.edu/eif/lmmdis.html.

[158] Ambler, S. W., "Agile Software Development," http://www.agilemodeling.com/essays/agileSoftwareDevelopment.htm.

[159] Wells, D., "Extreme Programming: A Gentle Introduction," Copyright © 1999, 2000, 2001, http://www.extremeprogramming.org/.

[160] Dowling, J., and V. Cahill, Department of Computer Science, Trinity College, Dublin, *K-Component Architecture Metamodel for Self-Adaptive Software*, http://www.cs.tcd.ie/publications/tech-reports/reports.01/TCD-CS-2001-50.pdf.

[161] Smith, H., chief technology officer (Europe) of Computer Sciences Corporation and cochair of the Business Process Management Initiative, and P. Fingar, executive partner with the Greystone Group, "The Next Fifty Years," *Darwin*, December 2002, http://www.darwinmag.com/read/120102/bizproc.html. (Discusses how computers have been seen as recordkeeping machines for 50 years, as opposed to being adaptable management machines. The need is now to use computers to gain actionable insight. For this, the authors say, corporations must shift their focus from "systems of record" to "systems of process." Moreover, "data processing" must give way to "process processing." The basic unit of automated support then will become the process, not data or the application system. The concept of databases thus will give way to "process bases," which will record and track past, present, and future business process structures, because, in the words of the authors, "business processes are the business." The authors describe how business processes will be made the central focus and basic building block of all automation and business systems in support of agility and responsiveness, and assert that the manual development of supporting information systems will be eliminated.)

[162] Oreizy, P., Ph.D. candidate, University of California, Irvine; M. Gorlick, research scientist, Aerospace Corporation; R. Taylor, professor, Department of Information and Computer Science, UCI, and Director of the Irvine Research Unit in Software; D. Heinsbigner, research associate professor, University of Colorado, Boulder; G. Johnson, Member of Technical Staff, Concept Shopping, Inc.; N. Medvidevic, assistant professor, Computer Science Department, University of Southern California; A. Quilici, associate professor of Electrical Engineering, University of Hawaii, Manoa; D. Rosenblum, associate professor, Department of Computer Science, UCI; and A. Wolf, associate professor, Department of Computer Science, University of Colorado, Boulder, *An Architecture Based Approach to Self-Adaptive Software*, 1999, http://ftp.ics.uci.edu/pub/c2/papers/ieee-is99.pdf.

[163] Robertson, P., Dynamic Language Labs, Andover, MA, "Self-Adaptive Software, Workshop on New Visions for Software Design and Productivity," White Paper, http://www.hpcc.gov/iwg/sdp/vanderbilt/position_papers/paul_robertson_self_adaptive_software.pdf.

[164] Scott, K., "Computer, Heal Thyself," *InformationWeek*, April 1, 2002, http://www.informationweek.com/story/IWK20020329S0005.

Mathematical Foundations: Set Theory, Number Theory, Category Theory, Theory of Functions, Lambda Calculus, Spaces and Their Properties, Borel Sets, and Tensors

[165] Cycorp, Inc., Austin, TX, "Mathematical and Logical Vocabulary," © 1996, 1997, 1998, all rights reserved, http://www.cyc.com/cycdoc/vocab/vocab-toc.html.

Mathematical Sets, Categories, Topoii, Groups, and Rings

[166] Siegrist, K., principal author, Virtual Laboratories in Probability and Statistics, Department of Mathematical Sciences, University of Alabama, Huntsville, "Sets and Events," http://www.ds.unifi.it/VL/VL_EN/prob/prob2.html. The Virtual Laboratories in Probability and Statistics project is a collaboration between the National Science Foundation and the University of Alabama. (Describes Set theory and Sigma Algebra.)

[167] Wikipedia encyclopedia (collaborative Web project), Set theory, http://www.wikipedia.com/wiki/Set_theory. (Describes the basic axioms of set theory.)

[168] Wikipedia encyclopedia (collaborative Web project), Basic Set Theory, http://www.wikipedia.com/wiki/Basic+Set+Theory.

[169] Wikipedia encyclopedia (collaborative Web project), Axiom of Choice, http://www.wikipedia.com/wiki/Axiom_of_choice. (Discusses creating sets by choosing elements from a collection of sets, even if they are sets with infinite members.)

[170] Wikipedia encyclopedia (collaborative Web project), Power Set, http://www.wikipedia.com/wiki/Power_set. (The power set of any given set is the set of all possible subsets of the set.)

[171] Wikipedia encyclopedia (collaborative Web project), Axiom of Regularity, http://www.wikipedia.com/wiki/Axiom+of+regularity. ("No set belongs to itself, . . . otherwise [it] would violate the axiom of regularity.")

[172] Wikipedia encyclopedia (collaborative Web project), Mathematical Class, http://www.wikipedia.com/wiki/mathematical+class. (Describes the differences between classes and sets, and how the mathematical concept of *class* subsumes the mathematical concept of *set*: "A class is a collection of sets that can be unambiguously defined by a property that all its members share.")

[173] Wikipedia encyclopedia (collaborative Web project), Category Theory, http://www.wikipedia.com/wiki/category+theory. ("A category attempts to capture the essence of a class of structures, instead of focusing on individual objects . . . the structure preserving maps between these objects are emphasized.")

[174] Baez, J., professor of mathematics, University of California, Riverside, "Categories, Quantization, and Much More," August 7, 1992, http://math.ucr.edu/home/baez/categories.html. (Although it is written primarily for mathematical physicists, the paper is a good source of information on category theory, groups, and morphisms, including higher order morphisms and categories, as well as their application in diverse areas.)

[175] Hillman, C., Ph.D., mathematics, University of Washington, "A Categorical Primer," a tutorial paper, July 2, 2001, http://www.di.uminho.pt/~lsb/mmc_ap/Hilmann.pdf. (Presents a reasonably simple mathematical introduction to category theory and Topoii.)

[176] Brown, C. E., Department of Mathematical Sciences, Carnegie Mellon University, Goldblatt, "Topoii: The Categorical Analysis of Logic" http://www.andrew.cmu.edu/~cebrown/notes/goldblatt.html. (Provides an introduction to categories and Topoii, the need for them, and how categories and Topoii generalize the concept of set.)

[177] Baez, J., professor of mathematics, University of California, Riverside, "This Week's Finds in Mathematical Physics (Week 68)," October 29, 1995, http://math.ucr.edu/ home/ baez/week68.html. (Provides a relatively benign discussion of Topoii for beginners, and a nonmathematical description of how subobjects emerge from commonalities based on the logic of Topoii.)

[178] Vickers, S., Department of Computing, Imperial College, London, England, "Topical Categories of Domains," *Mathematical Structures in Computer Science*, Cambridge University Press, Vol. 11, © 1995, http://mcs.open.ac.uk/sjv22/TopCat.ps.gz. ("A geometric form of constructive mathematics ... enables toposes as 'generalized topological spaces' to be treated ... in a ... spatial way.... It is quite in order to treat a topos as a 'space' whose points are models of the theory and to treat a geometric morphism ... as a transformation of points of one such space to points in another.... A topos can be considered both as a 'generalized topological space' and as a 'generalized universe of sets'.")

[179] Heyting Algebra, http://publish.uwo.ca/~jbell/HEYTING.pdf. (Briefly introduces Heyting Algebra as a generalization of Boolean Algebra.)

[180] Mori, M., Department of Information Systems, Interdisciplinary Graduate School of Engineering Science, and Kawahara, Research Institute of Fundamental Information Science, both of Kyushu University, Japan, Heyting Algebra, http://www.i.kyushu-u.ac.jp/ ~masa/fuzzy-graph/node2.html. (Provides a mathematical but brief introduction to Heyting Algebra, without proofs.)

[181] Goldblatt, R., "Topoii: Categorical Analysis of Logic," *Studies in Logic and the Foundations of Mathematics*, New York: North Holland, Vol. 98, 1984. (Access the book via links http://www.mcs.vuw.ac.nz/~rob/ or http://www.library.cornell.edu/math/digital-books.php#index.)

[182] Pitts, A. M., Computer Laboratory, University of Cambridge, U.K., "Nontrivial Power Types Can't Be Subtypes of Polymorphic Types," *Proceedings of Fourth Annual IEEE Symposium on Logic in Computer Science*, Asilomar, CA, July 1989, pp. 6–13, http://www.cl.cam.ac.uk/~amp12/papers.

[183] Wikipedia encyclopedia (collaborative Web project), Mathematical Topos, http://www.wikipedia.com/wiki/mathematical+topos. ["A topos (plural, Topoii) in mathematics is a type of category that allows the formulation of all of the mathematics inside it."]

[184] Baez, J., professor of mathematics, University of California, Riverside, "Topos Theory in a Nutshell," © John Baez, January 3, 2001, http://math.ucr.edu/home/baez/topos.html.

[185] Wikipedia encyclopedia (collaborative Web project), Law of Excluded Middle, http://www.wikipedia.com/wiki/law+of+the+excluded+middle. ("The law of excluded middle states that for any proposition, either it or its contradictory obtains, for any proposition P, either P or not-P." This law may not be true for all Topoii.)

[186] Wikipedia encyclopedia (collaborative Web project), Functor, http://www.wikipedia.com/wiki/functor. ("In category theory a functor is a mapping from one category to another which maps objects to objects and morphisms to morphisms in such a manner that the composition of morphisms and the identities are preserved.")

[187] Wikipedia encyclopedia (collaborative Web project), Monoid, http://www.wikipedia.com/wiki/Monoid. ("The set of all morphisms from this object to itself, with composition as the operation [is an example of a Monoid]. . . . Categories [are] generalizations of monoids.")

[188] Wikipedia encyclopedia (collaborative Web project), Mathematical Group, http://www.wikipedia.com/wiki/mathematical+group. ("Groups underlie other algebraic structures such as fields and vectors . . . also important . . . for studying symmetry.")

[189] Wikipedia encyclopedia (collaborative Web project), Semigroup, http://www.wikipedia.com/wiki/semigroup.

[190] Wikipedia encyclopedia (collaborative Web project), Subgroup, http://www.wikipedia.com/wiki/subgroup. (Describes the abstract mathematical theories that support the concept of subtyping by partitioning sets, and shows that subsets are subtypes of supersets.)

[191] Wikipedia encyclopedia (collaborative Web project), Group Action, http://www.wikipedia.com/wiki/group+action.

[192] Wikipedia encyclopedia (collaborative Web project), Mathematical Ring, http://www.wikipedia.com/wiki/Mathematical+ring. (Describes a kind of mathematical roup that generalizes commutative and associative operations.)

[193] Wikipedia encyclopedia (collaborative Web project), Fundamental Group, http://www.wikipedia.com/wiki/fundamental+group. (Describes the mathematical structures that convey information on loops and the one dimensional structure of space.)

[194] Wikipedia encyclopedia (collaborative Web project), Group Representation Lie Algebra, http://www.wikipedia.com/wiki/group+representation.

[195] Wikipedia encyclopedia (collaborative Web project), Abelian group, http://www.wikipedia.com/wiki/abelian+group. (Describes the mathematics of commutative operators.)

[196] Wikipedia encyclopedia (collaborative Web project), Lie Group, http://www.wikipedia.com/wiki/Lie+group.

[197] Wikipedia encyclopedia (collaborative Web project), Lie Algebra, http://www.wikipedia.com/wiki/Lie+algebra.

[198] Wikipedia encyclopedia (collaborative Web project), Ring Ideal, http://www.wikipedia.com/wiki/ring+ideal. (Describes the mathematical theories behind "ideal," an abstraction, and generalization of numbers.)

[199] Wikipedia encyclopedia (collaborative Web project), Integral domain, http://www.wikipedia.com/wiki/Integral+domain.

[200] Wikipedia encyclopedia (collaborative Web project), Field, http://www.wikipedia.com/wiki/field.

[201] Wikipedia encyclopedia (collaborative Web project), Finite Field, http://www.wikipedia.com/wiki/Finite+field.

[202] Wikipedia encyclopedia (collaborative Web project), Countable, http://www.wikipedia.com/wiki/Countable. (A set is countable if it is either finite or the same size as the set of positive integers, a set with infinite numbers of members.)

[203] Wikipedia encyclopedia (collaborative Web project), Countably Infinite, http://www.wikipedia.com/wiki/Countably_infinite. (Describes countability in infinitely large sets.)

[204] Wikipedia encyclopedia (collaborative Web project), Continuum Hypothesis, http://www.wikipedia.com/wiki/Continuum_hypothesis. (Describes the set theoretic basis of a continuum based on the continuum of real numbers.)

[205] Wikipedia encyclopedia (collaborative Web project), Cantors Diagonal Argument, http://www.wikipedia.com/wiki/Cantors_Diagonal_argument. (Describes a logical argument that demonstrates that real numbers are not countably infinite.)

[206] Wikipedia encyclopedia (collaborative Web project), Cardinal Number, http://www.wikipedia.com/wiki/Cardinal_number. (Gauges the relative sizes of sets, even sets with infinite members.)

[207] Wikipedia encyclopedia (collaborative Web project), Number, http://www.wikipedia.com/wiki/Number. (Describes numbers as abstract patterns and links to definitions of numbers of different kinds.)

[208] Wikipedia encyclopedia (collaborative Web project), Dense, http://www.wikipedia.com/wiki/Dense.

[209] Blanch, J., University of Gavle, Gavle, Sweden, "Domain Representation of Topological Spaces," 1998, http://www.sm.luth.se/~jens/pdf/top.pdf. (Describes Scott-Ershov domains and their properties. Scott-Ershov domains can facilitate approximation of the infinite continuum of numbers in finite state machines.)

[210] Hitzler, P., "Scott Domains, Generalized Ultrametric Spaces, and Generalized Acyclic Logic Programs," February 1998. (". . . every object of interest can be arbitrarily closely approximated by [compact elements]")

[211] Davies, G., ITE, "Order and Value Assignment," Hösten: Decision Theory, 2000. (Provides a relatively benign discussion of ordinal value theory for those willing to brave it.)

[212] Wikipedia encyclopedia (collaborative Web project), Ordinal, http://www.wikipedia.com/wiki/Ordinal. (Provides a set theoretic discussion of ordinalilty.)

[213] Wikipedia encyclopedia (collaborative Web project), Total Order, http://www.wikipedia.com/wiki/Total_order. (Describes the mathematical basis of ordered sets and ordinal domains.)

[214] Wikipedia encyclopedia (collaborative Web project), Well-Founded Set, http://www.wikipedia.com/wiki/Well-founded_set. (Describes the set theoretic basis of the origin in a coordinate system, especially in an ordinal domain.)

[215] Wikipedia encyclopedia (collaborative Web project), Well-Order, http://www.wikipedia.com/wiki/Well-order. (Provides a set theoretic discussion of lower bounds on ordinal domains.)

[216] Wikipedia encyclopedia (collaborative Web project), Ordered Field, http://www.wikipedia.com/wiki/ordered+field. (Describes the set theoretic basis of the "natural zero" of a domain.)

[217] Wikipedia encyclopedia (collaborative Web project), Partial Order, http://www.wikipedia.com/wiki/Partial_order. (Provides mathematical descriptions of subtyping and their relationship to set theory, especially "posets.")

[218] Wikipedia encyclopedia (collaborative Web project), Lattice, http://www.wikipedia.com/wiki/Lattice.

Numbers, Functions, and Number Theory

[219] Wikipedia encyclopedia (collaborative Web project), Natural Number, http://www.wikipedia.com/wiki/Natural_number.

[220] Wikipedia encyclopedia (collaborative Web project), Rational Number, http://www.wikipedia.com/wiki/rational+number.

[221] Wikipedia encyclopedia (collaborative Web project), Irrational Number, http://www.wikipedia.com/wiki/irrational+number.

[222] Wikipedia encyclopedia (collaborative Web project), Real number, http://www.wikipedia.com/wiki/Real+number.

[223] Wikipedia encyclopedia (collaborative Web project), Complex Number, http://www.wikipedia.com/wiki/complex+number.

[224] Wikipedia encyclopedia (collaborative Web project), Transcendental Number, http://www.wikipedia.com/wiki/transcendental+number.

[225] Wikipedia encyclopedia (collaborative Web project), Hyperreal Numbers, http://www.wikipedia.com/wiki/hyperreal+numbers.

[226] Wikipedia encyclopedia (collaborative Web project), Hypercomplex Numbers, http://www.wikipedia.com/wiki/Hypercomplex+numbers.

[227] Wikipedia encyclopedia (collaborative Web project), Octonions, http://www.wikipedia.com/wiki/octonions.

[228] Wikipedia encyclopedia (collaborative Web project), Quaternions, http://www.wikipedia.com/wiki/quaternions.

[229] Wikipedia encyclopedia (collaborative Web project), Sedenions, http://www.wikipedia.com/wiki/sedenions.

[230] Wikipedia encyclopedia (collaborative Web project), P-adic Numbers, http://www.wikipedia.com/wiki/p-adic+numbers.

[231] Wikipedia encyclopedia (collaborative Web project), Surreal Numbers, http://www.wikipedia.com/wiki/Surreal_numbers.

[232] Siegrist, K., principal author, Virtual Laboratories in Probability and Statistics, Department of Mathematical Sciences, University of Alabama, Huntsville, "Functions and Random Variables," http://www.math.uah.edu/stat. (Provides an elementary introduction to the mathematical theory of functions.) The Virtual Laboratories in Probability and Statistics project is a collaboration between the National Science Foundation and the University of Alabama.

[233] Wikipedia encyclopedia (collaborative Web project), Function, http://www.wikipedia.com/wiki/Function. (Provides another easily readable introduction to the mathematical theory of functions.)

[234] Wikipedia encyclopedia (collaborative Web project), Injective, Surjective, and Bijective Functions, http://www.wikipedia.com/wiki/Injective,+surjective+and+functions.

[235] Wikipedia encyclopedia (collaborative Web project), Cartesian Product, http://www.wikipedia.com/wiki/Cartesian_product.

[236] Wikipedia encyclopedia (collaborative Web project), Direct Product, http://www.wikipedia.com/wiki/direct+product. ("In mathematics, one can often define a direct

product of objects already known, giving a new [object]." Focuses on mathematical groups.)

[237] Wikipedia encyclopedia (collaborative Web project), Recursion Definition, http://www.wikipedia.com/wiki/Recursion_definition.

[238] Wikipedia encyclopedia (collaborative Web project), Transfinite Induction, http://www.wikipedia.com/wiki/Transfinite_induction. (Transfinite Induction is a technique of proving that a property applies to all ordinals.)

Lambda Calculus, Functional Programming, and Semantics

[239] Cardelli, L., AT&T Bell Laboratories, Murray Hill, NJ, and P. Wegner, Department of Computer Science, Brown University, Providence, RI, "On Understanding Types, Data Abstraction, and Polymorphism," *Computing Surveys*, Vol. 17, No. 4, December 1985, pp. 471–522, http://research.microsoft.com/Users/luca/Papers/OnUnderstanding.pdf. (Provides a mathematical treatment of polymorphism and inheritance based on λ-calculus.)

[240] Lambda calculus, http://www.wikipedia.com/wiki/Lambda_calculus. (Briefly discusses λ-calculus, including emergence of functions, arithmetic operations, and recursion, as well as equivalence of rule expressions.)

[241] Henz, M., "The Lambda Calculus," http://www.kids.net.au/encyclopedia-wiki/la/Lambda_calculus#History. (Provides a brief description and history of λ-calculus.)

[242] Larson, J., JPL Section 312, "An Introduction to Lambda Calculus and Scheme," *Programming Lunchtime Seminar*, July 26, 1996, http://www.jetcafe.org/~jim/lambda.html. (Describes how polymorphism emerges from λ-calculus, and how λ-calculus is a universal model of computation. Describes also a programming language, Scheme, which facilitates application of λ-calculus.)

[243] Myers, A., Cornell University, Advanced Programming Languages, http://www.cs.cornell.edu/courses/cs611/2000fa/slides/lec09.pdf. (Provides a brief presentation on normalizing rule expressions with Lambda Calculus. "Two functions are equal by *Extension* if they have the same meaning: they give the same result when applied to the same argument.")

[244] Zhang, H., Iowa University, Lambda Calculus, http://www.cs.uiowa.edu/ ~hzhang/c123/Lecture5.pdf. (Provides a simple but mathematical definition of lambda calculus and normal form, with reduction algorithms and examples.)

[245] Dominus, M-J., Plover Systems Co., managing editor of http://www.perl.com 1999–2001, Church-Rosser theorem, Copyright 1999. (Provides a brief presentation of the Church Rosser theorem that reduces rule expressions to a normal form.)

[246] Clack, C., senior lecturer and MScCS course director, Department of Computer Science, UCLA, "The Lambda Calculus: A Deeper Look," http://www.cs.ucl.ac.uk/teaching/3C11/HTML_Lectures/lecture3_3C11/sld011.htm. (Provides another good presentation on the essence of the Church-Rosser Theorem.)

[247] Fenner, S., "Normal Forms and the Church-Rosser Theorem," 1996, http://www.cs.usm.maine.edu/class/cos370/handouts/lambda/node7.html. (Describes when Rule Expressions can and cannot be reduced to normal forms.)

[248] Selinger, P., "Functionality, Polymorphism, and Concurrency: A Mathematical Investigation of Programming Paradigms," Ph.D. thesis, University of Pennsylvania, 1997. (Provides both formal and intuitive descriptions of the normal forms and the Church Rosser Theorem.)

[249] Homeier, P. V., U.S. Department of Defense, Ph.D. in computer science, UCLA, "A Proof of the Church Rosser Theorem for Lambda Calculus in Higher Order Logic," 1995, http://www.cis.upenn.edu/~hol/lamcr/lamcr.pdf.

[250] Wikipedia encyclopedia (collaborative Web project), Entscheidungsproblem, http://www.wikipedia.com/wiki/Entscheidungsproblem. ("Entscheidungsproblem" is German for "the Decision Problem." In mathematics, Entscheidungsproblem addresses the issue of the same rule being expressed in different ways. It specifically proves that there is no general

algorithm that will show that algebraic expressions consisting of different terms are equivalent.)

[251] Wikipedia encyclopedia (collaborative Web project), First-Order Predicate Calculus, http://www.wikipedia.com/wiki/First-order_predicate_calculus. (Describes symbolic logic that is the basis of set theory, values, relationships, and arithmetic and logical operators.)

[252] Kanka, M., "Semantics," © Manfred Krifka, Institut für deutsche Sprache und Linguistik, HU Berlin, WS 2000/2001, http://amor.rz.hu-berlin.de/~h2816i3x/SemanticsI-07.pdf.

[253] Roy, A. J., Department of Computer Science, University of Keele, U.K., *A Comparison of Rough Sets, Fuzzy Sets and Non-Monotonic Logic*, Technical Report TR99-11, June, 1999, http://pages.britishlibrary.net/aroy/ant/revigis/Comparisonpdf.pdf.

[254] Wikipedia encyclopedia (collaborative Web project), Functional Programming, http://www.wikipedia.com/wiki/Functional_programming. (Functional programming expresses logic by combining functions instead of focusing on execution of computer commands. Arguments as well as results of functions can be functions.)

Spaces and Their Properties

[255] Weisstein, E. W., Eric Weissensteinn's Treasure Trove of Science, © Eric W. Weisstein, "Space," http://hades.ph.tn.tudelft.nl/Internal/PHServices/Documentation/MathWorld/math/math/s/s513.htm. (Provides succinct but very abstract mathematical definitions of various spaces, including metric spaces and state spaces.)

[256] Wikipedia encyclopedia (collaborative Web project), Tensor, http://www.wikipedia.com/wiki/Tensor.

[257] Wikipedia encyclopedia (collaborative Web project), Tensor/Old, http://www.wikipedia.com/wiki/Tensor/Old. ("Tensors are quantities that describe a transformation between coordinate systems, in such a way that the physical laws [are described in a way that is] . . . independent of the coordinate system chosen. . . . Tensors were introduced as specific representations of the group of all changes of coordinate systems.")

[258] Weisstein, E. W., Eric Weissensteinn's Treasure Trove of Science, © Eric W. Weisstein, "Tensor," http://hades.ph.tn.tudelft.nl/Internal/PHServices/Documentation/MathWorld/math/math/t/t078.htm.

[259] Weisstein, E. W., Eric Weissensteinn's Treasure Trove of Science, © Eric W. Weisstein, "Metric Tensor," http://hades.ph.tn.tudelft.nl/Internal/PHServices/Documentation/MathWorld/math/math/m/m217.htm.

[260] Wikipedia encyclopedia (collaborative Web project), Vector Space, http://www.wikipedia.com/wiki/vector+space.

[261] Wikipedia encyclopedia (collaborative Web project), Normed Vector Space, http://www.wikipedia.com/wiki/normed+vector+space. (Describes mathematical "norm" and isometry.)

[262] Wikipedia encyclopedia (collaborative Web project), Topology, http://www.wikipedia.com/wiki/Topology.

[263] Wikipedia encyclopedia (collaborative Web project), Pointless Topology, http://www.wikipedia.com/wiki/Pointless+topology.

[264] Wikipedia encyclopedia (collaborative Web project), Topology Glossary, http://www.wikipedia.com/wiki/Topology+Glossary.

[265] Cairns, P., principal investigator, and J. Gow, researcher, Interaction Design Centre at the School of Computing Science, Middlesex University, U.K., "The Definition of a Metric Space Based on Lecture Notes by Peter Collins," Elements of Euclidean and Metric Topology of the Interactive Mathematical Proofs research project, available at the Mathematical Proofs research (IMP) project (January 2001 to June 2002), funded by the Engineering and Physical Sciences Research Council (EPSRC), U.K., http://www.uclic.ucl.ac.uk/imp/. (Describes a simple definition of metric spaces.)

[266] Rusin, D., associate professor of mathematics, Northern Illinois University, The Mathematical Atlas: Spaces with Richer Structures, Especially Metric Spaces, http://www.math.niu.edu/~rusin/known-math/index/54EXX.html. (Provides a minimally mathematical definition of metric spaces, and discussion of a metric as a generalized concept of topological distance.)

[267] MacLennan, B., Computer Science Department, University of Tennessee at Knoxville, "Discrete Metric Space," 1996.

[268] Wikipedia encyclopedia (collaborative Web project), Manifold, http://www.wikipedia.com/wiki/Manifold. ("A manifold, in mathematics, can be thought of as a 'curved' surface or space which locally looks like Euclidean space and therefore admits the introduction of local charts or coordinate systems. Every manifold has a dimension, the number of coordinates needed in local coordinate systems.")

[269] Wikipedia encyclopedia (collaborative Web project), Hausdorff Space, http://www.wikipedia.com/wiki/Hausdorff+space. ("A Hausdorff space is a topological space in which any two distinct points have disjoint neighbourhoods.")

[270] Wikipedia encyclopedia (collaborative Web project), Tychonoff Space, http://www.wikipedia.com/wiki/Tychonoff+space. ("A Hausdorff space X is called a Tychonoff space if, for every nonempty closed subset C and every x in the complement of C, there is a continuous function f : X -> [0,1] such that f(x) = 0 and f(C) = {1}." This is, a Tychonoff space is a space of distinct points that may be partitioned into two mutually exclusive sets of points. This is the mathematical theory that supports partitioning objects and state spaces.)

[271] Wikipedia encyclopedia (collaborative Web project), Dimensional Analysis, http://www.wikipedia.com/wiki/Dimensional+analysis. (Provides a description of how other physical domains emerge from fundamental physical domains, and the use of this information in engineering sciences.)

[272] Wikipedia encyclopedia (collaborative Web project), Fundamental Dimensions, http://www.wikipedia.com/wiki/Fundamental+dimension. (Describes fundamental physical domains of this book, called "dimensions" in this publication. Reference [337] augments this list in Chapter 5, Section 3.)

[273] Wikipedia encyclopedia (collaborative Web project), Hausdorff Dimension, http://www.wikipedia.com/wiki/Hausdorff+dimension. (Provides a mathematical description of the dimensionality of complex metric spaces that subsumes the "normal" Euclidean concept of dimension.)

[274] Wikipedia encyclopedia (collaborative Web project), Infimum, http://www.wikipedia.com/wiki/Infimum. (Defines a type of lower bound. The Hausdorff dimension is related to this concept.)

[275] Wikipedia encyclopedia (collaborative Web project), Hamel Dimension, http://www.wikipedia.com/wiki/Dimension+of+a+vector+space. (Provides a mathematical description of the dimensionality of vector spaces that subsumes the "normal" Euclidean concept of dimension, and accounts for the cardinality—see cardinal number—of the space.)

[276] Wikipedia encyclopedia (collaborative Web project), Connectedness, http://www.wikipedia.com/wiki/connectedness. (Mathematically describes the concept of points in space being connected to points in their neighborhood, as well as the weirder concept of points being isolated from others.)

[277] Wikipedia encyclopedia (collaborative Web project), Simply Connected, http://www.wikipedia.com/wiki/simply+connected. (Provides a mathematical description of paths and connections in abstract spaces.)

[278] Weisstein, E. W., Eric Weissensteinn's Treasure Trove of Science, © Eric W. Weisstein, "Distance," http://hades.ph.tn.tudelft.nl/Internal/PHServices/Documentation/MathWorld/math/math/d/d325.htm. (Succinctly describes a generalized concept of distance in a manifold.)

[279] Weisstein, E. W., Eric Weissensteinn's Treasure Trove of Science, © Eric W. Weisstein, "Metric," http://hades.ph.tn.tudelft.nl/Internal/PHServices/Documentation/MathWorld/math/math/m/m213.htm. (Succinctly describes a metric as a generalized concept of distance.)

[280] Wikipedia encyclopedia (collaborative Web project), Measure, http://www.wikipedia.com/wiki/Measure. (Gauges the relative sizes of sets.)

[281] Coquand, T., professor, Computing Science Department, Göteborg University, Sweden, "How to Define Measure of Borel Sets," http://www.cs.chalmers.se/~coquand/riesz.pdf. (Provides a complex mathematical discussion of Borel Sets and Cantor Spaces.)

[282] Wikipedia encyclopedia (collaborative Web project), Borel Measure, http://www.wikipedia.com/wiki/Borel_measure. ("The Borel Measure is the measure on the smallest set algebra containing the intervals which gives to the interval [a,b] the measure b-a.")

[283] Tsuda, K., Electrotechnical Laboratory, Japan, "Machine Understanding Division: Subspace Classifier in Hilbert Space," *Pattern Recognition Letters*, Vol. 20, Issue 5, May 1999, pp. 513–519. (Uses Hilbert spaces to automate creation of classes and subtypes based on similarities between objects. The paper is a sophisticated mathematical discussion of how objects might be classified from a large number of samples using statistical methods.)

[284] Tan, C-I., Department of Physics, Brown University, "Notes on Hilbert Space," http://www.chem.brown.edu/chem277/Tan_on_Hilbert_Space.html.

[285] Megill, N. D., MIT Alumnus, "Hilbert Space Explorer," Copyright (GPL) 2000, http://us.metamath.org/mpegif/mmhil.html. (Provides a set of definitions, theorems, and explanations about Hilbert Space.)

[286] Sarfatti, J., "A Semi-Pop Non-Mathematical Tutorial on Hilbert Space in Quantum Mechanics," http://www.qedcorp.com/pcr/pcr/hilberts.html. (This paper focuses on representing quantum mechanical states with the help of Hilbert Spaces. "Hilbert space contains infinite dimensions, but these are not geometric. Rather, each dimension represents a state of possible existence for a quantum system. All possible states coexist." The book you are reading is about business systems, not quantum states, and the metamodel in this book focuses on purely deterministic systems. In contrast, the state of a quantum system is unknown, and merely querying it can change its state. However, mathematically astute readers will find interesting analogs that can be extended to describe the states of nondeterministic business systems in Sarfatti's paper—especially those that might change state by merely querying the information in them. This can happen in all real world systems, but is beyond the scope of this book. We can safely ignore Hilbert space in this book.)

Buckingham's Pi Theorem—About the Independence of Physical Laws from Their Units of Measure

[287] Hanche-Olsen, H., The Weizmann Institute of Science, "Sets and Events at Buckingham's Pi-Theorem," Version 2001-09-15, 1998. (Describes Buckingham's pi-theorem with illustrative examples of its use in finding solutions to physical problems. Includes a mathematical discussion of values, measurement, and units of measure—nonmathematicians beware!)

[288] *Harcourt Academic Press Dictionary of Science*, "Buckingham's Pi-Theorem," C. Morris, (ed.), New York: Elsevier, 1991. (Provides a concise description of Buckingham's pi-theorem.)

[289] Weisstein, E. W., Eric Weissensteinn's Treasure Trove of Science, © Eric W. Weisstein, "Buckingham's Pi Theorem from Eric Weissenstein's World of Physics," http://scienceworld.wolfram.com/physics/BuckinghamsPiTheorem.html. (Provides de- scription and mathematical proof of Buckingham's pi-theorem.)

Information Theory, Chaos Theory, and Miscellaneous Publications

[290] Wikipedia encyclopedia (collaborative Web project), Information Theory, http://www.wikipedia.com/wiki/information+theory. (Provides a brief introduction to Shannon's Information theory and measures of information.)

[291] Wikipedia encyclopedia (collaborative Web project), Sapir-Whorf Hypothesis, http://www.wikipedia.com/wiki/Sapir-Whorf+hypothesis. (Provides an overview of the impact of language on meaning and perception.)

[292] Wikipedia encyclopedia (collaborative Web project), Chaos Theory, http://www.wikipedia.com/wiki/Chaos+theory. (Succinctly introduces the theory of chaos.)

[293] Kanamaru, T., Dept. of Electrical and Electronic Engineering, Tokyo University of Agriculture and Technology, Japan, and J. Michael and T. Thompson, Dept. of Applied Mathematics and Theoretical Physics, Cambridge, "Introduction to Chaos and Nonlinear Dynamics," September 1997, http://brain.cc.kogakuin.ac.jp/~kanamaru/Chaos/e/. See Time Series of Logistic map at http://brain.cc.kogakuin.ac.jp/~kanamaru/Chaos/e/Logits/. (Provides an interactive site that gives the reader a hands-on experience in chaotic systems.)

Books

[294] Ross, R. G., *The Business Rule Book: Classifying, Defining and Modeling Rules*, Boston, MA: Database Research Group, Inc., 1994.

[295] Hammer, M., and J. Champy, *Reengineering The Corporation*, New York: Harper Collins, 1993.

[296] Herzum, P., and O. Sims, *Business Component Factory: A Comprehensive Overview of Component-Based Development for the Enterprise*, New York: John Wiley & Sons, 2000.

[297] Nijssen, G. M., and T. A. Halpin, Department of Computer Science, Un: Business Component Factory, University of Queensland, *Conceptual Schema and Relational Database Design: A Fact Oriented Approach*, Upper Saddle River, NJ: Prentice Hall, 1989.

[298] Harmon, P., and D. King, Ch. 4, "Representing Knowledge," and Ch. 5, "Drawing Inferences," in *Artificial Intelligence in Business*, New York: John Wiley & Sons, 1985.

[299] Fowler, M., *Analysis Patterns: Reusable Object Models*, Reading, MA: Addison-Wesley, 1997.

[300] Scheer, A. -W., ARIS, *Business Process Frameworks*, New York: Springer-Verlag, 1999.

[301] Scheer, A. -W., ARIS, *Business Process Modeling*, New York: Springer-Verlag, 1996.

[302] Rumbaugh, J., et al., General Electric Research and Development Center, *Object-Oriented Modeling and Design*, Upper Saddle River, NJ: Prentice Hall, 1991.

[303] *Structured Systems Analysis and Design Methodology, Version 4*, SSADM College, Ltd., 1996. (See http://www.comp.glam.ac.uk/pages/staff/tdhutchings/chapter4.html.)

[304] Fleming, C. C., and B. von Halle, *Handbook of Relational Database Design*, Reading, MA: Addison-Wesley, 1989.

[305] Maisell, H., and G. Gnugnoli, *Simulation of Discrete Stochastic Systems*, Chicago, IL: Science Research Associates, 1972.

[306] Finkel, R., *Functional Programming*, Reading, MA: Addison-Wesley, 1996.

[307] Taylor, P., Sec. 2.3, "Sums, Products and Function-Types," in *Practical Foundations of Mathematics*, Cambridge, England: Cambridge University Press, 1999, http://www.cs.man.ac.uk/~pt/Practical_Foundations/html/s23.html. (Provides a simple, physical explanation of lambda calculus, and the need for it in addressing practical real world problems. "[We] discussed how functions act, but they must also be considered as entities in themselves. Early ... problems arose in which the unknown was a function as a whole, rather than its value at particular or even all points: the Sun's light takes that path through

the variable density of the atmosphere which minimizes the time of travel; the motion of a stretched string depends on its initial displacement along its whole length.")

[308] Finkbeiner II, D., Kenyon College, *Matrices and Linear Transformations*, Ch. 1, Reading, MA: Addison-Wesley, 1966. (Includes a mathematical discussion of sets, set operations, functions, mapping between sets, relationships and domains.)

[309] Thomas, G., Department of Mathematics, Massachusetts Institute of Technology, *Calculus and Analytical Geometry*, 3rd ed., Reading, MA: Addison-Wesley, 1960. (Includes simple mathematical descriptions of functions, domains, ranges, existence, and continuity.)

[310] Parzen, E., Stanford University, *Modern Probability Theory and Its Applications*, New York: John Wiley & Sons, 1960.

[311] Siegel, S., research professor of psychology, Pennsylvania State University, *Nonparametric Statistics for the Behavioral Sciences*, New York: McGraw-Hill, 1956.

[312] Wagner, H. M., Yale University, *Principles of Operations Research with Applications to Managerial Decisions*, Englewood Cliffs, NJ: Prentice-Hall, 1969.

[313] Gillett, B. E., professor of computer science, University of Missouri-Rolla, *Introduction to Operations Research: A Computer-Oriented Algorithmic Approach*, New York: McGraw-Hill, 1976.

[314] Kreysig, E., professor of mathematics, Ohio State University, *Advanced Engineering Mathematics*, New York: John Wiley & Sons, 1967.

[315] Goodman, A. W., University of South Florida, *Modern Calculus with Analytic Geometry*, New York: Macmillan, 1967.

[316] Durell, W. R., Data Administration, Inc., *The Complete Guide to Data Modeling*, New York: Macmillan, 1967.

[317] Durell, W., *Data Administration: A Practical Guide to Data Management*, New York: McGraw-Hill, 1985.

[318] Pagnoni, A., *Project Engineering: Computer-Oriented Planning and Operational Decision Making*, Berlin, Germany: Springer-Verlag, 1990. (Describes various techniques for modeling and managing tasks, including complex stochastic, and models of repetitive processes, using techniques such as GERT and Petrinets.)

[319] Dymond, K. M., *A Guide to the CMM®: Understanding the Capability Maturity Model for Software*, Annapolis, MD: Process Transition International, Inc. YEAR?? (Describes the dynamics of Best Practices and processes needed to institutionalize change based on the System Engineering Institute's [SEI] Capability Maturity Model® [CMM®].)

[320] Duck, J. D., senior vice president, Boston Consulting Group, *The Change Monster*, New York: Crown, 2001. (Offers an excellent and very readable work on the social, emotional, and organizational dynamics of change.)

[321] Moore, G., *Crossing the Chasm*, New York: HarperCollins, 1991. (Discusses the acceptance of technological innovation in the marketplace.)

[322] Inmon, W. H., *A Brief History of Data Base Design*, New York, John Wiley & Sons, 1999. (Describes some changes in business environments and assumptions that have disrupted legacy systems.)

[323] Mullins, T., Department of Physics, University of Oxford; D. Holton, Department of Hydrogeology, Harwell Laboratory; R. May, Department of Zoology, University of Oxford; J. M. T. Thompson, Center for Nonlinear Dynamics and Applications, University College of London; P. L. Read, Department of Physics, University of Oxford; M. S. Child, Department of Chemistry, University of Oxford; and J. Keating, Department of Mathematics, University of Manchester, *The Nature of Chaos*, New York: Oxford University Press, 1993.

[324] Chamberlin, G. J., and D. G. Chamberlin, *Colour: Its Measurement, Computation, and Application*, London, England: Heyden and Sons, Ltd., 1980.

[325] Pekelis, V., *Cybernetics A to Z*, Moscow, Russia: Mir, 1974 (in English).

[326] Aburdene, M., Bucknell University, *Computer Simulation of Dynamic Systems*, Dubuque, IA: William C. Brown, 1988.

[327] Law, A., president, Simulation Modeling and Analysis Company, Tucson, AZ, and professor of decision sciences, University of Arizona; and W. Kelton, associate professor of operations research and management science, University of Minnesota, *Simulation Modeling & Analysis*, 2nd ed., New York: McGraw-Hill, 1991.

[328] Meyer, B., *Object-Oriented Software Construction Interactive*, Software Engineering, Inc., 1993–2001. All rights reserved. Key extracts are available at http://www.eiffel.com/ doc/ manuals/technology/oosc/inheritance-design/section_05.html.

[329] Fowler, M., and K. Scott, *UML Distilled: Applying the Standard Object Modeling Language*, Reading, MA: Addison-Wesley, 1997.

[330] Douglass, B. P., *Real-Time UML: Developing Efficient Objects for Embedded Systems*, 2nd ed., Reading, MA: Addison-Wesley, 2000.

[331] Rumbaugh, J., I. Jacobson, and G. Booch, *The Unified Modeling Language Reference Manual*, Reading, MA: Addison-Wesley, 1999.

[332] Rumbaugh, J., I. Jacobson, and G. Booch, *The Unified Modeling Language User Guide*, Reading, MA: Addison-Wesley, 1999.

[333] Muller, P-A., *Instant UML*, Birmingham, England: Wrox Press, Ltd., 1997.

[334] Blanchard E., *Introduction to Networking and Data Communications*, J. Drake, B. Randolph, and P. Ma, (eds.), Commandprompt, Inc., 2001, and Copyright © 2000, by Eugene Blanchard, http://www.linuxports.com/howto/intro_to_networking/book1.htm.

[335] Smith, H., and Fingar, P., *Business Process Management: The Third Wave*, Tampa, FL: Meghan-Kiffer Press, 2003.

[336] *The New Encyclopedia Britannica*, 15th ed., Chicago, IL: Encyclopedia Britannica, Inc., 2005.

[337] Mitra, A., and A. Gupta, *Creating Agile Business Systems with Reusable Knowledge*, Cambridge, England: Cambridge University Press, 2005.

About the Authors

Amit Mitra is a managing consultant in Headstrong's Information Management Optimization practice. He holds a black belt certification in the six-sigma process discipline, and is the author of two books on the nexus between component technology, business process management, and service-oriented architecture. He has assisted several Fortune 500 corporations to comply with the CMM® and to leverage it to improve their best practices. Mr. Mitra has helped align information systems with business strategy and developed metrics to measure and control the alignment on a continuing basis. He has applied and enhanced the Balanced Business Scorecard approach.

Mr. Mitra was the assistant vice president of the American International Group, a global insurance conglomerate. He had worldwide responsibility for the corporation's information systems methodology and headed an initiative to develop a strategic business knowledge architecture that cut across all of AIG's lines of business, spread over its 250 subsidiary corporations, operating in more than 130 countries across the world. He initiated an R&D program for developing a discipline for encapsulating business knowledge in reusable, technology-independent artifacts that can facilitate applications development.

Mr. Mitra left AIG to become director of systems architecture in NYNEX, then America's second-largest telecommunications company after AT&T. He was a part of NYNEX's leadership team, responsible for integrating the architecture of its many departments, divisions, and subsidiaries, as a part of an overall transformation initiative for the company. In that role, he extended and tested the new disciplines he had helped create in AIG. Mr. Mitra also has been a manager in KPMG and the manager for the information systems planning unit of AGS. He has consulted for Fortune 100 corporations for various software process improvement, measurement, and e-commerce initiatives and has been engaged to reengineer the IT process to make it more responsive to the business. Mr. Mitra is a vice president of the Data Management Forum and has spoken at several domestic and international forums, such as DAMA, the Computer Sciences Round Table in New York, Global Business Research, Technology Transfer Institute, and the CSI CIO summit. Mr Mitra can be reached at thebestfirm@hotmail.com and Amit@Sprybiz.com.

Amar Gupta is the Thomas R. Brown chair in management and technology; a professor of entrepreneurship and MIS; and the senior director for research and business development at the Eller College of Management of the University of Arizona in Tucson. Between 1979 and 2004, he was with the MIT Sloan School of Management. For one-half of this quarter-century period, he was the founding codirector of the Productivity from Information Technology (PROFIT) initiative at MIT.

Dr. Gupta holds a B.S. in electrical engineering, an M.S. in management from MIT, and a doctorate in the area of decision support systems. He has served in key technical and management capacities at MIT and elsewhere. In 1991 and 1992, he served as the associate director of MIT's International Financial Services Research Center. In 1995 and 1996, he served as the director of the MIT Research Program on Communications Policy and was instrumental in the establishment of the Internet Telephony Consortium, which was subsequently renamed the Internet and Telephony Convergence Consortium.

Dr. Gupta has served as an advisor to many leading corporations and several UN organizations, including WHO, UNDP, and UNIDO, on various aspects of national policy and large-scale information management in the context of the needs of both individual agencies and member governments. For example, in 1992 and 1993, he led a UNDP team to plan and implement a national financial information infrastructure in a Latin American country where 40% of the banks had gone bankrupt. More recently, he has served as an international advisor on a $500 million nationwide effort to get computers into every school in Brazil and as a World Bank advisor on a distance education endeavor in Mozambique.

When the IBM personal computer was introduced, Dr. Gupta served as an advisor to IBM, Boca Raton, and the president of that division (Don Estridge) contributed a chapter to one of his books. Subsequently, Dr. Gupta was one of the founders of Visual Communications Network, Inc., and served as its chief scientist and vice president for several years.

Dr. Gupta is the lead inventor of a patented approach for reading handwritten information with high accuracy, and has played a pivotal role in nucleating new ideas for nationwide paperless processing of bank checks. He was part of the team that developed ExecuVision software in early 1980s, which has been hailed by *Fortune*, *BusinessWeek*, and other independent observers as being the pioneer PC-based presentation graphics package. Dr. Gupta has received the Rotary Fellowship for International Understanding and an award from the U.S. Department of Transportation for distinguished performance on a project funded by the federal government. More recently, Business 2.0 magazine conducted a survey of the top tech-savvy business schools and the key professors there; Dr. Gupta was cited as the first among three short-listed professors at the MIT Sloan School of Management.

In November 2003, Dr. Gupta and Professor Lester Thurow, eminent economist and former dean of the MIT Sloan School of Management, initiated a new endeavor on "Outsourcing of Professional Activities." Dr. Gupta's work in this area and in related areas has received coverage in *CNN-Money*, the *Wall Street Journal*, *BusinessWeek*, *Newsweek*, and over 100 other newspapers and magazines published from different countries around the world. Dr. Gupta can be reached at agupta@alum.mit.edu.

Index

A

Accuracy, 70, 144, 154, 156, 160, 165, 189, 197
Activity Cost, 204
Acyclic, 24, 99, 100, 151
Ad hoc polymorphism, 329
Agent, 126, 152, 226, 232
Aggregation, 37, 47, 56, 61, 89, 100, 102–5, 138
Antisymmetrical, 48, 78
Antisymmetry, 78
Arbitrator, 140
Array, 161, 189
Atomic rule, 3, 7, 9, 17, 29, 32, 33, 34, 35
Axiom of Regularity, 330

B

Baseline, 125, 156, 210
Bijection, 325, 326, 327
Bijective, 135
Borel Object, 109, 114, 116, 118, 119, 155, 161, 200, 209
Borel Set, 113, 114, 116, 119
Bunge, 113, 334
Business Process Management, *xix*
BWW, 334–37

C

Capability Maturity Model® (CMM®), 243, 257, 259, 310, 312, 317
CAPE, 220, 221
Cardinality, 32, 49, 50, 56, 58, 133, 160, 218, 327, 349, 350
Cartesian, 70, 118
CASE, *xxi*, 15, 221
    tools, *xxi*, 15, 220
Causal analysis, 219, 220, 311
Chief knowledge officer, 312, 313, 314, 318
Chief information officer (CIO), 312, 313, 317
Chief technology officer, 314
Church-Rosser theorem, 344
CMM® level, 264–311

CMMI®, 310–12, 317
Coercive polymorphism, 15, 329, 330
Colorimetry, 347
Commutative, 327, 328, 345,
Completeness, 70, 160, 189
Constraint, 10, 31, 34–38, 49–51, 55, 58, 63, 116, 134, 159, 162–64, 176, 177, 194, 341
Contrafund, 202, 204, 206
Contract, 33, 34, 172, 192, 193, 194, 266, 268
Contractor, 142, 266, 268
CORBA, *xxii*, *xxv*
CPFR, 149
Cycle time, 12, 158, 161, 189, 201, 261, 301, 338
Cyclic, 99, 100, 320

D

DARPA, 233, 234
Demand chain, *xxv*, 41, 199–202, 213
Deterministic, 70, 71, 322, 338, 349, 350
Distributive, 328
Distributor, 140, 151, 152, 153, 194,
Double-entry bookkeeping, 202, 204, 206

E

Effect, 159
Eiffel, 339
Essence, 98, 103, 105, 157, 229
Expert systems, *xxi*
Extension Inheritance, 340
Extreme Programming, 224

F

Facilitator, 49, 137, 140, 141, 150, 233
Feature Group, 150, 199, 201
Formativeness, 58, 107, 108, 133, 148
Functional Programming, 162, 344, 346

G

GAAP, 183, 184, 204, 208, 211

Practical Insight into CMMI®, Tim Kasse

Practical Software Process Improvement, Robert Fantina

A Practitioner's Guide to Software Test Design, Lee Copeland

The Requirements Engineering Handbook, Ralph R. Young

Risk-Based E-Business Testing, Paul Gerrard and Neil Thompson

Secure Messaging with PGP and S/MIME, Rolf Oppliger

Software Configuration Management, Second Edition, Alexis Leon

Software Fault Tolerance Techniques and Implementation, Laura L. Pullum

Strategic Software Production with Domain-Oriented Reuse, Paolo Predonzani, Giancarlo Succi, and Tullio Vernazza

Successful Evolution of Software Systems, Hongji Yang and Martin Ward

Systematic Process Improvement Using ISO 9001:2000 and CMMI®, Boris Mutafelija and Harvey Stromberg

Systematic Software Testing, Rick D. Craig and Stefan P. Jaskiel

Testing and Quality Assurance for Component-Based Software, Jerry Zeyu Gao, H. -S. Jacob Tsao, and Ye Wu

Workflow Modeling: Tools for Process Improvement and Application Development, Alec Sharp and Patrick McDermott

For further information on these and other Artech House titles, including previously considered out-of-print books now available through our In-Print-Forever® (IPF®) program, contact:

Artech House	Artech House
685 Canton Street	46 Gillingham Street
Norwood, MA 02062	London SW1V 1AH UK
Phone: 781-769-9750	Phone: +44 (0)20 7596-8750
Fax: 781-769-6334	Fax: +44 (0)20 7630-0166
e-mail: artech@artechhouse.com	e-mail: artech-uk@artechhouse.com

Find us on the World Wide Web at: www.artechhouse.com